The Philosophy of MALEBRANCHE

The Philosophy of

MALEBRANCHE

A Study of his Integration of Faith,
Reason, and Experimental Observation

by

BEATRICE K. ROME

HENRY REGNERY COMPANY
Chicago 1963

To

SYDNEY

Contents

Contents

Contents

Contents

The Philosophy of MALEBRANCHE

Introduction

In 1660, at the age of 22, the frail, gentle, and modest Nicolas Malebranche entered the *Oratoire*, a society founded by Cardinal Bérulle, the friend of Descartes. But in 1660 Cartesianism was not in favor at the *Oratoire*. The members of the congregation were free to investigate it, but were expressly forbidden to teach it. Hence, during the next four years an obedient Malebranche devoted himself exclusively to preparation for the priesthood, showing no apparent interest in the "new" philosophy. Yet, curiously, on the eve of, or on the day following, his ordination, he suddenly and unexpectedly became a convert to Descartes. Walking along the street of St. Jacques, he came across Descartes' *L'Homme*, just published by Clerselier. In addition to Descartes' manual, the volume that Malebranche purchased contained other pieces. M. Gouhier tells us [1] that its contents included:

1. A letter from Clerselier to Colbert.
2. A preface by Clerselier.
3. *L'Homme* by Descartes.
4. *La description du corps humain*, a treatise that Clerselier called: *De la formation du foetus.*
5. The remarks of Louis de la Forge on *L'Homme*.
6. The French translation of the Preface placed by Schuyl before the Latin edition of *L'Homme*, published at Leyden in 1662.

Descartes' own writings in this volume are primarily scientific, although they assert the metaphysical distinction between the soul and body and allude to its importance for ethics. Those of Clerselier and Schuyl stress Descartes' contribution to the cause of religion and his accord with Augustine.

Whether Malebranche's extraordinary elation was prompted by the purely scientific contents of the book or whether he found in it the revelation of a solid Christian philosophy, is anybody's guess.[2] This

[3]

much is clear: for the next ten years, from 1664 to 1674, Malebranche devoted himself feverishly and voraciously to mathematics, to the natural sciences, and to Cartesian philosophy.

The initial result of this intellectual ferment was the monumental *Recherche de la vérité*, the first volume of which appeared in 1674, followed by a second volume in 1675. In this work and in all his subsequent writings, Malebranche reveals himself to be a faithful disciple of Descartes and Augustine and yet at the same time an intrepid, revolutionary, original innovator and reformer. And this means that his philosophy well deserves the independent designation that it enjoyed in the last quarter of the seventeenth century: Malebranchianism; for it is both timeless and ultramodern. For example, one of his best contemporary interpreters, M. Paul Mouy, writing in the nineteen-thirties, maintained that Malebranche's physics anticipates in many striking ways recent developments: before Euler and Young, he discovered the frequency theory of color. His reformulation of Descartes' vortices enabled him to develop a theory surprisingly anticipatory of those of the kinetic theory of gas and ionization.[3] His conception of light and weight as interchangeable properties of a field had to await twentieth-century developments before it could be adequately evaluated. Had it not been for Malebranche's inherent modesty, argues M. Mouy, and the unfortunate identification of Cartesianism with the hack-work of Régis, Newton would never have been glorified at the expense of Descartes.[4] Whether Mouy's claims concerning the scientific greatness of Malebranche are valid, I frankly am unprepared to determine. I cite them, however, to show that Father Malebranche is no moribund figure but a true giant among the geniuses of the seventeenth century.

Yet not alone in physics did this man display his unusual talents. From the time of the publication of the *Recherche* in 1674 to his death in 1715, Malebranche was the storm center of intellectual controversy.[5] Theologians were shocked by his rationalistic incursions into the realm of grace and by his bold interpretation of theological dogmas. The *avant-garde* of philosophic truth, the storekeepers, inheritors, and disciples of Descartes, were horrified by Malebranche's anti-Cartesianism, by his unashamed appeal to faith in the sphere of nature and reason. Arnauld the Jansenist accused him of Molinism; the Molinists charged him with Jansenism. While Fénelon and Lamy enrolled him in their camp as a quietist, mystic and advocate of a pure, self-less, disinterested love of God, Arnauld labeled him an Epicurean. To the skeptical academician Foucher, Malebranche was betraying the cause of philosophy by employing theological dogmas. Régis and Arnauld, the Cartesians, were scandalized by his "scholasticism" (his mingling of faith and reason), while the scholastics were feverishly working, and succeeded, to place him on the Index.

Now, it is a great pity that the only major study in English, that of Mr. R. W. Church, should convey nothing of the greatness, originality, fecundity, and unity of Malebranche's thought. From Mr. Church's study, Malebranche emerges as a philosophical lame duck, a mass of hopeless inconsistencies and pious frothings.[6] My purpose is to show the extraordinary degree of unity and coherence that obtains between Malebranche's methodology, epistemology, metaphysics and religious faith. Now, M. Gouhier aptly describes Malebranche as a Christian philosopher, and he rejects those interpreters who see Malebranche's system of philosophy as a hodge-podge, a mere juxtaposition of Cartesian science and Augustinian metaphysics. Gouhier is entirely correct as we shall see; Malebranche does not simply superimpose Augustine on Descartes. But yet M. Gouhier does not, it seems to me, adequately penetrate into the philosophical core of this Christian philosophy, namely, Malebranche's view of God as Being. And while M. Gouhier, moreover, notes Malebranche's experiments on insects and his love for the natural sciences, he does not explore the extent to which this Christian philosophy is indebted to the spirit of Bacon. Conversely, those writers like M. Mouy and Labbas, who have concentrated on Malebranche as scientist, ignore the profound effects of his mastery of the science of his day on his epistemology and metaphysics.

It is my contention that an illuminating approach to Malebranchianism is from the point of view of his conception concerning the role and nature of scientific method. Accordingly, I begin by showing why and how Malebranche combines the mathematical rational method of Descartes with the empirical inductive method of Bacon. This methodology entails a relational view of necessary and contingent truths. The empirical emphasis, furthermore, entails a revision in the nature of a scientific hypothesis: a true and intelligible hypothesis is one grounded in fact, expressible in mathematical equations, and corroborated by predictive results. Next, I claim that this view of methodology and his attitude toward the intelligible and toward the contingent, descriptive aspects of science led Malebranche to formulate an inductive epistemology and a Platonic version of universals. Then I show how, in conformity with the empirical aspect of his method, Malebranche goes beyond Platonism to the realistic conception of God as Being. Subsequently, in the light of the method and of the nature of God, I argue for a reinterpretation of Occasionalism as a metaphysical account of the origin and nature of beings: creatures are a synthesis of essence and existence; reality is more than a system of essences, and the real, in so far as it exists, acts. Creation proper belongs to God, but the gift of existence permits the occasional cause to act. Moreover, because, unlike Descartes, Malebranche emphasizes the existential, I indicate how the will becomes the core of human personality and how the existence of the self as a dynamic process is known to consciousness. After this, in the light of his method, of his metaphysics of participation and of the distinction between essence and existence, I show how Malebranche develops a theory of veridical perception as a direct natural revelation of the existence of the external world. Finally, his employment of faith in our knowledge of the external world, I claim, is grounded on reason; and I point out how the mutual interconnection between faith and reason is parallel to the initial vision of the interplay between reason and science, between general principles and brute matters of fact, between essence and existence.

Malebranche thus emerges as a heroic figure. In an age when men's loyalties are bitterly divided between the book of nature and the book of God, when, like Pascal, they renounce reason to embrace the occult, or like Spinoza they castigate the heart in behalf of the intellect, or finally like Thomas Browne they oscillate between one sphere and another, Malebranche establishes an extraordinary synthesis of science, philosophy and hard-headed faith, a synthesis inspired by the methodological requirements of science itself.

Chapter I

Scientific Method

To his critic, Foucher, Malebranche wrote that his entire *Recherche de la vérité* had been written in order to prepare his readers for and to justify the account of scientific method contained in the sixth and last book, entitled, "De la méthode." [1] This disclosure to Foucher reveals Malebranche's principal objective in writing the *Recherche*. My thesis is that his entire system on the nature of man, on God, and on human knowledge can and must be interpreted as oriented towards his method. Accordingly it is necessary to become clear concerning what method means to Malebranche, and this is what I propose to do in the present chapter.

Malebranche's philosophy oriented towards his method.

I. Intuitive and Deductive Aspects of Malebranche's Method

(*a*) *Malebranche Follows Descartes with Respect to Mathematical Aspects of Method.* Malebranche's sixth and last book of the *Recherche* (on method) is divided into two parts. The first part is devoted primarily to an analysis of the import and structure of the various branches of mathematics; the second part formulates seven rules for the attainment of truth, with illustrations of their application to metaphysical, physical and moral problems. These latter rules, as Toesca and Church properly observe,[2] are borrowed from Descartes. They show us that, as for Descartes, method for Malebranche consists in a double and continuous movement of analysis and synthesis, of decomposition into simples and subsequent orderly combination of simple elements into complex wholes. We may therefore say that in setting out to justify his own method, Malebranche, even though this may not be all that he is trying to do, is, at the least, in fact seeking to

Analysis into simples and synthesis into complex wholes.

[7]

justify major aspects of Descartes' method. Moreover, the very division of the book on method into the two parts just noted further indicates his affiliation with Descartes; for he begins with an analysis of mathematics prior to the enunciation of the rules, because, like Descartes, he considered mathematics to be the true logic and very key to method. His rules then, like Descartes', are obviously inspired by the procedures of mathematics. For this reason, it is necessary to scrutinize what Descartes and Malebranche mean by mathematics itself and by mathematical procedure, in order to determine the relevance of these to Malebranche's scientific method. Let us begin by considering Descartes' views on mathematics and on mathematical procedure.

Descartes, it will be remembered, believed that the best application of his method was to be found in his *Geometry*.[3] When Descartes set out to discover his method, it was to the ancient Greek mathematicians that he turned for aid—to Pappus for geometry and to Diophantus for algebra. In their works, he tells us, he found the secret of what constitutes the true method and the certainty of mathematics. Descartes came to the conclusion that all those branches of knowledge classified as parts of mathematics—astronomy, optics, mechanics, music, geometry, arithmetic—were so defined because they all shared the two common features of order and measurement.[4] The reasons why indubitable propositions can be ascertained in these sciences are two: first, that in them any given problem is set forth according to a certain order, namely, the order that follows from the resolution of the problem into its simplest terms or elements,[5] and second, that by the comparison of the simple elements with some given measuring unit, a composition or synthesis of quantitative relations is achieved which corresponds to the required solution.[6]

Furthermore, Descartes, having observed the significance of relational order and measurement for achieving certainty in these mathematical sciences, proceeded to the generalization that this method of order and measurement is the sole method to be employed in all the provinces of strict knowledge.[7] He accordingly denominated the total science of order and measurement, "Universal Mathematics."[8] Universal Mathematics yields truth and certainty, because, being a science exclusively of quantitative relations, it is conversant with exact relations of comparison. Consequently, as Milhaud shows, it is not simply that mathematicians use long chains of reasoning that impresses Descartes. Nor is Descartes exclusively impressed by the sheerly formal logical procedures used in mathematics, although he does summarize these procedures in the four rules of the *Discourse*. The key to mathematical truth and certainty for Descartes really lies in quantitative relation.[9] According to the method of Universal Mathematics, knowledge consists in the intuition of absolute or simple, unanalyzable rela-

Order and measurement.

Exact relations of comparison.

[8]

tions, together with the subsequent combination of these simples into complex relations by a continuous process of deductive comparison. When a true proposition is attained, or when a truth is discovered, the net result consists in the apprehension of equality or inequality among the known and unknown relations in respect of some unit of measurement.[10] In so far as knowledge is thus defined as a comparison of the relations of equality and inequality, it holds of all branches of mathematics. It goes without saying that this conception of knowledge is *par excellence* a generalization of algebraic procedure; the equation in algebra is its prototype.

Subsequently, in his own *Geometry*, using techniques borrowed from the ancients, Descartes goes on to show how the great variety of curved lines can be classified in terms of quantitative complexity and represented by equations of varying degrees.[11] We can now see why Descartes regarded his *Geometry* as the best exemplification of his method. In his sixth Rule, Descartes discloses what he calls "the chief secret of method." This secret is: ". . . that all facts can be arranged in certain series, not indeed in the sense of being referred to some ontological genus such as the categories employed by Philosophers in their classification, but in so far as certain truths can be known from others . . ." He goes on to say that this method does not regard things as isolated realities, but compares them with one another in order to ascertain their interdependence.[12] Thus his method consists not in considering each thing in isolation, but instead in seeking the series involved in knowing them. And Descartes' *Geometry* best exemplifies this methodological "secret," for it shows that the path to truth or the knowledge of truth or truth itself lies in quantitative relations.

Relational knowledge ordered serially.

The *Geometry* shows too that the variety of geometric lines are to be classified not in terms of genera and species but in terms of their complexity, where this complexity can be specified as more or less. The variety of figures is not a distinct multiplicity, with separated, isolated examples, but an *organized system*. The various figures are not arranged hierarchically as in the Tree of Porphyry but instead are given at once as aspects of a single continuum.[13]

And by degrees of complexity.

(*b*) *Geometry Essentially Algebra for Malebranche* (*Step beyond Descartes*). In consideration of the foregoing, Brunschvicg concludes that Descartes' geometry, unlike that of Euclid, is essentially a science of purely intellectual relations.[14] It is from algebra, he notes, that Spinoza borrows the model of perfect intelligibility: the intuition of the adequate proportionality between simple numbers.[15] The example used by Spinoza is also employed by Descartes in the *Rules*.[16] Since this work was not published until 1701, I do not know whether or not Malebranche or Spinoza had access to it in manuscript.[17] What is significant, however, is that in the *Recherche* Malebranche also uses examples of the same sort in his sixth book on method.[18] In fact, Malebranche does more than use the examples. He devotes two entire chapters in the first part of the book to an analysis of the utility of geometry, arithmetic and algebra. The discussion on geometry occurs in Chapter IV of Part I, which is entitled, "De l'usage de l'organisation pour conserver l'attention de l'esprit, et de l'utilité de la géométrie." Chapter V is entitled, "Des moyens d'augmenter l'étendue et la capacité de l'esprit. Que l'arithmétique et l'algèbre y sont absolument nécessaires."

These titles are significant. Geometry in the ordinary Euclidean sense of fixed images is useful for arresting and conserving the attention of the will, according to Malebranche, although it belongs to the sphere of the imagination. Descartes writes that an infinitude of figures suffices to express all differences in sensible things.[19] Malebranche similarly explains at length how useful a crutch the imagination can be. Lines and figures, he says, are even marvelous aids for apprehending clearly and distinctly.[20] How? Malebranche's answer to this question shows what he really understands by geometry. The lines and figures of geometry, he writes, serve to represent to the imagination the relationships that obtain among magnitudes or things that are capable of more or less, such as space, time and weight.[21] Thus what geometric figures imply or signify is always a ratio or proportion, something more and other than merely the static sensibly fixed image itself. Geometry is the science that teaches one to make comparisons in order to uncover relationships among lines. Hence, astronomy, music, mechanics and all the exact sciences which deal with extensive magnitudes can be related to geometry; for—Malebranche tells us—all speculative truths consist exclusively in the relations of things and in the relations which occur between their relations; hence, they can all be referred to lines.[22] Because geometry is thus a science of relationships and because exact speculative scientific knowledge consists in the apprehension of relations, geometry may be treated as a sort of universal science.[23] From this it is clear that Malebranche must mean that in a sensible geometrical construction, such as a line, the relationship sensibly symbolized by the line and thus present to the senses is nevertheless a purely intelligible content to be grasped by the understanding alone. The line itself is no intelligible meaning. Yet the function of the line, its role or office, is to convey such a meaning. A sensible figure thus *contains*, as it were, an intelligible meaning. For this reason, an object like a line is useful not only in provoking or arresting or sustaining one's mental vision in its search for the truth, but also in that the sensible figure actually

Geometrical images embody intelligible meanings.

embodies in a palpable and concrete manner the very truth sought for.[24]

What Malebranche is maintaining, then, is that in geometry the sensible figure is an embodiment of an intelligible meaning. One understands or knows the figure in so far as one grasps this ideal signification. And this ideal import, symbolized by the fixed and static figure, is a relationship. Finally, while the figure embodies the meaning, in the last analysis the understanding of that intelligible import is an operation of the pure understanding, not of sense.

Perhaps the following may help clarify what is here involved. A circle drawn on paper and thus palpably present to the senses is a fixed, inert appearance which in itself has no resemblance to the intelligible meaning of circularity, as conveyed by the algebraic expression, $x^2 + y^2 = c^2$. The latter expresses the idea or essence of circularity. This algebraic equation, furthermore, expresses a relationship. Circularity as understood by the mind is thus a proportion, whereas the circle present to the senses is a crystallized entity. Hence between the image and the algebraic meaning there is no resemblance. The intelligible nature of the circle—the idea itself—is not a configured image. And conversely, the image, the circle on paper, is no fair reproduction or picture or copy of the intelligible relationship. On the other hand, the circle on paper does have a connection with the essence of circularity conveyed by the algebraic expression. The seen circle is isomorphic with or equivalent to its intelligible algebraic counterpart. One can go further. One may say that the seen circular image is really a participation of or an embodiment of its algebraic meaning, that without resembling or copying the equation, it nevertheless "contains" it. The seen circle is, as it were, the objectification of the algebraic meaning.

In a later work, the *Entretiens sur la métaphysique,* Malebranche devotes the fifth dialogue to a discussion of the function of sense in the sciences. Here he offers a number of geometric constructions to show how these are useful for conveying knowledge. Merely open your eyes, Theodore suggests to Aristes, and gaze upon the following figure. Does not one immediately see that the square on the diagonal of a square is double the squares on the sides? The truth "saute aux yeux." [25] Yet it is not the senses that convey the truth, but reason combined with the senses.[26] It is the idea or meaning of extension that enlightens the mind; colors make it perceptible. Moreover, the geometric figure drawn on paper may not be a perfect square; the lines may not be perfectly straight, nor the angles exactly right angles.[27] Hence, strictly speaking, the squares of which geometricians speak, and whose properties and relations they understand, are the ideal squares, not the crude images of the senses. "These crude images may

Examples.

[11]

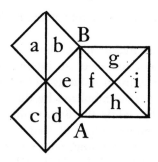

perhaps sustain their attention, giving bodily form, so to speak, to their ideas," concludes Malebranche. "But it is the ideas wherein they find sure foundation, which convince them of the truth of their science." [28]

An adequate grasp of the true nature of Cartesian geometry thus discloses to us that it at once discredits the senses as far as knowledge is concerned and at the same time elevates the sensible in the knowing process. According to the philosophies of Descartes and of Malebranche, it is necessary to hold that uncritical acceptance of sense testimony would present the sensible circle as no more than an arrested image without thus penetrating into its real inner core, its nature-engendering nature or Form, to use Bacon's expression. On the other hand, for a sensibility enlightened by reason, the seen circle is now apprehended as the crystallization of an intelligible proportion. The seen circle is thus the Word made flesh, the intelligible rendered incarnate.

It may be said, then, that for Descartes and Malebranche strict knowledge, that is, mathematical knowledge, is never of concrete existing things in themselves but of their relational pattern or structure. When the mathematician studies magnitudes, it is always as relational complexes. We do not know, writes Malebranche, what absolute size, or shape, or figure, is.[29] In arithmetic, too, whole numbers express relationships. Thus the entire enterprise or science of mathematics consists in analyzing complex relationships into the more elementary or simple ones and then by a process of gradual combination arriving at the more and more complex.[30] The mathematician, thus, is never conversant with terms, but always with relations; and the simple terms of his deductive system are really the laws that govern the generation of complex relations. As Schrecker says, the equation of the parabola (a relation of groups of spatial relations) is for Malebranche the law which expresses the distances of each point on the curve from the coordinates.[31] In so far as exact knowledge means a system of intelligible relations, the senses are confused and unreliable, because they present extension in discrete, separated forms. On the

Sensibility and reason.

Relativity: —exact knowledge relational.

other hand, these fixed geometric figures really do embody and really do express or convey an intelligible content. In so far as they do, geometry, for Malebranche, is useful in the search after truth. And this, of course, likewise implies that sense and imagination are instrumental in and do function in knowledge. In this respect, geometry not only arrests attention and sustains the will; it actually serves to convey the truth. Hence we may say that sense perception implicates understanding or conception. To see is to understand.

What, then, can we say of Malebranche's notion of truth? At the beginning of his discussion on the nature of arithmetic and algebra, Malebranche offers us a precise and elaborate statement concerning his view of truth. Truth, he tells us, is nothing else than a real relation, whether of equality or inequality. It is that which is, and one is never deceived when one sees relations which are. Hence, he affirms, "Les vérités ne sont donc que des rapports, et la connaissance des vérités la connaissance des rapports." [32]

Truths consist in real relations.

These truths which are exclusively real relations fall into three groups: relations among ideas, relations between things and ideas, and relations among things. "$2 \times 2 = 4$" is an example of a relationship among ideas. The proposition that there is a sun expresses a relationship between an idea and a thing. And the assertion that the earth is larger than the moon expresses a relationship between facts. Of these three groups, only the first, the relationships among ideas, are eternal and immutable. Because of this immutability, these exact relationships constitute the rule and measure of all the others, for every rule or measure must be invariable. It is with these alone that arithmetic, algebra and geometry are concerned, for these general sciences regulate and contain all the particular sciences.[33] Moreover, whereas the discovery of contingent truths depends upon the senses, it is only within the realm of eternal truths that one seeks to make discoveries by the simple exercise of the mind. Only mathematical truths or relationships can be grasped by the mind with infallibility and grasped by it alone, without the use of the senses,[34] although some sensible imagery always accompanies even the purest and most abstract acts of thought.[35]

Thus, inasmuch as the truth conveyed by a geometrical figure is intrinsically a system of intelligible meanings and exact proportions, it remains correct to say that in its purity and strictness, in its clarity and distinctness, knowledge of geometrical figures for Malebranche belongs to the understanding alone. A sensible figure, for example, a circle, is after all, only an approximation to or adumbration of what the algebraic formula connotes. Hence, Malebranche writes, it is only the pure understanding that can grasp the perfect square and the perfect circle.[36]

[13]

Because the perfect circle is indeed no fixed image but a proportion, Malebranche considers arithmetic and algebra to be superior to geometry in training the mind for the acquisition of truth.[37] Malebranche is here taking a significant step beyond Descartes in his conception of mathematics. Milhaud tells us that Descartes did not emphasize the tradition represented by algebraicists like Diophantus, so much as he did that of the classical geometers, like Pappus. The algebra of the Diophantian tradition Milhaud describes as "une sorte de prolongement de l'Arithmétique; les solutions des équations sont des valeurs numériquement calculables à l'aide de formules." According to the other tradition, that of Pappus, "ce sont des longeurs qu'il faut construire." [38] Descartes, from the very beginning of his work in mathematics to the time of the *Geometry*, clung tenaciously to the latter tradition, always insisting on the use of lines rather than on the use of formulae. This he did, because he believed that number could not represent continuous quantity or the relations among incommensurables.[39] But, Milhaud observes, ever since Descartes, the infinite has penetrated more and more into mathematical thought, and the notion of number as a continuum is no longer avoided.[40] As a matter of fact, it is Malebranche who greatly furthered this tendency in mathematics which Milhaud finds to have had its halting beginnings in Descartes.[41]

For Malebranche, every magnitude is a relation, since nothing, he insists, is ever absolutely large or small. Arithmetic has the virtue that in it whole numbers are just as much relational as are fractions. 4 is a relation, just as much as are $\frac{4}{1}$ or $\frac{8}{2}$, Malebranche tells us, since 4 is equal to $\frac{4}{1}$ or $\frac{8}{2}$. He concludes that because every magnitude is a relation and every relation is a magnitude, we can express all relations by numbers [42] and represent them to the imagination by lines.[43] Of these two latter opportunities, Malebranche prefers the first, for he holds that ordinary geometry does not perfect the mind so much as it does the imagination; the truths discovered by this science are not always so evident as geometers surmise. For example, says he, they think that they have expressed the value of certain magnitudes, when they have proved that these magnitudes are equal to certain lines which are subtended by right angles whose sides are exactly known, or to others which are determined by some conic section. But it is clear that they are deceived; *for the subtended lines are themselves unknown.* For this reason, Malebranche claims that one knows $\sqrt{8}$ or $\sqrt{20}$ more exactly than one knows a line that one imagines or that one describes on paper. One knows at least that $\sqrt{8}$ approaches 3 and that $\sqrt{20}$ is about $4\frac{1}{2}$. Besides, one can, by certain rules, constantly approach closer to their infinitely precise value ("approcher toujours à l'infini de leur véritable grandeur").[44] If one cannot actually

Arithmetic and algebra superior to geometry.

Conceiving infinity.

arrive at this precise value, the fault does not lie with the intrinsic nature of algebra and of arithmetic. The limitation arises only because the mind cannot comprehend the infinite. In geometry, on the contrary, one has only a very confused idea of the magnitude of subtended lines, and one is even obliged to have recourse to $\sqrt{8}$ or to $\sqrt{20}$ to express them. Thus, Malebranche affirms that geometric constructions which are used to express values of unknown quantities are less useful to regulate the mind and to discover the relationships or the truths that one is looking for, than to regulate the imagination.[45] In contrast, while we cannot actually comprehend infinity, as we shall note later, nevertheless arithmetic and algebra enable us to go as far as *to conceive* and *to understand infinity.*

Hence Malebranche is able to assert a theory of truth as a system of infinitely complex relations. From the very first appearance of his *Recherche*, Malebranche affirmed:

Truth a system of infinitely complex relations.

Mais non-seulement il y a rapport entre les idées, mais encore entre les rapports qui sont entre les idées, entre les rapports des rapports des idées, et enfin entre les assemblages de plusieurs rapports et entre les rapports de ces assemblages de rapports, et ainsi à l'infini; c'est-à dire qu'il y a des vérités composées à l'infini.[46]

This view of mathematics, as an infinitely complex system or continuum of relations of relations, Malebranche designates in subsequent writings as an "Intelligible Extension"; and we shall later examine this notion more closely. Church and Arnauld claim that in the *Recherche* Malebranche speaks of a plurality of separate ideas and that later he changed his mind.[47] Malebranche himself denied this charge. If Church and Arnauld had paid serious attention to the fact which was emphasized at the very beginning of this essay, that the entire *Recherche* was written to prepare for and to justify Malebranche's method as presented in the sixth and last book, wherein the notion of "vérités composées à l'infini" occurs, they would have understood that, while Malebranche did not use the *term* Intelligible Extension in the *Recherche*, its content had already been delineated and established.[48] As the present essay proceeds, we shall find that this error in the interpretation of Malebranche by Arnauld in the seventeenth century and by Church in our own century vitiates most of their allegations concerning the deficiencies of Malebranche's philosophy. For these reasons Malebranche's preference for arithmetic and for algebra over geometry not only is historically significant in its own right, but also it possesses great significance for an adequate understanding of Malebranche's own philosophy.

From Descartes' *Geometry* and, more especially, from Malebranche's analysis of the role, function and interconnections of geometry and

Intuitive and deductive conclusions.

algebra together in the pursuit of truth, we may infer important consequences regarding Malebranche's conception of method. First, Malebranche is quite faithful to the spirit and method of Descartes in so far as Malebranche insists that mathematics is a system of quantitative intelligible relations and that these are to be obtained by pure intuition and deduction. Further, from the manner in which Malebranche treats geometry, it is apparent that while sense and imagination do not yield knowledge in its purity, they nevertheless do play an important epistemological role—they not only arrest attention, but they really can represent in a sensible manner an intelligible truth. In fact, sense can even be taken as the springboard to knowledge proper. For notice that in the training of the mind in its pursuit of truth, geometry must precede algebra; the sensible must be prior to the purely intellectual. Yet, in studying geometry it is the intellectual component alone that matters—in studying geometry the mind is being disciplined to comprehend the intelligible in the sensible.

Thus from the *Geometry* we learn that the proper method in science is *not* to regard things in isolated fashion or to search for some accidental or external similarities among them; but rather it is to look for their inner law, the serial order, that unites descriptive facts into an organized, coherent system, and to regard the facts themselves as variants of one and the same law.

The *Geometry* further teaches that the senses are to be distrusted only to the extent that the latter present things as if they actually were completely isolated and distinct realities, hopelessly fragmentary, pluralistic, and radically unlike or heterogeneous. It does not, however, teach the total denial of the senses. And in so far as geometry makes use of sensible constructions, there is the further suggestion that the intelligible laws and relations sought for by the understanding are immanently embodied in the sensible objects themselves.

Thus in setting out to defend his method, Malebranche is seeking to defend major elements of Descartes' method. By the latter is meant the intuitive, deductive, relational method, a method which extols the intellect, but which does not altogether condemn the senses. Nevertheless, it must be admitted that the senses do not occupy a central role in mathematics, particularly in so far as mathematics is conceived as an algebra. Mathematical figures help to convey a truth but not to confirm it. Had Malebranche and Descartes, then, conceived of method entirely in terms of mathematics, they should have culminated in the *a priori* rationalism of Spinoza, for Spinoza's metaphysics was entirely inspired by the method and character of mathematics. His conception of the unicity of substance, with the mode an aspect of substance, is a philosophy in which the universe is an organism of organisms, an individual of individuals, a system of systems, and the mode has no reality apart from its status as aspect of the whole. But more, Spinoza's is really a system of essences of essences. In terms of the foregoing account of the intuitive and deductive aspects of Malebranche's method, Spinoza's entire universe is an infinitely complex system of relations of relations, held together by coherence and consistency. Did Descartes and Malebranche, however, like Spinoza, conceive method as *exclusively* deductive, as entirely independent of sense? The later Descartes did indeed go far in that direction, but the methodology of the earlier Descartes has another side, an experimental side, and it is this, we shall now see, that occupies special prominence in Malebranche's writings.

II. Empirical and Experimental Aspects of Method

(*a*) *Descartes and Bacon.* In his remarkable work, *Descartes savant,* Milhaud devotes two chapters to Cartesian science, that reveal a side of Descartes hardly ever remarked in histories of philosophy. These two chapters are entitled "Descartes expérimentateur" and "Descartes et Bacon." In his former chapter Milhaud contends not only that Descartes was passionately concerned with experiments, but also that he was very much aware of the nature of an experiment. Citing as example a letter in which Descartes describes his experiment on the circulation of the blood, Milhaud calls attention to the careful manner and detail of Descartes' procedure.[49] But what is even more important, says Milhaud, is the path that led Descartes to the experiment: we do not see him here proceeding from simple *a priori* principles, nor do we see him here preoccupied with the entire human organism. Rather, we see a Descartes instinctively following the methods of Harvey. In this connection Milhaud cites other instances of Descartes' experimental work, all of which indicate that in addition to a natural tendency to soaring *a priori* speculation and generalization, Descartes also possessed an uncanny capacity for the piecemeal, detailed, observational techniques of the laboratory. One cannot, Milhaud concludes, compress Descartes' genius into any simple formula:

"Descartes expérimentateur."

> A côté du savant ambitieux qui aspire à tirer de son cerveau et de quelques principes *a priori* la science intégrale, à côté du savant philosophe et métaphysicien, il y a le savant tout court, disposé, à un degré qu'on ne soupçonne pas, à suivre d'instinct la marche objective et spontanée de la science de son milieu et de son temps.[50]

In his subsequent chapter on "Descartes et Bacon," Milhaud shows at great length that this "savant tout court" was not so far removed from Bacon as we think and that Descartes himself was not conscious of any fundamental opposition between himself and the Englishman.

I shall here briefly review and enlarge upon some of Milhaud's interesting discoveries concerning Descartes and then investigate how these discoveries can be used for developing an adequate interpretation of Malebranche's views on experimental method.

In 1630, in letters to Mersenne, Descartes cites Bacon's method as the proper one to follow in conducting useful experiments. In 1632, Descartes writes to Mersenne expressing the wish that someone would undertake an exhaustive description of celestial phenomena, following the method of Bacon and without making any presumptions or hypotheses. But it is not simply Bacon's method as an instrument for the collection of data that Descartes admired. Bacon was opposed to any method that was based upon what he called the distorting rays of the intellect; he denounced fantastic speculation; he insisted on observation and respect for brute data. Had Descartes really found these aspects of Bacon's method diametrically antagonistic to what he conceived to be proper scientific method, why, asks Milhaud, did he never indicate his opposition? Not only did Descartes never disparage Bacon, but, claims Milhaud, careful attention to the rules that Descartes offers for the pursuit of truth will reveal that, in point of actual fact, they are not very different from those of Bacon.[51] Descartes' refusal to abide by authority, his insistence upon order, upon the avoidance of precipitation, upon making complete enumerations, upon omitting no required steps in the ascent to truth—all this is entirely in the spirit of Bacon, particularly in the spirit of the latter's objection to hasty generalizations and of his demand for middle principles.

Yet will it not be said, argues Milhaud, that, after all, Descartes' rules as presented in the *Discourse* are inspired by the procedure of mathematics, that they simply summarize the mathematical method itself? But, in answer to his own query, Milhaud reminds us that while

Descartes considered the *Geometry* to be the fruit of his method and its best illustration, nevertheless both the rules and the method were intended as *universal* in scope.[52] At the same time that the *Geometry* appeared, Descartes also published the *Dioptrics* and the *Meteors*, and the *Discourse* as well.[53] The latter is concerned with metaphysics and also contains a section on physiology. Descartes' method and rules, then, were intended to be adaptable to all branches of human knowledge, not merely to mathematics proper. By this method, he says, "there can be nothing so remote that we cannot reach to it, nor so recondite that we cannot discover it."[54]

But how is such adaptation and generalization of the method possible, when from mathematical deductions we want to pass to the concrete world? In the *Rules* Milhaud finds his answer. Milhaud grants that most of the examples of the *Rules* are indeed borrowed from mathematics, and that mathematics serves as model for the demonstration and certainty of propositions. Nevertheless, he asserts, Descartes' actual language in formulating the rules is sufficiently general to include experimental procedure as well as the deductions of geometry.[55] Especially significant in this connection are the second and fifth Rules. The second Rule affirms that, "Only those objects should engage our attention, to the sure and indubitable knowledge of which our mental powers seem to be adequate." [56] Milhaud notes that in explaining this rule Descartes points out that there are *two* roads to knowledge: experience [57] and deduction. Instruction from experience is frequently fallacious and hence not so trustworthy as are deductions, which can never err, except by inadvertance. Nonetheless, it is to be noted that Descartes does speak of experimental induction as a road to knowledge, and, while he stresses its fallible character, he yet does not say that it is always fallacious. Descartes does, in truth, here hold up arithmetic and geometry as the very prototype of indubitable certitude, because these sciences, in his words, "need make no assumptions at all which experience renders uncertain, but wholly consist in the rational deduction of consequences." [58] However, this statement simply erects arithmetic and geometry as *models* of exact knowledge. It does not assert that experimental work is always wholly defective and uncertain.

Like Lalande, Milhaud finds Descartes' Rule V and his commentary on that rule especially reminiscent of Bacon.[59] The Latin conveys the alliance even better than does the English translation:

Descartes' scalae gradibus.

Tota methodus consistit in ordine & dispositione eorum ad quae mentis acies est convertenda, ut aliquam veritatam inveniamus. Atque hanc exacte servabimus, si propositiones involutas & obscuras ad simpliciores gradatim reducamus, & deinde ex omnium simplicissimarum intuitu ad aliarum omnium cognitionem per eosdem gradus ascendere tentemus.[60]

In explaining this rule, Descartes affirms that those who neglect it "act like a man who should attempt to leap with one bound from the base to the summit of a house, either making no account of the ladders [vel neglectis scalae gradibus] provided for his ascent or not noticing them." [61] As Lalande and Milhaud both affirm, there surely can be no doubt that here Descartes has in mind Bacon's Middle Principles. Furthermore, Descartes cites as examples of those who make precipitous leaps and neglect the "scalae gradibus":

(a) the astrologers (they do not make "proper observations of the movements of heavenly bodies. . . ."),

(b) those who study mechanics apart from physics, and

(c) "those philosophers who, neglecting experience [neglectis experimentis], imagine that truth will spring from their brain like Pallas from the head of Zeus." [62]

[19]

Realize now that for Descartes this fifth Rule expresses the very quint-essence of his method. He himself evaluates it in these words: "In this alone lies the sum of all human endeavor." [63] For him, then, this rule which demands analysis and orderly synthesis is a rule of universal scope; and when so taken, it implies further, as the body of the rule shows, that in the pursuit of orderly investigation experiments must not be omitted.

Again, in his exposition of 'simple natures' in the twelfth Rule, Descartes says that they can be known either by the natural light or by "experiences." And, of course, the title of this rule speaks for itself: "Finally we ought to employ all the aids of understanding, imagination, sense and memory, first for the purpose of having a distinct intuition of simple propositions; partly also in order to compare the propositions to be proved with those we know already . . . ; partly also in order to discover the truths, which should be compared with each other . . ." [64]

On the basis of these and many more observations, Milhaud concludes that notwithstanding the origin of Descartes' method in mathematics, notwithstanding his numerous examples that favor arithmetic and geometry, notwithstanding that the rules seem to exclude experience, actually, all these rules can be transposed into the language of Bacon. Their sense is in each case sufficiently large to be applied to all scientific domains. [65]

A critic who might be opposed to such an interpretation of the early Descartes might perhaps point to Rule III where Descartes asserts unambiguously: ". . . those propositions indeed which are immediately deduced from first principles are known now by intuition, now by deduction . . . These two methods are the most certain routes to knowledge, and the mind should admit no others." [66] Milhaud and Lalande are both fully aware of Descartes' insistence on the primacy of intuition, but there is another side to their argument that Descartes is Baconian in his early years, one which bears significantly on the specific nature of Baconian sense observation. They hold, namely, that Bacon is much less the passive empiricist than is commonly supposed. Notwithstanding Bacon's emphasis on observation, what he really sought in experiment was a synthesis of Vulcan and Minerva, a synthesis of sense and of intellect. [67] In turn, Descartes, at least the early Descartes, for all his stress on intuition, did not intend to separate intuition from sense. Intuition may indeed be taken as the only avenue to knowledge, according to the early Descartes; yet this intuition may, as with Bacon's interpretation of intellect, have as its objects or data the elements presented by sense in experience.

Furthermore, Milhaud might have pointed to additional facts to support the foregoing claims concerning Descartes' experimentalism

Bacon's rationalism.

and Bacon's rationalism. Truth, for Descartes, consists in the intelligible order and connections of things, the general and universal laws, the relations of equality and of inequality.[68] As such, truth lies always within the sphere of intuition. Inasmuch as sense presents things in isolated, discrete fashion, while knowledge consists in grasping the facts in their widest generality, intuition is the only instrument to knowledge of matters of fact. In this respect Descartes could very well say that intuition is the sole mental operation that it is permissible to employ in order to obtain truth. But this conclusion would not militate against the use of sense and of experiment, provided that Descartes understood sense and experiment as did Bacon; for after all, Bacon, in carrying out the inductive procedure, acknowledged that it was the function of the intellect to grasp the Forms.[69] Also, in checking upon the Middle Principles by further experiments, Bacon recognized that it was still the intellect that did the checking. And again, the reason why Bacon insisted so much on incessant experimentation is that he too regarded the naked senses to be erroneous in their manner of presenting the facts, since they offered merely a plethora of unrelated particulars.[70] For Bacon, the purpose of experimental observation was to allow the intellect to penetrate into this chaotic welter and find therein the Forms or the nature-engendering natures.[71] These were the laws or causes or essences that governed the formation of the multiplicity of particulars.[72] In his search for Forms, Bacon rejected the scholastic method of classification by genera and species as much as did Descartes. And when he turned to sense data for corroboration and confirmation, it was not because he thought that brute facts could speak for themselves, *but rather because he believed that the Forms which he sought are immanent in the very facts.*[73]

Moreover, we may refer to what Lalande so carefully notes, that Bacon did not only not oppose mathematics, but highly extolled it. He placed it within metaphysics or the study of Forms. He recommended it as a remedy for the dull intellect and as a cure for too-great reliance on sense.[74] What he opposed was simply the abuse of mathematics, that is, he rejected the views of those who would subordinate physics to mathematics, who would seek to deduce the laws of nature in *a priori* fashion from mathematics. Mathematics was to give definiteness to, but not generate, natural philosophy.[75] Begin, he counseled, with physics; but end with mathematics.[76] Bacon truly sought the marriage of the rational and experimental faculties.[77]

We may say that just as Bacon was really opposed not to the understanding as such, but to the naked, unaided, unmethodized, uncritical and hasty intellect, so Descartes was not inimical to the senses, but only to the naked senses—naive, hazardous, unexamined.

It seems clear, then, that Descartes' method, in its early stages, envisioned both deduction and experimentation; that at that period Descartes conceived of knowing as involving both sense and intuition; that, in fact, like Bacon, he construed knowing as a single, uninterrupted and interdependent process, passing from sense to intellect and back to sense and again to intellect.

Furthermore, Milhaud and Lalande could have argued their case on still another ground, although one which at first sight might seem paradoxical. Descartes in the *Rules* could employ the auxiliaries of sense and of imagination because of the very reason that at that stage of his development *he did not doubt the intrinsic finality of intuition.* The method of the doubt and demon came later. The very scaling of the ladder from sense to intuition was possible because that process was in itself an implicit employment of and trust in intuition. This is suggested by Descartes himself when in Rule VIII he argues that once in one's lifetime one should make an exhaustive analysis of the various capacities of the soul to see how and to what extent they can function in the acquisition of knowledge. He there indicates that such an analysis involves the employment of intuition upon the immediately observable data of consciousness. There is no intrinsic *denial* of sense in the employment of intuition, and the knowledge obtained by intuition must be attributed to the real world that is the object of sense.

On the other hand, the Descartes of the *Meditations* is no longer the Descartes of the *Rules.* In the *Meditations*, Descartes, for reasons which we shall consider presently, introduces his method of antecedent doubt and thereby does take an attitude of sweeping skepticism towards sense, towards imagination, and even towards the ultimate validity of intuition itself.

(*b*) *Malebranche's Mitigated Doubt.* Malebranche, we must note carefully and at once, in his own "search after truth," is never *radically* skeptical toward sense and certainly not toward the ultimate validity of intuition. It is notable, in view of the Cartesian origins of his philosophy, that he nowhere employs Descartes' device of the universal doubt in order to provide a more ultimate grounding of intuition than intuition itself. The demon he labels an extravagant supposition, and even that does not infect or jeopardize the domain of immediately perceived mathematical truths.[78] The existence of the real world, furthermore, he does not question.[79] For him, as for Spinoza [80] and Bacon,[81] the process of knowledge is not from darkness to light, from absolute skepticism to certainty, but a progress from the less clear to the more clear, from the obscure to the perspicuous.[82] He would agree with Descartes that there is need for a method to discover the truth, but, like Spinoza, he would remind Descartes of his own assertions in Rule VIII, that there is no need of a preliminary method to find the

[22]

method and that no preliminary device is necessary to improve the understanding other than the self-corrective use of the understanding itself.[83] Had not Descartes, following Bacon, maintained that intuition is not acquired except through practice? Had he not said that through such practice it forges its own instruments? [84]

Malebranche does not actually repeat this observation of Descartes and Bacon; better than that, he puts their sage advice into actual use. That he does this can be readily established by examining the general structure of the *Recherche,* which is divided into six books, on sense, imagination, understanding, will, passions, and finally method. Malebranche is thus following the program laid down by Descartes in Rule VIII, to which I have already referred just above. Descartes had said:

> But let us give the most splendid example of all. If a man proposes to himself the problem of examining all the truths for the knowledge of which human reason suffices, . . . he will, by the rules given above, certainly discover that nothing can be known prior to the understanding, since the knowledge of all things else depends upon this and not conversely. Then, when he has clearly grasped all those things which follow proximately on the knowledge of the naked understanding, he will enumerate among other things whatever instruments of thought we have other than the understanding; and these are only two, viz. imagination and sense. He will therefore devote all his energies to the distinguishing and examining of these three modes of cognition, and seeing that in the strict sense truth and falsity can be a matter of the understanding alone, though often it derives its origin from the other two faculties, he will attend carefully to every source of deception in order that he may be on his guard. He will also enumerate exactly all the ways leading to truth which lie open to us, in order that he may follow the right way.[85]

Descartes thought that in the very process of carrying out this search the essential character of true knowledge of the true method would come to light.[86] And, as I have already noted, such an undertaking implies the confident focussing of the intellect or intuition upon what is introspectively given. Hence it is a process of reflection and observation simultaneously. Through such self-examination, carried out in the light of truth, and without recourse to the doubt that he was later to introduce, the early Descartes thought the mind could determine to what extent its various capacities—understanding, imagination, sense —are reliable, as well as the causes that might lead them astray.

This is the procedure that Malebranche actually follows. Trusting his understanding, he uses it to detect the causes and the kinds of error to which mind is subject in sense, in imagination, and in understanding. The analysis is itself based on the fundamental presumption that reason or intellect, although weak, is nevertheless inherently sound and efficient, i.e., that it needs no artificial, violent means or external sign like the universal doubt to insure itself. All that it needs is to become, so to speak, conscious of itself, to become clearly aware of its own nature, structure and procedure. What mind has to do is to know itself—as Malebranche says, know itself in its entirety—in relation to body and in relation to God.[87] Therefore the *Recherche de la vérité* is not a quest for means by which we can know that we know or how we know. Before we know that we know, we must first know, as is likewise the case for Spinoza.[88] For this reason, Malebranche's discussion of method properly comes at the end rather than at the beginning of his "search," although for us, whose task it is to understand Malebranche, our discussion of Malebranche's method properly comes at the start of our work. Hence it becomes clear that *method for Malebranche is simply a product, or rather a reflection or mirror, of a complete, orderly system of knowledge,* just as it is for Spinoza. The very rules that Malebranche offers as helps—*secours*—for improving the perspicacity and penetration of the mind, he regards as themselves founded upon and revealing the nature of the mind.[89] Since the early Descartes had not yet questioned or doubted intuition, had described this act of intuition as the undoubting conception of an unclouded and attentive mind,[90] and had not yet completely renounced the senses, the overall structure of Malebranche's *Recherche* indicates an affiliation in these respects with the early Descartes.

Recherche
criticizes,
but does not
deny, both
sense and
intellect (as
for Bacon).

And, because the early Descartes is not in any significant disagreement with Bacon, it is no paradox that the *Recherche* also exhibits a direct allegiance to Bacon, one that is equally as striking as the affiliation with Descartes. In the opening paragraph of his book on method, Malebranche tells us what he thinks he has accomplished in the preceding books:

> On a vu, dans les livres précédents, que l'esprit de l'homme est extrêmement sujet à l'erreur; que les illusions de ses sens (Livre I); les visions de son imagination (Livre II) et les abstractions de son esprit (Livre III) le trompent à chaque moment; que les inclinations de sa volonté (Livre IV) et les passions de son coeur (Livre V) lui cachent presque toujours la vérité, et ne la lui laissent paraître que lorsqu'elle est teinte de ces fausses couleurs qui flattent la concupiscence. En un mot, l'on a reconnu en partie les erreurs de l'esprit et les causes de ses erreurs; il est temps présentement de montrer les chemins qui conduisent à la connaisance de la vérité, et de donner à l'esprit toute la force et toute l'adresse que l'on pourra pour marcher dans ces chemins sans se fatiguer inutilement et sans s'égarer.[91]

The Baconian flavor of this passage is unmistakeable. Just as Bacon devoted the first part of the *Novum Organum* to eradicate false idols and to explain their causes, and thus to prepare his readers for his positive inductive method, so Malebranche first undertook to purge the mind prior to offering the positive route to truth. This he affirmed to Foucher. To pursue the truth, he wrote, two things are necessary: the removal of prejudices and of common errors, and secondly a good method.[92]

The very manner in which Malebranche loyally comes to Descartes' defence for employing the doubt in the *Meditations* and his own appraisal of the value of such a doubt, in fact, reveal how much more moderate and Baconian is Malebranche's own antecedent skepticism than is that of Descartes: "Savoir douter par esprit et par raison n'est pas si peu de chose qu'on le pense," he tells us in the conclusion to his first book on sense; "car, il faut le dire ici, il y a bien de la différence entre douter et douter." The remainder of this passage is eloquent and bears repetition:

> On doute par emportement et par brutalité, par aveuglement et par malice; et enfin par fantaisie, et parce que l'on veut douter. Mais on doute aussi par prudence et par défiance, par sagesse et par pénétration d'esprit. Les académiciens et les athées doutent de la première sorte, les vrais philosophes doutent de la seconde: le premier doute est un doute de ténèbres, qui ne conduit point à la lumière, mais qui en éloigne toujours; le second doute naît de la lumière, et il aide en quelque façon à la produire à son tour.[93]

(*c*) *Truth Immanent within Experience.* Now Bacon's purgation, as I said, was intended to "humiliate" both sense and intellect, but it was not Bacon's purpose to advocate pyrrhonism or to condemn or renounce either faculty in favor of the other. On the contrary, his method presupposed the "true and lawful marriage between the empirical and the rational faculty,"[94] a marriage, as we saw, furthermore, in which Bacon assigned an honorable role to mathematics. It was this goal and method of Bacon, as well as his program, which, it will be recalled, were adopted by the early Descartes.

What of Malebranche? The design of his last book on method, he tells us, is to seek to afford the mind every perfection that it can naturally acquire. The book will do this: ". . . en lui fournissant les secours nécessaires pour devenir plus attentif et plus étendu, et en lui prescrivant les règles qu'il faut observer, dans la recherche de la vérité, pour ne se tromper jamais, et pour apprendre avec le temps tout ce que l'on peut savoir."[95] What are these aids for increasing the attention and scope of the mind? We observed that Descartes said in the twelfth Rule that while knowledge properly speaking belongs to the understanding, yet every expedient should be used in the search

Malebranche's rules and method.

[25]

for truth. It was for this reason that Descartes advised the utilization of sense, imagination, memory. Similarly, Malebranche advises that *every capacity of mind* be employed. Despite the fact that the soul is so often led astray by turbulent passions, fluctuating sensations and fanciful excesses of the imagination, nevertheless, since the soul cannot exist without them, one should make a virtue of necessity and with adroit skill and proper circumspection put them to good advantage.[96] Passions are useful as a stimulus, to goad and sustain the mind in the pursuit of truth. But sense and imagination are useful, not only in awakening attention, but for purposes of comprehension. Sense and imagination express the truth by embodying it in a palpable way. For this reason geometers express proportions among magnitudes by sensible lines. By tracing the lines on paper, they, so to speak, trace in the mind the corresponding ideas. In this manner, they not only conceive the truth, but feel it. This is the method for teaching children difficult abstract truths: in looking at sensible objects their eyes behold not only colors, tablets, images, but their minds also behold the abstract ideas that correspond to the sensible things.[97]

We see that Malebranche is here adhering closely to Descartes and Bacon. The senses embody the truth and are thus useful in knowledge. At the same time it is equally true to say that whatever truth there is to be found in sensible things, discovery and comprehension are the work of intuition alone.

These statements are, however, still not sufficient to show that Malebranche's positive conception of method involved the role of sense to the extent that Bacon advocated. Moreover, the further aids that Malebranche offers for increasing the attention and the penetration of the mind are to be found in mathematics—in geometry, arithmetic, algebra, the differential calculus. These, he says, constitute the true logic and method, especially algebra.[98] In the light of this statement, how can we say that Malebranche's method has more than a superficial relation to Bacon's insistence on experimentation?

Yet we noted that while Descartes' method was inspired by mathematics, while he held that mathematics was the prototype of certainty, while he used a great many mathematical examples to illustrate his conception of truth, and while his *Geometry* was the fruit of his method, nevertheless Descartes' method itself went beyond mathematics for it was universal in scope, and it included experimentation. We find this very situation in Malebranche. We have already seen that truth for Malebranche is a system of intelligible relations, either between ideas, between ideas and things, or among things. The former alone constitute the sphere of mathematics. These relations are eternal, immutable, and, as such, the inviolable rule and measure of all other sciences. For Malebranche, then, as for Descartes, mathematics serves

Malebranche's rules and method, like Descartes', universal in scope.

as the very model and ideal of certainty, for here only intuition and deduction are at play. But mathematics is not the whole domain of science, nor does the procedure of mathematics alone constitute scientific method. Were his aim, to improve the capacity of the mind, carried to its ultimate perfection, Malebranche writes, the result would be a "universal science"—"car on tâche par ce traité de rendre les esprits capables de former des jugements véritables et certains sur toutes les questions qui leur seront proportionées. . . . La véritable science," he continues, "qui seule peut rendre à l'esprit de l'homme la perfection dont il est maintenant capable, consiste dans une certaine capacité de juger solidement de toutes les choses qui lui sont proportionées." [99] Immediately following these declarations, Malebranche enunciates Descartes' rule for evidence as the primary and fundamental one and the one upon which Malebranche's other six are based.

Obviously, then, like Descartes, Malebranche conceives these rules to be universal in scope, for he is laying the foundations of a universal science. The rules are to be adequate for and adaptable to all the sciences. But how? Must we conclude, by reducing all the sciences to mathematics or to an *a priori* deductive system? Not at all. To understand why not, it is necessary to examine the reasons which Malebranche adduces for studying mathematics.

In extolling mathematics and in calling it the true logic and method, Malebranche means simply that it is the supreme example or model of certainty and evidence. If we wish to know what it means to have knowledge that is exact and rigorous, we ought to turn to mathematics as a standard or ideal. If we wish to discipline the mind to acquire the habit of seeking certainty, then too we ought to turn to mathematics. Malebranche's goal is to lay the foundations of a universal science, to perfect the mind so that it can pass sure and swift judgements on all things. To achieve this result, we should *begin* with the study of mathematics.[100] And why should we so begin? For three reasons. Mathematical notions are:

Value of mathematics: Model of certainty.

1. *Evident.* Ideas of number and extension are the most clear and evident of all ideas. (If, in order to avoid error, we find it necessary to conserve every shred of evidence, then the improvement of the mind should commence with the exact sciences, rather than with physics, ethics, mechanics or chemistry.)
2. *Exact.* Our mathematical ideas, especially those of arithmetic, are our most distinct and exact ideas. (Arithmetic and geometry engender a desire for precision in knowing relationships among things. The mind thence acquires an exactitude lacking to those who remain content with conjectures; and the other sciences are replete with conjectures.)
3. *Standards.* The third and principal reason for studying and for

beginning with mathematics is that its ideas are "les règles immuables et les mesures communes de toutes les autres choses que nous connaissons et que nous pouvons connaître." (The perfect knowledge of the relations of numbers and of figures— or, above all, the art of making the comparisons that are necessary for knowing relations—yields "une espèce de science universelle." Here we have a means for achieving with evidence and certitude whatever is within the normal limits of the mind. Whoever lacks this art, no matter how clear his ideas may be, cannot discover with any certainty relations of more than only a very small degree of complexity.) [101]

Note that not one of these reasons for extolling mathematics makes any claim for the *exclusive* employment of intuition or of deduction, or for the identification of method with these processes. Physics, mechanics, chemistry, involving the senses, are defective, but, for all that, Malebranche does not renounce the senses altogether. In fact, even though the improvement of the mind demands that we begin with mathematics, nevertheless, Malebranche hastens to add, it is actually *dangerous* to pursue these sciences for too long. We should really scorn and neglect them for the more useful sciences of ethics and physics! [102]

And why is mathematics so great a source of danger? We know that Bacon went so far as to scorn certain uses of mathematics. In fact, this is often alleged to be his major fault. Yet the unqualified charge that he "scorned" mathematics is a gross injustice, as we have noted and as Lalande has shown.[103] Bacon opposed mathematics only in so far as mathematics might be employed to impose upon and to anticipate nature. What of Malebranche? Why does he counsel any disparagement of mathematics?

In the course of his discussion of the utility of geometry, which he describes as a *kind* of universal science, because all quantitative relations are expressible by lines, Malebranche bluntly warns that this very science, precisely on account of its exactitude, can be the source of many errors. So preoccupied do we become with its evident demonstrations, that: ". . . nous ne considérons pas assez la nature." Malebranche continues:

> C'est principalement pour cette raison que toutes les machines qu'on invente ne réussissent pas, que toutes les compositions de musique où les proportions des consonnances sont le mieux observées ne sont pas les plus agréables, et que les supputations les plus exactes dans l'astronomie ne prédisent quelquefois pas mieux la grandeur et le temps des éclipses. *La nature n'est point abstraite* . . .[104]

This is an extraordinary statement, the testament of a genuine empiricist. Granted that geometry in itself is an incontestable science and useful to express the quantitative order in reality; nevertheless, we must beware lest we make a false application of this science, lest we become reductionists who interpret nature as nothing but a mathematical order.

This same attitude concerning the concrete character of reality is again manifest in Malebranche's stubborn, and frequently iterated, distinction between necessary and contingent truths. Relations among essences or ideas are for him eternal and immutable. These comprise the sphere of pure mathematics. But relationships between essences and existence or among existents are contingent, and these require the senses in order to be discovered.[105] William James said that the perceptual order contains the conceptual order but much more besides. So for Malebranche, to the extent that nature is mathematical, geometry, arithmetic and algebra constitute the true logic and method, and are a *sort* of universal science—"une espèce de science universelle." But in so far as nature is not abstract, but concrete, the purely *a priori* conceptual procedure of mathematics is not sufficient. For example, there are many truths in metaphysics, in ethics, and in physics which can be known with certainty and yet are not representable by geometric figures.[106] Again, in astronomy one assumes that the planets describe perfectly regular circles and ellipses, which is not at all true. The supposition is useful for reasoning purposes, but one must ever bear in mind that it is no more than an approximation or supposition.[107] Similarly, in mechanics one supposes that the wheels and levers are perfectly hard, are similar to lines and to circles, are without weight and without friction; or rather one does not take fully into account their weight, friction, mass, or the relationship of these to one another. One does not consider that hardness and magnitude increase weight, that weight increases friction, that friction may diminish the strength of the machine, or wear it down, or break it. Comparing mechanics with abstract mathematics, then, one fails to realize that what may succeed on a small scale may fail completely on a large scale.[108]

Because nature is not abstract, Malebranche, after telling us that the physicist need not be concerned with the existence of bodies, inasmuch as his province includes no more than the axioms of geometry and the distinct ideas of extension, figure and motion, nevertheless immediately issues this warning: We must take care that ". . . les raisonnements que nous faisons sur les propriétés des choses s'accordent avec les sentiments que nous en avons, c'est-à-dire que ce que nous pensons s'accorde parfaitement avec l'expérience, parce que nous tâchons dans la physique de découvrir l'ordre et la liason des effets avec leurs causes . . ."[109] Sense and experiment, then, play an indispensable part in Malebranche's conception of scientific method.[110]

For still further corroboration of this view concerning Malebranche,

Physics must conform to experience.

let us take a glance at the manner in which he treats his rules for the pursuit of truth. The primary, most general, and overriding rule is a combination of Descartes' first and third rules of the *Discourse*. Since we are never to give complete consent, except to propositions that are so evident that we cannot refuse it without feeling internal pain, the fundamental rule is this:

> We must reason only about those things of which we have clear ideas; and hence we must always begin with the simplest and easiest things, and attend to them at length before undertaking the search for the more complex and the more difficult.[111]

After this general prescription, Malebranche offers six subordinate rules, the first two of which are of special interest. The first is this:

> One must conceive very distinctly the state of the question to be resolved, and have sufficiently distinct ideas of its terms, in order to be able to compare them, and in order thus to recognize the relations between them that one is looking for.[112]

But when relations among things cannot be apprehended by an immediate comparison of terms, then this second rule is to be observed:

> It is necessary to discover, by some effort of mind, one or several middle ideas (*idées moyennes*) which can serve as a common measure by means of which to recognize the relations which obtain between them.[113]

Malebranche's commentary and discussion of these two rules are most illuminating for showing his allegiance to Bacon. With regard to the first rule, Malebranche cites, as illustrative examples, problems in riddle solving. To solve riddles, the mind must sometimes conscientiously demand the elimination of ambiguities and irrelevant detail; but sometimes it must do much more—search for additional peculiar conditions that might satisfy the requirements of the problem. Take this fantastic example: how could you render a man immobilized by putting his little finger in his ear? The solution of this riddle appears at first sight to be impossible, for some relevant condition has been omitted. The mind must therefore stubbornly, repeatedly and persistently look for this neglected condition that would, if expressed, remove the difficulty. In the present case, although the humor is outrageous the answer is significant—the condition is that the man have his arm about a marble column or iron post. This example and others like it, Malebranche admits, are foolish and trivial. Nevertheless, he writes that they are not too different from natural questions, for natural effects are also, by their very nature, surrounded by obscurities and shadows, and it is necessary to dissipate these shadows *by the attention of the mind* and *by experiments* which are *species of demands* ("par l'attention de l'esprit et par des expériences qui sont des espèces de demandes") that one makes to the author of nature.[114]

This statement visibly proves all that I have been saying. First, it shows that Malebranche, like Descartes, conceives his rules to be universal in scope, and adequate for all the sciences. It establishes, secondly, the fact that his view of scientific method is broad enough to include experimentation. In ferreting out nature's secrets, both the attentive mind and experimental data are required. Thirdly, it shows that Malebranche has a very clear view concerning the role and function of experiments. An experiment is a demand—but a demand for what? Truth, be it remembered, is a relationship of equality or inequality. The function of experiment is to find the laws or causes of apparently discrete and discrepant facts. These laws are hidden from the naked senses. Hence, to uncover them, both attentive discrimination and experimentation are required, for experiments are a form of judicious interrogation, species of demands.

This very conception of the nature and role of experiments is obviously a reflection of Bacon's influence. The latter believed that nature had to be constantly goaded, vexed, hunted down in order to yield her hidden causes: "The secrets of nature," Bacon declared, "reveal themselves more readily under the vexations of art than when they go their own way." [115] By "vexations of art" Bacon meant experiments.[116] Experiments, furthermore, are not, according to Bacon, to be conducted in haphazard fashion, but instead with meticulous care and investigation, for "a faculty of wise interrogating is half a knowledge." Bacon quotes with approval Plato's remark, "Whosoever seeketh, knoweth that which he seeketh for in a general notion; else how shall he know it when he hath found it?" [117] These declarations ought surely to silence those carping critics who assume that Bacon intended the scientist to collect random data or to carry out research without any purpose or controlling idea. Such undirected experimenters Bacon compared to ants.[118] He sought experiments that were "fit and apposite." [119] He was not opposed to the use of reason, but to its abuse. He rejected only such reasoners who like spiders make cobwebs out of their own substance.[120] What he demanded is, in his own words, a ". . . closer and purer league between these two faculties, the experimental and the rational . . ." [121] And such cooperation is precisely what Malebranche is asking for in investigating the riddles of nature. What is required to dissipate nature's shadows, for Malebranche, are both attention of the mind and experiments.

In the eighth chapter of the second part of the book on imagination, Malebranche shows clearly his kinship with this priest of the senses and with his inductive method. Like Bacon, he affirms that "les expériences visibles et sensibles prouvent certainement beaucoup plus que les raisonnements des hommes." He has nothing but praise for "la philosophie expérimentale" and its practitioners. At the same time he calls them to task, and finds six abuses in their procedure, all of which findings are distinctively Baconian. Malebranche's very mention of these flaws in *defective* experimental work reveals his concern for *valid* experimentation. The six abuses are:

1. Conducting experiments haphazardly, rather than directing them by the light of reason.
2. Preoccupation with more extraordinary and curious phenomena to the neglect of the more commonplace.
3. Pursuing experiments which promise practical gain, at the expense of those which would provide illumination alone.
4. Failing to observe with precision special circumstances. For example, the word "wine" is highly ambiguous; an experimenter who began experiments on "wine" without specifying varieties would be likely to overlook important considerations.
5. Inferring too much from a single instance. Almost always, on the contrary, it is many experiments that are required in order to draw a single conclusion. A single experiment admits of a variety of conclusions, in most instances.
6. Failing to rise above particular effects as these actually occur in nature. Most physicists, Malebranche observes, and chemists, consider only specific natural effects; they never ascend to first notions of the things which compose bodies. Nevertheless, it is indubitable that one cannot be clearly and distinctly acquainted with the particular things of physics, if one does not solidly possess what is more general and if one fails to raise oneself even to metaphysics.[122]

Notice the use of the word, metaphysics, and Malebranche's assertion that one should *ascend* or *rise* to first notions and to metaphysics. Would it be extravagant to find in this Bacon's conception of the sciences as a pyramid, in which metaphysics as the science of Forms comes after physics which is the genetic science of latent efficient causes?

Malebranche's attitude toward experimentation is even more clearly brought forth in his discussion of the second rule, quoted in full above,[123] which speaks of "idées moyennes." Church opposes Toesca's interpretation of this rule. Toesca considers it to be derivative from Descartes' second rule, the rule of analysis. Church, on the contrary, finds this difficult to accept, because Descartes does not there speak of "mediating ideas." [124] It is possible to show that both these authors are right and both wrong. Descartes, as Church correctly observes, does not speak of "middle ideas" in the *Discourse;* on the other hand, he does, however, voice Bacon's notion of Middle Principles in his

Rule V. Hence Toesca is not refuted by the reference to "mediating ideas." Malebranche's second rule regarding the need for "middle ideas" is indeed derivative from Descartes' conception of analysis, provided that, with Milhaud, we interpret analysis in a broad sense.

That Malebranche's "middle ideas" reflect Bacon's Middle Principles, on the other hand, is also very clear from Malebranche's exposition of this rule and from the examples he offers. As his first example to illustrate the need for Middle Ideas in the resolution of complex ideas, Malebranche analyzes the problems of the attraction and repulsion of two magnets. What can be the cause of such magnetic attraction? How can the two magnets move each other without direct contact? To solve this problem, one must have recourse to no hidden or occult quality, form, entity, nor even to an intelligence; for the problem concerns the natural cause of motion in the magnets and that is certainly another body. Now it is a law of nature that bodies move one another only by local contact. Motion by impulsion is clearly conceivable and effectively established by experience. But neither reason nor experience can demonstrate clearly motion by attraction. Therefore, magnetically engendered motion ought to be explained by means of some unperceived particles. It is not enough to trust the naked senses, for they will impose upon reason. We remember too that the wind is also not visibly perceived. Hence it will not be difficult to maintain this very clear and intelligible notion of imperceptible particles as an explanatory principle of magnetic motion. One must cling to this principle and examine with care all the effects of magnets to discover how they can endlessly emit particles without becoming diminished. This latter difficulty can be solved by experiments, ". . . car les expériences que l'on fera découvriront que ces petits corps, qui sortent par un côté, rentrent incontinent par l'autre." Experiments will thus serve to explain all the difficulties that may be made against this resolution of the question.[125]

Malebranche is aware that this explanation by means of imperceptible particles and the principle of impulsion upon which it is based may not be the most adequate account. However, what is important in this case is his refusal to fly to some soaring or vague generalization. He insists on a limited principle or Middle Principle, in this case, imperceptible particles, and upon a general law well attested by experience.

Malebranche's second example is even more significant. Suppose the problem is to find the natural and mechanical cause for the movement of our limbs. The first step, in accordance with the first rule, is to analyze these motions into various kinds, such as voluntary, natural and convulsive. Let us attend to voluntary motion, and, for further simplification, to motion of the arm. To decide what is the cause of motion in the arm, writes Malebranche, I inform myself of its composition through some book of anatomy or rather I have a skillful anatomist dissect the arm, so that I can have a direct and sensible view of its fibers and tendons. Then I continuously put questions to the anatomist, questions so designed that they might eventually arouse in my mind the means wherewith to solve the problem.

Since anatomical observation shows that the movement depends on the contraction (*accourcissement*) of the muscles, the first hypothesis that suggests itself is that this motion arises from the fermentation of animal spirits within the muscles. The motion seems analogous to that of cannon powder or to the combination of liquids filled with alkaline salts and mixed with acids. Yet this hypothesis is to be rejected, for it is based on too hasty an analogy. Furthermore, fermentation is not a case of voluntary motion. Thus, it is evident that the present question is really analogous to the following problem in mechanics: to find by pneumatic machines the way to overcome a force of 100 pounds by another small force, the application of which is voluntary.

This problem can now be easily resolved and demonstrated. Malebranche proposes that we inflate a balloon half way, rest a very heavy rock or a man upon it, and then continue to breathe into it. The balloon will raise the heavy object aloft. He concludes that the action of the animal spirits in the muscles is similar to that which causes the inflation of the balloon. This explanation, affirms Malebranche, is not to be taken as complete and perfect, for there may be many other contributing causes.[126] It is, however, an adequate solution, and is offered as an example of a Middle Idea.[127]

Let us carefully note Malebranche's procedure. He begins with meticulous anatomical observation. He rejects hasty comparison. He has the idea, however, of turning to mechanics. And when he does, he offers a limited principle which he then corroborates by concrete observation.

We need not follow Malebranche's further attempts to explain convulsive and natural motions. His procedure is analogous to the previous case. What is important and extremely illuminating, however, are the general final remarks. One must not, he warns, resolve particular questions by ascending immediately to first or ultimate causes, for this is not the most correct or the shortest method of philosophizing. There are two sorts of problems. One type is concerned with the discovery of the general nature and properties of things. The second sort seeks to determine whether a given thing has a certain property or what may be the cause of a given property. Problems of the first sort, being very general, Malebranche tells us, must be resolved by considering things with respect to their origin, and by always conceiving them as being engendered by the simplest and most natural means. In problems of

Malebranche's conclusions concerning Middle Ideas.

the second type, the road to follow is that of supposition such as is used by geometers. To determine whether an object has a given property or a given cause, assume that it does and then see whether the supposition leads to any manifest absurdities or to veritable results.[128]

Suppose, for example, that a man wants to discover the nature of a chicken. What procedure shall he follow?

> . . . pour cela il ouvre tous les jours des oeufs qu'il a mis couver; il y remarque une vésicule qui renferme l'embryon du poulet et dans cette vésicule un point saillant qu'il découvre en être le coeur, que de là, il part de tous côtés des canaux de sang qui sont les artères, que ce sang retourne vers le coeur par les veines, que le cerveau paraît aussi d'abord, et que les os sont les dernières parties qui se forment. Il se délivre par là de beaucoup d'erreurs, et il tire même de ces observations plusiers conséquences d'un très grand usage pour la connaissance des animaux.[129]

Thus to determine the nature of a chicken, one makes no high-flown abstract suppositions, but follows the Baconian injunction of careful observation to uncover the latent processes and hidden mechanisms. In fact, it is just this sort of biological experimentation that led Malebranche to repudiate as early as 1674 Descartes' conception of the mechanical formation of living embryos in favor of his own doctrine of seminal seeds. Descartes' over-bold hypothesis or conjecture failed because of inadequate experimental observation.[130]

Or suppose again that the problem is to discover the nature of fire in general and of the various fermentations that are the most universal causes for natural effects. Here too the shortest and surest procedure is, as in the previous example, to examine the problem "dans son principe," that is, in a limited manner. Whereas, if one wanted to treat this matter by suppositions in order to ascend thus to the very first causes and even to the laws of nature according to which *all* things are formed, Malebranche writes, one would fall into many false suppositions that would be vain and useless.[131]

To appreciate the significance of these conclusions that Malebranche reached concerning Middle Ideas and to understand better their role in Malebranche's experimental method, I shall turn now to consider how the conception of an experimental hypothesis underwent development from Descartes to Malebranche.

(d) *Nature of an Experimental Hypothesis, for Malebranche.* Descartes, as Lalande maintains, speaks of "hypothesis" in two different senses.[132] First, by hypothesis Descartes means a "supposition," an explanatory principle sufficient to save the phenomena. Such a principle is not necessarily true or false; rather it is the sort of principle that one might utilize at will, that one might call upon as a useful fiction or convention for purposes of analysis. Such a principle saves the

Two senses in which Descartes uses "hypothesis."

phenomena by *conserving* them, that is, by showing how they could follow from the assumed supposition. In this view, a phenomenon is rescued or salvaged by being subsumed under the sheltering cloak of the hypothesis. The fact that it can be known to follow consistently from the hypothesis renders the phenomenon explicable and intelligible. Yet, the hypothesis itself is fundamentally a device, an arbitrary construction, making no claim to objective validity. This is the way in which Descartes uses "hypothesis" in his explanation of the formation of the world, for example. He uses it thus in the *Rules* and in the *Principles*.[133] (One might also draw the conclusion that, since for Descartes physics was but a concrete geometry, then mathematics itself was no more than an indifferent convenient construction that might or might not apply to a real world. Descartes did not draw this conclusion. But the threat to his system was that he *could* have done so, upon this usage of "hypothesis.")

But Descartes also uses hypothesis in another sense. When in the *Discourse* he describes the movement of the heart, and when in the *Principles* he maintains that his account of the world has a "moral certainty," then Descartes is no longer speaking of a hypothesis as a convenient, arbitrary indulgence. Here "hypothesis" means a *true cause* or true principle, to be based upon and to be confirmed by real observation and experiment.[134]

Lalande traces the development of the notions of "hypothesis," showing that in the seventeenth century and thereafter the second meaning gradually supplants the first, so that for Boyle and Newton, during the last third of the century, the search for hypotheses means the pursuit of *verae causae*. Thus when Newton rejects hypotheses, he is rejecting them in the first Cartesian sense of a mere *ad hoc* arbitrary explanation. It is interesting that this change of meaning in the notion of hypothesis is inspired in England by Bacon, who sought true Forms, and on the Continent by Pascal and Huygens.

Now, so far as I know, Malebranche nowhere discusses in so many words what a hypothesis is. And he does say that Descartes' physics in its description of the formation of the world is not contrary to scripture—that it is a supposition. As such it is nonetheless a legitimate explanatory supposition, although not entirely true. On the other hand, recall Malebranche's warning that nature is concrete and therefore is not to be imposed upon by abstractions of mathematics. In that discussion on the limitations of geometry, he also points out that the suppositions of physics cannot be supplied by mathematics. Once the suppositions have been established on the basis of fact, then mathematics is useful for clear reasoning.[135] Moreover, when one reads his strictures against Aristotle's *Physics* as well as against Cartesian phys-

Malebranche seeks verae causae.

ics, it seems fairly clear that what Malebranche wants are not mere arbitrary convenient explanations in physics, but true causes.

If so, his opposition to Descartes' epistemology and metaphysics will become of foremost importance. Descartes' notion of hypothesis as free supposition fits well with Descartes' doctrine of innate ideas and of arbitrary created truths. The human mind makes or invents its own hypotheses, as God does, and their truth is guaranteed by their own inner clarity and consistency. However, since hypotheses in this sense have no objective validity, there can be no guarantee that human thought in metaphysics or in any other sphere corresponds to the order of reality as made by God. There can be, furthermore, as many systems as there are minds, with their own powers to construct hypotheses. Truth then becomes either an empty formal system of abstractions, divorced from concrete reality, or else a pragmatic convention. This is the danger that is latent in Descartes.

But if, on the other hand, hypothesis is a search for true causes, this demands a unity of mind and a subordination of minds to reality, together with a unity of truth. Now Malebranche was acquainted with many scientists who, like Newton, reject the notion that hypothesis is fanciful construction. While, for all I know, Malebranche just possibly may never have read Bacon in the original, despite his numerous direct references to Bacon, this is unimportant. He did know the experimental physicist Rohault whose work he recommends. And Rohault's conception of an experimental hypothesis is very much along the lines of Bacon's. For Rohault a hypothesis is an intelligible principle engendered by numerous and meticulous observations; and when these predicted novel results are realized, then the hypothesis, the supposition, is not merely probable, but is very nearly certain.[136] And then, of course, Malebranche was intimately acquainted with the works of Huygens. In 1666 Huygens was asked by Colbert to draw up a program for the Academy of Sciences then projected. He replied: "La principale occupation de cette assemblée et la plus utile doit être, à mon avis, de travailler à l'histoire naturelle à peu près suivant le dessein de Verulamius." Only by means of such a Baconian natural history can one acquire knowledge of natural effects, such as weight, heat, magnetic attraction, light, colors, *etc.* Some years later he stated that in physics: "Il est possible toutefois d'y arriver à un degré de vraisemblance qui, bien souvent, ne cède guère à une évidence entière: savoir, lorsque les choses qu'on a démontrées par ces principes supposés, se rapportent parfaitement aux phénomènes que l'expérience a fait remarquer . . ." Above all does this apply when there is a large number of observed phenomena, when one can formulate and predict (*prévoit*) new phenomena that must follow from the employed hypothesis, and when one finds that the prediction actually does take place. Huygens' conclusion was:

> Que si toutes ces preuves de la vraisemblance se rencontrent dans ce que je me suis proposé de traiter, comme il me semble qu'elles font, ce doit être une bien grande confirmation du succès de ma recherche, et il se peut malaisément que les choses ne soient à peu près comme je les représente.[137]

Not only was Malebranche thoroughly acquainted with Rohault and Huygens, but also with Mariotte, Swammerdam, Boyle, Kepler, Galileo, and many others, and most probably with Bacon himself.[138]

It seems most likely, then, that when Malebranche quotes with hearty approval Bacon's remarks regarding the distorting intellect and when he insists so much upon experimentation, he is striking out against the "Cartesian" Descartes. At least it may be true to say that just as Descartes thought that he was simply improving upon Bacon, as I shall observe just below, so Malebranche may have felt that without becoming anti-Cartesian, he was simply redirecting Descartes' effort and thus being a more faithful Cartesian than was Descartes himself. Thus in his physics Malebranche rejected Newton on the grounds that the latter offers a merely arbitrary, fictional, abstract view of nature in his account of the force of attraction.[139] Nevertheless, while Malebranche clung to Descartes' *'tourbillons,'* he made, in the course of time, considerable reformation in that theory to render it more harmonious with empirical facts.

The first serious and impressive modification of Cartesian physics that Malebranche proposed, he offered, significantly, in his final chapter of the book on method; and he offered it in order to illustrate the general utility of the method. His task is to uncover the nature of hardness and of cohesion. The problem is this: Descartes explained solidity by appealing to rest as a distinct force. Malebranche will want to know, does a body at rest really involve, as Descartes claimed, a distinct force or is rest merely the negation or cessation of motion? Malebranche opposes Descartes on this score.[140]

First he argues that the attribution of hardness to bodies is at variance with the principle of clarity and distinctness. Hardness is an occult quality.[141] Secondly the assumption of hardness is contrary to experience. If bodies are hard by their *nature* or *essence*, then elasticity, divisibility and disruption of bodies could not be explained. Hence he rejects the indivisible, hard atom of Lucretius and Cordemoy.

Shall we then say with Descartes [142] that the only conceivable "cement" that unites the particles of matter and thus renders them hard is their own intrinsic rest? But this is no explanation. It is true that the parts of hard bodies remain united when at rest. But, exclaims Male-

The nature of physical hardness and rest—a consequent reform in Cartesian physics.

branche, that is not what I am concerned about—"Je prends le change."
I am not asking why the parts of hard bodies are at rest; what I want
to know is, why do these bodies have the force to remain at rest, and
how is it that they can resist an effort to move them? [143]

Shall we then say that bodies remain hard and at rest so long as
there is insufficient motion to vanquish their rest? But this assumes that
rest is an intrinsic, independent force. Such an assumption, avers Malebranche, is plausible but by no means certain.[144] Moreover, it is actually useless and vain. For according to Descartes, it is the will of
God that constitutes the moving force of bodies. In which case, it is
not necessary to assume a second additional will to explain rest. If a
ball is in motion, it suffices for God to cease willing the agitation and
this cessation will bring the ball to rest. Hence rest has no intrinsic
force that causes it. It is no more than a pure privation.[145]

Let us, on the other hand, assume that rest is a positive force. Here
is a ball at rest. God ceases to will that it be at rest. What will happen?
The answer is, nothing at all. We cannot conceive that it will move
with any specific movement. Movements are capable of more or less,
but not so with rest. Thus rest can be explained as the cessation of
motion, without erecting it into an independent principle.[146]

Now notice: Malebranche is not content to offer this important
revolution of Cartesian physics on merely speculative grounds. No;
immediately after presenting an elaborate theoretical argument, Malebranche at once adds:

> Mais il faut démontrer par des expériences sensibles ce que nous
> venons de prouver par des raisonnements abstraits, afin de voir si
> nos idées s'accordent avec les sensations que nous recevons des
> objects; car il arrive souvent que de tels raisonnements nous
> trompent . . .

Thereupon, Malebranche presents a number of experiments to confirm and check his abstract reasoning that rest has no power to resist motion.[147]

Subsequently he turns to his initial question concerning the nature
of hardness. He suggests that hardness is due to the violent agitation
of an invisible subtle matter that surrounds and compresses bodies.[148]
And once again he defends his speculative hypothesis by experimental
data and by sending the reader to the reports of the experiments of
others.[149]

Incidentally, these improvements in Cartesian physics occur in the
first edition of his work and, as Duhem and Mouy have brilliantly
shown, constitute but the first stage in a number of important subsequent reformulations. In all these changes, Malebranche scrupulously

adhered to the findings of the experimental scientists. Thus in his last work on physics he wrote:

> . . . Je ne fais aucune supposition arbitraire; je prends les corps tels qu'ils sont naturellement. J'examine quelle est la cause de leur dureté et de leur ressort, je tâche par ce moyen de rendre la raison physique des lois du mouvement que l'expérience nous a apprises . . .[150]

Descartes, continues Malebranche, established his laws of motion on the assumption that rest is a positive force and that the quantity of motion is constant. The first of these principles I have always rejected, he says, but until now I have failed to recognize the falsity and equivocation of the second. "Certainement on ne peut en ce cas découvrir la vérité que par l'expérience." The whole matter depends on the arbitrary will of God, and we cannot embrace the ends of the Creator except by a species of revelation such as is afforded by experience. How else shall we know whether He has decided to conserve or not to conserve an absolutely uniform quantity of motion in the universe, except by attending to the many observations of knowledgable and precise scientists studying the impact of bodies![151]

After this array of evidence, can one seriously accept the verdict of Ginsberg [152] or van Biema, of Blondel or Church,[153] or of any of the others who accuse Malebranche either of turning his back upon nature, or of having no interest in the experimental method for its own sake, or of ever seeking to disassociate reason and sense?[154] Is it not rather all too evident that Malebranche's conception of scientific method is sufficiently broad to include experimentation as well as deduction?

Bacon's insistence on experimentation is motivated by his demand for objective standards. In his search for Forms he is opposed equally to the champions of mind above all and to those of sense above all, that is, to subjectivism and to relativism. He demanded true Forms, not vain idols. And by true Forms he meant those that were like the Forms in the divine mind, those that God truly impressed upon nature, those that were immanent in the very things themselves.[155] Hence, to find them, he emphasized the use of the light of nature conjoined with experimental data.

It is to this side of Bacon that Malebranche is deeply indebted. Thus he quotes approvingly the "judicious" remark of Bacon that "all perceptions as well of the senses as of the mind are according to the measure of the individual and not according to the measure of the universe. And the human understanding is like a false mirror, which, receiving rays irregularly, distorts and discolors the nature of things by mingling its own nature with it."[156] Malebranche thus admits that the intellect can be as cloudy and confused as the senses, that the understanding can as easily go astray as sense.[157]

Because of this Baconian influence, strengthened by the authority of Augustine, Malebranche went on to develop some of his most characteristic theses, including his affirmation of eternal, uncreated truths (Chapter II), his metaphysics of Being (Chapter III), and his finalism (Chapter IV). Now these Malebranchian tenets are in complete opposition to Descartes' doctrine of created truths, to his notion of *Causa Sui,* and to his rejection of final causes. Because Malebranchianism is thus in collision with Cartesianism, it is important to examine the reasons for these three doctrines in Descartes and to consider their connection with Descartes' method. This I now do.

III. DESCARTES' EFFORTS TO GUARANTEE TRUTH

I have tried to show not only that Malebranche has been influenced by Descartes, but that the Descartes who most affected him is he who in turn is influenced by Bacon. Malebranche's method, in short, is a combination of deduction and induction. It is this method which he sets out to defend and which dominates his entire philosophy. But in defending it, he is at the very same time opposing another side of Descartes' thought, namely, the metaphysical doctrines in Descartes, which provide the guarantee for truth, but which are themselves the outgrowth of Descartes' excessive rationalism and a-priorism. For is it not true that in the end Descartes abandons experimentation? Lalande and Milhaud recognize that in the *Rules* Descartes already expresses a note of confidence in the natural light that far surpasses any trust that Bacon may have had in the intellect.[158] Already, there in the *Rules,* Descartes treats the natural light as a divine spontaneous vitality that can by itself develop the truth from within its own sources, that is, from divine seeds or germs implanted by God.[159] It is this notion which later Descartes as metaphysician begins to exploit and which allows him to abandon Bacon, or perhaps to feel that he is improving on Bacon.[160]

Descartes' a-prioristic method.

While Bacon said that nature to be commanded must be obeyed, for Descartes, to study nature is to study the order, dispositions and laws that God established and willed in created things. But Descartes' God is the arbitrary creator of all laws and eternal truths. God has implanted innate ideas. God is veracious. Therefore, Descartes came to feel that to study nature it is sufficient to develop those divinely installed and divinely guaranteed ideas. In this way, complete *a priori* knowledge of the universe becomes possible. To know that a true idea agrees with its *ideatum,* it is no longer necessary to seek out the *ideatum.* It is sufficient to turn inwardly towards the seeds divinely implanted and guaranteed within. Hence, as Milhaud concludes, to make contact with nature becomes for Descartes to make contact with God.

According to Milhaud, Descartes' final a-priorism is an emendation upon Bacon, an emendation that follows from Descartes' conception of the role and function of God. Descartes did not at this stage of his development feel it necessary to criticize Bacon, for he did not now, any more than before, feel any conscious opposition. He was simply fulfilling Bacon, by offering what he conceived to be a more adequate metaphysics.[161]

I do not quarrel with Milhaud's interpretation, yet at this point it does seem inadequate. For the further question naturally arises: why did Descartes conceive his ideas to be innate and God to be their arbitrary creator? And the answer is this: Descartes' conception of God is, as M. Gilson shows,[162] itself the result of Descartes' demand to ground his physics on an indubitable base, a demand which Descartes thought could not be fulfilled without eliminating finalism. Bacon said that final causes are like barren virgins dedicated to God, and he sought to remove the teleological method from physics. But yet Bacon did not banish final causes altogether.[163] Moreover, not only does Bacon's own description concerning the Form of heat lack the precision, exactitude and quantitative character of a mathematical law, but its very wording is still reminiscent of a qualitative and purposive universe.[164] Descartes was aware that the admission of sense testimony and experimental evidence carried with it a lurking danger of introducing finalism. Hence Descartes sought a physics more certain than that of the vulgar, a concrete geometry of efficient causes, the guarantee of which required nothing more than his own mind spontaneously developing itself. Consequently, Descartes' abandonment of, or if we will, his improvement upon, Bacon's method, cannot be said to have resulted from purely metaphysical considerations. For the metaphysics of innatism is itself constructed and postulated to justify a rigid certainty in physics.

(a) *Rejection of Final Causes*. The Cartesian conception of the unity of the sciences as a linear progression from idea to idea demanded that metaphysics or the science of first principles precede the science of physics. For the medievals, on the contrary, as for Aristotle, metaphysics was the summit of knowledge rather than the primitive foundation for knowledge. Descartes, building on metaphysics, could achieve certainty only by employing a logic of linear inference from intuitively apprehended premises. It was this complete reliance on deduction that left him no use for final causes.[165]

To Mersenne Descartes wrote regarding his *Meditations*: ". . . Je vous dirai, entre nous, que ces six méditations contiennent tous les

Metaphysics the foundation of physics.

fondements de ma physique. Mais il ne le faut pas dire . . ."[166] In view of the condemnation of Galileo and the execution of Bruno,[167] Descartes was reluctant to admit publicly that his metaphysics was so intimately allied with his physics; nevertheless he sought in his *Meditations* to prepare the minds of his readers in such a way that, without realizing it, they would by the end of the work be wholly receptive to the acceptance of his physics.[168] Descartes' interest in metaphysics, then, was primarily that of the scientist seeking some metaphysical system whose formulation and conclusions could serve as first principles of his science. To say that Descartes was principally a scientist is, however, not to deny his genuine interest in metaphysics or his profound conviction of the service of his metaphysics to religion. For example, writing to Mersenne of having begun a treatise on metaphysics, the principal points of which are to prove the existence of God and of the soul, he describes himself as "enraged" at atheists.[169] Only problems belonging to the sphere of theology proper, that is, founded upon revelation, did Descartes regard beyond the pale of his profession.[170] Nevertheless, it remains true that his concern with the existence and nature of God is oriented toward his physics.[171]

The kind of physics that Descartes sought to establish involved not only the dangerous Copernican principle of the movement of the earth, for which Galileo was condemned, but also Descartes' own very method of clear and distinct ideas of which this was alleged to be a consequence. In his *Principles* Descartes declared that he requires no other conceptions than those of geometry or abstract mathematics for his physics, because by their means all the phenomena of nature may be explained, and of them demonstrations are sure.[172] This is in effect the application to physics in particular of that general mode of procedure, best exemplified by mathematics, which develops from idea to idea as from cause to effect, or what Descartes called the analytical method.[173] For this purpose of achieving an exact mathematical physics, it was imperative for Descartes to discover a metaphysical foundation that would eliminate the pursuit of final causes, because the analytic method by which Descartes achieves certainty is a method of efficient or formal causes.

Physics founded on clear and distinct ideas of extension.

Medieval physics resorted to vitalistic, teleological, qualitative and anthropomorphic concepts to explain the nature of bodies, their variety of movements and positions, and of the construction of the world as a whole. Heavenly bodies move in circles because circularity is a superior form of motion. The universe of which the earth is the center is made for man and man for God as the final end. Descartes wrote to Burmann that such finalistic explanations do not disclose the real nature of any object.[174] Even more than this, teleological methods are not merely barren and sterile to Descartes; they are actually super-

[43]

fluous in Cartesian physics. In Descartes' view, the essence of all bodies is extension; from moment to moment the amount of motion and the extended nature of bodies are constant. Differences among bodies are then only differences of figures and configurations, and these latter are due to motion which is no more than locomotion.

Since the essence of matter is extension, the matter of the heavens and that of the earth are homogeneous; there is no vacuum; there are no atoms; there are no limits to this extended world; and extension is infinitely divisible and a *plenum*. Thus Cartesian physics eliminates substantial forms, eliminates qualitative differences among bodies, and reduces all motion to locomotion. Consequently final causes become superfluous.

As a result of identifying matter with extension, it is necessary to hold that the material world is boundless; and this conclusion permits Descartes to free himself from the geocentric, anthropomorphic, finite, as well as finalistic mentality of the medievals.[175]

To make sure that the properties of any physical phenomenon or of the entire material world would be explained solely in terms of extension and only by means of efficient causes Descartes cautiously maintained in the *Principles*[176] that the world is *indefinite* and that moreover it is presumptuous for man's finite comprehension to seek to grasp the infinite power of God. For similar reasons, he declares in the *Meditations* and *Principles* that it is erroneous for man to attempt to ascertain the ends that God has set himself in the creation of the world;[177] that although, for example, it may be a pious thought as far as morals are concerned, to believe that God has created all things for man's use, such a supposition would be certainly ridiculously inept in questions of physics, both because an indefinite world is hardly compatible with the notion that creation is for man and because such an account fails to explain what the world is like.[178]

The method of final causes in physics was sterile and useless to Descartes, not only because it did not explain the nature of things, but also because it was a method which, being *a posteriori*, was dependent upon conjecture. Although in ethics, wrote Descartes to Gassendi, conjecture is permissible, it is not allowable in physics where everything depends upon the most secure arguments.[179] Therefore, since it is absurd to suppose that any given one of God's purposes rather than any other is openly displayed to us, the method of final causes would endanger the whole fabric of science.[180] Here Descartes condemns finalistic explanation as dangerous, because he assumes that we cannot know God's motives and that this kind of explanation fails to tell us what the world is like.

(b) *Created Truths.* But Descartes' critique of finalism constitutes only the beginning of what Descartes found it necessary to do in order to guarantee truth in physics.[181] Descartes' doctrine of created truths or of divine liberty also bears closely on the problem, for this doctrine carries the consequence that Descartes' warning against the search for final causes is more than a warning against a difficult and uncertain attempt. It is rather a warning against a vain attempt, for created truths in effect render final ends utterly impossible even in metaphysics, and not simply, as we have noted thus far, in physics. Indeed, Gilson goes so far as to claim that Descartes expressly formulated his doctrine of created truths in order to eradicate finalism and that if it has any other advantages, these serve only to reinforce this elimination of final causes.[182]

We have just seen that Descartes' demand for certainty in the sciences led him to formulate a method which proceeds from cause to effect and thus renders finalistic explanation conjectural and sterile. But also we noted that for him all human knowledge is a unity. If Descartes finds final causes to be sterile in physics, the demand for a comprehensive unification of knowledge suggests that he is bound to find them equally vain in his metaphysics, for, although "il ne faut pas le dire," Descartes discovered his metaphysics because he needed a foundation for his physics. Accordingly, at the very source of his physics Descartes established a major metaphysical doctrine, that of created truths, which is in fact incompatible with final causes.

In a letter to Mersenne, as early as 1630, Descartes wrote that he intended to treat several metaphysical questions in his physics—particularly this one: that the mathematical truths which are called eternal have been established by God and depend entirely upon Him.[183] He begs Mersenne not to keep it secret but to proclaim everywhere and upon every possible occasion that God has decreed these mathematical truths just as a king establishes the laws of his country. Here, in his subsequent letters to Mersenne, Mesland, Arnauld, and, in fact, throughout his writings where this doctrine of created truths is expounded, the major reason that Descartes offers for this thesis is that to entertain the opposite theory, to maintain the autonomy of truths and essences, is to blaspheme and violate the power of God; it is to speak of God as of a Jupiter or Saturn and to subject him to the Styx and to the Fates. On the contrary, everything must be subjected to the immense and incomprehensible power of God. If truths, like those of mathematics, are declared to be independent and uncreated, it might suggest that even if God did not exist, they would. But the existence of God is the first and most truly eternal of all truths and the only one upon which the existence of all others depends.[184]

But may we not take "independent" in the mitigated sense? May we not assert ideas to exist *in* God's mind, but make a distinction between God's understanding of these truths and His will or power to create?

Created truths preserve the omnipotence and unicity of God.

To this Descartes gives a categorically negative answer. It is blasphemous to say that truths precede God's knowledge in any way, since in God it is a single thing to know and to will.[185] Even if no temporal, but only a logical, distinction is made between the divine understanding and the divine will, this too would place a restriction on God's liberty and omnipotence. It is a self-contradiction, declares Descartes, to the protagonists of the Sixth Objections, to conceive that the will of God has not been utterly indifferent with respect to what has or may come to pass. Hence, too, it is a self-contradiction to suppose that there are any ideas of truth and goodness in the divine mind, logically prior to their ordination by God's will, for then He would have been impelled to choose one thing rather than another, and this would curtail His freedom.[186] Had there been any predetermined essences of truth and goodness, God would have been compelled and determined to create what was best. On the contrary, God made the world in time, for example, and, therefore, simply because He happened to make it in His way, it is better than if it had been produced from all eternity. And although God willed certain things to be necessary, it by no means can be asserted that He has been necessitated to will them.[187] Consequently, affirms Descartes, no distinction must be allowed between the divine acts, not even "in order, or in nature, or in reasoned relation." [188] It is one thing in God to will, to understand, and to create, without the one preceding the other, *ne quidem ratione*.[189] Because there is no anteriority between the intelligence and the volition of God and therefore no priority of these truths to either the divine will or knowledge, writes Descartes to Mersenne, whether one conceives those truths as possible or as actual, one must affirm that they are such only because God knows them to be such and not that God knows them to be possible or actual because they are such.[190] And again since in God, to know, to will, and to create are unqualifiedly the same, it makes no difference whether we say that God willed, made, disposed, or created the essences and truths.[191] Later, in the *Reply to Objections II*, Descartes declares in a passage pregnant with Spinozistic monism and modern self-positing idealism, that one may consider the whole universe as an "entity formed by the divine thought," [192] because knowing and producing are identical. To Mersenne, as later in the *Reply to Objections VI*, Descartes states that God produced these truths by exactly the same species of causality as He created all other things, namely as the efficient and total cause,[193] for, although mathematical, moral, and metaphysical truths are not physical things, nevertheless God may be called their efficient cause in exactly the same way as a king is the efficient cause of the laws of his kingdom.[194]

When Gassendi in his comments on Descartes' Fifth Meditation asks how is it possible that there be immutable and eternal natures in addition to God, Descartes answers [195] very simply, as if this were hardly an objection, that these immutable natures, such as that of the triangle, are immutable because God has thus decreed them to be. Their immutability is only conditional. And it is useless to ask how God could have brought it about that four times two not be eight, or how He could annul the nature of the triangle.[196] The very fact that these truths are so clear and distinct and utterly comprehensible, whereas the power of God is wholly incomprehensible, shows that they must be inferior to and dependent upon that power.[197]

Incomprehensibility of the infinite.

The fundamental obstacle, according to Descartes, that prevents the mind from acknowledging the dependency of these truths upon the divine omnipotence is that that power, although knowable, is utterly incomprehensible, while these mathematical laws are so very clear and distinct that they appear to be intrinsically necessary and eternal. But, warns Descartes,[198] while it is legitimate to conclude that God has been able to produce whatever we can comprehend, we must not judge anything to be impossible to His power, however, from the fact that it may be incomprehensible to our finite mind. In fact, incomprehensibility is embraced in the formal concept of the infinite; [199] for although we do have a clear and distinct idea of God, by that idea we so to speak touch God and know that He exists, but we do not embrace the divine essence.[200] If these comprehensible truths and essences of things were not created entities, then since what is not a creature must belong to the Creator,[201] we should be compelled to affirm that the finite mind can comprehend the infinite essence of God —a manifest absurdity. "I announce" asserts Descartes categorically to Gassendi, "that it is a manifest contradiction that, when I comprehend anything, that thing should be infinite." [202]

God, thus, is the author of essences or ideas, of mathematical truths, of axioms [203] such as the whole is greater than the part—all of which are innate in the mind, as He is of the existences of the external world. But just as God has been free not to create the world, so has He been free to bring it about that the lines from the center to the circumference of a circle *not* be equal.[204] Admittedly, this is difficult to understand; nevertheless, since it is indubitably clear that nothing which falls under the category of causation can exist independently of God, it is highly irrational to doubt concerning what we do understand because of what we do not understand.[205] If then we attend to the immensity of God, Descartes holds, we shall be compelled to conclude that everything which subsists, every law, all order and every reason of truth and goodness depends upon the indifferent legislation of God.[206]

The Cartesian thesis of created truths, with its premises of the absolute identity of the divine acts, the absence of any predetermined

Conclusions:
Created
truths
eliminate
final causes.

or fixed essences of goodness or truth, and the utterly willful, arbitrary, motiveless, indifferent and incomprehensible liberty characterizing divine omnipotence, is thus a metaphysical position by which, as Gilson has shown, Descartes simultaneously achieves two important results for his physics. On the one hand, this conception of God banishes final causes from metaphysics, for to suppose that God acts for some end, however inscrutable it may be, is to admit some forethought, some idea, or some plan prior to the creative act. But this possibility has been unmistakably ruled out by the emphatic denial of any distinction among the divine attributes.[207] So confident was Descartes that final causes were absurd even in metaphysics that he considered it to be sheer anthropomorphism to conceive, for example, that God made the world for His own glory.[208]

In the second place, this doctrine of created essences and the incomprehensible libertarianism of God allowed Descartes to assert that we must not judge that the material world is finite, that it has

Created truths
require us to
conceive
infinity as
indefinite.

fixed boundaries, or that it contains atoms from the fact that infinite expansionality or infinite divisibility is not clearly comprehended by us. Let us say, then, that the world is *indefinite* and that for all we know it is finite to God.[209] Let us not dispute about the infinite and let us not circumscribe the power of God. A great many things may have been created which are not intended for man's use. Man may not be the monarch of the universe. The earth may not be the center of the world. And because God's power is so incommensurate with human understanding, Descartes can resort to this very principle in his public utterances as a sufficient reason for turning men away from the pursuit of the ends of God to the establishment of a "perfect science" [210] which consists in a knowledge of effects through their causes.[211]

(c) *Causa Sui.* The question remains, however, whether, in this bold, ambitious demand for absolute rigor and certainty, Descartes does not undermine the very goal that he sought. This, we shall see, actually is the opinion of Malebranche. By making mathematics and physics the fruit of his own intellect—however divinely ordained—does he not reduce these sciences either to a fortuitous anthropologism or to the arbitrary status of mere fiction or of pragmatic convention? For if God is the arbitrary creator of truth, then truth loses all objective significance. And if the mind can develop or construct science from within itself, then it is theoretically possible that there can be as many different systems as there are minds. There is no longer any absolute, objective, public reference as immutable standard.

Descartes was not unaware of this problem and of its gravity. Well did he realize that if an arbitrary, indifferent will is the source of truth, then he, Descartes, would have to find some way of curbing such power. Put differently, Descartes realized that he had to find some means of guaranteeing first, that what his mind apprehended as true was true and, second, that it would remain true permanently. Descartes had to guarantee not only the soundness of his intellect but also the continued existence of its structure. He had to show not only that the mind could think truly but that it would always think in the same way or always possess the same innate ideas. Descartes could not possibly say that truth was permanent because God could not alter it, or that the essence of man was to be rational, and therefore capable of knowing the truth. He could not make such statements since his conception of God was one of unlimited power. This, coupled with the Cartesian doctrine of time as pulverized into disconnected instants, made it necessary to find some instrumentality that would preserve the mind with its essences or truths from instant to instant. Thus the validity of the light of nature and the stability of the ideas or natures known required that the power or efficient cause at their origin be veracious and also constant.[212]

To Mersenne Descartes wrote that if anyone should ask whether God, like a king, could alter his decrees, the answer is no, because the divine will cannot change.[213] Gilson maintains that in appealing to an immutable will Descartes is utilizing a scholastic principle without however providing any metaphysical justification for it.[214] *Causa Sui invoked to guarantee truth.* For the medievals, God can not deceive because His intelligence is restricted by fixed truth, because the objects of the divine understanding are unalterable; and God can not vacillate in His volitions or creative acts, not merely because, being 'pure actuality' He is not subject to change, but also because His will and power are guided by a reason whose objects are permanent. Having espoused the doctrine of created truths and the unqualified identity of the divine attributes defined in terms of an arbitrary, indifferent power, to what can Descartes appeal to guarantee the immutability of that power with respect to its decrees? I believe that by the principle of *Causa Sui* Descartes did attempt to provide a justification, and that, indeed, under these circumstances, it is the only metaphysical tool by which he can even attempt to supply a justification. *Causa Sui* is the vehicle that Descartes uses to establish divine veracity, and thus the validity of the human light of nature, and divine immutability, and thus the stability of truth.[215]

To explain the existence of created ideas in the mind, Descartes, even though he denied final causes, could none the less have postulated a creative energy. But the conception of sheer creativity without purpose would afford no guarantee of the veracity or constancy of the ideas which it might create. Such a creativity could be purely volatile and capricious, and if so, defective and irrational beyond even the *The threat that the creative God reduces to the deceiving demon.*

point of creative indifference. Descartes' hyperbole of the evil demon is precisely of such an unprincipled, wayward, and fickle creative energy, that can alter the truth even in the very instant in which the mind seeks to grasp it.[216] Now the only means to avoid the charge of actually having this demon, who is potent enough to be indifferent with respect to what he pronounces to be good and true, but not sufficiently powerful to possess the perfections of veracity and immutability, is to conceive a far more immense power, which cannot fail to own every conceivable perfection or aspect of reality.

Measured against such a conception of towering perfection, mere creativity is not simply unprincipled; it is defective in potency. As a creator it is even evil, for it may not restrain itself from deceiving us on some or all occasions, and its creative potency is subject to a continual ebb and flow. The evil demon as an arbitrary power is evil precisely in so far as he *may* change essences and thus in so far as he *may* make and unmake his decisions. The evil demon does not necessarily have to change or deceive, but the fact that he may is for Descartes a sign that he is not really all powerful; it indicates a lack in self-restraint or a lack of stability or a lack of knowledge. A power stronger than that of the demon would be sufficiently potent to guarantee that what seemed to be true is true and would remain true. Descartes' problem then is to guarantee certainty in the sciences by a Deity more perfect than a mere creative force, without sacrificing His indifference. Having denied final causes, he had only power or efficient causality remaining by which to constitute this Diety. Descartes attempted to achieve greater perfection than that of a mere generative impetus by the device of doubling that power back on itself.

Descartes believed that any being so potent as to be the efficient or formal cause of its own existence was capable of endowing itself with every other perfection, for no perfection seemed to Descartes so great as that of existence.[217] Descartes had only power to which to appeal to explain perfection, but he believed that self-creation was power without limit. A *Causa Sui* was all that Descartes could appeal to in order to satisfy his scientist's demand for certainty, but a *Causa Sui* must have appeared to Descartes as quite sufficient to satisfy this demand. How?

Just as a mere cause or power, like the demon, will not of itself be equivalent to a veracious and immutable God, neither will an uncaused power. Such an uncaused power may expend itself and cease to be; it may be of a limited nature, unable to preserve its effects. Hence, writes Descartes to Caterus and to Arnauld, unless we pursue the principle of causality to its very limit, unless we seek the cause of everything that may exist, including God, we shall never arrive at a

Why an uncaused power is inadequate to insure certainty.

First Cause at all. On the other hand, considering the immense, incomprehensible power which exists in the idea of Him, we at once recognize that this power, by being its own source, requires no assistance to exist or to continue to exist.[218]

Now, one of the most common statements in Descartes, present in his early as well as in his late works, is that any being capable of giving himself existence and of preserving that existence possesses in this capacity a perfection so great that it includes every other perfection.[219] To Descartes it is axiomatic ("the light of nature makes it very clear") that if he were able to create himself he would give himself infinity, that is, infinite understanding, immutability, and omnipotence. Truth for Descartes falls under the category of being; error is non-being.[220] For God to err or to deceive is, to use a Cartesian expression, to tend toward non-being or nothingness.[221] Accordingly, the capacity to deceive, declares Descartes, is by no means a mark of subtlety or power but rather a sign of feebleness and impotence.[222] But a God who gives and maintains His own existence cannot tend towards non-being. Hence He is veracious. This means that when the mind beholds the idea of a triangle, it is indeed beholding a real thing or a truth, not nothing.

Why Descartes held that his God is veracious.

In the second place, such a power that gives itself every predicate of being is self-sufficient. Nothing is lacking to its nature. As it has caused and maintained its existence from all eternity, so from all eternity has it possessed all of being. From all eternity it has been full, complete, perfect. Such a being cannot be subject to limitation. Irresolution, vacillation, cardinal passions and weaknesses of the human will,[223] arising from man's finite nature and incomplete understanding, cannot be ascribed to a power that has conferred upon itself the whole of being, to whom nothing is lacking; and since in God, to know, to will, to create are an identical, unique, simple act, there can be no change in the divine thought or power or volition, and therefore none in His mode of operation, for God's acts are identical with His nature. As He is constant and immutable in Himself by virtue of being His own cause, so will that causal operation be uniform in whatever it may determine to create.[224]

Nevertheless, granted that God's nature is immutable, how does this serve to prove that His laws or essences are also immutable? May He not have decreed from all eternity, and without any change in Himself, the perpetual permutation of essences? It is indisputable that He could, since He could even have made contradictories to exist together. However, *Causa Sui* has guaranteed divine veracity. Now, when we perceive that the angles of a triangle are equal to two right angles, we perceive it as an *immutable* nature or essence. Consequently

Immutable God implies immutable decrees.

it must forever be so. The only condition upon which that truth can cease is for God's will or power to change. But this is impossible. And thus Descartes is able to write to Mersenne: "On vous dira que si Dieu avait établi ces vérités, il les pourrait changer comme un Roi fait ses lois; à quoi il faut répondre que oui, *si sa volonté peut changer*." [225] Thenceforth, Descartes can be sure that his understanding is not a perverted [226] faculty so that whatever he perceives clearly and distinctly in science is indubitable, with a certainty that is more than pragmatic. It is absolute.[227]

Unfortunately, *Causa Sui* as developed by Descartes is an unhappy solution to the problem of guaranteeing the stability and objectivity of truth. For *Causa Sui*, though couched in terms of power, is really not the traditional view of God. It reduces God to an abstract essence that posits existence or entails it as a logical property. How does Descartes' God establish and secure His existence? Through the immensity of His power. This is true; however, for Descartes the divine attributes are absolutely identical and indistinguishable. Not even a distinction of reason is allowable for distinguishing them. Hence the immensity of God's power is not only equivalent to but the same as the intellect. This is why Descartes writes that God is the efficient cause of Himself and yet that in this very efficiency He is also a formal cause.[228] Thus God is an essence that involves or confers existence as a property. It is the eternity and permanency and immutability of the essence that guarantees the permanence of God's existence. Therefore, it is really as an immutable intellectual essence that God preserves the immutable character of all other essences that issue from His creative thought.

With such a view of God, it makes no sense to speak of an indifferent creation or free will or veracity. This Spinoza saw with great clarity. Hence Spinoza not only followed Descartes and renounced finalism, but also went far beyond Descartes to discard the entire traditional framework of creation, of independent existents, and of free will. Descartes, on the contrary, was not prepared to reach Spinoza's conclusions. Descartes wanted a God who would be at once a self-sustaining essence and an indifferent creative will. As an essence, He would guarantee the stability of the will. But as an indifferent will, what God would really be guaranteeing would be the autonomy and self-certifying creative power of Descartes' own finite consciousness. Descartes' God is an intellectual power, but one unrestricted in how it thinks or in what it thinks. Hence He is indifferent, a thought that blindly postulates or decrees truths. The truths do not emanate by any necessity from God's intellectual efficacy. He is not constrained to think that three plus two are five. He merely happens to think

Problems arising from Causa Sui.

that way. Now man is made in the image of God. By his own intellectual powers he too is capable of freely constructing a metaphysics
or physics or analytical geometry such that, once made, it is self justify-
ing by its own internal coherence and consistency. Just as God is not
compelled to determine the truth by fixed essences independent of
His thought, just as God need not look to anything beyond Himself
as a reference to which His thinking must be adequate, so the mind
need not seek for any signs external to itself to guarantee its own
thought processes. He who has a true idea, says Spinoza, knows it,
nor can he doubt the truth of it. A true idea agrees with its *ideatum,*
but the mind is a spiritual automaton that requires no more than its
own inner light to know when it adequately mirrors reality. Thus
speaks Spinoza, and this is what Descartes sought with the doctrine
of created truths, but with this difference: for Spinoza, the mind,
after all, mirrors reality. For Descartes, reality and God must conform
to and mirror his own inventive mind. Indeed, Descartes' doctrine
of created truths needs far more a justification of God's existence than
it needs God to justify the truths.[229]

Such fluid creativity as foundation for truth is precisely what Bacon
anticipated and rejected. He rejected ancient systems of thought as
idols of the theater, as so many wild human inventions, fantastic
plays, far removed from reality. Bacon's goal in science was instead
an objective reality; his Forms were to be the very ones that participated in the Divine Forms. Bacon thus sought a community between
human and divine thought, and to obtain it he was compelled to seek
a synthesis between sense and reason. Far from elevating the intellect
alone as a divine instrument, Bacon saw that sense too was of divine
origin and that both together, being equally fallible, required each
other. "There is a great difference," he wrote, "between the Idols of
the human mind and the Ideas of the divine. That is to say, between
certain empty dogmas, and the true signatures and marks set upon
the works of creation, as they are found in nature." [230] Bacon wanted
the senses to supply the facts and the intellect to uncover therein
the true signatures that shared in the divine Forms. Had Bacon been
alive, says Milhaud, he would have applied all his energies to combat
the intuitive method of Descartes and to show how difficult it is,
without the aid of experiments, to distinguish the divine traces in
Descartes' soul from empty phantoms.[231] Precisely so! But what Bacon
did not live to accomplish, we shall see, was left for Malebranche
to achieve.

Malebranche, in order to justify his deductive-experimental conception of method, was compelled to undo and reconstruct Descartes'
theory of knowledge. This he accomplished, by rejecting Descartes'

innate ideas and created truths, by eliminating every trace of a copy theory from Descartes' form of representative perception, and by adopting natural judgments of sense or natural revelation. In Chapter II, we now consider his reasons for rejecting all theories of ideas which imply that truth is a creature or is innate.

Chapter II

Vision in God

Je crois que tout le monde tombe d'accord que nous n'apercevons point les objets qui sont hors de nous par eux-mêmes. Nous voyons le soleil, les étoiles et une infinité d'objets hors de nous; et il n'est pas vraisemblable que l'âme sorte du corps et qu'elle aille, pour ainsi dire, se promener dans les cieux pour y contempler tous ces objets. Elle ne les voit donc point par eux-mêmes; et l'objet immédiat de notre esprit lorsqu'il voit le soleil, par exemple, n'est pas le soleil, mais quelque chose qui est intimement unie à notre âme, et c'est ce que j'appelle *idée*. Ainsi par ce mot *idée*, je n'entends ici autre chose que ce qui est l'objet immédiat, ou le plus proche de l'esprit quand il aperçoit quelque objet, c'est-à-dire ce qui touche et modifie l'esprit de la perception qu'il a d'un objet.[1]

With this vivid preamble, later claimed to be no more than a bit of literary, ornamental raillery and good humor,[2] Malebranche begins his serious epistemological inquiry into the nature of ideas, which, after the rejection of four alternative hypotheses, culminates in the Vision in God. This investigation occurs in Part II of Book III (on the pure understanding) of the *Recherche*, and the whole discussion occupies no more than nineteen or twenty pages. Such scantiness for so weighty and difficult a topic seems perplexing. What does Malebranche mean by an 'idea'? And what by 'representative'? Is this a copy theory in sense perception, or is it one that is concerned with essences or universals, or is it both? It is therefore no wonder that Church calls Malebranche to task for this dogmatic brevity.[3] Malebranche, however, is not entirely blameworthy.

Nowhere more than in his discussion on ideas is the influence of Augustine apparent, not only in the letter of the doctrine, but especially in the spirit of its presentation. Augustinianism is a philosophy of conversion. As such, it does not lend itself to a linear form of didactic presentation or argumentation. Centering as it does about God, its style is that of digression and diffusion, and its goal is to illumine rather than to establish.[4] So it is with Malebranche's treatment of ideas. He does not begin with definitions or with a precisely formulated vocabulary. Though cast in didactic form, the *Recherche* is really written in the spirit of a dialogue, or even of a soliloquy, wherein, beginning with shadows in the cave, the soul slowly ascends to the light. Again, Malebranche's method of writing is in Descartes' terms analytic, not synthetic. This makes unmerciful demands on the reader. He is expected to meditate, to pass backwards and forwards in a continuous, uninterrupted movement of thought, until the author's vision becomes his own.

In addition, Malebranche's teaching and literary technique is often that of conciliatory persuasion. Unlike Descartes, who arrogantly demands a complete *tabula rasa* for his philosophical enterprise, Malebranche is frequently disposed to start with current or prevailing concepts in order to establish a universe of sympathetic discourse between himself and his reader, preparatory to a gentle conversion.[5] Knowledge, for him, is a process of gradual dialectical refinement. For this reason, even though Malebranche is the advocate of clear and distinct ideas, nevertheless, like Bacon, he hesitates to commence with a rigidly precise or exact vocabulary, lest right off he outrage the sensibility of his listeners.[6] Furthermore, on his own admission, he sometimes hesitates to declare his views directly and openly,[7] for he intensely dislikes to indulge in philosophical dispute or to engage in frontal attack on any given philosopher.[8] Naturally, such a modest attitude necessarily leads him into ambiguities of expression and apparent inconsistencies. But he himself offers the reader the proper rule for understanding him:

> Lorsqu'un auteur semble se contredire, et que l'équité naturelle, ou une raison plus forte nous oblige à l'accorder avec lui-même, il me semble qu'on a une règle infaillible pour découvrir son véritable sentiment. Car il n'y a qu'à observer quand cet auteur parle selon ses lumières, et quand il parle selon l'opinion commune. Lorsqu'un homme parle comme les autres cela ne signifie pas toujours qu'il soit de leur sentiment. Mais lorsqu'il dit positivement le contraire de ce qu'on a coutume de dire, quoiqu'il ne le dise qu'une seule fois, on a raison de juger que c'est son sentiment, pourvu qu'on sache qu'il parle sérieusement, et après y avoir bien pensé.[9]

In beginning with Malebranche's method in Chapter I, I have deliberately gone forward to the light. In the present chapter it will be time to go back into the cave, for Malebranche maintained to Foucher that two things are necessary for the acquisition of truth: a positive method (which we have investigated) and a preliminary purification of the mind to rid it of prejudices.[10] We know that his method was the goal of the *Recherche*, that it was both experimental and intuitive in character, and that the early books of the *Recherche* were considered by Malebranche as containing the preliminary purification designed to prepare for this method. The surprising conclusion that emerges from the chapter on method is that Malebranche is at once a purer rationalist than is Descartes and also is a completely empiricistic philosopher with respect to scientific knowledge of matter of fact. The genius of Descartes, writes Léon Brunschvicg,[11] was to have envisioned "l'idée méthodique de l'intellectualisation de la quantité mathématique." This speculative notion gave birth both to Spinoza's *Ethics* and to Malebranche's *Recherche de la vérité*. But the sharp dividing line between Spinoza and Malebranche lies in the latter's recognizing an impassable barrier between the domain of mathematics, which is one of pure intelligibility, and the domain of physics, which is concrete and contingent. Malebranche and Huygens freed themselves from the Cartesian dogmatism that demanded perfect intelligibility. For Malebranche, in Brunschvicg's view:

> . . . la forme mathématique est un schème dont l'abstraction et la simplicité fournissent le moyen d'aborder la complexité des choses; mais ces caractères mêmes ne doivent pas nous faire illusion. Il ne s'agit nullement de subordonner la connaissance du contenu à la perfection esthétique ou rationelle du schème. Au contraire, nous sommes avertis, par cette perfection même, qu'il ne saurait s'appliquer avec exactitude à la réalité conrète. C'est à l'expérience qu'il appartient de mesurer l'écart entre ce qui se déduit par le calcul et ce qui se passe dans la nature.[12]

Now, to achieve this twofold demand of absolute rationalism and completely contingent empiricism, Malebranche will, on the one hand, find it necessary to purge reason of every last trace of imagery and of contingency. To this end he will assert intelligible ideas to be uncreated, immutable, real universals. But this very purification of intelligible ideas will, on the other hand, permit him to affirm radical contingency on the perceptual and existential level. He will sharply divide knowledge of existence from knowledge of universals, thus satisfying the empirical and experimental moment of his thought with a doctrine of sense perception and satisfying the intuitive and rational moment of his thought with a doctrine of universals.

Thus neither the extreme rationalism nor the extreme empiricism of his thought may be forgotten if we seek an adequate understanding of his philosophy. But an even more challenging problem is that of comprehending their integration. The remainder of the present essay will be required in order to grasp the great synthesis which his philosophy constitutes. Clearly, then, in order to view Malebranche's thought with a degree of completeness, it will be necessary to hold a number of considerations disentangled from one another.

First we have to understand that and why Malebranche has to treat ideas from the outset primarily as universals and only subsequently as components of sense perception. This is all the more perplexing initially, because Malebranche's scientific method is designed to afford truth concerning matters of fact through sense observation. Next, possessing this invaluable formula (that ideas are primarily universals) for analyzing Malebranche's study of the five alternative hypotheses concerning ideas, we have to determine what Malebranche accepted as established concerning ideas—we have to determine the orientation and uncriticized presuppositions that underlie his critique of ideas. We shall find that Descartes' formulation of the nature of ideas at once supplied the grounds of criticism that Malebranche took for granted and the impetus to reject Descartes' own innatism. Descartes was really the target of Malebranche's attack on ideas, but the weapons were Cartesian.

Knowing the answers to these two questions—why does he interpret ideas as universals? and what are the basis and objectives of his critique of the five alternative theories of ideas?—we shall be able to understand why no theory advocated in his century can fulfill his demands and why he felt it necessary in the end to adopt some version of real universals as central to his metaphysics and theory of knowledge.

An artificial device will aid us in answering the first question concerning why Malebranche, the empiricist, interprets ideas as universals, namely, to consider what *Bacon* would have written concerning theory of knowledge, had Bacon had the interest and concern to investigate metaphysical problems in an un-hysterical manner. We return briefly now to Bacon.

I. IDEAS AS UNIVERSALS

(*a*) *Central Role of Conception in Malebranche's Treatment of Ideas.*
Actually, of course, Bacon was neither an epistomologist nor a metaphysician. While he insisted on experiments for the reason that the naked senses were suspect, he afforded no clear-cut theory concerning the nature of sensible qualities or concerning the relation between mind and body. In his treatment of Forms, are we to say with Brunschvicg [13] that the sensible qualities like yellow, or density, are in the objects themselves, or merely sensations in the mind? There is no

Sense and
intuition in
Bacon—a
speculation.

explicit answer. With respect to the Forms themselves, they are God's own true signatures; they are in the individual things themselves; and only individual things exist. Yet he does not make clear precisely what is the relation between the Forms in God and the Forms in things, or what between the Forms and the concretely existing things themselves. Let us, however, be permitted to speculate. Had Bacon treated his doctrine of Forms from an epistemologist's point of view, what might he have said regarding the relation between sense and intellect?

Baconian induction and experimentation imply that the Forms are in the things. This much he himself acknowledges. Only individual things exist, he claims; [14] and the Forms are their nature-engendering natures; and hence they are immanent therein. We begin with particular facts, for Bacon, elicit the Forms, and then return to observation for further confirmation.[15] Does this not suggest that, if we regard Bacon's philosophy from the viewpoint of knowledge, we can conclude:

a) That the knowing process begins with sense perception and ascends to intuition?

b) That perceiving involves conceiving, that is, that the Forms are present in sense, although present in an obscure manner?

c) That through experimentation and rigorous attention of the natural light, what finally happens is that the specific sensible elements gradually fade or fall away, and that the pure, intelligible Forms stand revealed to naked intuition? Is this not what actually happens in his illustration of the inductive discovery of the Form of heat?

Moreover, Bacon maintained that this inductive process is applicable to primary notions as well as to the Middle Principles; and he attributes his induction to Plato.[16] Now, does not Plato's theory of knowledge precisely exemplify this procedure of beginning with the senses which remind—that is, put one in mind of—what is already known? The already-known, or the idea, is in perception, but in an obscure fashion. The process of dialectic consists in shearing away the sensuous elements, until the idea stands forth clearly and luminously. Yet, in so far as Bacon insists on experimental verification, he would demand a return from knowing back to perception, in order to confirm the fact that the universal Form apprehended by the intellect is really in the things themselves. Baconian induction would thus be a combination of an amended Platonism and of an amended Aristotelianism (amended in the sense that Bacon's Forms and ideas are real essences,[17] not based on hasty analogies or on an induction by simple enumeration).[18]

Such a theory of knowledge and of perception, as we shall see, constitutes a large part of the philosophy advocated by Malebranche.

This vital clue enables us to anticipate how Malebranche will treat ideas, for it shows why Malebranche's theory of ideas is involved in the discussion of how we perceive bodies, and yet at the same time is a doctrine concerning universal concepts or how we understand what we perceive. What Malebranche seeks to demonstrate is that there is an intimate connection between sense and intellect, not indeed of the sort present in Scholasticism, but one that is perfectly conformable to the Cartesian dualism of mind and body and to the experimental method of a Bacon or a Huygens. His problem is to analyze the relationship between conceiving and perceiving. His position will culminate in the claim that perception is a combination of conception and sensation; that in perception there is an intelligible content of ideas, which by means of sensations are directly apprehended as being in the external world and which, when grasped in their purity by the act of conceiving alone, are seen as the universal archetypes in God. Conception thus departs from perception. Beginning with sense, the mind by a continuous process of effort and attention eliminates the sensuous to arrive at the intelligible. Our problem at present is to determine how Malebranche proceeds to this position.

(b) *Nature of Malebranche's "Purification" of Sense and Reason.* Because error and prejudice are the sources of all human misery, Malebranche proposes to purify the mind, so to speak, by an anatomical investigation into the causes of error. Since, as we saw, the method which examines things by considering them in their birth and origin is the most illuminating, Malebranche decides to follow this very procedure in revealing the idols of the mind.[19] Accordingly, while he emphasizes that the human mind is really not to be compartmentalized into separate, discrete faculties or parts, nevertheless, to facilitate discussion he first distinguishes between the understanding and the will. This permits him to assert, as did Descartes, that the understanding is passive; its function is to perceive; while the free will is the active principle that affirms, judges, consents, chooses, deliberates [20] and is thus the seat of error and of truth. Nevertheless, in as much as the various ways or manners of perception provide us many opportunities for precipitation and hasty judgments, each mode of perception is an indirect source of error. And once again to facilitate analysis, Malebranche distinguishes three kinds of perception. The soul, he declares, perceives objects in three different ways, by the pure understanding, by the imagination and by the senses.[21]

Through pure understanding, the mind apprehends spiritual objects, universals, common notions, the idea of perfection, the idea of an infinitely perfect Being, and its own thoughts. Even material things fall under the domain of pure understanding, for it alone can apprehend a perfect circle, a thousand-sided figure, or the essence of extension. The distinctive feature of the pure understanding lies in its capacity to apprehend without physical images. By the imagination, the mind renders absent material things present to itself, by forming images in the brain. Finally, by the senses the mind perceives sensible objects, when, being present, they make an impression upon the external organs of the body, which impression is communicated to the brain.[22]

These three faculties may be regarded as the chief avenues of man's blind mistakes, but to them may be added the inclinations and passions.

Thus, as we have already noted, the structure of the *Recherche* has a great deal in common with Bacon and with Descartes. The first three books are intended to purify the mind by casting doubt on the veracity of the senses, of imagination, and of understanding. They are intended to show the errors to which the mind is prone. They thus constitute Malebranche's preliminary skepticism. Yet, not merely is this antecedent skepticism provisional and therapeutic, but also it is of a mitigated character, resembling far more the skepticism of Bacon than that of Descartes. With respect to his doctrine of idols, Bacon maintained that it was intended for the purpose of eradicating dogmatism, but it was not intended to establish *acatalepsis* or complete skepticism,[23] that its purpose was not to destroy the authority of sense and understanding,[24] but to supply them with the proper helps, in order that the mind may eventually get to know and perceive things, not relatively, but objectively.[25] Bacon thus sought to destroy the notion that man is the measure of things.

Malebranche's therapeutic skepticism.

Descartes also insisted that his antecedent doubt was provisional, that he too was no skeptic, that in emptying his mind of former beliefs he was acting as if he were emptying a basket of apples in order thereafter to pick out and return the good ones.[26] Yet Descartes' initial skepticism was far more sweeping and severe than that of Bacon. For he went as far as to doubt the existence of a real world and even the truths of mathematics. This he did, in order to achieve certainty. Yet the net result of his quest for certainty is that neither in fact nor in principle did Descartes achieve his goal. Descartes failed because innatism makes man, not the universe, the measure of truth. For all his obvious insistence that the light of nature is common to all men, including Polyander, nevertheless, in principle, his is a protestantism that lacks objectivity.

Descartes' radical antecedent skepticism.

Now Malebranche was fully and consciously aware that Descartes' doctrine of ideas was the Achilles' heel that had to be punctured if genuine certainty were to be had in science.[27] The problem of ideas, he wrote, is the most abstruse one in metaphysics.[28] Descartes found himself possessed of three innate ideas. Of these, the most important, in one sense, is the idea of extension, for it is the basis of mathematics and of physics. If this idea is innate and if innatism harbors skepticism, then mathematical truths are no longer the very prototypes of certainty, and with their downfall all exact science is at once undermined. This is why the initial theme of Malebranche's *Recherche* is how we know bodies.

We know from our survey of Malebranche's method that knowledge is for him not of discrete particular facts, of the existential as such, but of the intelligible order; strict knowledge is not of the *that* but of the essence or universal nature of things. It is not the specific circle on paper with which the mathematician is concerned, but with its universal meaning, or with the idea of the circle as conveyed by the algebraic equation. So too Newton held that the natural scientist is not concerned with specific matters of fact but with the laws or natures that govern the presence and generation of these facts.[29] Hence when Malebranche in Book III on the understanding raises the fundamental question as to how we perceive bodies, his query is principally addressed towards finding out the status of universals and the manner in which we apprehend or discover them. But unlike Descartes in the first Meditation, Malebranche does not question the reality of ideas; he does not question whether three plus two are five, or whether when he contemplates the sides of a square he might be deceived by an evil demon. In fact, the first step that he takes is to insist on the reality of ideas and the immutable character of mathematical truths.

Malebranche averts radical skepticism by assuming the reality of intelligible ideas.

When his critic, Foucher, asks Malebranche on what grounds he so boldly asserts the reality of necessary mathematical truths, Malebranche replies: Because that is more certain than anything else, and because there is nothing certain, if that is not so. For if twice two are necessarily four, if a whole is necessarily larger than its part, then there are necessary truths.[30] And when Foucher, the skeptic, says: Let us ignore mathematics; then where shall we find eternal necessary truth?—To this Malebranche answers: As for me, I insist upon speaking of mathematics; and it is evident that my critic has not read my third book (On the Understanding).[31]

It is evident then that Malebranche does not doubt the necessity of mathematical truths and it is these that his doctrine of ideas seeks to vindicate. But just as he does not begin with any doubts concerning the capacities of the intellect, so neither does he begin with a wholesale condemnation of the senses. One must be "extremely" defiant of the senses, he writes,[32] but extreme defiance is not absolute. Like Donne, Malebranche doubts, but he doubts wisely. And this is in keeping with the experimental aspects of his method. For we saw that there is some intimate connection between the seen circle and its intelligible content, between the universal and the particular, between concept and sense. Furthermore, we saw that the scientist who

Purification of sensuous knowledge.

would understand nature properly must be sure that his findings check with concrete experience and experiment. This implies that the ideas or essences of bodies are conformable to and verifiable by concrete existence. It implies that however much strict knowledge is a matter of universals, at some point the universal must be grasped *in re,* at some point the existential must be given and given with cognitive assurance. It implies that however much the universal is given to pure conception, it is also present in perception. This is indeed what Descartes said when he claimed that simple natures are knowable by experience. This is what he later in the first Meditation rejected by his wholesale condemnation of sense and his innatism, only of course to reinstate the senses in the sixth Meditation. Yet even after this reinstatement of the probable validity of sense, Descartes still does not unambiguously claim that sensation gives direct access to existential objects and to their natures.

Accordingly, we may say that Malebranche begins where Descartes ended. In his purgation of sense, Malebranche goes only this far.[33] He shows that naked sense is untrustworthy because:

a) Space, time and figure are relational.
b) Apparent size, shape and figure, and motion are relative to the percipient organism.
c) Latent, imperceptible configurations exist that are hidden from the naked senses. Hence on the basis of sense we often foolishly conclude that things are non-existent because unseen.
d) Dreams, hallucinations, optical illusions show that we often make mistakes concerning what does exist.
e) Secondary qualities are subjective states and as such give no knowledge about external objects.

Despite these illusions, Malebranche insists upon two positive affirmations: *one,* that bodies really do exist. Extension, motion, figure are real, he writes, not imaginary, even though in specific cases our senses may make mistakes.[34] *Secondly,* even in erroneous perception, the content beheld is real. Even in illusion or dreams, *what* the visionary beholds is real. Circles seen from a distance may appear as oval or elliptical, or not even exist at all, but the oval or ellipse that is seen is very real.

> What Malebranche refuses to subject to radical doubt in sense perception.

Malebranche therefore concludes that in perception the immediate object of thought is an idea. Henceforth, the problem is to determine the nature, origin, status and manner of function in perception, of ideas.[35]

(c) *Order of Issues in Malebranche's Treatment of Ideas.* Now, it must be confessed that his treatment of ideas at the beginning of the *Recherche* is extremely ambiguous. He talks of ideas as representative of bodies; and his metaphysical dualism, his insistence upon the need for ideas to intervene between the mental and the physical, and his remarks on errors and illusions suggest that like Descartes he too upholds a copy doctrine of perception. This, however, is in flat contradiction not only with his statement that the primary qualities given to sense are real, but especially with his later writings where he energetically advances a form of direct perceptual realism. Accordingly two explanations of his seeming inconsistency are possible. We may, with Church, argue that Malebranche, because of his metaphysical dualism, began as a representationalist and copyist in knowledge but was compelled to abandon this position at a later stage in order to make existential truth accessible.[36] Or else we may argue that his initial ambiguities, which permit an uncritical interpretation of perceptual duplicating representationalism, are propaedeutic only—that inasmuch as he is speaking to Scholastic and Cartesian audiences, each of which advocates, or at least seems to advocate, a form of copy theory, it is only natural for him to begin with current doctrines and current language. But this does not compel us to conclude that Malebranche's doctrines are even at the first the same as the old ones. We may argue instead that he begins with current doctrines *only in order to discard them.* We know that as a reformer Malebranche is modest and gentle, preferring always to speak as though he were purifying the work of others rather than revolutionizing their work.[37] Then we may claim that his *expression* is old and familiar, but that consistently his *theory* is actually radically different from both the Scholastic and the Cartesian theories. My own view is that Mr. Church is mistaken and that the latter is the proper interpretation, for these reasons.

We must remember that the expression, *representative idea,* is itself ambiguous and can be interpreted in at least three different ways:

Does "representative" necessarily imply duplication?

(i) An idea may "represent" an object in the sense of being a specific resembling surrogate of a specific particular.

(ii) An idea may be a universal concept which "represents" the particular by being itself a copy or model of what is general in the particular.

(iii) An idea may be a universal concept which "represents" the particular by being itself that in which the particular directly participates. In this sense, the universal represents not in a transcendent but in an immanent manner.

From the fact that Malebranche affirms that the immediate object of thought is an idea, or from the fact that he stresses dreams and hallucinations as sources of error, it does not necessarily follow that he uses representative idea in the first or second sense, as Mr. Church assumes uncritically.[38] On the contrary, what he wants to show is that even in erroneous perception a universal content is present, an intelligible general idea.[39] Nor does the fact of erroneous perception imply that in veridical perception the representative universal is to be construed in the narrow transcendent sense of a model or literal copy.

All questions of sense perception can wait for later treatment, when the issue of existential reference enters. There is no reason why Malebranche should treat this question right off, in his discussion of the errors of sense. And there is good reason why he should not. The problem concerning the actual existence of bodies is a complex issue involving, as it does, such complicated principles as creation, causality, God, "participation" of the individual in the universal, and the very meaning of existence itself. Nothing certain can be said regarding these problems until and unless the very foundations of certitude are examined, that is, the role of general ideas in knowledge. Now Malebranche's conception of method demands that one analyze problems and treat them in an orderly fashion. From Malebranche's point of view, this rule of order demands that the status of ideas be investigated prior to any question concerning their existential reference. And the reason for this is that ideas are essences, universals, general concepts. It is with these that the mathematician and physicist are concerned. Upon their *status* will rest the fate of science and the outcome of the problem of induction. For after all, even an empiricist does not proceed from instance to instance, from *Fall zu Fall.*[40] When he goes to particular facts to confirm his general laws, it still remains true to say that what he actually beholds or sees or finds in the facts are general concepts, which Malebranche calls ideas. Therefore problems concerning the manner in which universals "represent" particulars and how we get acquainted with the particulars must come later.

In the *Entretiens sur la métaphysique,* Theodore, who is Malebranche's spokesman, defends this very procedure which I am claiming against Church is the path that Malebranche followed:

> *Theodore.* I am saying that all that I think of *is,* or if you like, exists. The cabinet . . .

> *Aristes.* I understand you partly, Theodore . . . You are not talking of objects, but of the ideas of objects. . . . I thought you were speaking of the objects themselves.

> *Theodore. Of the objects themselves,* why, we have not got to them! I am trying to think the matter out in the proper order.[41]

The proper order, Theodore goes on to explain, is to attend to the status and reality of ideas and our manner of knowing them prior to questions concerning the reality of existential objects and how we get acquainted with them; for particular objects are contingent existents, whereas ideas are intelligible and immutable essences. What Male-

[margin note:] Problem of perception subsequent to problem of nature of intelligible ideas.

branche means to say is that, taken strictly, the object of knowledge is never the singular, the contingent, the existential, *the* brute arbitrary matter of fact; rather, the object for knowledge is the immutable essence. And this is why we must treat essences before we go to the objects themselves. Thus Theodore continues:

> Many more principles than you may suppose are necessary to prove what no one doubts. For where are the people who doubt whether they have bodies, whether they are walking on this earth, whether they are living in a material world? But you will know soon what few people understand well, namely, that if our body moves about in a corporeal world, our mind, on the other hand, transports us incessantly into *a world of intelligence* which touches it, and which thereby becomes accessible to the senses. Since men attach no value to the *ideas* which they have of things, they give to the created world more reality than it has.[42]

To understand an author adequately, wrote Malebranche,[43] one must ascertain his goal or purpose in writing. Also, an equitable approach to a writer demands that we consult his later works.[44] If we follow these two admonitions, as I have tried to do—investigate his method which is the goal of the *Recherche* and also consult such later works as his *Entretiens sur la métaphysique,* as his controversy with Arnauld, and especially as his tenth Éclaircissement—then it becomes amply clear that Malebranche's epistemology is concerned not so much with the question of perception as it is with that of conception. To be sure, Malebranche is indeed in the *Recherche,* as later on, trying to explain how we perceive bodies or external material natures, and we shall examine his explanation fully in the last chapter below. This question of perception is, however, secondary to the more crucial problem, namely, how do we conceive or understand the objects perceived? This more central and more significant problem revolves about the status, the origin and the role of general ideas or universal meanings. And Malebranche's fundamental task is to show that no knowledge is possible without *a priori* general terms. Then, while settling this issue, he is, as a consequence of his decisions in this connection, constrained to offer a specific theory of perception.

Once we realize that the problem concerning the nature of ideas is really a question of universals, we can avoid the interpretation of mental surrogates. For the problem, really, is not how the immaterial mind can know the physical, as Church supposes,[45] but instead how the mind knows that which is intelligible in the physical or in particulars. Even were mind extended there would still be need for ideas in the sense of universals, inasmuch as knowledge for him is of essences, of the reasons of things. Malebranche utilizes the Cartesian dualism of mind and body merely as a preamble to his theory of

Goal of
Malebranche's
epistemology is
knowledge of
universals.

[66]

universals; merely to show that in knowledge it is not bodies in their factual, existential concreteness that are known by ideas, but that by ideas only specific logical or intelligible natures of bodies are known.

In the tenth Éclaircissement, writing in defense of his own Platonic version of universals, Malebranche affirms that his view:

Function of intelligible ideas: to yield certainty and generality.

. . . me paraît si conforme à la religion, que dis-je? *si absolument nécessaire pour donner à quelque vérité que ce puisse être, un fondement certain et inébranlable,* que je me crois indispensablement obligé de l'expliquer et de le soutenir autant qu'il me sera possible. J'aime mieux qu'on m'appelle visionnaire, qu'on me traite d'illuminé, et qu'on dise de moi tous ces bons mots que l'imagination, qui est toujours railleuse dans les petits esprits, a de coutume d'opposer à des raisons qu'elle ne comprend pas, ou dont elle ne peut se défendre, que de demeurer d'accord que les corps soient capables de m'éclairer, que je sois à moi-même mon maître, ma raison, ma lumière; et que pour m'instruire solidement de toutes choses, il suffise que je me consulte moi-même ou des hommes qui peut-être peuvent faire grand bruit à mes oreilles, mais certainement qui ne peuvent répandre la lumière dans mon esprit. Voici donc encore quelques raisons pour le sentiment que j'ai établi dans les chapitres sur lesquels j'écris ceci.[46]

Herein lies explicit evidence concerning the real nature of Malebranche's epistemology. This statement epitomizes the aim of Malebranche's quest in his search after truth, and shows why he is displeased with Descartes. What he is seeking is an indubitable and inviolable foundation for public, objective knowledge. His problem is akin to that of Socrates in facing the sophists and to that of Kant: how is knowledge possible? How is *any* kind of truth possible? Upon what foundations can knowledge be had? I see for example—Malebranche writes[47]—that two times two are four, that one must prefer his friend to his dog, and I am certain that there is no man in the world who does not see it as well as I. Malebranche is certain that the truths of geometry and algebra and ethics are eternal, immutable, universal, that they are valid for the Chinese, the Greeks, as for himself. But his problem is to account for and explain that validity. Evidently Descartes' doctrine of ideas cannot guarantee that validity.

Delbos argues that in investigating the nature of ideas apart from the question of their existential reference, Malebranche is simply following Descartes' anti-scholastic procedure of going from knowing to being.[48] In part, this is true. Descartes did say that before we decide whether anything exists, we must first know what we are talking about—essence precedes existence. However, even the medievalist who begins with the *esse* prior to the *nosse,* even he in his theory of knowledge does not claim that in knowing it is the particular as particular which is the object of knowledge. Even for him *the object of knowledge* in perception is not the singular existential object itself in its naked existential particularity; for knowledge, the object present to the mind is the *form*. For him, also, to know things is to apprehend them *sub specie universali*. Of course, for the medievalist secondary qualities are in the thing itself. Therefore in seeing them he perceives the thing itself. But Descartes and even more especially Malebranche have, on the basis of the idea of extension, relegated the sensible qualities to the mind. This makes the problem of the existential referent more difficult and acute. Yet epistemologically the problem is the same. In so far as perceiving involves the apprehension, contemplation and understanding of a thing's intelligible character, its essence rather than existence, then Malebranche may quite properly feel that in knowledge the right procedure is to investigate the status and reality of essences prior to existence, that of the immutable prior to the contingent.

My conclusion then is this: the broad objective of Malebranche's purification of the mind is oriented towards the vindication of the method. This method is deductive and experimental. To preserve this method and to get at objective truth, Malebranche's purification in a more immediate and narrower sense is directed first towards the formulation of a proper theory of universals and then secondly to a doctrine of sense perception. Accordingly, in this chapter I shall concentrate on ideas chiefly as universal concepts, and in the final chapter I shall treat their role in sense perception (in existential knowledge).

Conclusion concerning Malebranche's treatment of intelligible ideas.

Bearing in mind, then, that Malebranche's representationalism is not Descartes' copy theory, we may, however, try to determine to what extent there is agreement between him and Descartes on the nature of an idea. To a large extent this has, of course, already been suggested, but in a negative manner, by emphasizing differences between Descartes and Malebranche. The next section will focus on their more positive agreements.

II. What Malebranche Accepts from Descartes

Philosophy never originates or proceeds in a cultural vacuum. When Malebranche "refutes" the first four hypotheses concerning ideas, he finds in the thought of his century the positions that he rejects, and finds there his own basic affiliations as well as his challenge or problems calling for solution. Since his initial "moniteur" or guide to philosophy is Descartes, we must now consider what he accepted in Descartes' theory of ideas. Knowing this and knowing the nature of his method, we can then appreciate what perplexities he found in Descartes.

(*a*) *Pure Thought.* In the first place, as psychophysical dualists, both Descartes and Malebranche deny that thinking is equivalent to physical movements in the body or to cerebral images in the brain. Descartes, throughout his duels with Hobbes and Gassendi, patiently reiterates that consciousness or thought is not to be confused with the corporeal imagination.[49] And in the definition of an idea, at the end of the replies to the second set of objections, he flatly announces that, to brain-images "I here decidedly refuse the title of ideas." Pictures in the brain may be said to be ideas, he declares, only if by idea is meant the form of the mind itself directed towards the brain.[50] Only imagination or sensation is an idea, but not the cerebral, physical image. Malebranche adopts this view of Descartes.[51] *[Thinking not a physical act.]*

Both Descartes and Malebranche, secondly, understand immaterial thought in a very wide manner which includes all the mental operations. Malebranche echoes Descartes' declaration. Descartes states: *[Immaterial thought includes all mental operations.]*

Thought is a word that covers everything that exists in us in such a way that we are immediately conscious of it. Thus all the operations of will, intellect, imagination, and of the senses are thoughts.[52]

Malebranche repeats that by the words thought, mode of thinking, or modification of the soul he understands in general all the things which cannot be in the soul without it perceiving them by the awareness that it has of itself. By inner consciousness the soul is aware of its own sensations, its imaginations, its pure intellections, or simply its conceptions, even its passions, and its natural inclinations.[53]

Although sensing, feeling, willing and imagining are thus all included among the modes of thinking, both Malebranche and Descartes conceive the *cognitive* function of thought to be set apart. It alone belongs to the pure understanding and not to the operations of sense and imagination. Knowledge proper is to be found solely within the realm of pure reason.[54] Sense and imagination may contain an intelligible content and thus serve to fix our attention upon it, as in the study of geometry; but it is pure reason alone which can be said to know that the angles of a triangle are equal to two right angles.[55] *[Cognitive thought.]*

This cognitive function of the pure intellect is an act of acquaintance similar to vision. Knowledge or the knowing process is conceived by both Malebranche and Descartes as an acquaintance with a content of ideas. This acquaintance is analogous to sight. Descartes speaks of the light of nature or pure intuition as an inborn light that perspicuously beholds ideas in mental vision.[56] And Malebranche speaks of perceiving or seeing ideas.[57] Because knowing is thus construed as being analogous to vision, it follows that the object known must be ever conceived as being present to the knowing subject, although not necessarily locally present at it. *[Pure intellection is acquaintance.]*

(b) *Pure Ideas.* Since knowing is thus a direct awareness of an object, anything of which the mind thinks or is conscious, like a feeling of pain, may be supposed to be an idea. Both Malebranche and Descartes, indeed, do use "idea" in this very wide sense. For example, Descartes declares that when he wills and fears, because at the same time he conceives that he wills and fears, volition and fear are placed among ideas.[58] Descartes defines the term idea in general as the *form* of any thought by the immediate awareness of which one becomes conscious of that same thought.[59] Malebranche, likewise, in one of his meanings of the term idea includes any object of which the mind thinks.[60]

Descartes'
pure ideas
are essences
or universals.

When Descartes uses the word form, however, it becomes clear on the contrary that not everything of which the mind is immediately conscious can without qualification be called an idea. Ideas in the strictest usage are only the pure perceptions, the pure essences, not the "sentiments" or sensations. The term "form" is a scholastic word of which Descartes retained only half of its original meaning. Since Descartes does not begin, as did the Scholastics with sensible objects, "form" does not signify the sensible form of an object. Nevertheless, as Gilson observes, the Cartesian idea conserves the *representative* character of the scholastic *form*. When it is a true idea it remains a representative similitude of the object. Thus it is the principle of the knowledge that we have of the object.[61] Inasmuch, then, as ideas are defined as forms of thought, and form signifies the representative character of ideas, and only true ideas, that is, ideas that are both clear and distinct, may be representatives,[62] it follows that sensations and imaginations which are "confused perceptions," possessing no representative function, are not strictly ideas, i.e., nothing in the world resembles them. Thus only "simple natures" or pure concepts, or essences are properly speaking ideas. Now, both the "confused perceptions," which Descartes in the sixth Meditation and in the *Traité de l'homme* calls sentiments, and the clear and distinct ideas of God, the soul, and extension are said by Descartes to be innate. However, the former are innate in the sense of belonging to the very constitution or nature of the soul; they are its states or the dispositions belonging to the soul in virtue of its union with the body. But the intelligible essences or the clear and distinct ideas, such as that of the triangle, are innate in the sense of having been deposited by God as a "content" or "treasure" in the mind even *prior* to its connection with the body.[63]

Malebranche's
'intelligible
idea.'

Malebranche likewise defines ideas as immediate objects of thought. As a result, like Descartes, he often speaks of ideas of sense and ideas of the imagination. But in the third *Éclaircissement* he warns us that

. . . ce mot *idée*, est équivoque. Je l'ai pris quelquefois pour tout ce qui représente à l'esprit quelque objet, soit clairement, soit confusément. Je l'ai pris même encore plus généralement pour tout ce qui est l'objet immédiat de l'esprit. Mais je l'ai pris aussi dans le sens le plus précis et le plus resserré, c'est-à-dire pour tout ce qui représente les choses à l'esprit d'une manière si claire, qu'on peut découvrir d'une simple vue si telles ou telles modifications leur appartiennent.[64]

Thus, as for Descartes, ideas taken strictly are the universals of the *pure* understanding. The word, understanding, covers indeed all acts of intellection, namely, sensing, remembering, imagining, desiring, and conceiving, because the soul is one and indivisible.[65] But it is only the pure understanding, freed from all sensuous consciousness, which is capable of knowing ideas with exactitude. For this reason, following Descartes, Malebranche often designates the objects of the pure understanding as *intelligible ideas*.[66] Thus references to "ideas of sense and of imagination" do not signify that the imagination and the senses actually produce ideas but merely refer to the fact that ideas are present amidst the flux of sensations and images. Intellectual ideas are not a special category of ideas, but ideas taken in their rigorous meaning. They are conceptual entities which are the immediate objects of thought and by the "representation" or mediation of which we obtain a knowledge of the external world,[67] although, as we shall see, Malebranche does not fall into the theory that in veridical perception ideas *duplicate* a real world.

Descartes, in conceiving knowledge of the external world as consisting in an acquaintance with a content of purely intelligible similitudes or ideas and in defining these representative ideas as "forms," consciously and avowedly acknowledged himself to Hobbes to be adopting for the human mind the kind of knowledge which the Scholastics attributed to God. The medieval Deity, by contemplating the eternal "forms" or archetypes within His own essence, possessed a purely intelligible or conceptual knowledge that is both *a priori* and representative of the actual world created by His will.[68] And Malebranche too writes in similar vein:

On connaît les choses par leurs idées lorsqu'elles ne sont point intelligibles par elles-mêmes. . . . Je veux dire que l'idée que nous avons de l'étendue suffit pour nous faire connaître toutes les propriétés dont l'étendue est capable, et que nous ne pouvons désirer d'avoir une idée plus distincte et plus féconde de l'étendue, des figures et des mouvements que celle que Dieu nous en donne.[69]

The world of clear and distinct ideas or simple natures for Descartes is a world of concrete realities and facts, not a world of tautologies or definitions.[70] Ideas are the very building blocks and elements of our knowledge.[71] For Descartes this reality of an idea is twofold. (We shall see that Malebranche rejects the first aspect, but makes the sec-

Ideas are real beings, for Descartes.

ond kind fundamental to his philosophy.) Ideas are at once states, acts, or modes of thought and the representing objects of thought.[72] As modalities ideas are not different from one another [73] and carry no reference to the truth and falsity of objects.[74] As psychological states of mind, in this manner, ideas do not function in knowledge. It is only in their capacity of objects of thought that psychologically existing ideas acquire an "objective reality" or "representative validity." In this latter referential or, according to the old usage, 'objective' capacity, ideas possess a quasi-substantial reality. This reality is attested to by the fact that the *res cogitata* possess concrete properties, whereas nothing has no properties,[75] and by the resistance which ideas offer whenever we attempt to modify or alter their definitions.[76]

(c) *A Priori Truth.* Descartes claimed three clear and distinct ideas, of the soul, of God, and of extension. Although the *Cogito* is method-

Mathematical truth in Descartes' thought.

ologically the very prototype of a clear and distinct and true proposition, and although the idea of God is metaphysically the most clear and certain of all, it nevertheless remains true that the "best evidence" [77] is to be found in mathematics. By his metaphysics, that is, by his non-deceiving, immutable and self-caused Deity, Descartes secures the foundations of his mathematics and mathematical physics; [78] by his *Cogito* he reveals the characteristics of an indubitable proposition, "what in a proposition is requisite in order to be true and certain." [79] But mathematics always is the purest expression of certainty. In the fifth Meditation he confesses that even if he has not yet demonstrated that everything which is clear and distinct is true and is "something," nevertheless the nature of his mind is such that when he contemplates the objects of mathematics—figure, number, and extension—he cannot prevent himself from regarding these as true and immutable natures.[80] And significantly, Descartes, in seeking to show how certain he is of the existence of God from the idea of Him, appeals as standard to the truths of mathematics which concern only numbers and figures.[81]

If it is true that Descartes believed his physics to be pure mathematics and if it is true that the principal aim of his metaphysics is to guarantee and secure the acceptance of his mathematics of extension, then we cannot but conclude that the most fundamental problem for Descartes concerns the "objective," representative reality and *a priori* certainty of the idea of extension.

Malebranche is equally as insistent as is Descartes upon the objective or representative reality of the ideas of extension. He asserts that

Malebranche takes as assured the certainty and reality of mathematics.

mathematics is the most certain of all sciences. With respect to the ideas of number and extension, Malebranche describes their existence as "incontestable." Their nature is immutable. Of all the ideas of which we can think these are the most clear and evident.[82] These ideas—he recalls—are the immutable rules and the common measures of all other

[72]

things that we know and that we can know. Those who know perfectly the relations of numbers and figures, or better the art of making the comparisons necessary for knowing the relations of them, have a kind of universal science. They have a highly assured means for discovering with reliability and certitude everything which does not transcend the ordinary limits of the mind.

Against the claims of some who acknowledge actual existence only in corporeal objects and deny that ideas are real, he argues on the same two grounds that Descartes used. First, each idea has its own intrinsic properties that distinguish it from every other idea; for example, the idea of a square is entirely different from the idea of a circle. How then can we assume that ideas are nothing, since, secondly, "nothing or non-being has no qualities"; "one non-entity cannot be different from every other non-entity." [83] These ideas or objects of thought are at least as real as physical objects, for to the mind they offer at least as much resistance and solidity as does the floor struck with the foot to the foot.[84] It is utterly impossible to alter the definition of a triangle. Thus when Malebranche thinks of a circle, of a number, of being, or of the infinite, all these objects of thought must be realities, for each has its own distinct and determinate properties.[85] To think of nothing is not to think at all, and conversely every object of thought is something real. For these reasons, even dreams and illusions convey something real. In dreams and in fevers, objects are seen which do not and have not ever existed. Yet what is seen or imagined or thought of *is*, or, if you like, exists—at least during the time it is thought of. The idea is real, although the objects themselves may not be. Accordingly, again like Descartes, Malebranche concludes that even if the external material world were completely annihilated or had never existed, we might still possess a knowledge of ideas, for these might still continue to be with us.[86] For this reason, Malebranche says: our souls do not leave the body in order to measure the size of the heavens; they see external bodies only through ideas which represent them.

Hence, the question, really, is *not:* how do we know external objects? It *is*, instead: how do we know the essences or ideas of external objects? Thus Malebranche has to treat problems of our knowledge of bodies as the initial theme of the *Recherche,* and yet the central interest that drives Malebranche to investigate this theme is not exclusively or even primarily an interest in sense perception, but rather an interest in immutable natures. While Malebranche will renounce Descartes' innatism, the clash between them will be over the issue regarding where and how ideas exist, not whether they exist. Malebranche accepts from Descartes what underlies Descartes' recourse to innatism; he embraces the *a-priorism* that is contained in innate ideas. Malebranche agrees with this much of Descartes without qualification, namely, that the

[margin note:] Malebranche assumes a priori universals.

mind, in order to know intelligible ideas, must encounter an already-existing intelligible content. But he will condemn and disavow the existential, subjective aspects of innatism; to believe that *a priori*, intelligible natures have finite psychological existence in created minds, he will hold, can issue only in a devastating skepticism.

To sum up, this is what Malebranche retains from Descartes concerning ideas, and this is what constitutes the underlying beliefs and purifications concerning intelligible ideas, which Malebranche uses as a basis for his critique of the five alternative theories of ideas:

Summary.

1. Ideas are known by acts of immaterial thought.
2. Acts of thinking include purely cognitive thought.
3. Pure, cognitive thoughts are acts of acquaintance.
4. Ideas are among the objects of thought.
5. Intelligible ideas are essences or universals.
6. Intelligible ideas are real being.
7. Intelligible ideas are known through acquaintance with an already-existing intelligible content.

What Malebranche retains from Descartes can be compressed into the statement that intuitive knowledge yields certainty and consists in acts of acquaintance with a content of real, intelligible, immutable, already-existing relational natures. Only one further belief is really to be included among Malebranche's underlying assumptions concerning ideas, a belief arising from the requirements of the new mathematics of the second half of the seventeenth century. This belief is that we can conceive, even though we cannot comprehend, infinity. It will be treated below.

III. THE ALTERNATIVE THEORIES OF IDEAS

Malebranche was deeply convinced that Descartes had found a sure road for discovering all the truths that a limited understanding could comprehend.[87] For this accomplishment Malebranche held Descartes in the highest esteem. Nevertheless, Malebranche is no docile, passive disciple. Repeatedly he cautions us that Descartes was a man, just like anyone else:

> . . . M. Descartes était homme comme les autres, sujet à l'erreur et à l'illusion comme les autres; il n'y a aucun de ses ouvrages, sans même excepter sa géométrie, où il n'y ait quelque marque de la faiblesse de l'esprit humain. Il ne faut donc point le croire sur sa parole, mais le lire, comme il nous en avertit lui-même, avec précaution . . .[88]

Had Descartes detached himself even more from the testimony of sense, Malebranche contended, had he dwelled even less in the everyday world, had he applied himself with even more scrupulous care to the search after truth, then he would have been able to develop the sciences which he treated to a much greater degree, and ". . . sa métaphysique ne serait pas telle qu'il nous l'a laissée dans ses écrits." [89]

The principal defect of Descartes' metaphysics lies in the specific form in which he cast his doctrine of ideas. In the *Recherche*, Malebranche discusses this doctrine in the second part of Book III, on the understanding, where he denies innatism and conceptualism. Yet, although it is Descartes and the Cartesians who are the principal targets of his attack, before Malebranche launches into his major battle, he conducts a preliminary skirmish against the Peripatetics. All in all, he treats five alternative theories on the nature, origin and status of ideas:

1. Ideas as images of external objects, received from the objects.
2. Ideas as produced by our mind, upon external stimulation.
3. Ideas as innate.
4. Ideas as modifications of the mind.
5. Ideas as existent in God and known by an act of the mind.

The first two are variations of the Peripatetic view, and the third and fourth of the Cartesian view. All four are rejected in favor of the fifth, his own Christian version of Platonic realism.

Why does Malebranche begin with the Peripatetics, if Descartes is really the target? There is good reason for this digression. *First,* when Malebranche asks about the origin or cause of ideas, it must be carefully noted that he is still raising a question that is distinctively Cartesian. To Descartes, because ideas are really existing, substantialized entities, they, like any other existent object, require some efficient cause; for Descartes holds that of everything that exists we may and must ask why it exists or what is the cause of its existence.[90] This causal axiom or common notion [91] applies not merely to objects outside the mind like the actual sun, but also to ideas present to the mind, like the idea of the sun and like the idea of the immutable and eternal triangle.[92] However, *secondly,* although Malebranche raises this Cartesian question as to the efficient cause of ideas, he does so with the evident intent of reducing it *ad absurdum.* He will, as we shall see, reject it and in the end thereby discover a case which will deny the artesian axiom or rather which will restrict the search for efficient causes to the sphere of mutable and temporal objects and exclude efficiency from the realm of immutable and eternal triangles. In advancing his own positive theory as the fifth and only possible alternative, Malebranche will finally bifurcate Descartes' identity of formal and efficient causality; he will show that the "existence" of essences, or what some modern philosophers call their "subsistence," does not fall under power.

Why Malebranche begins with the Peripatetic theories.

This explains why he begins with the Peripatetics. What Malebranche wants to show is that notwithstanding Descartes' attempt to cut the umbilical cord, to sever himself from scholastic "superstitions," and to begin afresh, actually Descartes' doctrine (or at least that of the Cartesians, such as Arnauld and Régis), is not, after all, far removed from that of his scholastic predecessors. Even though Descartes speaks of the reality of the immutable triangle and even though he denies that it or the idea of God are mere figments or constructions of his own mind, but rather are clear and distinct realities, nevertheless, by treating these essences as innate (Third Alternative) or as modes of thought (Fourth Alternative), his view remains fatally close to the conceptualism of the Scholastics. That this is so, in fact, can be seen for example, in Descartes' explanation to Caterus of his search for the cause of the idea of God: How does it happen that the mind should fashion such an idea? We may ask this question, says Descartes, just as we may ask how the mind should happen to *construct* the idea of a machine.[93] By treating the Peripatetic view of knowledge prior to treating Descartes' views, Malebranche, I surmise, is able to show that Descartes' conceptualism is open to the same charges of relativism as are possible against the Peripatetics. Both, as Bacon would have said, make man, not the universe, the measure of truth.

Furthermore, in beginning with the Peripatetics, ascending gradually to Descartes and to the Cartesians, and arriving finally at his own Platonic version of universals, Malebranche, it appears to me, is exemplifying Baconian induction in the realm of epistemology. Beginning with sense and with a sensualistic epistemology, he follows the "scalae gradibus" of sound experimental method, by slowly rising to what he holds to be the true essence or definition of a universal.

Malebranche's aim in treating the four alternatives is primarily to prove that no doctrine which ascribes a causal origin to universals or that in any manner localizes universals in each individual mind, can adequately explain the possibility of having objectivity and certainty in the sciences. In the first two alternatives, Malebranche shows the inadequacies that arise from the naive empiricist's attempt to render particulars or minds the causal source of universals. In the second two alternatives, Malebranche reveals the difficulties of the Cartesian doctrine of making God or innate power of thought the efficient cause of ideas as universals. In this manner, he presents a brief but adequately exhaustive enumeration of the major alternative views on universals. By pointing out the limitations and insufficiencies of each, as well as their mutual affinities, he is thereby preparing the reader for a conversion to Platonism.

IV. First Alternative: Physical Impression

According to the First Alternative, ideas are abstracted copies or images of external objects. As is commonplace in his day, Malebranche takes it to be the hypothesis of the Peripatetics. Thus in entertaining this alternative, Malebranche is returning to the options open to Descartes when the latter commenced his own investigation into the nature of the knowing process.

Gouhier observes that Malebranche, like Descartes, appears to apprehend the First Alternative in a crude form.[94] What does Gouhier have in mind? Actually, for the Medievals themselves, man is a single substance composed of two elements, a soul and a body. Neither of these two can exist by itself and their union is not accidental but a real *conjunctum*. Man is *unum per se*. Descartes averted this doctrine only with difficulty, but in one place—when he treated the interaction of body and soul [95]—he actually conjoined the two distinct substances. Although the soul for the Medievals is the principle or the seat of knowing and sensing, nevertheless these operations are ascribed not to a part of man but to the entire man, and in intellectual as well as in sense knowledge the body enters as an integral part of man. Yet the cognitive function is not ascribed to a physical organ as is sight to the eye. Thus the soul is treated both as the form of the body, and, in its cognitive or intellectual functions, as distinct from the body. Because the soul is the form of the body, because every form, intelligible essence, or quiddity is embedded in matter, knowledge for the Medievals always originates in sense perception. It starts from the particular and the individual revealed in sense to proceed by *abstraction* to the general and to the immaterial or intelligible incorporated in the individual sensible object. The intellect can grasp the universal *in re* only by the intervention of sense and corporeal images.

In such a Peripatetic, anti-Platonic doctrine, the body does not exercise a lethal, soporific, impeding function in the attainment of knowledge. The soul learns not in spite of the body but rather by means of it. For this reason, the concept of *phantasms* or species plays an important role. Knowledge is not an identification or confluence between the knower and his object. Instead, knowing consists in the passive reception by sense of the sensible form or intentional species of an object; this sensible species is the material which becomes acted upon and rendered intelligible by the active intellect; then the intelligible species is received into the passive intellect. Neither the sensible nor the intelligible species is conceived by St. Thomas as an exact material copy or duplicate of the physical object, although it is a similitude or representative of it; nor is the sensible form a physical Democritian atom.[96]

Actual doctrine of the Peripatetics—central role of sense perception.

Thus these phantasms are at once semi-corporeal and semi-spiritual, and neither. The phantasms occupy this ambiguous, twilight zone, because, like Donne's animal spirits, ". . . such fingers need to knit/ That subtle knot, which makes us man."

Gilson admits that the scholastic representative theory of perception, however coherent it may be with its own metaphysics, raises serious difficulties which are not solved by Thomas. Nor did this theory receive constructive refinement in the hands of his successors.[97] Instead, the phantasms became really the gross Democritian images or *simulacra*. It is in this degenerate form that Malebranche attacks the Peripatetic theory.

Malebranche's dualistic formulation of the Peripatetic hypothesis.

To understand why Malebranche could formulate it in no other form, notice that he approached it as a confirmed and radical psychophysical dualist. For him the function of the species and phantasms was to cross the chasm between mind and body, and these messengers had to be either mental or material, but not neither or both. Even more, the radical distinction between minds and bodies compelled Descartes and Malebranche to reduce phantasms and species to mere words,[98] because they stand neither for anything physical nor for anything purely mental, and there is no third nature. They also reduce to mere words, because in the Cartesian physics there is no provision made for such Democritian corpuscles. The four reasons, to which we now turn, why Malebranche rejects the First Alternative are concerned with showing that species and phantasms, interpreted as material idols, cannot function in knowledge. Additional objections involve their becoming spiritualized. While the four reasons given just below are significant, it is these latter additional objections, as we shall see, that are really crucial.

Malebranche's rejection of the First Alternative.

Malebranche formulates the First Alternative thus: External objects emit material copies or images or species, *espèces impresses,* which resemble them. These are impressed on the external senses, whence they are carried to the 'common sense' where they are rendered intelligible by the active intellect. Thus spiritualized they become *espèces expresses.*[99]

As one would sweep away a cobweb, so Malebranche, with a few deft strokes, brushes off these age-old phantasms. Here are his reasons:[100]

1. *Impenetrability of bodies.* Because (on Malebranche's assumption of psycho-physical dualism) no material object can send off images of a nature other than itself, these images or copies must likewise be material bodies. But the entire region between, say, the sun and ourselves is a *plenum* filled completely with bodies. Since bodies are impenetrable, these species, being incapable of penetrating this occupied region, will, in knocking against the other bodies, become broken and crushed; and thus, no longer

being intact copies, they will not be capable of rendering their objects visible.

2. *Size of images is a function of distance.* The nearer an object is seen the greater it appears, and therefore the greater its copy or image should be. But how can an image decrease or increase in size? What happens to its parts when it decreases? Where does it get new parts to increase?

3. *Circles, viewed obliquely, oval.* Thirdly, if bodies send off images of no other nature than their own, how can we account for the fact that in looking at a picture of ovals or parallelograms we see only circles and squares? This should suggest that it is not at all necessary for an object, in order to be seen, to send off images resembling itself.

4. *Diminution in mass from sending off material.* Fourthly, it is inconceivable that a body should be capable of continuously sending off small bodies without itself gradually diminishing.

Malebranche might also have pointed out that a relational doctrine of matter and figure, such as he himself holds, precludes the notion of resembling species.

As a matter of fact, the foregoing is all that Malebranche has to say against this "Portrait Theory." But he ends his discussion with these teasing words:

Mais on ne veut pas s'arrêter davantage à rapporter toutes les raisons contraires à cette opinion . . . Celles que nous venons de rapporter sont suffisantes, et elles n'étaient pas même nécessaires après ce qu'on a dit qui regarde ce sujet dans le premier livre, lorsqu'on a expliqué les erreurs des sens.[101]

Malebranche seems to be in a great hurry to dispense with this doctrine and to proceed to other matters. After all that he has accomplished in his discussion of the errors of sense, he seems to feel that a reflective mind could provide all these "other reasons" by itself. And, to tell the truth, he is correct—provided that we do stop to reflect. To do so we must realize not only that Malebranche is repudiating the notion that matter and motion can cause sensations, but that above all he is concerned with universals. Like Bacon, he is opposed to a naive empiricism which, trusting the naked senses, proceeds to form a general idea by treating it as a mere abstraction from or a summation of many particulars. He has already referred to Bacon and discussed the flaws of ordinary empirical investigation in his previous discussion on the imagination. Malebranche thus rightly assumes that the enlightened reader, that is, one versed in the scientific method of Bacon and Descartes, can make his own extrapolations.

What then are these "other reasons" that one could raise against the Peripatetic theory? Malebranche himself provides all the clues in his

Malebranche
opposes reduc-
ing universals
to confused
assemblages
of sensuous
images.

subsequent works. Malebranche is primarily disturbed over the status of mathematical ideas and mathematical truths. For the Scholastic, a concept is a construct of thought. For Caterus, who was a Scholastic, for example, the idea of a triangle is not a distinct reality that requires a cause, other than the mind, to construct it. But for Malebranche, as will soon become apparent, if the mind is to be constitutive of the mathematical order of reality the possibility of an objective science and of truth must be foresworn. Furthermore, the concept, for a Scholastic, is like an effigy expressing some common property of many seen objects. Having observed many circles and found that they all have this in common, namely, that their radii from the center to the periphery are, in each, all equidistant, then the mind frames a general picture of the circle as such. The scholastic concept of a universal is thus a Euclidean image, whose formation follows the classificatory method. But for a Cartesian and Baconian, who has denied the Tree of Porphyry, for whom the essence of the circle is that intelligible relationship (in Descartes' case) conveyed by its algebraic expression, and for whom a grasp of the true facts is a grasp of the relationships existing in them, it becomes absurd to speak of a universal as an abstraction literally excised from empirical sense data or sensorial images. Hence even if there were impressed species sent off like Epicurean idols, how could they be transformed into intelligible meanings? That is, how can the universal, the essence, be a mere collection or confused assemblage of many particular instances—for example, shapes such as circles or ovals, squares or parallelograms?

Thus, crude as may be Malebranche's treatment of the Peripatetic doctrine, that Malebranche presents it in the form that he does, is epistemologically more significant for his own development than is any question of its historical validity. And perhaps he may have presented it in this exaggerated fashion with deliberation. For in rejecting the doctrine which he actually delineates, Malebranche thereby refuses materialism and nominalism as well; and not only that of Democritus or of Lucretius, but that of his own contemporaries, Hobbes and Gassendi, and therefore Newton.

For neither the early materialists nor their modern successors recognized any other principle of existence than matter in motion. For Lucretius, the soul is a composition of atoms, and seeing is the result of a blow on the eye. As for the concept, it is not more than a superimposed confusion of idols. This amounts to the assertion that a universal is but an arbitrary name for a confusion of sensory images. Such is the position of Hobbes and of Gassendi.[102] Both Hobbes and Gassendi hold that thought and sensation are phantasms, appearances resulting from the impact of external objects on the body.[103]

Consequently, when Malebranche asks: how can material images change into intelligible entities?—he, like Descartes, is discarding not only a materialistic metaphysics, but nominalism as well. This is clearly exhibited in his later work, *Entretiens sur la métaphysique*. Aristes asserts: "It seems to me that the mind can make general ideas out of several particular ideas. When one has seen several trees, an apple-tree, a pear-tree, a plum-tree, etc., one gets the general idea of a tree." Theodore contests Aristes' assertion: ". . . You cannot rid your mind of the thought that general ideas are no more than a confused collection of certain particular ideas, or at least of the thought that you have the power to form them out of this collective whole . . ." Theodore denies this account of the formation of universals. In order to think of a circle in general, Theodore accuses Aristes: "You think, Aristes, now of a circle with a diameter of one foot, then of one whose diameter is two feet, three feet, four feet, etc., and finally you do not determine the length of the diameter at all; and you think of a circle in general." But this is to equate the idea of a circle in general with the confused collection of circles of which Aristes has thought. Vehemently does Theodore challenge this nominalistic attitude:

> This conclusion is certainly false. *For the idea of a circle in general represents infinite circles and is applicable to them all,* and you have only thought of a finite number of circles. What happens must rather be that you have discovered the secret of forming the idea of a circle in general out of five or six circles that you have seen, and this is true in one sense and false in another. It is false if you mean that there is enough reality in the idea of five or six circles to form the idea of a circle in general. But it is true in the sense that after having recognized that the magnitude of the circles does not change their properties, you have perhaps ceased to consider them one after another as having a determinate magnitude in order to consider in general only an indeterminate magnitude. Thus you have, so to speak, formed the idea of a circle in general by spreading the idea of generality over the confused ideas of the circles which you have imagined . . .[104]

The First Alternative yields at best, then, for Malebranche, a world that duplicates sense. In this respect, the First Alternative is indeed about sense perception. But Malebranche is *rejecting* this alternative. And he does so, because he takes it for granted that when we perceive a circle or a square, we know a system of intelligible relations revealed through appearances that are ovals or parallelograms or through images which vary in size. Mere passive reception of sense cannot explain intelligible understanding and general, formal, relational knowledge.[105] This knowledge of universals is what is crucial for him.

[81]

V. Second Alternative: The Mind Creates Ideas

If the hypothesis of vaulting physical simulacra leads to insoluble problems, a less unlikely hypothesis may be that the soul still responds to external impressions, but does so by producing its own ideas. The external physical stimuli are retained—the soul is excited to produce or to create the ideas of the things about which it thinks by the impressions which objects make upon the brain—but *these* impressions are not physical replicas of the bodies that cause them, as is assumed in the first alternative theory of ideas. The proponents of this view, says Malebranche, claim that in this creative power of thought man is made in the image of God.[106]

The second hypothesis arises naturally when the first view of an actual influx of physical entities is denied. Probably, the reason why Malebranche formulates this position precisely as he does is that such a conception is indeed entertained by Descartes' precursors. According to Gilson, both before and after St. Thomas many theologians attempted various reconciliations between the Aristotelian and the Platonic theories of ideas. One of these reconciliations is this: in place of considering the image-object as being introduced to sense by the material object itself, in perception, the soul instantaneously forms in itself the image of this object. The senses, according to this view, play only the role of stimulus, announcing the object and exciting the soul to represent the object to itself.[107] The second hypothesis is, in this way, an adulterated form of the philosophies of both Plato and Aristotle.

Malebranche raises two kinds of objections against this type of theory. One kind is argued on metaphysical grounds; the second upon epistemological grounds. The metaphysical objections are these. Ideas are real things, in that they have real and distinctive properties. Granted that ideas are not substances, they are nevertheless "des êtres, et des êtres spirituels." From physical motion, on the other hand, only further physical motion can be produced. Physical bodies can contribute nothing to the formation of an intelligible entity. Accordingly, if the second hypothesis is formulated as the supposition that the human mind can *transform* a physical process into a spiritual one, then this alternative is equivalent to the supposition that the mind can *create* something out of nothing, inasmuch as *there is nothing in common between matter in motion and ideas*. It is as difficult to create (even more difficult) an angel out of a rock than out of nothing at all says Malebranche.[108]

On the other hand, if the hypothesis is formulated as the supposition that the mind *creates* ideas upon the occasion of material impres-

Metaphysical
objection:
creation *ex
nihilo.*

sions, then again the hypothesis actually assumes creation out of nothing. But creation of something *ex nihilo* is for man unthinkable no matter what reason there may be for affirming it, not only to Descartes and to his critical disciple, Malebranche, but also to their contemporaries of almost all shades of opinion and to nearly all their forebears, except, of course, such materialistic sensationalists as Hobbes and Gassendi. With perhaps these latter in mind, Malebranche adds that creation *ex nihilo* is even less difficult to conceive than the creation of ideas out of physical movements.[109] He suggests that all those who advocate this creationist view do so only because they neglect and scorn the intrinsic reality of universals.

The epistemological assault is even more significant than the preceding one, even though this antecedent metaphysical argument depends upon the tenet of the reality of ideas. The present second attack is directly concerned with *a priori* certainty. Not limited, as is the first merely to the denial that man has the power to fabricate real beings, it instead probes more deeply to ask *how* the mind can be asserted to create ideas. Even were one to grant creative power to man to produce and to annihilate ideas, Malebranche argues, nevertheless man could never avail himself of this power. For just as a painter, however skilful, cannot draw an animal that he has never seen, just as he cannot be sure that his picture is a true resemblance without consulting the original object, so a man cannot will or create ideas unless he is already acquainted with them, that is, unless he already has the ideas. And if he already possesses the idea, he knows *it;* to create another becomes a vain activity.[110] Hence it is useless to attribute a creative power to the mind. In order to uphold the Second Alternative, men must already possess the ideas for which the alternative professes to account.

Epistemological objection: creativity assumes a priori model.

In the first of the *Entretiens sur la métaphysique,* Aristes asks Theodore, "what becomes of our ideas when we no longer think of them? To me it seems that they retire into non-being." To this Theodore replies:

> What, Aristes! Can you possibly believe, then, that in resolving to think of a circle, for example, you are giving being to the substance, so to speak, of which your idea is formed, and that as soon as you decide to cease thinking of it you are annihilating it? Be careful. If it is you who give being to your ideas, you do so by willing to think of them. But, now, how can you will to think of a circle, if you have as yet no idea of it and out of which to form and complete it? Can you will anything without knowing it? Could you make something out of nothing? Certainly, you cannot will to think of a circle if you have as yet no idea of it, or at least of extension, of certain parts of which you could think without thinking of others.[111]

Malebranche argues, then, that the mind does not produce ideas on the occasions upon which it needs them, because ideas, being resistant factual beings, are themselves the models which would be required to guide the fashioning of themselves. If man had the power to produce ideas, accordingly, it would be of no avail to appeal to this power.

Should one affirm that the soul has general *confused* ideas which it does not produce, but that it produces merely the particular, clear and distinct ideas, then rejoins Malebranche in the *Recherche:* just as a painter cannot draw the portrait of a particular man without having had direct acquaintance with him, so if the soul does not already possess a clear and distinct idea of a horse, it is incapable of producing one from the general idea of being as such or of an animal as such and of knowing surely that it is perfectly similar to the horse; but if it has this first idea, it has no need for creating a second.[112] And the problem concerns *the origin and nature of that first idea.*

Malebranche does not say just who might have supposed that from the general idea of an animal the specific idea of a horse could be derived. Perhaps he was acquainted with the seventeenth century philosopher Silhon who seems to have advocated such a view.[113] Or perhaps he had in mind Descartes himself. For in the third Meditation, Descartes suggests that from the notion of substance he might be able to derive not only the ideas of extension and figure, but that of a specific object like a rock.[114]

But whomever Malebranche may be here criticizing, the interesting feature of this objection lies in his seeming to use Aristotelian weapons to refute it. He seems to be saying that in order to apprehend a specific universal—the particular geometric shape such as is characteristic of a horse—, it must be given in sense; that it could not be directly derived from the more general notion of being as such.

On the other hand, immediately after raising the above objection, Malebranche hastens to add that ideas of sense and imagination are clear and distinct only to the extent that they conform to those of pure intellection.[115] Here he is using Platonic weapons. We can conceive a square by pure conception; we can also imagine it. But the imagined or seen square is not itself more clear and distinct than the one conceived. On the contrary, it is the intelligible square that serves as the rule and standard for judging the clarity, correctness, and precision of what is seen or imagined. It is the understanding that guides and regulates the imagination. It is impossible for the mind to imagine a square without at the same time conceiving it.[116] The mind cannot label, identify, grasp the imagined square without having a pure concept, squareness. On the contrary, the imagined square is itself judged by comparison with the concept.[117] Because it is the concept, idea, or object of pure intellection which regulates, governs, and judges the

Malebranche attacks the Second Alternative with both Aristotelian and Platonic weapons.

correctness of the image, the pure perception of it is far more clear and distinct than imagination or sensation. But now the whole problem before us is to determine the origin of this concept. If we have the concept there is no need to seek it in the image.

When Malebranche argued in this fashion, he of course had in mind Descartes' own attack against abstracting concepts from images. In the *Meditations* Descartes denies the content of the first two alternatives, that the idea of a triangle reaches his mind through the medium of his senses, upon viewing bodies triangular in shape. Descartes contends that he can form in his mind infinitely many figures without being able to conceive them ever to have been objects of sense.[118] Again, in his replies to Gassendi he declares: "Certainly we should not be able to recognize the Geometrical triangle by looking at that which is drawn on paper, unless our mind possessed an idea of it derived from other sources." [119] And Descartes also repudiated Hobbes' contention that the mind arbitrarily wills or makes concepts.[120]

Although Malebranche thus had in mind Descartes' strictures against the efficacy of sense in creating concepts, it seems to me that in offering the examples of the horse and of the painter, Malebranche is saying something other than and more than Descartes. He apparently is making two points. On the one hand, he evidently would defer to the empiricist, to the Aristotelian, by admitting that an object like a horse cannot be the spontaneous product of the mind; that it pre-requires the concrete perception of a horse to know precisely what universal the horse exemplifies. Without sense the mind could not know what universal to consider. On the other hand, he defers to Plato: it is the pure understanding that alone can recognize and fully comprehend what is presented to sense; and only because, logically speaking, the mind is already, *a priori*, acquainted with the perfect square, can it effectively comprehend it and judge it when it is contained in sense and in imagination. It is for these reasons that the ascription of creative power to the mind to form intelligible species is useless. Such a capacity is valueless, because universals must be initially present to sense to become discovered; and they must already pre-exist and be present to the pure understanding in order to be fully understood when disclosed by sense.

His criticisms of the present Second Alternative are thus consistent with his inductive method, which we examined in Chapter I: universals are first present in perception; there is nothing in the mind that is not first given in sense. Yet it is not by abstraction from sense or by any spontaneous mental creation that the universal is known. Rather, it is by a process of subtraction, so to speak. Through greater attention the mind uncovers what is first given confusedly.

[85]

Malebranche concludes his treatment of the Second Alternative with the claim that all those who attribute to the soul a power of creating ideas of things, a knowledge of which it does not have, deceive themselves; and Malebranche can explain their error. This error is precisely that of the men holding the previous alternative. It lies in their concluding from the frequent conjunction of two things that one is the *true* cause of the other. People conclude that their will which accompanies the presence of ideas is the true cause of these ideas, because they know of nothing else to which they can attribute the ideas, and because they imagine that ideas cease to exist as soon as the understanding ceases to apprehend them, recommencing to exist as soon as they become present to the understanding. For the same reason, namely, of confusing constant conjunction with causal connection, people conclude that external bodies send off resembling species; for, not being able to apprehend objects in themselves, but only through ideas, one judges that the mind produces the idea, because ordinarily the idea is present to the mind in sense perception when the object occurs.[121]

Thus in a single conclusion Malebranche criticizes the first two alternatives; they involve a corruption of the understanding with respect to the nature of causality and to the nature of ideas.

In rejecting the Peripatetic hypotheses of impression and mental creation of ideas through external stimulus, Malebranche has essentially argued that even if the mind can produce mental events in either manner this would be of no value for knowledge. At this stage Malebranche is satisfied that intelligible ideas cannot originate in passive sensation. There is, of course, nothing surprising in his rejection of passive sensation, since he really has assumed a theory of non-temporal universals all along; but it has been necessary for us to consider his objections in order to determine their nature. It is now perfectly apparent that while these criticisms do bear on sense perception, they are in the first instance arguments against the genetic origination of universals. Malebranche's counterclaims against the Peripatetics reduce to this, that no genetic account of universals can afford the absolute certainty and independent reality of mathematical ideas, of which Malebranche is antecedently assured because of his conception of mathematics and of scientific method.

VI. Descartes' Ideas "Equitably" Interpreted

To reiterate, Malebranche's fundamental antagonism to the Peripatetic views, of impressed species and of mental sensory response to external stimuli, stems from his mathematical a-priorism. Underlying his denunciation of the two alternatives is his pre-assumed notion that

Malebranche explains why one would propose this Second Alternative.

knowledge of universals is acquaintance with already-existing ideas. But why, then, will he be unsympathetic to Descartes? For Descartes' ideas are innate. When the finite mind is arbitrarily created, it is endowed with a treasure of latent ideas. Ideas are in the mind and are there without non-mental assistance. For Descartes, ideas exist in the mind prior to and independent of its unity with the body. They await only summoning forth or eliciting by reflection.[122] This innate view contains intrinsically within it the element of a-priorism that Malebranche could not find in the Peripatetics. With respect to major aspects of Malebranche's thought, innatism offers him everything that he could ask for, and in these respects he must find it impeccably sound. It permits psychophysical dualism and the purging of all material elements from the mind; acquaintance in knowledge, according to which, to know an object is to be intimately united with it; an idealism, in which every immediate object of thought is an intelligible entity; and ideaism, or the doctrine that ideas are real beings. And yet Malebranche claimed that Descartes did not analyze the nature of ideas "*à fond.*"[123] Why?

Descartes, we saw, maintained that ideas, as modes of thought, are all alike. Only in their "objective reality" do ideas differ from one another, in perfection and in their properties. By the objective reality of an idea, Descartes understands:

> l'entité ou l'être de la chose représentée par l'idée, en tant que cette entité est dans l'idée . . . Car tout ce que nous concevons comme étant dans les objets des idées, tout cela est objectivement, ou par représentation, dans les idées mêmes.[124]

Does Descartes identify act of thought with object?

And it is to this objective reality of an idea, to the idea as the image or similitude of an object to which, Descartes declared, the term *idea* must properly speaking be assigned.

Now a problem arises with respect to Descartes' doctrine. When Descartes considers the mind to be conceiving or intuiting the idea or the objective reality of a triangle, does he mean to identify the operation or state of mind that *thinks* with the idea-triangle which is the object of thought? Assuredly there must be some kind of distinction in an epistemology which holds thoughts to be real entities; for if the objective reality were exactly the same as the mode of thinking, then by no means could there be any distinction between the thought of a circle and that of a triangle; and Descartes is explicit that these two acts do not differ from each other in so far as they are acts.[125] They differ only as objects of thought. Moreover, Descartes defines a mode of thought as finite and transient; but he considers the similitude of the triangle or the idea of God to be an immutable nature. Yet Descartes uses the term "idea" indiscriminately for the transient modes or acts of thinking and for the immutable "objective reality" or representative similitudes of external objects.

Arnauld and Régis, in their own philosophies, maintained what undoubtedly is the orthodox interpretation of Descartes, namely, the identification of act and object.[126] They thus understood the Cartesian idea as a single metaphysical unit possessing, nevertheless, a radically dual function as well as a two-sided nature. An idea is not only simultaneously act and object, but it possesses radically distinct and contradictory properties in its separate offices.[127]

Now Malebranche could not see why one should suppose that Descartes would believe a thing to be one, when looking at it from two different points of view endows it with two incompatible sets of properties.[128] He therefore maintained that Descartes suffered from an unfortunate ambiguity of language in designating both thinking and also object of thought by the single term idea. Malebranche flatly asserts that for Descartes the word idea is not used univocally.[129] Upon the basis of Descartes' third Meditation where Descartes claims that modes of thought are not different from one another, that only in their objective reality do ideas possess a representative function, and that it is to these alone that the term idea is properly to be ascribed, Malebranche concludes not only that Descartes did intend to separate states of consciousness from ideas representing external objects, but also that this interpretation is intrinsically more equitable than that of Arnauld.[130] We shall see that Malebranche's fairness to Descartes in rendering him more consistent with himself than his writings explicitly support is not disinterested. Interpreting Descartes "equitably" constitutes a major step toward repudiating Descartes' claim that ideas are created. Malebranche believes that his own interpretation of Descartes' ideas is more just than is Arnauld's, not only because it renders Descartes more consistent with himself for the above-mentioned reasons, but also because it avoids *de jure* the consequences of certain subjectivistic tendencies which Malebranche finds in Arnauld's position. (It does not avoid these consequences *de facto*, because Descartes never developed the many implications which Malebranche finds to be implicit in that interpretation.) In Arnauld's theory Malebranche found defects which he did not wish to assert to be absolutely intrinsic to Descartes' doctrine. I shall show, however, that these alleged flaws are also indigenous to the more "equitable" interpretation. Nevertheless, rather than ascribe to Descartes a position that undermines the very nature of the Cartesian metaphysics, Malebranche preferred to let him rest in equivocation and ambiguity. He thus held the "Cartesians," rather than Descartes, responsible for openly holding the doctrine that act and object are identical.[131]

Because of Descartes' ambiguous position and because of Male-

Malebranche's "equitable" separation of act and object in Descartes.

branche's "equitable" re-evaluation of Descartes, when Malebranche considers the doctrine of innate ideas in the Third Alternative, he takes it as a "magazine" of ideas "in" the mind, without, however, naming Descartes as the protagonist. And in the Fourth Alternative he will consider what today may be called the "orthodox" Cartesian (Arnauld's and Régis') position that identifies act and object. Thus together the objections to the third and fourth alternatives constitute a refutation both of the more and of the less "equitable" interpretations of Descartes.

VII. THIRD ALTERNATIVE: IDEAS AS INNATE

(a) *Metaphysical Argument against Innatism.* Malebranche's first argument against innatism is this. The mind can conceive an infinite number of simple figures to belong to a family of figures, for example, the members of a family of regular polygons or of circles. Moreover, it can conceive an infinite number of different types or species of each of these simple figures, such as types of triangles or of ellipses.[132] In the philosophy of clear and distinct ideas, to know that a class contains an infinite number of members, it is necessary to perceive all these members at once, in some non-imaginative manner, that is, as a system of relations of relations.

Conceiving infinity.

Thus the mind has a general idea of an infinite number of figures. It cannot comprehend this infinite number, but it can conceive it. As Mr. Schrecker observes [133]—and indeed as Descartes himself did [134] —Malebranche makes a distinction between knowledge by comprehension and knowledge by conception. The mind, being finite and limited, cannot "com-prehend" the infinite, but it can clearly conceive it.[135] We saw, in our discussion of method, to what extent the notion of the infinite enters into his conception of algebraic truths. Hence, writes Malebranche in his discussion on innate ideas, the mind has:

> . . . un nombre infini d'idées; que dis-je, un nombre infini! il a autant de nombres infinis d'idées qu'il y a de différentes figures; de sorte que puisqu'il y a un nombre infini de différentes figures, il faut, pour connaître seulement les figures, que l'esprit ait une infinité de nombres infinis d'idées.[136]

Now, is it likely—on the metaphysical supposition of simplicity—that God should create an infinity of infinite numbers of ideas with *each* created mind? Notice that at this point Malebranche does not say that it is impossible. Instead, he merely questions its plausibility. In so doing he is quite in accord with the general spirit of Cartesianism, for Descartes constantly argued in his attack on Scholasticism against the useless multiplication of entities, striving to employ the *most simple principles* in his explanations of physical phenomena.[187] Similarly, Descartes substituted his own four rules in the place of scholastic logic on the ground that, like political laws, the fewer the precepts the more advantageous they are.[188] Thus Malebranche is Cartesian in so far as he believes himself to be capable of offering a metaphysical hypothesis that will account for the presence of an infinity of infinite numbers of ideas to each mind, without having recourse to the creation of countless counterparts corresponding to the number of possible minds. This argument from simplicity is at best a probable one; it is not a refutation of the doctrine of innate ideas.

(*b*) *Argument from Sense Perception.* Even if the soul should have a magazine of all the ideas, it would nevertheless remain difficult to explain how the soul would be able to choose among them to represent objects to itself, how, for example, it could occur that in the very same moment that the soul opens its eyes in the middle of a field, it should perceive all those various objects, the size, figure, distance and motion of which it discovers at once. Malebranche doubts that it would be able even to distinguish a single object like the sun, when the latter would be present to the eyes; for, since the image which the sun impresses on the brain does not resemble our idea of the sun (First Alternative), it is inconceivable that the soul could correctly select among the infinite number of ideas in this spiritual magazine the one candidate necessary for imagining or perceiving the sun, or for seeing it of some particular determinate size.[139]

Selecting the correct idea from the magazine of innate ideas.

This objection is similar to one advanced in the previous alternative against the suggestion that the mind could spontaneously create intelligible and sensible species, such as enter into the perception of a horse, that physical movements could excite the mind to produce the image of a horse. In the present alternative, the supposition is that the mind simply "elicits" the right idea, the one necessary for perceiving the sun. And, as in the former case, Malebranche's implied criticisms are: *first,* that unless the mind were already acquainted with the sun's image and unless this sense perception already contained a specific intelligible content (for example, a given size or shape), it would be impossible *a priori* to know what universal should be correlated with what sensations to give the perception of a particular object; and *second,* that unless the perceived object, like the sun, already carried with it an intelligible content, how would the soul know which purely mathematical relationship to select in order to get the proper insight into the perceptual field?

I find these contentions illuminating, because, once more, they seem to indicate both the empirical and the rational sides of Malebranche. On the one hand, he denies that mathematical relations are constructs derived from sense. But equally he seems to be saying that an intelligible meaning must be given with and contained within perception; otherwise there could be no proper correlation between the seen and the known. It is the algebraic equation of the circle, for example, that enlightens the mind in seeing a circular sun, but unless it first saw the circle and unless the circle embodied that relation, how would it know that it ought to attend to that equation rather than to any other? In the light of his method and of subsequent arguments, we may then say, that this criticism of innatism is equivalent to the rejection of any idealistic view that makes mind creative or constitutive in knowledge, a denial that essences depend upon being perceived or conceived.[140]

(c) *Argument against a More Liberal Interpretation of Innateness.* Suppose innateness to be interpreted more liberally, Malebranche goes on to suggest.[141] Consider that God produces at each moment as many new ideas as we perceive different things. Against this position Malebranche argues first that it is not compatible with simplicity. Secondly, at any time the mind can desire to consider any one or all of an infinity of ideas, as a family of circles. And, arguing as before, for the will to consider or attend to the properties of any idea such as that of a chiliagon, a necessary prerequisite is that the mind be already in some measure acquainted with the concept to which it wishes to apply itself. Thus at every moment the mind must be confronted with an infinitely vast number of ideas, for any idea involves infinite relations. Hence it is not *likely* that God creates at each moment the ideas as we will to think of them, inasmuch as then we must be acquainted with so many of them in order to will to think of any. *God supplies concepts as needed—difficulties over infinite relations.*

(d) *M. Gouhier's Claim.* If now we stop to take stock of the above three arguments, can we seriously maintain that they constitute an impeccable refutation of Descartes? We cannot. While they tell us a great deal about *Malebranche* and his notions of conceiving infinity and the need for *a priori* meanings, none of them attests to any inherently logical inconsistency in *Descartes'* position. And if there were no additional argument on the part of Malebranche against Descartes, we should be compelled to admit with Henri Gouhier that essentially there is no vital intellectual or logical disagreement between Malebranche and Descartes. *Gouhier holds Malebranche not in significant disagreement with Descartes' innatism.*

Considering solely the above three complaints and noting the fact that Malebranche claimed that Descartes did not identify the changing states or acts of thinking with the eternal, immutable objects of thought, Gouhier concludes that whereas there is a deep-seated opposition between Malebranche and the Scholastics (Alternatives I and II), on the one hand, and between Malebranche and Arnauld and Régis (Alternative IV), on the other hand, there is no more than a *religious* clash between Descartes and Malebranche. Innatism is **not** regarded by Malebranche as an intellectual vice or refuted on intellectual grounds. He simply considers it as an unnecessarily complicated hypothesis and therefore an unlikely one; he *prefers* his own as better and more economical. Malebranche, claims Gouhier, cannot accept Descartes' innate ideas in a *Christian philosophy*, for that doctrine does not make man sufficiently dependent on his Creator.[142]

Now I have no quarrel with Gouhier in maintaining that Malebranche's peculiarly religious bias,—one that seeks to make God the constant and sole center of man's devotion in every human activity,— would make Malebranche dissatisfied with Descartes' philosophy. As a matter of fact, when Malebranche finally comes to the exposition and defense of his own theory on the nature of ideas, he asserts that his own doctrine, unlike that of Descartes, "met les esprits créés dans une entière dépendance de Dieu et la plus grande qui puisse être." [143] Nevertheless, I insist that this is neither the sole nor the major reason for Malebranche's rejection of Descartes. Indeed, even this notion of "dependence" must be qualified. It is true, as the above passage indicates and as Gouhier affirms, that Malebranche wants man to be in constant communion with God and not merely, as in Descartes, dependent upon God as an effect is dependent on its efficient cause. There is another kind of dependency implied by this passage, however, that Malebranche seeks to establish between man and God. It is one which he himself discloses to Régis in a commentary on the very passage in question.[144] This second kind of dependency may be called "social" and rational. It consists in giving man and God a common sphere of interests. Descartes, by making God the legislator of the true and the good, erected an impassable frontier between human reason and will and those of God, thus allowing no other relation between God and man than that of cause to effect. Malebranche demands the more intimate conjunction of the existence of a common truth at once for God and man.

Gouhier, then, maintains that Malebranche does not *refute* Descartes. To accept Gouhier's opinion we must either assume that the Third Alternative is not at all directed against Descartes or else conclude that Malebranche erred. For Malebranche firmly believed that the Third Alternative involves a contradiction. In a letter to Arnauld he asserts that "all" the alternatives, and this includes the present one, embrace manifest contradictions.[145]

Gouhier errs in supposing that there is no theoretical clash between Malebranche and Descartes, because, first of all, he neglects a most significant statement, made by Malebranche at the very end of his treatment of Descartes' innate ideas, and because, secondly, he does not realize that every major objection that Malebranche employs against the proponents of the Fourth Alternative can in all its strength

Infinity and the "magazine" hypothesis.

be directed against Descartes. This second point I shall establish only after completing the discussion of the Fourth Alternative. At present I shall consider the following statement voiced by Malebranche at the end of his denial that God recreates ideas at every moment, as and when we perceive them:

> De plus, il est évident que l'idée ou l'objet immédiat de notre esprit, lorsque nous pensons à des espaces immenses, à un cercle en général, à l'être indéterminé, n'est rien de créé; car toute réalité créé ne peut être ni infinie ni même générale, tel qu'est ce que nous apercevons alors. *Mais tout cela se verra plus clairement dans la suite.*[146]

It goes without saying that if this is a legitimate objection against the recreation of ideas at every instant, it is equally valid against Descartes' supposition of their having been created at all. It is true that Malebranche added the paragraph just quoted after the first edition of the *Recherche*. Nevertheless, the very fact that he went out of his way to do so, shows that Malebranche held that whatever he had to say against the Fourth Alternative applies to the Third.

The decisive argument against innate ideas, then, is that we cannot contain within our finite created minds real beings which are actually general and infinite. This contention of Malebranche turns on a fundamental principle of the Cartesian epistemology. It forces us to re-examine the nature of Descartes' "representative" idea. We shall find that a Cartesian idea, in representing or objectifying the properties of an independent object of thought, must itself *actually be characterized by the properties represented.* Secondly, this admonition of Malebranche against innate ideas will force us to examine Descartes' notion of the "infinite."

(*e*) *How Cartesian Ideas "represent."* What does "representative" or "objective reality" mean for Descartes? That an idea for Descartes is *not* a physical image in the brain, we saw above, is clear. That it is not a physical miniature of an external object is also clear both from his definition of an idea and also from Descartes' rejection of scholastic physics. Whence it follows that ideas are spiritual entities. It is only in this respect that it is correct to say that no correspondence obtains between an idea and its object. Nevertheless the resemblance-theory of ideas is in one form still upheld by Descartes. For Descartes defines the objective reality of an idea as an "image," [147] a "similitude," a "portrait." [148] Because ideas are spiritual we cannot say of the idea of a triangle, for example, that it is triangular, or three-sided, in the way in which the corresponding concrete actual object may be. Yet, the idea, still remaining a counterpart, similitude or "picture," must, notwithstanding, *in some manner* encompass and be made of all the properties of the object of which it is a counterpart. It is in virtue of

Cartesian ideas spiritually contain what they objectify.

this requirement that we pass from the terms "objective reality" and "representation" to the terms "contain" and "composition." That Descartes does in fact make this transition in language is clear from his declaration that the "images" which "represent" substances "*are* something more, and *contain* so to speak more objective reality *within them . . .*" [149] Again when Descartes in the third Meditation considers the clear and distinct idea of corporeal substance, he speaks of this idea as being "composed" of the qualities of extension, figure, situation, and motion.[150] Of course, the manner in which ideas thus *contain* or are *composed* of physical properties is *ideal* or *spiritual,* or *intelligible.* Yet, while the ideas of extension contain extended properties in a spiritual manner, the properties which are thus ideally included are not themselves spiritual properties. For there is a vital distinction between the spirituality of Descartes' idea of a triangle and the spirituality of Descartes' idea of the soul. The former is spiritually or intelligibly figured, divisible, extended and the latter is not. This distinction is important, for upon it depends Descartes' dualism. Physical properties are contained spiritually or objectively in ideas without becoming spiritual properties.

Now, inasmuch as the objective reality of an idea or the idea as a representative similitude must be "composed of" or "contain" the properties that its actually existing corresponding counterparts may have, the question arises, how can a created finite entity, as is Descartes' innate idea, "contain" or be "composed of" infinite and, especially, general properties? How can the created, finite determinate idea of a triangle contain or possess the properties of "all" triangles? How can the finite idea of God "contain" the infinite properties of God? Malebranche's claim is that the finite idea *cannot* contain infinite, general, universal, and perfect properties. For, to contain them, the idea must be characterized by them. The idea, aside from its formal or objective (in the modern sense) properties in which it is distinguished from no other idea, is distinguished from any other idea only in its objective (in Descartes' representative or "containing" sense) properties. These sole distinctive characteristics are only the characteristics of the actual material object represented or objectified spiritually. Malebranche's argument in short is that for a Cartesian idea to represent or objectify something that is not an idea, the idea must really be characterized by the properties of the external thing.[151]

The objection might here be raised that the Cartesian general idea might be interpreted to be a real mental object which represents an independent object solely in virtue of the relation of *signification.* This

is the position of the extreme nominalists or "termists," a position which Berkeley later occupied, when he declared that while ideas can never be abstract, they become general by being made "to represent or stand for" other particular ideas of the same sort.[152] Now it is true that Descartes in the *Principles* declares that an idea or a word becomes universal by being used to represent several objects of similar kind:

> Universals arise solely from the fact that we avail ourselves of one and the same idea in order to think of all individual things which have a certain similitude; and when we comprehend under the same *name* all the objects represented by this idea, that *name* is universal. For example, when we see two stones, and without thinking further of their nature than to remark that there are two, we form in ourselves an idea of a certain number which we term the number of two; and when afterwards we see two birds or two trees, and we observe without further thinking about their nature, that there are two of them, we again take up the same idea which we had before, which idea is universal; and we give to this number the universal *name* 'two.' And *in the same way* when we consider a three-sided figure we form a certain idea which we call the idea of a triangle; and we afterwards make use of it as a universal in representing to ourselves all the figures having three sides.[153]

But while Descartes renders an idea or word universal in this manner, by using it to represent several similar objects, he does not leave the problem of the *similarity* of objects *in virtue of which they may be grouped under a single idea or name* unexplained.

To Hobbes, Descartes declares:

> . . . in reasoning we unite not names but the things signified by the names; and I marvel that the opposite can occur to anyone. For who doubts whether a Frenchman and a German are able to reason in exactly the same way about the same things, though they yet conceive the words in an entirely diverse way? And has not my opponent condemned himself in talking of conventions arbitrarily made about the meanings of words? For, if he admits that words signify anything, why will he not allow our reasonings to refer to this something that is signified, rather than to the words alone?[154]

Thus while Descartes (like Spinoza)[155] denies universals of the Aristotelian, abstractionistic kind and considers these alone in a nominalistic light, he assuredly believes in his own brand of universals. But for Malebranche the problem is precisely this: is the Cartesian innate universal pure and unalloyed? That is, can a general term be a created, particular entity? Like Descartes in the *Principles* and like Berkeley, Malebranche admits that in some instances the mind can form general meanings; it can classify objects into genera and species; it can thus let a particular "stand for" a whole set of instances; in short, the mind can generalize. But, insists Malebranche, this very capacity to generalize testifies to the presence of a real universal.

Malebranche's insistence on real universals.

Were there *no* universals this generalizing activity would be impossible.[156] I have already called attention to the passage in the *Entretiens sur la métaphysique* wherein Malebranche declares that the general idea of the circle cannot be framed from a collection of particular circles, except in the sense that the mind possesses the secret of "spreading the idea of generality" over the multiplicity of particular instances. He goes on to say:

> . . . Yet I submit to you that you can form general ideas at all only because you find in the idea of Infinity enough reality to give generality to your ideas. You can think of an indeterminate diameter only because you see the infinite in extension and because you can increase or diminish it *ad infinitum.* I submit to you that you could never think of the abstract forms of genera and species, if the idea of the Infinite which is inseparable from your mind did not naturally become united with the particular idea of which you are aware. You could think of a definite circle, but not of a circle in general. You could become aware of a certain definite equality between radii but not of a general equality between indeterminate radii.

> The reason is that no finite and determinate idea can ever represent anything infinite or indeterminate. The mind, however, without any reflection adds to its finite ideas the idea of generality which it finds in the Infinite. For just as the mind spreads over the idea of a definite extension, though it be divisible *ad infinitum,* the idea of indivisible unity, so it spreads over certain particular ideas the general idea of perfect equality.[157]

It must be noted, too, that while the above view is thus expressed so very clearly in this later work, it was also perspicuously expounded in his earliest work, namely, in the *Recherche,* in his book on method.[158]

Now, then, we are back at the main problem. If there are real universals, and there are, as Descartes acknowledges, can these be said to be innate and thus created? Descartes thought they could be, for he claimed that God arbitrarily willed the essences of things to be universal and immutable. But to Malebranche this innatism and creationism must have appeared as in principle equivalent to nominalism or abstractionism. For the sole difference lies in the legislating *agency:* for a nominalist like Hobbes, it is the human will that arbitrates or decrees general terms; for Descartes it is the arbitrary will of God or the eliciting power of the mind. Perhaps this is why Malebranche complained that Descartes was too much attached to the senses.[159] But let us see how Malebranche further discusses this notion of the infinite.

(*f*) *Malebranche's Infinite versus Descartes' Indefinite.* The single Cartesian idea represents more than one object, because it contains spiritually the property in virtue of which the objects represented form a group. And to represent or objectify the properties of an external thing, a Cartesian idea must, we saw, really be characterized by the properties represented. Seizing on this fundamental principle in Descartes' epistemology, Malebranche now argues that we do in fact know propositions which involve infinity. Since the Cartesian idea contains what it represents, Malebranche forces Descartes to the position of holding that a finite real entity contains something infinite. This possibility Descartes would not and could not himself affirm, although from Malebranche's point of view it would appear that he has to do so.[160]

Descartes admits that we possess the idea of the infinite God. Aside from this idea, Descartes argues, we do not have ideas of infinity, but, instead, we do have ideas of indefiniteness.[161] To Malebranche, Descartes' appeal to *indefiniteness* is an equivocation, for Descartes is the philosopher of clear and distinct ideas. The present argument against the "magazine" alternative of innateness depends in large measure on the forcible dissipation of this equivocation.

In the *Entretiens sur la métaphysique*, Aristes, speaking in Cartesian fashion, grants that the mind perceives an extension to which it can assign no limit, but denies that it perceives infinite extension; a finite mind cannot behold the infinite.[162] Theodore, or Malebranche, replies: The mind when it thinks of the infinite cannot indeed embrace, comprehend, or be equal to its object; its perception is indeed finite; nevertheless, it knows *that* its object of thought *is* infinite, and it knows this fact, not because the mind is unable to conceive a limit to its object, but because it conceives it as an object without limit.[163] Suppose a man, fallen from the clouds, starts walking in a straight line upon the earth. Has he the right, after any number of days of journeying, to conclude that the earth is infinite, because he can find no end to it? If he is wise and circumspect, he will conclude simply that the earth is very large, but not that it is limitless, because he can find no limit. It is otherwise, however, with the idea of extension. We know it clearly and without doubt; it is infinite and therefore inexhaustible, or without end. Additional examples of how we perceive the infinite are the following: While improper fractions multiplied once by themselves approach eight, they never become equal to eight. The branches of a hyperbola approach the asymptotes but do not reach them. Mathematicians confidently assert, without recourse to experience, that no part of the diagonal of a square, be the part as small as the tiniest grain of dust, can exactly measure, without remainder, this diagonal plus one of its sides. To mathematicians who are exact in their reasonings, affirms Malebranche, these examples are known to be true at once and without finite induction from particulars.

We can conceive, but not comprehend, the infinite.

Malebranche concludes:

> . . . The mind can see the infinite in the small as well as in the great; not by division or repeated multiplication of its finite ideas which could never reach the infinite, but by the infinity itself which it discovers in its ideas and which belongs to them. These ideas teach it that on the one hand there is no unity [no ultimately small element], and on the other that there are no limits.[164]

Thus the idea of space or extension that has no limits, or of infinite extension, is of a vast *reality*, for it is an idea, and yet it is immense, immeasurable, inexhaustible, and positively limitless.

(g) *Malebranche's First Crucial Argument against Innatism.* Recall that Malebranche offered a "more equitable" interpretation of Descartes, one which distinguished intellectual thought from intelligible object of thought. Having thus removed Descartes' "equivocation," Malebranche rejects innateness in this manner. It is not merely unreasonable and improbable that the mind contains an innate store of ideas, but it is impossible; it is an hypothesis inadequate to explain the following truth. When the idea or immediate object of the mind is that of an immense space, it is clear that this object of thought cannot be an actual entity created by another entity, for that no actual entity so created is ever infinite was a commonplace to Descartes and Malebranche.[165] Yet Descartes' ideas are created in this manner. *Hence every idea of an infinite object must be an infinite idea.* And for Malebranche there are infinite ideas, or, more properly speaking, there are conceptions of many different infinities. In fact, Malebranche can conceive an infinity of infinities and both finite and infinite relations among infinites.[166] The "magazine" hypothesis of innate ideas is accordingly deficient in two ways: it is improbable that an infinite store of infinitely different ideas exists in the mind to permit a perfect induction of an infinite idea, and it is not possible, even were this infinitely infinite store to exist, for the finite mind actually to contain even one real infinite idea or clear and distinct idea of the infinite. And Malebranche has convinced himself that indefinite ideas do not in every case replace infinite ideas.

These two arguments—that the mind probably does not contain an infinite assemblage of real entities, and that, if it does, it cannot contain an actually infinite entity—do not exhaust the list of objections against the "magazine" hypothesis. In the Fourth Alternative, to which we now turn, appear arguments against subjectivism, which also apply to the present "magazine" theory; these new criticisms are strong, and they reinforce the polemic based on infinity. Let us then consider the theory of innate ideas as still upon the table, awaiting further discussion. It will not be disposed of completely, until after the Fourth

[sidenote] Descartes cannot admit actually infinite ideas.

Alternative has been treated. Such a procedure has the advantage
that it does not depend solely on ruling out Descartes' appeal to indefiniteness. It will have this further important by-product: we shall
see that Malebranche is Machiavellian in conceding to Descartes a
"more equitable" interpretation of ideas, in which thought and thinking are distinguished. For I shall show how the arguments against the
Fourth Alternative may be employed to demonstrate that, even interpreted "equitably," Descartes at most merely makes a claim that
thought and thinking are distinct; he cannot substantiate this claim,
because he lacks an adequate cosmology. It will then be fully seen
that Malebranche's rejection of innatism as an unlikely hypothesis is
really equivalent to the assertion that it is a fiction, a merely convenient, fanciful construction, a supposition rather than a true explanation such as (we saw in Chapter I) a true hypothesis must offer.

Before turning to the Fourth Alternative, I wish to call attention to
an observation that I have already made in the previous chapter regarding Malebranche's notion of the infinite. Critic after critic,[167] and
notably Arnauld and Church, have maintained that in the *Recherche*
Malebranche speaks of ideas as if there were a distinct and separated
plurality of them. As evidence, Church, for example, calls attention
to the fact that in describing the reality and resistance of ideas, Malebranche appeals to their distinctive properties. Hence, when later on
Malebranche asserts that he does not and never intended to suggest
a plurality of essences, but only a single idea, which he calls intelligible
extension,[168] his critics charge him with a change of position.[169] Yet,
who but a carping and blind critic can not apprehend that this view
of an infinite extension is present *throughout* the *Recherche?* Does not
Malebranche's relational theory of extension, his treatment of truth
as a system of relations of relations *ad infinitum* in his book on method,
and his explicit references therein to the role of the infinite in algebra
and *again here in the treatment of innate ideas*—all show that he conceives of universals as a single interdependent and inter-connected
infinite continuum? How can anyone grounded in Descartes' method
which asserts that knowledge is not of isolated facts, but of their
serial order, and in Descartes' *Geometry* which treats ideas as relations
and which shows that a distinction among figures is only one of complexity—how can anyone knowing all this [170] assume that when Malebranche speaks of circles and triangles he is proposing a plethora of
isolated and unconnected ideas?

And what is equally amazing, how after Malebranche does make
his position on infinite extension clear, can anyone imagine that this
insistence on unity *obliterates* the notion of plurality altogether? For
Malebranche repeatedly insists that this idea is inexhaustible, meaning thereby, that it is not a homogeneous idea, but one that is replete

Malebranche's own notion of the organic unity of the infinite.

with a variety and diversity of mathematical figures. The denial of a distinct plurality is not equivalent to a rejection of manyness.

VIII. Fourth Alternative: Ideas Are the Mind's Own Modifications

(*a*) *The Position.* The Fourth Alternative proposes a position espoused by Arnauld, Régis and other "Cartesians." According to this hypothesis, the soul requires nothing but itself in order to understand objects; in considering itself and its own perfections, it can discover objects external to and different from itself; its ideas are solely its own modifications. When the mind knows truly, following this alternative, the mind modifies itself in some manner representative of the state of its object.[171]

The soul requires nothing but itself to understand objects.

That the mind can, immediately and without universals or representative ideas, know its own sensations, like heat and cold, pleasure and pain, and its own passions, volitions and pure intuitions, is to Malebranche indubitable. And he willingly acknowledges that all these operations truly are modifications, manners of being, dispositions, or particular affections of the mind. Through consciousness the mind does indeed, for him, become acquainted with its own states or operations. These subjective and private modifications, however, correspond to nothing that is external or objective. The difficulty is to determine whether ideas which *do* represent something other than the soul, such as the ideas of the sun, a house, a horse, a river, are no more than private states.

There are those people who maintain that the soul, having been made in order to think, has within itself, within its own perfections, all that is required to apprehend the nature of external objects; that, being more noble than all the material things which it can distinctly conceive, it can therefore contain their properties in some superior, spiritual or *eminent* fashion. Such a view, says Malebranche, stems from man's natural vanity, from a love for independence, from a desire to emulate God who does comprehend within Himself all things.[172] Malebranche may not be talking here directly against Descartes, yet assuredly he could not have been obtuse to the fact that this position which claims for the human mind what the Scholastics attributed to God is not only suggested in Descartes' *Meditations*,[173] but is precisely the position that Descartes defended in his *Reply* to Hobbes.[174]

But whether it be to Descartes or to the Cartesians, to whom he attributes this Faustian vanity, is not vital to the present essay. What is important is what he is arguing against. The Fourth Alternative maintains that the modifications or states of the soul can themselves represent external objects, so that the soul by considering its own operations can discover the nature of the external world. Recall that for Descartes, "to represent" means "to contain" or "to be composed of." Were the operations of minds to be thus representative of the properties of an external world, it would mean that mental states are in some manner composed of those very properties, and therefore can serve as their universal similitudes. For Malebranche's objections to this alternative that ideas are mental modifications, this proposition is central.

In the *Recherche*, Malebranche spoke only briefly against the modification-hypothesis. But his statements provoked severe criticism from Régis and especially from Arnauld. The latter engaged Malebranche in a controversy that was continued for over fifteen years. To examine this noted debate in detail would be beyond the scope of the present study. Malebranche offers a wide variety of objections to Arnauld's position, scattered through innumerable writings. These animadversions I shall now summarize and organize under a few leading heads.

(b) *Metaphysical Objections.* The first strictures that I shall treat are of a metaphysical nature. Among these, it is convenient to begin with the distinction which we have already considered, between infinite ideas and ideas of infinity. Unlike God's mind, Malebranche argues, the human mind is finite and limited. Hence it cannot contain within itself an infinite number of essences. Yet, as we saw above, it can know such an infinity. (1) Infinite ideas and ideas of infinity.

Malebranche repeatedly observes that the knowing process does not consist in merely a succession of one idea or object of thought after another, but that the mind is quite able to conceive or think of an infinity of numbers and an infinity of infinite members of geometric figures. The mind, although without clear and distinct *comprehension*, can "think of" the whole realm of extended objects simultaneously. This assertion we have already noted. It is applied to the present hypothesis in this manner. If ideas were identical with operations of the mind, as the present hypothesis asserts, then the soul would either have the capacity to exhibit an infinite state of mind or be modified by an infinite number of such states at once.[175] But each of these consequences is a manifest absurdity, since the soul, being finite, its states must also be only finite states. At no moment, furthermore, is it capable of more than a single, finite state. Just as a mixture of colors on a palette can produce only a single and unique color, so no matter how numerous or extensive are its objects of thought, the operation of thinking is always globular and limited. But when the mind inspects the idea of a triangle or circle, it conceives it as a mode of the idea of extension; and this idea, as we saw, Malebranche claims to be known clearly as infinite [176] and inexhaustible. This idea, accordingly, cannot be contained in or represented by a limited finite perception.[177] And what is true of the infinite idea of extension is true of any general idea like that of a triangle. The idea cannot be a state of the mind because every such state is particular.[178]

In the tenth Éclaircissement, Malebranche offers another and most significant reason why ideas of bodies are not states of the soul. This reason is that in the thought, intellection or perception of, say, the **(2) Exteriority.** idea of the sun, this idea presents itself with a certain mark of *exteriority* by which it is easily distinguishable from the internal states of the soul. As Malebranche puts it, ". . . nous voyons clairement et nous sentons distinctement que ce soleil est quelque chose de distingué de nous." [179]

This present objection against mental modifications, based on directly felt "exteriority," rests upon Descartes' understanding of substance and mode. Substance is that which can be conceived by itself, whereas a mode is that which cannot be conceived apart from its substance. Malebranche accordingly maintains that if the idea of body were a modality of the soul, we should not be able to think of it by itself as representing, containing, or presenting solely body. But ideas are not modes of the soul, because the soul is not extended or figured. A mode is a quality; it is a state or manner of being; it is a disposition of the soul in the way in which roundness is a state of the body. For a body to possess roundness means that the body *is* round. So for the soul to have a pain means that it is *in* a painful state. For the soul to have an intuition or intellection means that it is in an intellective state.

Now the problem is whether the idea of a square, of a number, of the infinite, can be a mode or state of the mind. If the idea of a square could be a mode of thought, then the soul would be in a square, four-sided state. If the idea of the infinite could be a mode of thought, then the soul would be in an infinite state of mind. Could the idea of extension be a mode, the soul would be in an extended state.

One attempt to avoid this difficulty utilizes the scholastic principle of *eminent* causality, according to which an object X can contain all the properties of an object Y in a manner superior to the way in which *they* are contained in Y. This method Descartes employed as a suggestion.[180] Just as God contains all the properties of the material world without being material, so the soul would be square without actually being four-sided. It would contain all the properties of extension without actually being divisible, impenetrable, figured. Now Malebranche's contention is that this type of eminent existence cannot characterize a finite creature; that it is not possible for a determinate, specific, limited nature like the soul to have the inexhaustible properties of every possible object within itself.[181] Instead it is directly apparent to Malebranche that some objects of thought are not mental modifications and cannot be states of mind.[182] This direct refutation of the theory of identification is not to be despised as simply denying a position; upon the direct observation that some objects of thought are not mental rests the strongest arguments against subjective idealism. In his reply to Régis, Malebranche appeals to "la conscience des lecteurs" on this score, for, he asserts, this is one of those basic and ultimate truths that can be demonstrated in no other way.[183]

(c) *Epistemological Arguments.* At the instigation of Arnauld to read his *Art de Penser* and to learn therefrom that perceiving is identical with what is perceived, Malebranche replies that Arnauld's work itself confutes Arnauld's thesis.[184] Arnauld maintains that the principle or axiom upon which all the sciences depend is the Cartesian condition of certainty, namely, that whatever the mind apprehends clearly and distinctly in idea, it may affirm of the object of that idea. Arnauld goes on to assert that such a passage from ideas to objects is valid, because our clear and distinct apprehensions do not express personal beliefs, nor are they statements about our thoughts but about the objects themselves, in so far as the objects are in the mind by way of idea.

(1) Reduces knowledge to mere opinion.

Either, retorts Malebranche, this passage is a direct confutation of Arnauld, or else, if the author really believes that ideas and states of perception are identical, then the passage, far from destroying Pyrrhonism, leads inevitably to it. For if modes of the soul are representative similitudes, if ideas are our own states of thinking or us in a state, then the assertion that the angles of a triangle sum to two right angles reduces merely to the assertion that *we think so.* While creatures correspond to the knowledge possessed by their Creator, while they participate in the attributes of God, still He did not create the world according to our mode of perceiving it or to resemble our states of mind. The answer to the further charge—that we know what God has created because He has created us with a knowledge of these things—is that upon the basis of our personal modifications we cannot construct a *proof* that God so endowed us. Even if the soul were a mirror of the external world, even if our perfections and qualities were to contain and represent the properties of an external world, we could never be certain of this fact, so long as every idea or object of thought is identified with our apprehension.[185]

The identification-theory reduces knowledge of the external world to mere opinion without corroborative evidence. It is precisely to avoid this that Malebranche gives Descartes the more "equitable" interpretation of distinguishing in principle the object of thought from thinking.

Agreeing with Descartes that ideas are immutable, Malebranche further contends that states or modalities are nevertheless radically

(2) Precludes
immutability.

changeable.[186] Let the object of thought be a triangle. In conceiving a triangle the mind apprehends the relation of equality between the sum of its three angles and that of any pair of right angles. Suppose that it be asserted that this object of thought is simply the manner, or way, or mode in which the mind thinks. But what is a mode of thinking? A mode of thinking is nothing more than a disposition or state or act of thinking. Like a state of pain or pleasure or a sensation of color, a state of thinking is particular, fleeting or temporal, individual, private or personal, and contingent. Then, of an idea or object of thought, like a triangle, if it is simply a mode of thinking, the truth is born and annihilated with every individual act of the mind. For it exists only when perceived. And should Peter think of the triangle while John would not, then that triangle and that truth might be said both to be and not to be at the same time. And if no mind had ever thought, then that nature would not have existed.

Founded on this central insistence on the mutability of modifications, Malebranche erects arguments which turn Arnauld's criterion of clarity and distinction back on itself. The principle that whatever is contained in an idea may be affirmed of its object is not only the first principle of natural science, Malebranche agrees, but of all sciences, especially of the purely speculative sciences of Arithmetic, Geometry and Pure Mathematics. This criterion tells us that two times two cannot be other than four. But within himself Malebranche beholds only mutable and arbitrary (not necessary) things. I may not exist, he exclaims, or not be such as I am.[187] To affirm that truth is mutable and arbitrary is to contravene the leading principle of Cartesianism; Malebranche is certain that there cannot be minds that see truths and laws different from those which he sees.[188] Arnauld's and Descartes' procedure of affirming of the object of an idea all that is in the idea entails, under the identification-theory, the affirmation of every vacillating phase of a psychological modification as a truth.[189] Hence, Malebranche most aggressively writes to Régis:

> Il y a un rapport d'égalité entre 2 fois 2 et 4, soit que j'y pense ou que je n'y pense pas. Car il n'est pas nécessaire que ce rapport d'égalité soit aperçu afin qu'il soit.[190]

(3) Destroys
universality.

Not only are ideas immutable, but also they are universal. Modifications are private states. The identification-theory at best reduces the assurance of universality not to the support of identical natures distributed in different souls but to dependence on resemblance. To Régis, who maintained the same thesis as that of Arnauld, Malebranche wrote that if ideas and modalities are identical, there can be no guarantee that all minds when they perceive the properties of a circle perceive an identical truth, for states of thinking like states of feeling are not open to one another's immediate inspection.[191] Thus the universality which must pertain to Cartesian certainty is buttressed by no more evidence than Descartes or Arnauld themselves possess of the states of other minds. At best this is a judgment of the resemblance of minds, since assuredly the modifications of different minds cannot be literally identical. And even the judgment of resemblance is not confirmed by any further supporting evidence.

When X and Y perceive the essence of a triangle, we do not know whether they both are living through the same intellectual experience; we do not know whether in this act of understanding the mind or soul of each is affected in the same way; we do not know whether this mental state, by which the essence of a triangle is apprehended, is related to X's antecedent states of mind in the way that it is related to Y's history. Yet the Cartesian appeal to generalized certainty convinces Malebranche that both X and Y know and mean the univocal thing by the essence of a triangle. If the essence or idea were identical with the individual operations or states of mind of X and Y, some particular revelation [192] would be required in order to know that X and Y were having the "same" truth and the "same" psychological states.

Malebranche would say that the judgment that two minds can know the "same" thing, or that they can live through the "same" intellectual state, can be made only on the assumption that the truth or object perceived is independent of X's and Y's observations and therefore can become the common possession of both. When X and Y apprehend the essence of a triangle and each affirms its angles to be equal in sum to the sum of the two right angles, it is the independent character of this essence that serves as the point of reference for judging that X and Y are enjoying the same experience. They meet at an identical terminus that belongs to both and to neither at the same time. But if the essence and state of mind become coalesced, then, since those states are fleeting, contingent, dependent upon the causal arbitrary will of God, one could no longer universalize or generalize anything without a distinct and separate assurance of identity or perfect resemblance.

The privacy of mental modifications Malebranche employs with even more generality to show that under the identification-theory, as Hume was later to prove, *demonstration* becomes impossible. States of mind are variable and fleeting, be they sensations or pure intuitions. As such they are arbitrary and contingent. If ideas are identical with states of mind, then no strict demonstration is possible, for, exclaims Malebranche:

(4) Makes strict demonstration impossible.

> Je ne pourrais plus être assuré que tous les esprits voient la même vérité que je vois, quand je découvre par exemple, les propriétés du cercle; car sans le secours d'une révélation particulière, je ne puis

découvrir quelles sont les modalités des autres esprits. Ainsi toutes les sciences, toutes les vérités de morale n'auraient plus de fondement certain. On ne pourrait plus rien démontrer, car il est impossible de démontrer que les esprits ont ou n'ont pas certaines modalités, puisqu'elles feraient arbitraires ces modalités, et dépendantes de la volonté de Dieu, et que toute démonstration dépend d'un principe nécessaire.[193]

Failure to distinguish between essences and psychological states of mind, reflects Malebranche, will inevitably lead to the Pyrrhonism of the English authors, Hobbes and Locke.[194]

Arnauld and Régis could never fully comprehend Malebranche's opposition to their theory that ideas are mental modifications, for neither was a metaphysician or mathematical scientist. Both, furthermore, loyal as they were to Descartes, were not adverse to mingling their Cartesianism with a good measure of scholastic empiricism, a mixture for which, of course, Descartes himself was partly responsible. Thus, Arnauld and Régis, inspired by Descartes' discussion of universals in his *Principles*, contended that general ideas and numbers are mere abstractions of the mind. The philosopher Thales, Arnauld insists, for example, forms the concept twenty only upon enumerating twenty particular objects. In similar fashion does one form the general concept of a triangle.[195]

To Malebranche these statements are sheer nonsense: Monsieur Arnauld imagines that the numbers with which mathematicians deal, *"les nombres nombrants,"* are abstracted by the mind from particular sense perceptions. He does not realize that this alleged power of abstraction is no more than the power of attention, that unless these numbers had an independent reality, and unless the mind were already acquainted with them, it could never perform this so-called process of abstraction. How can Arnauld's philosopher Thales form or conceive an infinite number, never having seen an infinity of objects? How can Thales be certain that the numbers two and three are not square numbers, that is, the product of a fraction multiplied by itself, since sensible experience could never lead him to a knowledge of this truth? The philosopher Thales can consider and attend to these numbers, but he can never produce them from his own mind. Thales can indeed cease to think of twenty objects and consider the number twenty by itself, but only because that number already exists prior to and independently of our thought. To enumerate twenty objects, one must already possess the idea of the number twenty.[196]

Neither this reply, however, nor any of the above-treated arguments concerning infinity, exteriority, immutability, universality, or the requirements of strict demonstration, ever converted his adamant and acrimonious opponent, Arnauld. Between Malebranche and Arnauld the conflict ended with neither victory nor peace.

IX. OBJECTIONS TO FOURTH ALTERNATIVE APPLIED TO THIRD

At the conclusion of my discussion on the Third Alternative, I claimed that in imposing a more "equitable" interpretation upon Descartes' theory of ideas, which consists in distinguishing thought from object of thought, Malebranche is really being very shrewd. He is driving Descartes to a position which Descartes cannot sustain for lack of an adequate metaphysical foundation. The magazine-hypothesis considers ideas to be objects, and the identification-hypothesis considers them to be modifications. In so far as ideas are real but finite beings for Descartes—and we saw that they are—ideas fall under one or the other of these two formulations.

No matter how broadly or how strictly we interpret the Cartesian idea it exists either in a mind which contains it as a "magazine" or else in a mind of which it is a state. Malebranche's arguments that ideas are not states of a mind are very strong. Now I shall show that they can be used equally well against the "equitable" assumption of an innate storehouse, although Malebranche himself does not explicitly make this application.

(*a*) *Exteriority.* In arguing against the modification-hypothesis, Malebranche holds that one can perceive in reflecting upon the idea of extension that it represents properties which do not belong to one's own self. Therefore this idea of extension cannot be a modality of the soul, but instead must be distinct from it.

What are the implications of this argument for the magazine-doctrine? The idea is a real being. *Its* properties are those which it shows itself to possess. The idea of extension presents on its surface, as it appears, characteristics in virtue of which we call it a real thing, which have a patent "exteriority" to the mind. It has non-mental characteristics. Then the idea of extension must be a real thing which upon inspection reveals no connection with the mind. Only prejudices, apart from it or from its nature, would lead us to attribute this idea to the mind. From the conclusions that upon inspection the idea reveals no mental properties, that it encourages an intimation of exteriority, and that only an *ad hoc* theory, not clear and distinct evidence, induces us to claim that it belongs to the mind—from these conclusions we must now infer that the idea of extension is altogether distinct from the self perceiving that idea. Not only does it follow that the idea can remain while states of the soul change and disappear, but it is also obviously absurd to locate ideas *in* the mind and yet permit them totally distinct properties independent of that mind; for at the minimum the phrase

[marginal note:] Hard to attribute to mind an idea possessing exteriority.

in the mind means "internally related to the mind," that is, X is in the mind if X cannot occur unless the mind occurs. Thus the argument from exteriority also constitutes a strong objection to innatism.

(*b*) *Immutability.* Consider now the four epistemological objections. The first, of course, does not apply to Descartes, given Malebranche's "equitable interpretation" of Descartes. If, as Malebranche insists, Descartes meant to distinguish *his* intuition of the triangle from the objective reality of the triangle, then assuredly when Descartes claimed to affirm a proposition about triangles he did not intend to express a mere opinion or personal sentiment. Nevertheless the next three objections reveal that Descartes cannot maintain in fact what Malebranche permits him to assert by right.

The second of the epistemological objections to the identification of act and object is that thoughts of the mind are mutable and perishable, whereas the object of thought is immutable. To identify thought and object is thus to destroy the permanency of the object. I submit that this objection holds also against the magazine-theory which attempts to place the *permanent* object within the *finite* mind. A finite mind or soul *may* be immortal, but even Descartes admits that immortality does not belong to the essence of mind. Descartes does affirm, however, that essences or concepts are made to be eternal by God. How, then, can an eternal object reside within a finite, mortal, enduring mind? What would happen to the *ideas* if their owner were to be annihilated, as Malebranche grants to be possible?

Finite mind not hospitable receptacle of immutable real ideas.

(*c*) *Universality.* The third argument against identifying thought and object is this: acts are private; the object is universal or public. Once again I submit that this holds also against the magazine-theory. If ideas are "in" the mind, one can no longer call them universal. At best one can only affirm that each mind has a set of ideas that resemble each other. We then are faced with the difficulty involved in this judgment of resemblance. Descartes might say that he has a distinct idea of the human soul by which he knows that every soul is created with a similar set of innate ideas, among them being that of the square. But here the same problem is renewed on another level. If the idea of all souls is in my mind, how can I tell that all would conform to that idea? Descartes would now be compelled to rely upon the veracity of God, that is, his idea of God. But here we are back at the question of how we can reach God, if our idea of Him is something finite and in the mind? How can I know that every intelligence is implanted with the similar idea of God?

Descartes' subjectivism renders universality inaccessible.

(*d*) *Strict Demonstration.* The fourth objection against the identification-theory is that strict demonstration can be based only upon a principle which is necessary. This means that the axiom or premise of an exact proof must be such that its opposite is strictly inconceivable

Opposites of contingent states of mind conceivable.

and strictly impossible. For this reason Malebranche declared that if ideas are states of mind we can prove nothing, for such states are contingent, their opposite is quite conceivable.

This objection holds against Descartes' conception of a magazine of innate ideas, arbitrarily placed in the mind. Descartes expressly acknowledged that the essence of a triangle could have been other than what it is, that God could have decreed contradictories to exist. Strict demonstration is impossible on such conditions.

Mr. Schrecker rightly points out that Descartes' innatism is really an anthropologism.[197] The mathematical truths as well as the idea of God, by being stored in the mind, become in effect no more than a description of the manner in which the human mind happens to operate. It suggests the possibility that the mind might have been created to think in other ways, and that it is simply an accident that it is constrained to think in the way that it does. This reduces the mathematical and metaphysical truths to laws of thought rather than laws of reality. Descartes thus becomes an example of those who suffer from the idols of the theater, whose philosophy is but a stage play, a product of the distorting intellect, as Bacon might say.

Thus, while Malebranche may have treated Descartes "equitably" by interpreting his innate ideas as immutable contents, distinct from acts of thought, it cannot be said with Gouhier that there is no deep-seated opposition between Malebranche and Descartes. It is especially difficult to accept Gouhier's interpretation in the light of what Malebranche has to say against "created truths" in the tenth Éclaircissement, which he directs not only against the Cartesians, but specifically against Descartes, whom he expressly names.[198] Here again Gouhier seems to suggest that Malebranche rejects created truths because such a doctrine is insufficiently Christian.[199] This is true enough, but it over-simplifies the matter. Malebranche rejects created truths because they undermine all science.

X. GENERAL CRITIQUE OF ARBITRARY ORIGINATION OF IDEAS

Cartesian ideas possess two principal characteristics: they belong to finite minds, and they are arbitrarily created. In denying that ideas enter the mind by impression, that they are caused or occasioned in the mind, that they are there from creation, or that they are the finite mind itself, Malebranche has been trying to show that certainty is inaccessible if ideas belong in any way to finite minds. Now, in the tenth Éclaircissement, he will further contend that blind creativity or voluntarism, that is, *the arbitrary origination of ideas*, also renders certainty unattainable.

God's arbitrary will, and certainty.

Malebranche's anti-Cartesianism stems from his being a more zealous Cartesian than the master himself. Descartes, by his metaphysical conception of God as a supremely omnipotent, arbitrary, indifferent but veracious and immutable power, sought to guarantee the certainty and immutability of all [200] essences of truth and goodness. To Malebranche, as before him to the protagonists of the fifth and sixth sets of objections against Descartes, and as after him to Leibnitz, the Cartesian conception of essence as the arbitrary contingent fact mysteriously endowed with the characters of necessity, universality, and immutability appeared to be a parody on the very meaning of truth. In a system which prides itself on clarity and distinctness, to make an arbitrary fiat of God the source and origin of the whole fabric of science is at the least paradoxical. More, such a doctrine contains within itself the seeds of skepticism. Descartes' *Cogito* is not the Kantian unity of apperception. It is not upon the "I think" that Descartes grounds the possibility of an exact mathematics and mathematical science. The *Cogito* is simply first in the order of existences. The "I think" accompanies every Cartesian judgment only in the sense that no judgment concerning anything is possible without the mind being aware of its own existence and nature. For Descartes, God, and not the self, is, after all, the real, or at least the alleged condition for the possibility of knowledge. The innate ideas are not Kant's categories that impose themselves upon the contents of sensibility and thus create a phenomenal world behind which there is an unknowable *ding an sich*. Yet, in anchoring the certainty of science upon the arbitrary power of God, in making the created innate ideas the contingent features of a contingent finite mind, science, without becoming wholly subjective, is dependent upon the fortuitous fortunes of that mind or rather upon the arbitrary fiat of the divine will.

What gives Descartes' claim of achieving certainty a passing plausibility is the subtlety of his initial predication. Descartes, it will be recalled, wrote to Mersenne, "On vous dira que si Dieu avait établi ces vérités, il les pourrait changer comme un Roi fait ses lois; a quoi il faut répondre que oui, *si sa volonté peut changer.*" [201]

The immutability of God's will no guarantee of certainty.

Now Malebranche has no quarrel with Descartes concerning the fact that God has an immutable will. Indeed the immutability of God's will is an indispensable feature of divine perfection in every Christian philosophy before Malebranche. But what Malebranche questions are Descartes' *metaphysical grounds* for an immutable will, and this for several reasons.

To begin with, a will that is entirely arbitrary and indifferent, however unchangeable, is, *at the time of creation,* not compelled to establish decrees the results of which are static. Malebranche's criticism is simple: God's will, though immutable and founding immutable decrees, just as Descartes insists, can still immutably will certain things for a certain time, for a certain place, for certain people, or for certain kinds of being and not for others.[202]

Malebranche's present argument is sound. Nothing can prevent the Cartesian God *ab origine* from making as many different sets of essences as the multiple languages that He made in the tower of Babel. This is why Malebranche regards the problem of ideas as of capital importance in metaphysics, for upon it depends the very definition of the nature of man as a rational animal.[203] Descartes' position is that truth is immutable because the divine will is immutable. But the sole metaphysical justification that Descartes offers for this proposition is merely this: that once God decrees, it is repugnant to a perfect self-caused Deity to change. Descartes holds that what distinguishes men from brutes is *reason*, that is, man's capacity to know essences or the *rationes* of things. But if every essence is arbitrarily decreed by God, Malebranche contends, then the definition or the essence of mind is also something that might have been different from what it is, or it might be other for different minds. Thus we have no guarantee that *every* mind knows that extension is no more than length, breadth, and depth, or that four times two equals eight, or that the soul is a pure thinking substance. In short, there is nothing in the nature of Cartesian divine omnipotence, regarded from the eternal "now," that can constrain it to will the same thing for all minds and for all times, however unalterable He may be with respect to any given single choice. Descartes has not afforded rational—clear and distinct—evidence that the content of immutable decrees is in turn necessarily universal or immutable. Furthermore, Malebranche argues against Descartes that if God arbitrarily willed essences, one cannot be certain that God may not by that same arbitrary will cease to will what He has previously decreed:

> Car enfin, s'il n'était pas absolument nécessaire que 2 fois 4 fussent 8, ou que les trois angles d'un triangle fussent égaux à deux droits, quelle preuve aurait-on que ces sortes de vérités ne seraient point semblables à celles qui ne sont reçues que dans quelques Universités, ou qui ne durent qu'un certain temps? Voit-on clairement que Dieu ne puisse cesser de vouloir ce qu'il a voulu d'une volonté entièrement libre et indifférente? [204]

However, the reason why Descartes could assume the position of a past tense, the reason which allowed him to maintain that, once established, God is restricted in his action by his maintenance of essences, is that this claim depends upon the existence of a *veracious* God. Once we know that God is no deceiver, we can trust every intrinsic feature with which an essence imposes itself upon the mind. Thus the idea of a triangle has determinate properties that resist any

God's veracity, and certainty:

attempt to alter it. We are hence compelled to accept it as eternal, immutable, universal. Thereafter its imperishability is guaranteed by God's will.

Can Malebranche present a respectworthy argument against this premise of veracity? I believe that he can, and I am going to show that he does so, by offering an interpretation of the following passage. Malebranche declares:

> . . . Je veux bien supposer que l'on voie clairement que Dieu, par une volonté entièrement indifférente, a établi pour tous les temps et pour tous les lieux les vérités et les lois éternelles, et qu'à présent elles sont immuables à cause de son décret. *Mais où les hommes voient-ils ce décret?* Dieu a-t-il créé quelque être représentatif de ce décret? Diront-ils que ce décret est une modification de leur âme? Ils voient clairement ce décret, car ils en ont appris que l'immutabilité est assurée aux vérités et aux lois éternelles; mais où le voient-ils? . . . Au fond ce décret est une imagination sans fondement.[205]

Le Moine claims that this argument is foolish and of doubtful value, particularly Malebranche's assertion that no one has ever seen this decree. Descartes does not pretend to have seen this decree, "mais simplement qu'il y a là un point de vue qui permet de concilier l'éternité des vérités et leur caractère de créatures." [206] But surely it is paradoxical for a philosophy that is founded on clear and distinct evidence to appeal for support of that evidence to "un point de vue." This would be to seek refuge in no more than a wild, ingenious supposition, incomprehensible in character, and bereft of logical support. I believe, on the contrary, that the above passage constitutes a three-fold attack on Descartes' appeal to divine veracity. (1) It claims in effect that Descartes ends by appealing to something of which, as guarantor, we have, not clear and distinct, but rather *obscure assurance;* and an assurance, moreover, *to which we have no access,* because (2) divine veracity conflicts with divine power and because (3) the *idea* of a veracious God is an arbitrary entity residing within a finite mind.

Descartes himself confesses that he is unable to comprehend how God could be able to bring it about that certain things which are true could be other than what they are from all eternity. In defense of his seemingly gratuitous procedure of positing divine arbitrary decrees without rational evidence for them, Descartes argued that denying God to be the arbitrary indifferent efficient cause of all truths contradicts his omnipotence, and of this omnipotence we do have indisputable rational evidence. Descartes' problem is this, and he faces it quite openly—this rationally indisputable power to create truth is incomprehensible. "It is useless to inquire how God could from all eternity bring it about that it should be untrue that twice four is eight, etc.;"

(1) Our assurance of God's veracity founded on obscure ideas.

he declares, "for I admit that that cannot be understood by us."[207]

Descartes therefore makes no positive attempt to render God's indifferent decree comprehensible. Either one of two contradictories can, for example, be decreed true. Descartes merely argues that God could easily act by indifferent power in ways inscrutable to man. Thus all that Descartes knows with certainty is that all essences depend solely on God and that God's ways can be incomprehensible. From these two certainties, however, he argues in conclusion that it is actually irrational to doubt what we correctly understand because of what we neither comprehend nor perceive a need to comprehend. But this is precisely what Malebranche denies. To Malebranche there *is* a need to comprehend, inasmuch as all science depends on clear and distinct evidence, and this evidence must be clear and distinct at its roots.[208]

Malebranche turns Descartes' very argument back against him. It may be difficult to reconcile freedom and reason in God, but this is no excuse for doubting the intrinsic necessity and self-evidence of such truths as that twice four are eight. The issue is perfectly sharp. Whereas Descartes holds that it is irrational to doubt that God creates truth arbitrarily, because we do not comprehend how He does so, Malebranche contends that it is irrational to doubt what we clearly and distinctly perceive:

Si l'on doute de la nécessité absolue de ces vérités, c'est que l'on détourne sa vue de leur lumière, que l'on raisonne sur un faux principe, et que l'on cherche ailleurs qu'en ces vérités, qu'elle est leur nature, leur immutabilité, leur indépendance.[209]

From the point of view of Malebranche we must either accept an essence, idea, or concept in its entirety, wholly upon its face-value or not at all. When we consider, by itself, the definition of a triangle, that essence does not bear any label affirming it to be an entity arbitrarily promulgated by a lawgiver. But once we deny with Descartes a particular aspect of it, namely absoluteness, then we may no longer trust its other apparent features such as immutability and universality. These latter qualities then require special letters of recommendation, declaring them to have been thus appointed or decreed by God. Hence Descartes' appeal to divine veracity to justify human cognition and to prove that an essence, say of a triangle, is really an immutable, universal nature, cannot be legitimate so long as Descartes insists that it is "easy for Him so to appoint that we human beings should not understand how these very things [essences] could be otherwise than they are."[210]

Malebranche would willingly grant to Descartes that many of God's ways are inscrutable. He would even go so far as to say that there may be instances in which two propositions are each indubitable and yet antinomial when placed side by side. An example of such a conflict would be the point at issue: God is absolutely free; essences are independent of God. In such a case he would declare that either human reason itself can distinctly perceive that the solution is beyond its reach or it will solve the antinomy by finding a mediating ground between thesis and antithesis.[211] But in no case would Malebranche strive to go beyond an essence to seek its guarantee, for then we should have no foundation for the very notion of veracity. Negatively, the foundation of Malebranche's opposition to Descartes is contained in the denial: "Quand on pense à l'ordre, aux lois et aux vérités éternelles, on n'en cherche point naturellement de cause." [212] And positively Malebranche's whole critique of Descartes is latent in kernel in the affirmation: "On aperçoit au contraire d'une simple vue et avec évidence, que la nature des nombres et des idées intelligibles est immuable, nécessaire, indépendante." In this pronouncement, Malebranche has driven his premise, that certainty is attainable in the immediate inspection of conceptual ideas, to its inevitable rational conclusion. According to one phase of Descartes' thought, intuition is truly self-guaranteeing; it is indubitable. Descartes formulated a postulate to this effect.[213] Clear and distinct intuition is of the quintessence of Cartesianism. Malebranche now fulfills the letter of this demand. Far from having rational evidence for the content of God's decrees, it is inconceivable to Malebranche that essences known clearly and distinctly *could* be other than what they are. To guarantee God's veracity we must appeal to obscure evidence, but the evidence of clear and distinct ideas is entirely patent.

(2) Divine veracity conflicts with divine power.

    Malebranche's query as to whether there is a distinct idea of a divine decree can be interpreted as being directed against Descartes' doctrine of divine veracity in still another way. In effect, Malebranche is asking whether we have some indubitable *sign* that the equality apprehended between four times two and eight, for example, is a relation that will subsist everlastingly. Descartes would say that we perceive that equality with the characters of immutability and universality, and, since we know that God is veracious, it is impossible that twice four be otherwise than what we perceive it to be. Nevertheless, Descartes, in his replies to the sixth set of objections, expressly admitted that it is easy for divine omnipotence so to appoint things that although it might be incomprehensible to man to understand how things could be otherwise, they still might be otherwise. In short, divine veracity does not in itself guarantee that what appears to be *is* wholly as it appears to be. Divine veracity merely guarantees appearances: it guarantees that four times two *appears* to be immutable and universal. To Leibnitz, Descartes' conception of created truths is "very strange." If God is indifferent to what we call just or unjust, then, "we cannot determine anything as to the justice of God, and it may be that He has made things in a way which we call unjust . . ."[214] Thus Leibnitz is saying with respect to ethical notions of good-bad, right-wrong, what Malebranche says with respect to truth—we cannot tell that what *appears* to us as just *is* just. So too Malebranche declares that when we judge Nero's murder as a crime, we have no way of telling that it *is* a crime.[215]

Malebranche himself does not doubt that four times two *are* eight, and that it is so for all minds and for all times. What he doubts is that Descartes' metaphysics can justify *Descartes'* beliefs in such propositions. The most that Descartes' appeal to veracity can serve to guarantee is that appearances are what they *appear* to be; it cannot serve to guarantee that appearances are *wholly* what they seem to be, or that they seem wholly to be what they *are*. Divine veracity collides with divine potency.

Moreover, if we do not accept an essence upon its face value, then even the veracity of God will be useless, inasmuch as this veracity itself depends upon our reliance on the idea of God. But if this idea, like all ideas, is an arbitrary effect, it cannot serve to support a strict demonstration, for every demonstration depends upon some necessary principle. <small>(3) Idea of a veracious God is a finite idea.</small>

Although in my first chapter I claim that *Causa Sui* is the only possible answer to Descartes' demand for certainty, I do not believe it to be an *adequate* solution. Malebranche's negative criticisms of Descartes' appeal to divine arbitrary decrees, to establish the absolute veracity of ideas, make this perspicuously clear. Thus, while it is possible to understand why Descartes had to appeal to *Causa Sui*—he had to do so, because he had nothing else to which to appeal—this same *Causi Sui* nevertheless might just as well from all eternity have decreed different truths for different people; hence the existence of a *Causa Sui* is compatible with a complete relativism which is nevertheless precluded by Descartes' very demand for universal *a priori* certainty.

Descartes, to be sure, appeared to Malebranche, his disciple, to be on the road to the truth. Descartes recognized that ideas were eternal, immutable natures, not framed by the mind, and that they were so prior to any act of perception or conception. Nevertheless, by attempting to localize these essences in finite, particular, limited, contingent minds, Descartes compromised his own method in two ways. *First*, he compromised his method by the fact that in the realm of *natura naturata* no object can be general, universal or necessary. This error of localizing ideas in finite minds in turn led Descartes to make an unwarranted bifurcation of the realm of creatures. It led him to assert that some creatures, namely, essences, can be contingent and yet neces- <small>Descartes' alleged errors and their consequences.</small>

sary, limited and yet general, an assertion manifestly not compatible with his method which demands that whatever is conceptually different be distinct. His dualism depends on this separation of concepts, but in the realm of essence Descartes is not averse to mixing his concepts.

Again, Descartes supposed that ideas would continue to preserve their characteristic features of eternality and immutability, by assuming that once established, God's immutable will would guarantee their maintenance. In this assertion Descartes compromised his method in still a *second* way. By the simple inspection of the idea of a triangle he finds it to be an eternal immutable nature, and no more than that. The alleged property of its having been made that way is not something that he can deduce directly from the idea.

Strict adherence to Descartes' method, we must conclude, forces Malebranche to reject any attempt to mix the concepts of particularity and generality, of the contingent and the necessary. The first, immediate consequence of Malebranche's more rigid obedience to Descartes' method is to eject ideas from finite minds. And the second consequence of relying on pure intuition alone is Malebranche's unequivocal acceptance of its deliverances, namely, that ideas are absolutely immutable.

To Malebranche there are two kinds of "prejudices," both equally dangerous. There is the "prejudice" which consists in the unexamined and unqualified acceptance of any testimony, and there is a second "prejudice" which consists in maintaining an attitude of perpetual doubt, that crippling state of mind which refuses to have any positive convictions.[216] Each type of "prejudice" he calls an abuse of man's free will. For Malebranche, not only does the doubt or the capacity to suspend judgment testify to man's freedom, but also, as Coleridge later said, man's freedom must declare itself in a "willing suspension of disbelief."

XI. FIFTH ALTERNATIVE—VISION IN GOD

I have now retraced Malebranche's advance from Cartesianism to the point where he is ready to make a willing suspension of disbelief.

Descartes defined intuition as "the conception which an unclouded and attentive mind gives us so readily and distinctly that we are wholly freed from doubt about that which we understand." [217] He further declared it to be an act of vision that possesses an "immediately presented evidence." That latter characteristic distinguishes it from deduction whose certitude is of a lesser degree, because memory enters into deducing. In conformity with these definitions Malebranche declares that "on aperçoit . . . avec évidence, que la nature . . . des idées intelligibles est immuable, nécessaire, indépendante." [218] Not even the evil demon can impugn these truths, any more than he can the *Cogito*. Notice, then, that from the point of view of Malebranche one cannot, strictly speaking, seriously doubt these truths, for the mere attempt to doubt them is to think them and thus know them. This is in perfect accord with Descartes' assertion in the twelfth Rule concerning intuitive awareness of simple natures and their necessary conjunctions. Here he tells us that doubt can enter only in cases where the object is complex and where there are some unknown elements. Only where there is ignorance is there doubt. Malebranche *knows* such a truth as that four times two equals eight; he perceives it as eternal, necessary, immutable. Accordingly he has *no* reason to doubt it, not even upon the extravagant supposition of the demon.[219]

Descartes' attempt at a real doubt arises from a false assumption concerning where these ideas are seen. Believing that they are finite entities in his own mind and knowing that God is the cause of all things, Descartes sought to guarantee them. So writes Malebranche.[220] From what we have already examined concerning Malebranche's philosophy, it is obvious what he must do to rectify Descartes' error. Accordingly, Malebranche affirms that the ideas or reasons with which rational beings are acquainted illumine every spirit—man, angel, or God—by constituting a single eternal, infinite, universal Reason.

To Malebranche, the Cartesian doctrine of created essences appeared as a simple failure of attention. In his view, Descartes could not prevent himself, as no mind can, from discerning the immutability of the truths of mathematics and of metaphysics. But Descartes allocated them to an improper abode. Hence, knowing that God is the cause of all things, and discovering his own mind to be confronted with a realm of clear and distinct ideas, in order to guarantee the immutability of ideas, he erroneously fancied the necessity of an immutable decree.[221] Thus actually, as Malebranche sees it, and as we have just noted, by the assignation of truth and goodness to an indifferent will, that very will becomes a refuge of ignorance. This is the nature of Descartes' error. It is rectified by making ideas necessary, eternal, infinite real entities.

Malebranche can now account theoretically for certainty. He has a theory of ideas that meets and overcomes every objection that he previously used to overthrow the first four alternatives.

As a result of our examination of his method, we know that Malebranche wants to be able to say: I am certain that *every* man knows that two times two equals four, that *every* mind knows that a triangle is a figure whose angles are equal in sum to two right angles. He can satisfy this demand for universality by affirming that "la raison que nous consultons . . . est une raison universelle." [222] A single domain

Malebranche claims that ideas are not thoughts, but immutable objects of thought.

(1) Universality.

(2) Immutability.

(3) Infinity.

Malebranche's Vision in God solves problems arising in Descartes' conceptualism.

(1) More truly rational.

of ideas is open to all and is the unique common object of our pure thought. At the same time, he affords rational grounds for psychological persuasion, since if, he declares, the reason that I consult were *not* the same that answers to the Chinese, it is evident that I could *not* be so sure as I am, that the Chinese perceive the same truths as I see.[223]

Again, in keeping with the objectives to which his method is dedicated, Malebranche wants to say: I am certain that the ideas of number and figure cannot be other than what they are, that they are immutable "par leur nature" and will be the same tomorrow as they are today. He can satisfy this demand for essential necessity and immutability by excluding the ideas from the realm of finite, limited, transient creatures: "Toutes les créatures sont des êtres particuliers; la raison universelle n'est donc point créé." [224]

Malebranche also wants to say: I am certain that the idea of extension and number that geometers deal with is positively infinite and inexhaustible; I am certain that the idea of a perfect square or of a triangle as such is exactly as I conceive it to be—a general idea. Once again he satisfies his demand, this time for a conception of infinity, by affirming simply that "la raison infinie . . . n'est pas seulement universelle et infinie, elle est encore nécessaire et indépendante." [225] When we know this infinite object, the act of knowledge is finite and our comprehension is finite, but the object of conception is an infinite object.

We have now concluded that part of Malebranche's epistemology which concerns itself with certainty and necessary truth. Malebranche offers an adequate foundation for certainty by reverting to a realm of Platonic essences. This is his doctrine of Vision of Ideas in God. Finite creatures know ideas in God by finite acts of thought, but the ideas that are known are neither private nor mutable nor finite.

Now we can understand why Malebranche asserts his own doctrine to be the only one which conforms to reason and to be the most adequate for revealing the dependence of minds upon God.[226] It is especially noteworthy that in defending this statement Malebranche simultaneously resumes his attack on Descartes. Here, he declares, are my reasons for proving that God wills to reveal the ideas that He contains rather than create an infinite number of these in each mind: First, because Vision in God is itself a rational hypothesis and because God does nothing that is useless and without reason. "Ce qui marque sa sagesse et sa puissance n'est pas de faire de petites choses par de grands moyens; cela est contre la raison et marque une intelligence bornée." [227] Hence, inasmuch as God can will to reveal His eternal ideas, ". . . il n'y a pas d'apparence qu'il le fasse autrement, et qu'il produise pour cela autant d'infinités de nombres infinis d'idées qu'il y a d'esprits créés." [228] Obviously, this rejection of Descartes is more than a simple renunciation of a complicated hypothesis. It is a condemnation of Descartes' view of an arbitrary, irrational Deity, and as such it declares innateness to be logically false.

The second reason against innateness and for Vision in God is that the latter puts minds in the greatest dependence on God, for it is God Himself who enlightens philosophers in this knowledge that they describe as *natural*. It is He who "docet hominem scientiam." Human knowledge is thus provided with an objective foundation, such as Bacon wanted. **(2) More truly objective.**

But the strongest of all reasons against innatism and for Vision in God comes from the manner in which the mind apprehends all things. Desiring to apprehend now one idea, now another, this is possible only if all ideas are present. Cartesian innatism fails to establish this omnipresence of ideas, for ". . . il semble que tous les êtres ne puissent etre présents à notre esprit que parce que Dieu lui est présent, c'est-à-dire celui qui renferme toutes choses dans la simplicité de son être." [229] And why is the divine omnipresence superior to the doctrine of a magazine? The next paragraph elucidates completely: **(3) Affords a true *a-priorism*.**

> Il semble même que l'esprit ne serait pas capable de se représenter des idées universelles de genre, d'espèce, etc., s'il ne voyait tous les êtres renfermés en un. Car toute créature étant un être particulier, on ne peut pas dire qu'on voie quelque chose de créé lorsqu'on voit, par exemple, un triangle en général. Enfin je ne crois pas qu'on puisse bien rendre raison de la manière dont l'esprit connaît plusiers vérités abstraites et générales, que par la présence de celui qui peut éclairer l'esprit en une infinite de façons différentes.[230]

Here Malebranche unites in one summation the issue of abstract truths with the question of universals. For they are for him but two aspects of the same problem. Truth, being a relation among ideas, there can be no immutable truths without immutable ideas. Unlike innatism, the presence of God to finite vision guarantees the absolute uncreated character of truth.[231]

Chapter III

God as Being

In this chapter I wish to investigate why Malebranche places ideas in God, why he believes in the existence of God, and what God he does have. In order to understand why he localizes the eternal ideas in God, and how they exist in God, it is first necessary to show that Descartes' view of God is not open to Malebranche.

I. The Nature of God

Descartes believed that the attributes of God—His knowledge, His power and His will—were absolutely simple and indistinguishable from one another, and that God stood in the peculiar relationship of efficient cause to His own existence. For Descartes, God's existence is derivative from and conferred by an essence. For Malebranche, on the other hand, God must be uncaused and to some extent heterogeneous. The reason will be that Malebranche guarantees the certainty and universality of necessary truths by depriving them of all connection with creativity or even with activity; and, as a consequence, an *a priori*, given, necessary element exists within the Godhead, distinguishable from His will.

(*a*) *God Heterogeneous in Nature.* We have noted that Malebranche has accepted the intuitive and deductive method of Descartes to this extent, that essences, such as the truths of pure mathematics, given in immediate intuition or inspection, disclose themselves to be absolutely necessary, universal, immutable, univocal and self-identical for every intelligence; and thereby they guarantee in the only way possible the rational certainty that is to be found within the sciences. We have also seen that to Malebranche this theory of essences com-

Necessary truths are necessary for God.

[120]

pels him to reject Descartes' claim that all truths are dependent on God's arbitrary will. Can they, on the other hand, be said to depend upon or to follow from God's thought? To Mersenne, Descartes wrote:

Je dis derechef que *sunt tantum verae aut possibiles, quia Deus illas veras aut possibiles cognoscit, non autem contra veras à Deo cognosci quasi independenter ab illo sint verae.*[1]

But Malebranche, on the contrary, could not agree that God's thought, if not His will, renders truths true because God thinks them. For if the essences could thus depend on the arbitrary will or on the thought of God, then to Malebranche only two conclusions, neither acceptable, would result: either immediate inspection would not reveal the essences to be necessary by their *own* nature or else immediate intuition would misinform. Since Malebranche rejects both these conclusions, he accordingly denies that God is indifferent or arbitrary in His pronouncements of what is true. God can neither will these truths nor think them in any other way. "Dieu même ne peut vouloir le contraire de ce que cet ordre prescrit." [2] "Dieu ne peut ni voir ni fair que deux fois deux soient égaux à cinq." [3] It is as impossible and contradictory for God to conceive them in any other manner as it is for man.[4]

In what sense can it be said that God is prohibited from conceiving something? There are ultimately only two possible meanings, mutually exclusive. It may be impossible for God to conceive, will or make something, because His nature is such that He is internally constrained to think, will or act in a certain determinate manner. On this view, eternal truths or essences would again be the results of divine causality and efficacy, as they are for Descartes, except that the operation of this agency would no longer be undetermined, but instead would be, as for Spinoza, determined. The second possible meaning is that of Malebranche—the correct relationship imposes itself on the divine mind as it does on the human mind. In this meaning, it is because an idea is of a determinate nature that God must understand in a certain way. To say that God is thus constrained does not mean that something within Him compels Him to think or act in a given fashion, so that the acknowledged truth would be a necessary product of God's thought. Rather, it means that truth is free from any sort of causal connection, either with a free will or with a creative mind.

How truths can be necessary for God.

Notice that this second meaning, that of Malebranche, can be accepted only on the condition that in some sense the absolute identity of all attributes in God be relaxed. As long as it is rigorously maintained that in God to conceive or to know and to create are unqualifiedly one, then we must adopt either Descartes' view of the arbitrary creation of ideas by will or else Spinoza's view of their necessary creation by the divine intellect. Equally, on either version of the absolute identity of divine attributes, essences belong to *natura naturata,* differing in these two systems only in their mode of creation.

The moderate conceptualism of God's thought for Scholasticism.

I may be accused of having omitted one other possibility concerning the relationship of ideas to God, namely, the Scholastic view of eternal forms as acts or ways of God's knowing Himself. This view is that of moderate conceptualism. It does not assert any causal relationship between the divine intellect and the forms, but it does identify these forms with divine comprehending rather than with the content apprehended. Or, to be more exact, Scholasticism makes no distinction between act and content in God, just as in human knowledge it does not rigorously separate within the concept any difference between act and content. This is why, for example, Caterus cannot understand Descartes' treatment of an idea as an entity that requires any cause other than the mind itself.[5] To the extent that the ideas follow from the way in which God thinks, this view might suggest that, as in Spinoza, God is compelled to think as He does because of the necessary nature of His thinking.

When Malebranche localizes ideas in God, however, he identifies them with the divine substance, with the being of God, and not with God's knowledge.[6] Conceptualism, however moderate, harbors a lurking creationism, in the sense that thought is productive of its own content. And to the degree that we interpret moderate conceptualism in this productive way, the view tends to the same result as that of Spinoza. But in all fairness it must be pointed out that Thomas was deeply concerned to preserve the static character of ideas. M. Gilson explains that on this score there is a notable divergency between Thomas and Bonaventure. While the two alike uphold exemplarism and the Word as eternally engendered by God, Bonaventure stresses far more the produced, created character of the ideas as "expressions" and effects of divine thought, and thus his philosophy leads directly to Descartes. For Thomas, on the contrary, as God thinks Himself, He by this very act sees Himself in the infinity of particular modes in which the creatures can imitate Him. Thus Thomism mitigates the creative role of divine thought, although it never absolutely denies creativity in such thought. Gilson tells us that the vision of and the distinction of the ideas in God belongs for Thomas above all to the perfection of the knowledge which God has of Himself.

Thomism, then, does not absolutely deny the creative role of divine thought, but it moderates this view in order to stress the closer tie between ideas and God's essence. Bonaventure, on the other hand, treats ideas as "eternally announced, spoken or expressed by the thought of God." Hence he even uses so vivid an image as "omnes enim rationes exemplares concipiuntur ab aeterno in vulva aeternae sapientiae seu utero." [7] Productivity thus enters more deeply into divine knowing for Bonaventure than for Aquinas.

For purposes of comparison, Malebranche's thought seems far closer to the position of Aquinas than that of Bonaventure. In terms of the medieval debate, and apart from the critique of ideas which issues in Vision in God, the Christian philosopher can hold the moderate Scholastic position that truths are true because they are the way in which God's reason freely moves, or else the Christian philosopher must pass toward one of two extremes. Either he must hold that certainty is grounded on the fact that God is compelled, determined, to think as He does and in no other way (thus ultimately ending in Spinoza's solution of the problem of guaranteeing rational apodictic certainty) or else he must hold that certainty depends on God's having to think of an *a priori* immutable given content. Because of the intuitive and deductive aspects of Malebranche's method, he can pass only to the direction of Aquinas and static concepts and must refuse the direction of Bonaventure and the creative expression of God. Actually, we shall now see that Malebranche has to be more of a purist than Aquinas. He expressly severs the ideas on the epistemological level from God's efficient causality and explicitly denies that the ideas bear any relation whatsoever to omnipotence, be it to a creative will or to creative thought. Why?

Malebranche starts with the conviction that man has certain, indubitable knowledge of extension and number. He starts with the concrete facts of a mind that exists and knows some things, and he attempts to account for these facts. His point of departure, then, is the fact of human knowledge; and his goal is to find metaphysical conditions that explain concrete fact. He has found that essences or ideas are necessary; this means that emendation may place a truth in a frame or may associate it with other truths, but neither it nor these other truths are qualifiedly true. To account for the absolute certainty which, in accordance with his intuitive and deductive method, he knows is attainable, he must affirm the accessibility of discrete immutable truths. But this implies that if an immutable truth is available to one man, then at least this truth is obtainable without modification, although perhaps with additions, to all men and to God, and can never be or have been otherwise. Thus Malebranche, at the start of the book of the *Recherche* that deals with ideas, declares that when we speak of what any mind is in itself, apart from sense and imagination, "ce que nous en dirons, se pourrait dire des pures intelligences." [8] What is said of one mind thus holds for all minds, whether human or divine.

Why God is no conceptualist for Malebranche: an interpretation.

Now, we saw in the preceding chapter that on the human level of knowing ideas, Malebranche finds no element of creativity. From the outset he held that rational knowing is an operation which consists in acquaintance with a separate content, that the will to know presupposes an antecedent, *a priori* familiarity with the object or content to be known, and that judgment is an act of the will. Knowing necessary truth is thus a vision or contemplation of an immutable object, for Malebranche. It is selective and not generative; it consists, in short, in attending to or noticing and discriminating its unalterable object, but not in making it. It is in this way that certainty concerning essence is attained, for the object is impervious to every vision of it.

Malebranche has thus rejected conceptualism in human knowledge and with it any form of idealism which asserts that the being of distinct ideas depends upon their being thought or conceived by the mind. But if knowing is not creative in man, must not the same be true of God's intellect? It must; otherwise the very foundations of certainty would be destroyed. For we have seen that an impermeable realm of immutable ideas gives certainty to man. And man knows truth by knowing the ideas; the content of each truth that a man knows is in the realm of pure ideas. This is *what* he knows when he knows intelligible truth. Then if discrete intelligible truth is identical for man and God, God likewise knows this truth in the realm of ideas. Now it follows that if knowing, understanding and willing are ascribed to God, then He must know an identical content. A given truth, if known by a man, must be known in at least this identical character by God. If, on the epistemological plane, the relationship between God and His ideas were one of creativity, this can mean, so far as concerns the logical question of knowledge, only that something is added to the idea known when God knows it. Consider this addition. If intrinsically an addition alters the very character of the idea known, then the objectivity of truth is dissipated. It becomes impossible for men to have a single truth without having in addition the factor introduced by the creativity that we are supposing to obtain between God and man. Thus to assert that on the epistemological plane adjectives describing knowledge are analogical when ascribed to man and God can only mean that the given content for God is conjoined with other quite distinct contents not discovered by man, such that their unison produces a more extensive whole or pattern. When God knows more about a particular thing that man knows, He does not know different things, but instead He knows infinitely more things or circumstances related to the given thing.

On the epistemological plane, then, the relation between God and the ideas involves no intrinsic creativity. Whether or not on some other level of analysis God engenders the ideas does not here enter. If it should turn out that there is a form of creativity on the metaphysical plane, this would not affect the epistemic situation, for the knowledge of an idea introduces no changes into it. It is appropriate to call Malebranche's kind of knowledge of ideas, whether in God or in man, "acknowledgment," or, as he calls it, "vision."

Malebranche's epistemology, then, with its demand for an inviolable foundation for knowledge, demands that pure intelligible truth be utterly independent of causal efficacy—be it that of an arbitrary will or of a thinking mind. Neither will nor intellect—if they exist in God— can be constitutive of ideas. Malebranche cannot therefore have a God in whom to know, to will and to create are indistinguishably identical. His epistemology demands a heterogeneous God; it absolutely requires in the name of truth that the divine attributes of knowledge and power, if attributed to God, be distinguishable, even if not separable.

God's will and intellect must be distinct.

Power or efficacy thus becomes a distinct attribute which does not function, or have any connection, with respect to divine intellect or to the objects of that intellect. Having begun with a finite mind knowing a realm of eternal objects distinct from itself and the Cartesian (non-Spinozistic) assumption of the distinction between knowing and judging, he cannot question, as does Spinoza,[9] the legitimacy of ascribing that type of intellect to God; it is the only kind which he can attribute to Him.[10]

Again, Malebranche accepts for man Descartes' definitions of understanding, volition and liberty. With Descartes he views the will as a movement toward or repose in what is right and what is good; he rejects the notion that indifference defines human liberty; and he considers freedom as action in conformity with the true and the good.[11] But, because his epistemology asserts that essences are eternal, Malebranche is compelled to affirm that meanings are, if not univocal, at least analogical for God and man. This permits power to be of the essence of God, but prohibits power from being constitutive of that essence. God's will can no longer be described as indifferent in its pronouncements or affirmations of what is true or good; instead, God is obliged to consent to what is true and good. God, for Malebranche, must be as dependent on truth and on the moral order among ideas as is any human mind.

What I am arguing here is not merely interpretation. Malebranche indeed does, for the reasons I offer, *have* to reach this important doctrine, which bears not only on the nature of ideas and of our knowledge of matters of fact, but also on the very nature of the Deity and on the foundations of his entire system. But Malebranche himself was perfectly aware of the problem and was so at an early date. In the *Conversations chrétiennes*, Theodore instructs Aristarque in these words: ". . . Reconnaissez, dis-je, que ces idées sont immuables, éternelles, efficaces, divines en un mot; communes à tous les esprits et à Dieu même *qui les trouve* dans sa substance . . ." [12] And notice that while the ideas are the objects *for* divine thought, they are not derivative from God's thought. They constitute a part of God's substance, but they are not engendered by God's knowledge. Thus even in God the reality of ideas does not depend upon a divine *concipi*. God *finds* essences in Himself. They are an attribute of His Being, but not the products of His thinking. Again, speaking to God directly, Malebranche writes:

> Vôtre volonté, Seigneur, n'est certainement que l'amour que vous vous portez à vous-même. . . . Vous n'avez point aussi de Loi étrangère, ou d'autre règle de vos desseins, que cette Loi éternelle que vous *trouvez* en vous-même, dans l'ordre immuable de vos attributs. [13]

Ideas and eternal truths are an indelible code that impose themselves upon divine thought as they do upon human minds. [14]

That Malebranche thus carries his doctrine of Vision in God even into the Godhead Itself is supported by, and in turn makes clear, passages such as the following:

> Non, non, Seigneur le juste et l'injuste est nécessairement tel; vôtre Loi est immuable, la règle de vôtre conduite n'est point arbitraire; elle est écrite dans vôtre substance en caractères éternels. [15]

> Mais la raison que nous consultons n'est pas seulement universelle et infinie, elle est encore nécessaire et indépendante, et nous la concevons *en un sens plus indépendante que Dieu même*. Car Dieu ne peut agir que selon cette raison, il dépend d'elle en un sens, il faut qu'il la consulte et qu'il la suive. [16]

To Régis Malebranche declared:

> Je ne puis me persuader que les idées dépendent de Dieu, comme de leur cause efficiente. Car étant éternelles, immuables et nécessaires, elles n'ont pas besoin de cause efficiente . . . [17]

And in the *Entretiens sur la métaphysique* we find this striking exchange between Aristes and Theodore:

> *Aristes.* . . . The extension which I see subsists without me, since you can contemplate it, without my having to think of it, you and all other men.

> *Theodore.* You can add without any fear, 'and God Himself.' For all our clear ideas are in God so far as their intelligible reality is concerned. . . . Yes, Aristes. God sees in Himself the intelligible extension . . . [18]

Thus the destruction of Descartes' doctrine of created essences necessitates a Deity who is heterogeneous in character and who is, at least
epistemologically, dependent on ideas.[19] Now we must see that such
a Deity cannot be viewed as self caused.

(*b*) *God Uncaused.* Because properties assigned to God and man
must possess, if not univocal, at least analogical meanings, because
understanding must precede volition and power, if ascribed to God,
Malebranche will not be able to accept Descartes' *Causa Sui.* Descartes was enabled to introduce power between the essence and existence of God by claiming that there was no need for conceiving an
efficient cause to be temporally prior to its effect.[20] But Descartes
could never have made such an assertion had he not identified indistinguishably the attributes of God. For consider what Descartes
says about an efficient cause in general, and about God's self-endow-
ment of all possible perfections.

One of the major reasons on the grounds of which Descartes excludes force from matter, or occult qualities such as gravity, is that
these notions logically implicate the notion of intelligence or mind.[21]
Even in the case of God, what renders His power so immense is the
fact that it is simultaneously a knowing power. God could have de- God's
efficiency and
intelligence
for Descartes.
creed that contradictories should coexist, because He could have con-
ceived them in that fashion; and God can be the cause of Himself and
endow Himself with every attribute, because He is also, however
indistinguishably, an intelligence. There is no limit to what He can
do, because there is no limit to what He can conceive. This intelligence,
moreover, is conceived by Descartes not simply in terms of what is
going on but in terms of 'knowledge about.' If gravity were a property of bodies, then not only would bodies be conscious of themselves
as moving, but they would have knowledge about the earth, the center,
the direction of motion. This knowledge would be a vision of intelligible ideas.

Now just as Descartes must affirm the identity of attributes in God
in order to make it logically possible for God to be the legislator of
essences, so this identity is also a strictly necessary condition for God
to be the cause of Himself. God can confer existence on Himself, because in this case the efficient cause is akin to a formal cause; that is,
because to create Himself is similar to a thought thinking itself or
to a will affirming and positing itself. Thus, once more, only because
Descartes assumes initially that to think, to know and to will are
indissolubly one, is it possible for him to identify formal and efficient
causation and to conceive of self-caused in a positive manner, as a
self-asserting productivity.

But Malebranche's epistemology of independent essences forces the
rejection of the identity of attributes. Accordingly Malebranche will

not be able to affirm a dynamic God in Descartes' sense. His Deity, if He exists, will have to be an immovable mover, ". . . il n'y a que Dieu qui soit véritablement immobile et moteur tout ensemble"; [22] or better, an uncaused Being (". . . son existence ne dépendant point d'une cause." [23]), one whose actuality is not derivative from any essence. For Malebranche, essences are uncaused. They are dependent neither on will nor on thought. How then could Malebranche claim God to stand as efficient cause to Himself? To create or will His existence, He would first have to have an idea of Himself. He would, as Arnauld wrote to Descartes,[24] already have to be and to know before He could make Himself—a manifest absurdity.

Furthermore, the separation of act and content, of knowing and willing from independent forms, prevents Malebranche from possibly reducing, as does Descartes, God's existence or substantiality to one or more attributes. For Descartes the being or existence of anything whatsoever is reducible entirely to and exhausted by its nature. That something *is* depends on *what* it is. The existence of body is in terms of the principal attribute of extension; that of the self in terms of thought. We do not, says Descartes, know bare being or existence.[25] Furthermore, the distinction between essence and existence, Descartes also says, is merely a distinction of reason.[26] Here again he is following his idealistic assumption of the validity of going from knowing to being. The *esse* is always swallowed up into the *nosse*. So, in the case of God, His being is wholly reducible to an essence—His being depends on His conceiving and hence creating Himself.

But in Malebranche's case, for God to exist, that actuality can in no way be derivative from a thought that thinks itself—thinking is not creative—, or from a will that wills itself or from a power that makes itself; for volition and power are dependent upon understanding, and the understanding on ideas that God *finds* in Himself. If therefore God exists, He can not do so through self-causation. Given his Cartesian background and his anti-Cartesian epistemology concerning the inviolable character of ideas and truth, Malebranche must reject Descartes' view of God as univocal and self-creative. What alternatives are open to him? May Malebranche, for example, consider God as a Platonic Demiurge, an architect separate from the eternal ideas?

II. God as Being

Recall that Gassendi asked Descartes how there could exist eternal and immutable beings in addition to and outside of God. Descartes replied that this was possible, since God had made them such.[27] However, Malebranche has shown against Descartes that these essences, endowed with the characters of eternity and immutability, can not be creatures. Since Malebranche will believe that there is an eternal God, he must accordingly take account of Gassendi's objection. If there is a God, the affirmation of an eternal realm "outside" and in addition to God would in effect be the recognition of two divinities; and it would indeed make God subjected to a kind of Styx or Jupiter, as Descartes claimed. But Descartes himself believed that whatever does not belong to the creature belongs to the Creator. Since Malebranche has denied essences to be created effects, he will have no other alternative but to make them or assert them to be God, which he of course does.[28]

But Malebranche does not make a simple identification, as so many critics suppose.[29] The vision of ideas is a Vision in God, but not of God, not of the absolute divine totality. The ideas constitute part of the divine Word which is consubstantial with God, yet God is more than the Word. This is the real nub of the problem. Malebranche does not simply reduce the Deity to the realm of essence and of abstract truth, but instead makes the Christian Philosopher of the *Entretien* proclaim to his Chinese colleague: My God is Being, unrestricted Being, *Celui qui est*.[30] In this pronouncement, Malebranche is openly averring his return to the God of *Exodus* and to that of the medievals.

The problem is, what in Malebranche's epistemology allows, or even perhaps necessitates, this conception of God as Being?

(*a*) *Ideas Refer Intrinsically to Existence.* First of all, let us realize the referential, super-essential character of ideas. In the *Recherche*, in Chapter VI of Part II of the third book, on the pure understanding, Malebranche warns us that in order to comprehend his own solution concerning our knowledge of external objects, an important principle must be borne in mind, to wit, that prior to the creation of the world, God had knowledge (ideas) of all the objects He created. Without such ideas, God could not have exercised His power to produce a world of things. Now, what is significant at the moment is how Malebranche describes the reference of the ideas, for ideas afford *a priori* knowledge of concrete things to God.

Ideas as potentials for actualization.

To Arnauld, Malebranche explained how he learned of immutable essences and eternal truths from St. Augustine and how from St. Thomas he learned that essences were the exemplars of creation.[31] Again in the Préface to the *Entretiens sur la métaphysique* he attributes his doctrine of essences to Philo, Thomas, Augustine and the Church Fathers.[32] This allegiance to Aquinas and to Augustine is significant. It shows that part of the meaning and illuminating character of Malebranche's ideas are their potentiality for actualization. Thus his ideas bear upon themselves, so to speak, the mark or stamp of what today might be called their "ingressibility." In intuiting or conceiving an idea, not only does one apprehend its unique properties, but at the same time the intuition is of a "nature-that-may-exist." But for an idea to be thus imbued with an existential reference is, I suggest, to be laden with the meaning of creation, of actualization, of realization. We may indeed have no distinct or separate idea of power, as Hume later insisted was the case when he asserted that we have no impression and therefore no 'idea' of causal efficacy; that is, we may not, for Malebranche, *comprehend the process* by which an essence becomes actual. Creative efficacy remains to that extent elusive and mysterious. Nevertheless, we know what we mean by power, for in comprehending any essence we conceive it not only in itself—as eternal, immutable, necessary—but also as referring beyond itself to the temporal, the mutable, the contingent, in a word, to existence and to creation.

Ideas enlighten the divine mind, because they are that aspect of God's essence or nature which is relative to creatures. Ideas are a source of intelligibility to God, because they possess the very special status of bearing existential reference and of being fraught with existential import. As the exemplars or models for creation, *they do not constitute the absolute essence of God.* Instead, they constitute only those perfections which are relative to creatures, those, that is, in which creatures may or do participate.[33]

Thus for Malebranche any idea carries upon itself the meaning of or implicit reference to power and creativity as a feature of its intelligibility. It remains true to say, and Malebranche will indeed insist upon saying it, that there is no logical necessity between essence and existence. This is beside the present issue. In apprehending the nature of a triangle, God is not, and we are not, apprehending an *actual* existence or *actual* potency.[34] We are, however, entertaining existence, as a sort of *terminus ad quem*. And what is important at this point is that, apart from this *notion* of existence, or actuality, essences do not signify, but are empty and fail to serve in knowledge. Now, regardless of the interpretation that may be given to the manner in which objects are declared to be participations or expressions of these archetypal models, the significant thing is that Malebranche, *as epistemologist,* considers the essences to be illuminating only because they have this extra-essential or super-essential import, this intentional or existential direction.

The issue can be drawn sharply if we contrast Malebranche's account of ideas seen in God with Santayana's philosophy of essence, for Santayana has been deeply influenced by Hume, while Malebranche carefully refrained from tolerating any formulation that could lead to skepticism. In terms of recent debate, comparing roughly, we may properly associate Malebranche's vision of ideas in God with Whitehead's account of eternal objects in the Antecedent Nature of

Malebranche's essences contrasted with Santayana's.

God, while a critic like Church would pair Malebranche with Santayana.

Whereas for Santayana essences acquire an illegitimate symbolic reference to fact through the rude, inexplicable shock of animal faith that reads existential meanings into them, Malebranche takes the non-idealistic position that an essence has a depth of its own beyond its surface nakedness. In the very intuition of an eternal essence, the essence of existence, if I may speak metaphorically, is given. Neither the divine intellect nor divine will projects existential meaning into the essences. An essence not only connotes itself, but also denotes itself. "Nothing given exists," but the meaning of existence is given along with the essence.

We may still wonder why Malebranche localizes essences *in* God, and we may still have questions concerning the character of this Deity. This remains the task of the present chapter, wherein we shall examine the intimate relationship between Malebranche's Platonic epistemology and his realistic metaphysics. But we already see that his theory of knowledge need not be a pure Platonism, that the category of existence looms large in the philosophical horizon of Malebranchianism, that the act of knowledge is about something other than itself.

So too the early Santayana asserted, before he landed in the solipsism of the specious moment.[35] In my interpretation, Malebranche never fell into such a solipsism. That he avoided it is perhaps owing to his Christian and Baconian heritage. The task of the *Recherche* is to justify the deductive-experimental method. Bacon, in *his* search for Forms, sought the true signatures of a real world. Malebranche too sought to explain how we perceive externally existing objects and how we conceive what we perceive. In the only interpretation of Malebranche that I can find that renders him coherent, the culmination of this search after truth is his realization of the *a priori* role of eternal concepts in the cognition of matters of fact. But no more than Bacon, Malebranche never loses sight of the fact that knowledge is knowledge of facts, actual or possible. He never forgets that the search for the foundations of knowledge is a search undertaken by an existent in behalf of existence.

To be sure, Santayana himself maintains that knowledge properly speaking is of facts and that intuition is not knowledge. But Santayana seems to believe that when one reaches the watershed of skepticism, the ultimate depths of doubt and despair, there is a complete loss and forgetfulness of any sense or meaning of existence. Not only are essences for him naked manikins divested of reference beyond themselves, but strictly speaking essences cannot even be said to be given, for within the instantaneous intuition there is no self or act of intuiting to which the essences present or reveal themselves. Within intuition there is utter confluence and identity of intuiter and intuited. Any distinction between them is an act of animal faith and thus the beginning of irrational knowledge of facts.

Hume, as Leibnitz before him, said of the Cartesian doubt that were it possible one could never emerge from it. How much more does this criticism pertain to Santayana! He appeals to the shock of existence, that is, to animal faith, to explain the rude awakening from intuition. Thus animal faith explains the belief in and skepticism of animal faith. Which is, as Mr. J. W. Miller observes,[36] no explanation.

The truth of the matter is that Santayana cannot, much as he would like to do so, banish the category of existence. Any doubt itself testifies to the primordial sense of existence, not simply because, as Descartes put it, to doubt is to exist, but also because one cannot doubt nothingness. One's very doubt is a doubt about reality, of reality, and by reality.

Malebranche, on the contrary, never doubts the legitimacy of the category of existence. For him, the process of knowledge is from natural revelation or sense perception. The discovery of ideas is an illumination by ideas of an existential self, at least of an existential act of intuition; also it is an illumination, because the ideas themselves are originally given and present in perception; and thirdly, when they are apprehended in their purity by conception alone, they are then known not as bare data or essences but as divine models referring to a possible or actual creation. In short, Malebranche never abandons the level of existence. Thus he tells us, in a passage that is significant for the whole of the present chapter:

> Mais de plus, quoique nous ne voyions immédiatement que les idées des objets, et que ces idées ne soient que la substance efficace de la Divinité; cependant comme elles ne sont point la substance de Dieu prise absolument telle qu'elle est, mais seulement prise en tant que très imparfaitement imitable par les créatures: *en voyant directement et immédiatement les idées, nous ne voyons point véritablement Dieu, l'être infiniment parfait, mais l'essence des créatures*. . . . C'est proprement les créatures que nous voyons . . .[37]

Malebranche tells us that he fell into doubt and bottomless despair [38] over the fact that, having separated sensations as well as the acts of pure intuition from the contents or ideas intuited, he could no longer assign to the ideas that type of existential reference which they have in Descartes. For Descartes ideas as objects possess objective reality. As such, they too refer to an existential world beyond themselves; but as acts of thought they are the modifications of the self. Now Descartes' theory, as we saw in treating the Fourth Alternative, jeopardizes certainty. But recall that it also endangers the existential reference of an idea. If ideas are modes of thought, states of the self, then they cannot possess those features of exteriority and of intentional reference to existents. Hence, Malebranche complains:

> Mais la difficulté est de savoir si les idées qui représentent quelque chose qui est hors de l'âme et qui leur ressemble en quelque façon, comme les idées du soleil, d'une maison, d'un cheval, d'une rivière, etc., ne sont que des modifications de l'âme; de sorte que l'esprit n'ait besoin que de lui-même pour se représenter toutes les choses qui sont hors de lui.[39]

It is this difficulty as well as the question of certainty that drove Malebranche into despair, until, through the help of St. Augustine and Aquinas he realized that essences which are self-sufficiently immutable (uncaused) are also candidates for existence, and must constitute an archetypal attribute of God.[40]

This Vision in God satisfies the requirements for a defensible doctrine of cognition and perception. The Platonism saves science from skepticism and relativism. It makes nature, not man, the measure of things. It preserves the eternal, necessary, immutable. The Christian character of this Platonism—the identification of reason with the Word as the divine exemplar for creation—prevents science from losing contact with the real, the concrete, the existential, for these essences are no bare essences. Finally, Malebranche's insistence, which I shall examine in detail in the last chapter, that cognition of the ideal begins with an awareness of it in sense perception not only keeps the ideal nailed down to matters of fact but preserves the very spirit of the experimental method.

Thus we see again that the structure of the alternative theories of ideas which culminate in the Vision in God is not haphazard. Not only does it constitute the application of the Baconian method *to* theories of knowledge, but this ascent from theory to theory is itself a reflection of Malebranche's very conception of the cognitive process. His theory of knowledge is rooted in ontology. In rising successively from nominalism and materialism to a Christian Platonism, the mind is making an inductive exploration of the real, the existential. This very induction is possible, only because when realized, the ideal intelligible essences to which the mind aspires are already embedded or immanent in the sensible, only because, as a condition for creation, they are the immutable Forms awaiting realization. The sensible is a stepping stone to and reminder of the ideal, but the ideal is no mere ideal; it is an ideal that looks to the real. Hence, in examining various theories of ideas, one does not fortuitously turn from one to another, nor does one abandon one after another. Rather, nominalism, abstractionism, innatism, conceptualism are so many phases (*scalae gradibus*) of one idea. Each is a more and more refined form of Christian "exemplarism," of essences that refer to creatures. And in this pursuit of truth, the living, concrete existential reality of the self as seeker and knower is never lost sight of by Malebranche. This is why attention plays so prominent a role in his theory of knowledge. The "self" will be treated more fully later, but we must pause for a moment to consider its bearing here.

(b) *Vision of Ideas Accompanied by Vision of Power.* Knowledge, for Malebranche, consists in a continuous process of uninterrupted attention from sense to idea. But the alternative theories of ideas, with their attendant arguments, criticisms, disproofs, and demonstrations, are more than abstract logical exercises. Actually they constitute together a living and dramatic experience. They attest to the inner struggle of a personality in its thirst for truth and the final triumph or conversion of the mind from darkness to light. Not merely do the successive alternative doctrines constitute a spiritual reawakening from and breaking with error, but also they constitute a dynamic journey and *progressus*. The mind does indeed discover intelligible truth, the nature of ideas, but it does so through an act of will, an effort, a searching; attention is a natural prayer of the soul.[41] In searching and attending, the soul enjoys illumination. Thus the pursuit of truth is a moral and historical undertaking in which the soul not only finds the ideas which, by their nature, illuminate, but the soul also, in its search for truth, experiences the dramatic event of becoming enlightened.[42] As the mind attends to, weighs, reflects upon the alternative hypotheses, it is enduring and undergoing a process of transformation; it is becoming enhanced, enkindled and liberated; thereby it is being acted upon and changed. In short, the epistemological analysis of truth is a searching, a finding *and hence the very awareness of a causal influence.* The essences and the truth that illuminate are themselves merely static and ideal; but their disclosure to the mind, their revelation and appearance to the attending inquiring mind, involve an act of power. An influence, a force is exerting itself upon the inquirer and making the ideas swim into his ken; a force is acting upon the sluggish attention, sharpening it, extending it, and making the truth become present and perspicuous to it.[43]

Thus the search after truth is itself an experience of causal power. The epistemological quest could not be fulfilled without the ontological experience. The intelligible realm of ideas could not be found or given without the concomitant givenness or finding of actual, existential power that is felt to be exerting itself upon the inquirer. In the moment when an essence is intuited, there is simultaneously the intuition of its becoming present; hence, of an event occurring or being caused.

Thus a critical epistemology leads not only to a vision of ideas in God, but also to a vision of divine will. For all his Platonism, Malebranche does not reduce God to the formal realm of essences. As in the case of Augustine, Malebranche's God is not only a personal Deity but the Maker and Creator. Which is to say that if we experience power anywhere, then God is Will as well as Reason. Yet this is not saying enough. We must now see that God for Malebranche is not simply the *Deus Duplex* that Brunschvicg ascribes to him. Malebranche's God is not a Platonic Demiurge; but the Power that enlightens is one with the realm of essences, with Reason, and is even more.

(c) *God, for Malebranche, Is Being.* M. Gilson, in his *Spirit of Medieval Philosophy*, draws a sharp distinction between the Greek and Christian conception of God. For the Christian, God is Supreme Being. **Christian** This means first that there is only one, unique divinity, and secondly **God unique.** that the proper name for God is Being.

Neither Plato nor Aristotle, argues M. Gilson, conceived of divinity as unique. Although both travelled far in that direction, Plato's Demiurge in the *Timaeus* is at the top of a hierarchy of Gods, the most important and the most powerful, nevertheless one among many. Aristotle's Unmoved Mover is, similarly, "first" in the order of divinities and to that extent supreme among them; yet the Unmoved Mover is not alone; there are other divinities. Thus neither Plato nor Aristotle ever reached monotheism, however far in that direction each may have moved. Gilson further substantiates his argument concerning the divergence between Hellenic and Christian philosophy by turning from the unicity of God to a consideration of His nature or essence.

For Christianity, not merely is God a one and only divinity, but in addition His name is Being, for this alone expresses His essence or nature. Do Plato and Aristotle conceive of God as pure Being? With **The Christian** respect to Plato, Gilson quotes from the *Sophist:* "the degree of divinity **God is Being.** is proportionate to the degree of being; that, therefore, is most of all divine which most of all is being; now that which most of all is being is the universal Being or the All of being." To this Gilson replies that for a Christian, strictly speaking, there are no degrees of divinity. What separates the Christian tradition from Plato is the fact that Plato in no sense ever uses "being" exclusively for God. That is why his god possesses divinity only in a supreme degree but not in the least as a unique prerogative, Gilson tells us. For Plato there is divinity wherever there is being, because there is no single being that claims the entire fullness and privilege of divinity.[44]

Now, in the case of Aristotle it is true that he focuses on being as being; this seems to be analogous to the Christian Deity. Analogous it is, but not identical, avers Gilson. For, as said before, Aristotle's

Unmoved Mover is supreme in the totality of beings, but he is not alone. But more importantly, even were Aristotle's *being as being* unique and singular, "it would still be true that this being is none other than the pure act of thought thinking itself." This is why the attributes of Aristotle's God are "limited to those of thought." "In good Aristotelian doctrine the first name of God is thought, and pure being is reduced to pure thought"; but "in good Christian doctrine the first name of God is being, and that is why we can refuse to Being neither thought, nor will, nor power, and why the attributes of the Christian God overflow the attributes of Aristotle's in every direction." [45]

Malebranche's God more than a realm of essences.

Now this distinction between the Greek and Christian conceptions of God is of capital importance for understanding Malebranche's view of God and the localization of essences in God, as well as his later doctrine of causal efficacy. Particularly pertinent for the understanding of Malebranche's vision *in* God is this passage just quoted. Whereas the Aristotelian god is essentially abstract, a principle of intelligibility, an act of thought thinking itself, for the Christian, the cornerstone of his philosophy is the conception of God as Being. Even in Plato being is subordinated to the Good as the principle of intelligibility. But for the Christian, Being is primary.[46]

Accordingly, the first point to notice is that when Malebranche discovers the realm of universal truths, of ideal essences, and identifies them with God, this identification is only partial or approximate. His God is indeed the Word or Pure Reason or the source of intelligibility, but He is more than that. He is *Celui qui est.*

Christian ontological realism.

The problem still remains. How does Malebranche, starting from a theory of knowledge, from an intelligible order, pass to ontology, to a Deity who is more than essence or whose very essence is existence? Now we cannot answer this question until we explore further the Christian conception of Being. Notice that M. Gilson asserts that the primacy of Being holds true of "good" Christian doctrine. We must therefore ask what does "good" here mean? Do all Christians have the same conception of Being or does Being mean something special for the "good" Christian? Gilson does not explicitly distinguish between the good Christian and what must presumably be impure or bad Christianity. He does, however, offer a hint, or rather several hints. Expounding on the meaning of *Ego sum qui sum* from *Exodus*, Gilson explains that this can only mean that God is the pure act of existing. This implies that "it is not as a concept that God would have us think of Him nor even as a Being whose content would be that of a concept," [47] but rather as concrete, positive and absolute actuality. For the Christian, then, the concept of Being or existence is the most meaningful and most primordial of all concepts, and at the same time it is such because it goes beyond any concept.

[136]

Now, says Gilson, in further exploring the significance of this concept of God as Being, Christian speculation followed two converging paths, one of which leads to the description of God as perfect, the other to a description of Him as infinite.

Because God is Being or pure actuality, He is self-sufficient. He exists *per se*. Since "being" designates the essence of God, because this is the name by which He denominates Himself, in God essence and existence are identical. For the good Christian, however, this identity or self-sufficiency means absolute independence. Not only is God's existence not derived from any external source, but neither is it derived from any internal source.

> Just as His existence is not derived from any other than Himself, so neither does He depend on any kind of internal essence, which would have in itself the power to bring itself to existence. If He is *essentia* this is because the word signifies the positive act itself by which Being is, as if *esse* could generate the present participle active *essens*, whence *essentia* would be derived. When St. Jerome says that God is His own origin and the cause of His own substance, he does not mean, as Descartes does, that God in a certain way posits Himself in being by His almighty power as by a cause, but simply that we must not look outside God for a cause of the existence of God. Now this complete aseity of God involves His absolute perfection as an immediate corollary. . . . Thus the perfection of the Christian God is that perfection which is proper to being as being, that which being posits along with itself; we do not say that He is because He is perfect, but on the contrary, He is perfect because He is.[48]

The Christian God, then, is an essence to whose essence it belongs to exist.

Now when Malebranche describes God as self-existent, he leaves no doubt as to his meaning, although Malebranche's critics have overlooked this feature of his thought.[49] He employs the text of *Exodus*, to which, so far as I know, Descartes refers only once. Malebranche further explains the meaning of this notion in the very language which we find Gilson now using. God as Being is inexhaustible reality, the plenitude of being. Unlike Descartes' *Causa Sui*, Malebranche's Deity does not in any sense stand as the cause of His existence. Malebranche uses *per se* in the traditional sense. For him, God's existence is not suspended from or secondary to a causal essence like power. The Christian Philosopher addresses the Chinese Philosopher thus:

Malebranche a Christian ontological realist.

> Le chrétien.—Le Dieu, que nous vous annonçons est celui-là même dont l'idée est gravée en vous, et dans tous les hommes. Mais faute d'y faire assez d'attention, ils ne la reconnaissent point telle qu'elle est, et ils la défigurent étrangement. Voilà pourquoi *Dieu*, pour nous

renouveler son idée, nous a déclaré par son Prophète, qu'il est *celui qui est;* c'est-à-dire, l'Etre qui renferme dans son essence tout ce qu'il y a de réalité ou de perfection dans tous les êtres, l'Etre infini en tout sens, en un mot l'Etre.[50]

Moreover, Malebranche, precisely as does Gilson, makes it clear that the God of whom he speaks and whose name is Being is unique and alone. In the dialogue, the Christian emphasizes the fact that the God whom he adores, the "Seigneur du ciel," is not a particular divinity, one among others. Once and for all, cries the Christian, get clear about our doctrine: I repeat our God is *He who is,* He is *l'Etre,* Being without restriction or limitation.—But, persists the Chinese Philosopher, is not your God "un tel être, un être particulier"? To this query comes the reply:

> Le Dieu que nous adorons n'est point un tel être en ce sens, que son essence soit bornée: il est bien plutôt tout être. Mais il est un tel Etre en ce sens, qu'il est le *seul* Etre qui renferme dans la simplicité de son essence, tout ce qu'il y a de réalité ou de perfection dans tous les êtres, qui ne sont que des participations, (je ne dis pas des parties) infiniment limitées, que des imitations infiniment imparfaites de son essence.[51]

In a subsequent commentary on this very passage, Malebranche further explains that, ". . . CELUI QUI EST, ou l'Etre infiniment parfait, est un nom absolu, qui exprime l'essence du vrai Dieu, et qui ne peut convenir qu'à lui." [52]

Now while the original question remains unanswered as yet, namely, how Malebranche passes from essence to God as pure Being who encompasses but also overflows essences, we can at this point, however, make the following observations. Whereas for Descartes the being or nature of eternal truths is derivative from God's will and whereas for Descartes God as *Causa Sui* is essential for guaranteeing the continued permanence and stability of those truths, Malebranche's doctrine of uncaused, uncreated essences permits him to return to the pure Christian doctrine of God as Being. In fact, not merely does his doctrine of immutable essences permit him to do this; it also necessitates such a reversion. If Malebranche is to consider his uncaused ideas as exemplars for creation and is to lodge them in a God who is to be more than ideas, then this Deity must exist *per se* in the absolute sense of being divorced from any external or internal efficacy. Exemplarism is incompatible with any view of a God whose existence is derivative from power. Were God's being derivative from and subordinate to an internal creative essence, as in the case of Descartes, then the ideas too would be subordinate to such power. But the entire

Rejection of philosophy of creative essence.

brunt of Malebranche's polemic against Descartes and the Cartesians is to establish the absolute independence and sufficiency of essences.

We may therefore conclude that Malebranche's epistemology which seeks to guarantee a deductive-empirical method demands a Deity who is free from and altogether independent of any external or internal dynamism. This does not, however, imply that Malebranche's God has to be an Eleatic, static, formal absolute. He would be that were He nothing but a realm of universals. But if Malebranche's God is indeed the traditional God Who is Being, then His existence may be uncreated and nevertheless creative—an uncreated creativity.

(*d*) *Infinity of God.* How does Malebranche arrive at such a view of God? To answer this question, we must explore, first, another aspect of Christian thought, the notion of infinity. Because God is Being and thus self-sufficient and perfect, Christianity further developed the notion of Being as an absolute and positive expansion, that is, infinity. According to M. Gilson, the perfection of being calls for all realizations. In addition, it excludes all limits and generates thereby "a positive infinity which refuses all determination." [53] From this it follows that no idea, no concept, no essence, no general meaning can designate this most general totality of being. God is super-essential; in brief, He is infinite.

God's infinity: God as supra-essential.

This point of view also characterizes the thought of Malebranche. And it is precisely this special feature that enables Malebranche to make the leap or transition from an epistemology of essences to a realistic ontology, from essences to God as Being. Thus the argument against Descartes considered above, that the mind can conceive, even if it cannot comprehend, infinity, becomes important. This argument functions not merely negatively, to reject Descartes' innatism and conceptualism, but also constructively, to allow Malebranche's positive doctrines in epistemology and ontology. To see how this is so, I must beg the reader's indulgence while I reiterate some familiar doctrine.

Essences or ideas are real. They *are*. They have distinctive properties. They are not things or substances, but they are not nothing. While they *are*, however, into their reality and being enters the notion of the general and of the infinite. This or that determinate essence is intelligible only in so far as it is seen to be an expression of the general, the indeterminate, the infinite. [54] Essences do not constitute a garrulous, pulverized realm of windowless monads. For Malebranche there is no fragmentized plurality of separate ideas. To Arnauld, Malebranche stoutly denies that he ever held that a distinct enumerable collection of archetypes exists in the divine reason. This or that idea of this or that figured extension is an aspect of a single infinite intelligible extension.

This doctrine of the unity of essences is, remember, an extension of the doctrine of Descartes. Not only did Descartes affirm a single idea of an infinite extension, but also he maintained that before we can have the idea of the finite, we must already possess that of the infinite as a standard for comparison.[55]

Moreover, for Malebranche, in the sphere of essence, not only does the mind conceive the idea of an infinite extension, it also conceives the idea of an infinite numerical continuum ("les nombres nombrants") and the hierarchy of moral perfections.[56] But from Malebranche's point of view, no one of these infinites can be fully grasped apart from the conception of an infinitely infinite reality.

The important point is—How does Malebranche interpret this reality? Can this infinitely infinite reality be a super system of intelligible essences like Santayana's, organized under the general essence which he labels Being? Or like Duns Scotus' conception of *this* infinite— *haecceitas*—,[57] which again is the adoration of God as an essence, albeit a unique essence? Ginsberg says that for Malebranche God is not a self-conscious personality, but a system of Ideas such as we find in the philosophy of Plato.[58] And Ollé-Laprune compares Malebranche's Deity to the One of Plotinus, an impersonal abstraction.[59]

That Malebranche has taken an Augustinian route to God, there can

Augustinian
formulation. be no question. He explicitly formulates such an ascension:

> L'étendue intelligible infinie n'est point une modification de mon esprit; elle est immuable, éternelle, nécessaire. Je ne puis douter de sa réalité et de son immensité. Or *tout ce qui est immuable, éternel, nécessaire, et surtout infini, n'est point une créature, et ne peut appartenir à la créature. Donc elle appartient au Créateur, et ne peut se trouver qu'en Dieu. Donc il y a un Dieu, et une Raison;* un Dieu dans lequel se trouve l'archétype que je contemple du monde créé que j'habite; un Dieu dans lequel se trouve la Raison qui m'éclaire par les idées purement intelligibles qu'elle fournit abondamment à mon esprit et à celui de tous les hommes.[60]

Although Malebranche formulates this approach to the Divine in this clearly Augustinian manner, however, the vital point is that he does not halt with Augustine's *Deus Essentia*. For the foregoing formulation has been put between the lips of *Aristes* whom Theodore is instructing, and Aristes prefaces it with the words: ". . . j'ai cru que, sans manquer au respect que je vous dois, je pouvais aller seul dans le chemin que vous m'avez montré." True, Theodore accepts the formulation: "Vous ne vous êtes point égaré, mon cher Ariste." But— he warns Aristes—

> Mais ne vous imaginez pas qu'elle vous ait découvert la nature de l'Etre suprême auquel elle vous a conduit. Lorsque vous contemplez

l'étendue intelligible, vous ne voyez encore que l'archétype du monde matériel que nous habitons, et celui d'une infinité d'autres possibles. A la vérité, vous voyez alors la substance divine, car il n'y a qu'elle qui soit visible, ou qui puisse éclairer l'esprit. Mais vous ne la voyez pas en elle-même, ou selon ce qu'elle est. Vous ne la voyez que selon le rapport qu'elle a aux créatures matérielles, que selon qu'elle est participable par elles, ou qu'elle en est représentative. Et par conséquent, ce n'est point Dieu, à proprement parler, que vous voyez, mais seulement la matière qu'il peut produire.

When Theodore seeks to help Aristes to ascend as near as possible to the Divine itself, this infinitely infinite reality that Malebranche attains is at once identified with the God of *Exodus*. Let us consider what Theodore affirms.

Says Theodore:

The God of *Exodus*.

. . . La substance divine dans sa simplicité, où nous ne pouvons atteindre, renferme une infinité de perfections intelligibles toutes différentes, par lesquelles Dieu nous éclaire sans se faire voir à nous tel qu'il est, ou selon sa réalité particulière et absolue, mais selon sa réalité générale et relative à des ouvrages possibles.

No human can enter into the inner sanctuary of the Deity to comprehend there His particular and absolute reality. Ordinarily the human mind can perceive only those aspects of God which have reference to the created world. Yet Malebranche does make the attempt to overreach human limitations. "Cependant," Theodore continues, "tâchez de me suivre; je vais vous conduire le plus près de la Divinité qu'il me sera possible."

L'étendue intelligible infinie n'est l'archétype que d'une infinité de mondes possibles semblables au nôtre. Je ne vois par elle que tels et tels êtres, que des êtres matériels. Quand je pense à cette étendue, je ne vois la substance divine qu'en tant qu'elle est représentative des corps et participable par eux. Mais prenez garde: Quand je pense à l'être, et non à tels et tels êtres, quand je pense à l'infini, et non à tel ou tel infini, . . . il n'y a que Dieu, que l'infini, que l'être indéterminé, ou que l'infini infiniment infini, qui puisse contenir la réalité infiniment infinie que je vois quand je pense à l'être, et non à tels ou tels êtres, ou à tels et tels infinis.

But the idea of Being—of reality, of unlimited perfection,—is not of created things: ". . . L'idée de l'être sans restriction, de l'infini, de la généralité, n'est point l'idée des créatures, ou l'essence qui leur convient, mais l'idée qui représente la Divinité, ou l'essence qui lui convient."

Aristes: Il me semble que je vois bien votre pensée. Vous définissez Dieu comme il s'est défini lui-même en parlant à Moise: *Dieu, c'est celui qui est.* . . . L'être sans restriction, en un mot l'*Etre*, c'est l'idée de Dieu . . .[61]

Essence, existence, and Being.

In leading the mind up to the notion of the infinitely infinite Being, Malebranche has thus gone far beyond the sphere of abstract essences to the very Christian view of God as Existence itself. We may say, in other words, that for Malebranche the Platonic realm of essence, the realm of *static* universal intelligibility, is itself a bare, partial, limited abstraction and to that extent not completely and fully intelligible or meaningful. Complete intelligibility demands a notion of utmost generality. For him this requires that the dimension of static meaning be recognized as wedded to that of power and that the two together be characteristic of actuality itself. Complete intelligibility demands the unification of essence. But essences, universals, number can illuminate and clarify, can "explain" this and that existence, only because they are embedded in existence and wedded to it, only because existence is primary. Being or existence is the fountainhead and source of meaning. Without existence, essence is a chimerical abstraction, a bloodless, unintelligible category. Without the "idea" of existence nothing else is meaningful. Essences, for Malebranche, are thus super-essential, because they reveal themselves not only as referring to existence, but also as aspects of existence.

Moreover, Malebranche held this view from the very start. In the first edition of the *Recherche* he succinctly and forthrightly signalized the extent and limit of his agreement with Augustine. Whereas, wrote Malebranche, for Augustine God is identical with eternal truth, so that in beholding the immutable verities we are directly beholding God, I hold a somewhat different position. In my doctrine it is true to say that we see God when we contemplate eternal truths, *but not because God is no more than or exclusively truth,* but rather because the ideas that determine the relation of truth are *in* God. And, perhaps, he adds, this is what Saint Augustine himself had in mind. First Malebranche formulates the reasons by which Augustine proves that we have knowledge of God:

Il y a dans saint Augustin une infinité de passages . . . par lesquels il prouve que nous voyons Dieu dès cette vie par la connaissance que nous avons des vérités éternelles. La vérité est incréée, immuable, immense, éternelle, au-dessus de toutes choses. Elle est vraie par elle-même; elle ne tient sa perfection d'aucune chose; elle rend les créatures plus parfaites, et tous les esprits cherchent naturellement à la connaître. Il n'y a rien qui puisse avoir toutes ces perfections que Dieu. Donc la vérité est Dieu. Nous voyons de ces vérités immuables et éternelles. Donc nous voyons Dieu.

Malebranche comments:

> Ce sont là les raisons de saint Augustin, les nôtres en sont peu différentes, et nous ne voulons point nous servir injustement de l'autorité d'un si grand homme pour appuyer notre sentiment.

Malebranche's own position is stated thus:

> Nous pensons donc que les vérités, même celles qui sont éternelles, comme que deux fois deux font quatre, ne sont pas seulement des êtres absolus, *tant s'en faut que nous croyions qu'elles soient Dieu même.*[62]

Thus Malebranche concludes:

> Ainsi selon notre sentiment, nous voyons Dieu lorsque nous voyons des vérités éternelles: *non que ces vérités soient Dieu,* mais parce que les idées dont ces vérités dépendent sont *en* Dieu; peut-être même que saint Augustin l'a entendu ainsi.[63]

Hence, in pursuing his epistemological quest concerning the nature and possibility of knowledge, the nature of truth, Malebranche is led to the discovery of infinite Being or God as the locus of all significance and enlightenment. We can know nothing, grasp nothing, understand nothing, without this first and fundamental acquaintance with God or Being. Banish the category of existence and you destroy all knowledge, certitude and truth.

(*e*) *The Ontological Proof.* We can begin to appreciate why Malebranche asserts that mathematics is a direct approach to God and why he says that the best proof and way of knowing God's existence is by his doctrine of eternal ideas, or rather, through the idea of the infinite.[64] It is the best proof, not because it is a proof, but because it reveals through an analytic approach (analytic as Descartes used this term) the necessary foundation of proof and the nature of knowledge. It is the best way of reaching God, not because it identifies God with ideas, but rather because it is a critical and rational exploration concerning the meaning of meaning and the foundation of knowledge; because it shows that in the name of clear and distinct ideas one must go beyond ideas.

Realistic function of the proof.

By reverting to the view of God as Being, Malebranche's alternative theories of ideas may, when taken as a whole, be interpreted as an *a posteriori* proof of the existence of God. Taken together they show that to know, to conceive, or to understand anything is to conceive it as an aspect of Being; that nothing can be understood or conceived apart from God as Being. Not only is all knowledge knowledge in and of God, but all knowledge is in and of the real, of existence.

Just as Plato, the rationalist, was led to organize his multiple ideas under the one supreme idea of the Good, and just as the twentieth-century Plato, Santayana, united his garrulous realm of essences into one realm of being, so our seventeenth century Plato, Malebranche, was led by the same rationalistic love of order and unity to recognize the essential unicity of essences. As a universal is the *ratio essendi* of innumerable particulars, so the plethora of universals themselves must be further grounded on a most-general or all-general principle, the infinitely infinite, or Being. But Malebranche is more than a Platonist. Hence for him this all-embracive principle is no abstraction, but is instead *Celui qui est*.

In other words, Malebranche, in rejecting Descartes' doctrine of innate and created ideas as destructive of the foundations of science, is now pursuing his analysis even further. He is in effect asserting that an enlightened or critical epistemology will discover its dependence on ontology, and that the primordial principle of ontology is Being or existence. Accordingly, if we pursue the query: how is certain knowledge possible?—how is mathematics possible?—we find that such certainty must be grounded in an objective, non-mental, non-psychological, non-created realm of intelligible natures or essences. But this is only half the story. The epistemologist's task is to probe further. He must now realize that these ideal concepts can function in knowledge, that they can yield truth only because they belong in reality, only because they are aspects of that which is.

Essences as real beings are dependent on Being.

Spinoza said that the medievals begin with creatures, Descartes with the self, and I with God.[65] Malebranche, with proper qualifications, might have asserted the same principle. He might have said that the Scholastics, in beginning with the senses, begin with particular sensible beings, and that Descartes, in beginning with the *cogito* wherein he finds a magazine of ideas, is also starting from a limited perspective, either with his own finite and limited consciousness or with intelligible beings. But the proper point of departure is not *this* or *that* sort or aspect of being, neither sensible nor intelligible being, but Being as such.

However, a rectified Cartesianism is superior for an understanding of God's existence to Scholasticism. Anything, Malebranche states to Régis, can prove the existence of a superior power,[66] but this power may be a demon and not the true God. But once we purify Descartes' doctrine of ideas and show their uncreated character, then it is that their aspect of reality becomes central. Then we find that the meaning of meanings lies in Being.

André, the biographer and disciple of Malebranche, fully appreciated the import of this ascent to God and the sort of Deity whom Malebranche sought to establish. In two of his own discourses, André arrives at God in the following manner. He begins by considering the idea of the infinite as it enters into mathematics, in number, in extension, in the comprehension of generals and universals.[67] However, as far as God, the true infinite, is concerned, as long as we remain within the sphere of mathematics, declares André, ". . . nous ne sommes encore, si j'ose ainsi dire, que dans le vestibule du temple de la vérité. Entrons dans le sanctuaire." [68] But in entering the sanctuary, we go beyond mathematical infinites, to the infinitely infinite Being, that is, to the God of *Exodus*.[69] Thus André asserts:

Car, Messieurs, prenons-y garde, ces infinis mathématiques ne sont pas infinis en tout: chacun d'eux ne l'est que dans les bornes d'une espèce particulière. L'infini en étendue ne l'est pas en nombre; l'infini en nombre ne l'est pas en étendue; l'infini en longueur ne l'est pas en largeur ni en surface; l'infini en surface ne l'est pas en solidité ni en profondeur. Dieu seul est infini en tout genre d'être et de perfection. Ces infinis mathématiques ne sont que des infinis subalternes, qui ne s'élèvent les uns sur les autres à l'infini que pour nous élever encore plus haut, c'est-à-dire jusqu'à l'infini suprême au delà duquel on ne peut plus monter. Les nombres finis disparaissent devant les infinis numériques, les étendues finies s'anéantissent devant les infinis géométriques; mais tous ces infinis disparaissent à leur tour et s'anéantissent devant l'infinité de Dieu. Telle est sa grandeur; il est seul de son ordre. Il est seul grande, parce qu'il est seul absolument infini. On peut dire même, en un sens très-réel, qu'il est le seul être et le tout être, parce que cette infinité absolue, qui le caràctérise, renferme tout éminemment.

. . . Quand le plus fameux des prophètes prit la liberté de lui demander son nom, son nom propre et incommunicable, le nom le plus expressif, pour le représenter à son peuple dans toute sa majesté: *Si dixerint mihi: quod est nomen ejus, quid dicam?* La question était hardie, la réponse fut divine: *Ego sum qui sum.* Tu me demandes mon nom? je m'appelle *Celui qui est.* . . . Voilà donc, selon Dieu même, la vraie définition de Dieu. Celui qui est, l'existant, l'Etre; ou, comme il parle ailleurs, *le seul Etre.*" [70]

But now the full impact of Malebranche's ontological argument must be met. Granted that no knowledge, truth or meaning is possible without the "idea" of utmost inclusiveness or generality, without, in short, the *"idée"* of Being—how can we pass over the ontological gap between meaning and reality? What allows us to affirm that the "idea" of existence or of Being is more than an idea, that such Being *is?* This is the *cul-de-sac* of Descartes' ontological argument, as it is of Bradley who attempts to legislate for reality in terms of what must satisfy the intellect. Malebranche, we shall see, will avoid the difficulty by showing that strictly speaking we have no idea of Being. And in doing so he will be pointing up the critical limitations of an epistemology that begins and ends with ideas; he will be showing, too, that ontology

No passage by consequence, from idea of Being to Being.

is prior to epistemology, that before we can know that we know or how we know, we must first know.

Before entering into an analysis of the ontological argument and to appreciate its significance, we must first face a few side issues. Why, it may be asked, does Malebranche turn to the ontological argument at all? Surely, he was acquainted with the objections against it, at least with those that were made against Descartes' use of it! Yet Malebranche does not hesitate to assert that, "la preuve de l'existence de Dieu la plus belle, la plus relevée, la plus solide et la première, ou celle qui suppose le moins de choses, c'est l'idée que nous avons de l'infini." [71]

Malebranche's proofs of God different from Descartes'.

When, in the dialogue between a Christian and a Chinese Philosopher, the Christian completes the exposition of the ontological argument, then the Chinese Philosopher, complaining that this is too abstract for his understanding, begs for a more palpable proof.[72] The proofs which the Christian philosopher then offers are from efficient causality and from design: God as the author of our perceptions and sensations, and as that infinite Geometer, who with His knowledge of the laws of motion and optics can alone explain the order, uniformity, and simplicity of the material and spiritual worlds. Again, in the *Conversations chrétiennes*, Theodore, the voice of Malebranche, declares condescendingly to the debonair man of the world, Aristarque, that he would like to advance proofs that are the most simple and the most conformable to a rational soul, but that out of deference to the limitations of the vulgar, untrained, carnal mind, he will employ sensible, palpable proofs. The proof that Theodore offers is the same as that of the Christian philosopher [73]—the movement of bodies and the soul's sensations are caused and their true, creative cause is God. In the second work, the argument from design, that is, from the uniformity, regularity and order of the world, is barely mentioned, for even this is deemed too sophisticated for the learned but un-Cartesianized mind of Aristarque.[74]

These instances indicate that Malebranche employs proofs from efficient causality only as a condescension to the vulgar. Now, in view of the fact that Malebranche considers this type of proof to be especially useful for morality,[75] in view of the fact that he agrees with Descartes that there is not a single effect or creature in nature which may not lead to establishing the existence of God, and above all, in view of Descartes' insistence that the method of efficient causation is the fundamental, not to say the only one, of demonstrating God's existence, since the concept of efficient causality or power is involved even in Descartes' ontological argument, it goes without saying, that if Malebranche prefers the ontological proof to that of efficient causality, not only must his "idea" of God as an infinite perfection differ radically from that of Descartes, but also his conception of these proofs themselves.

Malebranche has several major objections against proving God by efficient causality. One objection is directed against the causal *argument;* the second is aimed at the *causal principle* itself. These two are intimately interconnected. Their difference is the difference between a principle of explanation or an individual concept and the argument which employs this concept.

Malebranche's objections to proofs from efficiency— dependence on memory.

Malebranche accepts Descartes' answer to his critics, that the existence of God is necessary to guarantee, not the clear and distinct ideas themselves, but the memory of them. But, argues Malebranche, all reasoning involves memory; consequently inferential proofs for the existence of God are untrustworthy, so long as we entertain the hyperbole of an evil demon who might willfully join our memory to the wrong principles. Since it is God who must guarantee memory, no philosopher is justified, continues Malebranche, in relying upon the evidence of a chain of reasoning to reach God, for this would require that the conclusion be more evident than the premises upon which it is based.[76]

Herein then lies the first difficulty with all *a posteriori* causal proofs, —they all involve long chains of reasoning which are not convincing on the assumption of an evil, deceiving demon. Secondly, because of the supposition of a demon, any proof based on efficient causality merely serves to prove some or other potent author but not God or a being infinitely perfect who is omnipotent and rational.

Is this objection against Descartes legitimate? Malebranche's claim that reasoning involves memory is unquestionably orthodox Cartesianism. Descartes' fourth rule in the *Discourse on Method* is an exhortation to vigilant enumeration and multiple reviews over our deductions, until any whole deductive chain becomes a single intuition. Does this, indeed, not testify to Descartes' ceaseless preoccupation with the fallibility of memory, and, what is more important at the moment, to his admission that any discursive process whatever involves memory?

As a matter of fact, Descartes, in his third rule of the *Rules for the Direction of the Mind,* states unambiguously that we distinguish "mental intuition from deduction by the fact that into the conception of the latter there enters a certain movement or succession, into that of the former there does not. Further deduction does not require an immediately presented evidence such as intuition possesses; its certitude is rather conferred upon it in some way by memory."[77]

If reasoning, then, involves memory, and if it is memory that must be guaranteed by God, *ipso facto* Descartes' first two proofs of God are invalidated. This dismissal, however, is too facile and peremptory. There is greater significance to Malebranche's rejection of demonstrative proofs than is apparent on the surface. To appreciate Malebranche's criticism, we must re-examine Descartes' conception of the evil demon.

Continued existence of truth.

For Descartes, the problem of memory as it concerns the proofs of the existence of God is largely a question concerning the continued existence of a truth, formerly perceived, from moment to moment. Recall than in his *cogito* argument his defiance of the demon is expressed within the duration of an instant: "I am, I exist, is necessarily true each time that I pronounce it, or that I mentally conceive it." [78] Thus, when Descartes asks for the cause of his own existence, he is not seeking for a past cause but for one in the immediate now. The evil demon cannot alter the truth or the fact that I am something as long as I think that I am. Neither can he falsify that truth in the future. What has been has been. The demon cannot "some day cause it to be true to say that I have never been, it being true now to say that I am . . ." [79]

When Descartes asserts that he might be deceived each time that he adds 2 and 3 or every time he counts the sides of a square,[80] when he declares that we must be sure that when we perceive things clearly and distinctly they "are true in the very way in which we think them," [81] it would make Descartes more consistent with himself to interpret these statements in the following way. When I consider the angles of a triangle, I cannot doubt at that moment that they are equal to two right angles. When I add 3 and 2, in that very instant I cannot doubt that their sum is 5. But ordinarily, when we maintain that it is true that 3 plus 2 are 5, the meaning is that the proposition is true *for all time*, that it will be immutably and forever true. However, a demon or God who can do all that he desires or conceives may annihilate that truth in the very next instant. However contradictory it may seem that 3 plus 2, which right now are seen to be five, should not be so tomorrow, it is precisely that of which neither believer nor atheist can be certain. And because the doubt is thus prospective, it is also retrospective. During a process of reasoning which involves a succession in time, there is no guarantee that from instant to instant a given truth might not disappear like the images of Dedalus, since truth is a creature for Descartes.[82]

We saw that it was precisely this problem that led Descartes to introduce the notion of *Causa Sui*, of a God who by virtue of being self-caused would lack no perfections and therefore be immutable and veracious. Now, since all the Cartesian proofs reveal a God who indeed is self caused, since the ontological argument itself depends upon the notion of God as an immense, immeasurable might or power, it follows that in a subtle sense all of Descartes' proofs of God are proofs from efficient causality. For this reason, Descartes could write to Arnauld that, ". . . to consider the efficient cause is the primary and principal, not to say the only, means of proving the existence of God."[83] Descartes thought that the trouble with the ordinary, traditional causal proofs lay in that they merely established a First Cause, but did not prove the true God; the mind, becoming weary of pursuing an infinite regress of causes, simply stops at a First Cause.

When Malebranche repudiates arguments from efficient causality, he is actually turning against Descartes himself, and is thereby attacking the very conception of *Causa Sui*. Once you assume an evil demon, argues Malebranche, you can never reach a perfect Deity. Given the evil demon, no argument founded on efficient causality, not even, I may add, one that assumes a self-caused Deity, can prove more than merely a superior cause.[84] It cannot prove a God who is veracious. If you assume a God who can make contradictories to coexist, then you cannot rely on a chain of reasoning and be sure that in course of such reasoning your meanings remain identical from beginning to end.

Hence, on this basis, even Descartes' ontological argument is invalidated, for it involves the whole problem of innate ideas, created essences, a self-caused being who arbitrarily decrees truths. What we need therefore is a way of reaching the true God, that is, infinite Being, and not simply God as a causal power. We need therefore a way that will eliminate both the demon and Descartes' God, of whom the demon is only an image. And this can be done only by a direct proof.

Were one to know God directly and immediately, or as Malebranche says, *par simple vue*, one would then know that God as infinitely perfect will not and cannot be a deceiver, "puis qu'il ne peut que ce qu'il veut ou que ce qu'il est capable de volour."[85] The true God cannot practice deception, because He has no power over eternal ideas.

God known par simple vue.

Reasoning, then, is suspect. What avenue remains for reaching God? Descartes has declared that there are only two roads to knowledge, intuition and deduction. Since deduction is invalidated by memory as a means for knowing God, there remains only the possibility of intuition. This, it will be seen, is Malebranche's knowledge of God's existence "par simple vue."

To his critics, Descartes repeatedly maintained that his "cogito ergo sum" was not an inference but a direct perception of a particular fact.[86] Because this knowledge is non-inferential, not even Descartes' demon could make him into nothing each time that he thought of himself as something, that is to say, even the Cartesian demon is powerless to affect the truth of the intuitive proposition: I, as thinking, exist. Ultimate, self-sufficient, self-certifying intuition such as that which supports the *cogito* argument, Descartes describes in the *Rules* as "the undoubting conception of an unclouded and attentive mind." Malebranche likewise affirms that the knowledge of the soul's existence is non-inferential, not mnemonic, but indubitable knowledge by simple inspection. Seeking to avoid inferential knowledge of God, Malebranche declares that the ontological argument based upon the idea of the infinite is just such knowledge by intuition or simple inspection: ". . . Les preuves de l'existence et des perfections de Dieu, tirées de l'idée que nous avons de l'infini, sont *preuves de simple vue.*" [87]

What seems to be a paradox now arises. Since Anselm, the ontological argument has been advanced as a "proof." What kind of proof is it that does not involve reasoning? Mr. Wolfson, in his work on Malebranche's contemporary, Spinoza, maintains that none of the ontological proofs is directly a proof of divine existence. Instead, the ontological proofs, as given by Anselm, Descartes and Spinoza, consist entirely in only their respective views that our knowledge of God's existence is the immediate knowledge which is implied in the idea we have of God as the greatest, or as the most perfect, or as the self-caused Being. To set forth clearly that the ontological argument is merely a convenient explication of the immediate intuition of God's existence, Wolfson reduces the various ontological proofs to the following syllogism:

> If we have an idea of God as the greatest, or as the most perfect, . . . then God is immediately perceived by us to exist.
>
> But we have an idea of God as . . .
>
> Therefore God is immediately perceived by us to exist.[88]

The function of the ontological syllogism is merely explicative. It serves to analyze the content and meaning of having an idea of God; it states in formal language that the knowledge of God's existence is immediate, non-inferential. Malebranche is fully aware of this function of the ontological argument. Immediately after offering his own version in Book VI of the *Recherche,* he declares: All these truths are known by simple vision to attentive minds, although it seems that we are making use of reasoning to expound them to others.[89]

Thus, all the reasoning involved in the ontological argument is simply an indispensable didactic device for purposes of exposition. It is just a means of calling our attention to our direct perception of God's existence. The ontological proof shows *how* our idea or thought of God is direct non-inferential knowledge of Him. Hence, Malebranche can assert that the proof of God from the idea of the infinite is a *proof* by simple perception, meaning that all proving is extrinsic to the final direct vision, that all the reasoning is a Socratic device for eliciting

Is Malebranche's ontological argument a "proof"?

Malebranche's ontological proof not an *ergo* but a *vide.*

what we already know; that at the end of the demonstration the result is not in the form of an "ergo," but rather the imperative, "vide."

If the entire procedure for discovering God is thus not a rational demonstration, but instead a hunt, a search, in which Malebranche is the monitor or guide, there must be some clue or idea as to *what* is being sought, in order that when found, the object will be recognized. In a system of philosophy which starts from existence to prove some other existent, *what* that other will be is a matter for later discernment. But when the aim and direction of a philosophy is not to prove but to convert, not to establish a fact, but to recollect and to disclose it, one must know in advance what it is for which he is looking. Truth, declares Malebranche, quoting Augustine, always speaks lucidly, but we do not always hear it clearly. The difficulty of obtaining a distinct response comes from the fact that we do not know *what* we are asking.[90] Thus the opening sentence of Malebranche's *Entretien* of a Christian Philosopher and a Chinese Philosopher is cast in the form of a question on the part of the Chinese scholar: "Quel est ce Seigneur du ciel, que vous venez de si loin annoncer?"—"Le Dieu, que nous vous annonçons est celui-là même dont l'idée est gravée en vous, et dans tous les hommes. . . . Notre Dieu c'est *celui qui est,* c'est l'Etre infiniment parfait, c'est l'Etre." [91] Because the ontological argument is not a proof of God's existence, but the claim that our knowledge of Him is immediate, it necessarily serves to show at once the very character and nature of that existence, the knowledge of which is asserted to be non-inferential.

However, even if we consider the ontological argument as a claim to an immediate awareness, immediate in the sense of non-discursive and non-inferential, the difficulty still remains of how we can pass from an idea of God as such and such to the assertion of His real existence. This difficulty is particularly patent in Descartes, where the idea of God is an idea in the mind. How can we pass from a concept inside the mind to what is external? How does it follow, asks the Chinese Philosopher, that God exists, from the fact that we think of Him? [92]

Malebranche's solution of this difficulty is truly extraordinary. For with one bold stroke not only does he succeed in escaping from Descartes' dilemma, but what is even more important, in so doing he shows the inadequacy of Descartes' *Causa Sui;* and even more importantly than this, he shows that the method of clear and distinct concepts is not the sole avenue to knowledge, but that there is an immediate, direct, intuitive awareness of existence that is both prior to and subsequent to the ideational analytical process.

(f) *Immediate Knowledge of Being.* The most effective way to understand the far-reaching difference between Malebranche's and Des-

cartes' conceptions of God, and the difference in their ontological arguments, is to turn first to *Malebranche's* presentation of *Descartes'* ontological proof and to compare it with *Descartes' own* statements, and
then to note the sort of emendation that Malebranche offers.

Descartes, in his reply to the objections of Caterus, maintained that
one may affirm the actual, necessary existence of God from the fact
of our possession of an idea of perfection, although we may not conclude to the existence of an actual perfect body from our idea of
such a body. The reason which invalidates the second conclusion is
that this idea of a perfect body is a composite idea, not a simple nature.
Consequently, it has possible existence but not necessary existence.
Then Descartes immediately adds: "Nay, because when I examine this
idea of body I see in it no force by means of which it may produce
or preserve itself, I rightly conclude that necessary existence . . .
does not belong to the nature of a body . . ." On the other hand,
when the mind attentively considers the idea of God, it first of all
perceives that God may exist or that this idea has possible existence,
like any other distinct idea. But, warns Descartes, "because we cannot think of God's existence as being possible, without at the same
time, and by taking heed of His immeasurable power, acknowledging
that He can exist by His own might, we hence conclude that He
really exists and has existed from all eternity; for the light of nature
makes it most plain that what can exist by its own power always
exists." [93]

Now observe how Malebranche treats the idea of a perfect body
and that of an infinitely perfect God. One cannot conclude, he declares, the necessary existence of a perfect body from its idea, because,
being composite, it not only *may* be false and contradictory, but it
actually is contradictory, for one cannot conceive clearly an infinitely
perfect body; a particular and finite being such as a body cannot be
conceived as universal and infinite.[94] But the idea of God, or of Being
in general, of Being without restriction, of the infinite, is not a fiction
of the mind. It is not a composite idea which involves contradiction;
although it embraces everything which is and everything that may be.
But this simple and natural idea of Being or of the infinite implies
necessary existence, for it is evident that Being (I do not say such
and such a being) has its existence

> par lui-même; et que l'être ne peut n'être pas actuellement, étant
> impossible et contradictoire que le véritable être soit sans existence.
> Il se peut faire que les corps ne soient pas, parce que les corps sont
> de *tels êtres,* qui participent de l'être et qui en dépendent. Mais
> l'être sans restriction est nécessaire; il est indépendant; il ne tient
> ce qu'il est que de lui-même: tout ce qui est vient de lui. S'il y a
> quelque chose, il est, puisque tout ce qui est vient de lui; mais

quand il n'y aurait aucune chose en particulier, il serait, parce qu'il est par lui-même, et qu'on ne peut le concevoir clairement comme n'étant point; si ce n'est qu'on se le représente comme un être en particulier ou comme un *tel être*, et que l'on considère ainsi toute autre idée que la sienne. Car ceux qui ne voient pas que Dieu soit, ordinairement ils ne considèrent point l'être, mais un *tel être*, et par conséquent un être qui peut être ou n'être pas.[95]

That Malebranche nowhere in this exposition of what purports to be pure Descartes employs the term 'puissance' or 'force' clearly indicates that his expressions "par lui-même" and "de lui-même" are negative in meaning and that his conception of the substance of God is wholly unlike Descartes' *Causa Sui*. What Malebranche is saying is that this or that matter of fact may be conceived to exist or not to exist because its existence is received, conferred, dependent, but that absolute non-existence or non-being is unthinkable. Whereas for Descartes our idea of God is that of power, which idea, therefore, includes or implies existence as a unique predicate, for Malebranche, as he explains Descartes, our idea of God is that of Being itself, or that which *is*.

Because Malebranche's conception of God is that of Being, in his exposition of Descartes, he asserts it to be absurd that we should have this clear and distinct idea of God as Existence and yet maintain that God may not be, for it is a contradiction to think of Being as not being.

However, notwithstanding the fact that Malebranche's conception of God is that of Being, one may still question the legitimacy of passing from essence to existence, from an idea of God as Being to His actual existence. It is at this very point that Malebranche's ontological argument becomes distinctive; in fact, it is here that it ceases to be an ontologism. Throughout Descartes' three proofs of divine existence, the process is always from *what* God is to the fact *that* he is. Descartes asserted that *ab nosse ad esse valet consequentia*. This maxim holds good for the ontological proof, notwithstanding the fact that this proof becomes reduced to the status of an axiom, thus losing its inferential, discursive character. Although we have an immediate knowledge of God's existence, it is nevertheless representative or ideal knowledge. We know God's existence via His essence. Now, however clear and distinct is our idea of God, however much existence is included as a predicate in *what* we know God to be, however concrete, real, and factual ideas or objects of thought may be, how can we pass from these ideal objects "in the mind" to actual objects outside the mind? Malebranche was fully aware of these difficulties. In the *Recherche*, immediately after the above exposition of Descartes' argument, he modestly appends an *"éclaircissement"* to make Descartes more acceptable. The object of this appendix is to show that "nothing finite can represent the infinite," that knowledge of God is non-representative, non-ideational, non-essential, that when we intuit or perceive God, the object of our knowledge is identically the externally existing God Himself.

Malebranche has shown that on the basis of the Cartesian requirements of certainty minds cannot know bodies "in themselves," but only by way of ideas; that in order that his knowledge be certain, immutable, and common to all minds, ideas must not be identified with the fleeting, particular, finite modifications or states of mind; and finally that these ideas or objects of thought are general and universal and therefore contained in a general or infinite reason. In the course of this exposition he has indeed spoken of the "idea of an infinite extension" or of the "infinite idea of extension," of the "idea of an infinite being" or of the "infinite idea of being." However, Malebranche makes perfectly plain that while we "conceive" the infinite, we do not "comprehend" it by any determinate concept. Ideas or concepts, although universal and eternal, are exclusive and determinate. As such they cannot "contain," or "embrace," a limitless reality. Strictly speaking, there can be no "idea" of any infinite, that is, no definite concept that can *comprehend* or embrace infinity. Even a "particular" infinite, such as that of extension, eludes determination.[96] How much more true is this of Being infinitely infinite! Hence Malebranche writes:

> On ne peut concevoir que quelque chose de créé puisse représenter l'infini, que l'être sans restriction, l'être immense, l'être universel puisse être aperçu par une idée, c'est-à-dire, par un être particulier, par un être différent de l'être universel et infini; mais, pour les êtres particuliers, il n'est pas difficile de concevoir qu'ils puissent être représentés par l'être infini qui les renferme dans sa substance très efficace et par conséquent très intelligible. Ainsi il est nécessaire de dire, que l'on conaît Dieu par lui-même, quoique la connaissance que l'on en a en cette vie soit très imparfaite; et que l'on connaît les choses corporelles par leurs idées, c'est-à-dire, en Dieu, puisqu'il n'y a que Dieu qui renferme le monde intelligible, où se trouvent les idées de toutes choses.[97]

Moreover, the denial of created truths and innate ideas has transformed the metaphysical status of ideas. Whereas for Descartes they were inferior to and copies of external objects, for Malebranche they have become the models or archetypes of which the world is a participant. Thus for Descartes the idea of God, although a true and immutable image, is less than God Himself. As a mark of the workman upon his work, it is inferior to the workman. Since for Malebranche, ideas are the models of all possible created worlds, there can be no archetype of an uncreated existence. Whence, Malebranche concludes, "Il n'y a que Dieu que nous voyions d'une vue immédiate et directe." [98]

III. DIRECT VISION OF INFINITE BEING

Because our knowledge of God is thus direct, non-representative, non-conceptual, as well as non-inferential, and because too for Malebranche being or existence is the very nature, essence, or definition of God, he may speak of a proof derived from the idea of the infinite. Since the Infinite is His own idea, to apprehend *that He is* is at the same time to apprehend *what He is;* and conversely, to apprehend what God is is at the same time to apprehend that He is. With the elimination of representative archetypal ideas from the knowledge of God, there is then no longer any problem of passing from thought to existence, for there is nothing interposed between the mind and God. Hence to comprehend more distinctly Descartes' argument and to counter the objections made against it, asserts Malebranche,[99] one must remember that finite objects or creatures are known not in themselves or by themselves, but through their model, representative ideas. Thus it is possible to know the nature or essence of an object without knowing its existence. It is solely for this reason that necessary existence is not involved in the idea which represents it; for the relation between the archetypal essence and its ectypal appearance is wholly contingent. With respect to God, however, there is no archetypal, universal idea of Him. Wherefore one cannot apprehend His nature without at the same time apprehending His existence.[100] To say that God has necessary existence is to say that God is existence, without beginning or end. Thus to think the infinite, to conceive the infinite, is at once to possess it, to know it, to perceive it. Malebranche accordingly declares: "Si donc on y pense, il faut qu'il soit." "On ne peut voir l'essence d'un être infiniment parfait sans en voir l'existence." And, as was said before, "He must exist" is not a conclusion but merely an explanation of what it means to think of God. In the case of God, *to think about* His nature is to be in His very existential presence, because His nature is to exist.[101]

However, does one ever think of the Infinite? Assuredly one does think of it, Malebranche insists.[102] And if one were to ask Malebranche —How do you know that you are not dreaming when you claim to think of the Infinite? Malebranche would reply, as he actually does reply: I have an internal feeling that when I think of the Infinite I am actually thinking of the Infinite.[103] This answer is comparable to Descartes' assertions concerning simple natures, and it is also comparable to his answer to the second set of objections concerning the criterion of certitude: to doubt a clear and distinct idea is to think it, and to think

[margin note: Malebranche's ontological proof.]

it is to know it. And since the validity of clear and distinct ideas is itself founded on the fact that nothing is not intelligible, hence to doubt the infinite is to conceive it, and to conceive it is to know it.

Thus the knowledge of the existence of God is at least as certain as is our knowledge of our own existence. In fact, it is even more certain.[104]

Descartes, in the third Meditation, declared that the idea of God, of the Infinite, of Perfection, exists in his mind "earlier" than the idea of the finite, else he would not be able to recognize himself as deficient, limited and subject to doubt and desire. Hence not only is this idea of something positive, but, in order to become acquainted with the idea of a finite, particular being, it is necessary to delimit this general idea of Being. Malebranche accepts this Cartesian position. His entire theory of ideas showed how dependent we are on the knowledge of the infinite, in order to know anything finite. But since for Malebranche there is no idea of God and since ideas of finite objects are seen in God, his knowledge of the existence of God is even more certain than it can be for Descartes. Through his innate idea, Descartes only was able to touch God, without embracing Him.[105] Malebranche does not claim to "comprehend" God either,[106] but for Malebranche the mind is in a continual intercourse with God. Not to think of God is unthinkable and inconceivable.[107] Hume could assert that necessary existence is meaningless, for Hume treated God as any particular matter of fact. Hume's methodology of impressions and ideas and its concomitant nominalism prevents him from considering the notion of infinite being as real and concrete in its own right. But Malebranche is no nominalist. For Malebranche, the particular and the finite are limited expressions of the infinite, and a particular existence involves the awareness of Being as such. Hence, not to think of Being is tantamount to not knowing at all, and conversely, to think is to think of Being. The apprehension of any particular idea is only a retrenchment or curtailment of the general notion of Being. For this reason, the contemplation of any one clear and distinct idea is an avenue of approach to God; it is a central focussing on one of the perfections of God, to the temporary peripheral exclusion of all other perfections and ideas. It is impossible, declares Malebranche, that man rid himself entirely of this general idea of Being, because he cannot subsist outside of God. One may even exist without, for awhile, thinking of one's self, but one cannot subsist even for a moment without thinking of God.[108]

Malebranche thus escapes the pitfalls of the ontological argument by claiming that we have access to God by a direct vision of His presence. Our knowledge of God is *par simple vue;* it is immediate not only in being non-discursive and non-inferential; it is immediate too in being non-conceptual and non-ideational. Kowledge *par simple vue*

Malebranche's knowledge of God more certain than that of Descartes.

is a form of intuition that is *sui generis*. On the one hand, it is non-sensuous; but neither is it abstract and formal; it is an intimate acquaintance or union with the divine presence.

Descartes said that before we know whether anything exists we must first determine what it is. The proper procedure is from *nosse* to *esse*. Descartes follows this procedure in the case of the self and also in the case of God. From the idea of self-caused perfection, he tries to deduce God's existence. Now the significance of Malebranche's critique of ideas for his ontology is that as a result of it, he discards Descartes' principle in methodology. In reaching God we do not begin with *an* essence or *an* idea, for nothing can represent or define God; no specific or finite or definite concept can reveal what God is, because His essence is Being itself. God is His own idea. Hence to understand God's existence we do not start from perfection, causality, or from *any* kind of concept; but we begin instead with existence itself.

Malebranche's method based on realistic ontology.

Thus the analysis of the alternative doctrines concerning the origin and nature of ideas, despite Malebranche's central concern with universals, serves another purpose. It is essentially an argument in which Malebranche seeks to show that an epistemology which seeks certainty and which relies on nothing but clear and distinct ideas must, to be valid, acknowledge the primacy of a realistic, existential ontology.

Because of this, we can now fully understand why Malebranche says that the awareness of the independent, non-mental, non-willed and non-created status of ideas offers the surest and most powerful proof for the existence of God. It does so by bringing us up suddenly, as it were, with the recognition that what permits ideas to be meaningful and intelligible, what enables them to function as clarifying principles, is their participation in Being. The universal can serve as the criterion for judging and measuring the particular only because it first of all *is*. But clear and distinct concepts or ideas can define the nature of things with utmost evidence not only in so far as they are universal, objective, and uncreated, but more importantly, in so far as they share in reality or in so far as they are aspects of reality. The Cartesian dictum—that we may affirm of a thing whatever is clearly and distinctly contained in its idea or nature—could not be true, unless these ideas were recognized as belonging to reality.

Thus Malebranche's localization of ideas in God is not an accidental or bizarre solution. Were he addressing a Platonist, he might say: you are concentrating on the intelligible forms of things; you recognize that without universals and general notions, nothing becomes clarified or comprehensible. But you ignore the status of these intelligible forms and forget their actuality or being. Only a Christian Platonism can serve as a foundation to knowledge. There is no other possible solution of the problem of knowledge, than Christian Platonism, for ex-

Why Malebranche puts ideas in God—Vision in God.

istence is prior to essence. In point of fact, this is precisely what the
Christian Philosopher asserts to the Chinese. The Chinese Philosopher
claims that his God, the Li, is a sphere of abstract wisdom, of abstract
justice and goodness, of eternal laws, but that this Li cannot be described as a being who is just and wise and good.[109] You are deceived,
counters the Christian Philosopher, by vain abstractions:

> . . . vous vous imaginez qu'il y a des formes et des qualités ab-
> straites, et qui ne sont les formes et les qualités d'aucun sujet: qu'il
> y a une sagesse, une justice, une bonté abstraite, et qui n'est la
> sagesse d'aucun Etre. Vos abstactions vous trompent: Quoi, pensez-
> vous qu'il y ait une figure abstraite, une rondeur, par exemple, qui
> rende ronde une boule . . . ?[110]

Vision of God. While it is true that one could not exist for a moment without thinking of God and that properly speaking there could be no Vision of
Ideas in God without prior vision of God, nevertheless, this immediate
intuitive awareness of God *par simple vue* may, so to speak, be dor-
mant, unconscious and unclear. Hence, in order to become perspicuously aware of this presence of God an arduous sharpening and focussing of attention is required. One therefore begins with the existence
of the self and its knowledge of bodies as the hard data from which,
by a gradual induction, one reaches the summit of the vision of God.
If, therefore, we consider the vision of God in its conscious luminous
form, then we may say that such knowledge is not attainable at once,
that is, *a priori* to knowledge of sensible facts. From this point of view,
the ontological vision of God has a causal and inductive element in it.
One begins with self-existence, with knowledge of bodies, with a self
that perceives and conceives bodies. One asks for the cause of these
various perceptions and conceptions, for the origin and cause of ideas,
for the cause of the "idea" of the infinite, for the cause of thinking of
the Infinite,—until one arrives simultaneously at a vision in and of God,
as *Celui qui est.*[111]

Vision in God and vision of God. We must not therefore confuse Vision in God with vision of God,
as other interpreters of Malebranche do. Pang Ching-jen, for example,
interprets Malebranche as not distinguishing between our immediate
and direct view of God and our knowledge of God through the Word.
Says Pang:

> Il n'y a que Dieu que nous voyions d'une vue immédiate et directe;
> il n'y a que lui qui puisse éclairer l'esprit par sa propre substance.
> Dieu n'a pas d'archétype sur lequel il ait été formé, et rien ne peut
> le représenter que son Verbe qui lui est consubstantiel. Donc, si
> on veut voir Dieu par une idée, cette idée sera le Verbe. Car le fils
> de Dieu est l'expression de Dieu, expression parfaite et éternelle
> comme Dieu. Il est la raison universelle. Il est l'image de Dieu.

[158]

C'est en lui qu'on voit l'infini, c'est-à-dire qu'on voit Dieu, ou simplement, on voit Dieu. Nous voyons Dieu d'une vue immédiate et directe.[112]

Pang's statement is not false, but it is not altogether true. Knowledge of essences *in* God or our acquaintance with the universal reason, with the Verb, with eternal truths, is indeed a knowledge *of* God, inasmuch as the Word is consubstantial with the Father and inasmuch as it is the same reason that illuminates all minds. Nevertheless, vision of God *par simple vue* is super rational; it is intuition of God as *Celui qui est;* it is direct confrontation with Being. The intuition of God Himself is beyond ordinary comprehension and beyond ordinary concepts. Granted that it is not supernatural, that the vision itself as distinguished from its object is not a miraculous inspiration given to only a few elect, that it is open to all; still it passes beyond the ideas.

Those who fail to discriminate between Vision in God and vision of God fail to comprehend the most salient aspect of Malebranche's metaphysics. Either they reduce God to *la Sagesse*, Reason, or they bifurcate Him into an unstable *Deus Duplex,* a loose association of Reason and Will, neglecting the integral unity conveyed by the phrase from *Exodus, Celui qui est*, the unity of infinite Being.[113]

Is this vision of God the vision of a St. Theresa? Le Moine observes that Malebranche is a rationalist and not a mystic, in the sense that his union with God is not a "fusion amoureuse." The union with God, for Le Moine, is an act of intelligence,[114] that contains nothing "extra rational." [115] Perhaps we can agree with Le Moine; certainly this is no complete mystical envelopment. But I must add one last word before concluding the present study of God as Being. While vision of God may be rational, or at the least, human, it is not without its *O Altitudo.* There is something else besides Spinoza's intellectual love of God, a call of the heart as well as of the head. In the nineteenth of the *Méditations chrétiennes* we read:

"En la présence du Dieu vivant."

O Jésus, quand sera-ce que j'aurai enfin libre accès au Saint des Saints, et que je verrai à découvert vos sacrés mystères? Quand sera-ce que lavé dans le sang de l'Agneau, plein de confiance et de joie, je serai en la présence du Dieu vivant, tout environné de ses splendeurs et de sa gloire. Je me nourris jour et nuit de mes larmes, quand je pense à la grandeur de mes espérances, quand je pense que j'entrerai un jour dans la Maison de Dieu, et que j'y verrai son Tabernacle. O céleste Jérusalem comment peut-on vous oublier, comment peut-on vivre content, et chanter des cantiques de réjouissance dans le lieu de son exil? Peut-on se repaître des corps, et se réjouir à la vue des objets sensibles, lorsqu'on s'attend de voir des beautés intelligibles dignes de la Majesté de Dieu même: lorsqu'on espère de se nourrir de la substance du Verbe Eternel, et de *boire éternellement d'un torrent de voluptés et de delices.* O Jésus, que je ne sois pas frustré de mes espérances.[116]

This passage and many like it have led some writers to describe Malebranche as a mystic. Malebranche's vision or contemplation of ideas in God is a mystical ecstasy, suggests Rabbe.[117] In listening to Reason or the Word of God, Malebranche is heeding a "voix mystérieuse." Such, too, is the opinion of Blampignon.[118] Vidgrain, on the other hand, cannot quite make up his mind. Malebranche is a mystic, but not of the masochistic or sentimental variety. Malebranche's union with God does not entail the extinction of the creature. It does not involve any special rites or esoteric, occult trances.[119] For such reasons, Gouhier claims that mysticism is altogether an inappropriate designation for Malebranche's thought.[120] Still again, Cuvillier argues that genuine mysticism is not necessarily anti-intellectualistic, that there is what he calls a rational mysticism or a mystical rationalism.[121]

In my opinion, these divergent interpretations and vacillations arise from the fact that all these critics treat Malebranche's Deity as *Deus Duplex,* emphasizing now His Reason and now His Will. Thus the union with God becomes wholly intellectual—an adoration of or absorption into eternal truths; or else becomes the ineffable effacement in God's Will. In either case it seems to suggest the extinction of the self, either in that timeless Ideal Society of Santayana or in an irrational Bergsonian *élan vital.* But if we once understand that Malebranche's Deity is the concrete God of *Exodus* who is the very act of existing, then union is neither identity with pure reason nor with a blind creative advance. Union with God is the conjunction of two separate existents; a conjunction therefore that involves both knowledge and love: the love and understanding *by* and *of* a person *for* another. True, this knowledge is beyond concepts, but not irrational; true, it involves super-sensuous feeling, but it is not the negation of clear understanding. It is a joyous devotion to and contemplation of the living Creator by the living creature. This, however, requires further understanding of the relation of God to the world, to which we now turn.

Chapter IV

Occasionalism

Malebranche's theory of causality is known as Occasionalism. It is so called, because the central notion of this theory is the assertion that God alone is truly efficacious and that creatures are no more than "occasional" causes, which "determine" God's power but which are in themselves impotent.

In this chapter I shall demonstrate that Occasionalism is first of all a metaphysical account of finite being or existence; that by affirming it, Malebranche seeks to explain *whence* things originate and *why* things are or the purpose of creation. After showing how Malebranche treats the nature and meaning of the creative act and its ultimate justification in terms of his conception of God as Being, I then examine what it is for a creature to be. I establish that for Malebranche, unlike for Descartes, a concrete thing is a combination or composition of essence and existence. Then, in the light of the doctrine of creation and in the light of his distinction between essence and existence, I argue that his doctrine of the divine "immensity" is intended to set forth the dynamic character of existence.

This approach then enables me to re-examine his attack on the efficacy of creatures. It becomes evident that the exclusive or privileged efficacy which Malebranche attributes to God is solely the power of creation, the power to create existence and to conserve it; that occasional causes are inefficacious only in the sense that they are non-creative and not independent of God; also, that the occasional cause, being a composition of essence and existence, can be said to be in-active only with respect to essence; it does act in so far as it exists. My final conclusions are that however much Malebranche may have influenced Hume, Malebranche's Occasionalism has been misunderstood by everyone except Church in one respect and Gouhier in another, because most of the critics have read him prospectively rather than retrospectively. What I mean is, that they have failed to comprehend his vision of God as Being or *Celui qui est.* Far from being reduced to an inert non-entity or to dead sterility, the natural world in Malebranche's philosophy is permeated with the power of creative efficacy. It exists and is real precisely to the extent that it is alive and active, to the extent that body is process and that mind is will.

I. Being, Creativity, and the Glory of God

(*a*) *The "True Cause."* The first statement of Malebranche's theory of causality is given in the *Recherche,* in the course of his discussion of the second theory of ideas. After denying that the mind has the power to create essences or the ideas of objects, Malebranche goes on to assert that such false attribution of creative power to the will stems from the fact that:

Neither bodies nor wills are "true" or "principal" causes.

> . . . les hommes ne manquent jamais de juger qu'une chose est cause de quelque effet quand l'un et l'autre sont joints ensemble, supposé que la véritable cause de cet effet leur soit inconnue. C'est pour cela que tout le monde conclut qu'une boule agitée qui en rencontre une autre est la véritable et la principale cause de l'agitation *qu'elle lui communique,* que la volonté de l'âme est la véritable et la principale cause du mouvement du bras et d'autres préjugés semblables; parce qu'il arrive toujours qu'une boule est agitée quand elle est rencontrée par une autre qui la choque, que nos bras sont remués presque toutes les fois que nous le voulons, et que nous ne voyons point sensiblement quelle autre chose pourrait être la cause de ces mouvements.[1]

Notice that Malebranche *does not deny* that the communication of motion from one ball to another is directly experienced;[2] nor does he say in this passage that the influence of the will on the body *cannot* be directly experienced. Neither does he deny that the ball or the will is a cause. What he does say is that they are not the "true" and "principal" causes, and also that the true and principal causes are not sensibly apparent. We know from his method that essences are present in perception, that the infinite Being is so present but that we are only dimly aware of that presence in perception, and that full perspicuous awareness requires a slow and arduous discrimination by reason. So here in the case of the motion of the balls and the movements of the arm, the "true" and "principal" cause is present, but it requires attention for its nature to be precisely determined.

Now, the initial question is, what does Malebranche mean by the "true" and "principal" cause? Significantly, we find the answer in the

second part of Book VI of the *Recherche*, on method. After explaining
in Chapter I the rules to be followed in the pursuit after truth, Malebranche argues in Chapter II that Scholastic physics is vitiated by its
adherence to ambiguous notions like occult qualities and substantial
forms. As usual, his tirade is directed especially against Aristotle whose
entire physics, says Malebranche, rests on mere logical abstractions.
Following this attack on Aristotle and on Scholastic physics, Malebranche devotes Chapter III to a discussion of what he calls [3] the
most dangerous error in the philosophy of the ancients.

Error of
Scholastic
physics: forms
reified into
entities and
therefore into
efficient
agents.

What then is this most dangerous of errors? In a previous chapter,
Malebranche tells us that the Scholastic and Aristotelian employment
of genus, species, act, power, nature, form, faculties, qualities, is useless in science. To be sure, such statements as bread nourishes by its
nutritive qualities, as fire warms by its warming faculty, are not
false.[4] But they signify nothing clear, nor are such explanations helpful
to physics. However, philosophers with allegiances to the past are not
content to use these vague general terms as merely descriptive, for
the Scholastics

> . . . veulent, outre cela, que ces termes signifient certains êtres
> particuliers. Ils prétendent qu'il y a quelque substance, distinguée
> de la matière, qui est la forme de la matière, et une infinité de petits
> êtres distingués réellement de la matière et de la forme; et ils en
> supposent d'ordinaire autant qu'ils ont de différentes sensations des
> corps et qu'ils pensent que ces corps produisent d'effets différents.[5]

Thus arises that most dangerous of philosophic errors, which consists in giving entitative status or distinct existential significance to
these occult qualities and forms. Instead of using them solely to describe the behavior of bodies, the occult qualities are reified into determinate entities within matter, and then the Scholastics are led to
affirm that these are the *true* or *principal* causes of the effects that are
observed to happen.

> Que si l'on vient ensuite, à considérer attentivement l'idée que l'on
> a de cause ou de puissance d'agir on ne peut douter que cette idée
> ne représente quelque chose de divin. Car l'idée d'une puissance
> souveraine est l'idée de la souveraine divinité; et l'idée d'une puis-
> sance subalterne est l'idée d'une divinité inférieure, mais d'une
> véritable divinité, au moins selon la pensée de paiens, *supposé que*
> *ce soit l'idée d'une puissance ou d'une cause véritable.* On admet
> donc quelque chose de divin dans tous les corps qui nous environ-
> nent, lorsqu'on admet des formes, des facultés, des qualités, des
> vertus, ou des êtres réels capables de produire certains effets *par la*
> *force de leur nature.*[6]

This passage merits serious attention. Notice how Malebranche
couples true causality with divinity, for to the Christian, to cause is,

properly speaking, to create. Secondly, while Malebranche thinks that such terms as forms are otiose in science, their real danger is a metaphysical one. For a philosophy that insists on the primacy of Being, the danger of forms is two-fold. Either we treat forms and qualities as belonging to the essence of bodies other than extension, or as themselves real existents. Either way there is risk. If form is essence that creates existence, then we are really back in the intelligible, existenceless universe of Aristotle or of Suarez.[7] On the other hand, if forms are actual existents, nevertheless, to endow them with creative power is to make them self-sufficient powers; it is once more to return to the pagan world of a plethora of subalternate divinities and movers.

M. Gilson says that with Aristotle you seem to enter a concrete world of dynamism and efficacy. Here "to be" is an active verb. As M. Gilson puts it in his book, *Being and Some Philosophers:*

> . . . It still remains to be seen whether Aristotle is here talking about existence, but he certainly is talking about existing things; and, because, such as he describes it, reality is an actually real nucleus of energy, its very core lies beyond the grasp of any concept. Nothing is more important to remember in Aristotle's philosophy of being, and yet nothing is more commonly overlooked: in their innermost reality, substances are unknown. All we know about them is that, since they act, they are, and they are acts.

> Having reached this point, Aristotle had to stop, leaving his doctrine open to every possible interpretation and misinterpretation. He knew full well that to be is to be in act, that is to say, to be an act, but to say what an act is, was an altogether different proposition.[8]

M. Gilson concludes that in the final analysis, for Aristotle,

> . . . the *is* of the thing is the *what* of the thing, not the fact that it exists, but that which the thing is and which makes it to be a substance. . . . The "whatness" of a thing is its very being.

> . . . Obviously, if there is in a substance anything that is act, it is not the matter, it is the form. The form then is the very act whereby a substance is what it is, and, if a being is primarily or, as Aristotle himself says, almost exclusively *what* it is, each being is primarily and almost exclusively its form. . . . The distinctive character of a truly Aristotelian metaphysics of being—and one might feel tempted to call it its specific form—lies in the fact that it knows of no act superior to the form, not even existence. There is nothing above being; in being, there is nothing above the form, and this means that the form of a given being is an act of which there is no act.[9]

This position, as we shall see below, is what Malebranche cannot accept. He cannot accept the doctrine that the form or essence of a thing can be the same as the thing's existence or the same as the true cause of its existence, for it will conflict with his repeated claim that there is only one true cause, because there is only one true God.[10] This is why Malebranche rejects the supposition of multiple Gods or that God needs instruments for creation. Creation is a unique attribute of God, as unique as is His existence. Hence it cannot be shared or delegated.[11] In Malebranche's philosophy, genuine creativity never lies contained within the created world.

According to Mr. Church, Malebranche's theory of Occasionalism, even though it becomes a key doctrine in his system, is put forth entirely to serve a religious purpose and not for any philosophical reasons. Its aim is to prove that God alone is the veritable cause; it is not intended to solve any "philosophical" problems, such as the problem of the relationship between mind and body, as is the case with Cordemoy's Occasionalism.[12]

Church's charge: Occasionalism a purely religious issue.

We shall have to conclude before we leave this chapter that Mr. Church's charge is absurd. In advance of considering the detailed evidence, let us treat two preliminary points. First, we ought to have little patience with debonair philosophers who draw a fine distinction between religion and philosophy. Such a distinction assails the sincerity and the perspicuity of the philosopher under attack, especially so in the present case, because Malebranche makes a magnificent effort to integrate philosophy and religion. And secondly, who would dare assert that the problem of causality is not a philosophical problem? Church is correct and illuminating in so far as he notes that the issue of causality is for Malebranche an issue concerning creation. But precisely because causality *is* a problem of creation, *for that very reason* does it become of paramount philosophical importance to Malebranche and a key doctrine of his system. For the problem of causality is the problem concerning the origin of beings and the problem concerning the very meaning of existence. That this is a peculiarly Christian problem, inspired as it is by the Bible, there can be no doubt. But surely the genetic source of a theoretical principle should in no way prejudge its candidacy for a philosophical hearing. And were it not for the serious charges which Church subsequently levels against Malebranche's Occasionalism, there would be no need to labor this point. However, all the difficulties that Church finds in Occasionalism are directly traceable to his initial failure to grasp Malebranche's view of God as Being and as Creator, views which obviously are most significant beyond any narrowly religious boundaries.

We have seen how, to secure the foundations of knowledge, Malebranche was led to his Vision of essences in God, and how, in order to explain or justify essences, he was led to his vision of God as *Celui qui est* or Being. Beyond and encompassing the sphere of intelligibility is that essence to whom alone it belongs to be. We saw too that for Malebranche the necessary existence of God does not imply that His is an essence that entails or involves existence in the sense of a *Causa Sui,* but rather that He is one whose very nature it is to be. Malebranche is thus one of the very few philosophers in the seventeenth century whose God is not an essence-Deity. Church, following Hume, argues that inasmuch as existence is a contingent predicate in creatures, it is meaningless to speak of necessary existence in the case of God.[13] But this criticism betrays a lack of understanding of the very cornerstone of Malebranche's conception of God and therefore of Occasionalism. In creatures, as we shall see, existence is an adventitious and contingent factor, because the creature is a composite of essence plus existence. But in the case of Malebranche's God, His existence is necessary only because His essence is Being itself. And because He alone is true Being, hence He alone is the true or veritable cause.

The many repudiations of Church's criticisms, which I offer below, reduce to this: Church is essentially fighting against the metaphysics of Creativity and of Being, although he does not explicitly formulate his arguments this way. And my *general* rebuttal is primarily this: in matters so central to the position of an author as Being and Creativity must be admitted to be for Malebranche's thought, there is no point in *combating* them in a commentary on the author's work; in one sense they constitute the fundamental insights of the author. Rejection of the most basic doctrines of a writer is tantamount to rejecting that author; but when criticism becomes completely destructive of a philosopher's contributions through initial distaste for his position, as is so often the case with Church, the criticism ceases to be helpful.

Brunschvicg argues that Descartes and especially Spinoza introduced a new conception of God, even though they employed the traditional language of substance or Being. This new view of God finds Him to be dynamic; it is a view of sheer productivity. In contrast, for the Scholastics, Being is simply a static concept, an abstract logical principle. Brunschvicg thus elevates the conception of *Causa Sui* over the Scholastic notion; *Causa Sui* is a view of God as concrete and real, for it affirms an active essence, an essence that involves existence, whereas the Scholastic Deity is really static.[14]

Brunschvicg's claim: *Causa Sui* more concrete than the Scholastic Deity.

That Spinoza did conceive of God's substantiality as dynamic, there can be no doubt. Spinoza maintains that power is the essence of God. Nevertheless it remains true that, dynamic as is Spinoza's Deity, the existence of Spinoza's God is yet subordinated to His essence. Spinoza's Deity stands as an essence-Deity; and His dynamism is that of form, as it is for Aristotle. I have heard Mr. Wolfson say that Spinoza is the last Aristotelian. I am not sure that Spinoza is the last, but he is surely Aristotelian in so far as the energetic nature of his *natura naturans* is that of an essence.

On the other hand, if we follow Gilson's exegesis on the nature of the concept of Being for the medievals, it seems difficult to accept Brunschvicg's view that the medieval God is a merely static entity. Far from that, God as Being is the pure act of existing.[15] For the medievals, the declaration of God's *aseity* does not reduce Him to an abstract substratum; it affirms rather that His essence is such that to Him alone belongs the act, to be, the act of be-ing.[16] Here God's dynamism is rooted in existence rather than in essence. And precisely because God and only God is the very act of existing, He alone can be the creator of beings. Indeed, it has been said that the pure and simple production of being is the action proper to Being itself.[17] This is why in Christian philosophy every proof for the existence of God based on efficient causality is really a proof for creation.[18] For the Christian philosopher, causality is rooted in Being and in the case of God, to cause is to create being. Because God alone is Being, He alone can cause beings.[19] Such a God is surely not less concrete or less dynamic than that of Spinoza.

Malebranche lies squarely within this tradition of Being. He too affirms the God of Exodus: *Celui qui est.* Hence for him too there can be only one *true* cause, because there is only one true God. And that Malebranche should give an account of the *veritable* cause in the very course of discussing his method is most pertinent, for it indicates how concerned he was with finding not mere suppositions or hypothetical fictional abstract constructions, but as we saw in Chapter I, with finding true explanations. His method is oriented towards getting knowledge of the real. Accordingly, for him causality is *par excellence* an issue concerning what *is* and *how* things *are*.

Recall that in his discussion on method, Malebranche asserted that nature is not abstract and that the levers and wheels in physics are no mere abstract mathematical circles. But then, what is a lever or wheel concretely and existentially? What is it for it to be and whence does it come? Occasionalism, it is clear, will explain finite existence itself.

Again, recall that in his method he distinguished between necessary immutable truths, such as those of pure mathematics, and contingent truths. The former can be known by the mind alone, by pure reason; but the contingent truths pertain to existence and therefore require the senses in order to be known. However, the senses present only facts, but they do not explain what it is *to be* a fact. This is a metaphysical task.

Finally, let us recall that because nature is not abstract, we need

Production of being proper action of Christian (and Malebranchian) Deity.

The "true" cause the foundation of Malebranche's experimental method.

sense, but more than that, we need experiments. The naked senses do not reveal what Bacon calls the latent processes of the inner mechanisms of nature. And this is why Malebranche rejects scholastic physics with its sensible and occult qualities. They do not yet get into the latent hidden mechanisms of nature, the motion of its insensible particles.[20] But worse, these forms and occult qualities are abstractions; hence when used metaphysically as the true causes of things, *the danger is that nature will have become abstract*, that existence and its true cause will have been omitted.

Bacon, for all his insistence on the empirical-experimental method that was to come to grips with reality and its true Forms, nevertheless refrained from going to the summary law of nature, to the very peak of his pyramid of knowledge.[21] He looked for Forms, but not for existence. In fact, he even tended to treat the Form as a nature-engendering-nature, an active essence, a true cause that made the thing *be*. But Malebranche, in seeking the *true* cause of things, is being more true to the experimental method than Bacon himself. For Malebranche is looking not for any essence, but for the very "true" creative principle that is the source of existence.

(*b*) *Creative Power.* Still, what is the meaning of divine causality, and is such causality intelligible? We, who have become enamored of Hume's criticism, often assume that cause and effect are always two separable, distinct, self-contained entities between which no influence and no logical tie obtain. Instead of causality in the sense either of logical entailment or of metaphysical involvement, ever since Hume, it has been fashionable in many circles to regard the causal bond as merely that of the succession of consequents to antecedents. With such a view, not only is causality unintelligible as a transitive, active operation, but even more so is the notion of creative causality, for the latter involves transitive causality and much more.

What is creation? In answering this question, philosopher as well as critic must tread warily, lest he be impaled on the horns of a dilemma. One horn is that of skepticism, the other is that of unintelligible mysticism. But perhaps this fear of impalement is misplaced. May it not be that the real danger is, in Mr. Homans' phrase, to get caught in a false dichotomy?

The positions of skeptic and mystic have been dramatically portrayed by Hume in his characterizations of Philo and Demea respectively. Philo would have us believe that creation is an illegitimate and meaningless notion, since we have no distinct idea or impression of causal efficacy. At best, he is prepared to acknowledge, with Cleanthes, the existence of the Deity as an antecedent architect, but not as a genuine creator. Demea, the mystic, is as eager as the skeptic to admit

Hume's reduction of causality to causation.

the lack of any clear idea of God or of His attributes. But unlike the skeptic, he feels compelled to seek refuge in his very ignorance. Like Pascal, Demea finds consolation in a *Deus absconditus*. Precisely because causality is unintelligible, he finds it necessary to believe in it. Often the mystic believes in the obscure, paradoxical and impossible, just because it is ineffable.

Now if we wished to indulge in corrosive criticism, we could, by tearing passages out of context, easily transform Malebranche, now into a mystical obscurantist, and then again into a semi-enlightened precursor of Hume. Thus in the *Recherche*, Malebranche asserts that a true cause is a cause between which and its effects the mind perceives a necessary connection. In addition, he affirms that there is only the infinitely perfect Being between whose will and its effects the mind perceives a necessary connection.[22] Hence God is the only true cause. Malebranche explains that we apprehend this necessity between God's will and the effects because we apprehend that God's will is omnipotent and efficacious; because we see that if God wills something it must indeed come about. "When we think of the idea of God," he says, and I am using Church's translation, "that is to say, of an infinitely perfect Being, and consequently One all-powerful, we know that between His will and the movements of all bodies there is a connection such that it is impossible to conceive that He should will that a body be moved, and that it should not be." [23]

Church's attack: Malebranche denies any distinct idea of power.

On the basis of these citations, Church rightly concludes: "This conception of causality implies that in a clear idea of the divine will the ground of all possible changes would be revealed." [24] But this, Church goes on to claim, is nonsense. For does not Malebranche openly avow that we have no idea of omnipotence or of causal power? In the *Méditations chrétiennes*, the Word declares: I do not give to men any distinct idea which corresponds to the word power or efficacy. And again it says: Even if you believe that God makes what He wills, it is not at all because you see clearly that there is a necessary connection between the will of God and the effects, since you do not even know what the will of God is. But it is evident that God would not be omnipotent if His absolute volitions remained inefficacious.[25] Do we not then see Malebranche as an inconsistent mixture of Humian enlightenment and Christian obscurantism?

On the basis of the foregoing admissions or confessions by the Word, is it not apparent, as Church says, that Malebranche cannot legitimately argue that God is the sole true cause, for "since we have not any idea of the will of God, then certainly we cannot, and Malebranche says we cannot, in any way know that between this unknown will and whatever we may choose to call an effect, there is any connection whatever." Thus, in point of fact, Malebranche does *not* see any connection *between* omnipotence and its effects, for he does not know *what* omnipotence is. All he knows is *that* God is omnipotent, because He is perfect. Hence Malebranche's argument for God's causality does not properly rest on his definition of causality, but rather on his definition of God as perfect Being:

> For though Malebranche does profess that the primacy and uniqueness of the divine causality is based no less on his definition of a cause than on the omnipotence of God, it is plain, and Malebranche in effect admits, that such is not the case. As a cause has been defined, to know that God is the sole cause is to know a necessary connection between His will and effects. This knowledge we have admittedly not got.[26]

And naturally to argue that God is the sole true cause on the grounds that His perfection entails omnipotence is to reduce the whole argument to empty verbalism.[27] And the further fact that Malebranche persists in believing in divine causality shows that he is just indulging in a "compensatory dogma." [28] These views coincide with those of Mr. Ginsberg.[29]

On the one hand, Malebranche confesses that we have no distinct idea of power. On the other hand, he insists upon attributing an incomprehensible efficacy to an incomprehensible will of God. What a strange monster, then, is Malebranche! Yet if we examine the above pronouncements judiciously, without prejudice, and in their proper setting, a very different Malebranche emerges. In the third of the *Méditations chrétiennes*, the Word instructs his questioning disciple on *how* to interrogate Him and upon what subjects to interrogate Him, in order to receive His replies.[30] Men's attention is the 'natural prayer' of their souls and it will always be rewarded with knowledge, *"pourvu* qu'ils me demandent ce que je possède *en qualité de sagesse et de vérité Éternelle."* [31]

The Word then goes on to explain that He will answer all queries concerning mathematical truths and abstract moral truths, but questions concerning matters of fact require the use of the senses. As for future events and contingent truths that depend upon the will of God,

> . . . je ne les renferme point dans ma substance. Ainsi les esprits qui me contemplent ne les découvrent point en moi. Car encore que je sois la règle immuable de toutes les volontés divines par lesquelles toutes les choses ont été produites; ces volontés n'étant point des émanations nécessaires de ma substance, on ne peut les reconnaître avec évidence en me contemplant, comme la raison universelle des Intelligences. Cependant, comme Dieu ne veut que selon l'ordre que lui prescrit sa sagesse, on peut en me consultant

Why the Word can give no 'idea' of power.

s'instruire non des êtres que Dieu a créés, mais de la manière dont il les a créés.[32]

Now, when the Word declares that we do not perceive a necessary connection between God's will and its effects and that we are ignorant of what power is, these pronouncements of the Word occur in that particular meditation wherein Malebranche's purpose is to refute Spinozism, that is, to show that the world is not a necessary emanation from God,[33] and that therefore creation is possible. We know that creation means that God originated the world by a free, spontaneous act of His will, an act not necessitated by any inner essence or nature. Hence, when the Word declares that we perceive no necessary connection between the divine will and its effects, since we do not even know what the will is, we must realize that there are several different issues involved here.

First, there is no necessity between the will and the world in the sense that there is no necessity for God to create as such. Nothing in the nature of God compels His will to act. In this respect, no reason, no cause and no necessity are perceived between God and the world. This does not mean, however, that if God *does* create that then we are not able to grasp the essential connection between His will and its effects. We cannot deduce the world *a priori* from God. *But once we know that something does in fact exist, we do apprehend its essential dependence upon and connection with the divine will.* We apprehend it at once as something suspended directly from God's power.

But how can this be? Does not the Word say that we have no idea of power? This is indeed true. Nevertheless, the Word who is speaking is *la Sagesse*—the realm of essence. As such it comprises the order of eternal truths. Furthermore, the divine Word, as the realm of essence, is that aspect of divine substance which is relative to creatures; it is that which refers to a possible existence. Accordingly, in comprehending essences and their relationships, quantitative and moral, we are understanding the nature of things, not the absolute substance of God. A knowledge of essences is a Vision in God; it is not a vision of God as such. All this we have seen in the previous chapter on Being. Small wonder, then, that we cannot have a distinct idea of creative efficiency. Creatures are not endowed with creativity. Causal power in the sense of creative power can belong only to God as Being, not to contingent beings. Hence we cannot possess the distinct idea of efficacy by consulting the divine Word or the archetypal essences that refer to particulars. This is why the Word declares that the request to understand causal efficacy is an indiscreet demand:

Tu voudrais bien comprendre comment la volonté de mon Père a tant d'efficace, qu'elle donne et conserve l'être à toutes choses. Mais c'est en vain que tu te tourmentes pour le savoir. Ne t'ai-je pas déjà dit que tu ne devais me consulter que sur ce que je renferme en qualité de Sagesse Éternelle, et de Raison universelle des esprits? Lorsque tu m'as interrogé sur la conduite de Dieu, ne t'ai-je pas répondu à proportion que je te trouvais capable de porter ces grandes vérités. Tu me demandais alors ce que je te devais donner en qualité de Sagesse et de Raison universelle des esprits. Mais tu veux savoir pourquoi une chose existe de cela seul que Dieu le veut. Tu me demandes une idée claire et distincte de cette efficace infinie, qui donne et conserve l'être à toutes choses. Je n'ai point maintenant de réponse à te faire qui soit capable de te contenter. Ta demande est indiscrète. Tu me consultes sur la puissance de Dieu; consulte-moi sur sa Sagesse, si tu veux que je te satisfasse maintenant. Je ne donne point aux hommes d'idée distincte, qui réponde au mot de puissance ou d'efficace; *parce que Dieu n'a point donné de puissance véritable aux créatures, et que je ne dois donner des idées que pour faire connaître les Ouvrages de Dieu et la Sagesse de sa conduite.*[34]

Read in its proper setting, Malebranche's meaning is clear, but its clarity is totally alien to that of Hume. Malebranche is warning us that we must not seek the meaning of creation in the realm of essence, for that realm is a realm of concepts that gives enlightenment concerning the natures of creatures only. Essences, as we saw in the previous chapter, indeed have a reference beyond themselves. As such they suggest efficacy, but they do not themselves contain efficacy as a property. Furthermore, essences reveal the natures of things only, what they are; but essences say nothing about the origins or actual existence of things. We can infer nothing from the nature of bodies concerning how they originate, how they endure, whether they exist, or what it means to say that they exist. Thus essence and existence are distinguishable and separable in the case of finite objects, and there is no logical necessity [35] between the idea of a triangle and its actual realization. Malebranche affirms that God apprehends the natures of things in His Reason, but their existence in His Will.[36] As M. Gilson so well puts this sort of notion, God knows essences, but He says existence.[37] We simply cannot search for the meaning of existence or for creation in the realm of essence. Any attempt therefore to reach an "idea" of existence, to conceptualize it or essentialize it, is doomed to failure. And this is why Malebranche has the Word declare that we have no idea of efficacy or omnipotence. Indeed, even the attempt to reach an idea of existence, in order to draw some conclusion from the absence of such an idea, is misguided. To apprehend *true* causality, we must, instead, as in the case of God's existence, go to intuition, to vision *par simple vue.*

But, it will be objected, if we have no distinct idea of power, how may we attribute power to God's will, particularly since Malebranche has asserted that we do not even understand what that divine will is? In fact, how can we even talk of a will at all, since we have no idea of it?

To press this objection is a mark of the pitfalls and fallibility of the analytical understanding. It is a sign of what James called vicious intellectualism and of what Malebranche considers to be the greatest single cause of human errors. The universal and general principle or source of all errors, he says in the *Recherche*,[38] is that tendency to assume that things of which we have no idea do not exist. Expatiating on this human tendency, Malebranche points out further that when we consider an object, it is usually from some single aspect, but then we go on to assume that the object in its entirety is no more than is revealed in this one-sided view. Thus the absence of an idea of will, that is, a concept, is no sign of the non-existence of such a will. Conversely, the presence of an idea is not exhaustive of the actual reality so symbolized.

Recall that for Malebranche, God is Being and that our acquaintance with Him is *par simple vue*. We can have no idea, no concept of God, for the infinite is His own idea. We can have no representational (essential) knowledge of God. Instead, our apprehension of God as infinitely infinite Being is direct, immediate, intuitive. To be sure, this vision of God is partial and limited. We do not comprehend infinite Being with that complete and exhaustive acuity with which He comprehends Himself. Our intuitive knowledge remains limited and fragmentary; nevertheless, within its proper extent this fragmentary glimpse is direct and non-ideational; we may well say super-ideational. Hence, we can understand why Malebranche both denies our having an idea of creative will and why in the same breath he attributes will to God. As long as we move in the realm of concepts and of distinct ideas, there can be no idea of a creative will, any more than there can be an idea of God. But once we directly intuit Being as *Celui qui est* and are illuminated by His presence, we simultaneously become aware of God's omnipotency and efficacy and of His causality. Moreover, we do not apprehend this omnipotency, as Church says, because it follows from the *definition* of God as perfect.[39] We do not apprehend *that* God is omnipotent *because* perfection entails omnipotence, any more than we apprehend existence because His essence entails it. On the contrary, we apprehend God as Being and in that intuition we simultaneously apprehend—but not comprehend—His power and efficacy.

It is true that in one sense Malebranche finds God's power and will by consulting the idea of God. But let us not forget what such consultation means. When Malebranche in the eighth of the *Entretiens* on metaphysics proceeds to "deduce" the divine attributes from the "idea" of God, this deduction is not an inference of abstract properties from an abstract meaning. The idea of God is a direct illumination of God *par simple vue*. In such an illuminationistic doctrine, to apprehend *that* God wills or has potency is to be aware of that power directly, to feel its operation.

The foregoing can be understood in another light. For Malebranche, the attempt to grasp the nature of causality must be understood on the level of existence or of being itself, not on the level of abstractions. So long as we seek for an idea of causality, our task is doomed to failure, for then we shall find no more than either the static, intelligible hierarchy of Aristotle's cosmogony or Hume's intellectualized series of inert antecedents and consequents united by the inference-making force of our expectations. Which is to say that the quest for causality is not the search for a diagram, a symbol, an essence, an image, an impression, or for an archetypal concept. It is instead the search for the *true* cause, and the true cause is the transitive creative source and root of being or existence itself, which can be grasped only intuitively, *par simple vue*.

(marginal note:) Power a question, not of idea, but of existence and therefore of God as Being.

According to M. Gilson, if Aristotle's First Mover

> makes causes to be causes, it is not by any kind of transitive action which would make these second causes at once to be, and to be causes. It moves only by the love it excites—which it excites, observe, *but does not breathe in.* . . . Even if we suppose that Aristotle's God were a moving and efficient cause properly so called, which is by no means certain, his causality nevertheless would fall upon a universe which does not owe its existence to him, on beings whose being does not depend on his. In this sense he would merely be the first unmoved mover, that is to say the originating point in the communication of movements, but he would not always be the creator of the movement itself.[40]

The Christian philosopher, in contrast, is always moving on the plane of Being. In seeking to grasp the nature of causality or in seeking to prove God as the efficient cause, he is seeking the Maker and Creator and Breather of any and every mode of being, because: "for every Christian thinker, *the relation of effect to cause* that links up nature with God lies in the order and on the plane of existence itself." [41]

That this is also the view of Malebranche there can be no doubt. In the ninth dialogue of the *Entretiens sur la métaphysique,* Theodore undertakes to consider the Divine as going out of itself, as ready to externalize itself in the production of creatures. At once the dilemma of creation arises. To create, God must know and will the universe. But, Theodore asks Aristes: "Do you then believe, Aristes, that He who is self-sufficient is capable of forming any desire?"

Aristes is readily plunged into doubts:

> Very well then, Theodore, I do not doubt that God knows, but I do doubt whether He can ever will anything or whether He ever has willed anything; for what could He will, He who is fully suffi-cient unto Himself? We will, we human creatures, but the fact that we will is a sure sign of our poverty. Not having what we need, we desire it. But the infinitely perfect Being can will nothing, de-sire nothing, since He sees quite well that He is in want of nothing.

Theodore rejects this conclusion with one sweeping but poignantly simple declaration: "We are, or exist, Aristes; this fact is indisputa-ble." [42]

Here we encounter another side of the dilemma concerning the in-comprehensible character of divine efficiency and volition. As long as we remain on the level of God as self-sufficient Being, then the concep-tion of a creative will is difficult to grasp. For if God wills it would appear that He must be lacking in something. But this is to anthropo-morphize and to humanize the Deity, and it is incompatible with His self-sufficiency. Yet if we deny will, we run against the stubborn fact that we exist.

> *Theodore.* . . . We are; this fact is indisputable. God is infinitely perfect. Consequently, we are dependent upon Him. We do not exist despite of Him; we exist only because He willed that we should have being. But how could God will that we should have being, seeing that He has no need of us? How can a being who lacks noth-ing, who is fully self-sufficient, will anything? That is the difficulty. [43]

Let us note this difficulty well. It does not stem from any lack of awareness of God's power or will acting upon us; nor does it stem from any ignorance of our essential dependence on God. Causality, declares Malebranche, is something divine; and—we must never for-get this—since there is only one true God, there is only one true cause. It is from this point of view that anything that exists directly testifies the presence of the Creator and its necessary connection with Him. We may not as yet know what the self is; we may not even as yet com-prehend what it is to be an existent. But no matter, for any given state is a revelation of God's efficacy. Be it a sensation, a volition, a pure conception, or finally the state of pure vision, God's creative power is being directly experienced. His creative energy is felt everywhere and at all times. We are, as it were, bathed with God's power. Thus it is that when one ball hits another, even though we do not sensuously per-ceive any creative influence of one upon the other, we nevertheless have the unmistakeable sense that such causal influence is going on.

This primordial sense of creative causality may indeed lead us astray. Through prejudice and inattention we may attribute this felt causality to the colliding balls. Nevertheless the awareness of "true" causal efficacy is there. It remains only to become critically aware of its proper source. This is why, reluctant though Malebranche may be to employ cosmological arguments for God's existence, it seems none the less evident to him that anything at all can prove the existence of a Causal Power, even on the supposition of an evil demon. And whenever Malebranche does argue for God as an efficient cause, the cause that he proves is that of a Creator.

In pure intuition *par simple vue* we discover who God truly is—infinitely infinite Being, and as such, not only is He not a deceiver, but He is omnipotent and efficacious as well. In pure intuition we discover that the products of being or any manner of being belong to Being proper. For Being is Be-ing, the pure act of existing, and as such He is, if you like, an energy, a productivity, a vitality. Malebranche, we saw, does not, as Descartes, say that God first is a power who then appropriates existence for Himself. He *is* existence. He is *uncreated* existence. But this very uncreated existence is through and through a creativity or productivity. It is the infinite enjoyment of actuality; the infinite and eternal affirmation of efficacy and causality. Thus again we see why Malebranche writes that there is only one *true* cause as there is only one true God. For God alone is He to whose essence it belongs to be. Being and causality are inseparable. This is why it appears evident to Malebranche that to establish God as Being is simultaneously to establish Him as omnipotent and efficacious. To know God *par simple vue* as Being is to know Him as Creator, and to know that God alone is Being is to know that God alone is Creator of existents.

Our "simple vue" of God as Being is identically acquaintance with creativity.

The direct awareness of God's efficacy, let us recall, played an important role in his epistemology. While essences were uncreated, it was noted that it still remained to explain *how* ideas get themselves to be known, *how* ideas become revealed. Ideas are eternal and uncreated; but how do *we* get acquainted with them? What causes *our discovery* of ideas and what causes the ideas to become disclosed to our presence or awareness? Ideas are the truth, the logical source of intelligibility. They make things intelligible; they illuminate our minds; but they do not of their own accord swim into our ken. Intense effort or attention is required on our part. We must possess a passionate desire for the truth. But in addition, a power must, as it were, allow ideas to become unveiled to our gaze, and we are directly acquainted with the operation of this power.

For Malebranche this beneficent power is the loving will of God. God's will is the cause of our conception or discovery of ideas; He allows us to find ideas. And it is He too who brings ideas into our presence.

Thus the God that Malebranche seeks to prove is not only truth but power, not only ideal essences but potency, not only intellect but will, not only God as formal cause, but as efficient cause. The intuition of Being is an immediate and direct experience of God as Be-ing, that is, of the efficacious character of God. Not only is God's presence *revealed* to intuition, not only is it a *revelation*, but rather it is a *revealing*. In intuition, Being is exerting and acting upon the mind. Attention, declares Malebranche, is the natural prayer of the soul. In attending to Being, the soul is bending and groping and straining for the light. In finding Being, God is illuminating or responding to the soul. But what is the character of this illumination? True, we find God either shining upon the soul—the Platonic image of the Sun irradiating its rays of light—or else the Word directly addressing the mind. We find God as Reason, yes, but the imagery is more significant, for in finding Being we find the spiritual energy, as it were, that is the creative source of our very striving, attending and groping and of the final triumph of understanding itself. To find God *par simple vue* as Being is to discover God as *communicating* Himself, as the animating and life-breathing principle of our existence. We can exist, declares Malebranche, without thinking of ourselves. But we cannot exist for a moment without thinking of God. This is because while we have no distinct idea of the nature of the soul, yet our sense of existence is, if we only reflect upon it, the intimate awareness of God's creative power making and sustaining us. It is His will directly pouring and communicating itself into us.[44]

> Power is God communicating Himself.

This would, once again, explain why Malebranche should consider the proof of divine existence by way of ideas to be the best. It is supreme because it submits to Occam's razor. It is the simplest and the clearest; with one cut it permits the discovery of God in the fullness of His attributes—as existence, as reason and as will.

A true cause, says Malebranche, is such that between it and its effect the mind perceives a necessary connection.[45] Now in perception we perceive no necessity between the movements of two colliding balls and no "true" causal influence. We do not, because perception does not ever disclose any necessity in the intrinsic existence or operation of the balls. Finite things are through and through contingent. We cannot say of them that their essence is to be. Their being and every mode of being is dependent. Ball A is not the true efficient cause of the motion in ball B, for ball A is not even self-dependent for its existence, nor is it therefore the creative cause of the existence of ball B or of the latter's change of position.

> Answer to Church's charge of "compensatory dogma."

Yet, while there is no awareness of an essential creative tie *between* the balls, this does not imply that we are not aware of a necessity and causal power as such. For constant conjunction is a fact—a way of being, a way of existence. But this very constancy, this particular mode of being, is no more self-sufficient or self-explanatory than any other fact. Therefore its ultimate justification, too, lies in the creative power of God as Being.

Accordingly, when Malebranche turns from constant conjunction to God, it is not through any compensatory dogma. To be sure, constant conjunction reveals no necessity and therefore no true cause between the conjoined events. To this extent Church is right. But because Church does not realize that Malebranche, unlike Hume, has developed an epistemology that goes beyond empirical perception, beyond even ideas to intuition, and that as a metaphysician Malebranche, via his intuitionism, is always moving on the plane of Being, for that very reason, unlike Hume, he cannot and does not stop with mere finite constancy. For Malebranche, constant conjunction serves only to explain why we erroneously impute creative power where it does not belong. But it does not account for our notion of power. Our query concerning our notion of power is not, for Malebranche, as it is for Hume, a search for an original impression. The search for true power is a search for the creative origin of existence itself, or of any mode of existence, such as constant conjunction. And the place to localize that power is not in any finite impression, were such to be had, but in God only. For Malebranche's search for true efficient causality is for the sort of transitive and communicating activity whereby things get born and made and preserved. But when Hume looks for an impression of causal power, not only is he demanding a static image of power, but this very demand shows that he conceives of the causal relation itself as a reified Bradleian external relation. Were one to find that link of dependency between two existents, one would then embark on an impossible track of infinite relations, for one would seek to find power in relations of comparison. Hence when Malebranche denies that perception reveals causal power, his very indictment of perception comes from the fact that the true kind of efficient causality can be only creative and therefore pertinent to Him alone whose *esse* it is To Be.

This explains why Malebranche rejects the conception of fashioning a world out of pre-existing matter. An architect can mold and fabricate out of pre-existing material. A Prime Mover can allow motion to drop, as it were, into an already-existing receptacle. But a Creator-God is He who is above all the cause of the very existence of things and so of movement itself as a mode of existence. Hence, writes Malebranche: ". . . si Dieu ne donnait point l'être à la matière, il ne pourrait point la mouvoir, puisque pour donner l'être de telle ou telle manière, il faut premièrement pouvoir donner l'être." [46]

(c) *Necessary Connection between Effect and Cause.* Hume said that no matter of fact implies any other, and Kant applied this to God. How can we say that God's will is the cause for the existent world? The divine will is something; granted; but the world is something *quite different,* that is, a distinct thing.[47] So how can we say that the one is *dependent* on the other? How can we find any real connection or relation among distinct existents?

This criticism is well taken when applied to a Cartesian God. The divine will of Descartes' God is precisely such a separate and distinct, self-contained existent. Malebranche, however, insists that while no logical tie is to be found between the two striking balls, it is to be found between God's will and the world. Why?

To answer this question it is necessary to become clear concerning Malebranche's understanding of a true cause as one which involves logical necessity. Malebranche does not say that a true cause is nothing but logical necessity, or that causality reduces to a logical concept, for the reason that his is not an essence-God. Far from affirming that the world can be deduced from any essence, Malebranche holds, on the contrary, that the existence of the world depends entirely on God's will. Malebranche is looking for a Creator, not an idea. Thus, conversely, the presence of logical necessity does not itself testify to causality proper. His polemic against Descartes' doctrine that God is the Creator of immutable truths and essences does seek to show that this essential kind of truth is eternal, necessary, uncreated, and stands in no need of a creator. The very character of the ideas involved dictates their immutable truth. But such logical necessity, on the other hand, is quite distinct from creative causality, from the origin of matters of fact.

Causality does not reduce to logical necessity.

Therefore when Malebranche asserts that in the case of a true cause there is logical necessity between effect and cause, he means (1) that absence of logical necessity indicates the absence of creative causality proper. Necessity is a necessary condition for the operation of causal creative power. And presence of true causality implies logical necessity. But (2) where we do find logical necessity, we cannot *ipso facto* infer that true causality proper is present.

How a true cause is logically necessary.

Now in a case of antecedent and consequent, such as two colliding balls, no logical necessity is perceived. Therefore no true creative causal power is present. In the case of God's will, we perceive a logical necessity, *but we do not therefore infer His causal power.* On the contrary, *it is from the awareness of the active presence of God's causal will that we infer a unilateral necessity.* When we attend to the operation of God's will, what we perceive is not a distinct existent, God, followed by another existent, creature. Rather, what we apprehend is a will *in operation.* We apprehend a will that is willing and making the very thing willed; we experience true creative causality. And because the divine will is actually creating and operating to produce a given effect, *for this reason* is it inconceivable that the effect not be or not have the character that it has. The experience of causality is akin to that of true understanding. In the latter, God is illuminating. So in the former—to be aware of His causal power is to be aware of His will truly influencing, impressing, agitating—of its being received, of its being applied. While we cannot pass by necessity from cause to effect as would be required in a philosophy of efficient essential causality, we can, with true causality, as Malebranche construes it, pass from effect to necessary cause.

> Mais lorsqu'on pense à l'idée de Dieu; c'est-à-dire d'un être infiniment parfait et par conséquent tout-puissant, on connaît qu'il y a une telle liaison entre sa volonté et le mouvement de tous les corps, qu'il est impossible de concevoir qu'il veuille qu'un corps soit mû et que ce corps ne le soit pas. . . . Il suffit qu'il veuille afin qu'une chose soit, parce qu'il y a contradiction qu'il veuille et que ce qu'il veut ne soit pas. Sa puissance est donc sa volonté . . .[48]

And to the phrase, "il suffit qu'il veuille" in the foregoing, Malebranche appends a line as footnote, to make perfectly clear the kind of will that he is attributing to his Deity: "Il est clair que je parle ici des volontés pratiques, ou de volontés que Dieu a lorsqu'il prétend agir."

Creativity, then, is the kind of potency which concerns existence. Now no finite entity can originate or produce or sustain being. This kind of operation is pertinent to God or Being alone. Hence creation remains incomprehensible, although not inconceivable. The *how* of creation is a mystery, for no creature is endowed with such a power. Yet its meaning and nature are intuitively clear. It is the engendering and conserving of beings by Being.

Creative power distinctly conceivable but incomprehensible.

In the seventh dialogue of the *Entretiens sur la métaphysique* Aristes declares: ". . . Now that the world is an accomplished fact, let God but leave it there; it will remain for ever." To this Theodore replies:

> . . . You judge of God and His works by the works of man, which presuppose nature and do not make it. Your house continues to exist, though its architect be dead. That is because its foundations are solid and *because it has no connection with the life of him who built it.* It does not depend upon the latter in any way. The ground of our being, on the other hand, depends essentially upon the Creator. . . . The universe, . . . having been created out of nothing, depends so much upon the universal Cause that it would relapse into non-being necessarily if God ceased to conserve it.

Theodore concludes this reply in terms that are almost presumptuous: "For God does not will, and indeed cannot make, a created thing which is independent of His volitions." But Aristes refuses to leave off his cross examination. He admits "an essential relation, connection, or dependence" obtains between Creator and created things; "but," he persists, "cannot one say that to retain for the created things their dependent nature, it is enough that God should be able to annihilate them whenever He pleases?" The dialogue continues thus:

> *Theodore.* "No, emphatically no, my dear Aristes. What greater mark of independence is there than unaided self-subsistence? To speak accurately, your house does not depend upon you. Why? Because it subsists without you. You can put it to the flames whenever it pleases you, but you do not sustain it. That is why there is no essential relation of dependence between you and it. Thus, though God could destroy all created things whenever it pleased Him, so long as they could subsist without the *continual influence* of the Creator, they would not be essentially dependent upon Him. . . . If bodies are essentially dependent upon the Creator, they need, in order to exist, to be *sustained* by His *continuous influence,* by the efficacy of the same will which has created them." [49]

Thus for Malebranche any fact whatever testifies to the continual and continuous operation of God's power and influence. Because Malebranche's Deity is not the God whom Hume had in mind, we can understand both why Hume's criticism of God's necessary existence does not apply to Malebranche and also why Malebranche does not go where Hume does in his view of causality. Hume argued that no essence involved its own existence. Hence every matter of fact is a distinct, arbitrary existence that implies no other existent. Hence too, if God exists, His existence is arbitrary too. Like any other essence, His does not involve existence. And if efficacy is unintelligible in the creature, it is unintelligible in God.

But Malebranche's God is not an essence that involves existence. His God is an Existence who is His own essence, His own idea. Being such, He can be the creative sustaining source of all other existents. This is why Malebranche can plead with the Word: "Vous êtes notre Chef, *influez* en nous." [50] And addressing God directly, he can write in terms that seem almost of our century rather than his in their insistence upon concrete duration:

> Mon Dieu, *faites-moi continuellement sentir la dépendance* où je suis de vôtre volonté toute-puissante. Mon être est à vous, et la durée de mon être ou mon temps est aussi à vous. Que je suis injuste! Mon être est, pour ainsi dire, l'être de Dieu: mon temps est véritablement le temps de Dieu, car je suis plus à Dieu qu'à moi, ou plûtôt je ne suis point de tout à moi, je ne subsiste point par moi, et

cependant je ne vis, et je n'employe le temps de Dieu que pour moi. Hélas, que je me trompe! Tout le temps que je n'employe point pour vous, ô mon Dieu, je ne l'employe point pour moi, je le perds: et je ne me cherche, et je ne me trouve, que lorsque je vous cherche, et que je vous trouve.[51]

Shall we dismiss these utterances as merely compensatory dogma? By no means. Malebranche is able to speak thus because his vision of God reveals to him God's power breathing upon him.

The real difficulty of grasping the notions of creation, efficacy, power and will do not stem from ignorance as to what these mean, or from lack of apprehension of the essential connection between God's will and His effects. The real difficulty with respect to the divine will lies in seeking to understand the *why* of creation. We feel and experience God as our Maker, but the puzzle lies in understanding the ultimate meaning of this creation. And this, too, can only be solved by a more intensified concentration upon God as Being. What therefore remains is to unfold the nature of that production and the reason for finite existence. Why does creation take place?

(*d*) *Purpose of Creation.* In the *Méditations chrétiennes*, the disciple, seeking to comprehend the creative act, declares to the Word:

Creation neither by indifferent will nor by necessary emanation.

I am in a difficulty that embarrasses me. How is it possible that you drew this world out of nothing? Is there any relation or connection between nothing and the world? Or can anything emerge or be made out of nothing? How can nothing and being be joined together? To these questions, the Word replies: "Il n'y a point aussi, mon cher Fils, de rapport entre le néant et l'être; et ce n'est point du néant que tu tires ton origine. C'est moi qui suis le Principe de toutes choses; et c'est par la puissance infinie de Dieu que les créatures reçoivent leur existence." [52] Moreau interprets this declaration as a frank admission on the part of Malebranche of his affiliation with Spinoza. Malebranche here denies creation *ex nihilo*, says Moreau, because, like Spinoza, he is admitting that creation comes out of God's substance.[53] On the contrary; nothing can be further from the truth than Moreau's allegation. Creation *ex nihilo* is indubitable to Malebranche.[54] What Malebranche is denying, however, is creation from blind chance, what we might today perhaps call emergent evolution. He plainly is asserting that at the root of creation lies both reason ("le Principe de toutes choses") and will ("la puissance infinie de Dieu"). Hence the import of this assertion is that he is in effect at once rejecting both Descartes and Spinoza with respect to the origin of the world.

To say, as does Descartes, that God acts by an indifferent and arbitrary will is equivalent, it seems to me, to the assertion that there is no intelligible connection, no "Principe" whatsoever between God and His effects—neither with respect to their existence nor with respect to their character. Arbitrariness implies that there is no community, no sharing, no participation, no similarity, no intercourse or interrelationship at all between Being and beings. Were such the case, God and His effects would be both utterly "windowless" with respect to each other and completely separated. Just as in the *Leviathan*, Hobbes' sovereign is the arbiter who issues edicts by brute force, but himself shares no community of interest with his subjects, so Descartes' Deity is a remote, mercurial potentate on the metaphysical level. Such a view not only reduces causality to a series of Humian external conjunctions, but opens it to all the serious objections of Bradley's attack on external relations. How can creatures be described as being dependent on God and conserved every moment, if the connection between God and them is one of completely indifferent transcendence? There may indeed be a disproportion, infinite, if you please, between Infinite Being and the finite beings; but the very disproportion itself must be rooted in something held or shared in common. It is because Malebranche believes this, it seems to me, that he refuses to agree with Descartes' denial of final causes and insists instead that there must be a sufficient reason for the existence of the universe. To say that there is no reason for the finite modes is to admit blind chance. And this in turn is to admit a rugged fragmentation or bare, static succession.

Spinoza also believed this, and, to avert it, introduced immanent causality in the place of transcendence. Spinoza's deterministic solution then provides the intelligible principle that Descartes lacks. But still it is unacceptable to Malebranche. Why? Some critics seek to offer personal rather than philosophical reasons for his rejection of Spinoza. They attempt to psychoanalyze Malebranche, appealing to the ninth of the *Méditations chrétiennes*, where the disciple writes of how he feels himself led to believe that his substance is eternal, that he constitutes part of the divine Being, and that all his thoughts are only modifications of the universal Reason. Bouillier, Ginsberg, and Ollé-Laprune feel that these are confessions to a fatal temptation towards pantheism.[55] They say that Malebranche is admitting an unconscious flirtation with Spinozism from which he is saved by fear, or by the guiding hand of Augustine, or by his "bon sens chrétien." [56]

Despite this verdict, we can readily see as a result of my previous chapters that Malebranche's rejection of Spinozism actually rests on the most fundamental issues. Determinism provides a unity that is too rigid and extreme for Malebranche, one that precludes not only the empiricism of his scientific method, but also his view of God as Being. The crucial issue between Spinoza's determinism and Malebranche's creationism is that Malebranche's metaphysics and his method require both causal necessity and contingency, and neither alone is sufficient for him. The intuitive aspect of Malebranche's method demands the recognition of independent, self-sufficing Platonic universals, or archetypes, or uncreated truths. The experimental aspect of his method requires, in addition, an allegiance to brute fact, because nature is not abstract. Neither of these requirements is compatible with Spinoza's conceptualism or with his extreme *a priori* rationalism. Moreover, for Spinoza God is a *Causa Sui*, an absolute nature that entails existence; and God's power is that of an *active essence*.[57] For Malebranche Creation is an act of will, because His God is He who exists. Thus for Malebranche creation is *par excellence* a notion that is inextricable from time; and, however difficult to comprehend, both time and creation he sees as clearly following from his view of God as self-sufficient Being.[58] Precisely because God is the fullness of Being, that is, existence, emanation is an impossibility. ". . . All that may be legitimately inferred from the self-sufficiency of God," we read in the *Entretiens sur la métaphysique*, "is that the world is no necessary emanation from the divine Being." [59]

From a wider perspective than our view of Spinoza alone, we ought further to note that the two extremes of Cartesian indifferent voluntarism and Spinozistic essentialistic determinism are actually not so far apart as they may seem. Spinoza himself admitted that the notion of an indifferent arbitrary will is "at a less distance from the truth than the opinion of those who affirm that God does everything for the sake of the Good." [60] Spinoza thus acknowledged that indifferentism is not far from necessitarianism. For this reason it is significant that Malebranche, because he seeks a synthesis of creative power and essential reason that limits each, has to reject the one and the other of the two extremes.

If indifference, efficiency, necessity, and emanation are not acceptable, Malebranche, as metaphysician, must explain the world in terms of finality. He construes the creative causal act as one of love and liberality.[61] The *why* of this outpouring or overflowing is the glory and goodness of God. Here is indeed a reason or motive that makes finite existence intelligible, that is, one that unifies the infinite and the finite, and accounts for the origin of the finite. But this principle of divine goodness, although it is the source of all intelligibility and clarity, is itself understandable only when grasped intuitively, only, that is, when it is not hypostatized into a specific concept or entity. The reason for creation is thus not an inner constraining drive, or a cosmic Freudian *Id*, or any other *mechanism*, but is instead to be found in the creative act itself. The reason for creation is the spontaneous enjoyment of and love for what creation achieves. Creation is the dissemination of Being into beings.

How can we interpret this emergence of beings? Malebranche reverts to the medieval description of creation as self-diffusion and self-

[margin note:] Creation purposive—to incarnate God's goodness and glory.

communication. Creation is a continuous overflowing, a movement from God to creature. Although there can be no idea of this activity any more than there can be of that activity which characterizes God's Be-ing, yet, if we should persist in denying creation, says the Word, on the grounds that we have no distinct idea of it, and if we carry this demand out to its logical conclusion, we should be forced to deny all change and movement, for even motion as change of place is a mode of being. We would thus have an existenceless universe.[62] Thus Malebranche not only repudiates Eleaticism as an absurd position, but does so in the same manner as Bergson did two hundred years later. As long as we are confined to static ideas, to the realm of essence, then change, motion, finite existence and creative power are apparently impossible and meaningless. But just as Bergson demanded a reform in metaphysics, a return to fluid symbols, so Malebranche, to explain creation, returns to the familiar notion of divine purpose and supremely generous love.

In reintroducing finality, Malebranche is fully conscious of his deliberate departure from Descartes and the gravity of his endeavor. God created the world because it is *better* than nothing.[63] Final causes are useless in physics, but absolutely necessary in metaphysics.[64] Glory is the motive for creation. No wonder Aristes exclaims: How naive and anthropomorphic a notion! *Is finalism anthropomorphic?*

Nevertheless, with the candor and sense of awe that Socrates felt in ascending to the Good, Malebranche attempts to explore the meaning of the glory of God. He actually utilizes a figure of speech reminiscent of Socrates' "waves." Caution and vigilance are imperative, he insists, lest in approaching the divine glory one founder on the rocks.[65] The perils and pitfalls are numerous. For instance, there is the dangerous tendency to transform God's glory from a motive into an irresistible necessity. Malebranche's method for struggling against this current is by no means original, but it is perfectly harmonious with his own philosophical spirit. God is self-sufficient Being; hence glory is an end to be achieved, not an impetus from behind.[66]

But is this not to humanize God? And what, after all, as Bergson later asked, is the difference between finality and efficient causality? Is not this view of finality an inverted mechanism, as Spinoza thought when he wrote: "This is indeed nothing else than to subject God to fate." [67] But Malebranche does not construe God's glory as a static plan or model that attracts God as a needle to a magnet. Finite man has needs and lacks, and so he constructs conscious goals which he seeks to achieve. But God is a divine artist who creates for sheer delight. Like an excellent architect who enjoys building, because his commodious structure expresses his skill, exemplifies his talents, and mirrors his abilities, so God rejoices because His creation bears the character of the attributes which He esteems and loves: "God finds His glory and His satisfaction in a work which in some way expresses His excellent qualities." [68]

This comparison of God to an artist is in several ways a strategic metaphor. *First,* only poverty of language and the difficulty of comprehending the infinite compel one to imagine God as an efficient householder who compares various plans and their means of execution and then chooses the best. Malebranche will himself make such descriptions in trying to account for evil. [69] Nevertheless, even this suggestion is mitigated by the fact that the divine choice is an eternal act involving no succession of thoughts and hence no wavering, deliberation or hesitation, as in man. Moreover, the view of God as choosing the best design is intended against those who like Descartes or Hobbes assume an utterly indifferent power or blind nature acting lawlessly or by chance. Even Bergson's view of the *élan vital* carries with it, we know, the dangerous implication that neither the product created nor the manner of creation matters; what is important is the explosive bursting of the rocket and the novelty of each new burst. While Malebranche's version of what Santayana calls the epic of Christianity does not minimize the element of time, nevertheless, his conception of God as the divine artist lays stress on both the end and the manner in which creation takes place. Malebranche's Deity acts in the classical, not the romantic, tradition. His God is not "carried away" by an irrational madness, nor does He conceive the end to justify the means. The manner, method, or means of execution are as important as the product.

There is a *second* significant feature in the comparison of God to an artist. God makes a work of art that expresses Himself, but is not Himself. This is why, as we shall see, Malebranche cannot accept or understand Spinoza's complete immanentism. We must not, he says, confuse the divine worker with His works. The work is stamped with the divine signature; it is an image or likeness of God in that it embraces God's qualities, nature and skill; but the analogue constructed is its own reality. [70]

But what is an analogue? The answer to this question indicates a *third* major feature of the comparison of God to an artist. It is sometimes assumed that imitation, likeness, resemblance, participation are to be construed in terms of photographic reproduction, in terms of vision. Yet the symbol of God as an architect or artist surely does not imply that a building or painting is a fair reproduction or copy of its inventor. It is a likeness in the sense that it "participates" in the character and skill of the maker. To take an example. Beethoven's last symphony reflects the turbulence, musical mastery, struggle, loneliness and moral principles of Beethoven's life. Hence it reveals Beethoven

The world as analogue.

himself. He himself appears, so to speak, in his work; and, in a very real sense, the merit and value of the symphony lie in the degree to which the work of art succeeds in being an expression of its author. Moreover, paradox though it be, from the point of view of participation, an artist truly finds self-satisfaction and self-glorification just to the extent that he becomes selfless, disinterested, and wholly concerned with the product itself. Only the fallacy of simple location has foisted the erroneous notion of crude semblance, anthropomorphism and monstrous egoism on the theme of creation. Inasmuch as the glory of God is the motif for creation, and self-glorification bespeaks a divine artistry, Malebranche looks upon the natural world with reverence. Nature as God's handiwork is good—*valde bona*.[71] At the same time, nevertheless, he maintains that: ". . . the universe, however grand, however perfect it may be, is still finite, is still unworthy of the action of a God whose worth is infinite." [72]

Although Malebranche's philosophy of creation is not anthropomorphic in a bad sense, his efforts to deny anthropomorphism bring him to the brink of what he calls the most perilous of all metaphysical pitfalls. His necessary reservation that the universe, being finite, is not worthy of God's creative efforts, leads to a sharp division between the self-sufficient infinity of God or infinite Being, on the one hand, and the intrinsic reality of the finite on the other. How reconcile these two orders of existential reality? The glory of God is not sufficient to untie *this* metaphysical knot. Infinity, writes Malebranche, is the most essential of God's attributes. How then can God rejoice in a world which, created *ex nihilo*, is limited and finite? How can the finite be an analogue of Him who is infinite? However noble, excellent or numerous the creatures may be, yet they are zero in comparison with the infinite majesty of God. How then can God find satisfaction in His creation? [73] The problem is also an ethical one. God is just. His wisdom embraces not merely speculative truths but an order of moral values. A natural, profane world cannot honor God.[74] God must therefore find the way to spiritualize and to sanctify the world.

Malebranche reconciles God and the world by uniting the two with a divine Personality. Through the incarnation of Christ, God found the secret of rendering His work divine. Through Christ, God "sanctified the whole of nature." [75] Thus Christ, as man-God, is not only, or even primarily, the Redeemer. He is the true realization of divine glory.

Malebranche is plainly aware that in this solution of his problem of the relation between the infinite and the finite he is resorting to faith. But he insists that this procedure is not unphilosophical. I go to truths of faith, admits Theodore, "because without them I can find no solution for thousands upon thousands of difficulties." [76] Male-

The One and the many.

branche is here following a perfectly valid philosophical or scientific procedure. He is seeking a principle that can order the world, unify facts, render them systematic and harmonious. In Scripture he finds a fecund idea, but its philosophical validity stems from its conformity to reason. Not that the incarnation is a clear and distinct concept or that we understand *how* it takes place. Yet, mysterious as it is in content, reason finds it acceptable, because by means of it an intelligible, sufficient reason has been afforded for otherwise immeasurable paradoxes. A full exploration of the interconnection between faith and reason will be undertaken in my last chapter, but here we must consider the momentous metaphysical implications of his doctrine of incarnation. And I pause here deliberately to consider these implications, in order to prepare the mind of the reader, as Descartes would say, to comprehend the occasional cause; for what relates God's reason and power to the world clearly is deeply relevant to the nature of that world.

God, Christ, man and nature.

It is often alleged that Malebranche is God-intoxicated, that his system centers about God and is theocentric.[77] Yet we learn that God, without needing it, nevertheless actually finds His Glory by making the Word become Flesh. This has suggested that Malebranchianism can be considered as Christo-centric.[78] But this label, if taken alone, is again inadequate. For it is not purely and simply Christ as the Word who glorifies God; it is Christ-man, "l'homme-Dieu." It is Christ in the capacity of *man* who is the dispenser of grace and the builder of the City of God.[79] May we not therefore equally well designate this system as humanistic, as homocentric? Does not the Incarnation actually stress the greatness and nobility of the human being? Through Christ we become Godlike and His coheritors.[80]

Let us advance another step. Even humanism is an inadequate designation. It is not uncommon to cavil at Malebranche, contending that his God is a monstrous egoist, because He makes the Incarnation the purpose of creation. This, it is said, obliterates the traditional tender and redemptive office of Christ. Hence, in seeking such self-glorification, God's creation is not really an act of love. Such is the verdict of Blondel and of Church, for example.[81] Yet the criticism is unfair. It ignores that fact that Malebranche does not renounce the redemptive role. What he does claim is that the redemption is a subordinate motive and that even if Adam had not sinned the Incarnation would have taken place.[82]

Est-ce que le Verbe ne peut s'unir à l'ouvrage de Dieu sans s'incarner? Il s'est fait homme; mais ne pouvait-il pas se faire ange? Il est vrai qu'en se faisant homme, il s'unit en même temps aux deux substances, esprit et corps, dont l'univers est composé, et que, par cette union, il sanctifie toute la nature. C'est pour cela que je ne crois point que le péché ait été la seule cause de l'Incarnation du Fils de Dieu.[83]

Thus, it seems to me, what is primarily significant about the Incarnation is that its function is to "save" or to sanctify the whole of nature. This implies that the natural world is an object worthy of reverent respect.

In the Jansenist universe of Arnauld, by contrast, the world is utterly worthless and corrupt through Adam's fall. Neither sense nor reason is valuable. For Pascal the study of nature is worthless. Only a learned ignorance can achieve salvation. Against this doctrine, Malebranche's account of the Incarnation affirms the essential glory of the natural universe, of the realm of sense and of secular learning. Is this not naturalistic? Not pure pagan naturalism, of course. The Incarnation adds a moral dimension to the universe. Christ is the director of the celestial Jerusalem. His task is to build a triumphant church. As man he is the occasional cause for the distribution of grace. The realm of grace is added to the realm of nature. However, this celestial Jerusalem or realm of grace is no mere external addition or juxtaposition to the realm of nature. The supernatural is already present in the natural. One uses but does not abandon nature to reach grace.[84] The Incarnation is thus a glorification of this natural world itself.

Furthermore, Christ is the Word—*la Sagesse éternelle*. The Incarnation then implies that the world is good not only for being the handiwork of God, a product of His creative power, but good by being permeated with or containing a rational order and structure. The Incarnation sanctifies nature by declaring the world of nature, the realm of sense and of finite fact, to contain and embody the divine reason. This is why the Incarnation would have occurred even without Adam's sin. For the world of sensible fact would be blind energy without reason, without general principles, without intelligence, without essences. Hence Malebranche will say that faith and sense will pass but reason will remain.[85] But on the other hand general principles and concepts without sense and creative power are empty. The reason that will remain is no system of abstract essences. It is man-God who remains. Therefore the intelligence that will remain and to which faith and sense are a guide is the sphere of concrete persons united with God.[86]

The Incarnation renders essences concretely actual.

Again, notice that Christ as the occasional cause of grace is Christ in the capacity of man, not the Word that is consubstantial with God. Thus the building of the celestial Jerusalem is the work of the creature, of finite man. Upon man thus rests the responsibility and the honor of cooperating with God in accomplishing the glorification of God. Here Malebranche's naturalistic and humanistic concerns are united. And here is where the redemptive role of Christ becomes most apparent. God permitted the Fall, because he saw that the world, reformed and regenerated through Christ, was superior to its primitive state. In the Christian universe of Malebranche, stress is on the inner man and on a spiritual cult. Hence, says Theodore: "I believe, Aristes, that God loved us so much that He has given us His only Son, . . . that He loved His Son so much that He has given us to Him as well as all the nations of the earth. . . . For this in a few words is the order of things: All belongs to us, we belong to Jesus Christ, and Jesus Christ belongs to God . . ." [87] Yet again, this ethical achievement is also a work in time.

In conceiving the Incarnation as the glorification of God, Malebranche opens a temporalistic dimension to this drama of creation. The coming of Christ is the beginning, not the end, of God's glory. Christ's role is to build a spiritual temple that will endure for eternity, but his achievement is in time and subject to constant change. Whereas in the universe that Bradley was to affirm, the Absolute knows no progress, in Malebranche's philosophy the world that will glorify God is a world in the making. Through Christ's efforts, grace is distributed and men are "called" to become the living stones of the celestial edifice. But who is called is not predetermined, for while there is an order of grace and an order of nature, yet Christ's choice is free in many situations.[88] In the *Méditations chrétiennes*, the Word explains: ". . . Je puis souvent remettre à un autre temps ce que j'exécute." Such delay, too, is unavoidable, for: ". . . Les matériaux dont je me sers ne sont pas également propres à mon dessein actuel, à cause de la combinaison de la grâce avec la nature: combinaison qui reçoit à tous moments des changements infinis." [89] History, novelty, contingency and time are thus of the essence of Malebranche's view of creation.

Finally, the Incarnation is required in order to do justice to the infinity of God. But what exactly is this attribute of infinity? We saw in the last chapter that infinity for Malebranche really means the positive expansion and limitless plenitude of God as *Celui qui est*. God is Be-ing. It is because God is the very act of existing that His attributes overflow; and it is because God alone is Being that He alone is the *true* cause—He alone can create. Now the Incarnation is intended to express God's infinity, that is, His act of existing and creating. By the union of the Word with man, Christ *as man* becomes the occasional or instrumental cause for the distribution of grace. Christ as man and as occasional cause thus becomes the analogue of God's existence and creative efficacy. Christ as the Word is the universal static Reason; but when this Reason becomes concretely embodied, incarnate, in an *existing* creature, man, then in this capacity does man

[margin note] History, novelty, contingency and time.

[margin note] A speculation concerning the occasional cause.

exercise the power of determining the distribution of grace. But the Incarnation, remember, is for the purpose of sanctifying the whole of nature, not merely man and the angels, but all creatures. May we then not speculate that for Malebranche all objects in varying degrees and to the extent that they exist become occasional causes and as such centers of *action*? If this be so, we shall understand why Malebranche believes the mystery of the Incarnation to be indispensable for metaphysics.[90] For while there is only one true cause who is God, and while God needs no instruments for creation, and while He cannot create subordinate independent self-existing energies or deities, nevertheless, it well may be that through "l'Homme-Dieu" God found the secret of how to make the occasional cause an active analogue of His own power and thereby to render His work divine.

II. Essence and Existence in Creatures

If God is Being, the pure act of existing, and if He creates spontaneously for His own glory, that is, to express Himself, His essence and attributes, what is the ontological status of the created objects that come forth from this spontaneous, self-diffusive energy? Creatures, says Malebranche, are made in the image of God and are participations of God's Being.[91] What is the meaning of such participation?

The process of creation and the nature of creatures.

Creation is, for Malebranche, a spontaneous act—as he says in *L'Amour de Dieu*, the liberal gift of being.[92] But now let us concentrate on the creature that, as a result of this liberal act, receives his existence or being from Being. What does reception of existence mean? We must not be misled by the metaphor. There is no aboriginal matter, stuff, or receptacle into which existence is inserted as into a box. The recipient of existence is an essence. Creation of beings is the actualization or concretization of essence. Still, the crux of the matter is, what is such concretization? What is it for an essence *to be*, to exist?

Now according to Malebranche, while the creative act is a free outpouring of Being, this outpouring is none the less intelligible, orderly. In Malebranche's language, God is not necessitated to create, but if He does create a world, His conduct must not belie His attributes or His nature. He must act in a manner that is fitting to a God who is universal Being. But this implies that there must be regularity, order, simplicity not only in the *process* of creation, but also in the contents or effects produced. The objects themselves must bear the likeness or image of God. That nature be methodized, the *what* is as important as the *how*. The results themselves must be consistent with God as Being.

God is unrestricted Being, that is, we saw, the pure act of existing.

God's Being is through and through a dynamic energy, a productivity, an activity. Now if creation is self-diffusion, self-communication, a self-giving or outpouring, does it not necessarily follow that the resultant being is itself an activity? Creation is self-communication; but what can God communicate other than what He Himself is, His very being, which is also causality? In Descartes' system, God could will, conceive, create anything whatever in any manner whatever. But in Malebranche's system, creation is, so to speak, a responsible activity. God need not create, but if He does, His conduct must reflect or bear the character of His attributes.[93] Ordinarily, says Malebranche, we judge causes by their effects. Properly, we should judge the effect in terms of the cause.[94] Let us therefore heed Malebranche's advice, as he asks us to do. We have the right to decide on *a priori* grounds, that is, by consulting the idea of God, as to what the world must be like. We may then accept Malebranche's statements that beings are participants, analogues, resemblances of God as Being. Then, to probe into the meaning of such participation, we must obey Malebranche's injunction and interpret this participation in terms of the idea of Being. Once we do that, we see that the gift of creation, the gift of Being, the self-diffusion and communication of Being, can be none other than the communication of an act of existence. *Henceforth we may say that creation is the addition of an act of existence to an essence, and that finite existence is finite activity.*

(a) *The Tradition of Essentialism.* Now I can hear my reader protest. What! Malebranche believes that to exist is to exert activity! But has Malebranche not rejected this in perfectly clear terms in denouncing the efficacy alleged to secondary causes? Let us, at least temporarily, postpone acceptance of this objection, and instead, to substantiate my interpretation of Malebranche's philosophy, let us focus on what he himself actually says concerning the existence of a material, extended object. Like Descartes, Malebranche asserts that the essence of matter is extension, the varieties of figures and configurations of which originate in motion.[95] Now Descartes conceives of the *existence* of extension as of a vast, indefinite, created substance, wholly inert, nothing but a concrete geometry. This substance is capable of movements, but not of force. Its motions are changed positions. The motive force responsible for the changes issues from God. That is, a transcendent external power insinuates itself into and exerts force upon the inert mechanism which is extension. For Descartes, then, God first creates an inert matter and subsequently exerts His influence upon it.

What can be the actual existence of a body, in Descartes' system? The physical world for Descartes is no more than a concrete geometry,[96] as I have said. By the word, concrete, Descartes means this:

[Marginal note:] Identification of existence with essence in Descartes.

out of an infinity of possible geometrical forms, certain forms have been selected by God to be actual. However, if we ask, in the spirit of Leibnitz, what difference is there for Descartes between, say, an ideal triangle and an actual, existing triangle,[97] it is quite clear that no difference exists between the two, unless we assume that body or matter is some sort of stuff or material support. In so far as Descartes defines extension as the principal attribute of body and this attribute as a subject of inherence, he would seem to be entertaining such a view.

But then movement is required to differentiate this solid mass. However, Descartes conceives of motion as a mode and he asserts that extension can be conceived as infinitely divisible and apart from its modes.[98] Well, since God can produce everything of which we have a clear and distinct idea,[99] does it not follow that He can create an immobile extension with real divisions prior to motion, which yet is alleged to be the source of all the variations and divisions?[100]

But then, if matter is inert and infinitely divisible, what constitutes the unity of a given body? And before movement is introduced,[101] what difference is there between the actual, created, inert extension with its divisions and the idea of extension with its ideal divisions? We are therefore forced to say that there is no intrinsic difference between an ideal triangle, the immutable essence or nature of the triangle, and its concrete actual existence. Concrete existence is completely exhausted by the ideal existence.

That Descartes could hold such a view is obviously owing to his view of God as *Causa Sui* and as the legislator and creator of immutable essences. Upon this view, to speak as Descartes does of the world as a concrete geometry, we must not even suppose that the concreteness refers to a selection from a *possible* realm, as my statement above may suggest. The concrete geometry that constitutes the physical world is concrete only in the sense that it is *this* geometry and no other that God happened arbitrarily to will. It is clear, then, that no difference whatever is to be found between the ideal triangle created by God and inserted innately into his mind, and the actual concrete triangle that "exists" outside his mind. Both are pure, formal, inert, intelligibilities. This is why Descartes could say that there is no real distinction between essence and existence, but merely a distinction of reason.[102]

Descartes is here following the tradition of Duns Scotus and Suarez, neither of whom allows a real distinction between essence and existence. For Duns Scotus, wherever we find essence we find being; whatever would be called existence is a definite mode of being, but this is of an essence when it has received full determination. For an essence to be, is nothing new; essence always is. When we say that an actually

The tradition of essentialism.

existing essence is, we mean that it exists as soon as it is fully constituted.[103] For Scotus, then, existence is nothing unique that is added to an essence. It simply is a definite or intrinsic quality, predicate, or modification or "degree" [104] of a given essence. This being so, essence is prior to existence *and is its intrinsic cause.*[105] To be an actually existing thing is to be an actually complete essence. Existence in this doctrine is no principle of individuation, since it is utterly inseparable from and a mode of essence.[106] Moreover, while Scotus agrees with Aquinas that God alone can create, it is not for the same reasons. For Aquinas, God alone is creator *ex nihilo,* for He only is the act of existence and therefore He alone can be the source of existence. For Duns Scotus, on the other hand, God creates in the same sense that He is the cause of essences. But inasmuch as existence is nothing over and above an actualized essence, whenever an efficient cause operates, since what it produces is a real essence, it also produces a real existence. When two animals beget a third animal, for Scotus, M. Gilson tells us, "all that enters the essence of an actual animal is actually given, and so what they beget is an actually existing animal. Hence, any efficient causality is productive of *esse,* and it cannot be said that God alone can do it." [107]

Suarez too denies any real distinction between essence and existence.[108] For him also an essence is the quiddity, the whatness or nature of a thing. This nature or essence is the innermost determining principle of a thing's operations. Not only does it make a thing be what it is, but this very whatness makes a thing to be and is thus the cause of its existence and its operations. As for Scotus, so for Suarez, an actual existing thing is simply an actualized essence. The distinction between essence and existence is a mere distinction of reason. Essence is either actual or possible, and the sole distinction that can be made between these two conditions is that what is actual is, whereas what is merely possible is not. For an essence to be a true actual being, such an essence must actually exist; it is. For Suarez it is the same for an essence actually to exercise its act of essence and for it to exist. There is no real distinction between actual existence and an actual, existing essence.[109]

M. Gilson takes sharp issue with Suarez. What Suarez does not realize, he contends, is that in creation God does not give an essence the actuality of an essence, for that it already possesses; any essence is completely actual *qua* essence. To create is, on the contrary, to confer upon essence another sort of actuality which is that of existence. The central claim of Gilson's *Being* is one that contests Suarez: "Creation thus does not actualize the essentiality of the essence, *but it actualizes that essence in another order than that of essence, by granting it existence.*" [110]

(*b*) *Opposition to Spinoza's Essentialism.* Suarez's influence was deep and widespread in its effect upon the Scholastic philosophers of the seventeenth century. To Descartes, for example, Scholastic Philosophy was Suarez.[111] I am indebted to M. Gilson for the foregoing acute account of essentialism in Scotus, Suarez and Descartes, for it enables me to formulate differences between Malebranche and Descartes with precision. The significant and crucial point that must be established for my present account of Malebranche's Occasionalism is that whereas Descartes followed the Scotist-Suarezian position on essence and existence, Malebranche rebelled against it and repudiated it; and in this Malebranche was followed by his Jesuit biographer and disciple André. André complained that Descartes' principal trouble in metaphysics arose from his failure to distinguish between essence and existence, a failure that André himself directly attributed to the "Scholastics." [112]

(margin: Malebranche distinguishes existence and essence.)

Malebranche makes of the distinction between essence and existence the very core of his repudiation of Spinozism and of his defense of creationism. He insists upon it throughout his writings. Thus in the *Méditations chrétiennes,* the Word declares:

> Il faut, mon cher Disciple, juger des choses par leur idées: on ne doit en juger que par là. Mais cela regarde leurs attributs essentiels, et nullement *les circonstances de leur existence.* L'idée, que tu as de l'étendue, te la représente divisible, mobile, impénétrable: juge sans crainte qu'elle a essentiellement ces propriétés. Mais ne juge pas qu'elle soit ni immense, ni éternelle. Elle peut n'être point du tout ou avoir des bornes fort étroites. Tu n'as pas raison de croire qu'il y ait seulement un pied d'étendue matérielle, quoique tu aies présente à l'esprit une immensité infinie d'étendue intelligible; bien loin que tu en doives juger que le monde est infini, comme font quelques Philosophes. Ne juge pas non plus que le monde est éternel, à cause que tu regardes l'étendue intelligible comme un Etre nécessaire dont la durée n'a point de commencement et ne peut avoir de fin. Car, quoique tu doives juger de l'essence des êtres par les idées qui les représentent, tu ne dois jamais juger par elles de leur existence.[113]

Towards the end of Malebranche's career an extraordinary exchange of letters took place between Malebranche and a young disciple of Spinoza, by name of Dortous de Mairan. These letters are truly illuminating, because they reveal the two radically opposed philosophies of being, the essentialism of Spinoza and the existentialism of Malebranche. In his first letter, the ardent Mairan confesses that on the one hand Spinoza's system fills him with sadness and compassion for humanity, but on the other hand, he cannot resist Spinoza's demonstrations. Show me, he pleads with Malebranche, the paralogisms of

(margin: Correspondence with Dortous de Mairan— Spinoza's cardinal error.)

Spinoza's system or at least the first erroneous misstep that led him to the fateful precipice of his undoing.[114]

In reply, Malebranche asserts that Spinoza's error stems from his definition of God, which taken in one sense is true, but taken in Spinoza's sense is false. But the principal cause of his mistakes issues from the fact that Spinoza does not distinguish between essences and concrete things.[115] With respect to Spinoza's definition of God, Malebranche says little. He simply advises Mairan to reread his own work, the *Entretien d'un philosophe chrétien avec un philosophe chinois,* in order to ascertain the proper nature of God. Mairan follows the advice of Malebranche, but he can find no difference between Malebranche's definition of God and that of Spinoza or of Descartes. Spinoza, protests Mairan, proves the existence of God exactly as Malebranche does in the *Recherche,* namely, from the fact that necessary existence is contained in the idea of God as "l'Etre par soi." [116] Mairan obviously fails to understand that Malebranche's Deity is Being, *Celui qui est,* not a *Causa Sui,* not, that is, an essence that confers existence.

Mairan's failure, in turn, prevents him from appreciating Malebranche's stubborn insistence upon the importance of distinguishing between essence and existence in things and his equally pertinacious emphasis upon the plurality of distinct existents. Completely imbued with Spinozism, the youthful Mairan writes:

1° Quand on parle de distinction en métaphysique, cela se doit presque toujours entendre de celle qu'on appelle réelle, c'est-à-dire de celle qui consiste dans ce que l'esprit aperçoit en deux ou plusieurs choses, qui fait que l'une peut être conçue et exister indépendamment de l'autre . . .

2° L'être ou l'existence des substances n'est distingué de leur essence que par abstraction, dans l'esprit seulement; et il n'y a nulle distinction réelle, hors de l'entendement, entre le propre être d'une substance et son essence, car elle n'existe que par cela même qui constitue son être.[117]

Herein lies the key to the crucial opposition of Malebranche against Mairan, Descartes, and Spinoza. For Mairan, there is a contradiction in assuming a real distinction between essence and existence in things. Hence, he cannot understand how two objects of the same nature or attribute can be described as distinct and separate substances.[118]

Malebranche, in reply, insists that the essences are eternal and belong to the divine Reason. Intelligible extension, that is, the infinite continuum of essences, is in God, and it is God Himself. By consulting it we can determine the properties of things but nothing whatever regarding their existence.[119] Moreover, a cubic foot of extension is not a modification but is itself a substance or rather an infinity of substances or 12 × 12 × 12 bits of substance, for each can be conceived to exist by itself.[120]

Je sais bien qu'un pied cube est de même nature que toute autre étendue; mais ce qui fait qu'un pied cube est distingué de tout autre, c'est son être propre, son existence. Qu'il y ait des êtres de même ou de différente nature, si cela se peut, ou qu'il n'y ait rien qui l'environne, il sera toujours ce qu'il est.[121]

Mairan is not content. Once more he writes with utter bewilderment:

Mais je vous avoue, mon Révérend Père, que je ne saurais comprendre comment plusieurs substances pourraient être distinguées par leur être propre ou par leur existence, indépendamment de leurs essences. L'existence sans l'essence n'est pas, ce me semble, un signe de distinction réelle, parce que, entre elles, je ne vois qu'une précision et une distinction de raison, qui n'a aucune réalité hors de l'entendement. Car les substances n'existent qu'en cela même qui constitue leur être ou leur existence; cet être, cette existence et l'essence qui la constitue *sunt in re ipsa unum et idem.* Et quoiqu'en supposant que les substances proprement dites n'existent pas nécessairement, *on puisse distinguer leur essence idéale et en puissance d'avec leur existence actuelle,* du moins sera-t-il toujours vrai de dire que *l'existence actuelle d'une substance n'est pas distincte réellement de son essence actuelle.* C'est pourquoi, si plusieurs substances existent actuellement ou sont distinctes entre elles, cette distinction ne peut consister que dans la différence de leurs essences actuelles. Or l'essence est partout ici la même; il n'y a donc nulle distinction.[122]

To this Malebranche replies once more that he cannot accept Spinoza's fifth proposition of the first book of the *Ethics,* for:

C'est à la troisième ligne: *Concedetur ergo,* etc. Je ne l'accorde pas; car Paris n'est pas Rome; la boule A n'est pas la boule B; ce sont deux boules, et, par conséquent, deux substances.—Non, dirait l'auteur, ce sont deux boules; mais c'est la même substance, car l'une et l'autre sont étendues.—J'en conviens; *l'idée de l'une convient à l'idée de l'autre; mais elle peut être sans l'autre,* elle peut être conçue sans l'autre.—Oui, dirait-il, mais elle ne peut être conçue sans étendue.—Il est vrai; mais c'est qu'une substance ne peut être conçue sans ce qui la constitue substance.[123]

In conclusion Malebranche affirms that the Cartesian principle, that everything that is conceived clearly and distinctly *is* necessarily, is a principle that holds for pure mathematics, which is conversant only with ideas, but it is not the first principle in physics.[124]

This exchange of letters is most instructive. It shows that for Malebranche there is *first* a real distinction between essence and existence in things; and *second* that existence is the principle of individuation. An essence makes a thing be *what it is,* but it is existence that makes a thing *be.* Malebranche is thus a pluralist as well as a realist. Mairan, on the other hand, maintains that existence is meaningless, that it adds nothing to an essence. For him, the difference between the idea or possible and the concrete or actual is that the former is pure essence, the latter an actualized essence.

Nor must we suppose that this realistic metaphysics of Malebranche, this insistence on the vital distinction between essence and existence, is made by Malebranche for religious reasons. Such is the accusation made by a recent critic, Bridet,[125] and such did Mairan too assert.[126] But the charge is in error, for as Gilson points out in a different application,[127] the distinction between essence and existence cannot be a theological one, inasmuch as many a good Christian theologian, notably Scotus and Suarez, did *not* subscribe to it. He, therefore, who insists upon this vital difference does so for other than theological reasons, for philosophical reasons. In Malebranche's case, we may notice further how well this distinction conforms with his experimental method as treated above. That method is oriented towards getting knowledge of a real world. But, however much one may focus on essences *qua* essences, this does not bring one to what really is. And this is why Malebranche insists that the reality of ideas does not constitute the first principle in physics.

It is often alleged that Malebranche misunderstood Spinoza. He himself admits that he read Spinoza but briefly and only in part.[128] Yet is it not significant that Malebranche should have touched upon the most crucial elements of Spinoza's system—the definition of God, the fifth proposition denying plural substances and the distinction between essence and existence? Is it not likely that Malebranche, having read Suarez, saw only too clearly the dividing line between himself and Spinoza? Spinoza insists that creation is impossible. This is for Malebranche the source of all the errors which he finds in Spinoza. But is not Spinoza's denial of creation the inevitable consequence of the Suarezian metaphysics? Once existence is advanced as a modification of essence and God is affirmed to be an essence that involves existence, then obviously creation is meaningless, and so is any plurality of existents. But for Malebranche creation is no merely dogmatic article of sacrosanct faith. Faith may have provided the origin of that notion and its initial recommendation for serious consideration, but the validity of creation for Malebranche rests on his intuition or vision of God as Being. If God is Being, then the universe cannot but have a beginning in time.[129] But if God is an essence that involves existence, then time and history are meaningless. This is why Malebranche could say that while Spinoza's definition of God taken in one sense is true, in

Essentialism in Spinoza and existence in Malebranche.

Did Malebranche understand Spinoza's God?

another it is false. And this is why in his letters to Mairan he advances so rapidly from the definition of God to the distinction between essence and existence in creatures. For Malebranche they are but two aspects of the same problem.

(c) *Existence the Principle of Individuation.* In God essence and existence are identical because His essence is to be. But the creature is a composite in whom essence and existence are distinct. Such a distinction or *compositum* means two things: *first*, that in every object the existential factor is distinguishable from its own essence; *secondly*, that each object, in virtue of its own being, is distinct from every other object.[130] But this further implies that *it is the existence, not the essence, which properly speaking, is the efficient cause of an object's actuality.* As Malebranche says, and this bears repetition, "ce qui fait qu'un pied cube est distingué de tout autre, c'est son être propre, son existence." Existence *makes* an essence be and be distinct. On the other hand, were there no essence to receive existence, there would be no object. Hence, writes Malebranche, the essence or extension is that which constitutes an object, that is, it is that which determines the nature or state or the what of the object.

Creatures as composites of essence and existence.

Because the distinction between essence and existence is no simple expedient for Malebranche, but a genuine, philosophical position, he can avoid Descartes' predicament of an inert extension, without going to Spinoza. Descartes, as we saw, had a created extension that was an inert mass which in no way could be distinguished from its ideal counterpart. Hence, as Spinoza alleged, Descartes had to seek refuge in God to impose movement upon it.[131] As bare inert created extension, matter was otiose, and the further recourse to God to infuse imposed movement into the inert world was a sheer *tour de force.* Spinoza sought to avoid Descartes' predicament by introducing motion into extension as an infinite mode and thereby to account for the variety of things.[132] However, for Spinoza no attribute of substance can be conceived that makes substance divisible. The attribute of extension, therefore, is not conceived as conceptually involving divisions. Hence the infinite mode of motion after all fails to produce real, distinct separations. Instead it makes the creatures be modes or internal adjectival expressions of a single extension.

Extension, motion and existence.

Malebranche pursued a different route toward individuality. He retained Descartes' view of extension in so far as concerns the idea of extension. Thus with Descartes he asserted that the idea of extension involves an intelligible divisibility. For him number and divisibility are no superficial, abstract, empirical concepts arising from the obscure senses or imagination, as they are for Spinoza.[133] Moreover, the idea of extension as infinitely divisible has full Platonic reality, for Malebranche. Thus he declares to Mairan:

[199]

Pour moi, Monsieur, je conçois clairement dans l'étendue intelligible infinie, une infinité de parties intelligibles; et que, si l'étendue créée n'était qu'une masse informe sans mouvement, il y aurait une infinité de parties différentes dont on pourrait former Paris, Rome, des cubes, des sphères, qui seraient toutes des substances particulières de cette substance infinie, et toutes de même attribut, c'est-à-dire toutes étendues et de même nature, toutes des substances, mais plus ou moins grandes.[134]

Note well the word "parties." Because Malebranche conceives the idea of extension as a continuum of inexhaustible and infinitely divisible parts, as a plenum of *virtual* plural distinctions, he can further conceive any one of those parts as a candidate for real substantiality, provided that God gave it existence. The fact that these different parts share the same attribute is of no moment to him, since it is existence that accounts for *real* distinctions.

On the other hand, if we can perceive the idea of extension as infinitely divisible, it does not follow for Malebranche that in fact actual extension is such. Hence he affirms:

Je sais aussi que l'idée de l'étendue est infinie, que l'esprit ne peut l'épuiser; *mais l'idée de l'étendue n'est pas le monde:* c'est l'idée de la substance étendue, substance dont le souverain Ouvrier, après l'avoir créé, a composé l'univers avec un art infini. Car il lui fallait une substance divisible à l'infini pour perpétuer la génération des animaux et des plantes, sans arrêter le cours uniforme et majestueux de sa Providence.[135]

For Malebranche, in the happy words of Moreau, existence puts a limit in fact to the infinite divisibility of essence.[136] Thus existence can be the principle of individuation, and thus we cannot judge of the circumstances of existence by contemplating the essence. When we conceive of an infinite extension or extension as infinitely divisible, we are considering only the ideal essence of things, not extension as it in fact exists. When existence is conferred upon an essence, then real distinctions, limitations and individuations take place. And hence again he tells Mairan that for a finite entity to exist it requires no other principle of determination but itself:

Je puis concevoir la boule A, et elle peut exister toute seule.—Non, dirait-il, cette boule serait infinie: car qui est-ce qui la terminerait? —Rien, lui dirai-je. Car, pour la terminer, il ne faut rien: il suffit qu'elle soit telle qu'elle est . . . —Mais ne concevez-vous pas que l'étendue est infinie? . . . —Oui, l'idée de l'étendue est infinie; mais cela n'empêche pas que la boule ne soit une substance, une partie de la substance, fût-elle infinie, dont le monde est composé. L'idée de l'étendue est infinie, mais son *ideatum* ne l'est peut-être pas.[137]

But how, scientifically speaking, does existence really individuate and distinguish? Here Malebranche's originality is revealed. He abandons Descartes' view of created extension as an inert mass into which movement is subsequently introduced. When God confers existence upon essence, He at once creates movement itself. To confer existence is simultaneously to confer movement. Movement issues from existence. The two are conjoint or solidary. Do not imagine, says the Word, that God creates bodies and that *thereafter* He communicates to them a moving force to put them into motion.[138] Thus, whereas motion is for Descartes an *ad hoc* afterthought, and whereas Spinoza's immanent dynamism, in the final analysis, renders the modes into a procession of timeless essences that follow from God, for Malebranche movement is very real and dependent upon that act of creation which confers existence.[139]

To summarize, for Malebranche existence is an absolute, conferred upon, but not a modification of, an essence. While it may depend upon God to originate and to conserve it, the existent so engendered is irreducibly unique. Ball A's existence depends upon God's power to   Summary. make it come into being and to continue to be, but this existence of ball A is something intrinsically its own that separates it from everything else. It is a principle of individuation. Objects may share the same nature, essence, attribute or universal. But the factor of existence is singular.

III. EXISTENCE OF CREATURES AND THE IMMENSITY OF GOD

Granted, then, that for Malebranche a creature is a composition of essence and existence and that existence is something added to an essence in the act of creation, what more can we say about existence?   God's How do objects exist? What is it for a thing to be movement? In rais-   immensity. ing these questions, we are obviously not asking for a definition of existence which, we have seen, is for Malebranche *sui generis*. What we seek therefore is not to conceptualize existence but to describe it further.

This, I believe, is precisely the task that Malebranche set himself in the eighth dialogue of the *Entretiens sur la métaphysique*, entitled, "God and His Attributes." It opens with a recapitulation of our direct knowledge of God as Being and an enumeration of His attributes, an enumeration that follows not from a definition of but from a vision of God. Since God is unrestricted Being, He is independent and immutable, for God is independent of the activity of causes.[140] He is also eternal, necessary, and *immense*. But why, asks Aristes, do you call God immense? What do you mean by immense?

> *Theodore.* I mean that the divine substance is everywhere, not only in the universe, but infinitely beyond. For God is not contained in His work—rather is His work in Him and subsists in His substance, which conserves it by its omnipotent power. It is in Him that we have being. It is in Him that we have movement and life, as the Apostle says, *in ipso enim vivimus, movemur et sumus.*[141]

Malebranche is thus asserting, *first* that the immensity of God is that attribute which describes the omnipresence of God; *secondly,* that God's works subsist in His immensity, wherein, *thirdly,* they are conserved by His power.

In the same dialogue, Malebranche goes on to assert that we must be careful to distinguish between ideal or intelligible extension and the divine immensity. For:

Intelligible extension.

The immensity of God is His substance itself spread out everywhere, and all of it is present everywhere, filling all places without local extension . . . Intelligible extension, on the other hand, is only the substance of God in so far as it is representative of bodies, in so far as it is capable of being participated in by them, . . . and which this intelligible extension represents, being their idea or archetype.[142]

Here again we meet with the important distinction between essence and existence, but now the distinction is presented in a new light. Elsewhere, in the *Recherche,* Malebranche says that God knows the natures of things in His reason but that He sees their existence in His will. In the present context in the *Entretiens sur la métaphysique* this dichotomy receives amplification. It seems to me that what Malebranche is doing here is describing not only how existence is produced but the very "stuff" or content of existence. Intelligible extension, constituting the divine reason, represents the essence of things; but the divine immensity which belongs to God's being is the "filling," the "where-of" of existence, that which God communicates when He creates.

It is really misleading to speak of God's immensity as stuff or as something static, however. For Malebranche warns us that this immensity or divine omnipresence is not to be confused with any imaginary space.[143] Perhaps this is an allusion to Newton's 'sensorium' or absolute space. In any case, he makes it clear that this divine immensity is to be taken in a dynamic sense. God is everywhere and everywhere is His entirety, precisely because His immensity is His influence and operation.

> *Theodore.* . . . Do you dare to deny that God is everywhere?

> *Aristes.* He is present through His operation. But—

Theodore. How through His operation? What sort of reality can attach to the operation of God if it be distinguished and separated from His substance? By the operation of God you do not mean the effect which He produces; for the effect is not the action but the termination of the action. By the operation of God you mean apparently the act whereby He operates. But if the act whereby God produces or conserves this chair is here, assuredly God Himself is here; and if He is here, He must be here wholly and entirely, and similarly in all other places where He operates.[144]

Descartes also speaks of the immensity of God as an inexhaustible power or energy.[145] But for Descartes, this divine immensity is equated with *Causa Sui.* The divine immensity is the positive efficient cause or active essence whereby God creates and conserves Himself. God's immensity is thus really reducible to the amplitude or exfoliation of essence. For Malebranche, on the other hand, the divine immensity is derivative from God's Being. Because God is existence, He therefore is an energy that can penetrate, be immanent and operate everywhere at once.

We now have to face a difficult issue. If creatures exist in and through God's immensity, if God is everywhere and the world is in Him, is not Malebranche going far in the direction of Spinoza and of the identification of the world with God? Many critics have alleged that there is a strong pantheistic tendency in Malebranche, and they have made their claim partly because of this view of things existing in God's immensity and partly on the grounds that Malebranche seemingly denies all efficacy to creatures. Thus Ginsberg, for example, writes:

Is immensity consistent with pantheism?

> Malebranche here ignores the proofs furnished by Spinoza of the impossibility of creation consistently with the definition of Substance. And he himself often speaks of finite things as *participations* in the divine substance. It is difficult to see what advantage this word has over the term "mode" or "modification." Participations are, no doubt, distinguished by him from parts, but then Spinoza would never have said that Substance had parts, and indeed he showed clearly that it could have none. All that Malebranche says with regard to the divine immensity applies equally well to Spinoza's notion of Substance. The former term is, in fact, used by Spinoza in the *Cogitata Metaphysica.* The comparison of immensity with eternity and the denial of temporal succession and local extendedness to God find a close parallel in the distinction that Spinoza makes between duration and eternity and his description of quantity, number, etc., as mere aids to the imagination and as not belonging to Substance *sub specie aeternitatis.*[146]

And again Ginsberg claims that, inasmuch as Occasionalism is a view that attributes efficacy to God only, then clearly, "along this line of thought Malebranche's position leads to a thoroughgoing pantheism such as was worked out by Spinoza." [147]

Mr. Ginsberg, like Mr. Church [148] after him, assumes that Malebranche takes refuge in creation as a refuge of ignorance, because Malebranche holds that we do not comprehend causal efficacy. He further assumes that because Malebranche speaks of the world as being in the divine immensity and because the manner of God's creation is not arbitrary, but rational, that therefore Malebranche's doctrine is really Spinozistic. [149] It makes no sense to Ginsberg to speak of creation by a free will. [150] What both Ginsberg and Church do not seem to realize, however, is that Malebranche's metaphysics is intended to justify his method, that unlike Spinoza, he is a firm believer in the necessity of experimentation for scientific knowledge, and that therefore his metaphysics demands contingency. Suppose, accordingly,that we take Malebranche's doctrine of God as Being and as Creator and his distinction between essence and existence as constituting a serious philosophical position, then is divine immensity a concealed Spinozism?

That Malebranche's view on divine immensity bears some resemblance to that of Spinoza goes without saying. Like Spinoza, he too is maintaining that whatever is, is in God, and nothing can be or be conceived apart from God. [151] Nevertheless this resemblance is one of language alone, not of doctrine. Malebranche rejects Spinoza's metaphysics, and with good reason. Spinoza denies creation and the multiplicity of substances. He denies a God whose essence it is to be. His is a God whose essence involves existence; existence for him is a property of essence. And in his finite modes, existence is identical with an actualized essence. [152] Therefore, in Spinoza's system, the modes are functions of a single essence. The *conatus* or power by which each thing endeavors to persevere or do anything or act is "nothing but the *actual* essence." [153]

But Malebranche's God, on the contrary, is Being, not essence. And when He creates, He communicates being, existence, to essence. He makes an essence become an existent. He adds something to an essence that is radically different from it. But what can such a becoming mean, unless the particular existence conferred is in the final result an expression of will and Being? In a system where God is Being, the expression that constitutes finite reality cannot possess the status of an adjective. God as Existence cannot *but* create separate existents. This is why Malebranche is struck with dismay at the impiousness of Spinoza who would reduce God to a collection or aggregate:

. . . How could he have believed that all created beings are but parts or modifications of the Divine? Is it a perfection to be unjust in one's parts, unhappy in one's modifications, ignorant, foolish, impious? . . . What disorder, what a conflict between the divine Being and its parts! What a monstrous, frightful, and ridiculous chimera this is! A God of necessity, hated, blasphemed, despised, or at least ignored by the majority of all beings! . . . A God of necessity, unhappy or unfeeling, throughout the greater number of His parts or modifications, a God who punishes Himself, and avenges Himself upon Himself—in a word, an infinitely perfect Being, who is nevertheless composed of all the disorders in the universe! [154]

In point of fact, as Brunschvicg shows, Spinoza does not reduce God to an aggregate.[155] But Malebranche cannot even begin to understand the unity of Spinoza's God, since to him God is not essence but Being; and creation is not the self-determination of an essence, but the communication of Being into beings. This is why for Malebranche, as for Aquinas, the creature is an analogue, a likeness of God. To be an analogue is to be like God but still distinct from Him.

As a matter of fact, I sometimes suspect that Malebranche deliberately "misrepresented" Spinoza's position in the above passage, rather than misunderstood him. He could have misrepresented him in the sense that Malebranche's objective here is to stress poignantly and eloquently the existential, historical reality of creatures, as opposed to Spinoza's logical universe where the finite mode vanishes when perceived *sub species aeternitatis*. For Malebranche, who believes in creation, duration is no crutch to the imagination. Thus when Malebranche talks of things as being *united* with God or when he talks of God's presence in things, he never construes that union or presence in terms of organic identity. There is union, because there is separateness and difference, and union does not reduce to identity.

Granted that Malebranche's notions of Being and Creation are, opposite to Spinoza, pluralistic and communicative, how shall we interpret the divine immensity? M. Gilson's exegesis on Thomism is of help here. Gilson makes three statements regarding the God of St. Thomas that are useful for understanding Malebranche.

First, God's action is compared by Aquinas to *sunlight.* Just as the sun is the cause of brightness in the air, so God is the cause of existence. But just as brightness never gets permeated with air, never can remain in the air if light is removed, so God's will is required to maintain a thing in existence. As Gilson so forcefully puts it: "God does not grant things an existence which they could keep, be it only for one moment, if He suddenly ceased to give it. . . . Existence has no root in even actually existing things." [156] Thus existence is *in* the world, like light in the air at noon— ". . . But the existence of the world never is *its* existence." [157] We can consequently see that for Aquinas God's

Immensity interpreted as Malebranche's account of particular existence.

[205]

being and will and power, according to Gilson, must be omnipresent and everpresent for the creature to exist.

Secondly, Aquinas speaks of this omnipotent presence of God and light as an *influx*. As light pours brilliance into the air, so God penetrates and fills the creature with existence. Existence is breathed into it.[158]

Finally, this existence, this "to be" which the creature receives from God's influx is described as an act of existence. To be is to act, to exert causal action, although not to create.[159] It is by this reception of an act of existence that, in St. Thomas' words, "Each and every created being shares, so to speak, in the nature of existence: *quodcumque ens creatum participat, ut ita dixerim, naturam essendi.*" On this, M. Gilson comments: "which of course does not mean that 'to be' is itself a nature, and still less that it *has* a nature, but that, as Saint Anselm had already said, God is the very *natura essendi* in which each and every being, so to speak, participates." [160] The Thomistic Deity is thus, in this way, both immanent and transcendent.

Now Malebranche, we saw, insists upon distinguishing essence from existence. Moreover, in his theory of ideas, he explicitly refers to Aquinas on this point. In the letters to Mairan too he argues that existence *makes* the actuality of an object. Further, Malebranche insists that from essences we can not deduce existence, or anything whatever regarding the *circumstances* of existence. Lastly, he distinguishes intelligible extension from God's immensity and he talks of that immensity as an *influence*.

Given all these elements, plus the fact that God for Malebranche is quite explicitly *Celui qui est*, is it not likely that his doctrine of divine immensity is far removed from that of Spinoza? May it not even be that Malebranche employs the notion of divine immensity to describe just what it is for a thing to be and how it is? Let us take a step further. Inasmuch as he attributes the division between essence and existence to Aquinas, is it not possible that, notwithstanding his strictures against substantial forms and his opposition to the Peripatetic epistemology, he may nevertheless have felt that no real difference exists between himself and Thomas in the sphere of metaphysics? Just as the early Descartes felt no opposition between himself and Bacon on method and therefore readily incorporated Baconian elements, so may it not be that Malebranche's view on God's immensity is in the tradition of Augustine and of Aquinas?

This suggestion seems to me all the more probable for the following reasons. Gilson asserts that between Augustine and Aquinas there is no real conflict on the role of God in nature. "St. Augustine's God does nothing that St. Thomas' God does not, and the Thomist creature can do no more without God's aid than the Augustinian creature can." [161]

The difference between Augustine and Aquinas is not a doctrinal difference but rather a matter of degree or emphasis. Philosophically both agree on the exclusive creative character of God's power and both agree that the natural world, being an analogue of God, is endowed with efficacy or potency. However, Thomas' Deity is more generous than that of Augustine, for Thomas's God saturates nature with causality.

In addition to the support that we can find in Gilson, we have further evidence to be found in the testimony of the eminent French critic, M. Henri Gouhier, who has written extensively on Malebranche's theology. On the problem of grace, M. Gouhier points out, Malebranche carefully distinguishes between "Thomists" and St. Thomas. With his dislike for erudition, Malebranche apparently did not read Thomas extensively. On this particular matter he cites Aquinas only twice. For, Gouhier states, "Aux yeux de Malebranche . . . saint Thomas est le disciple de saint Augustin." When Malebranche attacks the Thomists, "il est manifeste que Malebranche ne pense pas à saint Thomas; le vrai saint Thomas comme le vrai saint Augustin est celui qui n'admet pas la grâce invincible . . ." [162] Thus with respect to this crucial theological dilemma as to whether divine grace is wholly invincible or whether man's will has the power to accept or resist, Malebranche rejects Jansenism and accepts the view of man's free will.

Inasmuch, then, as Malebranche saw Thomas as the true disciple of Augustine and inasmuch as Gilson finds no more than a difference of degree between their respective metaphysical systems, is it not probable that with his view of God's immensity Malebranche is adhering to the Augustinian-Thomistic doctrine? Augustine speaks thus of God in his *Confessions:*

Particulars exist by participation in God's immensity.

. . . Is there anything in me, O God, that can contain You? All heaven and earth cannot contain You for You made them, and me in them. Yet, since nothing that is could exist without You, You must in some way be in all that is . . . [163]

But if You fill heaven and earth, do they contain You? Or do You fill them, and yet have much over since they cannot contain You? Is there some other place into which that overplus of You pours that heaven and earth cannot hold? . . . It is true that all things cannot wholly contain You: but does this mean that they contain part of You? . . . Are You not in every place at once in the totality of Your being, while yet nothing contains You wholly? [164]

Could any man be his own maker? Or is there any other channel through which being and life should flow into us, save that we are made by You, Lord, to whom "being" and "being alive" are not two separate things, since infinite Being is identical with infinite Life? For You are infinite and in You is no change, nor does today pass away in You. Yet in another sense in You it does pass away, for in You are all such things—they could not even have any being that could pass away unless You upheld them in being. And because Your years do not pass, Your years are today; and no matter how many our days and our fathers' days have been, they have all passed in Your undying day and from it have received such being and measures as they had . . .[165]

God is in each thing, because that is what creation means—the giving of Himself to each thing. As for the statement that things are in God, rather than God in the world, I interpret this to mean that while God is indeed present wholly and entirely in each creature, nevertheless each is entirely separate from every other, and no one creature or collection of them is equal to the Being of God. A work of art, as I said before, receives the full character, spirit and vision of the artist, for what else can it be? Again, the philosophical intuition of a thinker, say of Bergson, is completely present in each of his works. Yet each of his books has a life, message, an *élan*, an existence of its own; still, the entire aggregate falls far short of that philosopher's vision. Each is limited in extent; and no one of them really lives apart from the philosopher's impetus. For these reasons, would it not be more apt to describe the works of this philosopher as living in him than he in them?

I suggest accordingly that we interpret Malebranche's doctrine of God's immensity not apart from or despite his theory of creation, but in the light of that theory. If we do so, the divine immensity can serve to explain the "circumstances of existence," that is, what it means for a thing to be. For a thing *to be* is to receive God's presence, His Being

Immensity interpreted in the light of Malebranche's philosophy of creation.

and immense power; that is, the sensible world exists by participation in the divine immensity. Malebranche is claiming that for an essence to become concrete or for a body to exist or to be, it must dwell in or share of divine Being and immensity. The nature or essence of body is extension, and this consists in relations of distance. This nature can be known in God's reason, the realm of ideas. But for this nature to be, to exist, to be actual, it not only requires God's will to create and conserve it, but also requires that existence be added. This addition means that this very divine will should confer or *constitute* its being. Not only is God's will the *originating* creative, efficient cause of the being of objects, but His immensity is the "material" cause as well—it is the very being of their being, their "natura essendi."

This immensity which establishes the metaphysical sameness and equality of all existents does not preclude the greatest possible variety in their details. God's immensity, declares Malebranche, is immutable, indivisible, unchangeable. Yet this immensity is described as being everywhere, at all times, and as a whole in any one place or time. Just as Spinoza asserts that each attribute completely, though not exhaus-

tively, expresses the entire essence of God, so Malebranche maintains
that within each finite entity God is completely and wholly present.
Thus he says that God is in this chair and at the same time and wholly
in the heavens. This is possible, proclaims Malebranche, precisely because God is not corporeal; hence He is not confined by any temporal
or local limitations.[166] But, we saw, Malebranche also says against
Spinoza that the earth is not the sky, Paris is not Rome, ball A is not
ball B. To me this is meaningful only on the assumption that God's
will, however simple and indivisible, is nevertheless not a bare homo-
geneity, but one which encompasses and expresses itself in the greatest possible heterogeneity and difference. In which case, every object
and each body may be viewed as a total and unique embodiment of
the divine will. Each grain of dust involves and presents and discloses
the whole substance and will of God, although no one thing exhausts
its infinite richness, designated by the term immensity. Each thing is
replete and wholly filled by God, and yet each is only a participation
and hence a limited, partial and separate expression.[167] To exist is to
share in God's will and Being.

We are back therefore at the crucial question: having taken the position that God is He who is and that creation is self-communication,
what is the status of an *existent?* Unless we assume that Malebranche **Rejection of**
was philosophically inept or else blatantly inconsistent, it seems to me **pantheism.**
that we must assume that his pronouncements against the efficacy of
creatures are not intended to reduce them into utter non-entities; and
that his doctrine of divine immensity and his very conception of God
do in fact establish the creature as genuinely an act of existence. For
if a body, like a chair, dwells within the immensity of God, if it is
created and conserved by God's will, may we not then infer that the
very being of such a body lies in its participation of God's Being? And
what is God's Being? It is, we saw, the pure act of existing; it is caual-
ity itself. Is it not likely, then, that what constitutes the being or actual
existence of an object as distinct from its ideal nature, lies in this crucial
difference—as an essence, it does nothing; but as an existent the object
is an activity, a potency, a will?

If this interpretation be correct, and no other fits the entire corpus of
Malebranche's writings, then Occasionalism must be viewed in a new
light.

IV. OCCASIONALISM

(*a*) *"True" Efficacy.* In his rejection of the efficacy of secondary
causes, Malebranche asserts that causality is a divine characteristic,
and since there is only one true God, there can be only one true cause.
Secondary causes then are merely the occasions for the display of

divine power. Malebranche has been vehemently denounced for this doctrine. His critics, including M. Gilson,[168] have been eager to point out that he too-readily sacrifices the finite creature for the sake of glorifying God. Some, on the other hand, contend that Malebranche cannot consistently hold that God does everything, inasmuch as the second cause, occasional though it be, nevertheless is said by him *to determine* divine efficacy.[169] Are these adverse criticisms justified? I hold that in a very significant sense they are not.

To understand Malebranche's views, we must move slowly and step by step from his crucial doctrine of God as Being. Failure to take this key notion as fundamental has been responsible for the widespread misunderstanding of his Occasionalism and the attendant bitter attacks upon Malebranche. In the present section of this chapter I shall show that there are three stages or moments in Malebranche's doctrine of Occasionalism, all dependent on his view of God as Being. First, there is the notion of *creation:* the occasional cause does not create. Second, the occasional cause does *not* act in virtue of an *essence* or form. Third, the occasional cause *does act,* but its power to act is derivative from God's will and requires the continuous sustaining presence of that will. These three elements are constantly intermingled in Malebranche's arguments, so that when he opposes the efficacy of creatures, the subtlety of these distinctions is not always apparent. If we can understand them clearly, however, Malebranche's Occasionalism assumes a new and impressive cogency.

There is only one true God; hence there is only one true cause—we must begin to treat the nature of the occasional cause by repeating this statement. I propose now to show that whenever Malebranche thus speaks of God as the sole and "true" cause, he has in mind the special meaning of creativity that follows from his view of Being. Malebranche's Deity, be it recalled, is infinitely infinite Being. He is not a god among gods, not the first among a plethora of beings. He is, on the contrary, simply Being: *Celui qui est* or the *Ego sum qui sum* of *Exodus.* As such, God is perfect, infinite, and one; not a collection or addition of beings, but a complete unity; immutable, unrestricted and unchanging. He is divine existence *per se.*

"True" efficacy and creativity.

Certain corollaries of this conception of Being follow in the case of Malebranche, as they do for the entire Christian tradition. If solely God is Being, if only in Him are essence and existence the same, if He alone exists *per se,* then nothing else can be eternal or necessary. All else must be contingent; that is, whatever else exists must have its being, nature and origin dependent upon and derivative from God. God is the cause not only of the nature of things, but of their very being and existence. According to Gilson, for the Christian philosopher, God as Being therefore implies that God alone is the Creator. Plato's god is, in contrast, an artificer, but not a creator; Aristotle's god is a mover but not the creator of the long series of movers. ". . . The first principle of all being, as Plato and Aristotle conceived it, integrally explains indeed why the universe is what it is, but does not explain why it is." Contrariwise, in the philosophy of which Gilson is speaking, "the pure and simple production of being is the action proper to Being itself." Aristotle and Plato failed to arrive at the notion of creation, for the reason that both lacked the view of God as *Ego sum qui sum.*[170]

Now, I am not concerned here with the validity of Gilson's present contention that the Greek and Christian views of Being basically differ in this fundamental respect. What is of concern is that this very difference *is* the source of Malebranche's denial of the efficacy of secondary causes. If we make a judicious and impartial examination of the various writings in which Malebranche attacks the attribution of efficacy to secondary causes, there can be no doubt that creationism is the issue. There can be no doubt, further, that the philosophical enemies against whom he is writing are Aristotle in particular and the Greeks in general. And finally, he is writing against any philosopher, such as Suarez or Descartes, who fails to distinguish between essence and existence, or who would somehow or other reduce existence to essence. Let us glance then at some of the basic writings in which inefficacy is the issue, or rather, at the major arguments given over and over in the various writings.

First there is the familiar argument based on the definition of causality: a true cause is such that between it and its effect the mind perceives a necessary connection. Because no such necessity is apparent between matters of finite fact, such as one ball hitting another, therefore one is not the true cause of the other. But we have already seen that in employing this demonstration, Malebranche is simply rejecting the assumption that finite existents have true efficacy in the sense of creative potency. No creature is its own being or existence, as God is. Hence neither can it confer existence on any other, nor any mode of being, such as actual motion. Ball A is not requisite to the existence and operation of ball B, because it is not the creator of B.

Malebranche's arguments for inefficacy of creatures: (1) No necessary connections between creatures.

Second, when Malebranche talks of God as alone the Creator, he equates this with the claim that God alone is motor. Since God alone can create, He alone can move.[171] But this should offer no difficulty. Creation of unorganized bodies takes place through generation and corruption, that is, through motion:

(2) Creatures do not originate motion.

> Il est constant que c'est par le mouvement des corps visibles ou invisibles que toutes choses se produisent, car l'expérience nous apprend que les corps dont les parties ont plus de mouvement sont toujours ceux qui agissent davantage et qui produisent plus de changement dans le monde.[172]

If God alone creates, He alone is the genuine cause of motion itself. This is why not even the human or angelic will can be the *true* cause of movement in a body. For if an angel were a true cause, then it would be capable of creation and annihilation.[173] Hence, when Malebranche insists that it is inconceivable and contradictory for God to communicate power to creatures, it is always with the reservation that God cannot make *true* or creative causes:

> Je dis de plus qu'il n'est pas concevable que Dieu puisse communiquer aux hommes ou aux anges la puissance qu'il a de remuer les corps, et que ceux qui prétendent que *le pouvoir* que nous avons de remuer nos bras est une véritable puissance, doivent avouer que Dieu peut aussi donner aux esprits la puissance de créer, d'anéantir, de faire toutes les choses possibles, en un mot qu'il peut les rendre tout-puissants . . .[174]

Clearly what is at stake here is the power to create motion.

This aspect is especially well brought out in his reply to Suarez in the fifteenth Eclaircissement. Absurd it is indeed, writes Malebranche, to have recourse to God for the explanation of particular effects. How ridiculous it would be to say that God dries the earth or turns water into ice. Particular causes must be given for particular effects. But:

> . . . lorsqu'en raisonnant on est enfin venu à un effet général dont on cherche la cause, c'est encore fort mal philosopher, que d'en imaginer quelque autre que la générale . . . Par exemple, quand on demande d'où vient qu'il y a des corps en mouvement, ou d'où vient que l'air agité communique son mouvement à l'eau, ou plutôt d'où vient que les corps se poussent les uns les autres; comme le mouvement et sa communication est un effet général dont tous les autres dépendent, il est nécessaire, je ne dis pas pour être chrétien, mais pour être philosophe, de recourir à Dieu, qui est la cause universelle.[175]

It is to God that one must turn rather than, like the pagan, to some blind nature, first mover, or universal soul.

Malebranche is here obviously moving on the plane of existence itself. He is asking for the cause of the very being of movement. This only the God of *Exodus* can explain.[176]

Again, we have the argument based on Descartes' description of extension. "Pour juger de l'efficace des créatures, il faut rentrer en soi-même et consulter leurs idées: et si l'on peut découvrir dans leurs idées quelque force ou quelque vertu, il faut la leur attribuer: car il faut attribuer aux êtres ce que l'on conçoit clairement être renfermé dans les idées qui les représentent." [177] If we examine the clear idea of body, however, says Malebranche, we find in it no idea of power, or more specifically, of self-movement:

(3) No efficacy intrinsic to ideas (or essences) of bodies.

Écoute-moi: un corps petit ou grand, carré ou rond, ou si tu le veux, blanc ou noir, froid ou chaud, peut-il se mouvoir par lui-même? *Ne dis que ce que tu conçois. . . . Dans l'idée que tu as de la matière y découvres-tu quelque puissance?* [178]

But what does this argument really prove? What it proves is that existence is not reducible to an *essence*, or derivable from one. No power is to be found in the *idea* of a body.

Descartes, we have repeatedly noted, makes no genuine distinction between essence and existence in creatures, but only a distinction of reason. In this, we saw, he is following Suarez, according to whom the essence of a thing not only makes it be what it is, but makes it really be. In other words, that a thing *is* and *acts* comes wholly from *what* it is. Now in the fifteenth Éclaircissement, as we shall soon see, Malebranche unambiguously opposes that doctrine and mentions Suarez by name, as well as some later Scholastics who apparently followed Suarez's doctrine. The fact, then, that Malebranche utilizes Descartes' notion of passive extension to show that creatures are impotent does not prove that as existents they are altogether powerless, inert nonentities. All it proves, on the contrary, is that the essence of body, its nature, its *what*, consists in relations of distance, and therefore, such being the case, mere quantitative relationships cannot confer actuality on an object, or even its motion which is a way of being or of existence. Malebranche is thus using Descartes' own notion of extension as a weapon against Descartes himself. He is refusing to identify the nature of bodies with the conditions of their existence. If essences were active forces or potencies, then they would be instrumental causes of their own existence and action. No longer would God be the sole true creator of existence.[179]

Malebranche's polemic against the efficacy of secondary causes occurs throughout his writings, but it is to the fifteenth Éclaircissement that we must turn for a proper understanding of the arraignment. For here Malebranche reveals the names of his opponents. Among these are Suarez and philosophers cited by Suarez, such as Scotus, Paludan, Perer, Aristotle. In addition he briefly mentions and rejects the opinions of Avicenna, Fonseca, Rubio, Averroes. The significant question is quite specific, that of creation or of the relation of essence and existence. For our purposes it is fortunate that we have the independent research of M. Gilson on this issue, and I shall accept his account of the attitudes of the more notable figures, Avicenna, Scotus, Suarez, as definitive. We know that for them the actuality of a real essence requires no separate existential act in order to become an existential actuality.[180] We know that for them existence is an accident or appendix of essence, that essence and being are identical. We know that for a disciple of Suarez the essence is: "'the root, or the innermost bottom

(4) The major attack on efficacy of creatures in the fifteenth Éclaircissement.

and the first principle of all the activity as well as of all the properties of things.'" [181] But we also know that *Malebranche* carefully distinguishes between essence and existence. In the light of this knowledge, let us follow Malebranche's discussion on the inefficacy of creatures as given in this éclaircissement.

The inquiry opens with the declaration that God and His operations are hidden from the senses. Hence, even though the mind encounters God at all moments and even though it is He alone who produces and conserves all beings, the mind has difficulty in recognizing Him. Hence some philosophers, rather than make a serious effort to acknowledge "la main de celui qui fait tout en toutes choses," [182] prefer to worship a blind *nature* and *faculties* as the cause of natural effects. Thus far Malebranche is simply reiterating his opposition to a pagan philosophy that does not adore the true God as the Maker and Creator.

But now follows a discussion of the variety of conflicting opinions among those who attribute true power to secondary causes. Some philosophers, writes Malebranche, and here he refers us to the text of Suarez,[183] assert that secondary causes act by their matter; some say by their substantial forms; others claim that it is by their accidents; some say that accidents derive their power or causal influence from the form; some assert that accidents are instrumental causes only, but these men explain neither what they mean by an instrumental cause nor the nature of that power that it receives from the principal cause. Moreover, philosophers do not even agree on the action by which secondary causes produce their effects. Some allege that *causality* is not something that can be produced, since it produces. Others claim that secondary causes act truly by their own action. "Voilà une grande variété de sentiments," Malebranche exclaims, "quoique je n'aie point rapporté ceux des philosophes anciens ou qui sont nés dans des pays fort éloignés." [184] What all these opinions have in common, it seems apparent, is that they are the opinions of essentialists. Either, like Suarez, these are writers who make forms or natures the source of efficacy or else they are those who maintain that causality needs no explanation, that creatures are by themselves true causes. But for Malebranche the true cause is God, the creator, and He alone explains existence itself.

When Malebranche next turns to the "ancients," among these he singles out for rejection Avicenna, Averroes, Aristotle and a man named Rubio. The latter's views, as presented by Malebranche, are especially worth noting. According to Malebranche,

Il prétend que Dieu produit immédiatement une substance spirituelle très parfaite, que celle-ci en produit une autre moins parfaite, et celle-ci une troisième, et ainsi de suite jusqu'à la dernière, laquelle produit toutes les substances corporelles, et les substances corporelles produisent les accidents.[185]

Here we are transported back again to the sphere of the abstractionists, to Plotinian emanations or to an Aristotelian series of movers.

After examining these ancient and modern philosophers, Malebranche concludes that the power of creatures is but a fiction of the mind, whereupon he once again sets out to show that only God "fait tout en toutes choses." Only God is the *true* cause of motion; only He can create and annihilate.[186]

Now is it not apparent, from the views he cites, that the basic issues in Malebranche's attack on secondary causes are creationism and its concomitant essentialism?[187] Why should he not assert that efficacy is a fiction when its exponents are Suarez and others who do not distinguish between essence and existence! It has been said that in the seventeenth century Scholasticism meant Suarez. And my point is that in attacking secondary causes, Malebranche is evidently rejecting a particular, partisan view of Thomism. Notice that in this condemnation the name of St. Thomas is never mentioned. Is this an accidental oversight, or can it be that here, as in his theology, he again distinguishes between St. Thomas and Thomists?[188] On the one occasion when he does refer to Aquinas, it is in a footnote against Aristotle's claim, mentioned by Aquinas, that "sol et homo generant hominem."[189]

Again and again, then, Malebranche's opposition to efficiency centers about creation. God, says Malebranche, has no need of instruments. He alone is efficacious. To assume that God endows objects with forms that can create and move is idolatry. This argument is first developed by Malebranche in Book Six, Part Two, Chapter Three of the *Recherche*, entitled, "On the Most Dangerous Error in the Philosophy of the Ancients." The fifteenth Éclaircissement is intended to do no more than amplify this statement. After all, if God alone creates by His will, and if movement is the source of all effects, what need is there to postulate specific natures or forms to explain the existence or action of things? Some philosophers, notably Suarez, would object that without forms and natures as "inner principles of action," living things could not be distinguished from non-living, or the action of fire from water.[190] Malebranche rejoins that it is God's will that animates and vivifies all things: ". . . C'est sa volonté qui est la force mouvante des corps, et qui fait aussi la communication de leurs mouvements."[191] This statement occurs immediately after Malebranche's denial of a first mover or universal soul as the general cause for natural effects. Hence, read in that context, it simply reasserts the fact that creation belongs exclusively to God.

Still and all, why not say that form describes a palpable fact, namely, that bodies once created can, so to speak, exist by their own power?

Inefficacy of creatures means creatures not creative.

Existence
never belongs
to creatures
in their own
right: Creation
and conserva-
tion.

Malebranche can no more accept such a view than can either Augustine or Aquinas. May I avail myself once more of M. Gilson's independent commentary on this issue: he observes that for the Christian, creatures cannot have creative efficacy because they have no independent
existence. Therefore their *esse* or nature does not imply 'to be.' Hence
they have no power to produce being. Moreover, existence, once be-
gotten, still never belongs to objects in their own right. If 'to exist'
meant something inalienable from the object, then to destroy the object God would require a positive will to non-being. Existence is continually dependent on God, therefore, for recreation. And this is not
continual rebirth at each moment, since it is a continuation of the same
will.[192]

This is precisely the position that Malebranche adopts. Says the
Word in the *Méditations chrétiennes:* You imagine that divine creation is comparable to human fabrication. You imagine that after God
has created a body, He can leave it *to itself,* that having been made, it
can continue to subsist *by itself.* When man makes an artifact, that
object can subsist without any further labor on man's part. However,
human and divine action are not comparable, *for men do not give
being to the matter that they fashion;* they find it made. But God
makes all and presupposes nothing. Hence a body exists, because God
wills it to be; and it continues because God continues to will that it be.

> Car si ce corps continuait d'être, quoique Dieu eût cessé de vouloir
> qu'il fût, il serait indépendant: mais tellement indépendant que
> Dieu ne pourrait plus l'anéantir. Afin que Dieu pût anéantir ce
> corps, il foudrait que Dieu pût vouloir que ce corps ne fût point:
> il foudrait que Dieu fût capable d'avoir une volonté, dont le néant
> serait le terme. Or le néant n'a rien de bon ni rien d'aimable. Dieu
> ne peut donc l'aimer ou le vouloir d'une volonté positive.[193]

In the *Entretiens sur la métaphysique,* it will be recalled, Aristes asks
Theodore: granted that things are dependent on God, is it not a sufficient mark of dependency that God can destroy them whenever He
pleases? No, replies Theodore, for, "What greater mark of independence is there than *unaided* self-subsistence?" [194]

These last passages are remarkable, not only for showing to what
extent creationism is the real issue in Malebranche's attack on secondary causes, but also because they contain elements that will be of
help in understanding to what extent creatures *are* potent.

In the fifteenth Éclaircissement, Malebranche develops the notion of
conservation, which we are now considering, in a very interesting way.

Meaning of
divine
concourse.

Remember that in the Scotist or Suarezian metaphysics creation means
the actualization of an essence and it is the essence that makes a thing
be. Accordingly, creation and conservation amount to no more than

this: God concurs with an essence in its becoming realized and in its operations. But in Malebranche's metaphysics, God by His will breathes existence upon an essence and what He conserves or sustains is this act of existence.

Thus at one and the same time Malebranche attacks the Scholastic notion of divine "concurrence" and yet tries to show that his own position is compatible with that doctrine.[195] First he criticizes the principle of divine concurrence as being equivocal and ambiguous. It is ambiguous for two reasons: It suggests either that the world, once created, can, so to speak, stand on its own and survive unaided and by itself, or else that the action by which creatures operate is derivative from essence and is thus different in character from the divine will:

> La plupart des hommes s'imaginent que Dieu a créé d'abord toutes choses, et qu'il leur a donné toutes les qualités ou facultés nécessaires pour leur conservation, qu'il a, par exemple, donné le premier mouvement à la matière, et qu'ensuite il l'a laissée à elle-même produire par la communication de ses mouvements, cette variété de formes que nous admirons.[196]

On the other hand, Malebranche is quite ready to accept the notion of divine concourse, provided that all "essential" intermediaries between God and the creature are removed. Once it is granted that God alone is truly the immoveable mover, then, says Malebranche, I am prepared to say that bodies act with the concourse of God, for then the body's action is immediately derivative from and dependent upon God's will.[197] Theologians say that the action of secondary causes is not different from the action by which God concurs with them. They allege that God acts in creatures by the same action as do the creatures. This, they are indeed obliged to believe:

> . . . car si les créatures agissaient par une action que Dieu ne fît point en elles, leur action comme action efficace, serait, ce semble, indépendante; or ils croient, comme ils le doivent, que les créatures dépendent immédiatement de Dieu, non seulement quant à leur être, mais aussi quant à leur opération.[198]

Herein, then, lies the secret of Malebranche's opposition to efficacy in the creature. He does not deny that the creature can and does act. What he does deny is that this action is ever anything that the creature possesses in its own right or nature, or that it can exercise independently or apart from the divine presence that immediately, directly and continually sustains it. Theologians who appeal to divine concourse do so out of deference to Aristotle who "croit que Dieu ne se mêle point du détail de ce qui se passe sous le *concave* du ciel de la lune . . . et que la *nature* qu'il suppose dans tous les corps, suffit pour produire tout ce qui se fait ici bas." [199]

Le *concours simultané* n'a été introduit dans la Théologie qu'après coup, je veux dire que pour rendre plus supportable ce préjugé des sens, ou ce principe de la Philosophie des Païens, que la nature et les lois naturelles sont différent de l'efficace et des volontés générales du Créateur.[200]

Like the ancient prophets, Malebranche is ceaselessly and continually warring against idolatry, against the substitution of nature for God. The vulgar majority, he poignantly complains, are ready to recognize God in extraordinary situations, but they worship nature in their daily lives.[201] But it is not nature whom man should fear, adore, and love. It is not nature that is his source of joy and nourishment. It is not nature that regulates the seasons. Nor is it nature and God, but God alone: [202] *Soli Deo honor et gloria.*[203] Yet God, be it remembered, created the world for His glory; created it so that the world and man share in that glory. Thus far we have concentrated primarily on the divine. It is now time to consider the creature itself. But before we continue to explore those writings in which Malebranche expresses the power of creatures in even more striking and positive terms than we have yet encountered, I would like to make a relevant digression.

It may be asked: Is it not a perceived fact that bodies act on one another and that minds act on bodies? To such a query the Word in the *Méditations chrétiennes* replies that while the senses are adequate guides with respect to facts, neither external senses nor internal senses reveal any *true* power in bodies or in minds.[204] For, assuming that bodies are *true* causes, how will they know in which direction to move, with what speed? If a body meets another, what will it do, not knowing the opponent's size or weight? So with minds. When we examine the idea we have of all finite minds, we see no necessary connection between their will and the movement of any body whatever, and on the contrary, we see that there is no such connection and that there can be none.[205] Why does Malebranche exclude necessity from minds? For the same reason as from bodies. To perceive necessity is to apprehend a creative influence. How can we move our arm?—he asks. To move it we have to have animal spirits; we have to dispatch them via certain nerves to certain muscles in order to extend and contract them, for it is thus that the arm is moved. Hence the effort of will cannot be the true cause of moving our body.[206]

We cannot perceive true power by the senses.

Now, with respect to the will, it has been pointed out against Hume, who but repeats Malebranche, that it is not necessary to be a physiologist and anatomist in order to move the body. And as a matter of fact, Malebranche himself acknowledges this. Men who do not even know whether they have spirits, nerves or muscles, move their arms, he says, and do so with greater address and facility than the most

knowing anatomists.[207] Mr. Church maintains that in this admission
Malebranche is in flat contradiction with himself. The fact that certain physiological conditions connected with bodily movements are unknown, says Church, ". . . is to emphasize our ignorance of the conditions of volition, it is not to demonstrate the impotence of the will." [208]
I would agree with Church that Malebranche is in contradiction with
himself and that the criticisms against Hume and Malebranche are
well taken, provided that Malebranche and Hume are saying the same
thing. But if, as I claim, Malebranche is arguing against creative
powers in the will, then the criticism is unjust, when applied against
Malebranche.[209] *Of course a creator needs to be a competent geometer
and physiologist!* Of course he has to know the movements of the
animal spirits and an infinity of details, if he is to create them out of
nothing and conserve them continually. Hence the fact that the will,
in moving an arm, has no knowledge of its bodily conditions shows
again that the will is not the *true* or principal cause. Whether it is a
cause in some other sense we shall treat when we come to consider
the "occasional" cause proper. The important point is to realize once
and for all that power and efficacy, taken strictly, can mean only one
thing: creation. And this is precisely why the Word declares that we
must carefully distinguish our internal awareness of effort, Hume's
animal nisus, from efficacy: But dost thou not often feel that thine
efforts are powerless? Effort, then, is one thing, and efficacy is another.[210] Indeed, if our efforts were creative, they would never fail.
Our very failures indicate that our will is not a creative one.

In all these writings, then, Malebranche is rejecting the view that
anything other than God possesses creative power—the power, that is,
to confer existence, being, or the various modes of being, such as motion. Yet if God alone is creative, does this necessarily imply that the
creature is wholly passive, inert, and destitute of all power or activity?
No one can deny that Malebranche's language in which he describes
the utter dependency of the world upon God is frequently so eloquent
in behalf of God that one can understandably conclude that the finite
entity is left completely bereft of any sort of activity. So often does
he say that we have no idea of power, that the door to Hume seems
wide open.

Is the creature, then, totally inert?

Yet again caution is required. Concerning the utter dependency of
the world upon God, so good a Thomist as M. Gilson himself asserts:

> As soon as the sensible world is regarded as the result of a creative
> act, which not only gives it existence but conserves it in existence
> through all successive moments of its duration, it becomes so utterly
> dependent as to be struck through with contingency down to the
> very roots of its being.[211]

Again, he says:

> Nothing exists, nothing develops, nothing acts, but it receives exist-ence, development and efficiency from the motionless subsistence of the Infinite Being.[212]

> . . . Contingent beings are never more than second causes; they are no more than second beings. Their causal activity is strictly limited to the transmission of modes of being and to the alteration of the dispositions of the subjects on which they act; *it can never go so far as to cause the very existence of the effects produced,* and, in a word, *homo faber* can never become *homo creator* . . .[213]

Gilson evidently feels that there is no contradiction in these statements. On the one hand the sensible is through and through dependent upon God for its existence and for its modes of existence, while, on the other hand, finite beings are none the less described as active—their very ex-istence is described in terms of energy and this very activity is itself dependent upon God. Elsewhere Gilson says God is Be-ing, creativity; and therefore in conferring existence He confers not indeed the power to create being but its analogue, the power to transmit and thereby produce or generate being.[214]

Now my claim is that there is nothing in Occasionalism which is re-pugnant to this doctrine. In fact, Malebranche's occasional cause which determines the divine efficacy is active in the very sense signified by Gilson.

(*b*) *Malebranche, the Alarmist.* To be sure, Aquinas expresses the dynamic character of created things in language that is unambiguous and clear-cut, whereas in the case of Malebranche, the opposite is the case. For the latter, the extent of God's omnipotence is clear and that of the power of the universe is ambiguous. This is because Aquinas and Malebranche are writing in different eras and are therefore con-fronted with different problems. Malebranche himself insists that to understand an author we must read him in the milieu in which he wrote.[215] We must understand his problems and his opponents. At the time of Aquinas perhaps it was not God but nature that needed em-phasis. But in the seventeenth century, God's role was in jeopardy. A brief glance at the climate of opinion in the era of the Great Renewal makes it clear that, beginning with Copernicus, Kepler and Galileo, up to and including Newton, God was becoming less and less operative in the world described by the successive thinkers. While no one in the century (except Hobbes, who makes His existence depend upon the fiat of the magistrate) is quite ready to dispense with God as is La-place in the nineteenth century, nevertheless the Deity of the new sci-ence is not the living, breathing, vital and moral Spirit of the Bible.

Changing cli-mate of opinion regarding God in the 17th century.

I cannot forgive Descartes, Pascal writes,[216] for trying to dispense with God, after according him a fillip to put the world in motion.

God in the seventeenth century is, on the whole, either an architect of a fashionable, neatly contrived edifice, or a first cause, a remote land-lord, an unmoved mover resembling an engineer's central power house, or a geometer, a *Causa Sui*, a guarantor of distinct ideas; in short, God is an abstract intellectual principle that explains all the intelligible aspects of the universe, except its very being.

These intellectual features of God play a prominent part in Male-branche's system, too, as we would expect. However, when Male-branche extols the divine efficacy, the perfect independence and om-nipotence of God, and insists upon the utter dependency of the world upon Him, he is focussing on the central metaphysical problem, the problem of existence. What Malebranche seeks to emphasize in his Occasionalism, then, is the total and constant dependence of beings upon Being. Occasionalism is thus *par excellence* a preoccupation on the part of Malebranche with the metaphysical problem of Being. His foremost concern is to concentrate on what appears to him to be the one and proper task of metaphysics, namely, an inquiry into the con-cepts of creativity and Being. This is *the* issue that the Cartesians seem to have neglected.

Paradoxically, while God was in great jeopardy on the one side, it is equally true that at the time of Malebranche science was also being attacked. In many quarters the study of nature was considered a use-less pastime, if not a downright carnal sin. The middle of the century still needed sorely Bacon's defense of learning. Now, what better way could the interest of science, of the study of nature, be furthered than by supernaturalizing and sanctifying it? In his *Great Chain of Being*, Mr. Lovejoy suggests that if the world is the handiwork of God, one would think that man could find no better way to glorify his Creator than by studying His creation.[217] Malebranche is no less conscious of this aim.[218]

Unfortunately, it must be admitted that in seeking to rectify an error of omission, Malebranche himself committed a compensatory error of excessive exaggeration. So concerned was he to emphasize the vital role of God, that he tended to *write* in a manner that seems to pervert and to overlook the role of God's effects. As a result, we get such ex-traordinary statements as that which so shocked Berkeley: "In truth, it is not I who breathe"—Theodore is speaking—"I breathe despite my-self. It is not I who speak to you; I merely wish to speak to you." [219]

It is important to bear in mind, however, that Malebranche is an extraordinarily perceptive teacher and psychologist. Like his great predecessor Augustine, he is aware of the heart's frailty and weakness. Malebranche's Malebranche knows that however noble and resolute the will may be, literary devices.

its span of concentrated attention and absorption is limited. Accordingly, just as in the sphere of grace fallen man requires the aid of a holy concupiscence, a saintly joy and exhilaration, that agitates the will and helps the just man to persevere in righteousness, so too in the natural sphere, abstract truths must be sensibly clothed to touch the heart and sustain its attention. In the *Méditations chrétiennes,* we find the disciple ardently beseeching the Word to penetrate his mind with the glory ("éclat") of His light: Burn my heart, the disciple cries, with the ardor of Your love, and give me, in the course of this work, expressions that are clear and true, vivid and animated.[220] For all his disdain of sense and passions, Malebranche keenly understands their power, and he is eloquently adroit in utilizing every sensible device for purposes of reform and piety. As a result, like Socrates, he is a gadfly, an irritant, an enthusiast, frequently indulging in irony, gentle raillery, cajolery, and sometimes provoking his reader with exaggerated, dramatic, intemperate expressions deliberately calculated to shock, alarm, and intoxicate.

But Malebranche shares with us the secret of these techniques. In the *Conversations chrétiennes,* for example, he proposes the Socratic method of interrogation as the most persuasive instructional technique. Its value lies in the fact that the teacher assumes the air of a disciple, so that the student thus fancies that he has mastery over the teacher. With a sense of superiority achieved in this manner, the student feels that the truth he has obtained is his own invention, and he is more readily convinced.[221] The more violent and heady method of persuasion Malebranche exposes in his *Entretiens sur la métaphysique* through the statements of Theotimus and Theodore. There are three characters in this work: Aristes is the tutee; Theodore represents Malebranche; and Theotimus, who enters abruptly towards the middle of the work, seems to be the moderating voice of Malebranche. It is noteworthy that the last makes his entry in the seventh dialogue where the issue of causality first arises. When Theodore announces that the mind is not at all united to the body and has no power to act over it, Theotimus pacifies the dismayed Aristes with this significant remark: "Theodore maintains part of the truth, and if he exaggerates a little, it is in order to set us right."[222] As a matter of fact, Theodore himself has already admitted as much:

Aristes. I see that I have made a very bad beginning.

Theodore. Very bad indeed. I did not expect this sort of beginning . . . But prejudices will always return to the attack and deprive us of our conquests, if we do not know how to maintain our position by our vigilance and good intrenchments. Oh well! I submit to you that we are not united to our body at all, much less are

Theotimus.

we more intimately united to it than to anything else. *I am using somewhat extreme expressions* so that they shall leave a vivid impression . . .[223]

Elsewhere Malebranche tells us that in his pristine purity Adam's life was in a state of perfect equilibrium, like a well-balanced scale. Since the Fall, the body and the senses weigh him down. Unmistakably then, Malebranche uses violent invective against the creature, the world, the body, nature and its powers, only in order to readjust the scales, to recall his contemporaries from libertinism and materialism to the cult of the true God.

Nevertheless, if we go behind the letter to the spirit of Malebranche, it seems to me that the charge against him of sacrificing the whole of nature to God is an uncharitable and on the whole unwarranted one. Far from sacrificing the finite to the infinite, I should say that Malebranche seeks to sanctify and divinize the finite by making it indissolubly united to and inseparable from the creative infinite.

(c) *The Occasional Cause. First,* let us return to the question of the conservation of the world. Recall that conservation is a continuous creation. "If, then, the world subsists," Theodore instructs Aristes, "it is because God continues to will that there should be a world. The conservation of created beings is, therefore, so far as God is concerned, their continuous creation." [224] *Conservation as continuous creation.*

But how shall we understand this continuous creation? It is commonly assumed that Malebranche's conception of conservation is identical with that of Descartes. But is it? Descartes asserted that time is made up of instants, no one of which is dependent on any other. Hence at each instant God "produces me anew." Conservation is thus a continual reproduction.[225] Now Malebranche, in the first place, rejects the notion of time as a series of instants. ". . . Il n'y a point d'instant dans la durée, comme il n'y a point d'atomes dans les corps . . ." The "parties de durée" are infinitely divisible.[226] Duration is an infinitely compact continuum, then, for Malebranche; there are no instantaneous 'nows.' *(1) Duration a continuum.*

After asserting that, *as far as God is concerned,* conservation is a continuous creation, Malebranche goes on to explain this phrase:

I say so far as God is concerned; for so far as the created beings are concerned there is a difference, since in and through the act of creation they pass from non-being to being, whereas through the act of conservation they continue to be.[227] *(2) Conservation sustains continuously enduring finite existence.*

This subtle distinction between the two points of view calls for special notice. From the point of view of the creature, conservation is not a reproduction of existence. Creation confers existence upon an essence. But conservation is that act by which God sustains that existence.

From the divine point of view, conservation and creation are the same, because they involve the same will. Nevertheless, from the point of view of the creature, its continued existence is not a rebirth. Having received existence, it thereby endures, although to be able to continue and to endure it must be sustained by God's continuous influence. When an architect builds a house, the arrangement of the stones depends upon his will, but the house has no vital tie with the life of the architect. Hence the house can exist independently of its builder. The architect does not sustain it. That is why there is no essential connection between them. But the world does have an essential relation to God, because it cannot endure without His sustaining will.[228]

This leads to a *second* observation. Malebranche is not denying self-subsistence of the creature. All he denies is its *unaided* self-subsistence. He does not, that is, deny that the object created possesses a being in (3) Self-subsistence of creatures. its own right. The effect produced, he says in the *Entretiens sur la métaphysique,* is different from God's operation that produces it.[229] The existent creature is thus "other" than God. Its existence is its own. Nevertheless this proprietorship whereby each existence has its own existence is not an inalienable right. It enjoys its existence and endures only because God permits and continually wills that it do so. This view of self-subsistence entails a reconsideration of what we mean by a creature. Indeed, the crucial question concerning the efficacy of creatures depends on the more fundamental question of the existence of creatures, their very being.

But if such is Malebranche's view of conservation, does it not throw new light on Malebranche's assertions that God alone can be the mover of bodies? For a body to exist and continue to be, it must receive the constant sustaining influence of God's will. But equally for a body to move, that is, to change in spatial position, it requires the sustaining and permissive will of God to preserve it throughout its spatial positions. From this point of view, it is indeed as Malebranche claims, a (4) Conservation sustains the movement of bodies. contradiction to say that one body can move another. For, if we grant that only God's continuous will can create and preserve a body's existence through duration, then it also follows that strictly speaking it is only God's will that can sustain its spatial transportations. Just as each particular object stands in an immediate relation to God in time, so it does in space. No object depends for its gift of existence or continued existence upon anything other than God. So neither can it depend on anything for the spatial movements that befall it. Did God not actively will that, upon impact, a body be moved, that movement would not occur. Theodore sums up these observations in the seventh dialogue of the *Entretiens sur la métaphysique:*

> La création ne passe point, la conservation des créatures n'étant de la part de Dieu qu'une création continuée, qu'une même volonté

qui subsiste, et qui opère sans cesse. . . . Il y a contradiction qu'un corps en puisse remuer un autre. Je dis plus: . . . il y a contradiction que tous les Anges et les Démons joints ensemble puissent ébranler un fétu. . . . Il y a contradiction que Dieu veuille que ce fauteil soit, qu'il ne veuille qu'il soit quelque part, et que par l'efficace de sa volonté il ne l'y mette, il ne l'y conserve, il ne l'y crée. Donc nulle puissance ne peut le transporter où Dieu ne le transporte pas, ni le fixer ou l'arrêter où Dieu ne l'arrête pas, *si ce n'est que Dieu accomode l'efficace de son action, à l'action inefficace de ses créatures.*[230]

This last phrase is significant: ". . . *unless God accomodates the efficacy of His action to the ineffective actions of His creatures.*" Creatures do act, but they act ineffectively—this is the plain, albeit strange, sense of the passage. We know that the term, ineffectively, basically, signifies non-creatively. But in what sense do they actually act? And how does God accommodate His efficacy to the action of creatures?

In what sense do creatures act?

Let us realize that, while in denouncing the potency of creatures Malebranche is rejecting the view that creatures are the *true* or *principal* causes, nevertheless he does not deny that they are in some sense causes. Creatures are causes, but, unlike the true cause, they are *occasional* or *natural* causes: ". . . Outre la cause générale," he says, "il y en a une infinité de particulières: outre la cause véritable il y en a de naturelles, et que tu dois appeler *occasionnelles,* pour ôter l'équivoque dangereux qui naît de la fausse idée que les Philosophes ont de la nature." [231] One danger of using the term, natural, is that it countenances polytheism. A second danger is that it suggests a universe that can subsist or act independently of God's conserving will. A body has the power to transport another, but only on condition that God wills that transaction to take place. A body can transport only because God wills that it have such a power.

God is the true cause. His alone is the power to create and to conserve. But God is also a general cause, which means that He creates in the most simple and efficient manner.[232] To act in a simple and general manner means, as Mr. Church so ably puts it, that "although God does cause all things, He provides the power only, and does not determine what is to be the nature of the effects He does cause." [233] On the other hand, it is the function of the occasional or natural and particular cause to determine what particular effects should be created. The occasional cause determines God to create and what to create. In what manner does the occasional cause act, that is, in virtue of what can the occasional cause so act?

The answer is this. When God created the material world, He set it in motion. I have already observed that Descartes' view of created extension is that of a concrete geometry into which movement is in-

Motion of
bodies stems
from their act
of existence.

sinuated. But in Malebranche's doctrine, there cannot be a "created" geometry. For a created geometry would by itself be no different from the uncreated geometry present in the divine reason, and, moreover, would be a contradiction in terms, since essences qua essences are not created. Conversely, uncreated essences are not actual finite existents. Hence when Malebranche speaks of imparting motion into extension, he means imparting motion into ideal or intelligible extension. Motion vitalizes, animates, concretizes extension.[234] Movement thus constitutes the actuality of bodies; it issues from their very act of existence.

No doubt, this is why Malebranche rejects the notion of an uncreated, eternal matter and why he insists that God could not move matter, were He not the author of its being.[235] For Malebranche, motion is coextensive with the very being or actuality of matter. To create a body is to create movement. He rejects explicitly the opinion of those who try to make a distinction between creation and the production of motion.[236] To say that God created matter is to say that He created a fluid universe, a world of whirlpools (*tourbillons*), processes, movements and energies. Thus the Word says: ". . . La matière est une *nature* impuissante, qui *n'agit que par l'efficace du mouvement que je lui imprime.*"[237] Thus the *essence* of matter is its immutable, inert, quantitative relations; but its *existence* is sheer process or movement: matter . . . acts only by the efficacy of the movement that I impress upon it. Again Malebranche declares: "Matter is essentially movable. It has, by its *nature*, a passive capacity for movement. But it has no active capacity; it is actually moved only by the continual action of the Creator."[238]

Now bodies, as whirlpools of movement, do indeed depend on God as creator and conserver; but also, being movements, they can impart, although they cannot create, movements. And in fact they do so. For when God created this plenum of movements, this vast turbulence, this process, His interest was to obtain the greatest diversity of effects in the simplest possible way. To that end, He established at the beginning of creation general laws for the communication of movements and in accordance with which He always acts. However, and note this well, prior to the laws of nature He created the occasional cause, for "without an occasional cause there can be no general law." Thus the first step of creation was to create actual existents and movements.[239] Then God established laws to govern and to regulate this process.

Bodies do
communicate
motion through
the aid of laws.

Now, all this being granted, the Word says: when a body is in movement, it certainly does have the force to move another in consequence of the laws of the communication of movements that God constantly follows: "Cela supposé, lorsqu'un corps est en mouvement, il a certainement la force d'en mouvoir un autre en conséquence des

lois des communications des mouvements que Dieu suit constam-
ment." [240] Does this mean that a body can *create* movement? Of course
not. Hence Malebranche adds: It can be said that this body is the
physical or *natural* cause of the motion it communicates, because it
acts in consequence of the *natural* laws. But Malebranche does not
say that it itself is in any way a true cause. He tells us: it is not in
the least a natural cause in the sense of the philosophy of the pagans;
it is absolutely only an *occasional* cause which determines by the
collision of bodies the efficacy of the general law according to which
a general cause ought to act. Thus we may say that the sun is the
cause of many admirable effects, because its force is the movement
that animates it. However, God is the true cause of the movement,
and hence the sun is an occasional or natural cause, for its active
power comes from God's laws.[241] And is not this description of the
occasional cause precisely that of M. Gilson's generative and productive, but non-creative, cause? Occasional causes do move, for Malebranche; they do communicate and impart motion; and they do so
because God, through His laws which are but expressions of His
will, empowers them to act thus. The Word instructs:

> Car, Mon fils, retiens bien ceci, *Dieu ne communique sa puissance
> aux créatures, qu'en les établissant causes occasionnelles pour pro-
> duire certains effets, en conséquence des lois, qu'il se fait pour
> exécuter ses desseins d'une manière uniforme et constante, par les
> voies les plus simples, les plus dignes de sa sagesse, et de ses autres
> attributs.*[242]

Can we wish for a more distinct statement concerning the active
powers of the occasional cause?

Does this mean, however, that the power of the occasional cause,
once given, belongs to it intrinsically, that is, that the occasional cause
can exert power apart from the sustaining influence of God? Certainly
not. Hence Malebranche writes:

> . . . lorsqu'une boule qui se remue en rencontre et en meut une
> autre, elle ne lui communique rien qu'elle ait, car elle n'a pas *elle-
> même* la force qu'elle lui communique. Cependant une boule est
> cause naturelle du mouvement *qu'elle communique.* Une cause
> naturelle n'est donc point une cause réelle et véritable, mais seule-
> ment une cause occasionalle et qui détermine l'auteur de la nature
> à agir de telle et telle manière en telle et telle rencontre.[243]

Notice that ball A does indeed impart motion to B. And this communication is given to perception. However, A is not the creative cause
of the motion it imparts; and secondly, A's power to communicate is
not something that it has by itself. A can act and determine God to
create only because this power to act is continually maintained by

God's will. This is brought out even more clearly in a passage which occurs just after the above. *Natural* causes, Malebranche here declares, are not true causes at all. They are only *occasional* causes which act solely by the force and efficacy of the will of God. Thus the occasional cause remains active, but its activity depends on God's creative and conserving power.[244] So equally in the case of the will. We are conscious of an effort to move an arm. This effort is indeed an exertion that does something, but: I deny—writes Malebranche—that the effort is *by itself* capable of giving movement to the animal spirits or of determining them.[245] Thus the will acts, but not unaided and not creatively. In the *Entretiens sur la métaphysique*, Malebranche says that God's will is the *source* of his power and faculties. His efficacious decrees—Malebranche is talking: "endow me with the power which I have over my body." [246]

It is all too often assumed that when Malebranche appeals to perception to deny efficacy in the creature, that he is denying influence between two objects. Mr. Church, for example, seems to hold such a view,[247] based on this following passage in the *Méditations chrétiennes*. The Word has just asserted that the senses are reliable witnesses to

Inconsistency imputed by Church. facts, but He continues: do not judge that bodies have in *themselves* a moving force, nor that they are able to spread it in those that they encounter, for of this you see nothing . . .[248] Now this passage occurs where Malebranche discusses *true* causes. Thus what the senses do not show is that the influence between A and B is a creative one. Hence, secondly, the senses do not show that when A imparts motion to B it does so *in itself* or *by itself*. In other words, sense does *not* show that A can act in an *independent* or *intrinsic, unaided* manner. Neither, for that matter, do the senses show the *dependent* character of the occasional cause. Senses simply reveal influence between A and B. But to know *how* A operates and *that* it operates or acts through the communicating and sustaining power of God belongs to a metaphysical vision. Hence Malebranche writes that God's operation is invisible.[249]

I say that Mr. Church seems to believe that for Malebranche transitive causation is not given in perception on the basis of the foregoing passage. To be scrupulously fair, however, I must admit that he does not quote that passage. He does, however, refer to another passage a few pages further on, which he translates thus: "Renounce, my son, thy prejudices, and never judge with respect to natural effects that one thing is the effect of another because experience teaches you that it never fails to follow it. For of all false principles, that one is the most dangerous and the most fruitful in error." [250] But Mr. Church fails to notice or to acknowledge that this passage too occurs in a context where Malebranche is explaining what is a "true" cause as distinct from the occasional cause. By the time we reach this passage we already know or should know that true causality means creation and conservation; we know or should know that occasional causes act, but only through the sustaining power of God. *Therefore* the most dangerous error in philosophy lies in confusing occasional causes— that is, dependent, imparting, distributive causes—with the creative conserving power of God. In point of fact, Mr. Church himself *eventually* admits that this is the correct interpretation of Occasionalism. But despite the acuity of his ultimate proper interpretation, he then makes a volte-face and charges Malebranche with inconsistency.[251] Having first gratuitously assumed that Malebranche's definition of true causality implies the *total* impotence of the creature and having little sympathy for the notion of creativity in any case, Church thinks it uncritical for Malebranche subsequently to assert the active character of occasional causes.

Granting that occasional causes, taken as ideas realized in process, and existing as power, do move and do communicate and impart motion, we may ask why God established occasional causes at all and why He communicates His power to them. God has specific reasons for doing so, according to Malebranche, namely, to produce the greatest diversity of effects. God, if He creates, must do so in a manner that befits His attributes. He is a General Cause who must act in a general, orderly, uniform manner. This explains the establishment of general laws to which God always conforms. But these general laws are only half the story in describing the ways of Providence. The laws guarantee order and regularity, but they do not of themselves determine the variety and diversity of the particular effects. The particulars determine the particularity of the particulars that follow them. For His glorification God wants an infinitely rich and variegated universe. That God's creative power be thus diversified, the occasional cause is established. It is the role of the occasional cause to determine the specific ways in which God's creative power shall display itself. While the laws guarantee the stability of the divine conduct, the occasional cause provides the means for inexhaustibly full and rich results. The occasional cause thus determines not only the efficacy of God's laws, but also their manner of operation:—not only does the occasional cause determine God's creative power to display itself, but also to display itself in a specific manner. Malebranche says: "To the end that the General Cause should act through laws or general volitions, and that this action should be regulated, constant, and uniform, it is absolutely necessary that there be occasional causes which determine the efficacy of these laws *et qui servent à les établir*."[252] Thus the occasional cause is necessary in the sense that if God wills to create, then to preserve generality in His conduct He makes use of the occasional cause as the medium through which a diversity of

[margin note:] Occasional causes diversify effects.

effects is obtained. Again, when two bodies meet, it is the occasional cause that determines the specific results of this encounter: As we saw above, a natural cause is not a real and true cause, but only an occasional cause which determines God to act in such and such a way, on such and such an encounter.[253]

But why, it may be asked, if the occasional cause plays so important a role, does Malebranche keep reiterating that it is not a *true*, but only an *occasional* cause? This occasional cause does so much. Through the laws of motion it becomes empowered to move bodies. Through the same laws it is empowered to prescribe the specific results that are to follow. Yet, calling a creature an occasional, as distinct from a true cause, is of no small significance. The import is twofold. First, by describing the creature as a natural or occasional cause in a non-pagan sense, Malebranche means to designate the fact that the power to impart movement is a divine gift, divinely sustained. Just as the origin and continued existence of a body depends on God's creation and continued conservation, so is its power to induce movement. In fact, on my interpretation, the two are nearly indistinguishable. A body exists in so far as it *is* in the active sense of the verb, *to be*. This existence is coextensive with process, which is an effect and analogue or expression of God's will. From its very being of movement follows its capacity to communicate movement. And this capacity becomes exercised, maintained, and regularized through the laws of motion.

While Church does not share my views on the nature of God's existence as *Celui qui est* or that of the material world as essence plus existence, he does, however, recognize that the occasional cause is an active cause. And, while he uses this recognition to attempt to find confusion in Malebranche, the recognition itself is well taken, and I am therefore pleased to call upon him for additional support. Indeed, the very fact of his incessant attack on Malebranche throughout his study makes this present point of agreement all the more impressive. Says Church: "Bodies and souls are powerless only if conceived of as completely self-dependent. When their dependence on God is admitted, they may then be said to possess power; to possess power, that is, not intrinsically, but in virtue of the will of God." [254]

Yet, while Church recognizes the genuine potency of the occasional cause, he nevertheless insists that Occasionalism involves a twofold contradiction: "That God should be determined by His creatures contradicts His omnipotence; that His creatures should effect this determination contradicts their asserted impotence." [255] Here, having employed Church to correct the critics who claim complete inertness in occasional causes, I find it necessary to call upon Gilson once more, in order to rectify the mistakes of Church. Church finds inconsistencies, because he does not understand the nature of Malebranche's God,

Why natural causes are called occasional causes.

Church's correct claim that creatures possess power.

that He is Being, and thus He alone possesses creative powers. Thus the second significant import of calling a creature an occasional cause is that however active and dynamic it may be, its power is never that of creation proper. A body does not cause the *existence* of another; and while upon impact body A may communicate movement to B, the actual power that confers motion upon B comes from God. Recall Gilson's statement: a second cause "can never go so far as to cause the very existence of the effects produced." [256] So with Malebranche. The occasional cause may determine God to act and to act in specific ways; Church is correct in insisting upon these aspects of the occasional cause. It may even be said to *move* another body, that is, impart motion; but it can never be said that the actual presence of movement in an object can come from any source other than God. So Malebranche declares that for God to communicate efficacy to man or to an angel, can only mean that when a man or an angel wills that some body should be moved, God wills that this body should be *actually* moved.[257] Thus when it comes to conferring existence, this is God's prerogative. The occasional cause can determine God to create; it can determine the when and how of creation; but that final, irreducible, unique act which creates being belongs to God only. This again is why God remains the true and only cause. Thus the contradiction that Church finds in Occasionalism vanishes.

How, asks Church, further, can Malebranche on the one hand affirm that God, being omnipotent, needs no instruments to act and yet, on the other hand, how can Malebranche allow the occasional cause so important a role as to diversify God's conduct and determine Him to create? [258] It is plain that Mr. Church does not distinguish, as Malebranche does distinguish, between creation and alteration or distribution. God, says Malebranche, need no instruments to create, but He does need them for the governance of the world.[259] This involves no contradiction. God has no need, as in Aristotle or in Plotinus, of a chain of intermediaries by which to create or to communicate power to the occasional cause. He em-powers each creature immediately and directly. And precisely because each creature does receive its existence and power to act directly from God, can it interact with others. What Malebranche demands is for each creature to be in immediate and direct contact with God, and God to serve, through His laws, as the intermediary or tie among creatures:

God's instruments.

—Dieu a établie toutes les puissances, les causes secondes, les hiérarchies visibles ou invisibles immédiatement par lui-même ou par l'entremise d'autres puissances afin d'exécuter ses desseins par des lois générales, dont l'efficace soit déterminée par l'action de ces mêmes puissances.—Car il n'agit pas comme les rois de la terre qui donnent des ordres et ne font plus rien. Dieu fait généralement tout ce que font les causes secondes. La matière n'a pas par elle-même la force mouvante dont dépend son efficace et il n'y a pas de liaison nécessaire entre la volonté des esprits et les effets qu'elle produit. Dieu fait tout: mais il agit par les créatures parce qu'il a voulu leur communiquer sa puissance pour exécuter son ouvrage par des lois dignes de lui.[260]

God, then, needs instruments to this extent—if He is to impart His creative power, He needs creatures as the recipients of His power and as the means for diversifying His unique act in a plurality of occasions. But we must not argue by means of a pun on the word, instrument. The occasional cause is not an instrument in the sense of creation and conservation, but in the sense of distributing and imparting God's power. Thus Malebranche declares:

> . . . Dieu a établi ces lois pour plusiers raisons considérables qui toutes néanmoins ont rapport à son grand ouvrage. Il les a établies pour unir les esprits à des corps, et par leur corps à ceux qui les environnent: et par là les unir tous entre eux et former des Etats et des Sociétés particulières: et par là les rendre capables des sciences, de discipline, de religion: et par là fournir à Jésus-Christ et à ses membres mille moyens d'étendre la foi, d'instruire et de sanctifier les hommes, et de construire ainsi son grand ouvrage l'Église future . . .[261]

It might of course be asserted that this distinction between creation and distribution is spurious and is an illegitimate one. Perhaps this is the brunt of Church's criticism. To which I answer that the problem of causality is similar to the problem of existence itself. If we begin with God as the only true, self-sufficient Being, then it becomes a paradox that anything besides God should exist. And if we begin with mere finite existents, it becomes difficult to find a necessary existent. But this is a false dichotomy. Properly speaking, the ontological realist begins with both. So with causality. The theory of Occasionalism is not intended to impale one on the horns of a dilemma, but to help one to escape a false dichotomy; it is put forth to harmonize reason and the senses.[262] Reason shows that God alone is the Creator and therefore alone the true cause. Reason reveals necessity. The senses, nevertheless, are witnesses to facts. They reveal change, movement, constant conjunctions, and concomitancies. The business of the metaphysician is to reconcile the two.

Or, as Malebranche says, we must go from the sensible to the intelligible.[263] What this means is that we must go from the facts of observation to general principles. It is the latter which give knowledge, because they explain and unify the facts. Church imposes a Humian view on Malebranche which is entirely alien to the Oratorian and which Church himself recognizes to be foreign! But his formidable analytic prowess prevents him from seeing Malebranche's Occasionalism as a whole.

Again according to Church, Malebranche fails to see that by his definition of causality, perception fails to disclose *any* cause. What Malebranche *said* was that a *true* cause is such that between it and its effect there is necessary connection. Now he acknowledges that experience fails to disclose any such connection of necessity. When one ball hits another, no necessity is revealed, but only constant conjunction. But from these assertions Church argues that *no cause whatever* is apparent. Yet Malebranche no more draws this conclusion than did Berkeley after him. Instead, Malebranche maintains that in perception there is causal power, but that that power is the power of an occasional cause and that true power and necessity belong to God's will. Malebranche, therefore, according to Church, is indulging in a "compensatory dogma." On the one hand Malebranche maintains,—so Church alleges,—that the belief in necessity is engendered by constant conjunction, and, as such, it is a mere habit, as Hume would claim, without rational validity. Only through habit do we erroneously infer that A is the true cause of B. Yet, on the other hand, Malebranche seems to say that while belief in necessity is habit engendered by constant conjunction and therefore without foundation, nevertheless it is not really erroneous belief, for behind the conjunction there is really present the efficacious and uniform will of God. Therefore constant conjunction does mean necessity and causal inference, and Malebranche accordingly is arguing in a circle. To demonstrate the inefficacy of creatures, he applies the definition of causality as necessity. But to justify his dogma that there is real causality in God's will and then to explain the working of that will, Malebranche has to appeal to the constant conjunction of occasional causes, thus transforming the conjunction into a necessity and endowing the occasional cause with power.[264]

Is true causality meaningless because inaccessible to perception?

Let us examine some of these accusations. Malebranche does say that there is no perception of necessity in experience. Also, he says that from constant conjunction we infer erroneously that an antecedent A is the true cause of its concomitant B. Strictly speaking, according to Malebranche, there is no perception of a true causal tie between A and B in perception. The inference from a conjunction to a true causal connection arises from habit. Why, then, does Malebranche not stop there as Hume does? It is not because of any compensatory dogma, but rather because Malebranche is more strict or more deeply philosophical than is Hume. First of all, Hume makes no distinction between necessity and transitive influence in his negative account of causality, although he does have "gentle forces" of association (natural relations) in his constructive theory of causal inference. Hume assumes that, because no matter of fact implies any other matter of fact, therefore, there can be no conjunctive, transmissive influence between them. He equates the absence of logical necessity with the absence of causal efficacy. But we have no right to read Malebranche through the eyes of Hume. All that Malebranche asserts is that a *true* cause is such that between it and its effect the mind apprehends necessity. *Hence the absence of necessity indicates the absence of a true cause,* for Malebranche; and as I noted above, this is all it indicates. A true cause is a creative cause, for him. And the absence of necessity indicates that finite events or finite creatures are not creative entities. This does not mean that they are not causes in some other sense. The theory of Occasionalism explains *in what sense they are causes,* namely, as distributive, transmissive, dependent powers.

Furthermore, for Hume the very belief in necessary connection, the very notion of necessity, is mere psychological habit, engendered by constant conjunction. For Hume minds engage in causal inference: *we* project our habits of necessity into nature. Such is not the case with Malebranche. For Malebranche, perception does indeed disclose no necessary connection and hence no true causes. But the belief or inference from conjunction to the presence of real, true, creative power and necessity is not made on the basis of the absence or presence of causality within perception. The basis of the belief and of the causal inference is that constant conjunction is a mode of being that cannot be conceived apart from the Infinite Being. Therefore, once more, the inference is really made in terms of our acquaintance with God as Being and with His unilateral necessity. That from the perception of constant conjunction and psychological habits we should make the apparently unwarranted leap to necessary connection is an exemplification, in another sphere, of Malebranche's theory of knowledge. It indicates the priority of concept to percept and of intuition of God to all forms of knowing. Constant conjunction "reminds" us of necessity and of causal power, for it reminds us of God as Being. Properly speaking, we do not discursively arrive at causal power. And we do not derive any idea of true causality and necessary connection from perceived conjunctions or any number of conjunctions. For there is no *idea* or concept of power. But constancies do suggest necessity; they elicit and recall what we intuitively know in *a priori* form, and they do so because they are themselves hard, given facts.

Thus it is not true to say either that Malebranche discursively infers the presence of a divine will from observed conjunctions or that he appeals to God as a compensatory dogma. Conjunction reminds us of the presence of necessity and of creative causal power. What the theory of occasionalism does is serve to make clear the locus of that necessity, just as the alternative theories of ideas serve to make clear the presence of God as Being and Reason. After seeing A and B together a number of times, we become dimly but *intuitively* aware of creative causal energy being exerted. We do not perceive this efficacy sensuously, nor do we conceive it through ideas. But we are aware intuitively of its presence, for we are aware by simple vision of God as Being. Haste and prejudice make us erroneously attribute this intuited creative efficacy to the particulars. Attention, examination and reflection enable us to localize this efficacy where it properly belongs. Then we behold it by simple vision as an attribute of God.

Thus it is not surprising that Malebranche should argue that perception reveals no causal tie or connection between the impact of two balls and at the same time assert that a causal influence is indeed present. For the truth of the matter is that for him the mere presence of the colliding balls testifies to the presence and exertion of God's causality. The ball is an existent; its change of position is a form of existence. How then, or whence, can such occurrences take place except through and by the creative sustaining power of Being? For Malebranche, the principle that every effect must have a cause is axiomatic, because creativity is evident. And creativity is evident, because Being is so.

Antecedent and consequence, and causality.

As for the claim that, given God's uniform will, Occasionalism really transforms the causal nexus into necessity, so that, in Church's formulation, "given one experience of two conjoined events, we must henceforth believe that an occurrence of the one event will necessarily determine God to produce the other" [265]—as for this claim, Church forgets that, for Malebranche, God always reserves the right to suspend the laws of nature by a particular will or to act in conformity with other laws. Thus miracles are possible. Furthermore, while God's uniform will does guarantee uniformity as such in nature, nevertheless, alternative orders are possible and alternative possibilities within a given order.[266] Then again, we know *a priori* that God acts in the simplest, best and most uniform manner, and therefore we know that He has established laws that He will ordinarily follow in regular fashion. Yet since the laws are derivative from God's will, they are in principle arbitrary, depending on God's pleasure, as Malebranche said to Leibnitz; and since they govern existential behavior, since nature is not abstract, what these laws are must be discovered *experimentally*, and no single experience of two conjoined events provides an adequate basis of induction. Church's efforts to drive Malebranche into this seeming consequence are simply not fair to one of the salient features of our author's thought.

Lucien Labbas offers an interpretation of Malebranche's theory of causality that is far more sound.[267] Concerning the originality of this theory he tells us that:

La causalité occasionnelle est une liason constante, mais non nécessaire, un rapport synthétique, non analytique et déductif. C'est une liason qui n'est connue de nous qu'a *posteriori* par l'expérience. La causalité naturelle n'est donc pas la liason mathématique qui est analytique, nécessaire, déductive, explicative. . . . La causalité naturelle n'est cependant pas aux yeux de Malebranche un rapport tout contingent. Simple relation inintelligible du point de vue de l'expérience, la causalité naturelle est intelligible du point de vue divin, elle a sa valeur, sa réalité objective dans la volonté de Dieu, elle est déterminée par la Providence. Sans la comprendre, nous savons qu'elle ne vient pas du hasard et nous croyons qu'elle est stable par le décret qui la consacre. Elle n'est pas une simple juxtaposition, une pure agglutination comme dans l'associationisme anglais. La causalité naturelle repose sur Dieu. Elle est constante, non pour l'effet d'une répétition, non parce qu'elle fait naître une habitude dans l'esprit, mais parce qu'elle est déterminée par une volonté générale de Dieu.[268]

Malebranche, thus, as Labbas observes,[269] does indeed advance beyond the positions of Bacon and of Descartes, who treat knowledge as the search for explicative, necessitating, determining causes. For Malebranche, on the other hand, the relation between the occasional cause and its effect is neither fortuitous nor capricious, nor is it rigorously determined. The relation is constant, invariable, yet, at the same time, metaphysically brute and contingent, inasmuch as it depends on the arbitrary will of God.[270]

Mr. Church seeks to drive Malebranche farther still into absurdity and contradiction. According to him, not only is Occasionalism a self-contradictory theory, but worse, it is purely verbal. Can any meaning, he asks, be found for its two major propositions: (1) that God is determined by the occasional cause, and (2) that God is the sole "real" cause?[271] He answers, no, to his query. Why?

Siding with Arnauld, Church (like Ginsberg, Bouillier and Blampignon)[272] maintains that for occasional causes to be able to determine God

Are occasional causes inconsistent with divine power?

is plausible only if, in fact, these causes do possess an efficacy of some sort. They must possess not only the power to determine God, but also a power to determine themselves; a power to will, if the cause be a volition, and a power to produce motion, if the cause be a body. For to constitute the occasion for God's intervention, the angel or the man must will inefficaciously; and to will thus is to be capable of volition. The divine volition and the finite volition are not, and cannot be, the same, and leave to the term 'occasional cause' any meaning. To constitute an occasional cause the finite will must in its own right have the capacity to choose what body it inefficaciously wills to move. Yet, that the will should be even so much as able to choose is precisely what, consistently with the impotence of creatures and the omnipotence of God, Malebranche cannot admit. Hence, if it is to be maintained that God is the sole real cause, the finite will must be denied all capacity to exercise itself in any sense by itself; and without that capacity, the inefficacious volition that is an occasional cause cannot be.[273]

Church and Arnauld are in error in supposing that Malebranche cannot admit the capacity of choice to the will. All that Malebranche actually affirms is that this intrinsic capacity on the part of the human will to choose is an aptitude that is God-given and divinely sustained. The human will is indeed man's will. To say that it is no different from God's is to say that it is an analogue of God's. Or better still, it is to say that each will is a participant that in creation expresses God's will in its entirety but in its own way. Hence, quoting St. Paul, Malebranche can say that all our force and aptness come from God.[274]

Creatures are embodiments of God's will.

Malebranche does say that the will is invincible in the sense that it is a love or search for happiness, for union with God. It is not in our power to seek or not to seek God. We are born that way. God incessantly pushes us towards Him, for He continually sustains our longing for the Infinite. It is however in our power to arrest the will, to stop and be content with false, finite goods. It is in our power *not* to stop; we are free to suspend judgment and free to choose those finite means that will lead us to God. Our freedom is something of which we are directly conscious.[275] Actually, it is this doctrine of a free will that troubled Arnauld, the Jansenist. He had no interest whatever in human liberty and therefore sought to confute Malebranche by claiming that Occasionalism really deprived man of freedom. To Arnauld Malebranche's insistence that with respect to grace man was free to accept or reject the divine gift was pure Molinism.[276] Since Arnauld, critic after critic, including Church, but with the exception of Gouhier,[277] has assumed that God is the cause of each individual volition and that therefore man is not free. Yet this Malebranche expressly repudiates. What he does say is that man's self-determination and choice are made possible by the fact that God continually impresses him with the power or will wherewith to do it.[278]

And what is true of the will is true of bodies. According to Church:

. . . God moves bodies only on the occasion of an impact. But this would be plausible only if bodies came into contact of their own accord. If, as Malebranche holds, their impact is due to a volition of God, then the rôle of bodies as occasional causes loses all meaning. Hence Malebranche must either render superfluous the intervention of God by granting to occasional causes the efficacy proper to causes, or he must maintain that God is the sole cause in every sense, and thus deny to occasional causes all meaning.[279]

[237]

On my interpretation, bodies do indeed come into contact "of their own accord," and not through *a* volition of God. *For bodies are themselves expressions of God's will.* They are analogues of His will. Thus *their very existence is to be cores of energies.* But again their very aptness to come together is owing to their having been thus made and thus sustained. The crucial question is this: when two bodies, A and B, are in collision, *what* are bodies A and B? Throughout most of the critical literature on Malebranche, this question is not asked nor is the proper answer understood, although no question is more important for comprehending Malebranche's philosophy. If we look at their essence or nature—their idea—then indeed bodies are empty, impotent geometrical configurations. As such they can indeed do nothing. Not only can they not create movement or even transmit motion, they cannot even be said to be. They are truly bloodless essences. Only when bodies A and B are taken concretely and actually are they real existents. But this we saw meant to be participants in and infused by the will of God. *Only as they are will are the bodies really bodies.*

This does not mean, of course, that bodies are free in the manner of humans. Nevertheless, living bodies, like plants and animals are organisms that in their development and growth from seminal seeds display purpose in the interpendence and co-functioning of their parts.[280] Only inanimate bodies are described by Malebranche as "necessary causes." [281] But even with respect to the latter Malebranche does not assert that their impact is due to the specific intervention of God, or to *a* volition, as Church declares. This is why Malebranche can assert:

> Le choc des corps étant la cause occasionnelle des mouvements et ma volonté celle du mouvement de ma langue, cela épargne à Dieu un nombre infini de volontés particulières. M. Arnauld n'en peut douter qu'en supposant que les corps ne se choquent jamais que Dieu ne les meuve auparavant par des volontés particulières. Si cela est et si Dieu, par des volontés particulières, inspire toujours aux hommes tous les désirs pratiques qu'ils ont de prononcer quelques paroles, alors, je l'avoue, les lois générales de l'union de l'âme et du corps et des communications des mouvements ne seront propre à épargner à Dieu des volontés particulières.[282]

The function of the formal order.

Still God may be said to be the sole cause in the sense that He alone creates and sustains. Accordingly, we may interpret the occasional cause in either of two ways. If we consider the particular objects in purely conceptual terms, they are being viewed in their formal properties only. As such the bodies are indeed occasional only —they are the occasions, the conditions, the formal circumstances, the structural fabric within which events occur in conformity to general laws. Then, when Malebranche speaks of the occasional cause as non-creative and non-efficacious but as *determining* the creative power of God, we may understand him to mean that divine efficiency or potency manifests itself through and within a geometric medium. The presence of a geometric medium is the necessary condition for the display of power. Thus mechanism, as such, does not possess efficacy; it "determines" not by way of force but in the sense that it is the vehicle through which or upon the presence of which, force is effected. This would explain why Malebranche says that God needs occasional causes. If the occasional cause is taken as a mathematical, formal, logical order, then for God to require such order implies that creative and efficient causality possesses an intelligible structure, that is, a structure understandable in mathematical and logical properties. As a formal pattern, the occasional cause is inert; *it* does not exercise potency.

If, however, we view the bodies as existents, as vital expressions of God, we may then consider them as genuine, although not creative, causes. Body A is divine; it incorporates God's will in Its entirety, albeit in a limited manner. But equally this is true of body B. Hence body A may be described as actually transmitting and communicating of itself to B and of eliciting or producing a change in B. _{Bodies are acts of existence.}

This total situation recurs in Hume's philosophy, as historically it has to occur, projected on a naturalistic plane. In causation, cause and effect are simply the philosophical relations of comparison; formally there is no tie of any kind to be found between the cause and the concomitant conjunctive effect. There is nothing in the nature of the cause (Malebranche said the idea or essence of the cause) which entails the effect. And yet cause and effect is for Hume a natural relation; indeed, the only natural relation that permits him to transcend the present moment. As natural relation, a gentle force, the force that actually produces expectation, operates between cause and effect for Hume; and in practice we always find the extreme skepticism mitigated by the very natural forces of animal expectancy.

Critics who are prejudiced against Scholasticism can find no greater praise of Malebranche than to call him a positivist, that is, the philosopher who prior to Hume destroyed the notion of transitive causality, who, in Brunschvicg's phrase, banished even the search for causes, who reduced the world to a system of successive events or phenomena governed by regular laws. So say Brunschvicg, Mouy and Labbas, to cite a few examples.[283] But what is this transitive causality that he has abolished? Lalande's *Vocabulaire de la philosophie* defines a transitive cause as the action or modification of one agent by another. And in a note, M. M. Drouin writes that it is worthwhile to add that transitive causality has been understood in a realistic sense: ". . . l'action étant conçue comme une *chose* qui de la cause passerait dans l'effet." Precisely this notion, he says, is what Malebranche and Hume attacked.[284] _{Conclusion.}

That Malebranche eliminated the view that causality consists in the transmission of one *thing* from another is absolutely right, and if this is all that the other critics intend, they too are correct. There is no passage of any fixed, inert properties or qualities for Malebranche, and hence no transmission of occult forces, if force means an inert nature, essence, or form. Thus in the *Entretiens sur la métaphysique* Malebranche asserts that a body cannot move another without communicating to it its moving force. But this moving force, he insists, ". . . is not a quality which belongs to the body itself. Nothing belongs to it but its own modifications; and modifications are inseparable from substances." [285] In other words, the moving force that animates concrete matter and which gets communicated is no fixed inert modality or thing that belongs to the essential nature ("substance") of extension. "God has linked together all His works, though He has not on that account produced in them *entities* charged with the function of union," Theodore announces in the *Entretiens sur la métaphysique.*[286] "He has subordinated them to one another without endowing them with active *qualities*." If force were a static predicate, then communication would not take place. But if causality or force is understood in the dynamic sense of process or influence, that issues from God's will and is communicated to the creature when it receives existence, then is not the occasional cause, on the existential plane, a core of energy that imparts its own motion into the motion of another? Motion flows into motion. To repeat the statement of the Word: Matter, by *nature* impotent, acts only by the efficacy of the movements which I impress in it.[287]

And if transitive causality means the action of one agent upon another, then are not occasional causes, in so far as they exist and are movements, just such agents? For the power of the occasional cause to move stems from the act of existence. Its own movement or energy and its capacity to move another in regular ways emerge from its ontological status of being an act of existence. And since this is the case, without derogating from the stature and originality of Malebranche, how does this view appreciably differ from that of the medievals, say of Thomas? There is no important difference, unless we equate Thomism with Suarezianism. This M. Gilson emphatically repudiates. Aquinas defines a cause as: "causa importat influxum quemdam ad esse causati." [288] But this causality is rooted in and stems from Being who is the act of existing and to whom it belongs to diffuse Himself. In this interpretation of causality, there seems to be no suggestion, as Drouin assumes, that the transmitted is a fixed element. An operation, a movement, a breath, a process, an influence is imparted, not a thing.

Mr. Perry calls "the fallacy of difference": "The tendency to conceive a sectarian doctrine in terms of its *special*, to the exclusion of its *ge-*

neric, characteristics." [289] M. Gilson, in my estimation, commits this fallacy in his evaluation of Malebranche, although he carefully avoids it in his appraisal of the differences between Augustine and Aquinas. He is ready to acknowledge that Augustine and Aquinas agree on the exclusive creative role of God, that the two agree that the natural world is endowed with efficacy. Thomas' God is simply more generous. [290] To support this view, Gilson considers three aspects of the problem— physical causality or the doctrine of seminal virtues, causality in the cognitive order or doctrine of truth, and causality in the moral order or doctrine of virtue. He asserts that in each case Aquinas does not disagree with Augustine, but simply "rectifies" him. [291]

Malebranche, on the other hand, says Gilson, "perverts" St. Augustine and is less faithful to him than is Aquinas, [292] for, "Malebranche will have it that the glory of God is chanted by a world without nature and without efficacy; a radical impotency attesting the omnipotence of its Author."

I believe that Gilson is unjust in his accusations against Malebranche. If it be true that St. Thomas' doctrine does not essentially conflict with that of Augustine, then we must be equally prepared to acknowledge that Malebranche is no *radical* opponent of Thomism. The crucial question is whether or not, for Malebranche, God's glory is, as Gilson alleges, manifested by a world radically bereft of efficacy. Is Malebranche's world wholly and altogether without power? This I have abundantly shown to be untrue. But let Malebranche once more speak for himself:

> By means of these laws ["the most general laws of nature and of grace"] He communicates His power to His creatures and gives them a share in the glory of the work which He accomplishes through their agency. Indeed, it is through this very communication of His power and glory that He does the greatest honour to His attributes . . .[293]

But it will be asked, does Malebranche have agents? Is the occasional cause a *substratum?* Moreau, for example, after showing brilliantly how the distinction between essence and existence is for Malebranche no *tour de force,* then insists upon foisting a wholly idealistic interpretation upon him. Because Malebranche rejects Descartes' inert substantialism or any notion of substance as a static subject of inherence, Moreau concludes that Malebranche is no realist, as if realism were synonymous with bare staticism. He then insists that the distinction between essence and existence is "non indispensable" to Malebranche's system; [294] that regardless of what Malebranche says, it need not be construed in a realistic fashion, that is, that existence need not be taken as distinct from and added to an essence. For after all, says

Moreau, existence is synonymous with movement and duration. It is therefore no more than a phenomenal appearance of the essence. Accordingly, the major difference between Spinoza and Malebranche reduces to this: For Spinoza essences and their actualization follow necessarily; for Malebranche the actualization of an essence is contingent and arbitrary. If I have understood Moreau properly, then it seems to me that he is imposing upon Malebranche a sort of Suarezian or Scotist interpretation. When God creates, all that He really does is actualize an essence. Existence is no new element, but the accidental or durational determination of an essence. Moreau does not realize that this view annihilates the very distinction that Malebranche seeks to erect. By thus reducing existence to no more than the contingent appearance of an essence, the distinction between essence and existence would become a distinction of reason. Yet Malebranche insists that it is a real distinction.

However, if it is not the idealism of Suarez that Moreau intends, then he would seem to be veering towards Hume, in so far as Moreau insists upon eliminating existence as a distinct element and reducing it to nothing more than durational phenomenalism.[295] This too I think would be a betrayal of Malebranche. For Malebranche the creature is an analogue of God. God as Being is the act of existence. His creative power and efficacy are rooted in and derivative from that dynamism. Yet God is no mere Heraclitian flux or even a Bergsonian *Élan*. Being involves utmost stability and a superabundant activity. He is an unmoved mover. What is true of God is true of the analogue. As it is existence that makes an essence to be, as it is existence that concretely and in fact arrests mathematical divisibility, and thereby gives unity to the created object, so it is that this very act of existence also limits or arrests infinite diversity or flux. This very act of existence, which enables the creature to act and change, at the same time gives it permanence and identity. No such view is open to Hume, because his matters of fact are no more than passing inert states. But for Malebranche, the world of process, mobility and change is rooted in existence, and it is this existence added to an essence that allows both action and stability.

Chapter V

The Self

As a result of our investigation of Occasionalism, which we have just completed, we now view creatures in Malebranche's philosophy as combinations of an intelligible meaning or essence and of the vital action of existence. In the present chapter we shall see how this distinction casts new light on Malebranche's theory of the self. What awaits us is the discovery that, while the essence of the self is unknown, we are yet capable of indubitably apprehending its existence through the *simple vue* of the *sentiment intérieur*.

I. Pure Thought the Principal Attribute of Mind

In Descartes' dialogue, *The Search after Truth,* Epistemon the Scholastic asks the Cartesian Eudoxus: ". . . You say that you are and . . . that you know it because you doubt and because you think. But do you know what doubting or what thinking is? . . . How can you be certain that you are by means of attributes so obscure and consequently so uncertain?" [1] The enlightened Eudoxus replies:

The nature of thought, for Descartes.

> . . . I declare that there are certain things which we render more obscure by trying to define them, because, since they are very simple and clear, we cannot know and perceive them better than by themselves. Nay, we must place in the number of those chief errors that can be committed in the sciences, the mistakes committed by those who would try to define what ought only to be conceived, and who cannot distinguish the clear from the obscure, nor discriminate between what, in order to be known, requires and deserves to be defined, from what can be best known by itself. . . . It is only requisite to open one's eyes and see the white; in the same

way in order to know what doubt is, or thought, it is only requisite to doubt and think.[2]

To Descartes, thought, existence, doubt are self-evidently clear, for they are what he calls in the *Rules* 'simple natures' which, merely to think of them, is to know them. Elsewhere, however, Descartes is not averse to giving, not a definition, but a fuller account of what he means by thought. Thus in the second Meditation he writes that he is a thing which thinks and accordingly he "is a thing which doubts, understands, conceives, affirms, denies, wills, refuses, which also imagines and feels."[3] In the *Principles* and in the *Reply to Objections II* he offers a similar description and identification of thought with consciousness. "*Thought* is a word that covers everything that exists in us in such a way that we are immediately conscious of it. Thus all the operations of will, intellect, imagination, and of the senses are thoughts."[4] Again:

> By the word thought I understand all that of which we are conscious as operating in us. And that is why not alone understanding, willing, imagining, but also feeling are here the same thing as thought. For . . . if I mean only to talk of my sensation [sensu], or my consciously seeming to see or to walk, it becomes quite true because my assertion now refers only to my mind, which alone is concerned with my feeling or thinking that I see and I walk.[5]

On the basis of these texts, Mr. Church interprets Descartes' assertion that the nature of thought is more easily known than that of body. Descartes makes this claim, according to Church, because he identifies thought with the total conscious life of the soul. Thus Church continues:

The principal attribute of mind, for Descartes— pure thinking.

> Every perception, every image, every act of the understanding, illustrates the claim of the *cogito* that the denial of the existence of thought only reaffirms it. And not only is it impossible to doubt the existence of the present thought, it must also be plain that in the occurrence of every single thought there is an awareness of the nature of thought itself. Thus, in our examination of a piece of wax, whatever we learn about the nature of the wax shows us something of the nature of our own mind.[6]

Now Church's interpretation is true, but not true enough. There is, as I shall show presently, an even more important reason for Descartes' pronouncement that the soul is better known than the body than his identification of thought with consciousness. But first I want to point out that while Descartes does identify thought with all states of consciousness and not merely with the intellect, nevertheless all those conscious states occupy a special position. For in the *Principles* he declares:

But although any one attribute is sufficient to give us a knowledge of substance, there is always *one principal property* of substance which constitutes its nature and essence, and on which all the others depend. Thus extension in length, breadth and depth, constitutes the nature of corporeal substance; and thought constitutes the nature of thinking substance. For all else that may be attributed to body presupposes extension, and is but a mode of this extended thing; as everything that we find in mind is but so many diverse forms of thinking. *Thus, for example, we cannot conceive figure but as an extended thing, nor movement but as in an extended space; so imagination, feeling, and will, only exist in a thinking thing. But, on the other hand, we can conceive extension without figure or action, and thinking without imagination or sensation, and so on with the rest; as is quite clear to anyone who attends to the matter.*[7]

Again, in the sixth Meditation he asserts: ". . . This power of imagination . . . is in no wise a necessary element in my nature, or in my essence, that is to say, in the essence of my mind; . . . we might conclude that it depends on something which differs from me. . . . This mode of thinking differs from pure intellection only inasmuch as mind in its intellectual activity in some manner turns on itself, and considers some of the ideas which it possesses in itself; while in imagining it turns towards the body . . ."[8] The power of understanding that is the essence of mind, hence, Descartes describes as "pure intellection."

It is to be noted, then, that while sensing, willing, imagining are included in thought, they are so as its modes. That thought which constitutes the principal and essential attribute of mind is pure thought, that is conception. Even in the example of the wax, the thought that Descartes claims to know so well is rational thought, for he asserts: ". . . I could not even understand through the imagination what this piece of wax is, . . . it is my mind [*entendement* F., *mens* L.] alone which perceives it. . . . Its perception is neither an act of vision, nor of touch, nor of imagination, and has never been such although it may have appeared formerly to be so, but only an intuition [*inspectio*] of the mind, which may be imperfect and confused as it was formerly, or clear and distinct as it is at present."[9]

Mr. Albert G. A. Balz points out, in his *Cartesian Studies*, that Descartes adopted the dualism of body and mind in the first instance in the interests of attaining certainty—his problem was primarily logical and epistemological. "The 'cogito' does not imply the fact of self-consciousness as the central element in the definition of mind," Mr. Balz declares decisively. "It is rather the affirmation of rational certainty." Thus the function of the dualism is initially to define the subject as distinct from its subject matter; and it is only the consequence of this

But thinking becomes all of consciousness for Descartes and for the Cartesians.

position, Mr. Balz continues, that forces Descartes to alter the contents of his dualism. This consequence is a mechanistic physiology. As a result, the substance, the very essence of which is primarily to think rationally, subsequently acquires other elements excluded from matter. "Mind becomes *res cogitans,* and thinking comprises anything and everything that, being incompatible with extended substance, is existentially of a different character." Thus thinking and thought become being conscious and conscious states. Balz echoes Brunschvicg: *Ego sum* degenerates into *ego sum Cartesius.*" In the end the field for psychology is defined, and epistemology turns on this psychology.[10]

Balz goes on to show that the Cartesians begin where Descartes arrived. For example, for Clauberg, he tells us, the mind is a *res cogitans,* and *cogitare* includes all the activities of which the mind is directly aware, such as ratiocination, volition, intellection, sensation.[11] For La Forge the essence of mind is apprehended by a *"sentiment intérieur,"* which Balz interprets as immediate awareness. Balz declares: "La Forge here virtually equates thought, consciousness, and spirituality. . . . The *sentiment intérieur* is present in every *pensée.* Hence, the substance that thinks is a being the essential nature of which is to perceive everything happening within itself." Thus, for La Forge, in Balz's interpretation, spirit perceives itself, perceives what happens within itself, and its being is in this perceiving.[12]

Now, we must conclude that Malebranche follows both the epistemological and psychological Descartes. He too uses thought (*la pensée*) to designate all conscious states. This Mr. Church acknowledges.[13] But Church fails to see that, *just like Descartes,* Malebranche goes on to make conscious states modifications of pure rational thought, and retains the latter as the primary attribute. And Malebranche does so for precisely the same reasons as those which move Descartes, namely, that sensing, imagining, desiring, all involve and depend upon conceiving. Thus at the beginning of Book III of the *Recherche,* on the Pure Understanding, Malebranche writes:

> Je ne crois pas qu'après y avoir pensé sérieusement, on puisse douter que l'essence de l'esprit ne consiste que dans la pensée, de même que l'essence de la matière ne consiste que dans l'étendue, et que, selon les différentes modifications de la pensée, l'esprit tantôt veut et tantôt imagine ou enfin qu'il a plusieurs autres formes particulières . . .[14]

As a note to the phrase, "l'essence de l'esprit," Malebranche later adds to the foregoing passage: "Par l'essence d'une chose j'entends ce que l'on conçoit de premier dans cette chose, duquel dépendent toutes les modifications que l'on y remarque." In this text, Malebranche uses *pensée* as does Descartes to designate all forms of consciousness. But

[margin note:] Malebranche follows Descartes: conscious states modifications of pure thought.

[246]

then, just as Descartes maintains that every substance is constituted by some principal attribute on which all its properties depend, so Malebranche continues:

> J'avertis seulement que par ce mot, *pensée*, je n'entends point ici les modifications particulières de l'âme, c'est-à-dire telle ou telle pensée, mais la pensée capable de toutes sortes de modifications ou de pensées; de même que par l'étendue l'on n'entend pas une telle ou telle étendue, comme la ronde ou la carrée, mais l'étendue capable de toutes sortes de modification ou de figures. Et cette comparaison ne peut faire de peine que parce que *l'on n'a pas une idée claire de la pensée, comme l'on en a de l'étendue; car on ne connaît la pensée que par sentiment intérieur ou par conscience,* ainsi que je l'expliquerai plus bas.
>
> Je ne crois pas aussi qu'il soit possible de concevoir un esprit qui ne pense point, quoiqu'il soit fort facile d'en concevoir un qui ne sente point, qui n'imagine point, et même qui ne veuille point; de même qu'il n'est pas possible de concevoir une matière qui ne soit pas étendue, quoiqu'il soit assez facile d'en concevoir une qui ne soit ni terre ni métal, ni carrée ni ronde, et qui même ne soit point en mouvement. Il faut conclure de là que comme il se peut faire qu'il y ait de la matière qui ne soit ni terre ni métal, ni carrée ni ronde, ni même en mouvement, il se peut faire aussi qu'un esprit ne sente ni chaud ni froid, ni joie ni tristesse, n'imagine rien, et même ne veuille rien; de sorte que toutes ces modifications ne lui sont point essentielles. La pensée toute seule est donc l'essence de l'esprit, ainsi que l'étendue toute seule est l'essence de la matière.[15]

It must be borne in mind that all these statements occur as a prelude to his discussion on the nature of ideas. Hence when Malebranche declares that thought alone is the essence of the soul, he means that the capacity to grasp universal meanings, eternal truths, and thus rational certainty is the defining characteristic of minds. Thus one cannot conceive an intelligence that does not think. Even the damned in hell are to that extent united to God, for even they are not unaware of eternal truths contained in the Word. This must be so, for it is impossible for God to make a mind that does not know Him, i.e., that is not enlightened by the Word, or one that is not, however vaguely, intuitively aware of Him as infinitely infinite Being.[16]

Moreover, such pure intellect is the essence or principal attribute of the soul, because there can be no sensing or imagining without intellection, but intellection can take place without imagery, as in Descartes' example of the chiliagon or in Malebranche's treatment of arithmetic. Thus Malebranche agrees with Descartes that the essence or principal attribute of mind is thought, that this thought includes all modes but is primarily rational or intuitive intellection; although he insists that this essence is not known through a distinct idea. Hence, like La Forge and like Descartes too, he is saying that this rational essence of mind, as well as all other modes of thought, can be apprehended or known only through the *'sentiment intérieur.'* The *sentiment intérieur* is not purely an epistemological or logical "I think" but is an act of conscious awareness or apprehension that accompanies or is present with every thought, be it a sensation or act of conception. And to this extent we shall find that for Malebranche, as for La Forge, the *sentiment intérieur* will constitute and disclose the *being* or existence of mind, although it does not perspicuously define its essence.

Church, resting his argument on the above passages which we have quoted from Malebranche, makes several unwarranted claims. First, he argues that when Malebranche talks of the modifications of thought, of this or that thought, he refers exclusively to states of *sensuous* consciousness.[17] Secondly, because of this alleged restriction, Malebranche, it seems apparent to Church, uses "substantial thought" in rigorous contrast to the sensuous consciousness, thus erecting a virtual dualism in the soul. ("This distinction becomes a virtual dualism within the soul . . .")[18] Thirdly, because Malebranche, unlike Descartes, divorces pure substantial thought from sensuous modifications, it follows that, contrary to Descartes, for Malebranche: "No modification of the soul in any way exhibits the fact that its nature is to be a modification of thought, or of anything at all. No amount of introspective analysis can discover more than certain states of consciousness. Therefore pure spirit is unknowable."[19] For this reason, says Church, self knowledge through introspection or through the *sentiment intérieur* is not regarded by Malebranche as real knowledge. "The issue between Malebranche and Descartes is clear," proclaims Church. Malebranche believes that all that we know of the soul are feelings, inclinations, passions and the images of sense and imagination. Church allows Malebranche to agree with Descartes that we know states of consciousness when we imagine or sense, "but he is concerned to deny that any state, or any collection of states of consciousness, affords knowledge of the nature of thought itself." Moreover, Church continues, whereas Descartes might admit that a taste like that of melon affords knowledge of thought itself, since it is a state of consciousness, "Malebranche points out that from the experience of the present moment nothing as to its source can be inferred."[20] Were we to ask Church where Malebranche does point this out, he would send us to Malebranche's eleventh Éclaircissement, where Malebranche asserts that even though we are actually feeling pain or seeing color, we cannot discover by introspection that these qualities belong to the soul.[21]

At this stage of his exposition of the philosophy of Malebranche, Church has the stage props all set for the dramatic performance of

Church alleges a dualism of substantial thought *vs.* sensuous consciousness in Malebranche.

Hume. Having separated pure rational thought from conscious states, and having claimed that for Malebranche introspection reveals no more than this or that sensuous state, then, concludes Mr. Church, "Had Malebranche shared Hume's desire to believe as little as possible in philosophy, his criticism of Descartes might well have carried him on to deny the existence of a thinking substance." What restrains Malebranche from becoming Hume, in Mr. Church's view, are Malebranche's deference to Descartes' authority and his "religious convictions!"—"But owing to his religious convictions and his faith in Descartes' authority, Malebranche stops where Hume's preoccupation with the foreground of consciousness should have arrested him." *And holds that sensuous consciousness precludes all knowledge of the self.*

Indeed, Malebranche even "anticipates Hume's sceptical analysis of personal identity," says Church with a patronizing flourish, for: "No less clearly than his successor, Malebranche sees that no examination of consciousness can reveal the nature of its substance, nor indeed that it has a substance at all." It is in this "important respect" that Malebranche even anticipates Hume.[22] *And destroys personal identity.*

Thus in Church's opinion Malebranche ought to have recognized that the *sentiment intérieur* or introspection yields no more than the prospect of the present moment, a "datum" from which nothing can be inferred. But out of what amounts to religious benightment and servile submission to Descartes, Malebranche nevertheless insists that while the *sentiment intérieur* yields no knowledge of the nature of the soul still it does incomprehensibly yield knowledge of the existence and personal identity of the soul. To be sure, with respect to this latter stubborn insistence, Church is prepared to praise Malebranche for being a better empiricist than Hume. The *sentiment intérieur* is indeed unlike any other feeling. It is a feeling of self consciousness, of self existence, and of self identity. But still and all, argues Church, the *sentiment intérieur* is no more and no less an immediate experience than any other conscious state; therefore: "like any other experience, it affords no ground for asserting the existence of more than itself."[23] Accordingly, Malebranche has no foundation for his dogged belief in the existence of a thinking substance.

Moreover, everything that Malebranche says about the substantiality of pure spirit makes it as unknowable as Locke's "I know not what." In fact, it is worse than that. For, by excluding pure spirit from sensuous consciousness, by describing it as passive and pure, Malebranche renders it other-worldly and inaccessible, bereft of all determinate character and therefore completely empty.[24] We cannot know pure spirit by the *sentiment intérieur*, for this is a feeling, and pure spirit cannot be felt.[25] But being wholly "pure" and "passive," it, the pure spirit, is like a wind without direction, and cannot be conceived as an actual existence.[26] *And reduces spirit to non-entity.*

The Philosophy of Malebranche

From Mr. Church's analysis we can only conclude that Malebranche is both a poor philosopher and a bigoted religionist. His religious zeal leads him to abandon Descartes, to divorce thought and sensuous consciousness, so that thought can be united with God. This line of reasoning, however, leads to Hume's sceptical conclusions concerning the impossibility of transcending the specious present. Thus on the one hand pure spirit is made into a non-entity absorbed in God. On the other hand, Malebranche is equally concerned to maintain a personal immortal soul, and hence he employs the *sentiment intérieur,* but this *sentiment* completely fails to perform the task for which it is introduced. Furthermore, having thus reduced Malebranche to the specious present, Mr. Church then criticizes him for offering a psychology of the soul. Malebranche can have no such psychology, for the soul is nothing but a succession of impressions, and the fact that Malebranche does offer one shows how dreadfully inconsistent he is. Finally, since Malebranche has so radically bifurcated pure spirit from sensuous consciousness, he can have no adequate theory of sense perception. Perception cannot include the understanding; it cannot therefore include any intelligible content. And the fact that Malebranche insists that it does and goes so far as to affirm that perception is a natural revelation of objects, but shows once again how incoherent, inconsistent and futile Malebranche can be.

From my point of view, Church's interpretation of Malebranche's doctrine concerning the self is misconceived from beginning to end, and it is unfortunate that the only important study of Malebranche in English is the result of this misinterpretation. The misunderstanding arises, moreover, at the very beginning of Church's *Study* and thus becomes the critically erroneous point of departure for his subsequent analysis of Malebranche's philosophy. I believe, further, that with regard to the self, Church's mistaken polemic issues first from his initial failure to understand those passages in which Malebranche claims that the essence of the soul is pure thought; secondly, from his failure to realize what are the *chief* grounds of Descartes' claim that mind is better known than body. Thirdly, having neglected Descartes and having misconstrued Malebranche right from the start, it was inevitable that Church should have read the important eleventh Éclaircissement wherein Malebranche criticizes Descartes through Humian eyeglasses.

Let us, then, first return to the crucial citations in which Malebranche warns that by the word thought (*pensée*) he means *substantial thought* and not the particular modifications of thought. Now, despite Mr. Church's allegation, there is no evidence whatsoever that in distinguishing substantial thought from its modes, Malebranche intends to do what Descartes did not do; that is, there is no evidence that Malebranche makes a *radical* separation between pure intellection and

Will and feeling inseparable from pure thought, for Malebranche.

sensuous states. That such is actually contrary to his intention is clearly evidenced by his treatment of volition. Immediately following his assertions that it is impossible to conceive a mind that does not think, although it is very easy to conceive of one that does not feel, imagine, or will, Malebranche goes on to say that really there can never exist a pure spirit without a will. A pure intelligence without a will, he declares, would be useless, for such a mind would be incapable of enjoying, loving, or uniting itself with the objects of its contemplation. Just as matter or extension without movement would be entirely useless and just as it would be incomprehensible that such motion-free matter would be created by an intelligent being, affirms Malebranche, similarly a spirit or thought that lacked will would be entirely useless, "puisque cet esprit ne se porterait jamais vers les objets de ces perceptions . . . : de sorte qu'il n'est pas possible de concevoir qu'un être intelligent l'ait voulu produire en cet état." [27] And, remember, when Malebranche affirms that something is vain, inconceivable or useless, this is equivalent to the assertion that it is an irrational and false assumption. For Malebranche's Deity is no indifferent dictator. He acts with purpose and reason. As it is impossible for God to create minds that do not know Him, so it is impossible to make minds that do not will or love Him.

But this is not to identify will with spirit—"Néanmoins, comme le mouvement n'est pas de l'essence de la matière, puisqu'il suppose de l'étendue; ainsi vouloir n'est pas de l'essence de l'esprit, puisque vouloir suppose la perception." [28] Malebranche clearly recognizes that a purely passive spirit would be utterly empty and thus no real existent. For this reason, he goes out of his way to add that whether or not the mind is united to a body, the will is *inseparable* from thought: ". . . Mais vouloir est une propriété qui l'accompagne toujours, soit qu'il soit uni à un corps ou qu'il en soit séparé; laquelle cependant ne lui est pas essentielle . . ." [29] If volition is a part of sensuous consciousness (and Church recognizes this to be so for Malebranche), then it is clear that, at least as far as willing is concerned, Malebranche does not exclude it from pure spirit, but rather insists upon its inseparability from it.

What, then, of other sensuous states, those of imagination and sensation? Malebranche concedes that all the feelings of pleasure and pain and all the sensations with which we are at present acquainted are occasioned by physical processes. Nevertheless, he says, it is reasonable to believe that in after life the soul will experience sensations far surpassing anything felt at present.[30] Why is it reasonable to make such a supposition? The easy answer is: because of a religious conviction. The true answer is that pure spirit is inseparable from will, and to be a will is to love and to enjoy. Feeling is as inseparable from spirit, then, as will. This is why in his treatise, *L'Amour de Dieu*, Malebranche lays such emphasis on the delectation of the saints and the pleasures of the saved and blessed life. These are different from those of our present existence, but the important point is that in principle Malebranche recognizes some kind of feeling to be an integral aspect of mind. Even God in the person of the Holy Spirit possesses love. This enables us to understand why Malebranche forcibly rejects the quietistic doctrine of Fénelon according to which the soul becomes wholly lost in God, totally oblivious of its own self, and indifferent to pleasure or well being.

Why, then, it will be asked, does Malebranche assert pure thought to be the essence of the soul? The answer is to be found, once more, in what he says of volition: to will is not the essence of the mind, since to will presupposes perception. Again: the will is not essential to thought (*la pensée*), because one can *conceive* a mind (*esprit*) without a will as one can conceive a body without movement.[31] Be it recalled (what I have been arguing for two chapters) that Malebranche distinguishes between essence and existence, between what a thing is and the circumstances of its being. In insisting upon the inseparability of the will from spirit, while at the same time making thought the principal attribute, he is, curiously, both following and departing from Descartes. While the Scholastics recognized inseparable attributes of substances, Descartes went much further. We saw that Descartes assigned to each substance an attribute which was in some way fundamental, which alone enabled the existence of the substance to be asserted, and which "du même coup" defined its essence, since the substance is, as existing, simply that attribute substantialized.[32]

But pure thought is the essence of the soul.

To the extent that Malebranche insists upon the will in a really existing mind, he is in profound disagreement with Descartes. Since for Descartes God can create anything of which we have a clear and distinct idea, since pure thought is the essence, and since existence adds nothing to the essence, then presumably God can actualize a purely passive thought, as He can an inert extension. But for Malebranche thinking alone does not make a thing really be. Hence Malebranche does not, when considering substance on the metaphysical, *existential* level, reduce it to the attribute of thought. However, when, as an epistemologist, he considers substance as that which defines the *nature* of a thing, as that which makes it be what it is, then, for him, as for Descartes, willing, sensing, imagining are all forms of thinking. For this reason they cannot be comprehended apart from thought. To imagine, will, sense—all these are included in thought not only in so far as thought embraces all states of consciousness, but also because they all depend upon some form of intellection proper. Thought is the essence of the soul, because it can be conceived as the primitive and primary notion. Thought is the substantial attribute, because there is no more basic or ultimate principle into which it can be further analyzed and because there is nothing else which it presupposes. And thought as intellection is primary, because, too, it is that aspect of mind which distinguishes it from beast and animal. Reason and cognition are the principal characteristics of the human mind as of all minds.[33] This is why intellection can be grasped apart from sense, imagination and volition; and why we can not conceive a mind that does not think but can conceive one that does not imagine, sense or will.

Thus, far from setting up a rigid divorce between pure spirit and sensuous consciousness, as Church claims, Malebranche, on the contrary, follows Descartes and makes spiritual thought the very ingredient and constituent principle of all that the soul experience in itself. Were Church correct, then we should be compelled to condemn Malebranche as a very loose thinker indeed, for if at the outset of the chapter, where he speaks of substantial thought, he intended to divorce spirit from consciousness, he is very quick to reunite them in the fourth paragraph and maintain their marriage straight through to the end of the chapter, which culminates thus: "Il nous suffit donc de savoir que le principe de toutes ces modifications c'est la pensée." I am certain, Malebranche continues, that one knows his soul only by thought (*la pensée*), or by the *sentiment intérieur:* "personne n'a de connaissance de son âme que par la pensée ou par le sentiment intérieur de tout ce qui se passe dans son esprit . . ." Malebranche is likewise assured that if one wishes to reason concerning the nature of the soul, he need consult only the *sentiment intérieur:* "il ne doit consulter que ce sentiment intérieur qui le représente sans cesse à lui-même tel qu'il est . . ."[34]

Pure thought the necessary condition and constituent of all consciousness.

Shall we assume that *la pensée* here at the end is no longer the same substantial *la pensée* as it is at the beginning? Church, of course, would be compelled to say this, for Malebranche refers to the *sentiment intérieur* at this juncture, but pure spirit, according to Church, cannot be felt. Yet in a later chapter Malebranche claims precisely the contrary:

> . . . par ces mots, *pensée, manière de penser,* ou *modification de l'âme,* j'entends généralement toutes les choses qui ne peuvent être dans l'âme sans qu'elle les aperçoive par le sentiment intérieur qu'elle a d'elle-même: comme sont ces propres sensations, ses imaginations, ses *pures intellections,* ou simplement ses *conceptions,* ses passions mêmes et ses inclinations naturelles.[35]

Now, if when Malebranche talks of modifications he means only states of sensuous consciousness, as Church alleges, then how shall we explain this unambiguous inclusion of acts of conception? And if the *sentiment intérieur* is a sensuous feeling that cannot be aware of pure acts of understanding, why does Malebranche claim that it can? And why when he defines the essence of thought as pure intellection does he assert that one can grasp it through the *sentiment intérieur?* It is evident that Church is too rash in his de-Cartesianizing of Male-branche. Moreover, even Clauberg and La Forge, if we follow Mr. Balz, as we saw, include acts of pure cognitive intellection within the scope of the *sentiment intérieur.* Again, we know that Malebranche first became acquainted with Descartes' writings through reading Des-cartes' *L'Homme. L'Homme* was published in 1664 by Clerselier and contained a preface by him.[36] In *L'Homme* Descartes describes the soul in language that resembles that of the second Meditation. But Clerselier in his preface does something more. He uses "thought" at once very widely to include all states of consciousness and simulta-neously he speaks of the soul in terms of its cognition or intellectual function.[37] Thus he uses thought as does Descartes to include all states of consciousness; at the same time in determining precisely the nature of thought he refers to the purely rational aspect of thought.

And so it is with Malebranche. In the *Entretiens sur la métaphysique,* he asserts:

> Nothing or Non-being has no qualities. I think, therefore I am. But what am I, I that think during the time that I am thinking? Am I a body, a mind [esprit], a man? As yet I know nothing of all this. I know only that during the time in which I think I am something that thinks. Now let us see. Can a body think? Can a piece of extension whether of length, width, or depth, reason, de-sire, feel? No, beyond a doubt, for all the modifications of such an extension consist only in certain relations of distance; and it is obvious that such relations are not perceptions, reasonings, pleasures, desires, feelings, in a word, thoughts. This "I" that thinks, then, my own substance, is not a body, since my perceptions, which cer-tainly belong to me, are entirely different things from these rela-tions of distance.[38]

These statements exactly echo Descartes' description of the mind in the second Meditation and in his *Reply to Hobbes* where he affirms that thought is the common notion or element of all perceptions. And when at the outset of the third book of the *Recherche* Malebranche warns that by *pensée* he means substantial thought, he is still follow-ing Descartes. Descartes affirms that the soul apprehends itself by an act of pure thought, that is, without physical imagery.[39] Augustine did likewise.[40] And for Malebranche the *sentiment intérieur* will play the same role. It will be a form of internal apperception by which the mind directly apprehends itself.

The Self

II. INTELLECTUAL THOUGHT AND EXISTENTIAL THOUGHT

Malebranche and Descartes then both use thought in a comprehensive manner, and, in so far as they do, there is no disagreement between them concerning the claim that mind is better known than body. But there is another reason why Descartes is so sure of knowing his mind more evidently than body, and it is this reason which forces Malebranche to abandon Descartes—from thinking to being, the consequence is valid—before we know whether anything exists, we must first know what it is. These pronouncements of Descartes are by now fully familiar. They are the basis of his conception of God as *Causa Sui.* They are also, as is well known, the basis of his *Cogito.* While Descartes maintains that the *Cogito* is not an inference but an immediate self-evident awareness of a particular existential thing or fact, nevertheless this awareness of his own individual existence is one that proceeds from what he is to that he is. Thus it is that the *Cogito* is for Descartes the very prototype of clear and distinct knowledge, for in the pronouncement, "I think; I am," it is thought that is entailing or positing its own existence. Thinking is not for Descartes a way of existing but the root and very cause of his existing. This is why he defies the demon—the demon cannot make me into nothing as long as I think I am something. Again, when Descartes asks how often is this fact of his existence true, the answer is: each time that I pronounce it or mentally conceive it.

(margin: Descartes, identifying thought and its objects, passes from knowing to being.)

Geneviève Lewis rightly insists that the *Cogito* does not affirm a timeless impersonal, universal subject, but a concrete personal self, for, she points out, what Descartes says is "Ego cogito, ergo sum, sive existo." This, she argues, is not equivalent to "Es denkt in mir." It is this stubborn emphasis on the *Ego cogito,* she claims, that kept Descartes from Spinozism, and it explains his vehement opposition to Averroistic pantheism.[41] When Descartes announces, "Sum ergo Deus est," [42] he does indeed find God immediately and directly and inwardly present to his mind, but not himself as a mode in God. The *cogito* remains an image and semblance of God, outside God, and is not an integral part of Him.[43]

All this is true; yet individual and separate from God as may be the *sum, sive existo,* its individuality nevertheless is something bequeathed. It is thought actualizing itself into an *existo.* It is an essence that generates or degenerates into the durational mode, which mode becomes the *sum.*[44]

Because the *Cogito* is thus an expression or illustration of the essence of thought entailing its own being, Descartes is able to say that he knows his own mind better than his body. The example of the wax is offered as testimony. When by a pure intuition or inspection of the mind he recognizes the wax to be something extended and moveable, this intuition is nothing but another example of pure thought exercising itself and thus affirming its own being. Moreover, since Descartes acknowledges no separation between act and content, each clear and distinct idea, be it that of the immutable triangle or the idea of God, is additional confirmation of the clarity with which he knows his own soul as a thinking thing. Finally, once again, inasmuch as Descartes rejects any real distinction between essence and existence, not only is thought the principal attribute that *defines* his existence, but it is primary and absolute in the sense that it *determines* his existence. This is why he declares that if he should cease to think he might cease to exist.

Since then his very existence is a determination of thought and the whole content of thinking—all the ideas—are intrinsic aspects of thought, it is with very good reason that Descartes claims to know himself with utter perspicacity. For what really is this intellection or thought that constitutes the primary attribute of mind and makes Descartes to be or exist? The soul, considered as pure thought, has the cardinal role of addressing itself to quantity. As Kepler said,[45] so Descartes believes too: that the real function of understanding is not to understand anything you please, but quantity. Now for Descartes this quantity means geometrical shapes, like the triangle, or its algebraic equivalent, and these are innate, lodged in the mind, even created by it. Because of this doctrine of innateness, Descartes can indeed assume that he has a distinct idea of the soul and even that it is better known than anything else. For, as again in the case of the wax, what the mind knows of the wax is its pure quantity lodged in and made by the act of pure intuition. In short, for Descartes the pure thinking thing, the epistemological *Cogito*, is a mathematically structured and self-causing spiritual automaton that in affirming itself at once generates all mathematical and eternal truths. To think in terms of quantity is the very essence of the soul. Hence Descartes can say that he knows its nature or has a distinct idea of it. For the mathematics apprehended and the mind that apprehends are really identical. Thus the discovery of analytical geometry was as much a discovery of his own mind as it was of body.

But Malebranche, as we saw, divorces content from act of conception. The triangle conceived, the geometric circle or its algebraic equation, is a distinct entity and no creation of thought. Hence, while it remains true to say that to think distinctly is to think quantitatively, for Malebranche this means to think of or about quantity, and not, as for Descartes, to be characterized by the content thought. The adverb, quantitatively, in "to think quantitatively" is used adjectivally by Des-

Malebranche separates thought and its objects.

cartes as an attribute of the soul; but quantity becomes a noun in the philosophy of Malebranche. Hence, Malebranche can no longer say that we have a distinct idea of the soul, for we do not have an algebra or geometry of thinking. There exists a quantitative or algebraic expression for the soul, but it is not disclosed to our inspection, and the quantity of which we do think is not innately constitutive of the soul. In Spinoza's philosophy this problem is eliminated by his making extension or body parallel to mind. The body for him is the mechanism and geometry of the soul. The mind is the idea of body. As knowledge of the body is transformed, so is self knowledge. But this "solution" is not open to Malebranche, for Malebranche remains a Cartesian dualist, and his God is *Celui qui est,* not Spinoza's *Causa Sui.*

As long, then, as Descartes holds a theory of innate ideas wherein idea as object of thought and idea as an act of thought are inseparable, Descartes can indeed assert that his knowledge of his own mind is superior to that of body. What Descartes ignores, however, is the fact that however much it belongs to the nature of mind to think in terms of exact mathematical relations and so far forth can be identified with the relations known, nevertheless this very mathematics does not of itself encompass all those elements that Descartes includes in his description of thought. As founder of analytical geometry, that body of truth pertains to his mind. Still it is not an account of his mind, in so far as that mind is a sensing, feeling, willing being. The analytical geometry still remains a geometry of matter and not that of thought. And for this reason sensations are embarrassing to Descartes. As a mathematician, he can be high handed about imagination, for imagination is thought directed to a corporeal figure, which in turn can be treated geometrically. But what to do with sensations of pain, of pleasure, of hunger, of colors and of sounds? In the *Rules* Descartes can suggest, we saw, that an infinitude of figures can represent an infinitude of things, including colors. Nevertheless the secondary qualities in themselves are not mathematically quantifiable, and once their exclusion from body is made, all semblance to quantification is abandoned. What is true of sensation is true of volition. No more than sensation, volition somehow or other escapes the formal, mathematicizing intellect. So that while willing is described as a mode of thought, nevertheless it is given a quasi-independent existence.[46]

Church, then, is partly correct. Descartes can say that he knows his mind better than body as long as he uses "mind" or "thought" to cover all states of sensuous consciousness. But conversely and more importantly, Descartes can also maintain that his knowledge of mind is more evident as long as he ignores volition and the actual sensuous modifications and identifies the mathematics of body with his own intellection, idea and act. Now it is just this latter negligence on the part of Descartes and his followers that marks the parting of the ways between Malebranche and the Cartesians. And it becomes a point of division precisely because, unlike them, Malebranche separates act of conception from the distinct mathematical ideas conceived. Once this separation is made, it becomes palpably clear that our knowledge of the nature of mind is not so complete or perfect as is our knowledge of body. Thus it is that his disagreement with the Cartesians on our knowledge of mind is first fully explored in the chapter of the *Recherche* that follows his discussion of Vision of ideas in God. In other words, there is no disagreement between Descartes and Malebranche concerning the knowledge of mind on the introspective level. By introspection, or the *sentiment intérieur,* we become, as Eudoxus said, clearly aware of our sensations, imaginations, acts of conception, volitions. By reflection on these various operations we recognize them to be modes of a single principle, thought.[47] "Elle [the soul] aperçoit par *l'entendement pur* les choses spirituelles, les universelles, les notions communes, l'idée de la perfection, celle d'un être infiniment parfait, et généralement toutes ses pensées comme ses inclinations naturelles, ses passions et ses perceptions." [48]

This passage occurs at the beginning of the *Recherche.* Yet, while Malebranche did amend it, he did so in such a way that there is no reason to suppose that in turning to the *sentiment intérieur* he meant to exclude the pure understanding from it. And this is why Malebranche can say with Descartes: *Je pense, donc je suis,* or: "Je conclus que je suis parce que je me sens, et que le néant ne peut être senti." [49] This is not, as Mr. Church would have it,[50] a reformulation of Descartes—that is, this is not a statement that regards sensuous states only and excludes pure thought. It is not this, because, as we saw, acts of conception are also felt by the *sentiment intérieur.* Hence the declaration is as comprehensive as Descartes' *Cogito.*

Nevertheless, after having shown that ideas of body are an eternal, immutable order, Malebranche is now compelled to assert, as did Epistemon in Descartes' *Search after Truth,* that our introspective and self-reflective knowledge of mind falls short of the knowledge of body; not that it is false, but that in comparison with what we know of the nature of extension, introspection is not so complete (*entière*) and perfect.[51] Through introspection we know our own *existence* better than the existence of body. But with respect to their natures, we know the *nature* of body better than that of mind. As a vindication of this position, Malebranche wrote the eleventh Éclaircissement. The message of this clarification is that, were psychology a strict science, it would be both *a priori* and mathematical, but in point of fact, it is not and cannot be.

In the case of body, our knowledge of its essence is clear, distinct

And therefore Malebranche has only obscure and indirect ideas of the nature of mind.

and exact, because it is both *a priori* and subject to precise mathematical or quantitative statement. Descartes himself acknowledged that the secret of that science called universal mathematics lay in its order and measurement. These two elements then became the core of his mathematical method, as we saw above. By order Descartes meant that in any investigation we should begin with those notions that are primary, those from which a deduction of properties could follow, such as would solve the problem at hand. The unknown was to be determined by an uninterrupted deduction from certain intuitively known elements. But in addition to order, there was measurement. The unknown was arrived at by a concise, rigorously quantitative comparison of the terms. Faithful to this description of what constitutes the secret of mathematical certainty and going even beyond Descartes, as we observed, to the claim that arithmetic and algebra have greater intelligible clarity than geometry, Malebranche challenges Descartes on our knowledge of the nature of mind. Malebranche examines the status of secondary qualities in order to prove that we have neither an *a priori* nor a mathematical cognition of mind. We can say, declares Malebranche, that we have a clear and distinct idea of body, because it suffices to consult the essence of extension to know right off by simple inspection (*de simple vue*) its properties and the exact relationships among them. Merely to consider extension is to know immediately that it can be round or square, at rest or in motion.[52] Extension taken in its precise signification as relations of distance at once excludes the secondary qualities. Furthermore, the relationships among figures are known with exactitude. We conceive without difficulty that a square can be divided into two triangles. Thus our knowledge of body, of its properties and relations, is both *a priori* and mathematically rigorous.

But it is quite otherwise with the soul. We have no idea of mind such that by simple inspection we can at once deduce what it comprehends and what it excludes:

> Si nous n'avions jamais senti ni plaisir ni douleur, nous ne pourrions point savoir si l'âme serait ou ne serait pas capable d'en sentir. Si un homme n'avait jamais mangé de melon, vu de rouge ou de bleu, il aurait beau consulter l'idée prétendue de son âme, il ne découvrirait jamais distinctement, si elle serait ou ne serait pas capable de tels sentiments ou de telles modifications.[53]

Furthermore, when the Cartesians attribute the secondary qualities to the soul, they do so not by directly examining the essence of thought but rather by the indirect process of excluding them from extension.

> Pour s'assurer si les qualités sensibles sont, ou ne sont pas, des manières d'être de l'esprit, on ne consulte point l'idée prétendue de

l'âme; les cartésiens mêmes consultent au contraire l'idée de l'étendue, et ils raisonnent ainsi. La chaleur, la douleur, la couleur ne peuvent être des modifications de l'étendue; car l'étendue n'est capable que de différentes figures et de différents mouvements. Or il n'y a que deux genres d'êtres, des esprits et des corps. Donc la douleur, la chaleur, la couleur, et toutes les autres qualités sensibles appartiennent à l'esprit.[54]

Such a circuitous detour shows that we have no distinct idea of the soul as we do of body. We know that roundness belongs to extension, not by excluding it from thought but positively by examining the nature of extension. But the immediate experience of a pain or color does not disclose *it* to be a property of thought. As a matter of fact, in experiencing pains and colors we instinctively attribute the sensed qualities to bodies, and we correct our mistakes by examining the essence of body, not that of thought. "Je dis plus, quoiqu'on sente actuellement de la douleur, ou qu'on voie de la couleur, on ne peut découvrir de simple vue si ces qualités appartiennent à l'âme." [55]

For Church this passage shows that Malebranche has completely abandoned Descartes and gone far in the direction of Hume. Because introspection fails to disclose the physical or mental nature of the sensed qualities, we must conclude, he argues, that for Malebranche introspection reveals *nothing* of the nature of thought or of consciousness; introspection or experience is not knowledge at all, because: "it consists in no more than the prospect of the present moment." [56]

But acts of perceiving attest existence of soul.

But what right have we to impose so narrow an interpretation on the above passage? All that Malebranche is asserting is *first* that apart from empirical experience we do not know the specific sensations of which the mind is capable, and *second* in sensing a color or in suffering a pain, we do not know whether the *qualities* sensed do or do not belong to the soul. *But what about the acts of sensing and of suffering?* May Malebranche not still agree with Descartes that the *tasting* of the melon, the *seeing* of red disclose themselves when experienced as ways of thinking and to that extent do reveal the nature of thought? Church's interpretation forces Malebranche to the unhappy predicament of having no psychology at all, and thus falling into hopeless inconsistency, for after all Malebranche does claim to know a good deal about the soul.

But if we distinguish between sensing and qualities sensed, between acts and content, we eliminate all these difficulties. Malebranche, by making this distinction, is enabled to agree with Descartes to the extent of avoiding Hume's prospect of the present moment and yet to disagree with Descartes to the extent that introspection, however much knowledge it offers, is imperfect when compared to the ideal of a rational mathematical psychology. After all, when Descartes in the second Meditation maintains that every state of consciousness reaffirms the *Cogito*, he does so on the grounds that the operations of doub*ting*, feel*ing*, will*ing* and imagin*ing* are immediately known to be forms of thinking. And this is the core of the answer to Gassendi, namely, that each time he is aware of anything at all, every such act is an expression of his thinking. Now there is no reason why Malebranche may not accept these statements of Descartes. And in point of fact he does when he describes what we know through the *sentiment intérieur:*

> De toutes nos connaissances, la première c'est l'existence de notre âme; toutes nos pensées en sont des démonstrations incontestables, car il n'y a rien de plus évident que ce qui pense actuellement est actuellement quelque chose. Mais s'il est facile de connaître l'existence de son âme, il n'est pas si facile d'en connaître l'essence et la nature. Si l'on veut savoir ce qu'elle est, il faut surtout bien prendre garde à ne la pas confondre avec les choses auxquelles elle est unie. *Si l'on doute, si l'on veut, si l'on raisonne,* il faut seulement croire que l'âme est une chose qui doute, qui veut, qui raisonne, et rien davantage, pourvu qu'on n'ait point éprouvé en elle d'autres propriétés; car on ne connaît son âme que par le sentiment intérieur qu'on en a. . . . Ainsi l'on connaîtra par simple vue ou par sentiment intérieur tout ce que l'on peut connaître de l'âme, sans être obligé à faire des raisonnements dans lesquels l'erreur se pourrait trouver.[57]

Notice that this knowledge through *sentiment intérieur* is described as knowledge *par simple vue.* Thus even though we are obliged to attribute the sensed *qualities* to the soul by indirect reasoning; even though in sensing a color we cannot know immediately the status of the quality, we do know *par simple vue* that perceiv*ing* belongs to consciousness.

Even the manner in which Malebranche attributes qualities to the soul indicates a distinction between act and content. Cartesians, he complains, are not in agreement on the status of the qualities assigned to the soul. Does the soul actually become sweet, peppered, salty? Does it become blue, red, yellow or tinged with the colors of the rainbow "lorsqu'elle le considère?"[58] Had we a distinct idea of the soul, we should know the answer. Nevertheless, it is to be noticed that on the basis of immediate experience we *do* discriminate between considering or sensing blue and the blue sensed. The qualities themselves are neutral; they say nothing about the nature of thought nor indicate that they are mental. And had Malebranche rigorously pursued this line of reasoning and had he not applied Occam's razor so acutely, he might have seen that there was no good reason for excluding them from body or including them in mind. Still and all, as mental acts, sensations can be said to reveal themselves as operations of the mind.

This distinction between sensing and the qualities sensed Malebranche makes clear in an undated letter published by Blampignon. You ask me (so Malebranche writes to P. de Villes) to tell you who consults the idea of extension to know whether color is a modification of the soul. My answer is that everyone does, including yourself, who is convinced that his soul is green when looking at a field. For I defy you to prove to anyone that green is a property of the soul, without consulting the idea of extension. ". . . Ne venez pas nous dire, qu'en se consultant soi-même, on voit bien que c'est l'âme qui sent la couleur; je le veux . . ." Although Aristotle and practically everyone else say that the soul senses, no one concludes from *this* that the color sensed may be a modality of the soul.[59] The issue then is clear. In introspection, Malebranche agrees, the mind can immediately know that it is feeling the color; and it can know immediately that the feeling or sensing belongs to it; but what it does not know immediately is what relates to the quality sensed.

It is perfectly apparent that Mr. Church violates the text. His procedure may be compared to that of a weird doctor who might amputate a patient's leg and then in defense of the unnecessary act argue that the patient never really was a two-legged creature. Thus, gratuitously assuming that in the eleventh Éclaircissement Malebranche does not distinguish between sensing and qualities sensed, he imprisons Malebranche within the prospect of the present moment, depriving him of the use of any noetic function for sensing. But then he finds that Malebranche does more with his acts of sensing than merely treat them as quasi-substantial matters of fact in the manner of Hume—he finds, that is, that Malebranche claims to know himself through the *sentiment intérieur*. And then Church, arguing consistently with his Humian interpretation of Malebranche, erroneously concludes that this self awareness, like any other feeling, "affords no ground for asserting the existence of more than itself." [60]

I shall have more to say later about self-existence. But to return now to the disagreement between Descartes and Malebranche, it is clear, then, that Malebranche's censure based on the ambiguity of the secondary qualities is intended to show that we have no *a priori* knowledge of the activity of thought.

Malebranche's second major criticism of the Cartesians is that the knowledge that we do have of the mind through introspection and reasoning is not so mathematically rigorous as that afforded by extension. No doubt Malebranche is here inspired by Gassendi's attack on Descartes.[61] While Malebranche does not, as did Gassendi, ask for a chemical analysis of thought, he does point out, as we just saw, that even though the sensible qualities are ascribed to the soul, there is still wide disagreement among the Cartesians as to whether the soul

How our knowledge of the soul is not by perspicuous ideas.
Objections to Cartesians.

is actually blue when it considers blue. But were agreement reached on this score, he persists, it would still not advance us to an adequate knowledge of the soul. Descartes declared that the more attributes one discovers in the soul, the better it is known. Hence each time the mind is conscious of a desire or sensation, for Descartes, the better it knows itself. That consciousness thus reveals a great variety of operations which one feels belong to the soul, Malebranche does not deny. What he does reject is the assumption that an unordered, uncoordinated multiplicity, heterogeneous as it may be, can be described as exact scientific knowledge. "Je puis *compter* qu'il y a dans mon esprit trois propriétés, celle de connaître que 2 fois 2 font 4, celle de connaître que 3 fois 3 font 9, et celle de connaître que 4 fois 4 font 16," Malebranche declares; and he observes that these three are distinct from one another. I may thus count in myself an "infinite" number of properties, he elaborates; but: ". . . Je nie qu'on connaisse *clairement* la nature des choses que l'on peut *compter*. Il suffit pour les compter de les sentir." Truly distinct knowledge of a thing is had when that thing can be compared with something else that is clearly known, or at least when the thing's properties can be compared with one another. Numbers and figures are thus comparable;

> Mais on ne sait point avec évidence, ni de combien, ni ce que c'est qu'être plus couvert et plus éclatant. L'on n'a donc point d'idée claire ni de l'âme ni de ses modifications; et quoique je voie ou que je sente les couleurs, les saveurs, les odeurs, je puis dire, comme j'ai fait, que je ne les connais point par idée claire, puisque je ne puis en découvrir clairement les rapports.[62]

Malebranche also takes seriously the criticisms raised by Hobbes, Arnauld, Gassendi, and by the Scholastics of the second Objections. How, they all ask of Descartes, can you conclude that you are nothing but a thinking thing separate from the body? May it not be that this attribute of thought which alone is inseparable from yourself should nevertheless be a property of body? To Arnauld Descartes answers that had it not been for the demon the mere doubt concerning the attributes of body would have sufficed to establish the real distinction between mind and body.[63] To Hobbes and Gassendi he declares that their real distinction is established only after he has examined the idea of body and has proved the existence of a non-deceiving Deity.[64] But clearly in both these replies he virtually acknowledges that the *actual* separation is based on the idea of body. When in the second Meditation he doubts that he is a man or an animal, that he walks or moves or takes nourishment, what Descartes is in effect doing is more than merely recognizing that sensing, feeling, willing, thinking are modes of thought. Right then and there he is also admitting that these modes of thinking are being excluded from the nature of body.

The real separation therefore is accomplished not on the basis of immediate introspection but indirectly through exclusion of thinking from extension. Thus the idea of body is really the cornerstone of Descartes' dualism, not any pretended clear and distinct idea of mind. Had Descartes possessed a distinct idea of mind there would have been no need for this circuitous route, no need to begin with the doubt, no need to examine the idea of body. And this is the brunt of Malebranche's criticism of the Cartesians:

> Si la nature de l'âme est plus connue que celle de toute autre chose, si l'idée que l'on en a, est aussi claire que celle qu'on a du corps, je demande seulement d'où peut venir qu'il y a tant de gens qui la confondent avec lui. Est-il possible de confondre deux idées claires entièrement différentes? Faisons justice à tout le monde. Ceux qui ne sont pas de notre sentiment, sont raisonnables aussi bien que nous; ils ont les mêmes idées des choses, ils participent à la même raison. Pourquoi donc confondent-ils ce que nous distinguons? . . . C'est donc qu'il y a quelque difficulté à reconnaître leur différence. C'est que cela ne se découvre pas d'une simple vue, et qu'il faut raisonner pour conclure que l'une n'est pas l'autre.[65]

In the *Méditations chrétiennes* the Word declares: ". . . Si tu y prends garde, ce n'est qu'indirectement et par l'idée claire que tu as du corps, que tu reconnais que ton âme n'est ni matérielle ni mortelle." [66]

But we must note carefully the import of Malebranche's criticism of the Cartesians. Malebranche does not deny that introspection reveals the mind as a thinking, willing, imagining, sensing being. What he does say is that the further assertion that these mental activities are non-physical and really separable from body is an assertion made, not on the basis of introspection, but on the basis of exclusion from body. In other words, just as introspection does not disclose the status of the secondary qualities, so introspection alone does not reveal the soul to be a *distinct* or *separate* substance.

This does not mean, however, that introspection confines us to the prospect of the present moment from which no knowledge whatever of mind is possible. Such an inference would be appropriate only in another philosophy and with another author. What it does mean is that this knowledge of mind is, in Descartes' language, plain or clear, but not distinct—it is imperfect and inadequate, compared to that of body. It means that if we had a distinct idea of mind, we could deduce at once its separateness from body, its containment of the tertiary and the secondary qualities. It means, further, that if we had such a distinct idea we would possess an exact topology of mind as we do of body. Just as we know the exact relations between ellipses and circles, just as we know how a circle must be modified to become an ellipse, so, if we had a structural topology of mind, we should know how thought must be affected to feel a pain and to feel such and such a degree of pain rather than any other.

Again, we understand clearly the mechanism of memory and of habit with respect to the body, but we do not know about the internal dispositions of the soul. When we speak of dispositions of the soul, we do not understand just what enables the mind to think or act with greater promptness. We cannot even conceive or comprehend just what constitutes a disposition or habit. We cannot prove positively, that is, demonstrate with mathematical precision, that, apart from the body, the soul is capable of spiritual habits and of a spiritual memory. "On voit sans peine en quoi consiste la facilité que les esprits animaux ont à se répandre dans les nerfs, dans lesquels ils ont déjà coulé plusieurs fois; ou pour le moins on découvre sans peine que les tuyaux des nerfs s'élargissant, et leurs fibres se couchant d'une certaine façon, les esprits peuvent aisément s'y insinuer," Malebranche acknowledges. "Mais," he asks, "que peut-on concevoir qui soit capable d'augmenter la facilité de l'âme pour agir ou pour penser?" Thus if we had a clear and distinct idea of the soul and if its nature were really better known than the body, we should not be in such utter darkness. Hence he concludes: ". . . Je jugerais en ne consultant que le sentiment intérieur, qu'il n'y a point dans mon âme ni d'habitude, ni de mémoire spirituelle." [67]

Taken in its preceding and total context this denial is not a blanket rejection of our capacity to be aware of habits and dispositions, for Malebranche admits that through consciousness we are vividly aware of that facility through which thoughts and acts are recalled and excited in us.[68] Moreover, since Malebranche does differentiate between acts and content, awareness of such a facility or ease is not reducible to a mere feeling that testifies to nothing beyond itself. Accordingly, all he is concerned to deny is that in consciousness we have any strict understanding of the "sub-conscious" mechanism of that readiness. Indeed, he even acknowledges that through the *sentiment intérieur* we are immediately aware that there are relations between thought, volition, sensation, passions. "The inner feeling which I have of myself teaches me that I am, that I think, will, feel, suffer, etc.; but it does not enable me to know what I am, or what is the nature of my thought, my will, my feelings, my passions, my pain, or what are the relations which subsist among these things," Theodore tells Aristes in the *Entretiens sur la métaphysique*. Yet these relations among modifications, Theodore is quick to add, "I feel vividly, though I do not know them." [69]

In this entire analysis concerning the lack of a truly clear and distinct idea of the soul and more especially in his insistence on the ob-

scurity of memory, Malebranche is following Augustine as his master.
Augustine confesses:

> Assuredly, Lord, I toil with this, toil within myself: I have become
> to myself a soil laborious and of heavy sweat. For I am not now con-
> sidering the parts of the heavens, or measuring the distances of
> the stars, or seeking how the earth is held in space; it is I who
> remember, I, my mind. It is not remarkable if things that I am not
> are far from my knowledge: but what could be closer to me than
> myself? Yet the power of memory in me I do not understand, though
> without memory I could not even name myself. What am I to say,
> when I see so clearly that *I remember forgetfulness?* . . .

> Great is the power of memory, a thing, O my God, to be in awe of,
> a profound and immeasurable multiplicity; and this thing is my
> mind, this thing am I. What then am I, O my God? What nature
> am I? A life powerfully various and manifold and immeasurable.[70]

Yet, despite Augustine's abysmal ignorance of his soul, he is nevertheless sure of its existence and personal identity on the basis of introspection. And Malebranche is likewise. Augustine in fact finds it in
the very obscurity of memory. He points out that *cogitation* is a "drawing together" in memory. "For *cogito* (I think) has the same relation
to *cogo* (I put together)," says Augustine, "as *agito* to *ago* and *factito*
to *facio*." [71] Time itself he considers as a distention. He interprets the
present moment as an act of attention that endures, for this act unites
past and future by anticipation and memory. The present moment of
consciousness is itself a kind of memory, a drawing together, a vital,
indivisible activity that distends backward and forward.[72] Etymologically, attention means *ad tendere,* a movement towards. For Augustine,
the present act of attention is a moving backwards and forwards.

Then, too, not only is memory the recall or drawing together of the
past, but there is also a memory of the present, that is a movement
forward from the unclear to the clear, as in the recognition of God's
presence and of eternal truths.[73] Finally, this entire directional movement or ascent to God is an act of will or love. It is this will that animates the soul and gives it life.[74]

These Augustinian elements are to be found in Malebranche. In his
discussion on method, Malebranche clearly affirmed that there can be

degrees of knowledge, with mathematics as the perfect norm. Ideal
knowledge implies exact definitions, for, he tells us, definitions ought
to explain the nature of things, and the terms that compose them
ought to reawaken distinct and particular ideas in our spirit.[75] However, in addition to truths that can be rigorously known, there are
others that can be known imperfectly.[76] These are called imperfect
only by comparison with mathematics. For example, one understands

"perfectly" that Paris is larger than the Place Royale, but only because we fail to know by how much, do we call our knowledge imperfect. Moreover, within this sphere of imperfect knowledge there is an infinity of degrees.

That introspection does not measure up to the standard of *perfect a priori* deductive knowledge does not therefore imply that it is altogether an abyss of shadows and darkness. The absence of an *a priori* deductive psychology, of an algebraic topological psychology, does not legislate against the possibility of another lesser degree of knowledge. While introspection does not say what the nature of mind is in the strict sense, it still reveals what mind is in another sense. Thus in the *Traité de morale* Malebranche declares: "La connaissance de l'homme est de toutes les sciences la plus nécessaire à notre sujet. Mais ce n'est qu'une science expérimentale, qui résulte de la réflexion qu'on fait sur ce qui se passe en soi-même." [77] The *sentiment intérieur*, then, which discloses what goes on in the soul is reliable and trustworthy, for it is the basis of an experimental science. In fact, it is so trustworthy that Malebranche even calls it infallible. The *sentiment intérieur*, he tells us, is not the same as exterior sense in that the latter sometimes deceives us when we accept its testimony. "Mais notre *sentiment intérieur*," Malebranche boldly asserts, "ne nous trompe jamais." [78] As an instrument of direct acquaintance with hard data, we thus see, the *sentiment intérieur* is unimpeachable. Analogous to the vision of God *par simple vue*, which is super-conceptual, the *simple vue* that we achieve through the *sentiment intérieur* may be described, I suggest, as infra-conceptual.

[margin note: Introspection yields positive information.]

III. THE SELF AS ACTIVE WILL, AND OUR EXISTENTIAL KNOWLEDGE OF IT

And now we reach the crucial issue concerning self existence. Malebranche agrees with the Cartesians that through the *sentiment intérieur* each of us can know his mind's existence with greater assurance than he can that of his body. The nature of body is better known than the nature of mind, but the mind's presence or existence is more palpably evident than that of body. But how should we know the mind's existence, its substantiality, identity and unity, if its nature were wholly unknown? Descartes said that bare existence is unknowable, bare substance is ungraspable. We know substance through its properties, especially through its principal attribute. For Descartes, not merely are thought and extension inseparable attributes of substance, they are the very stuff of substance. There is no substance or subject behind or in addition to thought and extension. Furthermore, while Descartes in his *Reply to Objections II* does speak of substance as a

[margin note: What the self knows by its sentiment intérieur: Neither bare existence,]

subject of inherence, his genuine conception of substance, as Brunschvicg argues, is in terms of causality:

> La relation tout imaginative, toute statique, entre ce qui supporte et ce qui est supporté, avait été posée par Aristote comme spécifique de la substantialité, et elle demeure telle j'usqu'à Descartes. La substantialité c'est surtout pour Descartes, c'est uniquement pour Spinoza, la fécondité tout intellectuelle qui est la racine de l'être, qui enveloppe, intérieures à l'unité de l'essence, la totalité de ses consequences. La substance se comprend par la causalité.[79]

Now we have already noted in our discussion of God that M. Gilson would take exception to this assertion, that until the time of Descartes substance was construed in static terms.[80] Quite the contrary, he insists, for Thomas, to be is to act. It is true, however, that when Descartes and Spinoza identify substance with activity, they do so, as Brunschvicg observes, in terms of "la fécondité toute intellectuelle." In other words, the activity or causality of substance is that of an essence affirming or entailing existence, whereas for the Thomist, the dynamism of concrete substance is derivate from the act of existence. As we saw, for Descartes there is no real distinction between essence and existence; not only does the attribute make a thing be what it is, it also makes it be. Given the concurrence of God, existence adds nothing to extension or to thought.

Nor an essence positing existence,

It is otherwise with Malebranche. Existence which depends on God's will vitalizes, animates the essence of body. It is existence which makes the essence of body be. It is existence from which movement issues, that transforms an essence into a concrete substance. For this reason we cannot go from essence to existence in the case of bodies. But conversely, for this very reason we can grasp our own self existence, even though we lack a strict ideational knowledge of what we are. To grasp our existence is to grasp or sense our vitality, our being alive, our activity. Descartes is right to this extent, that bare existence is not comprehensible. To know an existent is always to know a somewhat. In fact, for Malebranche, the self's existence cannot be barely and simply grasped, because, unlike God and like every creature, it is a composition of an essence and existence. In God alone do we find a Being whose essence it is to exist or to be. In God alone are essence and existence identical. Hence God as Being, as the act of existing, can be grasped intuitively, albeit only finitely. But in the case of the self whose existence is a received, created, conferred being, it cannot be grasped as such, apart from its essence. Yet its real inner nature in its purity is hidden.

But its own particular existence, that is, its spiritual activity.

Therefore we must fall back upon that much of its nature as is disclosed through introspection, that is, upon its operations. These are directly experienced. So in grasping our self and its substantiality, we do not grasp bare activity or vitality as such. Through the *sentiment intérieur* we discover ourselves as a desiring, loving, thinking, imagining, sensing being. In short, we may say that introspection reveals our self as will or doer. Hence, as we saw, Malebranche affirmed the soul's existence to be incontestable: ". . . Car il n'y a rien de plus évident que ce qui pense actuellement est actuellement quelque chose." Nor should the word *chose* mislead us. Etymologically to be a thing meant to be an activity, a causality, not an inert entity.[81] And each description that Malebranche offers of this thinking thing is in active terms, for example: "Si l'on doute, si l'on veut, si l'on raisonne, il faut seulement croire que l'âme est une chose qui doute, qui veut, qui raisonne, et rien davantage . . ."[82]

Were the *sentiment intérieur* no more than a "mere" feeling, a static datum of the present moment, then indeed Mr. Church would be correct in his assertion that self consciousness or the sense of being alive, like the feeling of solidity for Hume, is no evidence for the presence of a self or substance. But this interpretation, as Mr. Church admits, prevents Malebranche from having any sort of psychology. Yet, as psychologist Malebranche does not treat or regard self consciousness as a static solipsism of the present moment. When, for example, he asserts that each of us through internal feeling can become conscious of his mind as a continued circulation of thoughts, it is plain that for Malebranche this introspective awareness of change and succession is *not*, as Santayana will say, itself an immediate present. It is plain that for Malebranche introspection discloses real change, real movement, real activity.[83] Why should we seek to reduce Malebranche to a mass of contradictions when we can accept what he does say in good faith? The only obstacle has been the eleventh Éclaircissement, but this I have shown is no obstacle at all. And would Mr. Church be prepared to say that when Malebranche claims to have an internal conviction, through the *sentiment intérieur,* of his vision of God's presence, that this too is a mere feeling that attests to nothing beyond itself? Mr. Church's difficulty is that he always seeks data as grounds from which to make inferences, whereas Malebranche's philosophy moves within the orbit of illumination or intuition.

That Malebranche should so passionately insist that we know the soul's or the self's existence as an indubitable fact, notwithstanding our ignorance of its real innermost essence, implies that self consciousness, inadequate as it may be, is for him a far more significant and elaborate process than Hume ever dreamed of. To appreciate the role of the *sentiment intérieur,* of introspective consciousness, we must must bear in mind, nor be ashamed of the fact, that the consciousness of which Malebranche speaks is that of a Christian consciousness.

The complex structure of introspective consciousness.

When the Christian seeks to know himself, when he becomes aware of himself, what his consciousness discloses is himself as a likeness or participating similitude of God.

God is Being, the infinite plenitude of existence. As such He is also a three-personed Deity, at once One in Many. He is the Father, the Son, and the Holy Spirit. As Father He is the Creator and the principle of being, the act and power of existing. The Word is the divine reason, that which expresses God's Being to Himself. God knows Himself, His essence, in the Word. Finally God is Will or Love, a Will that loves Himself and glories in Himself and affirms Himself to Himself. It is through the Will that God pronounces of Himself: "Ego sum."

Now when man turns inwardly to find and know himself through consciousness, what he finds is himself as participation and analogue of God. Through the *sentiment intérieur* he becomes conscious of intellectual operations or pure conceptions directed toward the divine Reason; through self consciousness he becomes aware of his intuitive knowledge of God as Being—he is conscious of knowing Him *par simple vue*. Through introspection he finds a will or love moving in the direction of the infinite. Through consciousness he becomes aware of his will as an active principle, as both an effort of attention that elicits and evokes the presence of ideas and the principle of judgment.

The *sentiment intérieur* or consciousness is thus cognizant of multiple operations, analogous to those of God. Just as God knows His own essence in the Word, so the self knows itself through its operations. The Word informs us, in the *Traité de morale*, that: "Les trois personnes divines de la Trinité sainte impriment chacune leur propre caractère dans les esprits qu'ils ont créés à leur image." The Father, as power, affords them part of His power. The Son affords them wisdom and truths. The Holy Spirit animates and sanctifies them through an invincible impression for good and love of Order implanted in their hearts:

> Comme le Père engendre son Verbe, l'esprit de l'homme connaît qu'il existe; mais de plus, par ses désirs il est la cause occasionelle de ses connaissances: et comme le fils est avec le Père principe d'amour substantiel et divin, nos connaissances excitées par nos désirs, qui seuls sont véritablement en notre puissance, sont en nous le principe de tous les mouvements réglés de notre amour.[84]

Thus the *sentiment intérieur* or consciousness involves a judgment of its own existence. Consciousness is not only an act that is aware of a variety of operations but also an act that involves the intuitive judgment or assertion which claims or appropriates or affirms these operations to be mine, to belong to me. Hence the awareness of myself is not a simple or mere feeling; it is an apprehension that is *sui generis;* the *sentiment intérieur* is an awareness indissolubly accompanied by

Sentiment intérieur no mere feeling or datum, but a complex act of apprehension.

or involving judgment or an act of will that appraises or pronounces the data of consciousness to belong to itself. This judgment is not an inference from the data of introspection but concomitant with the introspective act. Self knowledge through the *sentiment intérieur* is an intuitive affirmation or judgment of the self to itself through the observed or experienced operations. Perhaps this is what Locke had in mind when he said that consciousness "makes" the self. But Locke's problem is that in the last analysis the self he found in consciousness and the self he looked for as an epistemologist were very differently conceived. As an epistemologist Locke was constrained to consider an object as a collection or congeries or troupe of simple, inert, unorganized elements. Hence he sought for but could not find that *je ne sais quoi*—that inert substance which could somehow or other serve as a magazine or filing cabinet in which the simple elements could be filed, arranged, and thus given some coherent frame or unity.

But, contrary to our twentieth century allegations, Malebranche's attachment to medieval realism, to his metaphysics of God as Be-ing, should warn us that his conception of substance is far removed from that of Locke. Not only is God as Be-ing an active, dynamic principle, for Malebranche, but also Malebranche's conception of God as a three-personed Deity is a conception of what is almost a society of selves, or is a conception, if we will, of a society of principles.[85] The use of the word, society, in the *Traité de morale* in this connection, is significant. God is not a juxtaposition of three different persons or principles. He is a society, an integrated whole. The complex substance of the self.

So it is with the self. Despite the fact that Malebranche, like Descartes, distinguishes between the passive intellect and the active will, he nevertheless sharply warns us against taking these distinctions in too literal a manner. These different faculties are not hermetically sealed off entities, separated from each other or from the soul itself. It is the soul itself that knows and wills. Moreover, while ordinarily one says that the will is active or the will is free; properly speaking it is the soul which is active and free.[86] Thus the self that is judged to be present and is felt through introspection is a many-layered, multi-faceted, integrated, dynamic system. Herein lies man's likeness or similitude to God. But herein, too, is the reason for man's incomprehensibility to himself. However much one knows God as Being, his trinitarian existence is still shrouded in mystery. *How* God is one and infinitely infinite, *how* the divine organization and unity is achieved, are beyond us.[87] For the same reason we possess neither a clear and distinct idea of the soul, nor is our self knowledge through introspection adequate. Being an analogue or image of God Himself we are as incomprehensible to ourselves as God is. Did we possess a clear and distinct idea of our essence, we should know at once and apart from all experience the formal, mathematical structure that constitutes the pattern of psychological unity and organization. This is why Malebranche says that we have no idea of the Trinity, any more than of ourselves.

But, as even Pascal confesses, while God is a *Deus absconditus,* He is not altogether hidden.[88] And, as Malebranche affirms, while God is incomprehensible, He is not altogether unknowable.[89] Beyond our awareness of God *par simple vue,* there remains an impenetrable mystery. Yet our vision of God is true as far as it goes. So with respect to our self, there are unfathomable depths and relationships into which we cannot penetrate. Yet what we learn through introspection is not false; it is simply partial and incomplete. We are aware of our unity, of our personality, even of our greatness and sublimity; nevertheless we remain an enigma. But it is of prime importance to notice that for Malebranche, as for Pascal, and for Augustine, the enigmatic, mysterious, elusive aspect of ourselves is discovered through an intense probing into our own consciousness. While much of our *positive* knowledge of the soul comes, as Malebranche has shown, through indirect reasoning on the nature of body, the revelation of how little we know of ourselves comes from our inner self-scrutiny. It is through the *sentiment intérieur* that we discover the length and depth of that abysmal darkness that surrounds us. But that inner probing is also an act of attention and will, and hence in that very act of exploring and of probing, the existence and unity of the self are given and made directly accessible as an indubitable (although incomprehensible) fact.

> Cependant il faut l'avouer, et on le reconnaît assez, je n'ai fait que bégayer dans la comparaison que je viens de faire de l'âme avec la Trinité sainte. Ce mystère est incompréhensible, et d'ailleurs je n'ai point d'idée claire de l'âme. Comment donc pourrais-je en marquer précisément les rapports? Dieu nous a créés à son image et à sa ressemblance. Le fait est certain: mais c'est une énigme réservée pour le ciel. Il est bon néanmoins d'entrevoir cette grande vérité, afin que l'esprit pense a l'excellence de son être, et qu'il souhaite de connaître clairement ce qu'il aperçoit confusément.[90]

Malebranche asserts: "Je conclus que je suis parce que je me sens, et que le néant ne peut être senti." [91] For Mr. Church, as we saw, this self awareness, this felt I, is no different from any other feeling. And just as Hume held that felt solidity is not solidity itself, so, says Church: ". . . The feeling that I exist is not the existence of myself. No more than any other feeling is the *sentiment intérieur* evidence for the existence of a self." [92] For him, self-consciousness cannot therefore offer assurance or ground for believing in the existence of a personal, self-identical thinking substance. However, for Malebranche, that peculiar and unique feeling or awareness that such and such activities

Does Malebranche's self-knowledge reduce to a congeries of sensations?

belong to *me* or are *mine* is more than a bare momentary feeling, indistinguishable from the content sensed. Self-consciousness is a complex process of distinguishable but inseparable factors. It is first an act of awareness whose contents are a variety of mental operations; and secondly it is an act of attention or will that intuitively judges or attributes or claims these activities to belong to itself—to the very existence that is itself engaged in examining and in judging.

Furthermore, this introspective knowledge of one's selfhood and personal existence is not the occurrence of a split second or a specious moment. Self-discovery, like the discovery of God, is the achievement of a long, arduous, lived experience. Introspection involves attention. Attention is an act of will. As such, attention is a slow, gradual elaborate, ever-deepening, ever-discriminating process. Attention, moreover, is no mere succession of non-significant perceptual contents. When, for example, through strenuous effort of attention the mind reaches a vision of God, the process of attending is akin to an ever-widening whirlpool in a surging river. Similarly, self-examination is an agonizing but continuous process of self-scrutinization. Precisely because Christian Socratism involves the perpetual commitment of the will and is never really complete until the mind arrives at the knowledge of God, this whole struggle to grasp one's self and one's existence can never be the datum of a present moment or a series of juxtaposed, unrelated simple events. Self-scrutinization is a lived, temporal, ever-growing, ever-burgeoning historical process.

Christian Socratism:

Attending, agonizing, committed will—

In his *Fragments de philosophie cartésienne*, Victor Cousin prints an account by Corbinelli of a discussion between the anti-Cartesian Desgabets and a group of Cartesians, including Malebranche. Desgabets argued that Descartes' *Je pense* was reducible to a succession of states, because duration meant succession. This Malebranche vigorously rejected. He insisted that duration and existence were continuous and indivisible. In fact, creatures endured because thereby they were participating analogues of God's duration.[93]

Groping, enduring, searching will—

Thus to Malebranche self-awareness is no awareness of a dead, passive, inert substantial I; it is the awareness of a dynamic, struggling, groping, enduring, searching will. Really for him the substantiality of my self is that of a moving center. The more I turn inwardly to grasp myself the more I discover interlocking movements or activities directed towards God. But in so moving or rising towards God, there is always the awareness of a single whole personality that is thus ascending. And in the final triumphant vision of God or union with God the act of vision is my act and the union is that between me and God as an enduring person. This is to say that for Malebranche the presence of God to the soul or the union of God with the soul is not ever the annihilation of one's personality. The vision of God is a per-

Seeking God.

sonal experience. And the communion or union with God is the union
of distinct beings.

Hence once again I must take exception to Mr. Church. Having
erroneously and gratuitously decided that pure understanding is distinct from consciousness and therefore that it cannot be felt by the
sentiment intérieur, he concludes that: "Pure spirit is actually present
only in meditation and prayer." This presence of the Word, he declares,

**Does the self
lose its self
identity in
transcendental
knowledge?**

> is not a presence in or to any modification of the soul. In meditation
> and prayer, all states of consciousness have 'fallen away,' and the
> pure understanding, being thus undisturbed by the body, is free, as
> was Adam, to participate in the Word. Yet this conception of an
> understanding denied all activity and any determinate character of
> its own must be said to be empty. A form of spirit which is in its
> purity other than all conscious states, cannot be conceived; and a
> spirit that is passive, like a wind without direction, is impossible.[94]

Apparently Church has forgotten, in making this attack on his author, that meditation and prayer are, for Malebranche, themselves
acts of attention and thus acts of will. Attention, declares Malebranche,
is the natural prayer of the soul. It is true enough that volitions as
desires relative to the body largely fall away together with those other
passions and feelings relative to physical existence, but the will as a
movement and love toward God never ceases. Hence, too, the final
participation by the soul in the Word is never the participation of a
non-entity.

Put differently, the union of the soul with God is not that sort of
participation that is the equivalent of absorption into and identification with God. Church has either willfully forgotten or else inexcus-
ably failed to appreciate Malebranche's constant opposition to pantheism. For Malebranche the soul is a created substance, separate from
God. It is not a part of God. Yet were the soul in its union with the
Word to become wholly passive and bereft of all determinate character, as Church says it must, would it not then follow that the soul's
existence could then no longer be differentiated from God's? What
then becomes of Malebranche's celebrated opposition to pantheism?
A mere verbalism, a gross inconsistency,—or another one of those timid
"compensatory" religious dogmas? If we take Malebranche's attack on
pantheism with philosophical seriousness, however, then, from this
standpoint, no intelligence, angelic or human, ever loses its personal
existence or identity.

Mr. Goheen tells us that "it is by the real distinction between essence and existence in created substances that Aquinas avoids pantheism. . . . It is in God that essence and existence are one. In all other
creatures there is the distinction between the two. . . ."[95] Mr. Goheen

**The existence
of the self as
active will.**

goes on to show that "all other creatures" includes all intelligences, angels as well as human souls.[96] And precisely because all created substances and intelligences are thus a mixture of essence and existence, they are not only not simple as is God, but also radically different from Him and from one another. What distinguishes their radical diversity and individuality, moreover, is their degree of being or existence, not their essence. This, says Mr. Goheen as does M. Gilson, is where Aristotle and Aquinas part company. It is the act of existence that actualizes, realizes and confers being upon an essence or form. And this act of existence enjoyed by the creature is a received existence— that conferred upon an essence by God.

Now we have already seen that Malebranche upholds the real distinction between essence and existence, that it is for him the core of his opposition to Spinoza, the very heart of his view of God as Being or as *Celui qui est*. And we have seen too that while Occasionalism denies creative power to the creature, it does not eliminate activity altogether. We must therefore conclude that for him the union of the soul with God is a union of distinct persons or existents and as such the existential soul is not an empty, passive non-entity, nor is it that "leere vereinigende Form der Bewusstseinserscheinungen" of Novaro.[97]

Because Malebranche thus emphasizes the act of existence in persons, attention, prayer, meditation play a most prominent role for him. Attention and meditation are preeminently assertions of will; and the will, both in man and in God, most adequately approximates the view of existence as act or energy. Accordingly, Malebranche describes the will as a movement or love that is a search for union with God.[98] The knowledge of this will through the *sentiment intérieur* is the direct experience or awareness of a continuous striving or longing. At the very time when man arrests his will and becomes satisfied with or finds repose in a particular object, he feels, declares Malebranche, that he has the capacity *not* to stop, the capacity to move on. "Nous sentons," he tells us in the first Éclaircissement, "qu'il nous est libre de nous y arrêter, *que nous avons du mouvement pour aller plus loin* . . ."[99]

But what is this tendency of which we are immediately conscious, this "mouvement pour aller plus loin?" Whereto does it aspire? The consciousness of this capacity to move on is not the awareness of a specific desire, not, that is, a desire for some other definite or finite object. Rather is it the awareness of limitless aspiration, that is, of a movement or yearning for the infinite, the indeterminate, and the universal, for "le bien en général," for "le bien universel."[100]

Thus, psychologically, man for Malebranche is not simply a succession of longings and desires, as Hobbes maintained, nor is man drawn to God by a "Pulley" that consists in a series of finite states of restlessness, as the poet Herbert described. What man perceives through the *sentiment intérieur* is an uninterrupted flow, a moving center or conatus of attention or an infinitely capacious will.[101]

The self is revealed as a moving center of attention also in another way. Being, Malebranche says, is an indelible imprint on the mind. That is, to think is to think of Being.[102] But this thinking is at first confused and hazy. Then slowly the scope of the mind's attention becomes enlarged and its object appears ever more clearly to it. Here we have in Malebranche a reversion to Augustine's memory of the present, a memory moving from the latent or unconscious to the conscious. The treatment of the *sentiment intérieur* is itself deeply suggestive of Augustine's description of remembering memory. Where do I recognize memory, Augustine asks in his *Confessions*, except in my memory? Remembering is in the forefront of his consciousness, yet consciousness is itself a kind of memory.

"Remembering memory."

Knowledge for Malebranche, then, is not panoramic—not like Bacon's idols of the theater, in which theory after theory, system after system passes in review and vanishes. Bacon's idols fit Hume's theory of mind as a theater and Hume's view of knowledge and causality. But for Malebranche knowledge is contractive and expansive. Each succeeding view of ideas is a qualitative intensification of a single experience. Here "Vision in God" and "vision of God" are apt as expressions, for the experience of sight is that of a qualitative organization. But this expansiveness and growth in understanding occur through the increase of attention, and attention is the exertion and the striving and effort of the will to become clear and clearer. Thus in the experience of attention and knowledge—an experience of which the *sentiment intérieur* is cognizant—there is found the unity of the volitional self.

Descartes himself asserted that it is in the infinite will that man is properly speaking made in the image of God.[103] The doubt itself is an act of will. And it is precisely in this power of attention and volition that Malebranche really discovers both the key to his existence and identity and the reason for its incomprehensible mystery. It is through the direct awareness or consciousness of himself as an inexhaustible purposive activity striving towards God that he knows his own existence better than that of the body. But compared to the mathematical clarity of extension, the nature of volition is an unfathomable mystery.

The volitional self as a fully concrete existent.

We are now prepared to evaluate Malebranche's rules for scientific method in their true metaphysical light. These rules for intellectual analysis and experimental verification are designed to amplify, fortify and augment the mind's capacity of attention, hence the power of the will. But does not this recognition of the will's power to augment or diminish its attention through its own effort suggest that in a most significant sense real selfhood is a moral and intellectual achievement through time? God incessantly and continually gives man the love and will to seek happiness, to seek Him. But man is free with respect to the manner in which he applies or determines that will. He is free to choose the means towards his pursuit of God. In these choices and sacrifices he forges his unique personality and character. Truth is eternal and objective, and the human mind is but "une lumière illuminée." Yet the attainment of the truth is not universal but through one's own personal efforts. God being infinite and the mind finite, each mind is afforded the opportunity to arrive at the truth in its own way.[104] And because truth and selfhood are achieved through time, the ultimate reward of well being or blessedness or union with God is construed by Malebranche in personal terms. Through Christ we become, not lost in God, but His co-heritors.

Malebranche's conception of scientific method faced two demands of the new physics: one deductive, mathematical and necessary, the other inductive, empirical and contingent (Chapter I). The deductive and Conclusion. formal aspects he satisfied with a theory of universals as immutable archetypes in God (Chapter II); the inductive aspects he grounded in an ontology of God as Being (Chapter III). Archetypes and Being were communicated to the material world and were exemplified in creatures that were composed of essence and existence. The two demands of the new physics were satisfied in Malebranche's Occasionalism by combining in bodies mathematically comprehensible essential natures and a derivative, continuously sustained but enduring, created dynamism of active efficacy. (Chapter IV.)

In the present chapter we face the problem which arises from Malebranche's disagreement with Descartes concerning the self. Whereas for Descartes the self is better known than the body, for Malebranche the nature of body is in principle completely knowable, but the nature of the self remains stubbornly incomprehensible. First we consider why Malebranche has to disagree with Descartes: Having denied Descartes' conceptualism of innate ideas existing in the finite mind, and having affirmed the Vision of archetypes in God as the beholding of immutable, independent ideas, the mind for Malebranche is deprived of a mathematical structure. It can no longer be Descartes' mathematical automaton. Positively, on the introspective level, Malebranche can and does accept every Cartesian pronouncement concerning our knowledge of our selves, provided that these are strictly interpreted as relating exclusively to spiritual, volitional *activity*. Such is the function of the *sentiment intérieur*. While the essence of the soul is unknowable, its existence is very well known, even better known than that of the body. This reflects Malebranche's scientific method, for what the *sentiment intérieur* affords Malebranche is indubitable access to a matter of fact, in this case, his own existence. We shall now also see that we cannot attain access to the existence of the external world by any *a priori* deduction; rationalism is not enough; Malebranche will turn to the natural revelation of sense and to the revelation of faith.

Chapter VI

Sense, Faith, and the External World

I. Why Immaterialism Is Not the Inevitable Consequence of Malebranche's Philosophy

In the *Entretiens sur la métaphysique*, Malebranche bases our knowledge of the existence of an external world on the evidence of our natural judgments or natural revelations of sense and also on the revelation of religious faith. His appeal to faith has in many quarters been regarded as a confession of philosophical ineptitude, as an appeal founded on philosophical fear, and therefore as an admission of the inaccessibility of external reality. Moreover, the testimony of faith depends on the evidence of sense for its reception. But Malebranche's denunciation of the senses, his persistent claims that the world is "invisible," that our knowledge is conversant with ideas only, that in sensuous experience the secondary qualities are deployed in an ideal extension, not in concrete matter, his "representationalism," and finally his Occasionalism—all these factors have seemed to render the existence of matter not only problematic but even, to many, superfluous. Such is the indictment of Church and Novaro,[1] for example.

> The claim that immaterialism is inevitable for Malebranche.

Thus too in an article in the *Review of Metaphysics* Mrs. Anita Dunlevy Fritz suggests that the ingredients of Berkeley's immaterialism are fully present in Malebranche's philosophy and that their explicit development is hampered by a lack of philosophical candor and fortitude. That Malebranche did not become a Berkeleian, she maintains, was because of his religious convictions.[2]

The reader will surely understand, at this stage of my argument, that

[279]

this impresses me as a facile explanation. Whether Malebranche did or did not directly influence Berkeley is not of concern here. But let us grant Mrs. Fritz all that she could hope for, that Berkeley actually was historically influenced by Malebranche, not merely with respect to his epistemology of ideas, but also with respect to his metaphysics, i.e., the denial of matter. A further question remains, one which she unnecessarily raises,[3] namely: was *Berkeley* right? Mrs. Fritz could have argued explicitly (as she does implicitly) that a special interpretation of Malebranche, dominated by metaphysical premises different from his and based on denying certain fundamental tenets of Malebranche's philosophy, led Berkeley to immaterialism. Such an argument has without doubt a large degree of historical validity—not only Locke, but also Descartes and Malebranche undoubtedly influenced Berkeley's metaphysical investigations. But now for our purposes it is important to understand Malebranche from the point of view of *Malebranche's* system and orientation. With this interest, our question must be, why did Malebranche himself not take the extreme step into subjective idealism? Religious faith cannot serve as a sufficient excuse for refusing to do so, because Malebranche conceives of faith as the source of indubitable data, facts, or "experiments," but it belongs to the understanding or reason to explain such data.[4] Moreover Berkeley also was religious, ultimately a bishop of the Anglican Church, but he found no difficulty, even from the first, to reconcile his position with the Scriptures. In view of the great subtlety and daring of Malebranche's thought, as it has been exposed in the foregoing chapters, we have no reason for not assuming that Malebranche could have been equally ingenious had he really believed on philosophical grounds that the external world was inaccessible or superfluous. Yet the fact remains that the more Malebranche denounces Descartes' proofs for the existence of a material world in his sixth Éclaircissement to the *Recherche*, the more fully Malebranche seems to insist upon its existence; and he does the same in the definitive *Entretiens sur la métaphysique.*

Malebranche says that if God creates, He, being wise and rational, must do so in the simplest possible manner.[5] Because of this principle of economy and because of the fact that we behold essences in God, declares Mrs. Fritz, Malebranche himself has destroyed any need for believing in matter, for matter becomes useless and functionless.[6] God Himself can cause our sensations and perceptions. It is therefore irrational to suppose that He would create useless entities. This, of course, is one of Berkeley's arguments, suggested by Malebranche himself,[7] and Berkeley actually directs it against Malebranche, as Mrs. Fritz correctly notes.[8] But as an argument *against Malebranche* its apparent strength rests on ignoring important aspects both of Malebranche's and of Berkeley's systems. By comparing the two systems we can not only avoid Mrs. Fritz's conclusions but, more importantly, also clarify our understanding of Malebranche's epistemology.

Berkeley's immaterialism is of a double sort. First, he believes that there are a plurality of separate, independent, immaterial active volitional spirits or souls. Secondly, he holds that natural objects, commonly called bodies, are nothing but ideas or mental objects. This twofold immaterialism is summarized by the pronouncement, "Existence is percipi or percipere." [9]

Berkeley's twofold immaterialism.

In so far as Berkeley conceives minds to be independent of their being known or being perceived by other minds, he is being a realist, that is, he is treating existence as a primary category, *sui generis*. When we understand another mind through 'notions,' the notion takes account of that mind, and we infer its existence from our ideas. Notions plus ideas tell us that certain beings probably exist and that these beings are minds like ours. Yet, realist though he be, in the sense of recognizing plural independent minds, I have the uneasy feeling that for Berkeley existence as such is not a fundamental category, in his view of mind. It seems to me as though minds exist for Berkeley to the extent that they think and will, rather than that they think and will because first of all they are. And indeed, in Part I of the *Principles* he declares:

> . . . In truth whoever shall go about to divide in his thoughts, or abstract the *existence* of a spirit from its *cogitation*, will, I believe, find it no easy task.[10]

The Berkeleian mind, human or divine, appears as a duplex entity whose existence is wholly exhausted by its capacities to think and to will.

Bodies, in any case, are no more than congeries of simple, passive, inert qualities. They can have no independent reality or existence apart from the perceiving mind, for they cannot think or will. From Berkeley's point of view, then, the independent existence of matter is both meaningless and useless. It is useless, for being wholly passive and inert, matter can do nothing. It would be in vain for a wise Providence to create functionless objects. Perception is treated as if it were the confrontation of a mental content and not the revelation of an independent existence. Being contents and not apprehensions, our perceptions can be given us by God without the need for a second, independently existing group of objects. But furthermore, Berkeley as metaphysician cannot even conceive such an independent matter, for he knows the qualities of bodies and these are all objects of thought. By his sensationalistic and nominalistic theory of knowledge, the result of his polemic against abstract ideas, every object of thought is either entirely reducible to a conglomerate or troop of sense qualities or else is spirit or relation. And since sensations or images are mental contents, their very being depends upon their being perceived—upon their presence in or to a mind.

Malebranche, in contrast, continues to insist that there are real universals apart from their being perceived and that there is a real distinction between essence and existence in the creature. This is the crux of the issue with Berkeley. Berkeley explicitly accepts what I have argued in my chapter on Occasionalism is the doctrine of Malebranche: That true causality is exclusively spiritual; that *natura naturans* is God; "that the divine conservation of things is equipollent to, and in fact the same thing with, a continued repeated creation: in a word, that conservation and creation differ only in the *terminus a quo*." It is not this that is at issue. Berkeley indeed describes this as the common doctrine of the Schoolmen and says "Druandus" alone held the world to be like a machine, "made and put in motion by God, but afterwards continuing to go of itself . . ." "The very poets teach a doctrine not unlike the schools," he continues, "—*Mens agitat molem*. . . . I am not therefore singular in this point itself, so much as in my way of proving it." Berkeley goes on to argue like Malebranche that God has no need of independent instruments or self-sufficient subordinate causes in preserving and governing the natural world, for ". . . all nature would shrink to nothing, if not upheld and preserved in being by the same force that first created it." Hence he concludes that the view "that all things necessarily depend on Him as their Conservator as well as Creator" is perfectly consistent with Holy Scripture.[11]

The point at issue, then, is not the direct and continual action of God; but instead it is the immutable subsistence of archetypes, on the one hand, and their relation to existence, or to creation and conservation, on the other hand. Berkeley accepts the tenet that God's ideas are archetypes of ours. "But," he says, in reply to the inquiries of the American, Samuel Johnson, concerning the above statements on divine conservation—"But I object against those archetypes by philosophers supposed to be real things, and to have an absolute rational existence distinct from their being perceived by any mind whatsoever." [12]

Malebranche affirms what Berkeley denies, that immutable essences exist absolutely in God, independently of being perceived by us or by Him. Furthermore, for Malebranche, God is Being. What He creates by His will is an analogue of Himself; what He communicates is being or the act of existing. Thus, if bodies exist, they cannot be for Malebranche entities whose being is in any way derivative from or exhausted by their essence. Extension is indeed the principal attribute of bodies—it determines *what* bodies are, but the existence of bodies lies in their possession of being, conferred by God's will and super-

The issue is the independent reality of essences and the distinction between essence and existence, for Malebranche

Existence of matter meaningful for Malebranche.

added, as it were, to what Berkeley calls the "absolute rational exist-ence" of their essence. Mrs. Fritz actually raises the question as to whether, for Malebranche, the being of bodies adds to extension; but, unaware of the true nature of Malebranche's God as *Celui qui est*, even though she actually quotes this phrase,[13] she erroneously con-cludes that existence adds nothing to extension.[14] This is a capital error.

From the distinction between essence and existence it follows fur-ther that should external bodies exist, they cannot be conceived by Malebranche in Berkeleian terms as inert passive substrata that do nothing, and certainly their vital process cannot be reduced to *percipi*, i.e., to the mere presentational appearance of ideas to a mind. If they exist, they do so as occasional causes. We saw that while the occa-sional cause is not creative, it is none the less active, and that in so far as it exists and acts, it does so in virtue of the fact that God does communicate His power to it.

Thus in Malebranche's system it is neither meaningless nor useless to suppose the independent reality of bodies. Such a supposition is not *useless*, for bodies as occasional causes have an important role and function in the divine economy. As occasional causes they serve to diversify God's conduct; they determine the laws of motion and through motion all change.

Nor is the assumption of independently existing bodies *meaningless*, or impossible, or inconceivable. It is not meaningless for three reasons: *First*, as we saw, Malebranche's conception of God as Being renders the idea of independent physical existence meaningful, inasmuch as existence adds something to the essence of extension. *Secondly*, his the-ory of Occasionalism explains how a perfect Deity must act in a manner that befits divine conduct. In this view, God acts as a general cause only, whose creative efficacy requires occasional causes to determine it. True, Occasionalism does not pre-judge what these occasional causes are. It is conceivable that other entities besides bodies should serve in the capacity of being the causes of sensations. But if Occasionalism does not demand bodies, it at least does not outlaw them. There is at least no contradiction in conceiving that bodies may be the occa-sional causes. Here again Mrs. Fritz goes astray, for she follows that standard interpretation and regards the occasional cause as a non-entity.

Thirdly and finally, Malebranche's theory of knowledge renders the *conception* of independent physical existence a perfectly self-consistent assumption. Unlike Berkeley, Malebranche can conceive extension apart from sensation and imagery. He can understand and separate the prick of a pin from the pain felt. Admitting abstract ideas or, better, essences, he can conceive extension as an object for thought and independently of its being thought. Hence for him there is no inconsistency in conceiving an independently *existing* extension. Given the independence *from* thought of the essence of bodies, it is possible to conceive that essence as receiving an existence that would belong to itself.

Thus far I have merely tried to show that immaterialism is in no way the ineluctable consequence of Malebranche's philosophy that Mrs. Fritz seeks to demonstrate, that the view of an independent material world is entirely compatible with his system; that the supposition of an external world can at least be entertained by him without contradiction; and that an external world is not necessarily superfluous in his philosophy. Whether we can prove that such an external material world does exist, and whether we can get across to it—these are important questions, but of another order. We must first agree that the notion of an independent world is, so far as Malebranche is concerned, a genuine possibility, regardless of the subsequent problems concerning its actuality. Malebranche, then, *can* believe in a real world. Now the question remains, does his system provide grounds for well-founded belief in it? To answer this question we must examine Malebranche's theory of sense perception, from its beginning as first formulated in the *Recherche*, through its subsequent stages of development.

II. Natural Judgments of Sense

Mr. Church claims that as first proposed in the *Recherche*, Malebranche's theory of perception treats perception as simply compound sensations.[15] This means to Church that Malebranche rigorously divorces understanding from perception.[16]

Malebranche comes to adopt this initial theory in the following way, according to Church: Malebranche wants to show how visual perception is sufficiently adequate for practical living. Notwithstanding the fact that visual perception cannot afford an exact knowledge of extension, inasmuch as extension is relational and nothing can be known as absolutely large or small in itself, nevertheless vision is not entirely erroneous. Accordingly, Malebranche wants to explain how distance and magnitude are perceived with an accuracy sufficient for pragmatic living. Hence, in Mr. Church's formulation, ". . . he describes five signs by which distance is *estimated* by the mind." [17] Again:

Malebranche's alleged epistemology of compound sensations.

> In Malebranche's view, a judgment is involved in every sense-perception; and it is this judgment that brings the percipient to *interpret* the sense-perception as being a real external existent of a definite magnitude, standing at a certain distance from him.[18]

Such judgments are not conscious, but "natural," involuntary and irresistible. Therefore ". . . Malebranche sometimes speaks as if they
were instincts or habits; and sometimes, also, as if they were *inferences*
in the sense of being the result of a sort of geometry 'natural' to the
mind." [19] Perhaps what Mr. Church has in mind is that this natural
geometry is some form of understanding that the mind imposes on a
raw sensuous manifold. In any case, as a first stage of his theory of
compound sensation, Church attributes to Malebranche the claims that
in visual perception the mind estimates distance by employing visual
signs as data, that the "sense-perception" is interpreted by acts of
judgment as being a real external existent, and that the interpretative
judgments are either instinctive or a sort of natural geometry.

However, continues Church, Malebranche cannot stop with such a
natural geometry of sensation. For in order

> . . . to fulfil their function of *adapting* awareness to the signs,
> natural judgments must become much more complex, as well as
> extremely variable; they cannot be a merely instinctive painting of
> colour upon object. The judgments must now *give* the data a com-
> plicated three-dimensional form . . .[20]

Still, however complicated, these natural judgments are in accord with
the laws of optics and that, says Church, is the reason why Malebranche finally claims these judgments to originate not in inference
or instinct but in God.[21]

But once God is declared to be the cause of these judgments, Malebranche has to admit that they are not, properly speaking, "judgments"
at all, but only compound sensations. For if God is the cause, the so-
called signs have lost all meaning. Occasionalism—God compounding
sensations—becomes a substitute for a theory of perception. ". . . Although angles and objects still enter awareness," Church tells us, "they
have no more meaning to the mind than has colour or any other simple
sensation. . . . Perception no longer even nominally involves judgment or in any way includes understanding." Church holds that Malebranche frankly admits this and it is for this reason that the theory of
compound sensations is introduced. Church's verdict is, " 'Since the
senses can only sense, and properly speaking never judge, it is certain
that judgment is only a compound sensation . . .' " [22] Church's conclusion is essentially that Malebranche cannot have any epistemology
at all. In effect, in his view, the epistemology collapses into an account
of simple, passive reception of congeries of inert sensations. In
Church's terms:

> The notion of divinely or 'naturally' directed judgment *organizing*
> the sense-manifold through forms of relation or understanding, is

[285]

no longer present; the understanding is rigorously divorced from perception, with the result that God simply 'compounds' sensations.[23]

Now, from this last statement as well as from the previous statements that I have quoted from Church's study, it is obvious that he reads Malebranche from a Kantian perspective. He treats Malebranche's five "means" for perceiving distance, his notion of judgment, and the role of understanding in perception as if Malebranche were first a Kant, but then a Christian dogmatist who, however, because of his unfortunate dogmatism, has completely emasculated perception.

Malebranche's alleged change of doctrine.

It is no wonder, then, that when Church later on discovers that Malebranche after all *has* included, and insists upon including, an intelligible content in perception, he charges him with a "radical change" and one for which Malebranche offers no reason whatever. And what precisely is this radical change that is alleged to occur in the *Entretiens sur la métaphysique?* Says Church:

> The statement that sense-perception is compound sensation defines perception in so far as it is made up of modifications of the soul. But Malebranche has come to regard sense-perception as involving an intelligible content; an idea of its occasional cause. He gives no reason for this radical change in his original theory of perception. Yet we may believe him to have seen that as no more than compound sensation, sense-perception can have no relation to thought; which is to say that in all experience nothing is intelligible.[24]

Actually, Malebranche insists from the first on conceptual essences in perception.

Now it is curious, indeed, to say that Malebranche *arrived* at this view of sense-perception in the *Entretiens sur la métaphysique* and that he did so for no apparent reason, in view of the fact that this doctrine is precisely the very foundation of his discussion on method in the *Recherche* and is one that conforms to his conception of method. Moreover, Church is fully aware that this view of perception—as constituted by sensation and conception of an idea—is presupposed in Malebranche's presentation of method in the *Recherche,* for when Church himself discusses the method, he accepts this very view of sense-perception.[25] But the book on method in the *Recherche* was written long before the *Entretiens sur la métaphysique!* Furthermore, the section which introduces the term "compound sensation" does not occur in the first edition of the *Recherche,* but is added later. While Lewis does not indicate when it was added, in Schrecker's volume, it can be noted that it was added to the second edition.[26] That would be in 1675. But 1675 is the date for the *first* edition of Volume II of the *Recherche,* where method is discussed. And, as I have said, in the presentation of method in Volume II, sense-perception is treated as it is in the *Entretiens sur la métaphysique,* i.e., as including both conceptual ideas and sensations. Moreover, this view of perception is

[286]

affirmed by Malebranche in Book III of the *Recherche*.[27] Of this too Church is perfectly aware.[28]

In the light of these facts, surely we cannot say with Church that Malebranche's view of perception as a natural revelation is one at which Malebranche arrived only in the *Entretiens sur la métaphysique*. Are we then to assume that he was simultaneously suggesting two different theories of perception? Are we to suppose that in his work on vision in Book I he was advancing a doctrine of compound sensations that was radically unlike what he was affirming in his third book of the *Recherche* on understanding and in his sixth on method? Humans are indeed fallible, and contradictions often occur within a single work. But it is genuinely difficult to believe that an author will be affirming at the same time two such radically opposed theories of such central importance to his system. If Church had not been misled initially by his Kantian and anti-theological approach to Malebranche and by his unwarrantable assumption that Malebranche seeks to divorce intellect and sense, he would have saved himself and his readers a great deal of confusion.

The reasons why Malebranche argues that the senses are deceptive and uses vision as illustrative are these: *First,* there is no absolute magnitude or time; these are relational. A body's size is relative; so is its movement and shape. Nothing is absolutely large or small. *Secondly,* magnitude varies with respect to the percipient. Thus an insect appears small to us, but seen under a microscope it has innumerable parts and from its own perspective it may appear large to itself or to its insect neighbor.[29]

Thus, when Malebranche argues that we do not see bodies in themselves, he means that we do not perceive them in absolute but in relational terms. Secondly, the relational aspects are not perceived with exactitude, for we perceive a body in so far as it enters into a new relation—in so far as it appears relative to us.

But now, the crucial issue concerns the status of these appearances. This relative appearance of an object—is it a true, real, independent appearance, or is it mind-dependent? When the moon appears relative to my body as two hundred feet away and circular in shape, are this apparent size and shape determined or constructed or so organized by me, or are they true of the moon in regard to me? Does the being of the apparent object lie in its *percipi* or is my awareness of it dependent on its being?

Visible appearances and 'natural judgments of sense.'

It is with regard to this issue that Mr. Church and I sharply disagree. He assumes that for Malebranche the apparent size or distance of objects is determined by the percipient's mind. He assumes that the cues for distance are *data* for a mind to organize, interpret. But when Malebranche speaks of means for judging distance, there is no evidence whatsoever that he considers the structure of perception as consisting of a manifold of chaotic sensations that are organized by an understanding into a perceptual object. There is not even any evidence that he regards sensations as the given *data* from which the mind subsequently *infers* to the presence of an object. In fact, there is a good deal of evidence to the contrary. With respect to construing the judgment of distance or of size in the Kantian sense of a mental construct, Malebranche's entire polemic against conceptualism and creationism of ideas should dispel any such illusion. Both in his theory of knowledge and in his Occasionalism, Malebranche is at great pains to disprove that the mind is genuinely creative. From this we may not conclude that understanding plays no role in sense perception. What this proves, on the contrary, is that whatever intelligible content or meaning is found in perception, why, then, it is indeed revealed or found. And this means too that whatever size or distance an object appears to have, it really does appear in that way.

In the second chapter of Book I of the *Recherche*, Malebranche explains that he uses "judgment" in two different senses. Properly speaking, he there says, judgment is an act of will. This voluntary act consists in free acceptance or rejection, in acquiescence or denial, of what is perceived, sensed, or understood. From the present point of view, the mind, whether it senses, imagines, or understands, never judges.[30] There is, however, another view of judgment. In this latter view, judgment consists in the apprehension of relations between things. When the mind perceives a simple object without any relation to anything else, this perception is called a simple percept; when it apprehends relations between two or more things, this apprehension is a judgment; and perception of relations among relations is called reasoning.

Now in the very passage that Church cites, in which Malebranche affirms that the senses only sense and never judge, so that properly speaking natural judgments are composite sensations, Malebranche offers the following example to illustrate his meaning:

> Lors, par exemple, que je regarde un homme qui marche, il est certain qu'à proportion qu'il s'approche de moi, l'image ou l'impression qui se trace de sa hauteur dans le fond de mes yeux augmente toujours, et devient enfin double, lorsque étant à dix pas il n'est plus qu'à cinq. Mais parce que l'impression de distance diminue *dans la même proportion* que l'autre augmente, je le vois toujours de la même grandeur. Ainsi la sensation que j'ai de cet homme dépend sans cesse *de deux impressions différentes*, sans compter le changement de situation des yeux, et le reste dont je parlerai dans la suite.[31]

Thus, even in the very passage upon which Church's entire argument depends, Malebranche's view of judgment and of signs by which we judge apparent distance or magnitude or shape is neither Kantian nor Berkeleian, nor is it a view which looks upon sensations as data from which inference is made. The mind neither interprets signs, nor organizes them, nor infers from them. What it does do is involuntarily, instantaneously or instinctively see, behold, become aware of a complexity of relations.

In short, the apparent magnitude, size and shape of objects is not determined by the percipient's mind. The soul does not use cues or signs to construct a visual object or an apparent distance. These means are tools, instruments or vehicles (but not data) through which the mind becomes automatically aware of the apparent relationship between external objects and its own body. Thus, when Malebranche calls natural judgments composite sensations, he does not mean that perception is a bundle or congeries of initially *unrelated* or non-intelligible items. He means that relative distance is an actual relation directly experienced. Thus, in his controversy with Régis, who claimed that the apparent magnitude of an object depended on the size of the retinal image, Malebranche insisted instead that it depended on the *felt* or *perceived* distance. He insists that a distance that is *not actually perceived by the senses* must be counted as nothing; an unperceived distance, he says, cannot serve as a foundation for the natural judgment. Again he tells us:

> Mais afin que l'inégalité de la distance produise de l'inégalité dans les apparences que nous avons de deux objets qui tracent des images égales, il faut que cette inégalité de distance soit actuellement aperçue par les sens. . . . C'est pour cela que les astronomes ne voient pas le soleil plus grand que les autres hommes, quoiqu'ils le jugent infiniment plus éloigné qu'on ne le croit ordinairement.[32]

Church, commenting on Malebranche's controversy with Régis, asks: of what use are signs for judging distance if distance itself can be perceived?[33] It is perfectly fair to retort: if by signs Malebranche has meant that distance is an intellectual relation created by thought, then they are patently useless. But none of the cues is an occasion for an intellectual construction. They are simply mechanisms that indicate a direct apprehension. There is no inferential judgment apart from the complexly related and ordered sensations themselves. In fact, Malebranche even compares the natural judgments for apprehending distance to the apprehension of the flow of time. The awareness of the passage of time is constituted by the intermingling and merging of successive mental acts. The sense of the apparent length or slowness of duration is no different from the actual "con-fusion" of the thoughts themselves. That is, the judgment of the elapsing of an hour or more is not separate in the sense of being an inference from the passing

The function of the visual signs of distance.

experiences. As these experiences are lived and felt, they involve an act of attention or application that immediately or intuitively testifies to or reveals their own span.[34] So it is with the judgments concerning distance. The soul does not employ signs or means to *fashion* or *fabricate* the apparent size or distance; it uses them to *find* or *discover* these appearances. But this capacity to make these responses or discoveries is not intrinsic to the soul, that is, the soul is not the creative source of its responses. This is why Malebranche describes natural judgments as instinctive, automatic, or a sort of natural geometry.

Signs and Occasionalism.

For Descartes, natural geometry implies innate ideas and created truths. It implies therefore a mind which can perceive as it does in virtue of its own inherent inventive structure. Since Malebranche rejects innate ideas, for him the manner in which the mind discovers apparent distance must be grounded on an objective foundation. This is why he declares that the senses do not judge. Appearances are not dependent on the human will, nor does the mind contribute anything to appearances. Hence his appeal to God and to the divinely ordained causal laws that govern the union of mind and body. Occasionalism thus does not replace the theory of vision through natural judgments and signs. Rather it serves to explain the ultimate metaphysical *true* cause that enables minds to use signs, that is, to apprehend the objective appearances.

The theory of signs or means for perceiving distance is advanced to describe the manifold particular ways of perception—how perception takes place. Occasionalism, the doctrine that God as Being is the true creative cause, explains why it so occurs. It is not enough, Theodore tells Aristes in the *Entretiens sur la métaphysique,* to fly at once to God's will as ultimate cause in order to explain a phenomenon. If, for example, upon being pricked by a sharp instrument, one explained the cause of the pain as being simply one of the laws of the Author of nature, this would be wrong. Says Theodore: "I ought to tell you that the prick cannot separate the fibres of my flesh without disturbing the nerves which propagate stimulation to the brain, and without disturbing the brain itself." And yet there is a limit to explanation in descriptive psychology, that is, in the field concerned with the "laws of the conjunction of soul and body." Theodore continues: "But if you wish to know how it is that when a certain part of my brain is disturbed in a given way, I feel the pain of a prick, this question concerns a general effect; and, as one cannot by tracing the matter further, find a natural or particular cause, one must have recourse to a general cause. For this amounts to a question as to who is the author of the general laws of the conjunction of soul and body." [35]

Now, once we discard a Kantian approach to Malebranche's theory of judgment and signs, once we realize that "composite sensations" means the awareness of relations among relations, there is no need to assume that his view of perception implies a divorce from the intellect. It is difficult, as Malebranche says to Arnauld, for a philosopher to explain everything at once. In his preliminary analysis of sense and imagination, Malebranche has not yet fully explained the nature and role of ideas. This is treated later, in Book III of the *Recherche*. Hence the full statement concerning perception, namely that it is a combination of concept and sensation, is not given until we come to this book, wherein essences and the Vision in God are set forth. We must not, however, be misled by Malebranche's artificial division of sense from understanding for purposes of analysis; we must not assume that the distinguishable is necessarily separable. Thus when he talks in Book I of perception as composite sensations, *it does not follow that perception is nothing but sensations.* Clearly, in seeing the apparent distance and magnitude of the moon, that seeing involves understanding, for it involves such meanings as angles and proportions. However, at this point in the *Recherche*, Malebranche has as yet discussed neither his doctrine of universals, nor their role in perception, nor their ontological status. But as soon as this latter doctrine has been treated, as soon as he has completed his discussion of the pure understanding, he immediately makes it known that sense-perception does indeed involve understanding. In Book III he explicitly tells us: When we perceive something sensible, *in our perception* are found a sensation and a pure idea. He there carefully states that the sensation is a modification of the soul, that the idea is in God, and that God conjoins the sensation to the idea when objects are present, in order that we believe in them.[36]

(margin note: Sense perception involves pure ideas as well as sensation.)

Thus sense-perception is a complex activity: it involves the act of conception, or pure intuition, and also sensation. Conception presents a universal meaning clearly and distinctly. The same meaning is present in perception. Through sensations we "judge," that is, become directly aware of the relation between idea and existence; we are aware that the immutable idea conceived really exists and that it exists as it appears, with the perceived relations of size or shape that it has.

Thus, in order to signalize that the visual or perceived object is a true appearance, Malebranche was led in the *Recherche* to assert that the natural judgments of sense are in us despite ourselves, that they are created by God, and that they are such as we ourselves *would* create if we were divinely versed in the laws of optics and geometry. What this shows, in other words, is that our sensory perception or awareness is not constitutive of the object, but a revelation or discovery of it in relation to us. We perceive as we do because the objects really appear as they do relatively to us.

Since, however, we know that God alone is the Creator and secondary causes are only occasional causes, we may say that external objects do not create our natural judgments but that they elicit or occasion such intuitive awareness.

Once again, then, Occasionalism is not called in to replace his original view on vision. Rather Occasionalism is called upon to present the ultimate metaphysical explanation. Whenever we seek for the cause of a general effect, we are then compelled to seek its general cause, namely God. The five so-called means for explaining the apparent distance and magnitude of objects are merely instrumental or particular accounts of the way objects appear in relation to our body. The ultimate reason for such appearances rests on God's will. He has deliberately willed the laws that govern the union of mind and body, and it is these objective laws that determine the relativity of perceptions. Malebranche's later writings do indeed, on many points, amplify his theory of perception and knowledge, but in no way do they indicate a radical change from the position of the *Recherche*. To assure ourselves that this is so, let us now consider, as a critical example, the tenth Éclaircissement.

III. INTELLIGIBLE EXTENSION

The tenth Éclaircissement is written, as its title indicates, to elucidate *how* one sees *all* things in God.[37] Its purpose accordingly is to explain not only our Vision in God of the eternal truths that constitute the sphere of mathematics and of ethics but also our knowledge of particular existents: how and in what sense they are seen in God.

Essential and existential knowledge of matters of fact.

The mind knows objects in two ways: by 'light' and by 'sentiment.' It knows a thing by light when it has a clear idea and when in consulting that idea it can discover its properties. It is by light and clear ideas that the mind knows the essences of things and numbers and extension. It is through sentiment, on the other hand, that the mind judges the existence of creatures.[38] Malebranche, then, reaffirms in this Éclaircissement that perception or our knowledge of existents is constituted by pure idea and sensation: ". . . car il y a toujours idée pure et sentiment confus dans la connaissance que nous avons de l'existence des êtres . . ."[39] He maintains, too, that while sensations, being the modifications of the soul, cannot represent anything distinct from ourselves, they can, nevertheless, represent the existence of things.[40] Thus on the one hand sensations do not "represent" the nature of things. It is the divine idea contained in perception that renders objects intelligible or knowable. Sensations reveal only what pertains to the soul. Nevertheless, while they do not disclose *what* things are, they do help to reveal *that* they are.

It remains to explain, however, how material particulars are seen *in*

God and how sense discloses that they are or exist. If Vision in God is meant to include a vision of all things, then how can movement and change and actual configurations be seen in God? Malebranche poses this objection in these words:

> Il n'y a rien en Dieu de mobile; il n'y a rien en lui de figuré. S'il n'y a un soleil dans le monde intelligible, ce soleil est toujours égal a lui-même, et le soleil visible paraît plus grand, lorsqu'il est proche de l'horizon, que lorsqu'il en est fort éloigné. Donc ce n'est pas ce soleil intelligible que l'on voit. Il en est de même des autres créatures. Donc on ne voit point en Dieu les ouvrages de Dieu.[41]

To answer this problem Malebranche employs the notion of 'Intelligible Extension.'

One must realize, says Malebranche, that God contains in Himself an ideal or intelligible Extension. Since the mind can apprehend a part of this Extension, then it is certain that it can apprehend in God all kinds of figures, for figure is the limit of extension. In other words, figure is determined by the relations of distance. A circle is produced by a line one of whose points is fixed and the other in continuous motion. God can comprehend the meaning of this figure, as conveyed by the algebraic expression, without Himself being figured or in motion. Hence, concludes Malebranche, there need be no sensible bodies in God or real or actual figures in Intelligible Extension, to enable us to see them in God or to enable God to see them in Himself.[42] He goes on to say that one must not suppose that:

> . . . le monde intelligible ait un tel rapport avec le monde matériel et sensible, qu'il y ait par exemple un soleil, un cheval, un arbre intelligible destiné à nous représenter le soleil, un cheval et un arbre; et que tous ceux qui voient le soleil, voient nécessairement ce prétendu soleil intelligible. Toute étendue intelligible pouvant être conçue circulaire, ou avoir la figure intelligible d'un cheval ou d'un arbre, toute étendue intelligible peut servir à représenter le soleil, un cheval, un arbre, et par conséquent être soleil, cheval, arbre du monde intelligible, et devenir même soleil, cheval, arbre visible et sensible, si l'âme a quelque sentiment à l'occasion des corps pour attacher à ces idées, c'est-à-dire si ces idées affectent l'âme de perceptions sensibles.[43]

In God there are no separate and distinct ideas for each individual object. For example, the idea of the sun is that of a circular extension; so is that of a penny. Hence there is no need for a different essence for the penny and the sun. Secondly, the essence of a circle is an ideal meaning, that conveyed by the algebraic expression. Hence there are no actual shapes or figures in God—essences are meanings, not images. Thirdly, in contemplating ideal meanings God can com-

prehend or conceive movement; He can conceive changes of position and therefore change in size or figure without suffering change Himself and without becoming configurated.[44]

Intelligible Extension is thus conceived by Malebranche as infinitely garrulous and yet ontologically neutral. The concept of a circle is equally appropriate to express the properties of a poker chip and those of a baby's bracelet. Hence, just as Bacon denies a plethora of Forms—the Form of man, the Form of lion—but insists instead on simple natures for yellowness, malleability, density and so forth,[45] so Malebranche is saying that various universal essences, each remaining identically itself and so unchangeable, can indifferently enter into the perception of objects. Hence in seeing the sun, now large and now small, now flat and now circular, these perceptions depend upon the manner in which the various aspects of Intelligible Extension are disclosed to the mind. Were there a distinct and specific idea for the real sun in the sense of a definite figure and size, then indeed we could not see it now large and now small, now circular and now flat.

Perception is constituted by idea or essence plus sensation. Since this is so, we may ask, if the essence of the sun is that of a sphere, then in seeing the sun as a flat disc, how can we obtain or apprehend the intelligible notion of a flat figure? Similarly, if the sun is of a given size, how do we apprehend the idea that it is larger than it appears? The answer to these questions is this: we know that there is no specific idea for each kind of object. Intelligible Extension is a system of various meanings—circles, ellipses, squares. In this system we can conceive changes in position and therefore in size. This ideal system itself, however, does not change. $x^2 + y^2 = r^2$ never alters. In perception we can see the sun as flat or circular, because now one meaning or essence and now another can be grasped, depending on what the occasional cause requires. If the actual body that strikes our senses be a round penny, that will occasion God to reveal to us in perception the concept of a circle. If the *apparent* size of the moon actually changes in relation to our body—then we will have different concepts of relative size when it is at the horizon and at the meridian.

Now, while concepts are particular in the sense that each has its distinctive properties, they are also universal, for they can enter into many different instances. How, then, do we tell when a general meaning, as that of a circle, belongs to or is characteristic of such and such an object as the sun or a penny? This we do through sensations.

> De plus on voit, ou l'on sent, tel corps, lorsque son idée, c'est-à-dire, lorsque telle figure d'étendue intelligible et générale devient sensible et particulière par la couleur, ou par quelque autre perception sensible dont son idée affecte l'âme, et que l'âme y attache . . .[46]

Universals in sense perception.

[294]

Mr. Church interprets this doctrine to mean that sensations individualize Intelligible Extension and thus render it specific and concrete. This he declares to be an impossible description of individuality. The reality which sensation is to render individual is other than, and independent of, sensation. Ideas, Malebranche insists, have no necessary relation to modifications of the soul. As thus essentially other than ideas, it is impossible that a sensation should have to an idea the necessary relation of being what differentiates that idea from every other idea. Even though it were accepted as true that when present in perception the intelligible extension is individuated by the sensations then spread over it, what individuates the intelligible extension when it appears in the pure understanding? [47]

Intelligible Extension both One and Many.

Church commits two errors. He assumes *first* that intelligible extension is a single, homogeneous, uniform idea.[48] He thinks that Malebranche's denial of a plurality of ideas, of a specific idea for each object, such as a tree or a house, is tantamount to a denial of plurality and individuality altogether. But, as M. Gouhier observes, and as we saw in the discussion on method and in Malebranche's replies to Mairan, Malebranche does not reject *plural essences* in the idea of extension. What he rejects is a plurality of *images*.[49] Church himself is aware of this distinction,[50] yet he persists in assuming that Intelligible Extension is undifferentiated. Because Malebranche in his reply to Arnauld compares Intelligible Extension to a block of marble that potentially combines all figures, but is itself uniform, it does not follow that this idea of extension is one of diaphanous simplicity.[51]

How can God apply this simple homogeneous extension, ask Church, Arnauld,[52] and Bouillier,[53] in such a way as to make the mind apprehend now one figure, now another, unless these individuated figures are in God in the first place? Now it seems to me that when Malebranche speaks of the single infinite Intelligible Extension, he is being once again faithful to Descartes' *Geometry*. There, as we saw in Chapter I on method, Descartes has shown that the variety of geometric curves, such as the circle, the parabola, the ellipse, do not constitute a distinct multiplicity. They are all related to one another, their differences being one of complexity, represented by equations of varying forms. Thus intelligible extension in its singularity is not to be understood as an undifferentiated homogeneous idea, but rather as a continuum of interrelated aspects. Intelligible Extension is one infinite system of relations of relations. As such it is at once both one and many. Intelligible Extension is a system of particular affirmative essences, to use an expression from Spinoza. Therein, the ideal triangle, though not separable from, is distinguishable from the ideal circle. Each has its own properties. In this respect, each universal is also particular and individual.

[295]

Why then does Malebranche use the figure of the marble and speak of ideas as being potentially in the divine reason? Does this mean that the variety of figures are not really in God? No, not at all. Potentiality does not refer to the manner in which the ideas are in God, but to the manner in which they are perceived. Now perception relates to concrete reality. The concretely real is for Malebranche the addition of existence to an essence. Existence translates an idea into a real entity. Thus ideas as aspects of an infinite Intelligible Extension are real therein, but only potentialities with respect to their concretization. That is, the idea of extension is an infinitely rich field of "exemplary" possibilities, out of which any number of worlds could be made. Hence with respect to existence it is like a block of marble from which all sorts of statues could potentially be fashioned. On the other hand, this idea of extension is no mere "blob;" it is definitely articulated into distinguishable and determinate aspects. Malebranche calls these articulations "intelligible" parts in order to indicate that, real though they are, these are no actual divisions in God.[54] In perception one becomes aware through sensations of that aspect of Intelligible Extension that has been willed to exist. Thus the particular intelligible idea has a threefold role: (1) it is an aspect of Intelligible Extension in God; (2) it is seen in God by an act of intelligible vision on our part; and (3) it is embodied, incarnate, in the object.

Church commits a *second* error in assuming that it is sensations that individuate. In an actually existing object, it is existence and movement which are the principles of individuality. Existence makes an idea to be; existence individuates an essence. It is existence that individuates the roundness of the sun from that of the penny. But *we* perceive this actual distinction between penny and sun by sensations. Our sensations do not render or cause these real distinctions; they reveal them. These assertions are supported by the following.

The principle of individuation and the perception of individuals.

In the case of God, He apprehends actual movement and change by consulting His will:

> Car Dieu ne voit point le mouvement actuel des corps dans sa substance, ou dans l'idée qu'il en a en lui-même, mais seulement par la connaissance qu'il a de ses volontés à leur égard. Il ne voit même leur existence que par cette voie, parce qu'il n'y a que sa volonté qui donne l'être à toutes choses.[55]

The divine will is the source of existence and therefore of actual movement. Existence is the principle of individuation. God knows *what* the essence of sun and penny are by consulting that part of His substance that relates to creatures, namely, Intelligible Extension. He knows *that* they are and *how* they are by consulting His will. Thus while the essence of the sun *as a circle* is always the same, God can understand intellectually that change is possible, and He is aware of real change by consulting His will.

Now in human perception we discriminate the existence and action of one object from another by means of sensations. Conceptually, the idea of sun and penny as $x^2 + y^2 = r^2$ are identical. What enables us to tell one from the other existentially is a difference of color. Colors are modifications of the soul, but they are attached to, projected on, or "painted over" ideal meanings.[56] When ideal meanings are conjoined with sensations, the ideal meaning tells us what the object is, and the sensation helps to reveal that this meaning really exists. In other words, we have no way of grasping that act of existence that constitutes the individuality of an object, except through sensations. God, who is their creator, sees a thing's existence, its received process, through His will. We see through sense. In this respect, the existence of things, or creative power incarnate in things, is invisible. And this is why Malebranche writes to Régis that our awareness of existence is indirect.[57] It is indirect in this sense: our sensations are directly attached to or conjoined with essences or ideal meanings, but at the same time they warn or admonish us of the actual presence of the object. And because sensations do announce or declare the actual presence of an object, are instruments for the discovery of the object, Malebranche boldly asserted in the *Entretiens sur la métaphysique* that sensation is a sort of natural revelation.[58] For these perceptions occur in accordance with the laws that govern the union of mind and body, and hence upon the occasion of what takes place in the body. Hence, it is not we or our sensations that individuate.

Once more Church is aware of this situation. He is aware that Malebranche in his reply to Arnauld has clearly explained what is the ontological source of individuation.[59] But Church's procedure here as everywhere else in his study on Malebranche consists in reading Malebranche in piecemeal fashion. In this he agrees perfectly with the method of Arnauld. As a result of treating some small portion of Malebranche's philosophy he first raises what appear to be insurmountable objections. Then when he finds them to be successfully explained by reference to other parts of the text, he accuses Malebranche of inconsistencies and of radical changes of position. The truth of the matter is that Malebranche's philosophy proceeds on many different levels which Malebranche tries to keep separate, but which necessarily often overlap. As he himself declares: "Il faut de l'équité dans les lecteurs, et qu'ils fassent crédit pour quelque temps, s'ils veulent qu'on les satisfasse; car il n'y a que les géomètres qui puissent toujours payer comptant." [60] Thus it is one thing to explain as an epistemologist how we know and how we perceive: through pure intellection we know universals; through sense, ideas become individuated and facts are perceived. It is, however, another thing to explain as an ontologist what it is for something to be a fact, what individuality is, and how God is the "true" cause of our perceptions. Hence when Malebranche is faced with problems relating to ultimate principles of explanation, he naturally goes to Occasionalism, and this constitutes his metaphysics.

Thus Malebranche develops a subtle theory of sense perception—a theory that may, paradoxically, be described as at once immediate and doubly mediated.

Revelation of existence through sense.

First, perception involves an act of conception. Conception gives knowledge about the object—it reveals its meaning, its import, its intelligible character, its *ratio* or idea. *Secondly,* conception is immersed in or accompanied by sensations by which we intuit that the object conceived actually exists. We have an immediate revelation of the presence of external reality. However, the reality perceived to exist is never grasped as it is for itself, but always relatively to our bodily needs. Upon this view, it may still be said that objects are neither visible nor intelligible in themselves. They are not intelligible in themselves, for their essence is beheld only in so far as it participates in God's reason. They are not visible in themselves, for they are beheld through sensations.

Revelation through sensation is a complex situation. First, sensations, being existent operations, reveal God as the true creative and sustaining power, the true source of the sensations. But in addition to the general cause, recall, there are occasional causes. These, in turn, exist and act through participating in God's immensity, will, and power. Sensations thus serve to reveal the presence and action of the occasional cause; through them is disclosed God's will embodied in and communicated to the occasional cause. Finally, through sensations God's creatures are revealed relatively to us, not as they appear to themselves or to an infinite point of view. At the same time, while the subjectivity of another's existence is concealed in the meaning that we cannot live it or be it itself, nevertheless, the *fact* of its existence is not opaque; and its nature or essence, while not completely knowable on the existential level, is yet not false. We perceive the object relatively to us, and hence in a limited or partial manner. Yet the appearance is the very object appearing.

We can now understand what 'Vision in God' means. Sense perception is a revelation of all things "in" God, because it is a revelation of

How we see existents in God.

God's efficacy in all things. The idea contained in perception is identically the same idea when apprehended clearly and distinctly. As such it is the divine archetype. When conjoined with sensations, the latter manifest God's will as their 'true cause' and the external object as the 'occasional cause.' Inasmuch as the occasional cause is itself an embodiment of God's will and sustained thereby, we may say that the existence of objects is seen in God's will as is their essence in God's reason. But since the object participates in God's reason and will, it is equally true to say that perception is a natural revelation of things.

When Arnauld asks Malebranche how, out of marble (out of Intelligible Extension), we can form the face of Augustine, without having previously seen Augustine, Malebranche replies that the issue is not one concerning the *origin* of ideas but instead one concerning their *nature*.[61] To become acquainted with particular existential facts, we of course need the instrumentality of sense, but to apprehend what is so presented, we need *a priori* universals.[62] Thus, knowledge, for Malebranche, has, in the word of Church, its "incipience" in sense perception.[63] Malebranche holds that perception contains sensations which "admonish" us of the existence of things. He speaks of them as a natural revelation of the presence of objects. At the same time, there is in perception an intelligible content which, when the sensations have become disregarded, stands forth as a pure essence.

IV. NATURAL REVELATIONS OF EXTERNAL EXISTENCE

After completing his analysis of the inadequacy of the senses, especially vision, for discerning the primary qualities of bodies—their size, distance and motion—Malebranche asserts that however inexact or relational vision may be, nevertheless, this much we do know, that bodies really do exist. He writes:

Malebranche affirms knowledge of the existence of external objects.

> Nous avons vu, dans les chapitres précédents, que les jugements que nous formons sur le rapport de nos yeux touchant l'étendue, la figure et le mouvement, ne sont jamais exactement vrais: cependant il faut tomber d'accord qu'ils ne sont pas entièrement faux; ils renferment au moins cette vérité, qu'il y a hors de nous de l'étendue, des figures et des mouvements quels qu'ils soient.[64]

In the *Recherche* itself, then, Malebranche maintains that while the senses do not reveal the *objective* size, shape or motion of bodies but only the *apparent* properties (where "objective" means either relative to the object's perspective or to an infinite perspective or to a usual perspective, and "apparent" means relative to our perspective or to the varying conditions of the perceiver),[65] yet, the senses do declare the objective presence or external existence of the object. In short, while the senses reveal an object's primary characteristics or qualities in a manner relational to us, at the same time they testify to its real actual existence as something independent of us.

Not only does Malebranche insist on the cognitive validity of perception with regard to external independent existence of bodies, but he goes on to treat that *enfant terrible* of direct realism, error, in a light, off-hand manner:

> Il est vrai que nous voyons souvent des choses qui ne sont point et qui ne furent jamais, et que nous ne devons pas conclure qu'une chose soit hors de nous de cela seul que nous la voyons hors de nous. Il n'y a point de liaison nécessaire entre la présence d'une idée à l'esprit d'un homme et l'existence de la chose que cette idée représente, et ce qui arrive à ceux qui dorment ou qui sont en délire le prouve suffisamment. Mais cependant on peut assurer qu'il y a ordinairement hors de nous de l'étendue, des figures et des mouvements lorsque nous en voyons. Ces choses ne sont point seulement imaginaires, elles sont réelles, et nous ne nous trompons point de croire qu'elles ont une existence réelle et indépendante de notre esprit, quoiqu'il soit très difficile de le prouver démonstrativement.[66]

This paragraph is of utmost importance. First, let it be noted that notwithstanding dreams, hallucinations or errors, Malebranche retains his allegiance to the natural revelations of sense. It cannot therefore be said that he ever changed his mind on that score. Even though on particular occasions and in particular circumstances the natural revelations may lead to error, ordinarily perception as such is trustworthy. In calling attention to dreams and illusions, Malebranche is not asserting the absolute unreliability and bankruptcy of the senses; he is merely sounding the warning that mistakes are made. As he says in the *Entretiens sur la métaphysique:* it is certain that we are often deceived, *but it is no less certain that we are not always deceived.*[67]

But, it may be asked, what right has Malebranche to trust the senses at all in view of his "representationalism?" How may he even

Alleged copy theory in Malebranche.

speak of a natural revelation? As I have commented already, Church, like Arnauld, supposes that Malebranche takes "representative idea" in a literal sense, namely, that external "invisible" objects are copies of the visible divine archetypes.[68] "Since the natural revelation of an idea is one thing," he writes,[69] "and knowledge that this idea represents a particular body is another, it remains to be explained how we can pass from the natural revelation of existence to the knowledge of an existent." What Church is asking is how we can know that corresponding to the idea given in perception there exists a specific object resembling that idea. In asking this, he must be interpreting Malebranche's epistemology as a copy theory, for otherwise, if the immutable idea known were literally embodied in the object, then having a "natural revelation of existence" *would reveal existence; it would* be identical with having "knowledge of an existent." His question is quite proper within the scope of his own interpretation of Malebranche. But must we accept such an assumption of epistemological, inferential dualism? Church is perfectly aware that Malebranche found it sufficient to answer the objection in this way:

> The particular process of attention which begins in a natural revelation is, throughout its development and concentration, the same process which finally occasions a pure perception. The idea then perceived clearly and distinctly can be no other than the idea revealed in sense-perception, because that idea has been constantly identified by a continuous process of attention.[70]

Once more Mr. Church is correct. This is precisely the sort of explanation that one would expect of an adherent to the experimental method of Bacon. Beginning with the perception of facts which dimly contain an intelligible meaning, one proceeds by a continuous process of elimination and identification to get at the clear view of the natures, essences, or forms contained in perception.

But if Malebranche is indeed offering a Baconian view of knowledge and perception, is it not possible that he does so because he also has in mind an ontology compatible with Bacon? Is it not possible that the ideas which Malebranche finds in perception and in God may also be immanent in the things themselves and that therefore there is no inference from idea to thing? In that case, Malebranche's explanation would be entirely valid, and Church's first objection would be dissipated.

But even if it is granted that *ideas* are not simply located, the objection may still be raised, how can we perceive *objects*—real bodies—when all that we apprehend are *ideas*? Critics beginning with Arnauld have repeatedly pressed this objection and have not understood its answer. Failing to permit Malebranche to discuss one issue at a time, they have made the error of taking a part of his philosophy as a doctrine complete in itself. To repeat, as an epistemologist, offering an account of sense perception, Malebranche is concerned with an anatomy of knowledge. He is concerned with dissecting the elements that enter into cognition. Malebranche is describing *how*, on his theory, we perceive things; and his answer is that perceiving is constituted by concepts and percepts. The critics who have followed Arnauld have confused the epistemologist's task with the ontologist's, and have gratuitously assumed that this description necessarily implies a duplication of entities, that the real object must be a copy of the idea. Having made this assumption, they naturally ask, how, in knowing an idea, we also know that the real object is like the idea? And how can we infer the existence of the real object from the existence or knowledge of the idea?

But in describing how we perceive, *Malebranche is not committing himself in any way concerning the relation of idea to thing.* This question is a metaphysical one; *and it can be settled only after we understand how God creates and what it is for a thing to be and to exist.* Metaphysically, we know it turns out that a created thing is a composite of essence and existence, that it is a complete embodiment of the whole of God, and that God is immanent as well as transcendent. From this point of view, the essence known is *identically* in God and in things. Through sense, the existence revealed is the natural revelation of the very divine will and power that have entered into and have been embodied in the creature. The creature thus, on Malebranche's theory, becomes the occasional cause that acts in such a way as to provoke and stimulate both our sensations which announce its existence and our acts of conceiving which declare its essence.

All this is ignored by Arnauld and the critics who accept his objections. Instead, they commit a fallacy of misplaced concreteness, and assume that Malebranche is guilty of advocating the crudest form of copy theory, with quasi-substantial entities duplicating perceived entities. This Malebranche himself roundly denied.[71] Also, in the seventeenth century "to represent" was often used in the sense of "to present." And in the Neo-platonic tradition, objects were understood to be analogues of God in the sense of participation, not copies. Thus for Philo, for example, essences enjoyed multiple stages of existence. They were first in God and after creation in things also.[72] Precisely this theory I tried above to suggest is present in Malebranche's Occasionalism.

It is true that Malebranche appeals to fevers, dreams and illusions, to show that ideas may be present even though nothing "resembling" or "like" them may actually exist.[73] "Thousands upon thousands of experiences teach us that often the soul perceives as present objects which do not actually exist." And on grounds of scientific knowledge he holds:

Erroneous apprehension of essences no evidence for a copy theory in veridical perception.

> From a thousand experiences, and from the demonstrations of optics, it is certain that bodies are not seen directly or immediately, and in themselves. For some are seen that are not, and what is not, cannot be seen.[74]

However, from the fact that in non-veridical perception we apprehend essences that do not exist, it does not follow that in veridical perception there is any *duplication* between the divine archetypes and the essences of things. Almost every critic of Malebranche's theory of knowledge has naturally assumed that this duplicate-copy theory is the position of Malebranche. Yet I find no good reason for this assumption, and, on the contrary, insist that his metaphysics of participation leaves no room for it.

Nor, furthermore, does error affect the disclosure of existence in *veridical* perception. From the fact that in non-veridical perception we apprehend ideas that do not exist, it does not follow that real *existence is never* in some sense given. Mr. Church thinks that in turning to natural revelations in the *Entretiens sur la métaphysique* Malebranche is in fact exemplifying the inevitable failure of every representative doctrine: that sooner or later every representational theory has to turn to direct knowledge of existence in order to verify its mediating ideas.[75] But inasmuch as no change of position has occurred between the *Recherche* and the *Entretiens sur la métaphysique,* it does not follow that Malebranche ever thought that external existence was inaccessible through sense.

But it may be objected, is perception *ever* veridical, for Malebranche? Does not the relativity of perception indicate that we never get "direct" access to the object itself, that is, to the nature of the object as that nature is in itself? Does not Malebranche assert:

> . . . nous ne pouvons nous en assurer entièrement. Cependant sans la connaissance de la ligne on ne peut jamais connaître aucune figure, comme tout le monde sait assez.
>
> Voilà ce que l'on peut dire en général des figures qui sont tout proche de nos yeux et entre nos mains; mais si on les suppose éloignées de nous, combien trouverons-nous de changement dans la projection qu'elles feront sur le fond de nos yeux! [76]

And does he not make Theodore maintain:

> . . . you are not even certain that what you see is a square, and that this particular line is straight, or that angle a right angle. The relations which your mind conceives between the magnitudes are not the same as the relations of these figures.[77]

Citing these instances as evidence, Mr. Church concludes: "We must never believe the idea discovered in natural revelation to be the true idea of the occasional cause . . . It is plain that what attention discovers in perception, and renders present to thought, is not the archetype of the occasional cause, but some other idea." [78]

I do not agree, however, that the relativity of perception supports Church's conclusion. From the fact that the spherical sun and moon, seen at a distance, appear flat and circular, all that we may validly infer is that perception does not reveal the object *totally* and *completely.* It does not follow that what is immediately perceived is some new object totally alien to the real object. This is what Malebranche himself actually asserts: "De ce que nous avons l'idée d'une chose, il ne s'ensuit pas qu'elle existe, et encore moins qu'elle soit *entièrement* semblable à l'idée que nous en avons." [79]

Church ignores the important adverb, *entirely.* But there is a vast

How ideas "represent" in veridical perception— relativity of perception does not bar access to limited essential aspects of perceived object.

difference between not seeing an object *entirely* and not seeing it at all. For, after all, an intimate connection obtains between squares and parallelograms, circles and ellipses. We cannot afford to ignore Theodore's telling reply to Aristes, made after the latter complains of the inexactness of sensations:

> But at least you are sure that God is always exact in causing you to see the sun as becoming smaller in proportion as it gets further away from the horizon. This exactness means something, Aristes.[80]

Herein lies the answer to Church. Inasmuch as there are definite laws that govern and explain the appearances of an object, it cannot be said that what is given in perception is some idea *other than* the archetypal one. On the contrary, what is given in perception is the archetypal idea, the essence, with certain qualifications and limitations. And when from perceptions, say of an elliptical penny, we pass to a conception of it as circular and to an understanding of the laws of optics, we are then in a position to understand the interrelationship in Intelligible Extension between geometrical figures, for example, the interrelationship between circles and ellipses.

Church raises still a further problem concerning Malebranche's theory of perception. If, he argues, knowledge begins with natural revelation, or with sense perception which is supposed to culminate in the pure conception of an essence, then how can we assert that this essence is the essence of an actual existent? "For it entails the assertion that something proper to sense-perception, viz. the revelation of external existence, can be a datum of pure perception. This is difficult to admit on Malebranche's principles, because it denies the purity of that spirit which knows only the ideal, and it denies the statement that in God no existence is known." [81]

Are pure essences too pure for sense perception?

What Church forgets is that Malebranche's Platonism is a Christian Platonism, for Malebranche not only asserts an independent immutable reason like that of Plato, but, following Augustine and Aquinas, he identifies this reason with the Eternal Word. Not only do we apprehend eternal ideas, but we apprehend them in God. As we saw, ideas as archetypes are fraught with existential import. True, from the contemplation of a pure idea we cannot move to the affirmation of its *ideatum,* as Malebranche said to Mairan. Hence, if we started exclusively with an idea, it could not yield knowledge of existence. If, however, we begin with perception and by continuous attention ascend to conception, then there is no reason why the idea at which we arrive cannot give us knowledge of the thing from which we depart. Moreover, nothing prevents us from going back to perception, after the idea has been conceived, in order to check that it is the very prototype which has been sought. This is exactly why Malebranche insisted, as we saw in the chapter on method, that nature being concrete, we must revert to experimental verification for testing all abstract hypotheses.

V. THE INDEMONSTRABILITY OF THE EXTERNAL WORLD

Malebranche never utilized the phenomena of error and of dreams to discredit perception or to deny that perception does in part achieve access to existence. Why then does he call our attention to errors and dreams? Of course Malebranche's chief reasons for disparaging the senses are to eliminate the secondary qualities from extension, to eradicate the false notion of *nature*, i.e., to show that there is only one true God and one true cause, to show that we are immediately united to God and that all our knowledge of things is through or, if we will, mediated by our vision of and in God. In this way Malebranche seeks to establish that God is better known than anything else and that whatever else can be known must be so known through God. Now this principle must apply not only to the natures of things but also to their existence as well.

If we are to know *existence*, this too must be through God. But how? Here is where emphasis on illusion and dreams is useful. Malebranche insists on them in order to show (a) that perception, reliable as it may be, can never be treated as constituting a scientific proof of an external world, that its evidence is not of the same order as that of a mathematical demonstration; and (b) that the reason why perception cannot possess that sort of mathematical indubitability is because in principle no such rigorous proof is possible—in principle there is no necessary connection between essence and existence in creatures, for the world is a free, spontaneous, arbitrary creation. Therefore, no argument concerning an external world and no source of acquaintance with it can ever be regarded as a strict proof of its existence. Thus dreams and errors do not disprove the existence of an external world, nor do they prove any totally untrustworthy character of the senses; rather they serve to indicate that no "proof" of a real world is possible, and therefore sensory perception is a different sort of cognition. Even if there were no dreams or abnormal experiences, perception could not be held as strict knowledge, and the fact that we do commit mistakes only helps to reinforce this point in a more dramatic manner.

As I see it, in short, Malebranche's position is this. Malebranche is obliged to acknowledge that our intuitive judgments of existence or the natural revelations of sense, veridical though they be, nevertheless are lacking in the kind of irresistible self-evident clarity pertinent to mathematical truths or to our vision of God. Our judgments of external existence are, as such, sure and certain, yet no one of them ever bears

Existence of bodies neither demonstrable nor necessary.

that transparent truth that dispels all doubt. At no time is the mind necessarily constrained to accept such perceptual judgments as it happens to have. In the case of mathematical truths, there can be no doubt that $3 + 2 = 5$; the opposite is inconceivable and contradictory; even God is constrained to acknowledge it. But with every perceptual judgment there is room for wonder and doubt. And the reason is that in principle it is self contradictory to attempt any rigorous proof of a freely created universe or of one that is ever-dependent on God for its continued existence.

To justify this attitude, Malebranche wrote the sixth Éclaircissement. The aim of this appendix is to show that all the difficulties that stand in the way of a proof of the existence of bodies really stem from the single fact that in principle no proof is logically possible. Any attempt to demonstrate the existence of a material world must be ruled out on *a priori* grounds, because it implies a necessitarian universe and is thus contrary to the basic notion of a free, spontaneous creation.

The sixth Éclaircissement:

This assertion is stated by Malebranche almost at the end of the Éclaircissement and, upon hasty reading, it appears as a casual afterthought to a lengthy discussion concerning the unreliability of sense perception. Yet his view on the theoretical impossibility of demonstrating an external world is really the crown of his argument. His position makes sense only if every difficulty raised with regard to perception is understood as being used deliberately in order to establish this one claim. Thus the Éclaircissement falls into two parts with a single theme.

First comes a lengthy discussion of the various ways in which the senses may be misleading and deceptive. This, however, is not intended to destroy the validity of direct perception as such but rather to indicate that a source of knowledge which is open to doubt and to mistake cannot be regarded as an avenue of *indubitable certainty*. For perception involves a conceptual element, the idea, plus sensations (*sentiments*) that introduce us to existence. What is revealed are relations among relations. Through sense we are aware of a relation between an idea and its existence. But this relation is metaphysically an *arbitrary* one. There is no logical necessity between essence and existence. The relation between them is necessarily an external and contingent relation. Therefore, theoretically there is always the possibility of making a mistake, as in point of fact we do.

(1) Distinction between essence and existence precludes *demonstration* of existence.

Accordingly, as long as Malebranche distinguishes between essence and existence, as long as he views existence as something spontaneously added to and conferred upon an essence, then however united they become, in principle the object is a *compositum*. Hence our awareness of that union, even if highly reliable, forever remains beyond the pale of certainty. Certainty would mean the awareness of a necessary, intrinsic connection between an essence and its existence. This we saw obtains only with God, for He alone is *Celui qui est.*

> On ne peut avoir de démonstration exacte de l'existence d'un être que de celui qui est nécessaire. Et si l'on y prend garde de près, on verra bien qu'il n'est pas même possible de connaître avec une entière évidence, si Dieu est ou n'est pas véritablement créateur du monde matériel et sensible. Car une telle évidence ne se rencontre que dans les rapports nécessaires, et il n'y a point de rapport nécessaire entre Dieu et un tel monde. Il a pu ne le pas créer, et s'il l'a fait, c'est qu'il l'a voulu, et qu'il l'a voulu librement.[82]

I am insisting, accordingly, that when Malebranche has recourse to errors of sense he is simply using the more easy and convenient way to argue for his principal metaphysical thesis of creationism. By calling attention to problems of illusion and error, he is not denying the direct accessibility of a real world, nor is he arguing for a dualism in epistemology. His concern is primarily metaphysical and only secondarily epistemological. Given the arbitrary character of creation, perception is *ipso facto* ruled out as scientific knowledge. Phenomena of dreams, illusions, the subjectivity of secondary qualities—all these are simply further testimony to the imprecision of perception. Had Malebranche really been concerned with denying the accessibility of the external world or had he sought a dualistic theory of perception, then why in this very éclaircissement did he go on to reaffirm the validity of our natural judgments that disclose the existence of bodies? [83]

More importantly, for Malebranche not even God or the heavenly saints have knowledge of existence that can be described as rigorously evidential. Surely God and the saints are not subject to hallucination! Yet, while their knowledge of the *nature* of objects is certain and strictly evident, their knowledge of existence belongs to a different order altogether. God knows the existence of bodies by knowing His will, by seeing them in His will, and the saints by a revelation of that will to them.[84] The foregoing is the basis of Malebranche's rejection of Descartes' "demonstration" of the external world, which he does in these words:

> . . . on doit remarquer que comme il n'y a que Dieu qui connaisse par lui-même ses volontés, lesquelles produisent tous les êtres, il nous est impossible de savoir d'autre que de lui, s'il y a effectivement hors de nous un monde matériel, semblable à celui que nous voyons, parce que le monde matériel n'est ni visible ni intelligible par lui-même. Ainsi pour être pleinement convaincus qu'il y a des corps, il faut qu'on nous démontre non seulement qu'il y a un Dieu et que Dieu n'est point trompeur, mais encore que Dieu nous a assurés qu'il en a effectivement créés, ce que je ne trouve point prouvé dans les ouvrages de M. Descartes.[85]

In a commentary on this passage, Malebranche writes against Arnauld that it is madness to doubt the existence of bodies. Nevertheless one must distinguish between *proof* and *demonstration*. Thus Descartes' proof does not constitute a true and ineluctable demonstration. "Je prends . . . ," he tells us, "ce mot de *démonstration* dans toute la rigeur et l'exactitude géométrique . . . Et celui qui croit avoir une *démonstration* que Constantinople existe, est dans l'erreur, et ne sait point discerner entre simple *preuve*, et *démonstration*. Je crois donc qu'il y a des corps, mais ce n'est point par la prétendue démonstration de M. Descartes, ni par les huit preuves de M. Arnauld. Ce sont néanmoins de bonnes *preuves*, mais de fort méchantes démonstrations. Je le crois comme bien *prouvé*, et mal démontré." [86]

This commentary and the foregoing passage now serve to introduce a *second* aspect of the problem treated in the sixth Éclaircissement. Existence is precisely that metaphysical element which, to be obtained and understood, requires a form of disclosure that is *sui-generis*. It

(2) Natural revelation of the existence of creatures.

requires an inspection or revelation of God's will. Such revelation affords certainty in the sense of assurance, but not in the sense of rational, ideational evidence. We can now appreciate the full impact of Malebranche's repeated utterances concerning the "invisibility" of external objects. They are not directly and immediately visible, since their essence is not to be. Only God can be known immediately and intuitively, although always inadequately, for He is uncaused and uncreated. Hence knowledge of every other existence requires some arbitrary revelation of His will.

Now Malebranche affirms that the saints have a revelation that we lack. And in his later work he calls sense-perception a sort of natural revelation.[87] What can this mean? I interpret it thus. The saints penetrate into the very mystery and secret of creation. But to man creation is disclosed only in an adumbrated and obscure fashion. The senses do reveal existence to man. In perception we do get access—direct (unmediated), although obscure access—to actual existents. We really do know the things in themselves in their concrete actuality, for the existent encountered is indeed a spark or embodiment of God's creative power. At the same time such awareness is only a *sort or species* of revelation. It is not a full disclosure, because first, we still fail to apprehend the "how" of creation, and second we never completely penetrate to the very core of a given particular embodiment or concrete existent in the manner that God does. In the *Entretiens sur la métaphysique* Theodore declares that:

. . . to doubt the existence of bodies on the strength of reasons which show that one cannot doubt the existence of God or the incorporeal nature of the soul is some proof that one has put oneself above all prejudices, and instead of subjecting reason to the senses as most men do, one has recognised the right which it has to pronounce judgment authoritatively. That it is impossible to give an exact demonstration of the existence of bodies I can prove conclusively . . .[88]

This shows clearly that Malebranche's aspersions against sense are deliberately intended to establish the supremely evident character of God's existence as Creator and the consequent impossibility of proving a world that is metaphysically contingent.

An interpretation of Malebranche that would construe his "representationalism" as a copy theory would have to hold that in veridical perception, for Malebranche, we have an idea of an object, that this idea is seen in God, and that this idea serves as surrogate for the object. If this were Malebranche's doctrine, it would of course be untenable, giving rise to difficulties similar to those which Berkeley and Hume found in their interpretation of Locke. It would be untenable, because then, even if revelation would give us the *existence* of the object, we could never be sure that the essence apprehended in God would indeed be realized in the object so revealed. And certainly from a simple vision of no more than the idea in God, we could never infer the existence of any creature that embodies it. This is in substance the accusation of Arnauld and Church against Malebranche. But the fact that over more than a decade of controversy Malebranche never felt the force of Arnauld's objections may well indicate that Malebranche did not hold the theory of knowledge that Arnauld attributed to him. Perhaps it was Arnauld who took too naively Malebranche's position that the world is a resemblance of its divine exemplar.

The interpretation of Arnauld and of Church, in any case, is not open to us at the present stage of this study. If we take the metaphysical doctrine of the divine immensity in an immanent sense, participation means that the very essence in God is identically the essence of the created object. In that case, in veridical perception by natural revelation, when we apprehend an essence or idea in God, we are *in this very act* of Vision in God apprehending *identically* the essence of the externally created object. There is no duplication of essences. Granted that the archetype really has independent reality as archetype and is constituent in the substance of God, still this archetypal essence is logically identical with that pertaining to or belonging to the object. Moreover, when Malebranche appeals to natural revelation or judgments of existence, he is in effect affirming not only the givenness of an essence but the very givenness or presence of the object's existence.

Shall we then enroll Malebranche as a member of the neo-realists of the twentieth century? This would be difficult to do. For while, as I have argued, Malebranche never undergoes a change of position in his doctrine of sense-perception, while he always affirms existential accessibility, it nevertheless remains equally true that he always clings to the statement affirming the invisibility of the existent object.

But rather than looking upon these two claims as contradictory, I believe that Malebranche takes a now-familiar way out of this impasse. In upholding natural revelations Malebranche agrees with the direct realist in so far as the latter claimed direct access to the object's existence. But if existence is *accessible,* does it necessarily follow that it is through and through *penetrable?* I think not. For the neo-realist a thing *is as it is perceived.* But other than the fact that the thing perceived enjoys a status that is independent of mind, the neo-realists never distinguished an object's characters from its being or existence or reality. Being real added nothing to an object's being this or that. But for Malebranche, the qualities, properties, attributes of a thing never do more than determine its nature. For him existence is precisely that which is never reducible to or graspable by a description or definition. This does not make existence unknowable; it does mean that it is available in its own unique way, best rendered when we speak of the sense of existence.

Now, it seems to me that in a system where existence does add something to an object's character, it is possible to say that such existence is accessible and yet never wholly penetrable. As in the case of God we can intuitively grasp that He is without yet comprehending His Being as He comprehends Himself, so we can through natural revelation become aware of an object's being without ever penetrating its existential status to the point of grasping it as it exists fully for itself or to itself.

Existence, then, is in a measure encounterable but never wholly embraceable. Through the judgment of existence or natural revelation we greet the object's existence, acknowledge its presence as an occasional cause, as an expression of God's will or power. But in this salutation we never become so united as to effect a confluence that entails the loss of our own identity; we never become absorbed in it.

VI. Perceptual Evidence for the Existence of the External World

(a) *Probable Proofs of External Existence.* But if we have access to the created existent in veridical perception, how is error possible? Granted that we need *a* revelation to attain to a real world, on what grounds can perception be accepted as a sort of revelation, especially since it is at times deceptive? Aristes expresses the issue frankly:

. . . Since one cannot assure oneself of the existence of bodies by means of a clear proof, there is no other way left than the authority of a revelation. But this way does not seem to me certain. For though I find clearly in the idea of the most perfect Being that He cannot wish to deceive us, experience teaches me that His revelations are deceptive: two truths which I cannot reconcile with one another. For, after all, we often have feelings which reveal false things to us . . .[89]

In his reply to Aristes, Theodore appeals to Occasionalism. Sensations are a form of natural revelation, because they are caused in us by God upon the occasion of what takes place in our body and in accordance with the laws that govern the union of mind and body. Natural revelations are in themselves true, for general laws are not deceptive in themselves.[90] They are a source of error, only because they are improperly used. Their function is to serve as prompt, vivid, curt, automatic warnings, not of the exact natures of bodies, but of their properties in relation to our body.[91] They are thus swift reminders, vigilant guides to the preservation of life.

How does it happen, then, that sensations, so wisely ordained, should be the source of afflicting, evil and malignant errors? "Our senses disconcert our ideas and tire our attention," Malebranche tells us in the *Entretiens sur la métaphysique*.[92] Using Adam as a principle of explanation in philosophy, he continues: But to Adam they spoke with respect. Prior to the Fall Adam was in full control of his thoughts, at all times, even during his sleep. His will was master of his brain. Already in the *Recherche* Malebranche explained that properly speaking it is not our senses which have become corrupt by the Fall. Adam had the same senses as we have now. It is only the will and its power of attention that has become corrupt. His attention unimpaired, Adam knew enough to avoid having to be a gross and naive empiricist. He did not attribute secondary qualities to objects, nor did he ignore the function of sensation as a revelation of the existence of objects and of their properties in relation to his body.[93]

From the fact that this explanation occurs in the *Recherche* as well as in Malebranche's later writings and thus after the sixth Éclaircissement, it is clear that Malebranche is not appealing to Occasionalism to *establish* or vindicate perception. *If* we accept natural revelation, *then* we may appeal to Occasionalism to explain error. Reason can offer many good arguments for accepting perception, and as he declares in the *Recherche,* one must not absolutely scorn probabilities. Thus, wherever strict demonstration is impossible, as is often the case in physics, ethics and metaphysics itself, a sufficient number of converging and intercorroborative probabilities will yield reasonable assurance.[94]

Despite the fact of error, veridical perception continues to depend upon natural revelation.

In the case of the existence of an external world, strict demonstration is an impossibility, but there are many converging and sound reasons for accepting the revelations of sense. For one thing, reason cannot disprove the existence of an external world. Such a world *may* exist. There is no contradiction in that supposition. Again, reason cannot *disprove* the validity of perception, for, despite errors, we have *nothing* which proves that bodies do not exist.

> Mais il n'est pas facile de s'assurer positivement qu'il n'y a point de corps hors de nous, comme on s'assure positivement que la douleur et la chaleur ne sont point dans les corps qui semblent les causer en nous. Il est très certain qu'au moins il se peut faire qu'il y ait des corps au dehors. Nous n'avons rien qui nous prouve qu'il n'y en a point, et nous avons au contraire *une inclination* forte à croire qu'il y en a. Nous avons donc plus de raison de croire qu'il y en a, que de croire qu'il n'y en a point. Ainsi il semble que nous devions croire qu'il y en a. Car nous sommes naturellement portés à suivre notre *jugement naturel*, lorsque nous ne pouvons pas positivement le corriger par la lumière et par l'évidence.[95]

Thus while Malebranche is willing in the sixth Éclaircissement to grant the impossibility of a strict proof and while he is even willing to entertain the supposition that Berkeley later used against him, namely, that God, being omnipotent, could give us perceptions of an external world, even though no such world in fact existed, Malebranche always felt that there was more evidence *for* a world than against it.

And this position of the sixth Éclaircissement is reiterated in what Malebranche conceived to be his final metaphysical testament, namely, in the *Entretiens sur la métaphysique.* Says Theodore:

> Meanwhile, Aristes, despite all that I have just said, I do not see that there can be any good reason for doubting the existence of bodies in general. For though I may be mistaken with regard to the existence of a particular body, I see quite well that this is because God follows strictly the laws of the conjunction of soul and body; I see that it is because the uniformity of His mode of operation cannot be broken through the irregularity of ours, and because the loss which we have sustained through our own fault of the power which we had over our body cannot be supposed to bring about any change in the laws of its union with our soul. This reason is *sufficient* to prevent my being mistaken with regard to the existence of such a body. I am not inevitably led to believe that it exists. But *this* reason [i.e., a reason of *necessity*] is wanting, and I do not see any possibility of finding another, that would prevent me from believing in general that there are bodies, despite all the different feelings which I have of them—feelings which are so consistent and well connected, so well arranged, that it seems to me certain that God would be deceiving us if nothing of what we see really existed.[96]

When for Pascal reason found itself in a dialectical impasse with respect to demonstrating the existence of God, it could resolve its antimony either by an act of faith or by the probability of the wager. Likewise for Malebranche, the acceptance of natural revelation is basically a free commitment of the will. Not that this commitment is blind or irrational, for there is more weight for than against it. Thus the evidence and foundation for accepting natural revelation are based on probability. But having once taken the leap and freely consented to accept revelation, we may then seek the help of metaphysics, that is, of Occasionalism, to justify error. That Malebranche should have taken that leap into natural revelation is by no means surprising. Rather it was required in his system, for, as we saw in Chapter I, his own view of scientific method with its insistence on experimentation and factual corroboration was the very goal of his search after truth.

(*b*) *The Circle that is not Vicious.* Church detects a vicious circle in Malebranche. On the one hand, he appeals to Occasionalism to justify the validity of perception. But on the other hand, it is perception itself which discloses what specifically are the occasional causes.[97] There is a circle but it is not vicious. For Malebranche treats perception in two ways: *First,* as a source for data. In this sense, perception is not to be taken as a reliable source of evidence or knowledge or information but merely as the sensory stimulus that arrests attention and provokes the intellect. The senses thus offer food for thought. They yield the raw data for knowledge and speculation. But *secondly,* such sensible facts become intelligible when understood and explained by the intellect; that is, the facts become intelligible and explained when perceived under their universal aspect; or within a systematically coherent context. And to be thus grasped is a function or exercise of pure thought. To be understood, then, is not to be simply sensed but to be conceived and systematized. This is the function of Occasionalism.

And to the extent that Malebranche then views knowledge according to the latter, second sense, in terms of conception and explanation, he tends to disparage the senses. However, Malebranche is not a pure rationalist. He deprecates the senses primarily because he wishes to deny the objectivity of sense qualities. Hence, when he reinstates natural revelation of sense, perception does more than merely afford sensory data for knowledge. Its function is to be the stubborn test for the adequacy and relevance of intellectual explanation. The intellect must now conform to and be confirmed by sensible experience. Thus in his treatise on the laws of motion, these laws are founded on, generalized from, and verified by sensible experiments.

Similarly while Occasionalism explains on the metaphysical level how perception works, nevertheless, to know what laws actually do

Occasionalism explains how perception as such works, but perception discloses such occasional causes as we know.

govern the mind and body and what occasional causes God has actually created, we must turn to perception. ". . . Les vrais chrétiens ou les véritables philosophes," we read, "ne disent rien qui ne soit conforme au bon sens, à l'expérience." [98] The so-called circle is entailed by Malebranche's very methodology, and it is one upon which he goes out of his way to insist. Thus after enumerating the three general laws that God has established to regulate the ordinary course of nature, Theodore exclaims: "by means of reason and experience we are apprised of these three laws." Then Aristes observes of Malebranche's metaphysics: "All these principles seem to me so evident, so well linked with one another, so much in harmony with what we observe in actual experience." [99] Never for a moment did Malebranche abandon his initial position on method: general, internally coherent principles are required for explanation; but they must be in harmony with observation. This is very far from a vicious circle.

(c) *Error.* To return to Aristes' question: If we often have feelings which reveal false things, how can we assure ourselves of the existence of bodies by natural revelation?—or conversely, if revelation is reliable, how is error possible? Church asks the question thus: If the senses, then, never deceive, if they are governed by laws of the union of mind and body, if perceptions occur only on occasion of external objects, then must the senses not *always* reveal a real external existence? And if this is so, how can Malebranche account for hallucination and illusion? To this question, says Church, it is no answer to say that prior to the Fall Adam was not a naive realist, for what Aristes wants to know is how the true can be distinguished from the false in natural revelation.[100] And Malebranche's appeal to obscurity and lack of attention is no explanation of those instances where natural revelation discloses what does not exist.

Church is too hasty. Malebranche's Adam knew a lot more than Church realizes. Adam knew

> . . . that he ought not to judge of the nature of bodies by the feeling which he had of them, nor of their existence by those same feelings except when his brain was stimulated by a cause from without and not by a movement of the animal spirits excited from within. *Thus, he was able to recognise when an extraneous cause produced actual traces in his brain,* because the course of the animal spirits was in perfect submission to his will. Thus, unlike the mad or fevered or ourselves during sleep, he was not liable to take phantoms for realities.[101]

Thus Adam could, by consulting sensations, *recognize* when they had an external or internal reference. How? I think Occasionalism provides the answer.

Malebranche's theory of error itself depends upon truth as revelation.

When Malebranche speaks of sensations as *admonishing* us or *warning* us of an object's existence, this warning he denominates a revelation. As for William James an idea is what it does, so that warning serves to bring us to the object. Now, it is true that the body is always being agitated by some or other external object. When animal spirits lead us into error, it still remains true to say that their bizarre or fortuitous action is indirectly prompted by something in the external world. To this extent even imaginary experiences reveal a real outer reference, but an indeterminate one. In fevers or dreams the objects which set off or release the animal spirits have no real connection with them. In such cases the animal spirits do not act with the force and impact that they do when prompted by those objects by which they are naturally or normally regulated. Proper attention to the actions experienced in dreams and fevers would disclose that difference.

This power of attention is what has become diminished and corrupt since the Fall. Adam, says Malebranche, was awake even when he was asleep. He was master of his body. His mastery consisted precisely in this power to make delicate discriminations in the impact of animal spirits. Adam had the same senses as we do. No change has taken place there. But unlike ourselves, he had the power to attend to what the senses revealed. But ". . . as we have lost the power of restraining the traces which the rebellious animal spirits cause in the brain, we take these phantoms for realities." [102] With respect to dreams and hallucinations Malebranche, like the critical realist of the early twentieth century, may say that in such non-veridical perception a mere essence is apprehended. Through lack of attention and sharp discrimination, a mere subsistent elicited by animal spirits is erroneously affirmed to exist. Some existence or other is encountered, but the existent encountered is not that appropriate to the given essence concerned. Hence in such a case the erroneous judgment of existence is really a case of error with respect to content or essence. We apprehend some existent but impute the wrong character to it.

This is why, it seems to me, Malebranche asserts that in perception we do know that bodies as such exist. It is not the judgment of existence that goes astray but the mistake stems from a failure to make the correct identification. And for this the only remedy is greater attention. This interpretation would seem to be corroborated by Malebranche's statements on the nature of truth that we discussed in the chapter on method. There we saw that error for Malebranche is really nothing at all, and hence cannot be perceived, whereas truth is a real relation. Where truth is only a real relation, either of equality or inequality, falsity is only the negation of truth, an imaginary relation, he declares. "On se trompe toujours quand on juge qu'on voit certains rapports et

Source of error: diminished attention.

que ces rapports ne sont point; . . . puisque le néant n'est pas visible et que le faux est un rapport qui n'est point." [103]

Now as for Adam, because Adam had full voluntary control over his animal spirits, he could know whether a given stimulus exciting a sensuous response was external to him or whether it was the work of his own animal spirits. Hence where we, who passively suffer our sensuous modifications, might erroneously conclude upon the occasion of feeling a modification that some other object than the one really causing it does exist, Adam would have sufficient knowledge to withhold this erroneous conclusion. In practice Adam would always know when he had the truth, because he had the power to refrain from error.

But what does this prove? Not that the senses always revealed the truth to Adam, but only that Adam would not be inclined to err. He would not go beyond the testimony actually afforded him in sense perception. A power to withhold from error does not *per se* reveal truth. *If truth were revealed to Adam,* then he would not go on to err in addition to knowing the truth. And we err, not because we lack the truth, but because we superadd errors to the truth that we do have. *When* we have the truth, we have sound and justified intuitive awareness of external existence, upon the occasion of having a given sensuous modification. But from a sensation alone nothing can be validly inferred, neither truth nor error. Hence, having a sensation and not knowing its source, in error, we do not check our impulse to attend capriciously to some essence and to attribute existence to it, although we completely lack on this occasion metaphysically real, positive revelation.

Adam had truth, because he could resist error.

Thus, since truth as a relation of equality or inequality obtains not only among ideas but also between ideas and things, presumably false existential affirmations consist in perceiving illegitimate marriages between essence and existence, or in kidnapping an essence from its proper partner. But the only way to detect such mistaken relations would be, as the neo-realist claimed, in the light of perception itself. Similarly, Malebranche wrote in all but the last edition of the *Recherche:* Falsehoods are not; knowledge of the false or false knowledge is knowledge of that which is not:

> Mais les faussetés ne sont point et la connaissance de la fausseté, ou une connaissance fausse, est la connaissance de ce qui n'est point, si cela se peut dire; car comme l'on ne peut connaître ce qui n'est point que par rapport à ce qui est, on ne reconnaît l'erreur que par la vérité.[104]

Not only is Malebranche trying to explain here that truth is its own index, that we can determine the false only in the light of the true, but he is further suggesting that the false is really a limited or partial aspect of the truth. For truth may be complex. It may involve the awareness of relations among relations. And this situation holds for perceptual as well as conceptual truths. Just as vision, he writes, often casts us into error because we perceive only those faces of external objects that are turned towards us, so in conceptual knowledge we may be led astray because not all the aspects of the object are present to our mental vision. In short, error arises from not seeing all that there is to be seen.

Error would then consist in a limited or partial apprehension of the given relations. Through inattention, either relations would be seen in a misplaced order or else not all the relations would be apprehended, thus yielding an imperfect or distorted view. In discussing the pure understanding Malebranche wrote:

> . . . lorsque nous considérons quelque objet, nous ne l'envisageons ordinairement que par un côté; et nous ne nous contentons pas de juger du côté que nous avons considéré, mais nous jugeons de l'objet tout entier. Ainsi il arrive souvent que nous nous trompons . . .[105]

This view of truth as infinitely complex and of error as a partial or limited degree has two important and interesting consequences. Inasmuch as in Malebranche's system, the least things have among them an infinity of relations which only an infinite mind can comprehend, then to that extent man is by his very nature subject to error. Man can never arrive at absolute knowledge. That being granted, nevertheless, within his limited sphere man can avoid error through attention, that is, by never judging hastily; by never passing complete judgments except where full analysis has been made.[106] This proviso thus emphasizes the fact that, while human knowledge can never be absolute, it may, however, in its partiality be more or less adequate. Hence the need for a *method* to insure both critical examination and analysis and constant vigilant experimentation. Hence, too, the need for general principles, provided by metaphysics, and the corroborative evidence of fact afforded by natural revelation.

Finitude necessarily implies error.

VII. FAITH

> But, in order to deliver us entirely from our speculative doubt, Faith furnishes us with a proof which it is impossible to resist . . . It teaches me that Scripture is a divine book, and this book, or the appearance of this book, tells me clearly and positively that there are thousands upon thousands of created things. Thus, then, are all my appearances changed into realities. Bodies exist, this is rigorously demonstrated, faith being granted.[107]

To the formidable Arnauld, as to his twentieth century disciple Church and to the tender nineteenth century writer Blampignon, Malebranche's appeal to faith to establish the existence of an external world is the grossest and most vicious of errors.[108] How anyone can believe in bodies on the basis of appearances that assume bodies is to the author of the *Port Royal Logic* an absurdity so patent that—so he seems to imply—this error alone would suffice to condemn Malebranche to eternal scorn. But Arnauld, the Cartesian and the rigorous Jansenist that he was, could not appreciate the delicate subtlety of Malebranche's thought.

For Descartes, faith and reason were two independent and separate spheres of authority. Descartes set out to seek after truth by the light of nature which alone, without the aid of religion or philosophy, could teach all that a good man should know.[109] By philosophy, Descartes meant scholastic philosophy. And the rejection of this philosophy simultaneously with faith is no accident. For scholastic philosophy sought to unite and reconcile faith and reason, as it sought to unite sense and reason. But Descartes had to abandon faith for the same reasons that he tried to make a sweeping denunciation of sense. His search for certainty, we saw, led him to reject final causes, the probable and the experiential, and it led him to affirm innate ideas and created truths. The latter were implanted by God; yet, once they had taken root, Descartes' own mind was sufficient to guarantee their intrinsic validity and coherence. They were of a piece with Descartes' own mind and required no external or objective verification.

Faith was a separate and external empire. Being outside the natural light, it could serve neither as a source of knowledge nor as a guide to knowledge. It was a supernatural revelation accessible to an exclusive minority. Hence the contents of faith depended for interpretation on tradition and on the institution of the Church, on authority. Necessarily, then, faith and reason had nothing in common. And presumably when Descartes at the end of the *Principles* submitted all that he had written to the supervision of the Church, he did not do this for purposes of intellectual corroboration, for he was certain of everything that he had written because of its own internal coherence. But he submitted all his opinions to the Church in the role of believer, not knower.[110]

Unlike Descartes, Malebranche neither would nor could bifurcate reason and faith. Nevertheless, there are numerous passages in the *Recherche* where Malebranche appears to follow Descartes on this issue, where he seems to stress the essential differences between faith and reason. Hence it is necessary to consider them carefully. Thus, for example, he writes that in matters of faith it is not wrong to seek enlightenment from the opinions of St. Augustine or some other Church Father. It is even important to know whether Augustine is in agreement with his predecessors, ". . . parce que les choses de la foi ne s'apprennent que par la tradition, et que la raison ne peut pas les découvrir." In matters of faith, the most ancient opinions are the most true.[111] In theology truth and novelty are not compatible. Luther and Calvin were innovators, and they erred. In contrast, the innovations of Galileo, Harvey, and Descartes are not heresies.[112] For matters that depend upon reason are entirely unlike the dogmas and content of faith. Here, then, ancient opinion is of no avail. On the contrary, in philosophy novelty is to be loved and respected. In secular learning the ancients were more ignorant than the moderns, for:

> *le monde est plus vieux de deux mille ans, et qu'il a plus d'expérience que dans le temps d'Aristote et de Platon, comme on l'a déjà dit; et que les nouveaux philosophes peuvent savoir toutes les vérités que les anciens nous ont laissées, et en trouver encore plusieurs autres.*[113]

A few pages before the foregoing he declares: ". . . c'est la vieillesse du monde et l'expérience qui font découvrir la vérité." [114]

These sentences are a direct reflection of Bacon and show once again the latter's influence upon Malebranche. Read in that light, Malebranche is insisting that the contents of faith are subject neither to rational, conceptual discovery and analysis nor to experimental verification. Conversely, one must not use passages of Scripture to support or condemn principles in science. He refers with approval to Bacon's warning against seeking for the dead among the living and quotes what Ellis and Spedding translate as: "From this unwholesome mixture of things human and divine there arises not only a fantastic philosophy but also an heretical religion. Very meet it is therefore that we be sober-minded, and give to faith that only which is faith's." [115] Not only does Malebranche follow Bacon and Descartes on the separation of faith and reason, but he appeals to St. Thomas and Augustine as well.[116]

Again, at the beginning of the *Recherche* he announces that evidence does not accompany matters of faith, for:

> Il faut donc distinguer les mystères de la foi des choses de la nature. Il faut se soumettre également à la foi et à l'évidence; mais dans les choses de la foi il ne faut point chercher l'évidence avant que de les croire, comme dans celles de la nature il ne faut point s'arrêter à la foi, c'est-à-dire à l'autorité des philosophes. En un mot, pour être fidèle, il faut croire aveuglément, mais pour être philosophe il faut voir évidemment.[117]

Delbos thinks that these and like passages indicate that at the beginning of his philosophical enterprise Malebranche is visibly and

How faith and
reason are
united by
Malebranche.

strongly dominated by Descartes' view of the bifurcation of faith and reason, from which he only gradually and progressively detaches himself in his later works.[118] However, this is surely too sweeping a claim. For in the first place, Bacon's influence, not to say that of Aquinas and Augustine, is at least as dominating in the *Recherche* as that of Descartes. In the second place, Bacon never goes as far in the separation of faith and reason as does Descartes. After all, it is Bacon who says that while a little philosophy may turn a man into an atheist, the more philosophical he is the more religious he becomes. And this, we shall see, is the quintessence of Malebranche's position both in the *Recherche* as well as in his later works. Thirdly, from the beginning of the *Recherche* and throughout, Malebranche is constantly introducing "theological" doctrines as principles of philosophic explanation, such, for example, as original sin for the errors of sense. In fact he is accused by Foucher of mingling philosophy and religion. To this criticism Malebranche replies that while he sought to abstain from *confusing* faith and reason, he never intended *not* to employ theological doctrines wherever they might cast light on philosophical issues.[119] Conversely he never hesitated to employ reason for the intelligent explication of a mystery whenever it was feasible. Thus in an early fragment Malebranche wrote:

> . . . parce qu'il y a encore dans nos mystères quelque chose de si caché qu'il ne peut être connu et de si saint qu'il ne doit pas même être regardé, bien des gens prétendent qu'il faut que tout soit couvert de ténèbres mystérieuses. Ils veulent que la nuée ne cache pas seulement à nos yeux le propitiatoire et le Saint des Saints, mais tout ce qui est enfermé dans le sanctuaire.[120]

This passage reveals the true character of Malebranche's position in the *Recherche* and throughout his writings.

Malebranche, to be sure, says that to be faithful one must believe blindly, that one must not look for evidence before believing, and that the mysteries of faith are incomprehensible for lack of distinct ideas. However, not everything in them is occult. Moreover, we must realize that for Malebranche, unlike for Descartes, the absence of clear and distinct concepts does not render a notion meaningless or unintelligible. Hence belief in matters of faith is not necessarily nothing but blind brutal acceptance on the mere authority of the Church. Such notions as the Trinity are beyond conceptual understanding but not beyond the intuitive awareness of those who are capable of such awareness. Hence the reason for turning to the Church Fathers is not to enslave the mind into irrational obedience but to get from them the proper aids for intuitive intelligent illumination. Moreover the certitude of these articles of faith, and hence anything that the Church may affirm in their regard, rests ultimately on the knowledge of God:

> La connaissance de la cause universelle ou de l'existence d'un Dieu est absolument nécessaire, puisque même la certitude de la foi dépend de la connaissance que la raison donne de l'existence d'un Dieu.[121]

Malebranche describes this knowledge as natural, rather than an article of faith.[122] But, after all, this "rational" or natural knowledge of God is itself a form of revelation and illumination: it is an intuitive, non-ideational, non-comprehensive, non-conceptual, direct awareness. Thus, while for Malebranche the contents of faith are not subject to conceptual discovery or apprehension and in that sense are beyond or outside reason, yet, once found, the kind of intelligibility that we have in faith is in principle no different from what we have in our vision of God as *Celui qui est*. And as this vision is itself subject to rational explanation, and communication, so the contents of faith may be illumined by reason.

Finally, inasmuch as Malebranche in the *Recherche* abandons Descartes, both in his way of knowing God as well as with regard to the nature of God—God is Being, not an essence, and we know Him *par simple vue*—and inasmuch as our knowledge of things by way of concepts is itself a Vision in God—not by innate ideas—, then theoretically there is no longer any reason for upholding a double theory of truth. Henceforth there cannot be two truths or two spheres of truth, but only one indivisible truth that may, however, speak in two different ways.

This is what permits Malebranche to assert in the sixth book of the *Recherche*:

> . . . c'est la même sagesse qui parle immédiatement par elle-même à ceux qui découvrent la vérité dans l'évidence des raisonnements, et qui parle par les saintes écritures à ceux qui en prennent bien le sens.[123]

This formula for establishing a close rapport between philosophy and religion does indeed, as Delbos asserts, dominate all his later works.[124] Yet, it is not at variance with what Malebranche has to say in the preceding books of the *Recherche*. The first five books, as we noted above, are intended to remove intellectual prejudices. Moreover, on Malebranche's own admission to Régis, the *Recherche* is written for a wide and mixed audience. And we know that he has very definite views on techniques of teaching. Effective instruction lies in the use of gradual persuasion, in addressing men adroitly according to their own beliefs and capacities, in appealing to their self-respect by the "charitable dissimulation" of appearing to be an inquirer or seeker. "But when you see that the truth has impressed them, fight for it without any fear of their abandoning it." [125]

Accordingly it is important, as Delbos himself admits,[126] for Malebranche in the *Recherche* to stress the differences between faith and reason in order to prevent the stubborn, prejudiced mind from a paralyzing worship of ancient and scholastic authorities and to discourage the superstitious, fanatic zealot from identifying novelty with heresy in science. Once having humbled and chastened the pious and given new hope to the philosopher by a purified objective epistemology and metaphysics, Malebranche is now prepared for his own positive and constructive assertion: the Light of Nature and the Light of Faith are identical, but this Light speaks in two different ways. This, as Le Moine notes, is the real core of Malebranche's attitude.[127] And one, I may add, that Malebranche possessed from that first moment when, discovering Descartes' *L'Homme*, he became converted to philosophy and to science.

The truth of the matter is that Malebranche holds in equal contempt the excessive rationalists, those superbly arrogant skeptical minds who demand "que tout leur soit ouvert" [128] and the superstitious partisans of a "docta ignorantia." The aim of the *Recherche* is to eradicate both types of dogmatism. Yet, just as Bacon sought first to humiliate reason and sense and then to elevate the two, so Malebranche seeks now to defy reason in behalf of faith and then again to denounce faith in behalf of reason, only in the end, having tested and proved the two, to reinstate and reunite them. Hence Malebranche will say to Mairan that to lose faith is to lose all; [129] but equally he will assert that no man can divest himself of reason as of a piece of clothing.[130] Freedom to think is as necessary as air to breathe.[131] In the end, faith and reason are mutually interdependent, for they have one origin and they speak the same truth although in different languages.[132]

But why should wisdom speak in two different ways? It is to be noted that Malebranche's clear-cut insistence on the identity and unity of truth first occurs in that part of the *Recherche* where he discusses method and the role of sense in the pursuit of truth. The eternal wisdom or the Word of God chose to become incarnate, to present Himself to fallen man in a sensible and palpable manner, in order to teach him by sensuous words and convincing examples the path to salvation.[133] In a state of sin and corruption man is overwhelmed by the senses; he is incapable of grasping the abstract moral and speculative truths by the light of reason alone. He needs the stimulus of sense and of passion to awaken and arrest his at-

Wisdom speaks in two ways.

tention. This is why in teaching abstract truths to others we may imitate the example of the Word:

> . . . je dis qu'il faut exposer aux autres la vérité comme la vérité même s'est exposée. . . . La sagesse éternelle s'est rendue sensible, mais non dans l'éclat; elle s'est rendue sensible, *non pour nous arrêter au sensible, mais pour nous élever à l'intelligible* . . .[134]

There is a vast difference between faith and intelligence. The simplest of men is capable of faith, but only a few have the capacity for pure intellectual understanding. Hence the Word became incarnate and sensible in order to attract the vulgar by the very things which blind and captivate them. Acting with fools, He makes use of a species of folly to render them wise,[135] to elevate them to the intelligible.

Thus, the function of faith is to serve a role analogous to that of sense in science. It is to embody the truth in a concrete factual manner. At the same time the purpose of such embodiment is eventually to guide man, to raise him to the level of pure intelligence and contemplation. Again, as in epistemology one passes from perception to distinct ideas, and as in philosophy the senses provide facts, the stubborn data from which the metaphysician departs in order to find therein the ultimate general principles of explanation, so the content of faith must first be accepted, in order thereafter to grasp its true and inner significance. The latter kind of understanding is the work of intelligence. Hence Malebranche writes in the *Conversations chrétiennes*: Believe that which must be believed; but seek to understand that which can and should be understood. Wherever possible, the contents of faith should be illuminated by intelligent reflection. Libertines must be made to understand that reason incarnate is in perfect accord with the eternal wisdom: "Car il faut que la foi nous conduise à l'intelligence: il ne faut pas céder la raison au parti ennemi de la vérité."[136]

In insisting upon the fundamental accord between faith and reason and in adopting this formula of faith as a guide to intelligence, Malebranche, as Delbos notes, not only separates himself from Descartes, but at the same time suggests that the mysteries of faith possess a double genre of intelligibility.[137] First faith furnishes principles which, mysteries though they be, are nevertheless acceptable to reason, because by means of them countless difficulties and contradictions can be explained. Thus in the *Conversations chrétiennes* Malebranche writes:

Faith possesses two sorts of intelligibility.

> . . . le mystère de la Trinité s'accommode parfaitement avec la raison, quoiqu'en lui-même il soit incompréhensible; je veux dire qu'en le supposant, on peut accorder ensemble des faits qui se contredisent, et justifier la sagesse de Dieu, nonobstant le désordre

de la nature et la permission du péché, ce qu'on ne peut faire assurément par toute autre voie.[138]

Also in the *Entretiens sur la métaphysique* we read:

> How much philosophers are indebted to religion, my dear Aristes, for it alone can help them out of the perplexity in which they find themselves! [139]

Just as a scientist may have recourse to strange or even bizarre hypotheses or suppositions in order to save the phenomena, so reason finds many revealed dogmas true because of their metaphysical "utility."

But again mysteries of faith may possess a second type of rationality. After having been accepted as suppositions to save the facts, they in turn may be subjected to critical examination and explication by reason. Thus, for example, the doctrine of predestination is intelligible not only as an explanatory hypothesis for conflicting facts, but also because reason, in turn, can explain it in the light of philosophical truth.

> Il est permis d'expliquer même les mystères. . . . la prédestination n'est point un mystère en ce sens que l'esprit humain n'y puisse rien découvrir; car tous les décrets divins sont nécessairement conformes à l'ordre, à la raison, à la loi éternelle dont tous les hommes ont quelque connaissance.[140]

Since God does not act by caprice, predestination can be explained in terms of our knowledge of God and of the manner in which He must govern.

The incarnation of Christ possesses a similar two-ply intelligible structure. Not only is it a hypothesis or supposition that is in harmony with reason, but also it is one required by reason. Faith provides the dogma of the incarnation. The acceptance of this mystery can explain or give a sufficient reason for the creation. But more than that, reason itself by examining this dogma can establish its internal validity. For reason finds no connection between the infinite and the finite. It declares it to be a contradiction for God to create the finite, unless He can discover a way to sanctify it. The view of Christ as the Man-God is thus a notion that rescues reason from its intellectual impasse and is one the inner significance of which reason itself can illuminate.

We are now in a position to comprehend what Arnauld the Cartesian was unable to do. When Malebranche affirms that faith renders certain the existence of an external world, he does so not on the basis of mere sensible appearances that presuppose the existence of bodies. It is true enough that the Bible is a book to be touched by the hands and seen by the eyes. But it is to be read by the mind.

Sense communicates but does not confirm faith.

The Bible is only a set of appearances. This Malebranche candidly admits. But the crucial point is that for him these appearances, unlike any other, unlike the Koran, for example, possess an internal philosophical significance. To Malebranche not only does the Bible possess a remarkable internal coherence and structural consistency that attest to its divine validity and origin—such is Vidgrain's interpretation [141]—but more important than this self-contained internal unity is its rational import, its consistency with the insights of philosophical intuition. Here is a set of appearances which possess or convey philosophical truths. The Bible declares, for example, that God is Being, that He alone is the Creator and that He creates for His own glory. It expresses the fact, through the resurrection, that a profane finite world is not adequate to express the glory of an infinite, self-sufficient God. Now all these messages are philosophical truths, yet embedded in a set of sensory appearances.

Therefore, it is these philosophical revelations that induce reason to accept the Bible as a divinely authentic revelation. Hence Malebranche declares:

> Now, I read in the appearances of the New Testament about the miracles of a Man-God, His resurrection, His ascension to Heaven, the preaching of the Apostles, its beneficial success, the establishment of the Church. I compare all this with what I know from history, with the laws of the Jews, with the prophecies of the Old Testament.

Thus far he is stressing the inner structural consistency of the Bible. Then he continues:

> These are still but appearances. But now I am certain that it is God alone who gives them to me, and that He is no deceiver. Again, therefore, I compare all the appearances which I have just enumerated with the idea of God, the beauty of religion, the sanctity of morality, the necessity of a creed, and finally I am induced to believe in what our faith teaches us. In a word, I believe in it without insisting upon a rigorously demonstrative proof.[142]

What the Bible declares is thus both in accord with reason and grounded upon reason. Not only does the Bible speak of the incarnation; it also presents ethical truths, the very ones taught by reason.[143] Thus the appeal to faith for establishing an external world is in the final analysis an appeal to reason, not sense. Sense provides appearances; faith provides mysteries; but the function of the two is to lead to understanding. Faith will pass but reason will remain. It is reason which justifies the belief in the Bible as a divinely sanctioned book. The philosophical import of the Bible is the foundation and ground for our faith in it, although of course not the source of

Reason, not sense, confirms the revelations of faith.

this faith. Now, because of its philosophical and rational content, *this* set of sensory impressions can no longer be regarded as illusions or mere appearances. Here then, we have the sort of assurance for the existence of an external world that is lacking in Descartes. We turn to a set of appearances; then through attention and reflection we discover therein, the very truths we know intuitively *par simple vue.* Because we find those indubitable truths in the Bible, we therefore accept as veracious such other statements as that God created a heaven and earth and bodies. Note well the character of the proof. The rational acceptance of the Bible as divine is based on probable reasoning. But once accepted, then the existence of the world follows.

Because Malebranche believes that faith is to elevate man to enlightenment, because he is convinced that the revelation and dogmas of faith are in perfect accord with and even demanded by reason, Malebranche concludes that there can be not only no fundamental discord between philosophy and Scripture, but also none between reason and tradition or the authority of the Church. In the *Entretiens sur la métaphysique* we find Theodore announcing:

Philosophy and Scripture, reason and authority of Church, in fundamental accord.

I am convinced, Aristes, that one must be a good philosopher in order to gain an understanding of the truths of faith, and the more mastery one has over the true principles of metaphysics the firmer will one be in the truths of religion . . . For whether it be that Jesus Christ in his divinity speaks to philosophers in their innermost being, or whether it be that he instructs Christians by aid of the visible authority of the Church, it is not possible that he should contradict himself, though it is quite possible to imagine contradictions in his deliverances or to take what really are our own decisions for his deliverances. Truth speaks to us in different ways, but certainly it always says the same thing. Philosophy, then, should not be opposed to religion—unless it be the false philosophy of the Pagans, the philosophy which is based on human authority, in a word, all those non-revealed opinions which do not bear the character of truth—that irresistible certainty which compels all attentive minds to submission.[144]

The manner in which Malebranche seeks to establish the validity of an infallible and universal Church [145] is at once ingenious, consistent with his own metaphysics, and above all transparently honest. *First,* he considers the need for a Church. God, so Scripture declares, wants all men to be saved and to learn the truth. There are two ways to arrive at this goal, through critical examination and through authority. The former is suitable for the sophisticated cultured mind. The simple, the poor, and the ignorant need a palpable established authority.

Secondly, the contents of faith are often beyond ordinary human

The infallibility of the Church.

comprehension so that even the most enlightened minds need authoritative help to understand Scripture.

Thirdly, the claim of the infallibility and sacredness of Scripture itself rests on authority. But then either the Holy Spirit will reveal the fact to each individual or to the Church for all individuals. The latter is more simple and general. It is more conformable to the uniformity of God's and Christ's ways that there be a single, universal, infallible Church wherein decisions are achieved by a general assembly, or council, than that the truths of Scripture be infallibly revealed to each individual by a special particular revelation.

Fourthly, every society needs a government or authority, else it becomes a many-headed monster. Even heretical sects demand of their followers to abide by the decisions of their leader or synods.

Fifthly, all men are subject to error. Hence, even if the Church is not infallible, yet it is more probable that an assembly or council will arrive at the truth more easily than a private individual or the expert leader who relies on his own inspiration.

Sixthly, in speculative matters the judgments of the independent scholar or researcher are often superior to those of the multitude. But in the sphere of faith the more prevalent and the more commonly held doctrines are the more true.

> The more witnesses there are to attest a fact the more certainty does this fact possess. The dogmas of religion are not acquired by speculation but by authority, by the testimony of those who keep the sacred storehouse of tradition.[146]

Malebranche, like his friend, Richard Simon,[147] accepts the Scriptures as a body of facts and "experiments," because he believes them to have been well authenticated by historic and Biblical exegesis. The resurrection of Christ is so well attested that to doubt it is to renounce common sense altogether. To suppose Moses to have been an impostor is either vain ignorance or supreme madness, for a whole nation witnessed his acts. And would the Jews have submitted themselves to such harsh and difficult laws, if the Bible were not authentic?[148]

One may not be convinced as readily as Malebranche. But what is important is to realize that his acceptance of Scriptural facts is based on a reasonable foundation, not on mere blind acceptance. Or rather, he is ready to accept blindly and without reserve the authority of the Church, because reason permits and sanctions it. Reason provides the criteria for identifying another source of authoritative data.

Moreover, men generally fall into error or prejudice through some natural inclination of the heart or because it favors and pleases them.

[327]

But the Christian mysteries are such utter extravagance and folly: they shock the senses, astound the imagination and outrage reason! Hence, their very absurdity and their acceptance by countless people despite the absurdity indicate to reason their truth and supernatural origin. Accordingly, Theodore declares:

> . . . remember, Aristes, that the humble and submissive faith of those who yield to authority is neither blind nor injudicious; it is based on reason. Assuredly, infallibility is contained in the idea of a divine religion, of a society which has for its Head a being subsisting in the eternal Wisdom, a society established for the salvation of the simple and ignorant. Good sense, so it seems to me, demands that we should believe the Church to be infallible. We must, therefore, submit implicitly to its authority. But this is so only because reason tells us that there is no danger in submitting to it, and that the Christian who refuses to do so belies by his refusal the opinion which he ought to have of the character of Jesus Christ.

> Our faith is perfectly reasonable in its principle; it does not owe its institution to prejudice, but to right reason . . . [149]

Thus in the final analysis, it is reason which justifies, authorizes and explains the need of authority and faith. But, a doubting Thomas may ask, suppose that one should find one's self in a conflict between the Church or Scripture and reason? What method shall one use to reconcile the conflict? Shall reason be subjected to religion or religion to reason? Malebranche's answers to these questions are extraordinary.

What if conflict should arise between faith and reason?

> Those who study physics never argue against experience; but neither do they argue on the ground of experience against reason; they hesitate, not seeing the way of passing from one to the other; they hesitate, I say, not as regards the certainty of experience or the evidence of reason, but as to the way of reconciling the one with the other. The facts of religion or decided dogmas are my experiences in matters of theology. Never do I call them in question, they furnish me with rules and with guidance to intelligence. But, when believing myself to be following them, I feel myself in conflict with reason, I stop short, fully aware that the dogmas of faith and the principles of reason must, in truth, be in harmony with one another, however opposed they appear to be in my mind. I abide, then, by my submission to authority, full of respect for reason, but convinced of the weakness of my intellect and in continual distrust of myself. Finally, if enthusiasm for truth is kindled anew, I begin my researches once more; and, by alternately attending to the ideas which enlighten me and the dogmas which sustain and guide me, I discover, without having recourse to any other peculiar method, the means of transition from faith to understanding.[150]

Faith is not subservient to reason nor is reason a slave to faith. Faith is a guide to reason. The unintelligible mysteries of faith make the universe intelligible. Reason must serve faith, be its handmaiden in the sense of illuminating and explaining its data. But there is no question of sacrificing reason, "comme on se décharge d'un habit de cérémonie."[151] On the contrary, faith seeks illumination, and Malebranche rejects those persons of piety who attempt to prove by reason that one should renounce reason. He rejects those who assert that faith alone is an adequate guide or that blind obedience is the principal virtue of Christians. No; it is up to reason to decide and to rule.[152]

But, on the other hand, to lose faith is to lose all; for, as science worships facts because it recognizes that nature is concrete not abstract, that general principles must be *verae causae,* not monstrous suppositions, and are therefore to be checked by facts, so a true philosophy must not scandalize faith. Nothing, writes Malebranche, is more unreasonable or imprudent than to insist always upon geometrical precision.[153] Religion is the true philosophy.[154] By adhering loyally to the data of faith man will one day merit a perfect understanding of what now he merely believes.[155] Accordingly, in concluding his work on method Malebranche writes that the shortest and most assured path for discovering the truth is to live as a true Christian; the best method is to follow the precepts of the Evangel, to adhere to faith.[156] But the ultimate reason for this reliance upon faith is that it serves to check, strengthen, fortify, guide, and enlighten intelligence:

> . . . c'est par la fermeté de sa foi qu'on obtient de Dieu le don de l'intelligence. '*Intellectus merces est fidei,*' dit saint Augustin. '*Ergo noli quaerere intelligere, ut credas; sed crede, ut intelligas: quoniam nisi credideritis non intelligetis.*'[157]

In that way "La foi et la raison se soutiennent mutuellement l'une l'autre."[158]

Malebranche's conception of a single wisdom expressing itself in two different languages and his description of the means to be used for reconciling faith and reason and for their reciprocal checking reveal the living unity of his thought. They reflect the extent to which throughout his career he kept unswerving allegiance to his original conception of scientific method presented in the *Recherche.* Such a view could not have come from Descartes, or Spinoza, who, having abandoned Bacon's inductive method, would never have thought of theological dogmas as corroborative experimental checks upon reason.

Malebranche consciously and avowedly undertook to synthesize religion and philosophy on a Cartesian base, in order to convert the

Conclusion: Malebranche's synthesis of faith, reason and experimental evidence.

Cartesians themselves with Cartesian weapons.[159] But the success of this ambitious task depended not upon Descartes alone, but upon Descartes, Bacon and Augustine. Or rather it depended on his own metaphysical genius. For Malebranche the "new philosophy" held no terror; the Copernican revolution did not call all into doubt. Galileo's up-to-date, revised alphabet of circles and parabolas did not mean that all order and all coherence were gone, that "being's sum/ Is but the sum of dreams," that "our true existence/ Is decided by no one and has no importance to love . . ." Not being a reductionist or vicious intellectualist, Malebranche did not need to have his heart battered or his reason blinded, hypnotized or ravished. For, from that fateful moment when he became converted to Cartesian science, he knew that nature was intelligible and rational; but, too, he never forgot that it was concrete, not abstract. Thus he retained his faith and religion not through timorousness, but through the sincere conviction that therein lay the answer to disillusionment and the solution to innumerable philosophical perplexities.

He recognized that if science were to be more than ideal, if it were to apply to a real world, and if in that world men were not to lead a life that was nasty, brutish and short, then the deductive-empirical aspects of scientific method demanded the metaphysical distinction of essence and existence and this necessitated a reversion to the metaphysics of Being. Malebranche wrote his own "Search after Truth" (*Recherche*) to establish and defend his scientific method. But the method was not one of dogmatic rationalism. In behalf of truth and understanding, he found it necessary to worship not only reason, the candle of the Lord, but also brute empirical facts and laborious experiments. What he sought was an epistemology and metaphysics that would reconcile reason and sense, general principles and facts, intuition and experiment. Paradoxically, it is this very non-dogmatic tolerant attitude toward scientific method which permitted Malebranche to remain "always in submission to the authority of the Church, always ready to yield to reason" and "to throw upon the truths of faith that light which helps to reassure the intellect and fully to reconcile it with the heart." [160] We may therefore conclude that parallel to and concurrently with his initial undertaking to establish the deductive-experimental method was the attempt to guarantee a rational-theological method and the attempt to synthesize the two on the basis of the metaphysics of *Exodus,* the revelation of God as *Celui qui est.*

Bibliography

WORKS CONSULTED

References in the notes are made to short titles, listed at right below. To facilitate reference from notes to full titles, the alphabetical listing is in accordance with the short titles, wherever these occur.

For further relevant works, see the bibliographies of Vidgrain (*Le christianisme*), Bridet (*Connaissance*), Del Noce (*Bibliografia*), and Gouhier (*Philosophie de Malebranche,* 1948 edition).

FULL TITLE	SHORT TITLE
Malebranche, Nicolas. De l'adoration en esprit et en vérité.	*Adoration*
(1) In *Méditations sur l'humilité,* Cuvillier 1944 edition.	
(2) Œuvres complètes de Malebranche, Vol. 17-1, pp. 423-37, Vrin, Paris, 1960, A. Cuvillier, ed. Abbreviated: "O. C. xvii-1."	
———. Traité de l'amour de Dieu. Désiré Roustan, ed., Paris, 1922.	*L'Amour de Dieu*
———. Avis touchant l'entretien d'un philosophe chrétien et d'un philosophe chinois.	*Avis*
(1) In *Chrétien et chinois,* Le Moine edition.	
(2) O. C. xv, pp. 37-61, 1958, A. Robinet, ed.	
———. Entretien d'un philosophe chrétien et d'un philosophe chinois sur l'existence et la nature de Dieu.	*Chrétien et chinois*
(1) A. Le Moine, ed., Paris, 1936.	
(2) O. C. xv, 1958, A. Robinet, ed.	

The Philosophy of Malebranche

Bibliography

FULL TITLE	SHORT TITLE

Malebranche, Nicolas. Lettres du P. Malebranche touchant le IIe et le IIIe volumes des Réflexions philosophiques et théologiques. In Recueil . . . , Vol. 3, pp. 237 ff.

———. Lois générales de la communication des mouvements.   *Lois des mouvements*
(1) In *Recherche*, L. iii, pp. 269-298.
(2) O. C. xvii-1, pp. 7-197, 1960, P. Costabel, ed.

———. Méditations chrétiennes et métaphysiques.   *Méditations chrétiennes*
(1) H. Gouhier, ed., Paris, 1928.
(2) O. C. x, 1959, H. Gouhier and A. Robinet, eds.

———. Méditations pour se disposer à l'humilité et à   *Méditations sur* la pénitence (suivis du traité de l'adoration en   *l'humilité* esprit et en vérité et de divers opuscles, avec un essai sur la mystique de Malebranche).
(1) A. Cuvillier, ed., Paris, 1944.
(2) O. C. xvii-1, pp. 367-444, 1960, A. Cuvillier, ed. [Without the "essai"]

———. Traité de la nature et de la grâce.   *Nature et grâce*
(1) In Œuvres complètes de Malebranche, de Genoude and de Lourdoueix, eds., Paris, 1837, Vol. 2.
(2) O. C. v, 1958, G. Dreyfus, ed.

———. Polémique Malebranche-Le Valois [Louis de la   *Polémique avec* Ville] (1682-1712). A. Robinet, ed., O. C. xvii-1,   *Le Valois* pp. 445-531, 1960.

———. Première et deuxième lettres du P. Malebranche à M. Arnauld. In Recueil . . . , Vol. 4, pp. 363-400.

———. Réflexions sur la Prémotion physique.   *Prémotion*
(1) In Genoude edition, Vol. 2.
(2) O. C. xvi, 1958, A. Robinet, ed.

———. Prières avant et après la sainte messe.   *Prières avant et*
(1) In Méditations sur l'humilité, Cuvillier   *après la sainte* 1944 edition.   *messe*
(2) O. C. xvii-1, pp. 439-44.

FULL TITLE | SHORT TITLE

Malebranche, Nicolas. Quatre lettres du P. Malebranche touchant celles de M. Arnauld. In Recueil . . . , Vol. 2, pp. 1 ff.

———. De la recherche de la vérité, où l'on traite de la nature de l'esprit de l'homme, et de l'usage qu'il doit faire pour éviter l'erreur des sciences.
    (1) Geneviève Lewis, ed., 3 vols., Paris, 1946. Abbreviated: "L."
    (2) Francisque Bouillier, ed., 2 vols., Paris, *circa* 1880. Abbreviated: "B."
    (3) In Œuvres complètes de Malebranche, Paul Schrecker and Désiré Roustan, eds., Paris, 1938. (Consists solely of *Recherche*, Bks. 1 and 2.)

Recherche

———. Réponse à une Dissertation de M. Arnauld contre un Éclaircissement du Traité de la nature et de la grâce . . . In Recueil . . . , Vol. 2, pp. 247 ff.

———. Réponse du Père Malebranche au Livre des vraies et des fausses idées. In Œuvres philosophiques d'Antoine Arnauld, Jules Simon, ed., Paris, 1843.

Réponse au Livre des vraies, etc.

———. Réponse à M. Régis.
    (1) Recherche, L. iii, pp. 231-268.
    (2) In Polémique Malebranche-Régis, O. C. xvii-1, pp. 237-366.

Réponse à Régis

———. Réponse du P. Malebranche à la troisième Lettre de M. Arnauld . . . touchant les idées et les plaisirs. In Recueil . . . , Vol. 4, pp. 1-181.

Réponse à la Troisième

———. Traité de morale. Henri Joly, ed., Paris, 1882.

Traité de morale

———. Trois lettres au P. Lamy. In *L'Amour de Dieu.* Désiré Roustan, ed., Paris, 1922.

———. Trois lettres de l'Autuer de la Recherche de la vérité, touchant la Défense de M. Arnauld contre la Réponse au Livre des vraies et des fausses idées. In Recueil . . . , Vol. 1, pp. 321 ff.

Trois lettres touchant la Défense

Bibliography

FULL TITLE   SHORT TITLE

Albright, William Foxwell. From the stone age to
christianity: monotheism and the historical process. Baltimore, 1940.

Anderson, Fulton Henry. The philosophy of Francis
Bacon. Chicago, 1948.

André, Le Père. Discours. Sur les merveilles des idées.   *Des idées*
In André, Œuvres, Paris, 1843.

———. Discours. L'idée de Dieu. In Œuvres, Paris,   *L'idée de Dieu*
1843.

———. Documents inédits . . . , contenant la corre-   *Documents*
spondance . . . avec Malebranche . . . A. Charma   *inédits*
and G. Mancel, eds., Caen, 1844.

———. Œuvres. Victor Cousin, ed., Paris, 1843.

———. La vie du R. P. Malebranche, Paris, 1886.   *Vie du R. P.*
                                                             Malebranche

Anonymous. Nouveaux mélanges de littérature d'histoire et de philosophie. "D'un Centénaire, &c."
1769. Article: "Le Père Mallebranche."

Aquinas, Thomas. The summa contra gentiles of Saint   *Contra gentiles*
Thomas Aquinas. Translated by the English Do-
minican Fathers. London, 1923 ff.

———. The "summa theologica" of Saint Thomas
Aquinas. Translated by Fathers of the English
Dominican Province. Pt. 1, QQ. 1-26. 2 ed.,
London, n.d.

Arnauld, Antoine. Défense d'Arnauld contre la Ré-   *Défense contre*
ponse de Malebranche. In Œuvres philosophiques   *Malebranche*
d'Antoine Arnauld, Jules Simon, ed., Paris, 1843.

———. Des vraies et des fausses idées. In Œuvres   *Vraies et fausses*
philosophiques, d'Antoine Arnauld, Jules Simon,   *idées*
ed., Paris, 1843.

Augustine, Aurelius. The city of God. Marcus Dods,
trans. and ed., New York, 1948.

[335]

FULL TITLE	SHORT TITLE
Augustine, Aurelius. The confessions of St. Augustine. (1) Books I-X. Trans. by F. J. Sheed. New York, N. Y., 1942. (2) Trans. by William Watts, The Loeb Classical Library. London and New York, 1925.	*Confessions*
Bacon, Francis. The twoo bookes of Francis Bacon of the proficience and advancement of learning. In Bacon selections, Charles Scribner's Sons, New York, 1928.	*Advancement of Learning*
——. The great instauration. In Bacon selections, Charles Scribner's Sons, New York, 1928.	*Great Instauration*
——. Novum organum. In Bacon selections, Charles Scribner's Sons, New York, 1928.	*Novum Organum*
Balz, Albert G. A. Cartesian studies. New York, 1951.	*Cartesian Studies*
——. Idea and essence in the philosophies of Hobbes and Spinoza. New York, 1918.	
Baruzi, Jean. Leibniz et l'organization religieuse de la terre. Paris, 1907.	
Bayle, Pierre. Dictionnaire historique et critique. Amsterdam, 1784. Especially articles "Rorarius" and "Spinoza."	
——. Réponse de l'Auteur des nouvelles de la ré-publique des lettres à l'Avis qui lui a été donné sur ce qu'il avoit dit en faveur du P. Malebranche . . . In Œuvres diverses de M^r. Pierre Bayle, La Haye, 1737, Vol. 1, pp. 444-61.	
Berkeley, George. Philosophical commentaries (A. C. Fraser's "Commonplace book"). In The works of George Berkeley . . . , A. A. Luce and T. E. Jessop, Vol. 1, London, 1948.	*Commonplace Book*
——. The principles of human knowledge. In The works of George Berkeley . . . , A. A. Luce and T. E. Jessop, Vol. 2, London, 1949.	*Principles*

Bibliography

FULL TITLE	SHORT TITLE

Berkeley, George. Philosophical correspondence with Johnson. In The works of George Berkeley . . . , A. A. Luce and T. E. Jessop, Vol. 2, London, 1949.

Blampignon, L'abbé E. A. Etude sur Malebranche d'après des documents manuscrits suivie d'une correspondance inédite. Paris, 1862. *Etude*

Blanchard, Pierre. L'Attention à Dieu selon Malebranche. Desclée de Brouwer, 1956. *L'Attention à Dieu*

Blondel, Maurice. L'Anti-cartésianisme de Malebranche. Revue de métaphysique et de morale, Vol. 23, 1916, pp. 1-26. *L'Anti-cartésianisme de Malebranche*

Boileau, Nicolas. L'Art poétique. Paris, 1674.

Bouillier, Francisque. Histoire de la philosophie cartésienne. 2 vols., 3 ed., Paris, 1868. *Histoire*

Bossuet, Jacques-Bénigne. Œuvres philosophiques. Jules Simon, ed., Paris, 1844.

Boulenger, Jacques. Le grand siècle. 2 ed., Paris, n.d.

Boutroux, Emile. L'Intellectualisme de Malebranche. Revue de métaphysique et de morale, Vol. 23, 1916, pp. 25-36.

———. Des vérités éternelles chez Descartes. M. Ganguilhem, trans. Paris, 1927. *Vérités éternelles*

Bréhier, Emile. Histoire de la philosophie. Vol. 2, Fasc. 1, Paris, 1929. *Histoire de la philosophie*

———. Les "jugments naturels" chez Malebranche. In Malebranche, recueil publié par la *Revue philosophique,* Paris, 1938.

Bremond, Henri. Histoire littéraire du sentiment religieux en France. Vol. 3, Paris, 1930.

Bridet, L. La théorie de la connaissance dans la philosophie de Malebranche. Paris, 1929. *Connaissance*

FULL TITLE	SHORT TITLE

Brinton, Crane. Ideas and men. The story of western thought. New York, 1950.

Browne, Thomas. Religio medici. 1642.

Bruch, Jean-Louis. La méthode de M. Gueroult et son application à la philosophie de Malebranche. Revue de métaphysique et de morale, April-September, 1958, Nos. 2-3, pp. 358-373. — *La méthode de Gueroult*

Brunschvicg, Léon. Les étapes de la philosophie mathématique. 2 ed., Paris, 1922.

———. L'expérience humaine et la causalité physique, Paris, 1922. — *Expérience et causalité*

———. Le progrès de la conscience dans la philosophie occidentale. 2 vols., Paris, 1927. — *Progrès de la conscience*

———. Spinoza et ses contemporains. 3 ed., Paris, 1923. — *Spinoza*

Buffier, Père. Œuvres philosophiques de Père. Buffier. Francisque Bouillier, ed., Paris, 1843.

Burtt, Edwin Arthur. The metaphysical foundations of modern physical science. Revised edition. New York, 1922. — *Foundations of Physics*

Bury, J. B. The idea of progress. New York, 1920.

———. A history of freedom of thought. 1913.

Butterfield, Herbert. The origins of modern science. New York.

Callot, Emile. Problèmes du cartésianisme. Descartes, Malebranche, Spinoza. Annecy, 1956. — *Problèmes du cartésianisme*

Chevalier, J. Descartes. Paris, 1921.

Church, Ralph Withington. Hume's theory of the understanding. Ithaca, 1935.

———. Malebranche and Hume. Revue internationale de philosophie, October 15, 1938, pp. 143-61.

Bibliography

FULL TITLE	SHORT TITLE
Church, Ralph Withington. A study in the philosophy of Malebranche. London, 1931.	*Study*
Clarke, W. Norris. System: a new category of being? President's remarks, Proceedings, Twenty-third Annual Convention, Jesuit Philosophical Association. Woodstock, Maryland, 1961.	
Cloyseault, P. Généralats du Cardinal de Bérulle. R. P. Ingold, ed., Paris, 1882.	
———. Généralat du P. de Sainte-Marthe. Paris, 1883.	
Connell, Desmond. La passivité de l'entendement selon Malebranche. Revue philosophique de Louvain, Vol. 53, November, 1955, pp. 542-65.	*La passivité*
de Cordemoy, Geraud. Le discernement du corps et de l'âme. Paris, 1679.	
Cousin, Victor, ed. Fragments de philosophie cartésienne. Paris, 1855.	
———. Procès-verbal d'une séance d'une société cartésienne. In Fragments de philosophie cartésienne.	*Procès-verbal*
Crashaw, Richard. The poems. Oxford, 1927.	
Cuvillier, Armand. Essai sur la mystique de Malebranche. In *Méditations sur l'humilité*, Cuvillier, ed., 1944.	*La mystique*
Damien, A. Etude sur La Bruyère et Malebranche. Paris, 1866.	
Delbos, Victor. Etude de la philosophie de Malebranche. Paris, 1924.	*Etude*
———. Malebranche et Maine de Biran. Revue de métaphysique et de morale, Vol. 23, 1916, pp. 145-62.	
Del Noce, Augusto. Bibliografia malebranchiana. In Malebranche, nel terzo centenario della nascita. Supplement, Rivista di filosofia neo-scolastica, Milan, September, 1938.	*Bibliografia*

FULL TITLE	SHORT TITLE
Delvolvé, Jean, Religion, critique et philosophie positive chez Pierre Bayle. Paris, 1906.	
Demos, Raphael. The philosophy of Plato. New York, 1939.	
Descartes, René. Œuvres de Descartes. Charles Adam and Paul Tannery, eds. 13 vols., Paris, 1897, ff. Abbreviated: "A.T."	
———. The philosophical works of Descartes. Elizabeth S. Haldane and G. R. T. Ross, trans., 2 vols., Cambridge, 1931. Abbreviated: "H.R."	
———. Discourse on the method of rightly conducting the reason. In Haldane and Ross.	*Discourse*
———. La géométrie. In Adam and Tannery.	*Geometry*
———. Correspondance. In Adam and Tannery.	*Letters*
———. Meditations on first philosophy. In Haldane and Ross.	*Meditations*
———. Notes against a certain programme. In Haldane and Ross.	*Notes against a Programme*
———. The passions of the soul. In Haldane and Ross.	*Passions*
———. The principles of philosophy. In Haldane and Ross.	*Principles*
———. Reply to Objections I, etc. In Haldane and Ross.	*Reply to Objections I, etc.*
———. Rules for the direction of the mind. In Haldane and Ross.	*Rules*
———. The search after truth. In Haldane and Ross.	*Search*
Desgabets, Dom Robert. Critique de la Critique de la Recherche. . . , Paris, 1675.	
Dewey, John. The quest for certainty. New York, 1929.	

Bibliography

FULL TITLE	SHORT TITLE
De Wulf, Maurice. Mediaeval philosophy. Cambridge, Mass., 1922.	
Donne, John. The complete poetry and selected prose of John Donne. New York, 1946.	
Dreyfus, Ginette. La volonté selon Malebranche. Paris, 1958.	*La volonté*
Dryden, John. The poems. London, 1925.	
Ducassé, Pierre. Malebranche. Sa vie, son œuvre, avec un exposé de sa philosophie. Paris, 1942.	
Duhem, Pierre. L'Optique de Malebranche. Revue de métaphysique et de morale, Vol. 23, 1916, pp. 37-91.	*Optique*
Fénelon, Francois. De L'existence de Dieu. Paris, 1871.	
Fontenelle. Entretiens sur la pluralité des mondes. Paris, 1818.	
Fritz, Anita Dunlevy. Berkeley's self—its origin in Malebranche. Journal of the history of ideas, Vol. 15, No. 4, October, 1954, pp. 554-72.	*Berkeley's Self*
———. Malebranche and the immaterialism of Berkeley. Review of metaphysics. Vol. 3, No. 1, September, 1949, pp. 59-80.	*Malebranche and Berkeley*
Gamow, George. Turbulence in space. Scientific American, Vol. 186, No. 6, June, 1952, pp. 26-30.	*Turbulence in Space*
Genest, L'Abbé. Principes de philosophie. Paris, 1716.	
Gilson, Etienne. The philosophy of St. Thomas Aquinas. Second rev. and enl. ed., Cambridge, 1929.	*Aquinas*
———. Introduction à l'étude de Saint Augustin. 3 ed., Paris, 1949.	*Augustin*
———. Being and some philosophers. Toronto, Canada, 1949.	*Being*

FULL TITLE	SHORT TITLE

Gilson, Etienne. The philosophy of St. Bonaventure. New York, 1938. — *Bonaventure*

——. René Descartes Discours de la méthode, texte et commentaire. 2 ed., Paris, 1930. — *Discours*

——. Elements of christian philosophy. Garden City, L. I., 1960.

——. L'être et l'essence. Paris, 1948.

——. Etudes sur le role de la pensée médiévale dans la formation du système cartésien. Paris, 1930. — *Etudes*

——. Héloise et Abélard. Paris, 1938.

——. Jean Duns Scot: introduction à ses positions fondamentales. Paris, 1952.

——. La liberté chez Descartes et la théologie. Paris, 1913. — *Liberté*

——. The spirit of medieval philosophy. New York, 1936. — *Medieval Philosophy*

——. Painting and reality. New York, 1957.

——. The philosopher and theology. Cécile Gilson, tr. New York, 1962.

——. Reason and revelation in the middle ages. New York, 1939.

——. The unity of philosophical experience. New York, 1950.

Ginsberg, Morris. Translator's introduction. In Malebranche, Dialogues on metaphysics and on religion [Entretiens sur la métaphysique]. New York, 1923. — *Preface*

Girbal, F. Informations historiques et documents à propos de Malebranche et de Bernard Lamy. Revue international de philosophie, No. 32, Fasc. 2, 1955, pp. 288-290.

Bibliography

FULL TITLE	SHORT TITLE
Glaser, J. Vergleichung der Philosophie des Malebranche und Spinoza. Berlin, 1846.	
Goheen, John. The problem of matter and form in the *De ente et essentia* of Thomas Aquinas. Cambridge, Mass., 1940.	*Matter and Form*
Gouhier, Henri. Malebranche. 2 ed., Paris, 1929.	*Malebranche*
———. La philosophie de Malebranche et son expérience religieuse. Paris, 1926.	*Philosophie de Malebranche*
———. La vocation de Malebranche. Paris, 1926.	*Vocation*
———. Philosophie chrétienne et théologie: à propos de la seconde polémique de Malebranche. In Malebranche, recueil publié par la *Revue philosophique*, Paris, 1938.	
Grierson, Herbert John Clifford. Cross currents in English literature of the XVIIth century. London, 1929.	
Gueroult, Martial. Descartes selon l'ordre des raisons. 2 vols. Paris, 1953.	*Descartes*
———. Etendue et psychologie chez Malebranche. Paris, 1939.	*Etendue et psychologie*
———. Le cogito et la notion 'pour penser, il faut être.' Travaux du IXe Congrès International (Congrès Descartes), Paris, 1937, Vol. 1, pp. 53 ff.	*Le cogito*
———. Métaphysique et physique de la force chez Descartes et chez Malebranche. Revue de métaphysique et de morale, 1954, January-March, No. 1, pp. 1-37, and April-June, No. 2, pp. 113-34.	*L'idée de force*
———. Malebranche. 3 vols., Paris, 1955-9.	*Malebranche*
Hallet, Harold Foster. Aeternitas. Oxford, 1930.	
Haserot, Francis S. Spinoza and the status of universals. The Philosophical Review, Vol. 59, No. 4, October, 1950, pp. 469-92.	*Spinoza and Universals*

[343]

FULL TITLE	SHORT TITLE

Herbert [of Cherbury], Edward. . . . De religione laici. New Haven, 1944.

Herbert, George. The poems. Oxford, 1913.

Hobbes, Thomas. In The English works of Thomas Hobbes, Vol. 1, Sir William Molesworth, ed., London, 1839. "Elements of philosophy. Concerning body." *Elements*

———. Leviathan, or the matter, forme & power of a Commonwealth, ecclesiasticall and civill. A. R. Waller, ed., Cambridge, 1904. *Leviathan*

Huguet, Edmond. L'Evolution du sens des mots depuis le XVIᵉ siècle. Paris, 1934.

Hume, David. Dialogues concerning natural religion. Edinburgh and London, 1907.

———. Enquiry concerning the human understanding. L. A. Selby-Bigge, ed. 2 ed., Oxford, 1902. Impression of 1951.

Johnston, Charlotte. Locke's *Examination of Malebranche* and John Norris. Journal of the history of ideas, Vol. 19, No. 4, October, 1958, pp. 551-8.

Klopke, John Robert. Malebranche's theory of natural judgment. Dissertation, University of Toronto, Toronto, 1961. *Natural Judgment*

Labbas, Lucien. L'Idée de science dans Malebranche. Paris, 1931. *L'idée de science*

La Forge, Louis de. Traité de l'âme humaine. Paris, 1666.

Laird, John. Hume's philosophy of human nature. New York, 1931.

Lalande, André. Les théories de l'induction et de l'expérimentation. Paris, n.d. *Induction et expérimentation*

———. Vocabulaire technique et critique de la philosophie. Nouvelle édition, revue et augmentée, 2 vols., Paris, 1928. *Vocabulaire de la philosophie*

Bibliography

FULL TITLE	SHORT TITLE

Lamy, François. De la connaissance de soi-même. Vol. 5. Paris, 1698.

Lange, Friedrich Albert. The history of materialism. 3 ed. New York, 1925.

Laporte, Jean. La liberté selon Malebranche. Revue de métaphysique et de morale, July, 1938, pp. 339-410. *La liberté*

———. L'étendue intelligible selon Malebranche. Revue internationale de philosophie, October 15, 1938, pp. 7-58. *L'étendue intelligible*

Lecky, W. E. H. A history of the rise and influence of the spirit of rationalism. 2 vols. 1865.

Leibniz, Gottfried Wilhelm. (1) Démonstration courte d'une erreur considérable de M. Descartes. Nouvelles de la république des lettres, Sept., 1686. In Œuvres diverses de M^r. Pierre Bayle, La Haye, 1737, Vol. 1, p. 635.
(2) Courte remarque de M. l'Abbé D. C. [Catelan] où l'on montre à Mr. G. G. Leibnits le paralogisme contenu dans l'objection précédente. *Ibid.*, pp. 635-6.
(3) Réplique de M. L. Leibnitz à M. l'Abbé D. C. . . . touchant ce qu'a dit M. Descartes que Dieu conserve toûjours dans la nature la même quantité de mouvement. Nouvelle de la république des lettres, Feb., 1687. In *op. cit.*, Vol. 1, pp. 747-9.
Note: See bibliography of Vidgrain, "Polémique avec Leibniz," for remainder of this controversy, which issued in Malebranche's *Lois des mouvements*.

———. Discourse on metaphysics. Correspondence with Arnauld. Monadology. George R. Montgomery, trans., Chicago and London, 1931. *Discourse*

———. Essais de theodicée. 2 vols., Lausanne, 1790.

———. The philosophical works of Leibnitz. Translated from the original Latin and French. With notes by George Martin Duncan. 2 ed., New Haven, 1908.

Full Title	Short Title
Leibniz, Gottfried Wilhelm. New Essays. 2 ed., Chicago, 1916.	
———. Animadversions on Descartes' *Principles*. In Duncan.	*On Descartes' principles*
Leishman, James Blair. The metaphysical poets: Donne, Herbert, Vaughan, Traherne. Oxford, 1934.	
Le Moine, A. Des vérités éternelles selon Malebranche. Paris, 1936.	*Vérités éternelles*
Lewis, Geneviève. L'individualité selon Descartes. Paris, 1950.	*L'Individualité selon Descartes*
Locke, John. An essay concerning human understanding. A. C. Fraser, ed., 2 vols., Oxford, 1894.	
Lovejoy, Arthur O. The great chain of being. Cambridge, 1936.	*Great Chain*
McKeon, Richard. The philosophy of Spinoza. New York, 1928.	*Spinoza*
Milhaud, Gaston. Descartes savant. Paris, 1921	*Descartes savant*
Miller, James W. Critical realism. Unpublished thesis, 1927, in Harvard College Library, Cambridge, Mass.	*Critical Realism*
———. Descartes' conceptualism. The Review of metaphysics, Vol. 4, No. 2, Dec., 1950.	*Descartes' Conceptualism*
Milton, John. Of true religion, heresy, schism, toleration. 1673.	
de Montcheuil, Yves. Malebranche et le quiétisme. Paris, 1946.	
More, Henry. Enchiridion ethicum. English translation, London, 1690. Reproduced, 1930.	
Moreau, Joseph. Le réalisme de Malebranche et la fonction de l'idée. Revue de metaphysique et de morale. April, 1946, pp. 97-141.	*Le réalisme de Malebranche*

Bibliography

FULL TITLE	SHORT TITLE

Moreau, Joseph. Malebranche et le Spinozisme. In Correspondance avec J. J. Dortous de Mairan. Paris, 1947.
— *Malebranche et le Spinozisme*

Mouy, Paul. Les lois du choc des corps d'après Malebranche. Paris, 1927.
— *Lois du choc*

———. *Malebranche et Newton*. Revue de métaphysique et de morale, July, 1938, pp. 411-435.
— *Malebranche et Newton*

———. Le développement de la physique cartésienne, 1646-1712. Paris, 1934.
— *Physique cartésienne*

Newton, Isaac. Mathematical principles of natural philosophy. Florian Cajori, ed. Berkeley, Cal., 1934.
— *Principia*

Novaro, M. Die Philosophie des Malebranche. Berlin, 1899.
— *Malebranche*

Ogg, D. Europe in the seventeenth century. 1925.

Ollé-Laprune, L. La philosophie de Malebranche. 2 vols., Paris, 1870.
— *Malebranche*

Pang, Ching-jen. L'Idée de Dieu chez Malebranche et l'idée de Li chez Tchou Hi. Paris, 1942.
— *Malebranche et Tchou Hi*

Pascal, Blaise. The thoughts, letters, and opuscules. O. W. Wight, trans., New York, 1869.
— *Thoughts*

Perry, Ralph Barton. Puritanism and democracy. New York, 1944.
— *Puritanism and Democracy*

Pollock, F. Spinoza: his life and philosophy (1880, rep. 1899; 1911).

Prost, Joseph. Essai sur l'atomisme et l'occasionalisme dans la philosophie cartésienne. Paris, 1907.
— *Atomisme et occasionalisme*

Quesnel, Pasquier. Correspondance. Vol. 1. Mme Albert Le Roy, ed., Paris, 1900.

Rabbe, L'Abbé F. Etude philosophique sur l'Abbé Simon Foucher, chanoine de la Sainte Chappelle de Dijon. Paris, 1867.
— *Simon Foucher*

FULL TITLE   SHORT TITLE

Randall, John Herman. The making of the modern
mind. New York, 1926.

Régis, Sylvain. Système de philosophie. Paris, 1690.

Robertson, George C. Hobbes. Philadelphia, n.d.

Robinet, André. La vocation académicienne de Male-   *Vocation aca-*
branche. Revue d'histoire des sciences et de leurs   *démicienne*
applications, Vol. 12, No. 1, January-March, 1959,
pp. 1-18.

———. Malebranche et Leibniz: relations personnelles
présentées avec les textes complèts des auteurs
et de leur correspondants. Paris, 1955.

Rome, Beatrice K. Created truths and *Causa Sui* in
Descartes. Philosophy and phenomenological research, Vol. 17, September, 1956, pp. 66-78.

——— and Rome, Sydney C. Computer simulation towards a theory of large organizations. Chapter
22 of Computer applications in the behavioral
sciences, H. Borko, ed., Englewood Cliffs, 1962.

———, ———. Formal representation of intentionally
structured systems. Chapter 12 of Information
retrieval and machine translation, Allen Kent, ed.,
Vol. 3, New York, 1960-1.

———, ———. Leviathan, a simulation of behavioral systems to operate dynamically on a digital computer. Chapter 56 of *ibid.*

———, ———. Leviathan: an experimental study of large
organizations with the aid of computers. To be
published in the Proceedings of the First Con-
gress on the Information System Sciences, Mc-
Graw-Hill, New York, 1963.

———, ———. The Leviathan technique for large-group
analysis. Behavioral science, Vol. 6, No. 2, April,
1961, pp. 148-52.

Rome, Sydney C. Berkeley's conceptualism. The Philo-   *Berkeley's Con-*
sophical Review, Nov., 1946, pp. 680-6.   *ceptualism*

Bibliography

FULL TITLE	SHORT TITLE

Roth, L. Spinoza, Descartes and Maimonides. 1924.

Roustan, Désiré. Pour une edition de Malebranche. Revue de métaphysique et de morale, Vol. 23, 1916, pp. 161-175.

Santayana, George. The life of reason or the phases of human progress. New York, 1932.   *Life of Reason*

———. Scepticism and animal faith. New York, 1923.

Schrecker, Paul. Le parallélisme théologico-mathématique chez Malebranche. In Recueil published by the Revue philosophique, 1938.   *Le parallélisme chez Malebranche*

———. Malebranche et le préformisme biologique. Revue internationale de philosophie, October 15, 1938, pp. 77-98.

———. Arnauld, Malebranche, Prestet et la théorie des nombres négatifs. Thales, 1935.   *Nombres négatifs*

Smith, Norman. Studies in the Cartesian philosophy. London, 1902.   *Studies*

Smith, Preserved. A history of modern culture. Vol. 1, New York, 1930.

Sortais, Gaston. La philosophie moderne depuis Bacon jusqu'à Leibniz. Vol. 1, Paris, 1920.

Spingarn, Joel Elias. Critical essays of the seventeenth century. 3 vols., Oxford, 1908-9.

Spinoza, Benedict. Ethic. In Spinoza selections, Charles Scribner's Sons, 1930.   *Ethics*

———. On the improvement of the understanding. In Spinoza selections. Charles Scribner's Sons, 1930.   *Improvement*

———. The letters of certain learned men to Spinoza and his replies. In Spinoza selections. Charles Scribner's Sons, 1930.

———. A political treatise. In Chief works of Benedict de Spinoza, R. H. M. Elwes, ed., New York, 1951.

FULL TITLE   SHORT TITLE

Spinoza, Benedict. Short treatise on God, man, and his well-being. In Spinoza selections, Charles Scribner's Sons, 1930.

———. Theologico-political treatise. In Chief works of Benedict de Spinoza, R. H. M. Elwes, ed., New York, 1951.

Stephen, Leslie. Hobbes. New York, 1928.

Stout, A. K. The alleged 'petitio principii' in Descartes' appeal to the veracity of God. Travaux du IXe Congrès International (Congrès Descartes), Paris, 1937, Vol. 1, pp. 125 ff.   *Alleged "petitio"*

Strauss, Leo. The political philosophy of Hobbes. Oxford, 1936.

Tawney, R. H. Religion and the rise of capitalism. New York, 1926.

Tertre, du. Réfutation du nouveau systèm de . . . Malebranche. Paris, 1716.

Thamin, R. Le traité de morale de Malebranche. Revue de métaphysique et de morale, Vol. 23, 1916, pp. 93-126.

Thomas, E. Crewdson. History of the schoolmen. London, 1941.   *History of the schoolmen*

Van Biéma, E. Comment Malebranche conçoit la psychologie. Revue de métaphysique et de morale, Vol. 23, 1916, pp. 127-146.   *Comment Malebranche conçoit la psychologie*

Vidgrain, Joseph. Le christianisme dans la philosophie de Malebranche. Paris, n.d.   *Christianisme*

Wehrlé, Joannes. Préface [to Delbos' Etude]. In Victor Delbos, Etude de la philosophie de Malebranche, Paris, 1924.   *Préface*

Whitehead, Alfred North. Science and the modern world. New York, 1925.

Wild, John Daniel. Introduction to realistic philosophy. New York, 1948.

Bibliography

FULL TITLE	SHORT TITLE
Wiley, Margaret L. The subtle knot. Cambridge, 1952.	
Willey, Basil. The seventeenth century background. London, 1934.	
Williams, Roger. The Bloody Tenent. 1867.	
Wolfson, Harry Austryn. Crescas' critique of Aristotle. Cambridge, Mass., 1929.	*Crescas*
———. Philo. Foundations of religious philosophy in Judaism, Christianity, and Islam. Vol. 1, Cambridge, Mass., 1948.	*Philo*
———. The philosophy of Spinoza. 2 vols., Cambridge, Mass., 1934.	*Spinoza*

Notes

1. Gouhier, *Vocation*, p. 56.

2. On the basis of the contents of this volume, M. Gouhier is quite correct in taking to task those critics of Malebranche who explain his conversion to Descartes and to philosophy as simply an attraction for Cartesian science. "Pourtant s'il n'y avait eu que cela, imagine-t-on que *L'Homme* de René Descartes êut bouleversé sa vie?" asks M. Gouhier. If the scientific portions of this volume had been nothing but science, would Malebranche really have shown any interest in it and have become converted to it? No, answers M. Gouhier; what Malebranche found in the Cartesian man of *L'Homme* was the Christian man. In the separation of the mind and body, "le mécanisme cartésien éveille des résonances chrétiennes." The young oratorian was not looking for a physics or for a metaphysics at the time of his ordination. ". . . Ses croyances lui suffisent et il possède sur Dieu, l'âme, la destinée et l'origine des choses un système d'idées solidement enracinées qu'aucun doute n'a jamais effleurées et n'effleurera jamais. Il ne cherche pas la vérité, mais à mieux connaître la vérité dont il vit . . ." (Gouhier, *Vocation*, pp. 61-2.)

But Gouhier surely exaggerates. On the one hand we are to believe that in 1660 the *Oratoire* was anti-Cartesian, that Malebranche was an "écolier en théologie" uninterested in his philosophical comrades, that he was the very sort of person who would abide by the prohibitions and rules of Bourgoing not to study Cartesianism. We are on the other hand asked to believe that when on the eve or morning after his ordination, September, 1664, the young Malebranche, then 26 years of age, came upon Descartes' *L'Homme,* this young theologian was not interested in seeking the truth—that he already had it!—but only in the means of gaining greater understanding of what he already knew. He was overjoyed and overcome with this work because in it he found the principles of a Christian metaphysics. Now is it likely that a young man who *has* the truth and who is uninterested in philosophy and who is so scrupulously obedient to his superiors *would* pick up a book by Descartes? Why should he so much as glance at it, if, having not a shred of philosophical curiosity, he is wholly preoccupied with a well-worked-out system of truth? Does one turn to a prohibited work to seek greater understanding of the secure truths of religion? No doubt he found more than science to please him, and in this claim Gouhier is entirely sound. But there is no value in carrying this insight too far. If he did not already possess a philosophic and scientific curiosity, it is very unlikely that he would pay attention. The man who many years later wrote that faith will pass but reason will remain must have had a healthy and lively curiosity for reason from the outset.

3. ". . . Ces explications, certes, ne valent plus pour un moderne. Mais si l'on remplace les tourbillons par les atomes de la théorie de Bohr, et la rupture d'un tourbillon par la séparation violente des électrons, on aura les phénomènes de Hittorf, de Crookes, de Roentgen et de Becquerel. Il y a donc une très curieuse analogie entre l'ionisation dans l'atomisme moderne et la production du feu dans la théorie malebranchiste de l'éther." (Mouy, *Physique cartésienne*, p. 324.)

4. *Ibid.*, pp. 324-5.

Robinet, the assiduous and recent editor of Malebranche's *Correspondance, actes et documents, 1638-1689, 1690-1715* (Œuvres complètes de Malebranche, Vol. 18 and 19 (Vrin, Paris, 1961 [abbreviated: "O. C. xviii" and "O. C. xix"]), indicates that Malebranche's intellectual, scholarly, and scientific efforts were vigorously renewed in 1690, after a long period of controversy and polemic. From 1690 to 1715, Malebranche's scientific endeavors and experimentation were revolutionary in character, monumental in scope, and most comprehensive in range, covering the fields of chemistry, biology, medicine, navigation, mathematics, magnetism, and optics. Robinet concludes:

La vocation académicienne de Malebranche répond à l'exercice plein d'une tendance intellectuelle et pratique qui trouve son emploi optimum de 1690-1715. Il conviendra donc de rééquilibrier l'idée qu'on s'est faite trop couramment de la personnalité de Malebranche: sa vocation scientifique équivaut en portée et en profondeur à sa vocation philosophique et à sa vocation religieuse . . . Sa formation scientifique recommence en 1690: elle est caractérisée par l'éviction des formes mathématiques et physiques caduques héritées de la formation cartésienne, par l'imitation poussée au calcul de l'infini, par la prise en considération sérieuse de l'expérimentation. La nomination à l'Académie des Sciences [January 28, 1699] n'est qu'une illustration de cette compétence théorique et technique indubitable. (*Vocation académicienne*, pp. 15-16.)

5. *Cf. ibid.*, p. 5: "Les correspondances et les actes que nous avons collationnés nous permettent de vivre dans la pièce que Malebranche occupe à l'Oratoire du faubourg Saint-Honoré. Les amis présents racontent aux amis absents ce qui c'est dit, ce qui s'est fait. Les lettres du fonds Bernoulli regorgent d'indications de ce genre, et de multiples correspondances indirectes révèlent la vie quotidienne de Malebranche. Dans cette même chambre du Méditatif, du Religieux, il faudra faire une place très large au Savant. Il y a foule dans ce qu'on a pris trop longtemps pour une 'cellule' de philosophe ou de prêtre en prière. On dispute, on expose, on réclame l'arbitrage du maître. On lui soumet les questions de fait, de savoir, de personne. Cette chambre tient à la fois du salon, du laboratoire, de la salle de classe et de la bibliothèque."

6. In all fairness to Church, it must be acknowledged that he is not alone in his devastating criticisms of Malebranche. Many a European interpreter, including recent French compatriots, have been as sharp toward Malebranche, if not so vitriolic, as Church. To consider but one example at present, Gueroult (*Malebranche*, Vol. 1) complains that unlike the neatly defined notions of Descartes, those of Malebranche are ambiguous and frequently supported by equivocal reasoning; conclusions are con-

nected with premises only apparently or else harbor profound obscurities:

L'harmonie n'apparaît que si l'on contemple la construction de loin. Elle tend à se dissiper dés que l'on tente de l'examiner de prés . . . L'analyse fait tomber la façade d'idées claires et distinctes pour découvrir une vaste intuition qui se donne ou se refuse tout entière . . . Il y a là moins de logique que d'architectonique, moins de mathématique que de mystique.

According to Gueroult, the moment analysis is applied to Malebranche's thought, the apparent clarity vanishes and one begins to doubt whether his thoughts are as comprehensible to clear and distinct reasoning as Malebranche affirms them to be. (Pp. 25-6. *Cf.* p. 168, n. 54; pp. 186-7; p. 287: "le mysticisme de cette intuition unique permet d'assurer la fusion et la confusion de ce que la raison claire et distincte de son côté sépare." Also see Vol. 3, pp. 356-60.)

More than 15 years earlier, in *Etendue et psychologie*, Gueroult bewailed that the natural light, dear to Descartes, becomes transformed in Malebranche's thought into a suprahuman, supra-natural light. Intellectual knowledge yields to a divine illumination. (P. 36)

For an even more Gueroultian position than Gueroult himself is willing to condone, see *La méthode de Gueroult* by Bruch. An ardent admirer of Gueroult's rational method of analysis, Bruch takes Gueroult to task for entertaining a semi-Bergsonian intuitionism in his appreciation of Malebranche. Gueroult, he says, on the one hand is pleased to acknowledge the beauty, the metaphysical fecundity and even the coherence of Malebranche's architecture when he considers it from a distance and in a mystical or ineffable light. But, at the same time, when Gueroult regards that "philosophical cathedral" in close focus and begins to probe it with his rigorous analytical tool, then he is forced to conclude that, "Malebranche échoue presque partout dans son effort pour fonder sa doctrine en raison." (P. 367.) Bruch concludes:

La méthode de l'analyse des structures est donc justifiée: sans être *intégralement* fidèle à l'esprit du malebranchisme—il lui faudrait pour cela se faire complice de ses ambiguités—, elle l'est au *maximum*.

Mais il est, dès lors, impossible de juxtaposer en un jugement final ambivalent la critique des structures du système et l'admiration de son architecture métaphysique, ni de préférer celle-ci à celle-là. Aussi la réhabilitation du système de Malebranche, présentée par M. Gueroult au terme d'une analyse qui a exposé méthodiquement la fragilité de ses structures me paraît-elle difficilement acceptable . . . (Pp. 369-370.)

CHAPTER I. SCIENTIFIC METHOD

1. Malebranche, *Recherche*, Préface pour servir de réponse à la Critique du premier volume, L. ii, pp. 299-300.

2. Church, *Study*, p. 220.

3. Descartes, *Rules*, Rule 14, H. R. i, p. 57. *Cf.* letter to Mersenne, December, 1637, A. T. i, p. 478.

4. Descartes, *Rules*, Rule 4.

5. *Ibid.*, Rules 5 and 6.

6. *Ibid.*, Rule 14, H. R. i, pp. 56, 61, and 63.

7. *Ibid.*, Rules 2 and 5, H. R. i, pp. 5 and 14.

8. *Ibid.*, Rule 4, H. R. i, p. 13. *Cf.* Rule 6, H. R. i, p. 17.

9. Milhaud, *Descartes savant*, pp. 64-9. *Cf.* Descartes, *Discourse*, Pt. 2, H. R. i, p. 93.

10. Descartes, *Rules*, Rule 14, H. R. i, p. 55.

11. Milhaud, *Descartes savant*, pp. 124-32.

12. Descartes, *Rules*, Rule 6, H. R. i, p. 15.

13. Descartes, *Geometry*, A. T. vi, pp. 392-6.

14. Brunschvicg, *Spinoza*, pp. 260-1.

15. *Ibid.*

16. Descartes, *Rules*, Rule 6, H. R. i, pp. 17-18.

17. Vidgrain says that Malebranche was acquainted with it. (Vidgrain, *Christianisme*, p. 23, n. 1.)

18. Malebranche, *Recherche*, Bk. 6, Pt. 1, Ch. 5, L. ii, pp. 184-5 and note, p. 185.

19. Descartes, *Rules*, Rule 12, H. R. i, p. 37.

20. Malebranche, *Recherche*, Bk. 6, Pt. 1, Ch. 4, L. ii, pp. 168-9.

21. *Ibid.*, p. 176.

22. *Ibid.*, p. 175.

23. *Ibid.*, p. 177.

24. *Ibid.*, pp. 169 and 171.

25. Malebranche, *Entretiens sur la métaphysique*, Dial. 5, Sec. 1, Fontana i, p. 104.

26. *Ibid.*, Sec. 2, Ginsberg, p. 145.

27. *Ibid.*, Sec. 7, Ginsberg, p. 150.

28. *Ibid.*, Sec. 12, Ginsberg, p. 157.

29. "On prend donc dans chaque espèce de grandeur telle partie déterminée que l'on veut, pour l'unité ou la mesure commune; par exemple, une toise dans les longeurs, une heure dans les temps, une livre dans les poids, etc. Et toutes ces unités sont divisibles à l'infini." (*Recherche*, Bk. 6, Pt. 1, Ch. 5, L. ii, pp. 185-6.)

30. *E.g.*, *ibid.*, p. 184.

31. Schrecker, *Le parallélisme chez Malebranche*, p. 97.

32. Malebranche, *Recherche*, Bk. 6, Pt. 1, Ch. 5, L. ii, p. 183.

33. *Ibid.*

34. *Ibid.*, p. 184.

35. *Ibid.*, Bk. 5, Ch. 2, L. ii, p. 86.

36. *Ibid.*, Bk. 1, Ch. 4, Sec. 1, L. i, pp. 18-19.

37. *Ibid.*, Bk. 6, Pt. 1, Ch. 5, *passim*.

38. Milhaud, *Descartes savant*, p. 45.

39. *Cf.* Gilson, *Discours*, p. 219, note to p. 20, lines 16-17.

40. Milhaud, *Descartes savant*, p. 73.

41. According to Mouy, Descartes' physics, as that of his disciple, Rohault, is actually more dependent on the imagination than on the understanding.

"La physique cartésienne est une physique mathématique sans mathématiques," Mouy exclaims. "C'est une géométrie concrète, ce n'est pas une géométrie analytique, une algèbre de l'univers." (Mouy, *Physique cartésienne*, p. 144.)

Because Descartes wanted to *see*, to visualize, extension, he had to imagine it as hard and rigid, without rebound, or elasticity. This excessive dependence on geometric construction resulted in laws of motion that, not taking the direction of motion into account, failed to accord with experience.

Unlike Descartes, Huygens' physics, declares Mouy (*Ibid.*, p. 187), rests on calculation, not on imagination. As a result, he made important reformations in Cartesian physics, among them being the realization that it was not the quantity of motion but the algebraic relation that was constant in the impact of bodies.

Now according to Mouy (*Ibid.*, p. 214), when Malebranche began his scientific studies, Huygens was the best representative of Cartesian physics, and Malebranche was the *only* one who appreciated the significance of Huygens' contributions. (*Ibid.*, p. 217)

42. Jean Prestet (1648-1690) was servant and pupil of Malebranche. When in 1675 he published his *Elémens des Mathématiques, ou principes généraux de toutes les sciences qui ont les grandeurs pour objet*, this book, according to Schrecker (Schrecker, *Nombres négatifs*), was considered by Leibnitz, Bayle, and Collins as the work of Malebranche,

above all because "ces Elémens sont entièrement imprégnés des idées de la *Recherche de la Vérité* et la suivent souvent jusqu'au mot." (P. 84.) Schrecker discovered that the second edition (1689) of Prestet's work contains a controversy between Prestet and Arnauld concerning negative numbers. Arnauld, the orthodox Cartesian, believed with Descartes that negative numbers were a pure fiction; Prestet took an opposite position. According to Schrecker, not only may Prestet's theory be considered as the *first* theory on negative numbers, similar in principle, he says, to that given by Hankel in the nineteenth century, but Prestet's explanation "n'est évidemment autre chose que l'application d'idées malebranchiennes au probbleme en question." (P. 84.)

How so? For Prestet *minus* and *plus* are no more than ways or manners of conceiving magnitudes; that is, they are relations or operations among quantities. In this he follows Malebranche's theory that number in general is a relation among magnitudes.

43. Malebranche, *Recherche*, Bk. 6, Pt. 1, Ch. 5, L. ii, p. 184.

44. *Ibid.*, p. 185, n. 1, my ital.

45. Malebranche, *Recherche*, Bk. 6, Pt. 1, Ch. 5, L. ii, p. 185, n. 1.

46. *Ibid.*, p. 184. The omission of "des simples et" is obviously stylistic.

47. Church, *Study*, pp. 186-7; Arnauld, *Vraies et fausses idées*, Ch. 12, pp. 101-4, and Ch. 13, pp. 106 and *sqq.*

48. The very passage which Church here (pp. 186-7) quotes from Malebranche states this denial. Arnauld failed to understand that the basic issue in Malebranche's theory of knowledge relates to the foundation of mathematical truth. (See Chapter II, below.) My present claim, that the meaning of 'Intelligible Extension' is delineated from the very beginning and is no afterthought, is supported below. See Chapter II, Section VII, (g) Malebranche's First Crucial Argu-

ment against Innatism. *Cf.* Cuvillier's edition of the *Entretiens sur la métaphysique*, Dial. 1, note 23, pp. 80-1.

49. Milhaud, *Descartes savant*, p. 198.

50. *Ibid.*, p. 212.

51. *Ibid.*, pp. 213-18.

52. *Ibid.*, p. 218.

53. These appeared in 1637.

54. Descartes, *Discourse*, Pt. II, H. R. i, p. 92.

55. Milhaud, *Descartes savant*, p. 219.

56. H. R. i, p. 3.

57. Labbas (*L'idée de science*, p. 31) identifies Descartes' "experience" with the natural light, with pure intellectual intuition, with "the immediate consciousness of ideas which are in us." This identification is correct. However, Descartes also uses experience in the sense of experiments, and the function of intellectual vision is to discover what is presented by experiments. (H. R. i, p. 4, n.)

Incidentally, Labbas asserts (p. 33) that one must attribute the discovery of analysis to Descartes; that until Descartes, synthesis is regarded as the only truly scientific form of reasoning. This is not the case. Galileo's method of resolution is a form of analysis (*cf.* Burtt, *Foundations of Physics*, p. 70).

58. H. R. i, p. 5.

59. Lalande, *Induction et expérimentation*, p. 85; Milhaud, *Descartes savant*, pp. 219-20.

60. A. T. x, p. 379.

61. H. R. i, pp. 14-15; A. T. x, p. 380; *Cf.* Milhaud, *Descartes savant*, p. 220.

62. H. R. i, pp. 14-15; A. T. x, p. 380.

63. H. R. i, p. 14.

64. *Ibid.*, p. 35.

65. Milhaud, *Descartes savant*, p. 221.

66. H. R. i, p. 8.

67. Lalande, *Induction et expérimentation*, pp. 71-9; Milhaud, *Descartes savant*, p. 219.

68. See above Section I, (a) Malebranche follows Descartes.

69. Bacon, *Novum Organum*, Bk. 2, Aph. 5. *Cf. ibid.*, Bk. 1, Aph. 130 and Bk. 2, Aphs. 8 and 9.

70. *E.g., ibid.*, Bk. 1, Aphs. 18, 19, and 102-105.

71. *Ibid.*, Bk. 2, Aph. 1.

72. *Ibid.*, Bk. 1, Aph. 51 and Bk. 2, Aph. 2.

73. *Ibid.*, Bk. 2, Aphs. 4 and 13.

74. Lalande, *Induction et expérimentation*, pp. 71-9; Bacon, *Advancement of Learning*, Scribner, pp. 142-3.

75. Bacon, *Novum Organum*, Bk. 1, Aph. 96.

76. *Ibid.*, Bk. 2, Aph. 8.

77. *Ibid.*, Bk. 1, Aphs. 94 and 95.

78. Malebranche, *Recherche*, Bk. 6, Pt. 2, Ch. 6, L. ii, p. 239.

79. See *ibid.*, Bk. 1, Ch. 10, L. i, p. 53; *ibid.*, Bk. 6, Pt. 2, Ch. 6, L. ii, pp. 241 and 244; and below, Chapter VI, Sections V and VII.

80. Spinoza, *Improvement*, Scribner, pp. 12-16. Spinoza, of course, was an even more confident rationalist than either Descartes or Malebranche. He objected to Bacon's observation that the intellect can be a distorting ray. For Spinoza, he who has a clear and distinct idea knows it, nor can he doubt it. Hence strictly speaking Spinoza would admit of no preliminary purification of the understanding. He would purify the mind of the errors of sense and of the imagination, but the intellect would never come under any measure or slight degree of suspicion. He takes Descartes' Rule VIII to the letter.

81. Bacon, *Novum Organum*, Bk. 1, Aph. 126.

82. *E.g.*, Malebranche, *Recherche*, Bk. 1, Ch. 2, Sec. 5, L. i, p. 13; Ch. 3, Sec. 1, L. i, pp. 14-15.

83. Spinoza, *Improvement*, Scribner, pp. 13-14.

84. Descartes, *Rules*, Rule 8.

85. *Ibid.*, H. R. i, pp. 24-5.

86. *Ibid.*, pp. 25-6.

87. Malebranche, *Recherche*, Préface, L. i, p. xiv.

88. Spinoza, *Improvement*, Scribner, p. 12.

89. Malebranche, *Recherche*, Bk. 6, Pt. 1, Ch. 2, L. ii, p. 162.

90. Descartes, *Rules*, Rule 3, H. R. i, p. 7.

91. Malebranche, *Recherche*, Bk. 6, Pt. 1, Ch. 1, L. ii, p. 157.

92. *Ibid.*, Préface pour servir de réponse à la Critique du premier volume, L. ii, p. 299.

93. *Ibid.*, Bk. 1, Ch. 20, Sec. 3, L. i, p. 92.

94. Bacon, *Great Instauration*, Preface, Scribner, p. 15.

95. Malebranche, *Recherche*, Bk. 6, Pt. 1, Ch. 1, L. ii, p. 159.

96. *Ibid.*, Ch. 2, L. ii, p. 163.

97. *Ibid.*, Ch. 3, L. ii, p. 167.

98. *Ibid.*, Ch. 5, L. ii, p. 185. *Cf. ibid.*, p. 187. It was in a later edition (the fifth, in 1700) that he first added reference to the differential and the integral calculus, as Mouy observes (*Physique cartésienne*, p. 269). These additions occur in *Recherche*, Bk. 6, Pt. 2, Ch. 6, L. ii, pp. 242-3.

99. *Ibid.*, Bk. 6, Pt. 1, Ch. 1, L. ii, p. 158.

100. *Ibid.*, Pt. 2, Ch. 6, L. ii, p. 241.

101. *Ibid.*, pp. 241-3.

102. *Ibid.*, 243.

103. See above, Section II, (a) Descartes and Bacon.

104. Malebranche, *Recherche*, Bk. 6, Pt. 1, Ch. 4, L. ii, p. 176, my ital.

105. *Ibid.*, Ch. 5, L. ii, pp. 183-4.

106. *Ibid.*, Ch. 4, L. ii, p. 179, n.

107. *Ibid.*, p. 177.

108. *Ibid.*, pp. 176-7.

109. *Ibid.*, Pt. 2, Ch. 6, L. ii, p. 244.

110. Thus on the one hand Malebranche complains against ordinary philosophers who do not employ clear and distinct ideas in physics, and he praises Descartes for having tried to observe this fundamental rule of evidence in his own physics. (*Ibid.*, Ch.

4, L. ii, pp. 206-7.) But on the other hand, Malebranche, unlike Descartes, is not prepared to reduce physics to no more than a system of clear and distinct ideas, to a pure geometry. For him, the laws of motion are not mathematical principles that can be demonstrated on wholly *a priori*, rational grounds. As Mouy observes, for Malebranche, clear and distinct ideas dominate physics but do not constitute it; they leave an irreducible part to experience. (Mouy, *Lois du choc*, p. 11.) This recognition of the irreducible, concrete and contingent element in nature permitted Malebranche, at the instigation of Leibnitz, twice to change his views, in 1692 and 1698, on the laws of motion, in order to make them conform to more exact experimental observation. (*Ibid.*)

For this reason, too, after having developed his own frequency theory of color that far surpassed the theory of color of Newton he was nevertheless able to change his mind (*cf.* Duhem, *Optique*, pp. 85-9) on the nature of the color white to accommodate his doctrine to the experimental observations presented in Newton's *Optics*.

The correspondence between Lelong and Leibniz of September 4, October 23, and December 13, 1707 (O. C. xix, pp. 768-9) give evidence that Malebranche withdrew to the country with Newton's *Optics* to repeat a series of Newton's experiments on color. Robinet comments: "Il est vraisemblable que Malebranche a voulu vérifier ces expériences: il les a trouvées exactes puisqu'il écrira à plusieurs reprises que l'ouvrage de Newton est excellent; il modifiera en conséquence sa théorie du blanc et des couleurs simples en admettant que la blancheur est composée." (*Vocation académicienne*, p. 13.) *Cf.* Mouy, *Malebranche et Newton*.

111. Malebranche, *Recherche*, Bk. 6, Pt. 2, Ch. 1, L. ii, pp. 189-90.

112. *Ibid.*, p. 190. *Cf. ibid.*, Ch. 7, L. ii, p. 248.

113. *Ibid.*, Ch. 1, L. ii, p. 190.

114. *Ibid.*, Ch. 7, L. ii, p. 250.

115. Bacon, *Novum Organum*, Bk. 1, Aph. 98.

116. *Cf.* Bacon, *Advancement of Learning*, Scribner, p. 108.

117. *Ibid.*, p. 178.

118. Bacon, *Novum Organum*, Bk. 1, Aph. 95.

119. *Ibid.*, Aph. 50.

120. *Ibid.*, Aph. 95. *Cf. ibid.*, Aph. 51.

121. *Ibid.*, Aph. 95.

122. Malebranche, *Recherche*, Bk. 2, Pt. 2, Ch. 8, Sec. 4, L. i, pp. 172-3.

123. See above, Section II, (c) Truth Immanent.

124. Church, *Study*, p. 221.

125. Malebranche, *Recherche*, Bk. 6, Pt. 2, Ch. 8, L. ii, pp. 260-1.

126. *Ibid.*, pp. 264-7.

127. *Ibid.*, p. 259.

128. *Ibid.*, pp. 268-9.

129. *Ibid.*, Ch. 4, L. ii, p. 220.

130. *Ibid.*, Bk. 1, Ch. 6, Sec. 1, L. i, pp. 27-9. *Cf. Entretiens sur la métaphysique*, Dial. 11, Sec. 8, Ginsberg, p. 285.

131. Malebranche, *Recherche*, Bk. 6, Pt. 2, Ch. 8, L. ii, p. 269.

132. *Cf.* Lalande, *Induction et expérimentation*, pp. 93 ff., and Mouy, *Physique cartésienne*, p. 220.

133. Descartes, *Rules*, Rule 12, H. R. i, p. 40; *Principles*, Pt. 3, Prins. 44-7, A. T. ix, pp. 123-6; Pt. 4, Prin. 204, A. T. ix, p. 322.

134. Descartes, *Discourse*, Pt. 5, H. R. i, pp. 110-13; *Principles*, Pt. 4, Prins. 205-6, H. R. i, pp. 301-2.

135. Malebranche, *Recherche*, Bk. 6, Pt. 1, Ch. 4, L. ii, p. 177. "Les suppositions établies, elle [la géometrie] nous fait raisonner conséquement."

136. *Cf.* Mouy, *Physique cartésienne*, pp. 114-5.

137. *Ibid.*, pp. 185-7.

138. Gouhier (*Vocation*, pp. 66-88) lists the books contained in Malebranche's library on mathematics and

natural science. Among the latter are works by Gilbert, Kepler, Galileo, and Huygens, collections of experiments by Boyle, Harvey on the generation of animals, works on medicine, anatomy, physiology, plants, insects, *etc.*

Robinet (*Vocation académicienne,* pp. 6-7) states: "On trouvera au tome XX des *Œuvres complètes* [to be published by Vrin] l'édition intégrale du document [a listing by Lelong of the contents of Malebranche's library], un fichier des auteurs par ordre alphabétique et un fichier encyclopédique portant sur les 723 cotes relevées, qui concernent à peu près 1,050 volumes. . . . C'est là une bibliothèque parfaitement choisie, où rien n'est inutile . . ." Robinet divides the works into three kinds:

260 titles: bible, patristic, theology, controversy, ancient languages.
240 titles: philosophy, law, literature, history, arts.
280 titles: mathematics, physics, astronomy, biology, medicine (plus many collections of reviews, making a total of 350 volumes in the sciences).

"On s'aperçoit ainsi," Robinet continues:

que les livres rigoureusement scientifiques de Malebranche occupent à peu près la moitié de ses rayonnages. Ce n'est pas là un accident. Quand les jeunes chercheurs du groupe malebranchiste se retrouvaient chez le maître, ils avaient ainsi sous la main toutes les références de première nécessité. . . . Ce n'est pas la collection des ouvrages qui compte, mais le choix, très net, d'ouvrages d'avantgarde, de recherche, de révélation naturelle, dont la plupart sont l'œuvre d'amis intimes de Malebranche.

139. Mouy, *Physique cartésienne,* pp. 314 and 316.

140. Malebranche, *Recherche,* Bk. 6, Pt. 2, Ch. 9.
141. *Ibid.,* L. ii, pp. 276 and 278.
142. Descartes, *Principles,* Pt. 2, Prin. 55.
143. Malebranche, *Recherche,* Bk. 6, Pt. 2, Ch. 9, L. ii, p. 278.
144. *Ibid.*
145. *Ibid.,* p. 280.
146. *Ibid.,* p. 281.
147. *Ibid.,* pp. 282-5.
148. Later, about 1689, Malebranche abolished Descartes' distinction in physics between the first and second element, by throwing out Descartes' hard balls of the second element. Malebranche identified the subtle matter of the second element with vortices; and the vortices themselves consist of other vortices. Thus everything is fluid motion; hardness or solidity is the result of motion turning back upon itself. *Cf.* Mouy, *Physique cartésienne,* pp. 289-90. A popular account of the relevance of vortices (turbulence) to contemporary physical theories is presented in Gamow, *Turbulence in Space.* Gamow epitomizes the content of the theory in the following verse which he quotes:

Big whirls have little whirls,
That feed on their velocity;
And little whirls have lesser whirls,
And so on to viscosity.

149. Malebranche, *Recherche,* Bk. 6, Pt. 2, Ch. 9, L. ii, pp. 286 ff.
150. Malebranche, *Lois des mouvements,* Avertissement, L. iii, p. 269; O. C. xvii-1, p. 53.
151. *Ibid.,* L., p. 270; O. C., p. 55. Mouy, in his *Lois du choc* and especially in his brilliant *Physique cartésienne,* traces the successive stages in the evolution of Malebranche's physics, showing not only the extent of Leibnitz's influence, but particularly that of the contemporary experimental scientists. I am indeed deeply indebted to these works for helping me to appreciate the magnitude of Malebranche's experimental accomplishment and interests.

Chapter I. Scientific Method

There is one aspect of Malebranche's thought, however, that Mouy, it appears to me, does not sufficiently explore. Under the instigation of Leibnitz, says Mouy, Malebranche was led step by step to renounce all the characteristic features of Cartesian kinetism. He ended by accepting the idea of a matter that was not hard but elastic, and the movements of which conformed not to Descartes' principle of the conservation of motion but to Leibnitz's principle of the conservation of force. (*Lois du choc*, p. 80.) Yet Malebranche remained adamant toward Leibnitz's substantial forms in metaphysics. Why? In Mouy's opinion, this was because Malebranche was opposed to Leibnitz's rationalism and *a priorism*. For Leibnitz, the existence of the world was a truth of reason; for Malebranche it was a historic and contingent fact. (*Physique cartésienne*, p. 277.) According to Mouy, it made no difference to Malebranche what the laws of motion were, provided that they were rational. To be rational, they had to be both mathematical and to conform to the operations of nature, and above all to what Malebranche regarded as the chief core of Cartesianism, namely, that God alone is the efficacious source of motion. (*Lois du choc*, pp. 90-1.) This explains why Malebranche was not drawn to Leibnitz's neo-Aristotelianism. Yet, concludes Mouy, the controversy between Leibnitz and the Cartesians really proves that it is impossible to identify matter with extension and that one must appeal to something called force or energy, and which, as Leibnitz said, is fundamentally spirit. (*Ibid.*, p. 92.)

Mouy's analysis is entirely correct but incomplete. In my interpretation, Malebranche's occasionalism provided him with a more adequate theory than Leibnitz's monads. The Leibnitzian monad is still an essence. By distinguishing between essence and existence, as Malebranche does, Malebranche could retain the Cartesian principle that the essence of matter is extension and at the same time conceive of existence as a participant in God's will and thereby the real source of action. Thus the occasional cause, in so far as it exists, is active. See below, Chapter IV, Secs. II-IV.

See the important remarks of Pierre Costabel in his *Introduction* concerning the fiery and long controversy over Malebranche's views concerning the laws of motion. Especially see Costabel's comment on Mouy, O. C. xvii-1, p. 17.

152. *Cf.* Ginsberg, *Translator's Preface, Entretiens sur la métaphysique*, p. 31.

153. *Cf.* Church, *Study*, p. 51 and *passim*.

154. Although Vidgrain (*Christianisme*) is aware of the influence of Descartes' *Rules* on Malebranche's sixth book on method, he does not seem to appreciate the empirical and experimental aspects of this influence. He tends throughout his study to look upon Malebranche as one who seeks retreat, isolation, departure from the active natural world to contemplative rational solitude in a "cellule aux volets clos." (P. 31.) For Vidgrain, Malebranche's conversion to Cartesianism is exclusively to Descartes' mathematical method and mathematical physics (pp. 12-13), which Malebranche sought to complete by the addition of the Christian metaphysics of Augustine. (Pp. 17-19) This interpretation of Malebranche as a pious visionary interested solely in mathematics and the contents of faith, to the exclusion of natural sciences and the laboratory, is as widely prevalent as it is erroneous.

Blampignon goes even beyond Vidgrain (*Etude*). Not only is Malebranche converted entirely by Descartes' mathematical method, says Blampignon (p. 45), but he is a mystic like St. Theresa who hates the world (p. 190), not like Augustine

[361]

who esteemed science. (Pp. 133-8) He accuses Malebranche's method of an inflexible and excessive rationalism. Malebranche, claims Blampignon, adopted and pushed Descartes' mathematical rules to the point of sacrificing observation and fact. (Pp. 114-5.) Malebranche is no creative genius, ". . . il n'allume point le flambeau de la science." (P. 102.) Unlike Descartes, Malebranche not only defies the senses, but denies their validity altogether. (P. 105.) So great a mystic is Malebranche that he even rejects all human teaching as of zero value! (P. 129.)

While Blampignon regards Malebranche as a faithful, though errant and over-zealously rationalistic disciple of Descartes (pp. 45 and 103), led into wayward mysticism, and while Vidgrain attenuates this "sentimental" mysticism with a heavy dose of Cartesian rationalism (Vidgrain, *Christianisme*, p. 349), Blondel treats Malebranche as wholly anti-Cartesian! (Blondel, *L'Anti-cartésianisme de Malebranche*.) In Blondel's view, while Descartes seeks mastery and empire over nature, Malebranche seeks to vanquish eternity (p. 3); while Descartes is a man of action for whom science is a triumph and conquest of the human mind and will (p. 17) and who is not concerned with knowledge for its own sake but for the sake of power (p. 19), Malebranche seeks to disengage himself from the terrestrial and emigrate to the contemplation of the eternal (*ibid.*). While Descartes bows before God, only to go to the world, Malebranche turns his back on the world to find God. Malebranche is a contemplative that sees philosophy as a means for beatific salvation. (P. 45.) For Malebranche the methodic doubt is not provisional. He does not, like Descartes, seek an ultimate justification for sense and for other faculties, for these have been corrupted by sin. (P. 17.) Therefore for Malebranche only the pure sciences

of geometry and algebra are of importance; sense and consciousness play no role in knowledge. (P. 12.) Descartes reduces everything to motion for the sake of getting positive practical results and detailed explanations, but when Malebranche reduces all to motion it is for the sake of a speculative and general satisfaction. Malebranche does not suspect to what extent his explanations are up in the air. (Pp. 14-15.)

Then again, we have the evaluation of Van Biéma (*Comment Malebranche conçoit la psychologie*). He does, to be sure, call attention to Malebranche's experimental interests as revealed in his treatment on method in Book VI of the *Recherche*. ("Comment etc.", pp. 134-6.) But then Van Biéma concludes that Malebranche does not attend to the method of experimentation and observation for its own sake; in general it is only by accident—to prove something else—that Malebranche signalizes the value of experiments. In his philosophy, there is a relative effacement of the experimental method; Malebranche does not think of employing induction for new research. (Pp. 137-8.) This point of view is still widely prevalent. One of its recent advocates is Ginette Dreyfus. (See her *La volonté*, pp. 140-8)

What a paradox it is that while armchair philosophers have been preoccupied with de-naturalizing Malebranche's philosophy, it is the historians of science, like Duhem, Brunschvicg, Mouy, and Robinet, who have recognized Malebranche's scientific genius and contributions to physics. Moreover, their reevaluation has been made possible not merely by the changes in modern physics that put Cartesian physics in a more favorable light, but actually through a more scrupulous attention to Malebranche's methodology.

155. Bacon, *Novum Organum*, Bk. 1, Aph. 23.

156. *Ibid.*, Aph. 41.

157. Malebranche, *Recherche*, Bk. 2, Pt. 2, Ch. 2, L. i, p. 147.

158. For Spinoza the senses are limited and partial, hence inadequate. Intuition, however, can never go astray and therefore needs no external sign or confirmation whatever. In the deductive process, the mind is a spiritual automaton that requires nothing but its own strength. (Spinoza, *Improvement*, Scribner, p. 34.) And this is true for physics too. Hence, as McKeon has shown, Boyle's and Spinoza's discussion, *via* Oldenburg, on the nature of experiments, is a complete cul-de-sac. Spinoza abandons Bacon as in point of fact Descartes himself did. (McKeon, *Spinoza*, pp. 137 ff.)

159. Descartes, *Rules*, Rule 4, H. R. i, p. 12. *Cf. Discourse*, Pt. 6, H. R. i, p. 121.

160. Even at the end of his career, Descartes claimed in his *Principles* that his work was unfinished, owing to a lack of experiments. (Descartes, *Principles*, Pt. 4, Prin. 188, H. R. i, p. 289.) And he had to modify his hypothesis of round vortices in order to make it agree with the observed elliptical motion of planets. (Mouy, *Physique cartésienne*, p. 28.) Still and all, as Mouy says, experiments played a minor role in Descartes' physics. In the *Principles* Descartes first deduces his laws of motion and the general structure of the world—suns, stars, planets—from God and from his own mind; then only does he call upon experience to provide him with the concrete particulars. (*Ibid.*, p. 44.)

161. Milhaud, *Descartes savant*, pp. 225-7.

162. Gilson, *Liberté*, p. 94. *Cf.* pp. 104-6.

163. Bacon, *Advancement of Learning*, Scribner, pp. 140-1.

164. Bacon, *Novum Organum*, Bk. 2, Aph. 20.

165. Descartes, *Principles*, Author's Letter, H. R. i, p. 211. *Cf. Rules*, Rule 1, H. R. i, p. 2, and especially *Search*, H. R. i, p. 306.

166. "Car ceux qui favorisent Aristote feraient peut-être plus de difficulté de les approuver; et j'espère que ceux qui les liront, s'accoûtumeront insensiblement à mes principes, & en reconnaîtront la vérité avant que de s'appercevoir qu'ils détruisent ceux d'Aristote." Jan. 28, 1641, A. T. iii, p. 298.

167. Descartes was about to send Mersenne his book, *le Monde*, but he changed his mind when, through inquiring after Galileo's *Système du Monde*, he learned that it had been suppressed and its author incarcerated. If, wrote Descartes to Mersenne, the principle of the earth's motion is false, then "tous les fondements de ma Philosophie le sont aussi, car il se démontre par eux évidemment. Et il est tellement lié avec toutes les parties de mon Traité, que je ne l'en saurais détacher, sans rendre le reste tout défectueux." Nevertheless, continues Descartes, he prefers not to publish his book at all rather than incur the censure of the Church. (November, 1633, A. T. i, p. 271.) Descartes never abandoned this attitude. Even at the end of his *Principles* where he feels more than a moral certainty that every phenomenon in nature has been adequately and exactly determined, he yet concludes: "Nevertheless all my opinions are submitted to the authority of the Church." (Descartes, *Principles*, Pt. 4, Prin. 207, H. R. i, p. 302.)

168. See note 166 and *cf.* Gilson, *Liberté*, p. 95.

To a friend of Mersenne who urged him to publish his Physics, Descartes, in a letter of April, 1637, writes this concerning the *Discourse* and the three essays that accompanied its publication, the *Dioptric*, the *Meteors*, and the *Geometry*: "tout le dessein de ce que je fais imprimer à cette fois, n'est que de lui préparer le chemin, & sonder le gué." He goes on to say that if he can once make the world believe that his method, exemplified in the above treatises, "s'étend à tout," he will then no longer fear a poor reception for his physics. (A. T. i, pp. 369-70.)

169. Nov. 25, 1630; A. T. i, p. 182.

170. *Cf.* for example, the letter to Mersenne dated April 15, 1630; A. T. i, pp. 143-4.

171. *Ibid.*, p. 144: Descartes says he could not have found the foundations of his physics had he not begun with God.

172. Descartes, *Principles*, Pt. 2, Prin. 64, H. R. i, p, 269.

173. "Analysis shows the true way by which a thing was methodically discovered and derived, as it were effect from cause [*tanquam a priori*]." (*Reply to Objections II*, H. R. ii, p. 48.)

174. A. T. v, p. 158.

175. In a very early letter to Mersenne (December 18, 1629; A. T. i, p. 86), Descartes asks Mersenne whether there is anything *determinate* in religion concerning the extension of the created world, namely whether it is finite or infinite, for though he has no desire to treat this question, says Descartes, he fears that he will be constrained to do so.

176. Descartes, *Principles*, Pt. 1, Prins. 26 and 27, H. R. i, p. 230.

177. Descartes, *Meditations*, Med. 4, H. R. i, p. 173; *Principles*, Pt. 1, Prin. 28, H. R. i, p. 230.

178. *Ibid.*, Pt. 3, Prins. 2 and 3, H. R. i, pp. 270-1.

179. Descartes, *Reply to Objections V*, H. R. ii, p. 223.

180. Leibnitz, by the introduction of monadic forces into the world of extension, and under the influence of Malebranche's conception of God who acts with design and therefore in the wisest and simplest manner, maintained that physical phenomena could, without contradiction, be accounted for in a twofold way, by a consideration of final as well as of efficient causes. In fact, points out Leibnitz, although the method of efficient causes "goes much deeper and is in a measure more immediate and *a priori*," nevertheless, when it comes to details, the method of final causes "is easier and can be frequently employed to find out important and useful truths which we should have to seek for a long time, if we were confined to that other more physical method." According to Leibnitz, Snellius would have taken much longer had he used the method of efficient causes to discover the laws of refraction. (*Discourse*, Arts. 21 and 22.) But on the assumption of final causes he sought for the simplest direction in which light traveled and thus easily discovered the laws of refraction.

181. Descartes' aim to construct an *a priori* deductive physics not only requires the rejection of the *pursuit* of final causes but also makes it imperative that there be *no* final causes altogether. Why?

Consider his physics. It depends upon the idea of extension and the idea of an immutable veracious God. From the veracity and immutability, Descartes deduces *all* the laws which *must* govern *any* material world, and all the phenomena. This Descartes could not do if his God in creation acted with the purpose of glorifying Himself. How could Descartes know *fully* which laws were the best of all possible or which were the most suitable to God's designs? All that Descartes could know with certainty is that some set of laws is the best and that the best would and does govern the world. But his conclusions as to what these laws are *in toto* would only be conjectural. For the moment you introduce the notion of design, the divine predicate of veracity ceases to function in exclusive and categorical fashion. Without design, veracity can guarantee that everything discovered by a proper order and enumeration *is* as it is discovered and also *that there is no more to be discovered*. But if there is design in the world, veracity can guarantee no more than this, namely, that what is discovered does fit into the best of all possible schemes, but not the fact that there is no more to be discovered. But Descartes believed that his physical system was complete and exhaustive.

Moreover, notwithstanding the fact that Descartes spoke of his physics as a "fable" or "hypothesis," actually he held it as an indubitable demonstration for anyone who accepted his metaphysics. Thus, it is not sufficient for Descartes merely to renounce the *use* of final causes; the mere possibility that there is design would compromise his system.

182. Gilson states: It is because Descartes desires to destroy even in its foundation the finalistic conception of nature that he finds himself obliged to ascend as far as God and to modify profoundly the conception which the School made of his liberty.

While I agree with Gilson's thesis, nevertheless, my own point of view is that the doctrine of created truths has a much broader function, namely, to vindicate the general egocentrism of Descartes. For this doctrine, by destroying the possibility of utilizing the hazardous road of probable knowledge, implied by final causes, thereby once and for all barricades the human mind against any contact with God. Thenceforth there is no other avenue by which the mind can know the nature of the world except by turning to itself. By making a veracious but arbitrary Deity the efficient cause of ideas, Descartes achieves two results with one bold stroke. On the one hand, divine veracity gives him real knowledge, not merely phenomenal. But on the other hand, that knowledge is derivative from the isolation and security of his own mind. *Cf. La Liberté.*

183. A. T. i, p. 145.

184. To Mersenne, May 6, 1630, A. T. i, pp. 149-50.

185. *Ibid.*, p. 149.

186. *Reply to Objections VI*, H. R. ii, p. 248.

187. Letter to Mesland, May 2, 1644, A. T. iv, p. 118, and to Mersenne, May 27, 1630, A. T. i, p. 152.

188. *Reply to Objections VI*, H. R. ii, p. 248.

189. To Mersenne, May 27, 1630, A. T. i, p. 153.

190. To Mersenne, May 6, 1630, A. T. i, p. 149. "Je dis derechef que *sunt tantum verae aut possibiles, quia Deus illas veras aut possibiles cognoscit, non autem contra veras à Deo cognosci quasi independenter ab illo sint verae.*"

191. "Je dis que *ex hoc ipso quod illas ab aeterno esse voluerit & intellexerit, illas creavit*, ou bien (si vous n'attribuez le mot de *creavit* qu'à l'existence des choses) *illas disposuit & fecit.*" To Mersenne, May 27, 1630, A. T. i, pp. 152-3.

192. H. R. ii, p. 34.

193. "Vous me demandez *in quo genere causae Deus disposuit aeternas veritates.* Je vous réponds que c'est *in eodem genere causae* qu'il a créé toutes choses, c'est à dire *ut efficiens & totalis causa.* Car il est certain qu'il est aussi bien auteur de l'essence comme de l'existence des créatures: or cette essence n'est autre chose que ces vérités éternelles, lesquelles je ne conçois point émaner de Dieu comme les rayons du soleil." To Mersenne, May 27, 1630, A. T. i, pp. 151-2.

194. *Reply to Objections VI*, H. R. ii, pp. 250-1.

195. *Ibid.* V, H. R. ii, p. 226.

196. *Cf. Objections VI*, H. R. ii, p. 238 and *Reply to Objections VI*, H. R. ii, p. 251.

197. To Mersenne, May 6, 1630, A. T. i, p. 150.

198. To Mersenne, April 15, 1630, A. T. i, p. 146.

199. To Mersenne, May 6, 1630, A. T. i, p. 150. The incomprehensibility of God makes us esteem him all the more, just as a king has greater majesty the less familiarly he is known

to his subjects; provided, however, Descartes adds significantly, that they do not for all that think of being without a king, and that they know him sufficiently not to doubt of him. To Mersenne, April 15, 1630, A. T. i, p. 145.

200. *Cf*: ". . . on peut savoir que Dieu est infini et tout-puissant, encore que notre âme étant finie ne le puisse comprendre ni concevoir; de même que nous pouvons bien toucher avec les mains une montagne, mais non pas l'embrasser comme nous ferions un arbre . . . car comprendre, c'est embrasser de la pensée; mais pour savoir une chose il suffit de la toucher de la pensée." To Mersenne, May 27, 1630, A. T. i, p. 152. *Cf*. letter to Clerselier, H. R. ii, p. 130. Notice that Descartes distinguishes *savoir*, on the one hand, from *comprendre* and *concevoir*, on the other. Malebranche will agree with Descartes on *comprendre* but not on *concevoir*.

201. Consult Gilson, *Liberté*, p. 104-5; see reply to Burman, April 16, 1648, A. T. v, p. 166.

202. *Reply to Objections V*, H. R. ii, p. 218.

203. "These truths that are called eternal, as that the *whole is greater than its part*, . . ." (to Mersenne, May 27, 1638, A. T. ii, p. 138); also ". . . eternal truths . . . which are called common notions, as *it is impossible* [for a thing both to be and not be]" (to Burman, A. T. v, p. 167). Descartes does not give the complete statement of the axiom.

204. To Mersenne, May 27, 1630, A. T. i, p. 152. *Cf*. also letter to Mesland, May 2, 1644, A. T. iv, p. 118, where Descartes maintains that God could even have made contradictories to exist together.

205. *Reply to Objections VI*, H. R. ii, p. 251.

206. *Ibid.*, pp. 250-1. Supreme indifference is the very mark of divine omnipotence. But how, asked the theologians, may we assert indiffer-

ence as a perfection in God's will and a defect in human will, since the essences of things are indivisible? To this Descartes replied that the attributes of God and man are not univocal. Because man finds the nature of truth and goodness already determined for him, what constitutes a perfection in God would be an impiety in man. *Ibid.*, pp. 248-9.

207. Boutroux, Gilson maintains (*Liberté*, p. 94), tried to save finality in Descartes, by offering such an interpretation of Descartes as to oblige him to reintroduce that very distinction among the divine attributes that Descartes explicitly and in certain terms rejected. *Vérités éternelles*, Chs. 4 and 5.

208. To the anonymous Hyperaspistes he writes: "ce serait toutefois une chose puérile et absurde d'assurer en métaphysique que Dieu, à la façon d'un homme superbe, n'aurait point eu d'autre fin, en bâtissant le monde, que cella d'être loué par les hommes." A. T. iii, p. 431. French translation by Garnier, iv, pp. 273-4. *Cf*. also, correspondence with Burman, A. T. v, p. 158. On the other hand, in his letter to Chanut, Descartes does not hesitate to employ the glory of God as a reason for *disproving* a finite universe made for man. A. T. v, pp. 53-4.

209. *Principles*, Pt. 1, Prin. 26, H. R. i, pp. 229-30.

210. *Principles*, Pt. 1, Prin. 24, H. R. i, p. 229. *Cf. Reply to Objections V*, H. R. ii, p. 223.

211. Descartes' view of created truths and his banishment of final causes is intended, as Le Moine observes, to avert man's gaze from the supernatural to the natural and terrestrial: "La vie future? ce n'est pas elle qui saurait nous intéresser: occupons-nous de la vie présente, tâchons de pénétrer la nature et de nous en rendre maîtres. Dieu peut tout? nous aussi, dans notre domaine, soyons tout-puissants; et, puisque le ciel demeure fermé à notre spéculation, pos-

sédons la terre. (Le Moine, *Vérités éternelles*, p. 188.)" And this desire to become the master and possessor of nature (Descartes, *Discourse*, Pt. 6, H. R. i, p. 119) reflects, of course, Descartes' firm allegiance to Bacon (for example, *Novum Organum*, Bk. 1, Aph. 129).

212. Descartes, *Principles*, Pt. I, Prin. 30. Descartes, under criticism, claimed that the existence of God was necessary to guarantee, not our clear and distinct perceptions, but solely the memory of them. This was his reply to Arnauld and to the critics of the second set of objections who charged him with circular reasonings. Nevertheless, such statements as: I may be deceived *each time that I add 3 and 2 together* (*Meditations*, Med. 1, H. R. i, p. 174), make it difficult to accept Descartes' answer. Moreover, as Bréhier points out (*Histoire de la philosophie*, Vol. 2, Pt. 1, p. 81), and as Leibnitz did before him (On Descartes' *Principles*, "On Article 5," Duncan, pp. 48-9. *Cf.* "On Article 13," p. 50), memory remains as fallible subsequent to the knowledge of a non-deceiving God as before.

On the other hand, if Descartes did not seek to guarantee memory but really doubted in the immediate present what appears to be most evident, then, again as Leibnitz says, such a doubt would be absolutely insuperable and Descartes would be stymied at the very outset. (*Ibid.*) As a matter of fact, the problem of memory is really the problem of the continued existence of a truth formerly perceived. And in the presence of a proposition such as $4 + 3 = 7$, while Descartes maintains that the mind cannot indeed doubt its truth, nevertheless he does also assert that: "It is requisite that we may be assured that all the things which we conceive clearly and distinctly are true in the very way in which we think them." (*Meditations*, Synopsis of the Meditations, H. R. i, p. 140.)

Of course even this interpretation still has its difficulties. Even if we assume that the issue of memory is fundamentally a problem concerning the future permanent existence of a truth now perceived, Descartes would again be impelled to limit the sphere of the doubt. If the continued subsistence of every evident proposition, such as, what has been done cannot be undone, were doubted, Descartes would again be thwarted at the outset. Now, as a matter of fact, Descartes clearly claims in the *Principles* that "there is no doubt" that to those who are free from prejudices that class of propositions known as common notions or axioms are perfectly manifest. (*Principles*, Pt. 1, Prin. 50, H. R. i, p. 239.) Descartes distinguishes these axioms from our other cognitions in that they yield no knowledge of anything that may exist. (*Ibid.*, Prin. 10, H. R. i, p. 222, and Prin. 49, pp. 238-9.)

Because Descartes thus distinguishes between perceptions that have reference to possible existence and such general principles or "eternal truths" as *ex nihilo nihil fit*, Gueroult, Gilson and Levy-Bruhl maintain that the Cartesian doubt does not bear upon essences but only upon existential propositions. (See Gilson, *Discours*, p. 287; Gueroult, *Le cogito*, p. 57.)

I cannot, however, accept the interpretation of these authors. Consider Gueroult's claim. He says that Descartes does not doubt the internal, ineluctable necessity of such notions as $3 + 2 = 5$, or that the square has four sides, but that all that Descartes doubts is whether anything exists outside his thought comparable to these notions. Gueroult supports his claim by the fact that Descartes in the third Meditation asserts that ideas considered by themselves are not false, that falsity enters only into our judgments.

Yet if we attend to Descartes' statements in the first Meditation, there can be no question that Descartes doubts the intrinsic necessity of $3 + 2 = 5$ apart from any consideration of its objective external existence. There Descartes doubts the definition or essence of a square and not merely whether a square exists.

But, one will ask, what about this third Meditation which says that when we consider ideas in themselves "and do not relate them to anything else beyond themselves," they cannot be false? And what about Descartes' statement to Clerselier: I have not rejected the simple ideas or notions which contain no affirmation or negation, but only the judgments in which alone there can be error or truth? (H. R. ii, p. 127.)

Evidently there are two ways of relating ideas beyond themselves; there are two kinds of judgments that one can make about ideas. One kind of judgment, one way of relating an idea to something beyond itself, is to affirm that what is perceived in the present will hold for all times. Another kind of judgment or another way of relating an idea beyond itself is to affirm that something exists conformable to the idea. Thus I would suggest that while Descartes does exempt *some* non-existential propositions such as "what has been done cannot be undone" from the sphere of doubt, he nonetheless does not exclude all of them. Such propositions which do not involve relations among determinate representative ideas and which are indispensable for any discourse are free from doubt. On the other hand all such propositions as $3 + 2 = 5$, or a square has 4 sides, which involve simple natures are subject to a doubt, that is, to their continued existence.

213. April 15, 1630, A. T. i, p. 145-6.

214. Gilson, *Liberté*, pp. 51-56.

215. My supposition that Descartes' doubt concerning mathematical truths stems from the possibility of an all-powerful deity creating and altering these ideas in the future, and my claim that Descartes introduces *causa-sui* to combat this possibility were suggested to me by a reading of two texts. In his *Histoire de la philosophie* (Vol. 2, Pt. 1, p. 69), Bréhier declares that Descartes could hardly have imagined the evil demon had he not entertained the doctrine of created verities. Bréhier, however, offers no explanation of this correlation. On the other hand, Gilson in his *Etudes* asserts: "L'évidence peut se suffire et se suffit, mais elle ne garantit pas l'infaillibilité de la mémoire; elle ne garantit même pas la permanence de sa propre vérité dans l'intervalle de deux intuitions. Pour que ce qui *est* vrai, *reste* vrai, il faut donc une garantie distincte de l'évidence même, un principe stable de certitude . . ." (P. 237). But as long as we abstain, as Gilson does in this text, from considering Descartes' doctrine of created truths, it is by no means self-evident that a principle is required to guarantee the permanence of a truth once perceived and remembered. Once we do correlate created truths with the demon, however, then not only does it become clear that some principle is required to guarantee the future status of ideas, but also that *causa-sui* is the only possible principle.

Descartes' doctrine of *causa-sui* is ordinarily treated as being exclusively a metaphysical innovation. His attempt to drive the axiom of efficient causality to its last limits is sometimes interpreted as being the only effective means by which Descartes could reach an existence other than that of his own mind and at the same time do so through the traditional principle of efficient causality. Such is Gilson's interpretation for example. Sometimes in this principle of *causa-sui* one finds the influence of Descartes' mathematical training.

No one so far as I know has given it an interpretation in relation to the epistemology of Descartes. Yet when we consider that his metaphysics and mathematics are primarily oriented to his physics and all three are concerned with certainty, my epistemological approach to the doctrine of *causa-sui* seems more than justified.

216. *Cf.* Bréhier, *Histoire de la Philosophie*, Vol. 2, Pt. 1, p. 69.

217. *E.g.*, Descartes, *Reply to Objections IV*, H. R. ii, p. 111.

218. *Ibid.*, p. 109 and *Reply to Objections I*, H. R. ii, pp. 14-15.

219. Descartes, *Principles*, Pt. 1, Prin. 20, H. R. i, p. 227; *Meditations*, Med. 2, H. R. i, p. 168; *Discourse*, Pt. 4, H. R. i, pp. 102-3.

220. Descartes, *Meditations*, Med. 3, H. R. i, p. 166 and Med. 4, H. R. i, pp. 172-3. *Cf.* "La vérité consiste en l'être et la fausseté au *non-être* seulement, en sorte que l'idée de l'infini, comprenant tout l'être, comprend tout ce qu'il y a de vrai dans les choses, et ne peut avoir en soi rien de faux." To Clerselier, April 23, 1649, A. T. v, p. 356.

221. "Omnem fraudem à defectu pendere, mihi est lumine naturali manifestum; quia ens in quo nulla est imperfectio, non potest tendere in non ens, hoc est, pro fine & instituto suo habere non ens, sive non bonum, sive non verum; haec enim tria idem sunt. In omni autem fraude esse falsitatem manifestum est, falsitatemque esse aliquid non verum, & ex consequenti non ens & non bonum." *Ibid.*, A. T. v, p. 357.

222. Descartes, *Meditations*, Med. 3, H. R. i, p. 171; *ibid.*, Med. 4, H. R. i, p. 172; *Principles*, Pt. 1, Prin. 29, H. R. i, p. 231. *Cf.* preceding note.

223. *Cf.*, for example, Descartes, *Passions*, Pt. 1, Art. 48, and Pt. 3,

Art. 170, H. R. i, pp. 354 and 409. *Discourse*, Pt. 3, second maxim, H. R. i, p. 96.

224. Descartes, *Principles*, Pt. 2, Prin. 36 applies to essences; it does not apply to existences. God is potent in guaranteeing the immutability of truth, but the constant changes in created objects not only implies no variation in His power, but confirms it. (*Ibid.*, Prin. 42.)

225. April 15, 1630, A. T. i, pp. 145-6, my ital.

226. Descartes, *Principles*, Pt. 1, Prin. 30, H. R. i, p. 231.

227. *Ibid.*, Pt. 4, Prins. 205 and 206, H. R. i, p. 301.

228. Descartes, *Reply to Objections IV*, H. R. ii, pp. 108-10.

229. Perhaps another reason that impels Descartes to *causa-sui* is this. His method is to proceed not from the unknown to the known, but from the known to the unknown. A perfect science is to go from an efficient cause that is known to a deduction of its effects. If God is conceived in negative terms as uncaused, it is like proceeding from nothing to something. But *per se* in the positive sense implies starting from the known. Consequently Descartes asserts that just as the notion of the impossibility of an infinite regress is merely a negative doctrine revealing the limits of the mind, so self-originated in its negative meaning "proceeds merely from the imperfection of the human intellect." *Reply to Objection I*, H. R. ii, p. 15.

230. Bacon, *Novum Organum*, Bk. 1, Aph. 23. *Cf. ibid.*, Aph. 124.

231. Milhaud, *Descartes savant*, p. 227.

CHAPTER II. VISION IN GOD

1. Malebranche, *Recherche*, Bk. 3, Pt. 2, Ch. 1, Sec. 1, L. i, p. 234.

This passage may be an echo of Descartes, *Passions*, Pt. 1, Art. 33, H. R. i, p. 346: ". . . It is not more necessary that our soul should exer-

cise its functions immediately in the heart, in order to feel its passions there, than it is necessary for the soul to be in the heavens in order to see the stars there."

We must not be misled by this passage and hastily conclude that Malebranche is here denying direct perception of external bodies. Taken in its context, it makes merely these claims: *First*, we do not "see" bodies in themselves, because we discriminate one body from another through sensible qualities, which, however, do not belong to the bodies, but are modifications of the soul. Sensations are thus like vehicles, or like windows through which we distinguish objects. *Secondly*, Malebranche uses "perceive" in the sense of understand. In this sense, bodies as particular material facts are no more than brute isolated facts. As such, they are not intelligible in themselves, in their factuality. They become knowable only when grasped in their essence or through universals. Malebranche even uses a Platonic image—just as vision requires a good eye and an object and the sun, so the understanding must be sound, and it requires ideas to shine and act upon it. *Such Platonism does not necessarily imply a copy theory of perception*, although critic after critic has gratuitously assumed that the above passage necessarily entails a copy theory.

2. Malebranche, *Réponse au Livre des vraies, etc.*, Ch. 11, Sec. 7, p. 350 and Ch. 12, Sec. 7, p. 353.

3. Church, *Study*, p. 116.

4. See Gilson, *Augustin*, pp. 311-17.

5. Observe the procedure which Malebranche employs throughout his *Entretien d'un philosophe chrétien et d'un philosophe chinois* and note his statement in the *Avis au lecteur*, p. 95, Le Moine edition; O. C. xv, p. 39.

6. Bacon, *Advancement of Learning*, Scribner, p. 133. Malebranche, *Recherche*, Bk. 2, Pt. 1, Ch. 5, Sec. 1, L. i, p. 110.

7. Malebranche, *Avis*, p. 114, Le Moine edition; O. C. xv, p. 54.

8. See Malebranche's autobiographical sketch in his *Réponse au Livre des vraies, etc.*, Ch. 1, pp. 269-274.

9. Malebranche, *Recherche*, Ecl. 15, L. iii, pp. 141-2.

10. Malebranche, *Recherche*, Préface pour servir de réponse à la Critique du premier volume, L. ii, p. 299.

11. Brunschvicg, *Expérience et causalité*, p. 206.

12. *Ibid.*, pp. 244-5.

13. *Ibid.*, pp. 199-200.

14. Bacon, *Novum Organum*, Bk. 2, Aph. 2.

15. See above, Chapter I, Sec. 2, (a) "Descartes and Bacon."

16. Bacon, *Novum Organum*, Bk. 1, Aph. 105. *Cf. Advancement of Learning*, Scribner, p. 139: ". . . The speculation was excellent in Parmenides and Plato, although but a speculation in them, That all things by scale did ascend to unity. So then always that knowledge is worthiest, which is charged with least multiplicity; which appeareth to be Metaphysic; as that which considereth the Simple Forms or Differences of things, which are few in number, and the degrees and co-ordinations whereof make all this variety." Also compare *ibid.*, p. 137: ". . . It is manifest that Plato in his opinion of Ideas, as one that had a wit of elevation situate as upon a cliff, did descry *that forms were the true object of knowledge* [author's ital.] . . ." (*Cf.* Anderson, *Bacon*, pp. 129-30.)

17. *Ibid.* The passage just quoted, after affirming that Plato did descry that Forms were the true object of knowledge, continues thus: ". . . But [he] lost the real fruit of his opinion, by considering of forms as absolutely abstracted from matter, and not confined and determined by matter; and so turning his opinion upon Theology, wherewith all his natural philosophy is infected. . . . To enquire the Form of a lion, of an oak, of gold, nay of water, of air, is a vain pursuit: but to enquire the Forms of sense, of voluntary motion, of vegetation, of colours, of gravity and levity, of density, of tenuity, of heat, of cold, and all other

natures and qualities, . . . to enquire I say the *true forms* of these, is that part of Metaphysic which we now define of."

18. *E.g.*, Bacon, *Great Instauration*, Scribner, p. 22.

19. *Recherche*, Bk. 1, Ch. 1, L. i, pp. 1-2.

20. *Ibid.*, Chs. 1-2, L. i, pp. 1-12.

21. *Ibid.*, Ch. 4, Sec. 1, L. i, pp. 18-19.

22. *Ibid.*

23. Bacon, *Novum Organum*, Bk. 1, Aph. 67.

24. *Ibid.*, Aph. 37.

25. *Ibid.*, Aph. 41.

26. Descartes, *Reply to Objections VII*, H. R. ii, p. 282.

27. André, *Vie du R. P. Malebranche*, p. 15.

28. Malebranche, *Réponse au Livre des vraies, etc.*, Ch. 5, Sec. 1, p. 308.

29. Newton, *Principia*, Newton's Preface to First Edition, Cajori, pp. xvii-xviii; *ibid.*, Bk. 3, Rules of Reasoning, Cajori, pp. 398-9; *ibid.*, Bk. 3, General Scholium, Cajori, p. 547.

30. Malebranche, *Recherche*, Préface pour servir de réponse à la Critique du premier volume, Réponse a, L. ii, p. 303.

31. *Ibid.*, Réponse d, L. ii, pp. 303-4.

32. *Ibid.*, Bk. 6, Pt. 1, Ch. 1, L. ii, p. 157; *ibid.*, Préface pour servir de réponse à la Critique du premier volume, L. ii, p. 311.

33. *Ibid.*, Bk. 1.

34. *Ibid.*, Ch. 10, L. i, p. 53.

35. *Ibid.*, Bk. 3, Pt. 2, Ch. 1, Sec. 1, L. i, pp. 234-5.

36. Church, *Study*, pp. 202 and 184, and Ch. 10, especially p. 238.

37. *E.g.*, André, *Vie du R. P. Malebranche*, p. 189. *Cf. Réponse à Régis*, Ch. 2, L. iii, pp. 243-4 or O. C. xvii-1, pp. 280-1; and see above, first paragraphs of this chapter.

38. See below, Chapter 6, Section IV.

39. Pang Ching-jen, *Malebranche et Tchou Hi*, p. 20.

40. *Cf.* Bacon, *Novum Organum*, Pt. 1, Aph. 105: ". . . Induction which proceeds by simple enumeration is childish . . ."

41. Malebranche, *Entretiens sur la métaphysique*, Dial. 1, Secs. 4-5, Ginsberg, pp. 74-5.

42. *Ibid.*, Sec. 5, Ginsberg, p. 75, my ital.

43. Malebranche, *Conversations*, Dial. 6, p. 154, Bridet edition or O. C. iv, p. 134; *Réponse au Livre des vraies, etc.*, Ch. 24, Sec. 10, p. 432.

44. Malebranche, *Réponse à Régis*, Ch. 2, L. iii, p. 263 or O. C. xvii-1, pp. 309-10; *Entretiens sur la métaphysique*, Préface de l'auteur, Fontana i, p. 21.

45. Church, *Study*, pp. 116 and 119.

46. Malebranche, *Recherche*, Ecl. 10, L. iii, p. 75, my ital.

47. *Ibid.*

48. Delbos, *Etude*, p. 200.

49. For example, Descartes, *Reply to Objections III* and *Reply to Objections V*, H. R. ii, pp. 67, 215, 217, and 229.

50. Descartes, *Reply to Objections II*, H. R. ii, p. 53.

51. Malebranche, *Recherche*, Bk. 1, Ch. 1, Sec. 1, L. i, pp. 18-19.

52. Descartes, *Reply to Objections II*, Arguments demonstrating God, H. R. ii, p. 52. *Cf.*, *Meditations*, Med. 2, H. R. i, p. 153, and *Principles*, Pt. 1, Prin. 9, H. R. i, p. 222.

53. Malebranche, *Recherche*, Bk. 3, Pt. 2, Ch. 1, Sec. 1, L. i, p. 235.

54. Descartes, *Reply to Objection VI*, H. R. ii, pp. 252-3; *Meditations*, Med. 2, H. R. i, p. 155; *Rules*, Rule 8, H. R. i, p. 27. Malebranche, *Recherche*, Bk. 1, Ch. 4, Sec. 1, L. i, pp. 18-19; *ibid.*, Bk. 3, Pt. 2, Ch. 3, L. i, pp. 241-2; *Entretiens sur la métaphysique*, Dial. 5, Sec. 12.

55. Descartes, *Rules*, Rule 15, H. R. i, p. 65. Malebranche, *Entretiens sur la métaphysique*, Dial. 5, Secs. 1, 2 and 7.

56. Descartes, *Rules*, Rule 12, H. R. i, pp. 41, 45 and 46.

57. *E.g.*, Malebranche, *Recherche*, Bk. 3, Pt. 2, Ch. 1, Sec. 1, L. i, p. 235. *Cf.* his employment of Plato's simile of the sun, *ibid.*, Bk. 6, Pt. 1, Ch. 1, L. ii, p. 159.

58. Descartes, *Reply to Objections III*, H. R. ii, p. 68.

59. *Ibid., II*, Definition 2, H. R. ii, p. 52. *Cf. ibid., III*, H. R. ii, p. 68, and letter to Mersenne, July, 1641, A. T. iii, pp. 392-3.

60. Malebranche, *Recherche*, Bk. 1, Ch. 1, Sec. 1, L. i, p. 4.

61. See Gilson, *Discours*, pp. 318-21.

62. Ideas that are clear are sensations. If clear, but not distinct, they are confused perceptions. But ideas which present the nature of things must be both clear and distinct. Descartes, *Principles*, Pt. 1, Prins. 45 and 46, H. R. i, p. 237; *Meditations*, Med. 3, H. R. i, p. 159.

63. In the *Meditations* only the ideas of the soul, of God, and of extension are said to be innate. (Meds. 3 and 5, H. R. i, pp. 170 and 179.) In Descartes' *Notes against a Programme*, he speaks of sensations as innate. (H. R. i, p. 443.) But see his letter to Mersenne of June 16, 1641 (A. T. iii, p. 383) where he indicates unambiguously what is the comprehension of innate ideas: ". . . ut Idea Dei, Mentis, Corporis, Trianguli, & generaliter omnes quae aliquas Essentias Veras, Immutabiles & Aeternas representant."
Consult Gouhier, *Philosophie de Malebranche*, pp. 257-65.

64. Malebranche, *Recherche*, Ecl. 3, L. iii, p. 19.

65. *Ibid.*, Bk. 1, Ch. 1, Sec. 1, L. i, p. 4.

66. Malebranche, *Entretiens sur la métaphysique*, Dial. 1, Sec. 5, Ginsberg, p. 30.

67. ". . . Je ne puis avoir aucune connaissance de ce qui est hors de moi, que par l'entremise des idées que j'en ai eu en moi," writes Descartes to Gibieuf. (Jan. 19, 1642, A. T. iii, p. 474.)

68. Descartes, *Reply to Objections III*, H. R. ii, pp. 67-8.

69. Malebranche, *Recherche*, Bk. 3, Pt. 2, Ch. 7, Sec. 1, L. i, pp. 255-6.

70. In the *Rules* Descartes declares: ". . . Each individual can mentally have intuition of the fact that he exists, and that he thinks; that the triangle is bounded by three lines only, the sphere by a single superficies, and so on. Facts of such a kind are far more numerous than people think . . ." (Rule 3, H. R. i, p. 7.)

71. Descartes, in the *Rules*, declares that when he focuses upon the objects of the understanding, then his task is "to distinguish accurately the notions of simple things from those which are built up out of them. . . . We shall treat of things only in relation to our understanding's awareness of them, and shall call those only simple, the cognition of which is so clear and so distinct that they cannot be analyzed by the mind into others more distinctly known. . . . All others we conceive to be in some way compounded out of these." (Rule 12, H. R. i, pp. 40-1.)

72. *Meditations*, Med. 3, H. R. i, pp. 161-2.

73. *Ibid.*; to Regius, June, 1642, A. T. iii, pp. 566-7.

74. *Reply to Objections IV*, H. R. ii, p. 105.

75. *Meditations*, Med. 5, H. R. i, p. 180.

76. *Reply to Objections III*, H. R. ii, p. 66. *Cf.* Gilson, *Discours*, pp. 318-321.

77. *Meditations*, Med. 3, H. R. i, p. 170, and Med. 5, H. R. i, p. 179.

78. See above, Chapter I, Section III, "Descartes' Efforts to guarantee Truth."

79. Descartes, *Discourse*, Pt. 4, H. R. i, p. 101.

80. H. R. i, p. 180.

81. *Ibid.*, p. 181.

82. Malebranche, *Recherche,* Bk. 6, Pt. 2, Ch. 6, L. ii, pp. 241-2.

83. Malebranche, *Entretiens sur la métaphysique,* Dial. 1, Sec. 4, Ginsberg, p. 74.

84. *Ibid.,* Sec. 8, Ginsberg, pp. 79-80.

85. *Ibid.,* Secs. 4 and 5.

86. Malebranche, *Recherche,* Bk. 3, Pt. 2, Ch. 1, Sec. 1, L. i, pp. 234-5; *Entretiens sur la métaphysique,* Dial. 1, Secs. 4 and 6.

87. *Recherche,* Bk. 1, Ch. 3, Sec. 1, L. i, p. 15.

88. *Ibid.,* Bk. 3, Pt. 1, Ch. 4, Sec. 5, L. i, p. 233.

89. Malebranche, *Conversations,* Dial. 7, p. 192, Bridet edition; O. C. iv, p. 164.

90. Descartes, *Reply to Objections II,* Axiom I, H. R. ii, p. 55.

91. *Ibid.,* I, H. R. ii, p. 11.

92. *Ibid.,* H. R. ii, pp. 10-12.

93. *Ibid.*

94. Descartes says: ". . . Lorsque je vois un bâton, il ne faut pas s'imaginer qu'il sorte de lui de petites images voltigeantes par l'air, appelées vulgairement des espèces intentionnelles, qui passent jusques à mon œil . . ." *Reply to Objections VI,* A. T. ix, pp. 236-7. Gouhier, *Philosophie de Malebranche,* pp. 225-6.

95. To Regius, Descartes actually uses the phrase, *unum per se.* (A. T. iii, p. 508.)

96. Gilson, *Etudes,* pp. 20-21. But once the species have become intellectualized, then the mind forms or constructs the concept proper. This is distinct from the object and a substitute for it. Gilson, *Aquinas,* pp. 269-70.

97. Gilson, *Etudes,* pp. 23-5.

98. Schrecker in his edition of Malebranche (p. 430, note 119), points out that the *animal spirits,* which play so important a role in the mechanistic physiology of Descartes and Malebranche, were considered by the medievals as semi-spiritual and semi-physical, thus also serving as a link between mind and body. But Descartes rejected this dual character and treated the animal spirits entirely as material, as likewise did Malebranche.

99. Malebranche, *Recherche,* Bk. 3, Pt. 2, Ch. 2, L. i, p. 237.

100. *Ibid.,* pp. 237-9.

101. *Ibid.,* p. 239.

102. Descartes, *Objections III,* H. R. ii, pp. 76-7 and *ibid.* V, H. R. ii, pp. 182-5 and 190-2.

103. *Ibid. III,* H. R. ii, pp. 61-2 and 65: Hobbes, *Leviathan,* Pt. 1, Chs. 1-3; *Elements,* Pt. 4, Ch. 25; Descartes, *Objections V,* H. R. ii, pp. 137-51. Also *cf.* Newton's curious statement in the *Opticks,* cited by Burtt, *Foundations of Physics,* p. 258: "Is not the sensory of animals that place to which the sensitive substance is present, and into which the sensible species of things are carried through the nerves and brain, that there they may be perceived by their immediate presence to that substance?" Yet, of course, we must not lose sight of his statements concerning our knowledge of absolute space, time and motion. (Newton, *Principia,* Definitions, Def. 8, Scholium, Cajori, pp. 6-12.)

104. Dial. 2, Secs. 7-9, Ginsberg, pp. 93-4, my ital.

105. Malebranche begins his discussion of ideas with certain statements that appear inconsistent to Arnauld. These statements are: the mind does not take a walk in the heavens in order to perceive objects there; the immediate object of perception is an idea; minds and bodies cannot interact. Arnauld claimed that for an object to be known it was not necessary for it to act on the mind or to be united with it. (Arnauld, *Vraies et fausses idées,* Ch. 10, pp. 83-4; Ch. 12, p. 101; and Chs. 4 and 5.) But, as Le Moine observes (*Vérités éternelles,* p. 80), Arnauld completely failed to understand Malebranche. Neither does Church, I may add, and for the same reasons. For both Church

and Arnauld do not realize, as Le Moine does, that the basic issue revolved about ideas as essences and as eternal truths. It does not seriously matter for Malebranche whether minds and bodies cannot interact. The real problem is whether a particular body can act so as to engender a universal. Thus the relevant question is whether an essence is a manufactured, fabricated entity. On the first alternative it has to be, but Malebranche insists that this would destroy all possibility of truth.

106. Malebranche, *Recherche*, Bk. 3, Pt. 2, Ch. 3, L. i, p. 239.

107. Gilson, *Etudes*, p. 29.

108. Malebranche, *Recherche*, Bk. 3, Pt. 2, Ch. 3, L. i, p. 240.

109. *Ibid.*

110. *Ibid.*, p. 241.

111. Malebranche, *Entretiens sur la métaphysique*, Dial. 1, Sec. 7.

112. Malebranche, *Recherche*, Bk. 3, Pt. 2, Ch. 3, L. i, p. 241.

113. Gilson, *Etudes*, p. 39.

114. Descartes, *Meditations*, Med. 3, H. R. i, p. 165.

115. Malebranche, *Recherche*, Bk. 3, Pt. 2, Ch. 3, L. i, p. 241.

116. Malebranche, *Entretiens sur la métaphysique*, Dial. 5, Secs. 12 and 13.

117. Malebranche, *Recherche*, Bk. 3, Pt. 2, Ch. 3, L. i, p. 242. *Cf.* Malebranche, *Réponse à Régis*, L. iii, pp. 244-5 and 257; O. C. xvii-1, pp. 282-3 and 300-301.

118. Descartes, *Meditations*, Med. 5, H. R. i, p. 180.

119. Descartes, *Reply to Objections* V, H. R. ii, p. 228.

120. *Ibid. III*, H. R. ii, pp. 66 and 77.

121. Malebranche, *Recherche*, Bk. 3, Pt. 2, Ch. 3, L. i, p. 243.

122. Descartes, *Reply to Objections III*, H. R. ii, p. 73.

123. "Je prétens que ce grand Philosophe n'a point examiné à-fond en quoi consiste la nature des idées."

Malebranche, *Trois lettres touchant la Défense*, Let. 1, Recueil i, p. 362.

124. Descartes, *Reply to Objections II*, Arguments in Geometrical Fashion, A. T. ix, p. 124.

125. Descartes, *Meditations*, Med. 3, H. R. i, pp. 161-2.

126. So did Mersenne prior to Descartes. (Gilson, *Etudes*, p. 45.)

127. Arnauld defines the idea as possessing two relations. (Arnauld, *Vraies et fausses idées*, Ch. 5, Defs. 3 and 6, p. 51.) For the position of Régis, see Malebranche, *Réponse à Régis*, Ch. 2, L. iii, pp. 248-50; O. C. xvii-1, pp. 288-91.

128. Malebranche is not arguing against the view that a single existing entity can enter into two distinct offices in virtue of different sets of properties or relations. My claim is that his arguments constitute an attack against such an entity entering into *incompatible* offices. The proposition that in God the act of thinking and the object of thought are ontologically identical, a position that Malebranche will maintain, does not offer a similar difficulty, for in God there is no *succession* of passing, individual acts of thinking. There are no changing modes or manners or states of being in God. Thus the two offices are not in God incompatible. (*Trois lettres touchant la Défense*, Let. 1, Recueil i, pp. 368-9.)

129. Descartes, admits Malebranche, uses idea to designate modes of the soul, but the reason is that he does not employ the *word* in a univocal meaning. (*Ibid.*)

130. Malebranche, *Ibid.*

131. Malebranche, *Recherche*, Ecl. 10, Reply to First Objection, L. iii, p. 86.

132. *Ibid.*, Bk. 3, Pt. 2, Ch. 4, L. i, p. 244.

133. Schrecker, *Le parallélisme chez Malebranche*, p. 119.

134. Descartes, *Reply to Objections I*, H. R. ii, p. 17.

135. Malebranche, *Recherche*, Bk.

3, Pt. 2, Ch. 4, L. i, p. 244. *Cf. ibid.,*
Pt. 1, Ch. 2.

136. *Ibid.,* Bk. 3, Pt. 2, Ch. 4, L. i, p. 244.

137. *E.g.,* Descartes, *Principles,* Pt. 2, Prins. 201 and 203 and *Discourse,* Pt. 6, H. R. i, p. 121.

138. Descartes, *Discourse,* Pt. 2, H. R. i, pp. 91 and 92.

139. Malebranche, *Recherche,* Bk. 3, Pt. 2, Ch. 4, L. i, p. 245.

140. Church offers a very different interpretation of this argument. He claims that Malebranche's arguments about seeing a horse or about seeing the sun are indicative of a *confusion* in Malebranche's thought between images and ideas. The points at issue are so significant for a sound interpretation of Malebranche's entire philosophy and the differences between Mr. Church and myself are so profound on this score, that it will be necessary to repeat Church at some length, in order to treat the disagreement fairly. Says Church:

> This, and the argument of like tenor quoted above, Malebranche regarded as a refutation of any theory, including that of Arnauld, on which the mind is regarded as possessing the power to originate representative ideas of any kind. Yet it is a good example of the confusion between images and ideas which leaves Malebranche's writing only after he has introduced his theory of intelligible extension. When he presses the difficulty of explaining how, even though the soul should possess all ideas, it could ever choose the right one, he uses idea in what is, according to him, its proper sense; namely to mean a representative entity presented to the mind. But when it is asked how the soul could know how to compound ideas so as to present a landscape, the term 'idea' is used to mean an image of sense. Then the question does not turn on the representation of anything, but on how,

with its own powers and the 'ideas' given to it at birth, the soul could contrive the perception of a landscape. That objection has properly no place in the argument, however, since there is no question of innate images of sense, but only of innate ideas. At this point, however, Malebranche is not only urging that the soul cannot choose the idea proper to represent the sun, he is also urging that the soul cannot compound its own modifications so as to present to the senses a perception of the sun. And, as a consequence of this, he asserts that, even though the soul were by its own powers able to produce the compound of sensations that is the sense-perception of the sun, that sense-perception is so unlike the clear and distinct idea of the body itself, that all those sensations of heat and colour could afford no clue to the choice of that clear and distinct idea which represents the sun itself. In this way Malebranche meets a difficulty in his own primary objection to any theory of ideas as originating in the soul. For even though without a clear and distinct idea of the sun, is it not possible that we should know the sun through the senses? But, Malebranche insists, that objection overlooks the difference between images and ideas, a difference so radical that nothing in the sense-perception of the sun can even indicate the character of the idea of the sun. (Church, *Study,* pp. 122-3.)

I believe that it is necessary to disagree with everything in this page. There are at least five questions of interpretation wherein Church is in error:

First, Mr. Church interprets ideas as representative entities, and he means by this, surrogates. (*Cf.* pp. 117, 118 and 122.) In taking this interpretation for granted, he prejudges the true issue. One of the central themes of my entire present study is that Malebranche's "representative" ideas are universals. If my views are correct (and they constitute the only interpretation that I have been able to discover that is constructive, coherent, plausible, and that at the same time avoids reducing Malebranche to perfectly obvious contradiction), *the noun "representative" does not mean surrogate for Malebranche*. Since the plain meanings of "representative" in ordinary French usage do *not* reduce it *exclusively* to surrogate, the burden of proof for anyone applying such a Lockean and Cartesian interpretation to Malebranche's representative ideas rests on the person making the interpretation. It is noteworthy in this connection that Mr. Church does not even discuss Malebranche's first and crucial objection to innate ideas, namely, that they entail the presence in the mind of an infinity of mathematical truths. He likewise ignores Malebranche's explicit reference to universals at the end of the Third Alternative as well as such reference in the Second Alternative.

Second, Malebranche admits that he uses "ideas" loosely. But when he talks of ideas as images of sense, he means *ideas given or contained in* concretions of imagery and sensations. It is not true that this is a "confusion," or that this alleged confusion "leaves Malebranche's writing" upon some alleged subsequent introduction of his theory of intelligible extension. The presence of his doctrine of intelligible extension is perfectly clear in his treatment of method even as early as his first edition of the *Recherche*. It is true that he uses the *term* intelligible extension later, but the *doctrine* is intrinsic to his method. Hence this alleged "confusion" in doctrine (as distinguished from careless usage in terminology) vanishes when we commence our study of Malebranche's doctrine with a study of his method.

Third, it is not true that the argument is exclusively about innate ideas and not about innate images of sense. For (a) Descartes spoke of sensation as innate, and (b) there were "innatists" who did suggest innate images of sense, such as Suarez or such as Silhon, who seemed to make the mind creator of or elicitor of sensible species. (*Cf.* Gilson, *Etudes*, pp. 30-31.)

Fourth, sense-perception is not for Malebranche a mere compound of sensations. It is sensation *plus* intelligible content. Therefore the soul cannot produce it, for to do so the soul would need to have already seen and been acquainted with its object, for example, the sun.

Fifth, sense-perception does indicate the character of the sun, not in so far as it is a discrete image, *but in so far as it "contains" mathematical relations.*

Acceptance of the five foregoing objections to Mr. Church's interpretation of Malebranche's theory of representation precludes Church's idealistic and psychologistic interpretation of Malebranche's theory of knowledge; it eliminates any alleged initial fundamental confusion such as was claimed by Arnauld; and at the same time it permits an interpretation of Malebranche that is consistent, constructive, and coherent, rather than one that reduces Malebranche to inconsistency, and incoherence and one that is exclusively destructive.

141. Malebranche, *Recherche*, Bk. 3, Pt. 2, Ch. 4, L. i, p. 245.

142. Gouhier, *Philosophie de Malebranche*, pp. 227 and 272-8.

143. Malebranche, *Recherche*, Bk. 3, Pt. 2, Ch. 6, L. i, p. 249.

144. Malebranche, *Réponse à Régis*, Ch. 2, L. iii, pp. 253 and 261; O. C. xvii-1, pp. 294-5 and 305-6.

145. Malebranche, *Trois lettres touchant la Défense*, Let. 1, Recueil i, p. 333.

146. Malebranche, *Recherche*, Bk. 3, Pt. 2, Ch. 4, L. i, p. 245, my ital.

147. Descartes, *Meditations*, Med. 3, H. R. i, p. 162.

148. *Ibid.*, p. 163. *Cf. Principles*, Pt. 1, Prin. 17, H. R. i, p. 226.

149. Descartes, *Meditations*, Med. 3, H. R. i, p. 162, my ital.

150. *Ibid.*, p. 165. "Pour ce qui est des autres qualités, dont les idées des choses corporelles sont *composées*, à savoir l'étendue, la figure, la situation, & le mouvement de lieu . . ." A. T. ix, p. 35, my ital.

151. See Malebranche, *Recherche*, Bk. 4, Ch. 11, Sec. 2, pp. 53 *sqq*.

152. Berkeley, *Principles*, Intro., Sec. 12.

153. Descartes, *Principles*, Pt. 1, Prin. 59, H. R. i, pp. 242-3, my ital.

154. Descartes, *Reply to Objections III*, H. R. ii, p. 66.

155. Spinoza, *Ethics*, Pt. 2, Prop. 40, Schol. See Haserot, *Spinoza and Universals*.

156. Malebranche, *Entretiens sur la métaphysique*, Dial. 2, Sec. 9.

157. *Ibid.*, Ginsberg, pp. 94-5.

158. See above Ch. I, Sec. I, (b) "Geometry Essentially Algebra for Malebranche."

159. Consult Miller, *Descartes' Conceptualism*.

160. Malebranche, *Recherche*, Bk. 3, Pt. 2, Ch. 4, L. i, p. 245.

161. Descartes, *Reply to Objections I*, H. R. ii, pp. 17 and 18; *Principles*, Pt. 1, Prins. 26 and 27, pp. 229-30.

162. Malebranche, *Entretiens sur la métaphysique*, Dial. 1, Sec. 8, Ginsberg, p. 81.

163. *Cf.* Malebranche, *Réponse à Régis*, Ch. 2, L. iii, pp. 246-7; O. C. xvii-1, pp. 284-6.

164. Malebranche, *Entretiens sur la métaphysique*, Dial. 1, Sec. 9, Ginsberg, p. 82. *Cf. Recherche*, Ecl. 10, L. iii, p. 76.

165. Malebranche, *Recherche*, Bk. 3, Pt. 2, Ch. 4, L. i, p. 245.

166. Malebranche, *Méditations chrétiennes*, Med. 4, Sec. 11.

167. *E.g.*, Bouillier (*Histoire*, Vol. 2, pp. 67-72) accuses Malebranche of changing his original doctrine of Vision in God when he introduces intelligible extension in the tenth Eclaircissement. And Ollé-Laprune claims that intelligible extension obliterates all distinguishable aspects among ideas. (Ollé-Laprune, *Malebranche*, Vol. 1, pp. 199, 207, and 280.)

Ginette Dreyfus espouses a similar position. "La pensée malebranchiste se trouve, on le voit, comme suspendue entre deux apories," she declares (*La volonté*, p. 127),

ou affirmer l'homogénéité de l'intelligible conformément à la notion d'étendue, alors les formes archétypales s'évanouissent et la création devient inintelligible et aveugle; ou affirmer la spécificité des formes dans l'intelligible, alors l'homogénéité de l'étendue s'anéantit, et les formes finissent par perdre tout caractère d'intelligibilité géométrique.

She concludes that, contrary to his intentions, Malebranche's "gigantesque effort" of rationalization culminates in two "irrationels": the absolute indeterminacy of intelligible extension and the blind principle of determinacy and action that belong to the will. See also *ibid.*, pp. 120-39.

168. Malebranche, *Réponse aux Livre des vraies, etc.*, Chap. 15, Secs. 3-4, pp. 369-70.

169. Church, *Study*, pp. 139-40 and 187-89.

170. See above, Chapter I, Section I, "Intuitive and Deductive Aspects of Malebranche's Method."

171. Malebranche, *Recherche*, Bk. 3, Pt. 2, Ch. 5, L. i, p. 246.

172. *Ibid.*

173. Descartes, *Meditations*, Med. 3, H. R. i, p. 159.

174. Descartes, *Reply to Objections III*, H. R. ii, pp. 67-8.

175. Malebranche, *Recherche*, Bk. 3, Pt. 2, Ch. 5, L. i, p. 247.

176. Malebranche, *Réponse à Régis*, Ch. 2, L. iii, p. 245; O. C. xvii-1, pp. 283-4.

177. *Ibid.*, L. iii, p. 257; O. C. xvii-1, pp. 300-301.

178. *Ibid.*, L. p. 258, O. C. p. 302; *Entretiens sur la métaphysique*, Dial. 2, Sec. 10; *Recherche*, Bk. 4, Ch. 11, Sec. 3, L. ii, p. 61; *ibid.*, Ecl. 10, L. iii, p. 89.

179. *Ibid.*, Ecl. 10, L. iii, p. 90.

180. Descartes, *Meditations*, Med. 3, H. R. i, p. 165.

181. Malebranche, *Recherche*, Ecl. 10, L. iii, pp. 88-89.

182. *Ibid.*, Bk. 1, Ch. 10, Sec. 1, p. 54.

183. Malebranche, *Réponse à Régis*, Ch. 2, L. iii, p. 246; O. C. xvii-1, p. 284.

184. Malebranche, *Réponse à la Troisième*, Recueil iv, pp. 48-9.

185. Malebranche, *Recherche*, Bk. 4, Ch. 11, Sec. 3, L. ii, p. 58.

186. Malebranche, *Entretiens sur la métaphysique*, Préface, Fontana, p. 9; *Réponse à Régis*, Ch. 2, L. iii, p. 246, O. C. xvii-1, p. 284; *Réponse à la Troisième*, Recueil iv, pp. 33 and 38 ff.

187. Malebranche, *Recherche*, Ecl. 10, L. iii, pp. 75-6.

188. *Ibid.*

189. Again, ideas, when clear and distinct, have exact relations; perceptions and modifications are obscure; we do not know what they are. (Malebranche, *Réponse à Régis*, Ch. 2, L. iii, p. 248, O. C. xvii-1, pp. 288-9; *Recherche*, Bk. 4, Ch. 11, Sec. 3, L. ii, p. 61.)

190. Malebranche, *Réponse à Régis*, Ch. 2, L. iii, pp. 262-3; O. C. xvii-1, p. 309.

191. *Ibid.*, p. 261 or O. C. xvii-1, p. 306; *Recherche*, Ecl. 10, L. iii, pp. 75-6.

192. Malebranche, *Réponse à Régis*, Ch. 2, L. iii, p. 261; O. C. xvii-1, p. 306.

193. *Ibid.*; *Entretiens sur la métaphysique*, Dial. 8, Sec. 12, Ginsberg, p. 217.

194. Malebranche, *Chrétien et chinois*, p. 111, Le Moine edition; O. C. xv, p. 51.

195. Arnauld, *Vraies et fausses idées*, Ch. 6, pp. 62-7.

196. Malebranche, *Réponse à la Troisième*, Recueil iv, pp. 53-67.

197. Schrecker, *Le parallélisme chez Malebranche*, p. 111.

198. Malebranche, *Recherche*, Ecl. 10, L. iii, p. 81.

199. Gouhier, *Philosophie de Malebranche*, pp. 298, 300, and 302.

200. Malebranche voiced his opposition to Descartes' doctrine of alio-created essences (essences created by something besides themselves) and the arbitrary will of God most clearly in 1678 in the tenth Eclaircissement. This Eclaircissement formed part of the third volume accompanying the third edition of Volumes I and II of the *Recherche*. In this third edition an interesting variation occurs in connection with the doctrine of created essences. In Book I, *On Sense*, Chapter 3, the following statement occurs in the first and second editions of 1674 and 1675: I call necessary truths those which are immutable by their nature, and because they have been decreed by the will of God. Apparently, fearful lest this statement be taken to coincide with Descartes' doctrine, Malebranche in the third edition of 1678 amended it to read as follows: I call necessary truths those which are immutable by their nature, and those which have been decreed by the will of God.

For these variations consult *Œuvres Complètes de Malebranche* by Roustan and Schrecker, Vol. I, 1938, p. 55. These variations only serve to emphasize that from the very beginning Malebranche was conscious of his opposition to Descartes on this central thesis, namely, that some truths are necessary by their intrinsic nature, while others, pertaining to matters of facts but not ideas, are both arbitrary in origin and dependent on the will of God.

201. To Mersenne, April 15, 1630,

A. T. i, pp. 145-6, my ital. See above, Chapter I, Section III, (c) *Causa Sui.*

202. Malebranche, *Recherche,* Ecl. 10, L. iii, p. 77.

203. Malebranche, *Réponse à Régis,* Ch. 2, L. iii, p. 243; O. C. xvii-1, p. 280. *Cf. Recherche,* Ecl. 10, L. iii, p. 75.

204. Malebranche, *Recherche,* Ecl. 10, L. iii, p. 77. This criticism depends on the fact that Malebranche has a different conception of motion and rest from that of Descartes. To Malebranche rest is merely the cessation of a movement, a cessation that requires no new, activating principle and therefore produces no alteration or change in that which causes the rest. Similarly in man or God the cessation of the will, which is analogous to motion, is nothing positive. Thus, from the point of view of Malebranche, if the essence of a triangle were something arbitrarily willed by God, to obtain its annihilation God can merely cease to will it, without thereby producing any change within Himself.

205. Malebranche, *Recherche,* Ecl. 10, L. iii, pp. 77-8, my ital.

206. Le Moine, *Vérités éternelles,* p. 54 n.

207. Descartes, *Reply to Objections VI,* H. R. ii, p. 251.

208. To signalize how central is this argument of Malebranche against Descartes' support of indifferent and incomprehensible decrees, notice that immediately after Descartes declares that it is "irrational to doubt that which we correctly understand because of that which we do not understand and perceive no need to understand," he goes on to declare: "Hence neither should we think that eternal truths depend upon the human understanding or on other existing things; they must depend on God alone, who, as the supreme legislator, ordained them from all eternity." (*Reply to Objections VI,* H. R. ii, p. 251.) It is this latter declaration that Malebranche

attacks when he asserts that Descartes failed to perceive the alternative that ideas exist in God. The existence of ideas as eternal norms in God serves to explicate all the points which Descartes is here seeking to explain, and in addition possesses the feature that Descartes' account lacks, of being transparently rational.

Of course, as I shall show later, Malebranche was aware of the fact that Descartes in this very sixth set of replies, explicitly refused to admit the existence of ideas in a pre-existing realm in the mind of God, claiming that such a realm would curtail God's free power. But Malebranche's own doctrine strives to coalesce archetypal ideas with God's essence so that God is subject only to Himself in following these ideas and to this extent is free.

209. Malebranche, *Recherche,* Ecl. 10, L. iii, p. 78.

210. Descartes, *Reply to Objections VI,* H. R. ii, p. 251.

211. Malebranche, *Recherche,* Ecl. 8, L. iii, pp. 46-7.

212. *Ibid.,* Ecl. 10, L. iii, p. 78. *Cf. ibid.,* Ecl. 8, L. iii, pp. 44-5.

213. Descartes, *Reply to Objections II,* Arguments in Geometrical Fashion, Post. 7, H. R. ii, p. 55. *Cf.* Post. 4, preceding page. *N.b. Reply to Objections II,* H. R. ii, p. 41, paragraph beginning, "To begin with, directly we think . . ."

214. Leibnitz, letter to Philipp, Jan., 1680, Duncan, p. 3.

215. Malebranche, *Recherche,* Ecl. 10, L. iii, p. 80. *Cf.* Ecl. 8, L. iii, pp. 45-6.

216. Malebranche, *Recherche,* Bk. 1, Ch. 2, Sec. 5, L. i, p. 13.

217. Descartes, *Rules,* Rule 3, H. R. i, p. 7.

218. Malebranche, *Recherche,* Ecl. 10, L. iii, p. 78.

219. *Ibid.,* Bk. 6, Pt. 2, Ch. 6, L. ii, p. 239.

220. *Ibid.,* Ecl. 10, L. iii, p. 78.

221. *Ibid.,* Ecl. 8, L. iii, p. 45.

222. *Ibid.,* Ecl. 10, L. iii, p. 75.

223. *Ibid.*
224. *Ibid.*, p. 77.
225. *Ibid.*
226. *Ibid.*, Bk. 3, Pt. 2, Ch. 6, L. i, p. 248.
227. *Ibid.*
228. *Ibid.*, p. 249.
229. *Ibid.*, p. 250.
230. *Ibid.*
231. For a very different point of view from the one presented in this chapter, see Gueroult, *Malebranche*, Vol. 1, Chapter 9, *passim*, especially p. 174, and Chapter 11, pp. 211 ff., especially p. 249. Note Gueroult's characterization of Descartes' effort: "Il consistait à identifier l'essence des choses finies avec leur existence, l'une et l'autre créées, à réduire celle-ci à celle-là, l'existence n'étant rien d'autre que l'actualité de l'essence même, étendue géométrique ou intelligence pure." (P. 249. *Cf.* Gueroult, *L'idée de force*, pp. 119-20 and 124-5.)

Thus the very essentialism that, according to my position (see below, Chapters III and IV), Malebranche condemns is cited with approval when it occurs in Descartes. Small wonder, then, that Gueroult finds so many difficulties with Malebranche's ontological argument. (See, for example, his *Malebranche*, Vol. 1, pp. 262 ff., 270-3, 281 and 304.) Small wonder too that he fails to appreciate the truly revolutionary contributions of Malebranche towards a dynamic physics and metaphysics.

Gueroult does single out Malebranche's innovation: the elimination of Descartes' principle that rest requires a positive force. He then asks:

Mais si le repos est identifié au néant et le mouvement à l'être, ne faudra-t-il pas considérer que la substance des choses, ce doit être le mouvement et non ce qui est en repos . . . ? A ce primat du dynamique paraîtrait donc devoir se lier une nouvelle conception de la substance. . . . Il semble qu'on doive arriver, à l'inverse de Descartes, à mettre l'essence des corps dans le mouvement et non dans l'espace, à faire de la fluidité la propriété de l'espace immobile . . . (*L'idée de force*, p. 130.)

After pointing out that this was done by Leibnitz, Gueroult affirms that Malebranche does not accomplish this revolution. "Sa réforme de la physique s'en tient à des retouches partielles." His metaphysical conception of the substance of bodies remains that of Descartes, and "il persiste à réduire leur essence à l'étendue." (*Ibid.*, p. 131.)

Clearly, the magnitude of Malebranche's revolution in physics and in metaphysics escapes Gueroult for the very reason that Gueroult is not sympathetic either to the fundamental distinction of essence and existence or its role in Malebranche's philosophy. Malebranche does indeed offer a reformation of the notion of substance. Malebranche continues to say that the essence of body is extension, but he can do so, because, unlike Descartes, he makes this essentiality lie in an independent, objective intelligible extension. But he associates dynamic activity, fluidity and the movement of created bodies with their *existential being* derivative from the creative will of God.

See also Gueroult's *Descartes*, Vol. 2, Ch. 10, especially pp. 30-32, in which Gueroult defends Descartes' doctrine of created truths against Malebranche. Also see Vol. 1, pp. 383-4, for Gueroult's defense of Descartes' identification of essence and existence.

Chapter III. Being

1. Descartes, letter to Mersenne, May 6, 1630, A. T. i, p. 149.
2. Malebranche, *Recherche*, Ecl. 10, L. iii, p. 79. "Cet ordre" here means the hierarchy of perfections that obtain among the ideas of dif-

ferent creatures. (*Méditations chrétiennes*, Med. IV, Secs. 7-8.)

3. Malebranche, *Prémotion*, O. C. xvi, p. 99. *Cf. Recherche*, Préface pour servir de réponse à la Critique du premier volume, Rép. e and Rép. g, L. ii, pp. 304-5.

4. Malebranche, *Conversations*, Dial. 3, pp. 77 ff., Bridet edition; O. C. iv, pp. 70 ff.

5. Descartes, *Objections I*, H. R. ii, p. 2.

6. *E.g.:* Malebranche, *Recherche*, Bk. 3, Pt. 2, Ch. 5, L. i, p. 247 and note b; *ibid.*, Ch. 6, L. i, p. 248; *ibid.*, Ecl. 8, L. iii, pp. 44-5; *ibid.*, Ecl. 10, Réponse à la seconde objection, L. iii, p. 89.

7. Gilson, *Bonaventure*, p. 160.

8. Malebranche, *Recherche*, Bk. 3, Pt. 1, Ch. 1, L. i, p. 214.

9. Spinoza, *Ethics*, Pt. 1, Prop. 17, Schol.; *ibid.*, Pt. 2, Prop. 48 and Schol. and Prop. 49, Corol., and Schol.

10. *E.g.:* Malebranche, *Chrétien et chinois*, pp. 77 ff. or O. C. xv, pp. 24 ff.; *Entretiens sur la métaphysique*, Dial. 4, Secs. 17-18; *ibid.*, Dial. 8, Sec. 14; *ibid.*, Dial. 9, Sec. 12, Ginsberg, pp. 246-7; *Meditations chrétiennes*, Med. 19, Sec. 7; and especially *Recherche*, Bk. 3, Pt. 2, Ch. 9, Sec. 4, L. i, pp. 270-1.

11. Malebranche, *Recherche*, Bk. 1, Chs. 1 and 2.

12. Malebranche, *Conversations*, Dial. 3, p. 76, Bridet edition; O. C. iv, p. 69; my ital.

13. Malebranche, *Adoration*, Pt. 1, p. 156, 1944 edition; O. C. xvii-1, p. 425; my ital.

14. To be sure, Malebranche is no less concerned than is Spinoza with the rejection of anthropomorphism. (Malebranche, *Recherche*, Dernier Ecl., L. iii, p. 219; *Adoration*, Pt. 1, p. 164, 1944 edition or O. C. xvii-1, p. 429, note e; *Chrétien et chinois*, p. 86, Le Moine edition, or O. C. xv, p. 30; *Entretiens sur la métaphysique*, Dial. 9, Sec. 3 and Dial. 7, Sec. 5—see note of Cuvillier, Cuvillier, p. 228, n.

12.) He complains constantly against the dangerous tendency to humanize God. For this reason he insists on the ultimately incomprehensible character of God and of His attributes. Thus when we assert God to be Mind we are not to imagine that God knows or wills or thinks precisely as we do. In God there is no succession of thoughts. Divine knowledge consists in a single, all-encompassing intuitive act. (*Ibid.*, Dial. 8, Sec. 7.) Nevertheless Malebranche does not push the distinction between the human and the divine intellect to the point where, as in Spinoza, they differ *toto caelo* and have nothing in common but the name. (*Ethics*, Bk. 1, Prop. 17, Schol.) Malebranche does not render adjectives descriptive of God and man as pure equivocations. (*Entretiens sur la métaphysique*, Dial. 7, Sec. 16 and Dial. 8, Sec. 10.) They are not univocal, but neither are they equivocal. They are analogical. And on this basis, it seems reasonable to Malebranche to make distinctions among the divine attributes and to assume that if creation does not enter into human knowledge, neither does it in divine thought.

Descartes affirmed that his idea of God is like the mark of the workman upon his work. This idea is a true image. Whether this idea be taken as something distinct "in" the mind or as the very capacity of the mind itself, in either case Descartes admits the relation of resemblance between himself and God. Moreover, notwithstanding the fact that the idea of the infinite is declared by Descartes to be logically anterior in his mind to that of the finite, nevertheless it is at least upon the occasion of what he finds to be characteristic of his own mind that he is capable of eliciting the idea of God; and although Descartes denies, to Hobbes for example, that the idea of the infinite is arrived at empirically by amplification of the finite, yet his manner of cognizing the attributes of God is not free from analogical reasoning. It is by virtue of the mental operations that he discovers within himself that he is enabled to affirm certain predicates of God and to eliminate those, like passion or doubt, which he deems to be imperfections.

So far, then, as Malebranche utilizes analogical reasoning he is following Descartes. Where he abandons Descartes is at the top of the hill, so to speak. Descartes, after ascribing to God the properties he finds in himself, then refuses to maintain the analogy. He refuses to assert that these predicates have distinct logical meanings in God as they do in man, under the adroit pretense that such distinctions would destroy the unity of God. Descartes therefore affirmed that the predicates do not possess a univocal meaning or in other words a univocal truth.

But Malebranche has asserted that truth is one. Therefore, if the distinction between knowing and willing is valid for man, then it is valid for God.

15. Malebranche, *Adoration*, Pt. 2, pp. 168-9, 1944 edition; O. C. xvii-1, p. 431.

16. Malebranche, *Recherche*, Ecl. 10, L. iii, p. 77, my ital. *Cf. ibid.*, pp. 79, 81, and 82.

17. Malebranche, *Réponse à Régis*, Ch. 2, L. iii, p. 262; O. C. xvii-1, p. 308.

18. Malebranche, *Entretiens sur la métaphysique*, Dial. 1, Secs. 9-10, Ginsberg, p. 83.

Also consider the following passage:

La perception que Dieu même a de la matière, par exemple, en suppose l'idée, non comme un être représentatif hors de Dieu, ou distingué de son essence, ce que l'on a attribué aux Idées de Platon, mais comme une manière dont la nature divine peut être imparfaitement participée par la créature corporelle. Or, *la créature corporelle ne participe point à la nature divine en tant que cette nature est apercevante. Ainsi, la perception que Dieu même*

a de l'idée de l'étendue n'est point représentative de la matière en tant que perception. Ce n'est que l'idée de la matière qui en est représentative, c'est-à-dire que ce n'est que la nature divine, en tant qu'elle contient éminemment et divinement tout ce qu'il y a de réalité et de perfection dans la matière, qui est représentative de la matière. Recueil, IV, David, 1709 edition, pp. 104-5. Cited by Gueroult, *Malebranche*, Vol. 1, p. 163. My ital.

19. Brunschvicg claims that Malebranche has a *Deus duplex*, a God in whom reason and will are distinct. This conception, which is unlike that of Spinoza, says Brunschvicg, arises from Malebranche's initial distinction between a passive intellect and an active will. Malebranche, following Descartes, he asserts, does not appreciate Spinoza's rejection of this very doctrine; he does not realize that Spinoza rejects ideas as static images, that he emphasizes the active character of thinking and hence makes no division between the intellect and the will. It is this failure that is responsible for Malebranche's further misunderstanding of the relation between Spinoza's God and the world. (Brunschvicg, *Spinoza*, Ch. 11.)

Whether or not "Malebranche a laissé échapper l'originalité historique du spinozisme," as Brunschvicg claims (*ibid.*, p. 355), I shall not consider. Basically Brunschvicg recognizes the distinction between the idealistic metaphysic of Spinoza and the realism of Malebranche. But I take issue simply with Brunschvicg's claim that Malebranche did not thoroughly understand Spinoza's idealism. Rather, I would say that he comprehended its "essentialism" and rigorously combatted the latter, as we shall see when we come to his correspondence with Dortous de Mairan. Thus it is vital for Malebranche to preserve the Cartesian distinction between intellect and will. Malebranche's insistence upon the passivity of mind and its distinction from the will is formulated precisely in order to combat conceptualism and its implicit idealism. An idea for Malebranche is an archetype, a Platonic model, deliberately divorced from the operations of thought, human or divine, in order to guarantee an objective foundation to truth.

Malebranche will have no traffic with any sort of psychologism or subjectivism, whether on the human or on the divine level. Hence, Malebranche's adoption of the Cartesian distinction between a passive mind and active will and his attribution of this distinction to God are no accident. But as Laporte judiciously observes, this is not a "real" distinction in the sense of a separation, but neither is it a mere "distinction of reason" or a purely mental distinction as it is for Descartes. Laporte compares it to Duns Scotus's "formal distinction." (*La liberté*, pp. 354-5.)

20. Descartes, *Reply to Objections I*, H. R. ii, p. 14 and *ibid. IV*, H. R. ii, p. 110.

21. *Ibid. VI*, H. R. ii, pp. 254-5.

22. Malebranche, *Recherche*, Ecl. 15, Réponse, VIIe preuve, L. iii, p. 148.

23. *Ibid.*, Ecl. 10, L. iii, p. 85. *Cf. Entretiens sur la métaphysique*, Dial. 8, Sec. 2, Ginsberg, p. 204.

24. Descartes, *Objections IV*, H. R. ii, p. 89.

25. Descartes, *Principles*, Pt. 1, Prin. 52.

26. *Ibid.*, Prins. 62 and 63. See below, Chap. IV, Sec. 2, (a) The Tradition of Essentialism.

27. Descartes, *Objections V*, H. R. ii, p. 183; *Reply to Objections V*, H. R. ii, p. 226.

28. In doing this, Malebranche introduces the Augustinian doctrine of the Word as consubstantial with and as a necessary emanation from God the Father. (*E.g.: Réponse au Livre des vraies, etc.*, Ch. 24, Sec. 3, p. 426; *Recherche*, Ecl. 10, L. iii, p. 77;

Réponse à la Troisième, Recueil, Vol. 4, p. 138; *Méditations chrétiennes, passim.*) Hence he insists that this Reason which illuminates and which God is obliged to follow in no way enslaves Him, for it is one with God. Being His very own, God's independence is therefore not destroyed. (*Recherche*, Ecl. 10, p. 77; *Chrétien et chinois*, p. 78, Le Moine edition, or O. C. xv, p. 25.)

While the Word is a perfect and total reflection of God's essence, I have not found any text to suggest that for Malebranche the Word is engendered *by* God's knowing. He talks of the Word as an expression of God, but he does not explain how this is to be construed. I would suspect that for Malebranche the Word is engendered *when* God knows Himself but not *through* the process of knowing. In knowing Himself and His own essence, God finds immutable ideas and He finds, I would surmise, the Word.

29. *E.g.*: Le Moine, *Vérités éternelles*, pp. 73 and 205; Vidgrain, *Christianisme*, pp. 208-215; Blampignon, *Etude*, p. 143; Wehrlé, Préface, Delbos, *Etude*, p. xxiv. Wehrlé charges Malebranche with materializing God by identifying Him with infinite substance and geometric essences. This shows that Wehrlé failed to understand (a) that essences are ideal meanings, not images, for Malebranche and (b) that Malebranche's God is *Celui qui est* and as such beyond essences. See below, note 113.

30. Malebranche, *Chrétien et chinois*, p. 47, Le Moine edition; O. C. xv, p. 3.

31. Malebranche, *Réponse à la Troisième*, Recueil iv, pp. 100-4.

32. This preface is to be found in the Fontana and Cuvillier editions.

33. Malebranche, *Recherche*, Bk. 3, Pt. 2, Ch. 6, L. i, pp. 248-9.

34. *Ibid.*, Ch. 5, L. i, p. 247.

35. Santayana, *Life of Reason*, pp. 30-32.

36. Miller, *Critical Realism*, p. 69.

37. Malebranche, *Conversations*, Dial. 3, pp. 88-9, Bridet edition; O. C. iv, pp. 79-80, my ital.

38. Malebranche, *Trois lettres touchant la Défense*, Let. 1, Recueil i, p. 333.

39. Malebranche, *Recherche*, Bk. 3, Pt. 2, Ch. 5, L. i, p. 246.

40. Malebranche, *Réponse au Livre des vraies, etc.*, Ch. 24, Sec. 11; *ibid.*, Ch. 9, Sec. 15; *Entretiens sur la métaphysique*, Préface, Fontana, p. 15; André, *Vie du R. P. Malebranche*, pp. 15 and 20.

41. Malebranche, *Conversations*, Dial. 1, p. 3, Bridet edition; O. C. iv, pp. 11-12.

42. *Ibid.*, pp. 1-4; *Méditations chrétiennes*, Med. 3, Sec. 10.

43. Malebranche, *Recherche*, Bk. 3, Pt. 2, Ch. 6; *Conversations*, Dial. 3, p. 76, Bridet edition, or O. C. iv, p. 69.

44. Gilson, *Medieval Philosophy*, pp. 47-9.

45. *Ibid.*, p. 50.

46. *Ibid.*, p. 55.

47. *Ibid.*, pp. 52-3.

48. *Ibid.*, pp. 54-5.

49. Ollé-Laprune does call attention to Malebranche's God as *Celui qui est*, but then he goes on to misinterpret it by assuming that Malebranche's description of God as unrestricted being is equivalent to ineffable indeterminacy and hence nothingness. (*Malebranche*, Vol. 1, pp. 236-8.)

50. Malebranche, *Chrétien et chinois*, p. 47, Le Moine edition; O. C. xv, p. 3.

51. *Ibid.*, p. 56, Le Moine edition; O. C. xv, p. 10, my ital.

52. Malebranche, Avis, *Chrétien et chinois*, p. 101, Le Moine edition; O. C. xv, p. 44.

53. Gilson, *Medieval Philosophy*, p. 56.

54. Malebranche, *Recherche*, Bk. 3, Pt. 2, Ch. 6, L. i, p. 251.

55. Descartes, *Meditation*, Med. 3, H. R. i, p. 166.

56. Malebranche, *Méditations chrétiennes*, Med. 4, Secs. 3-12; *Entretiens sur la métaphysique*, Préface, Fontana, p. 11 and Dial. 2, Sec. 2; *Réponse à la Troisième*, Recueil, Vol. 4, pp. 53-9.

57. Gilson, *Being*, pp. 84-95; *n.b.*, p. 94. Thomas, *History of the Schoolmen*, pp. 553-8.

58. Ginsberg, *Preface*, p. 44.

59. Ollé-Laprune, *Malebranche*, Vol. 1, pp. 236-8.

60. *Entretiens sur la métaphysique*, Dial. 2, Sec. 1, Fontana, pp. 43-4, my ital.

61. *Ibid.*, pp. 43-6.

62. My italics. "Même" added after first edition. Critics have often noticed that Malebranche makes truth a relation and that he denies that it is an entity. No one, however, seems to have observed that in these significant passages, which have been so often commented upon, Malebranche is doing more than denying the entitative status of truth. In fact, in these passages he is refusing to *reduce* God to the sphere of abstract truth.

63. Malebranche, *Recherche*, Bk. 3, Pt. 2, Ch. 6, L. i, pp. 252-3, my ital.

64. *Ibid.*, Bk. 4, Ch. 6, Sec. 2, L. ii, p. 28; Bk. 3, Pt. 2, Ch. 6, L. i, pp. 250-1.

65. Cited by Brunschvicg, *Spinoza*, p. 297.

66. Malebranche, *Réponse à Régis*, Ch. 2, L. iii, p. 253; O. C. xvii-1, p. 295. "Tous les êtres créés dependent de la *puissance* du Créateur, esprits et corps . . ."

67. André, *Des idées*, p. 247-56; *L'idée de Dieu*, pp. 318-19.

68. André, *Des idées*, p. 256.

69. *Ibid.*, p. 258.

70. André, *L'idée de Dieu*, pp. 318-20. And this God is no *Causa Sui!* (See *ibid.*, pp. 320-2, for André's description of the divine attributes.)

71. Malebranche, *Recherche*, Bk. 3, Pt. 2, Ch. 6, L. i, pp. 250-1.

72. Malebranche, *Chrétien et chinois*, pp. 57 ff., Le Moine edition; O. C. xv, pp. 10 ff.

73. Malebranche, *Conversations,* Dial. 1, p. 8, Bridet edition; O. C. iv, p. 15.

74. *Ibid.*, p. 17, Bridet, or O. C., pp. 22-3.

75. *Ibid.*, p. 27, Bridet, or O. C., pp. 30-1.

76. Malebranche, *Recherche*, Bk. 6, Pt. 2, Ch. 6, L. ii, p. 240.

77. Descartes, *Rules*, Rule 3, H. R. i, p. 8.

78. Descartes, *Meditations*, Med. 2, H. R. i, p. 150.

79. *Ibid.*, Med. 3, H. R. i, p. 159.

80. *Ibid.*, Med. 1, H. R. i, p. 147.

81. *Ibid.*, Synopsis, H. R. i, p. 140.

82. A. K. Stout maintains that Descartes' distinction between immediately presented ideas and remembered ideas "would clearly fail in its purpose if it meant that clear and distinct perceptions are, as such, logically doubtful in retrospect but logically impervious to doubt while we attend to them." (Stout, *Alleged "petitio,"* p. 126.) It would fail according to Stout because "the only conceivable ground for holding clear and distinct perceptions to be doubtful in retrospect and yet indubitable while we are attending to them is that it may be *psychologically* impossible to apply the doubt to them at the same time as we are attending to them." (*Ibid.*) Stout would indeed be right if his "only" were correct. But Stout neglects the above alternative, concerning the permanency of ideas, which allows on logical grounds for the doubt to function merely in retrospect.

83. Descartes, *Reply to Objections IV*, H. R. ii, p. 109. *Cf.* Gilson, *Etudes*, p. 252.

84. Malebranche, *Recherche*, Bk. 6, Pt. 2, Ch. 6, L. ii, p. 240.

85. *Ibid.*, pp. 240-1.

86. Descartes, *Reply to Objections V*, Letter to Clerselier, H. R. ii, p. 127.

87. Malebranche, *Recherche*, Bk. 6, Pt. 2, Ch. 6, L. ii, p. 240, my ital.

88. Wolfson, *Spinoza*, Vol. 1, p. 176.

89. Malebranche, *Recherche*, Bk. 6, Pt. 2, Ch. 6, L. ii, p. 241.

90. Malebranche, *Conversations,* Dial. 1, p. 2 and p. 2, n. 4, Bridet edition; O. C. iv, pp. 10-11 and footnote, p. 11.

91. Malebranche, *Chrétien et chinois*, pp. 47-8, Le Moine edition; O. C. xv, pp. 3-4. Note that Malebranche is not offering a definition but rather a description or the name of God. Throughout the medieval ages and in the seventeenth century as well, it was debatable whether God, being a *summum genus*, could be defined. Even Spinoza expresses this hesitancy. *Cf.* Wolfson, *Spinoza*, p. 160, n. 1 and *Crescas*, p. 575.

92. Malebranche, *Chrétien et chinois*, p. 50, Le Moine edition; O. C. xv, p. 5.

93. Descartes, *Reply to Objections I*, H. R. ii, p. 21. For an even stronger expression concerning the intervention of power between essence and existence of God, see letter to Mersenne, March 4, 1641, A. T. iii, pp. 329-331.

94. Malebranche, *Recherche*, Bk. 4, Ch. 11, Sec. 2, L. ii, p. 55.

95. *Ibid.*, p. 56.

96. Malebranche, *Chrétien et chinois*, pp. 53-4 and 57, Le Moine edition; O. C. xv. pp. 7-8 and 10. *Cf. Réponse à Régis*, Ch. 2, L. iii, pp. 245-6; O. C. xvii-1, pp. 283-4.

97. Malebranche, *Recherche*, Bk. 3, Pt. 2, Ch. 7, Sec. 2, L. i, p. 256.

98. *Ibid. Cf.* Laporte, *La liberté*, pp. 360-1, and Callot, *Problèmes du cartésianisme*, Y a-t-il chez Malebranche une nouvelle preuve de l'existence de Dieu, pp. 179-90. Both Laporte and Callot are sensitive to the unique quality of Malebranche's ontological argument.

99. Malebranche, *Recherche*, Bk. 4, Ch. 11, Sec. 3, L. ii, p. 56.

100. *Ibid.*, p. 59; *Entretiens sur la métaphysique*, Ginsberg, Dial. 2, Sec. 5, p. 90.

In so far as the "idea of God" signifies an act of intuitive knowledge that is both non-inferential and non-conceptual, Malebranche is not opposed to its use. Thus he says that by the *sentiment intérieur* we are convinced "that we think actually of the infinite, or to speak as others, that we naturally have the idea of God or of being infinitely perfect." (*Recherche,* Bk. 4, Ch. 11, Sec. 3, L. ii, p. 61.)

101. *Ibid.,* p. 56. Gouhier understands well that Malebranche's proof for the existence of God is no mere elaboration, prolongation, or even a simple completion, as Malebranche himself modestly claimed, of Descartes' ontological argument. (*Philosophie de Malebranche,* p. 345.) Malebranche's proof is radically other than that of Descartes. (P. 348.) What, then, is the essential difference? For Malebranche, *to think of God* and *to know that He exists* constitute a simple intuition, not two separate propositions, one logically deduced from the other. Descartes, on the other hand, puts the ontological argument in the form of a syllogism (*Reply to Objections II,* H. R. ii, p. 57), because his proof requires an analysis of the relation that unites necessary existence to God's essence. The syllogism thus remains for Descartes a series of three different intuitions that never collapse into one. But for Malebranche analysis disappears together with the idea to be analyzed; hence the argument can no longer assume the syllogistic form. Gouhier declares:

Malebranche ne déduit pas un attribut de l'essence divine et il n'a pas à éclaircir la mineure d'un raisonnement: il a pour mission de mettre l'âme devant sa vraie nature et de lui faire sentir la présence de Dieu; *nous ne démontrons pas avec des raisonnements l'existence d'une statue:* nous conduisons devant elle celui qui ne croit pas en notre parole; ainsi le 'moniteur' conduit les âmes devant Dieu, devant le Dieu qui habite en elles. (P. 347, my italics.)

I have italicized what seems to me a very crucial sentence in Gouhier's description but one which he himself does not fully explore. Who is this Deity to whose presence Malebranche seeks to guide us? Gouhier is aware that it is *Celui qui est,* that it is, as he says, "une chose existante." (P. 348.) But then he goes on to assert that Malebranche had only to reflect on Augustinian principles to rediscover the argument as he presents it, and from this point of view, his source would be Augustine's demonstration of God's existence by eternal truths rather than Descartes' third proof in the *Meditations.* (*Ibid.*) But if Augustine is the source of Malebranche's inspiration rather than Descartes, is the God that Malebranche seeks to establish that of Augustine? The answer would seem to be both yes and no. The God whom Augustine adores in the *Confessions,* according to Gilson, is the existential creator-God of the Bible, but the God whom he establishes as a philosopher is the essence-Deity:

Chaque fois qu'il tente de nouveau l'une de ces ascensions mentales, c'est bien vers le Dieu de l'*Exode* qu'Augustin se met en marche, mais toutes ses routes le conduisent à ce qui, pour sa raison, constitue l'être dans sa plénitude: la stabilité dans l'essence, l'immutabilité, cette éternité, enfin, qui n'est pas seulement pour lui un attribut de Dieu, mais sa substance même: *Aeternitas, ipsa Dei substantia est.* (Gilson, *Augustin,* p. 27.)

Now one may say that Malebranche also proceeds on the level of essence, as we have noted before. And he does so because Descartes placed him in a dilemma. Descartes' view of God as power and arbitrary creator of truths compelled Malebranche to find a path to God that would be *par sim-*

ple vue, that would eliminate reasoning; more, one that would justify reasoning by disclosing a God who was reason and truth Himself. This is why, as we saw above, Malebranche ascends to God through the alternative hypotheses on the nature of ideas and eternal truths. Nevertheless, if the road to God is on the level of essence, the God whom he apprehends by *simple vue* is more than essence. And perhaps this is why Gouhier felt impelled to cite Gilson's text on St. Bonaventure for purposes of casting light on Malebranche. (Gilson, *Bonaventure,* pp. 127-138 in the English translation; pp. 128-139 in the original French text.) But this text suggests that the Deity whom St. Bonaventure discovers is no *Deus Essentia* but God as the very act of existing.

And my claim is that Malebranche can and does arrive at this Existential Deity because, while proceeding on the plane of abstract truth and immutable essence, Malebranche recognizes that the supreme truth is that which involves an existential affirmation; and I claim that he did so because of his profound recognition that nature is not abstract. Put differently, Malebranche never loses sight of the fact that the search after eternal truth is being undertaken by his own individual concrete self and for the sake of illuminating and controlling a concrete universe.

102. Malebranche, *Recherche,* Bk. 4, Ch. 11, Sec. 3, L. ii, p. 59.

103. *Ibid.,* p. 61.

104. *Ibid.; Entretiens sur la métaphysique,* Dial. 2, Sec. 5, Ginsberg, p. 90.

105. *E.g.,* Descartes, *Reply to Objections V,* Letter to Clerselier, H. R. ii, p. 130.

106. Malebranche, *Recherche,* Bk. 4, Ch. 11, Sec. 3, L. ii, p. 59. *Cf. Réponse à Régis,* L. iii, p. 247; O. C. xvii-1, p. 286.

107. Malebranche, *Recherche,* Bk. 3, Pt. 2, Ch. 8, Sec. 1, L. i, p. 260.

108. *Ibid.*

109. Malebranche, *Chrétien et chinois,* p. 72, Le Moine edition; O. C. xv, p. 21.

110. *Ibid.,* p. 73, Le Moine edition; O. C. xv, p. 22.

111. Although Malebranche claimed to have direct access to God, to know Him *par simple vue,* and to apprehend essences in God, nevertheless he insisted that this vision is of a limited character. He insisted that the absolute essence of God is unknowable. (*Recherche,* Bk. 3, Pt. 2, Ch. 6, L. i, p. 249 and Ecl. 10, L. iii, pp. 93-8.) To many critics this appears to be an equivocation (*Cf.* Le Moine, *Vérités éternelles,* pp. 220-2) or else equivalent to the statement that we know God's existence but not His essence (*Cf.* Pang, *Malebranche et Tchou Hi,* pp. 20 and 25). But their charges are groundless. They fail to see that for Malebranche there are degrees of clarity in knowledge. We do know some truths exactly as God knows them. This constitutes Vision in God. Further, we do apprehend God's presence face to face. We do know His essence, for His essence is to exist. Yet we do not understand all that there is to know in God, nor do we understand Him in the manner that He understands Himself:

Theodore. Je ne vous nie pas qu'on ne voie la substance de Dieu en elle-même. On la voit en elle-même, en ce sens que l'on ne la voit point par quelque chose de fini qui la représente. Mais on ne la voit point en elle-même, en ce sens qu'on atteigne à sa simplicité, et que l'on y découvre ses perfections. (*Entretiens sur la métaphysique,* Dial. 2, Sec. 7, Fontana i, p. 49. *Cf. Conversations,* Dial. 3, pp. 79 and 88, Bridet edition; O. C. iv, pp. 72 and 79-80.)

This is why Malebranche insists that God is incomprehensible in every way. (*Entretiens sur la métaphysique,* Dial. 8, Sec. 7, Ginsberg, p. 211.) This in turn has led to the charge of mysticism and obscurantism. But Malebranche does not insist upon God's total ineffability. We cannot love and worship a nonentity. Thus for him it is as false to say that God is so far beyond us that He is entirely inscrutable as it is to say that He is wholly comprehensible. Certain minds demand either all or nothing. Malebranche cogently insists upon an intermediate position. See *Prémotion, O. C. xvi*, pp. 24-5.

112. Pang, *Malebranche et Tchou Hi*, pp. 21-2.

113. Ginette Dreyfus also discerns in Malebranche's God "une dualité ineffaçable . . ." (*La volonté*, pp. 28-9.) While paying homage to the originality of Malebranche's views on divine and human freedom, nevertheless, page after page of her scholarly study is a chiselled exposé of dilemmas, problems, antinomies, contradictions, and irreconcilable conflicts. See for example her final summary on pages 379-87. I contend that her difficulties are directly traceable to three failures: (1) Inadequate attention to the experimental character of Malebranche's method and neglect of the algebraic character of Malebranche's physics as a hierarchy of relations of relations (e.g., pp. 127, 137). (2) Cavalier dismissal of Malebranche's vital distinction between essence and existence (e.g., pp. 77-9). (3) Total oblivion to Malebranche's view of God as *Celui qui est*.

Blampignon asserts that the Vision in God and the vision of God are identical. (*Etude*, p. 144.) This Gouhier rightly claims, is a gross oversimplification. (*Philosophie de Malebranche*, p. 321.) And yet, it seems to me that the interpretation which Gouhier offers is still oversimplified. The vision of God, Gouhier affirms, expresses the *essential* relation that unites the understanding to God; vision of God is the definition of the understanding in its nature or in its

function. (*Ibid.*) Given that God cannot create man without orienting him towards Himself, "voir Dieu" defines the nature of man on the intellectual level. Just as man's will is primarily a movement of love directed towards God, so the vision of God is the intellectual equivalent of this tendency. (Pp. 319-21.) Vision *in* God then becomes: "la définition de l'entendement dans son *fonctionnement*." (P. 321, my ital.) In other words, Vision in God expresses or explains what it is precisely and specifically that the mind actually apprehends in seeing God. It is the essence of man to see God; now if we seek concretely to explain what it is to see God, we must then say that we see God when we see the ideas or the Word.

Moreover, we know God, says Gouhier, as God knows Himself. And how does God know Himself? He knows Himself by expressing Himself in the Word. (P. 334.) Hence, when we know the Word, we know God as directly and immediately as He knows Himself.

Now Gouhier's interpretation is absolutely sound as far as it goes, for it is founded on Malebranche's own statement to Arnauld, (*Réponse aux Livre des Vraies, etc.*, Ch. 24, Secs. 1 and 3, pp. 424 and 426):

> J'ai dit expréssement . . . qu'a l'égard de l'infini, on le connaissait par lui-même et non par une *idée;* parce que je sais, qu'il n'y a point d'*archétype* sur lequel Dieu ait été formé, et que rien ne peut représenter Dieu que son *Verbe* qui lui est consubstantiel. . . . Je veux néanmoins qu'on voie l'infini: qu'on connaisse Dieu par une *idée;* mais certainement cette *idée* sera Dieu même; car il n'y a point d'autre *idée* de Dieu que son *Verbe*. Le Fils de Dieu est l'expression et la ressemblance parfaite de son Père. Je veux bien qu'on voie Dieu ou l'infini par une idée, mais une idée qui lui soit consubstantielle, une

idée qui renferme toute sa substance, une idée qui ne représente
point l'Être divin en tant qu'il peut
être participé imparfaitement par
ses créatures.

Malebranche then admits that we see
God in the universal Reason, in the
Word. This statement, however, Malebranche makes in order to save himself from ontologism—from Arnauld's
charge that man cannot in this life
know the absolute essence of God and
therefore requires an idea of Him. It
in no way proves that when Malebranche speaks of knowing God "par
simple vue" he identifies this process
exclusively with knowing God through
the Word. Furthermore, it is to be
noted that the Word, in so far as it is
the total and adequate and complete
reflection of God's *substance*, is far
more than the ideas relative to the
creatures and seen *in* the Word. If,
therefore, we are to treat the Word
as the source of our immediate knowledge of God, we must be careful *not*
to restrict the Word to the sphere of
intelligible abstract concepts. Our vision of God through the Word is then
something far more than our Vision
in God. In focussing on the Word *as
such*, we are then apprehending that
which contains the whole of God's
substance. We then see God *in* His
reason but what we see thus is more
than reason or essence—we behold a
reason that is consubstantial with
God, we behold an essence to whose
essence it belongs to exist.

114. Le Moine, *Vérités éternelles*,
pp. 238-9.

115. *Ibid.*, p. 236.

116. Malebranche, *Méditations
chrétiennes*, Med. 19, Sec. 1, pp.
387-8, Gouhier edition; O. C. x, p.
214.

117. Rabbe, *Simon Foucher*, p. 37.

118. Blampignon, *Etude*, pp. 137-
9.

119. Vidgrain, *Christianisme*, Ch.
4.

120. Gouhier, *Philosophie de Malebranche*, p. 409.

121. Cuvillier, *Le mystique*, p. 56
and *passim*. Cf. also Gueroult, *Malebranche*, Vol. 1, especially pp. 25-6
and 287, and see above, Note 6, Introduction.

Chapter IV. Occasionalism

1. Malebranche, *Recherche*, Bk. 3,
Pt. 2, Ch. 3, L. i, p. 242, my italics.
Italicized phrase added after first edi-
tion, to replace "qui lui arrive."

2. Mr. Church mistranslates this
passage (*Study*, p. 93), although he
refers to the Bouillier edition where
the phrase "qu'elle lui communique"
occurs and where Malebranche says:
"nous ne voyons point sensiblement
quelle autre chose pourrait être la
cause de ces mouvements." Church
translates: "C'est pour cela que tout le
monde conclut qu'une boule agitée
qui en rencontre une autre est la véritable et la principale cause de l'agitation qu'elle lui communique," as:
"For that reason everyone concludes
that a moving ball which strikes another is the principal cause of the
movement of the one struck." As a
result, his rendition fails to disclose
that for Malebranche, unlike for
Hume, there is communication of
movement from ball *A* to ball *B* and
that Malebranche's question is solely
whether ball *A* is the *true cause* of
the movement of ball *B*.

3. Malebranche, *Recherche*, Bk. 6,
Pt. 2, Ch. 3, L. ii, p. 198.

4. *Ibid.*, Ch. 2, L. ii, p. 196.

5. *Ibid.*, p. 197.

6. *Ibid.*, Ch. 3, L. ii, p. 198, my
ital.

7. Thomas, *History of the Schoolmen*, Ch. 30. Cf. Gilson, *Being*, pp.
96-107.

8. Gilson, *Being*, p. 44.

9. *Ibid.*, pp. 46-7.

10. Malebranche, *Recherche*, Bk. 6,
Pt. 2, Ch. 3, L. ii, p. 200.

11. *Ibid.*, p. 203.

12. Church, *Study,* p. 90.

13. *Ibid.,* p. 78.

14. Brunschvicg, *Spinoza,* Chap. 9, *passim.*

15. Gilson, *Medieval Philosophy,* p. 52.

16. *Ibid.,* p. 57.

17. *Ibid.,* p. 71.

18. *Ibid.,* p. 74.

19. *Ibid.,* p. 90.

20. Malebranche, *Recherche,* Bk. 6, Pt. 2, Ch. 2, L. ii, p. 193.

21. Bacon, *Advancement of Learning,* Scribner, p. 138.

22. Malebranche, *Recherche,* Bk. 6, Pt. 2, Ch. 3, L. ii, p. 203.

23. *Ibid.,* p. 201; Church, *Study,* p. 91.

24. Church, *ibid.*

25. Malebranche, *Méditations chrétiennes,* Med. 9, Sec. 2, pp. 167-8, Gouhier edition; O. C. x, p. 96. Church, *Study,* pp. 91-2.

26. Church, *ibid.,* p. 92.

27. *Ibid.,* p. 93.

28. *Ibid.,* p. 111.

29. Ginsberg, *Preface,* p. 57.

30. Malebranche, *Méditations chrétiennes,* Med. 3, Sec. 2, p. 39 ff., Gouhier edition; O. C. x, pp. 27 ff.

31. *Ibid.,* Sec. 10, p. 44, Gouhier edition; O. C. x, p. 30; my ital.

32. *Ibid.,* Sec. 16, p. 46, Gouhier; O. C., pp. 31-2.

33. *Ibid.,* Med. 9, Sec. 13, p. 175, Gouhier; O. C., pp. 100-101.

34. *Ibid.,* Sec. 2, pp. 166-7, Gouhier; O. C., p. 96; my ital. *Cf. Prémotion,* O. C. xvi, p. 132: ". . . Comment Dieu est-il Tout-puissant. . . . La liaison necessaire de l'acte avec son effet, nous passe . . . Nous ne voyons pas l'influence même de la cause, qui produit les effets."

35. *E.g.,* Malebranche, *Méditations chrétiennes,* Med. 9, Sec. 2, pp. 167-8, Gouhier edition, or O. C. x, p. 96; *Recherche,* Ecl. 6, L. iii, p. 32.

36. *E.g., ibid.,* Bk. 3, Pt. 2, Ch. 5, L. i, p. 247, and Ecl. 6, L. iii, p. 30.

37. Gilson, *Being,* p. 177: "God *knows* essences, but He *says* existences, and He does not say all that He knows."

38. Malebranche, *Recherche,* Bk. 3, Pt. 2, Ch. 9, Sec. 1, L. i, pp. 267-8.

39. Church, *Study,* p. 92.

40. Gilson, *Medieval Philosophy,* p. 75, my ital.

41. *Ibid.,* p. 73, my ital.

42. Malebranche, *Entretiens sur la métaphysique,* Dial. 9, Sec. 2, Ginsberg, pp. 226-7.

43. *Ibid.,* Sec. 3, p. 228.

44. Malebranche, *Méditations sur l'humilité,* p. 108, Cuvillier 1944 edition; O. C. xvii-1, pp. 391-2. See below, note 50.

45. See above, note 22.

46. Malebranche, *Méditations chrétiennes,* Med. 9, Sec. 6, p. 171, Gouhier edition; O. C. x, p. 98.

47. *Cf.* Gilson, *Being,* p. 123.

48. Malebranche, *Recherche,* Bk. 6, Pt. 2, Ch. 3, L. ii, pp. 201 and 203.

49. Malebranche, *Entretiens sur la métaphysique,* Dial. 7, Secs. 7 and 8, Ginsberg, pp. 186-7, my ital.

50. Malebranche, *Prières avant et après la sainte messe,* p. 208, Cuvillier 1944 edition, my ital. The editor, M. Cuvillier here notes: "*Influer* est pris ici en sens étymologique: *couler dans, s'insinuer dans,* mais au figuré. Bossuet l'emploie ainsi dans les *Méditations sur l'Evangile,* la Cène, 86ᵉ jour: 'Jamais homme n'a été Dieu comme lui (Jésus), ni n'a eu sur tous les esprits cette autorité naturelle qui fait que, sans s'y efforcer, . . . elle y influe si doucement et si intimement qu'on lui cède sans violence.'—Dans le titre de la XVI *Méditation chrétienne,* Malebranche lui-même prend le mot au sens *actif:* 'Jésus-Christ a des désirs passagers et des désirs stables et permanents. Les premiers influent la grace actuelle, et les seconds l'habituelle.'"

To the title of the sixteenth Meditation of the *Méditations chrétiennes,* Gouhier, as editor, appends this note to the word, *influent:* "Influer: 'Verbe *actif. Communiquer par une vertu* secrète.' Dictionnaire de l'Académie, 1694, *qui le réserve surtout pour 'les impressions que les astres répandent sur les corps sublunaires.'* "

51. Malebranche, *Méditations sur l'humilité*, pp. 108-9, Cuvillier 1944 edition; O. C. xvii-1, pp. 391-2; my ital. *Cf.* p. 151, 1944; O. C. xvii-1, p. 412.

52. Malebranche, *Méditations chrétiennes*, Med. 9, Sec. 2, p. 166, Gouhier edition; O. C. x, p. 96.

53. Moreau, *Malebranche et le Spinozisme*, pp. 6 and 87-8.

54. Malebranche, *Entretiens sur la métaphysique*, Dial. 7, Sec. 8, Ginsberg, p. 186 and *Chrétien et chinois*, pp. 88-9, Le Moine edition, or O. C. xv, p. 32.

55. Bouillier, Histoire, Vol. 2, pp. 60-1. Ginsberg, *Preface*, p. 50. Ollé-Laprune, *Malebranche*, Vol. 1, pp. 358-63, 544-8, and also 236-8.

56. Ollé-Laprune, *Malebranche*, Vol. 1, p. 548.

57. Spinoza, *Ethics*, Pt. 2, Prop. 3, Schol.

58. Malebranche, *Entretiens sur la métaphysique*, Dial. 9, Sec. 7, Ginsberg, p. 235.

59. *Ibid.*, Sec. 3, p. 229. See *Prémotion*, O. C. xvi, pp. 93-101 and 133 for Malebranche's strictures against the worship of a Deity who is no more than a blind, brute, bizarre, omnipotent force that acts like a terrible phantom without reason or motives. Specifically he singles out Hobbes and Locke.

60. Spinoza, *Ethics*, Pt. 1, Prop. 33, Schol. 2, end of schol.

61. Malebranche, *L'Amour de Dieu*, p. 77.

62. Malebranche, *Méditations chrétiennes*, Med. 9, Sec. 3, p. 168, Gouhier edition; O. C. x, pp. 96-7.

63. Malebranche, *Conversations*, Dial. 2, p. 43, Bridet edition; O. C. iv, p. 43.

64. *Ibid.*, Dial. 3, p. 64, Bridet edition; O. C. iv, p. 60. Actually he says here that final causes are neces-

sary for religion, but of course for him religion is the true philosophy. (See *Entretiens sur la métaphysique*, Dial. 6, Sec. 2, Ginsberg, pp. 163-4.)

65. *Ibid.*, Dial. 9, Sec. 4, Ginsberg, p. 230.

66. *Ibid.*, p. 231. In his *Nature et grâce*, Malebranche himself raises a telling objection against his own doctrine:

Dieu suit necessairement les regles de sa sagesse, il fait necessairement ce qui est le mieux. Or du moins il estoit mieux que le Monde fût créé dans le tems, que de ne l'être point du tout. Certainement il étoit à propos, selon les regles de la sagesse de Dieu, que le Monde fût produit dans les circonstances selon lesquelles Dieu l'a produit. Donc la Création du Monde dans le tems est absolument necessaire, Dieu n'est point libre à son égard, il n'a pû s'empêcher de le produire.

To resolve this difficulty, Malebranche declares:

Il faut prendre garde, que bien que Dieu suive les règles que sa sagesse lui prescrit, il ne fait pas neanmoins nécessairement ce qui est le mieux; parce qu'il peut ne rien faire. Agir & ne pas suivre exactement les règles de la sagesse, c'est un défaut. Ainsi, supposé que Dieu agisse, il agit nécessairement de la manière la plus sage qui se puisse concevoir. Mais, être libre dans la production du Monde, c'est une marque d'abondance, de plenitude, de suffisance à soi-même. Il est mieux que le Monde soit, que de n'être pas: l'Incarnation de Jesus-Christ rend l'ouvrage de Dieu digne de son Auteur, j'y consens. Mais comme Dieu est essentiellement heureux & parfait, comme il n'y a que lui qui soit bien à son égard, ou la cause de sa perfection & de son bonheur, il n'aime invinciblement que sa propre substance; & tout ce qui est hors de Dieu, doit être produit par

une action éternelle & immüable, à
la verité, mais qui ne tire sa neces-
sité que de la supposition des De-
crets divins. (Disc. II, Art. 54,
O. C. v, pp. 111-12.)

As Laporte observes (*La liberté*,
pp. 358-60), Malebranche is carefully
distinguishing in the above passages
between essence and existence. God is
free to create or not to create existents, but *if* he creates, *then* he must
observe principles of rationality.

67. Spinoza, *Ethics*, Pt. 1, Prop. 33,
Schol. 2, end of schol. *Cf.* Part 1,
Appendix.

68. Malebranche, *Entretiens sur la
métaphysique*, Dial. 9, Sec. 4, Ginsberg, p. 230.

69. *E.g., ibid.,* Sec. 10.

70. Malebranche, *Correspondance
avec Mairan*, pp. 106 and 140, Moreau
edition; O. C. xix, pp. 855 and 886.

71. Malebranche, *Recherche*, Bk. 4,
Chap. 1, Sec. 2, L. ii, p. 2.

72. Malebranche, *Entretiens sur la
métaphysique*, Dial. 9, Sec. 4, Ginsberg, p. 231. *Cf. Prémotion*, O. C.
xvi, pp. 119-20, 127, 129, 135, 137-8,
144-5.

73. Malebranche, *Adoration*, Pt. 1,
pp. 155-9 and n. 2, p. 155, Cuvillier
1944 edition or O. C. xvii-1, pp. 425-7,
including note b, p. 425; Appendix to
Cuvillier edition of *Méditations sur
l'humilité*, letter to Lamy, p. 217, or
O. C. xviii, p. 479; *Conversations
chrétiennes*, Dial. 2, p. 47, Bridet edition, or O. C. iv, pp. 46-7.

74. *E.g.,* Malebranche, *Conversations chrétiennes*, Dial. 2, pp. 48-50,
Bridet edition, or O. C. iv, pp. 47-9;
Entretiens sur la métaphysique, Dial.
9, Secs. 4 and 5.

75. Malebranche, *Entretiens sur la
métaphysique*, Dial. 9, Sec. 5, Ginsberg, p. 232.

76. *Ibid.*

77. Le Moine, *Vérités éternelles*,
see Chapter 4 of Part 3, entitled, "Le
Théocentrisme de Malebranche."

78. Cuvillier, *La mystique*, pp.
17-19.

79. *E.g.,* Malebranche, *Traité de
morale*, Pt. 1, Ch. 8, Sec. 3, p. 82.

80. Malebranche, *Méditations chrétiennes*, Med. 17, Sec. 14, p. 359,
Gouhier edition; O. C. x, pp. 198-9.
Cf. Recherche, Bk. 2, Pt. 3, Ch. 4, L.
i, p. 194; *Adoration*, Pt. 2, pp. 176
and 178, Cuvillier 1944 edition, or O.
C. xvii-1, pp. 435 and 436; and
Entretiens sur la métaphysique, Dial.
9, Sec. 6, Ginsberg, p. 233.

81. Blondel, *L'Anti-cartésianisme
de Malebranche*, p. 10. Church,
Study, pp. 108-9.

82. Malebranche, *Entretiens sur la
métaphysique*, Dial. 9, Secs. 5 and 8;
Recherche, Ecl. 8, L. iii, p. 49; *Conversations*, Dial. 1, p. 29, Dials. 2 and
5, *passim*, Dial. 8, pp. 199 and 220,
Bridet edition, or O. C. iv, pp. 32-3,
168-9, and 184-5. *Cf.* André, *Vie du
R. P. Malebranche*, p. 189. André
quotes Malebranche as follows:

"Il y a environ dix ans que j'ai
composé un petit livre qui a pour
titre: *Traité de la nature et de la
grâce*. Mon dessein est de justifier
la sagesse et la bonté de Dieu dans
la construction de son ouvrage,
nonobstant les désordres de la nature et le dérèglement des moeurs.
J'avais principalement en vue certains philosophes qui outrent la
métaphysique et qui prétendent que
Dieu fait le mal comme le bien;
on un mot, qu'il est auteur du
péché et qu'il ne veut point le salut
de tous ceux qui périssent. J'ai
combattu ces philosophes en me
servant de leurs principes et leur
parlant un langage qui paraît nouveau; mais c'est celui qu'ils enten-
dent. Si je les eusse combattus par
les principes et par le langage de
l'école, mon ouvrage n'aurait point
eu l'effet qu'il a eu et que je voulais
qu'il eût . . . Car, enfin, il faut
parler aux hommes selon leurs
idées . . ." O. C. xix, pp. 547-8.
Cf. Malebranche, *Réponse au Livre
des vraies, etc.*, Ch. 4, Secs. 3-4,
p. 292.

83. Malebranche, *Entretiens sur la métaphysique*, Dial. 9, Sec. 5, Fontana ii, pp. 200-1.

84. *Ibid.*, Dial. 12; *Méditations chrétiennes*, Med. 8, Secs. 19-23; *Recherche*, Bk. 5, Ch. 1, L. ii, p. 80; *ibid.*, Appendice, L. iii, p. 302.

85. Malebranche, *Traité de morale*, Pt. 1, Ch. 2, Sec. 11, p. 20.

86. Malebranche, *Entretiens sur la métaphysique*, Dial. 9, Sec. 8, Ginsberg, pp. 236-7.

87. *Ibid. Cf. Méditations chrétiennes*, Med. 11, Secs. 7-9.

88. Malebranche, *Méditations chrétiennes*, Med. 12, Sec. 20, p. 235, Gouhier edition; O. C. x, p. 132.

89. *Ibid.*

90. If my speculation is correct, it would explain why Malebranche finds it difficult to accept the incarnation as an expiation for man's sin. *Cf.* Malebranche, *Fragments et correspondance*, letter to Lamy, Jan. 18, 1688, pp. 102-3; O. C. xviii, pp. 478-9.

91. Malebranche, *L'Amour de Dieu*, pp. 75-6.

92. *Ibid.*, p. 77.

93. Malebranche, *Méditations chrétiennes*, Med. 5, Sec. 15, p. 87, Gouhier edition; O. C. x, p. 53.

94. *Ibid.*

95. *E.g.*, Malebranche, *Recherche*, Bk. 3, Pt. 1, Ch. 1, Sec. 1, L. i, pp. 214-5.

96. Descartes, *Principles*, Pt. 2, Prin. 64, A. T. ix, pp. 101-2; *cf.* Mouy, *Physique cartésienne*, pp. 220-1 and especially Gilson, *Etudes*, pp. 128-9.

97. *E.g.*, letter of Leibnitz to Malebranche, Jan. 13, 1679, Malebranche, *Correspondance de Malebranche et de Leibnitz*, pp. 371-2 or O. C. xviii, p. 143; Leibnitz, *Discourse*, Arts. 12 and 18.

98. Descartes, *Principles*, Pt. 1, Prins. 53 and 61, H. R. i, pp. 240 and 244.

99. *Ibid.*, Prin. 60.

100. *Ibid.*, Pt. 2, Prins. 23 and 36, H. R. i, p. 265 and A. T. ix, pp. 83-4.

Cf. Moreau, *Malebranche et le Spinozisme*, pp. 55-6.

Gueroult disagrees entirely with the present interpretation of Cartesian physics. See *L'Idée de force*. Also see above, Chapter II, note 231, and below: notes 139 and 257, this chapter, and note 29, Chapter V.

101. The letter of Descartes to Newcastle, October, 1645 (A. T. iv, p. 328. Cited by Lewis, *L'Individualité selon Descartes*, p. 53, n. 72), suggests that for Descartes God began to move matter in different ways "dès le premier instant qu'il a créé la matière."

102. Descartes à X***, August, 1641 and Descartes à X***, Egmond, 1645 or 1646, A. T. iii, p. 435 and A. T. iv, pp. 349-50. *Cf.* Gilson, *Being*, p. 110.

103. Gilson, *Being*, p. 86.

104. *Ibid.*, p. 91.

105. *Ibid.*, p. 87.

106. *Ibid.*

107. *Ibid.*, p. 90.

108. *Ibid.*, p. 96.

109. *Ibid.*, pp. 101 and 103.

110. *Ibid.*, p. 102, my ital.

111. *Ibid.*, pp. 105 and 109.

112. Marginal note to Proposition 9, "Propositiones prohibitas a congregatione 15ª. Generali Jesuit," André, *Documents inédits*, pp. 217-8.

113. Malebranche, *Méditations chrétiennes*, Med. 9, Sec. 12, pp. 174-5, Gouhier edition; O. C. x, p. 100, my ital.

For Malebranche, eternity, immensity, infinity—these are descriptive of existence, God's existence, or of ideas as existing in God, but say nothing concerning the existence of creatures. With respect to creatures we may *a priori* affirm of them only those properties contained *in* the idea, *e.g.*, divisibility, but not the "whether" or the "how" of existence. An actually existing world cannot be deduced from essence; and therefore an actual, concrete world may have existential circumstances that distinguish it from essence proper. Thus a created actual world may be limited and finite, even though the idea of extension is infinite.

114. Malebranche, *Correspondance avec Mairan*, pp. 102-3, Moreau edition; O. C. xix, p. 853.

115. *Ibid.*, pp. 105-6, Moreau; O. C., p. 855.

116. *Ibid.*, p. 110, Moreau; O. C. p. 858.

117. *Ibid.*, pp. 125-6, Moreau; O. C., pp. 873-4.

118. *Ibid.*, p. 127, Moreau; O. C., p. 875.

119. *Ibid.*, pp. 135-6, Moreau; O. C., p. 883.

120. *Ibid.*, p. 139, Moreau; O. C., pp. 885-6.

121. *Ibid.*, "Son être propre" omitted in the Cousin edition.

122. *Ibid.*, p. 156, Moreau; O. C., p. 899; my ital.

123. *Ibid.*, p. 169, Moreau; O. C., p. 909; my ital.

124. *Ibid.*, p. 171, Moreau; O. C., p. 911.

125. Bridet, *Connaissance*, pp. 300-305, 347-8.

126. Malebranche, *Correspondance avec Mairan*, pp. 129-30, Moreau edition; O. C. xix, pp. 876-7.

127. Gilson, *Being*, p. 63.

128. Malebranche, *Correspondance avec Mairan*, p. 105, Moreau edition; O. C. xix, pp. 854-5.

129. Malebranche, *Méditations chrétiennes*, Med. 9, Sec. 10, pp. 173-4, Gouhier edition; O. C. x, pp. 99-100. See above, note 58.

130. *Cf.* Gilson, *Being*, p. 171.

131. Spinoza, letters to Tschirnhaus, May 5, 1676 and July 15, 1676, Scribner, pp. 475 and 478.

132. Spinoza, *Ethics*, Pt. 1, Props. 21-3; *ibid.*, Pt. 2, Prop. 13, Axioms and Lemmas.

133. *Cf. ibid.*, Pt. 1, Prop. 15, Schol.

134. Malebranche, *Correspondance avec Mairan*, p. 140, Moreau edition; O. C. xix, p. 886. *Cf. Recherche*, Ecl. 10, L. iii, pp. 91-2, and *Réponse au*

Livre des vraies, etc., Chap. 17, Sec. 8, pp. 383-4:

". . . Monsieur, prenez garde que vous vous trompez encore, de croire, que pour concevoir quel est le mouvement propre à tracer une ligne courbe, il faut déjà la connaître; car il n'en est pas de même des vérités nécessaires que des faits, et des sciences que des histoires. Il faudrait avoir vu le visage de saint Augustin, pour savoir comment il était fait. Mais pour former des lignes géométriques, et en découvrir les propriétés, il ne faut que consulter l'étendue intelligible, et contempler les rapports exacts qui sont entre les grandeurs. Si, par exemple, une ligne droite et un point étant donnés immobiles sur un plan, je veux m'imaginer qu'un autre point quelconque se meuve sur ce plan, en conservant toujours le même rapport de distance à ce point et à cette ligne immobiles; alors j'aurai les trois lignes parabole, hyperbole et ellipse, sans que j'en aie jamais oui parler."

135. Malebranche, *Correspondance avec Mairan*, pp. 139-40, Moreau edition; O. C. xix, p. 886; my ital.

136. Moreau, *Malebranche et le Spinozisme*, p. 48. But in an earlier article (*Le réalisme de Malebranche*) Moreau seems to chide Malebranche for not having been a Plato, for not having sought refuge in principles of an indeterminate matter and determinate forms to account for the natural world. Here Moreau assumes that for Malebranche ideas are entitative hypostatizations and that the created material world is a duplicate imitation or copy (p. 131). He seems to ignore the fact that intelligible extension is a hierarchy of relations of relations (p. 133, n. 2). As such it serves as a system of laws or functions that regulate and, in a mathematical sense, generate the formulas for the configuration of physical objects and their interactions. Thus created matter is a participation of intelligible extension, and existence is its principle of

individuation. Surely, with this distinction of essence and existence, there is no need for Malebranche to be other than Malebranche.

137. Malebranche, *Correspondance avec Mairan*, pp. 169-70, Moreau edition; O. C. xix, pp. 909-10. Consult Lovejoy, *Great Chain*, Ch. 5, for seventeenth century attempts to escape Spinozism by limiting the principle of plenitude. Malebranche, by maintaining in his letters to Mairan that existence is arbitrary and that it may be finite in extent, is doing precisely this.

138. Malebranche, *Méditations chrétiennes*, Med. 9, Sec. 6, p. 170, Gouhier edition; O. C. x, pp. 97-8.

139. Malebranche, *Recherche*, Ecl. 16, *passim*.

It is true, as Moreau observes (*Malebranche et le Spinozisme*, p. 67), that Malebranche did not arrive at this identification of existence with movement at once. Thus in 1675 when he wrote the second volume of the *Recherche* he still adhered to Descartes' view of created matter as an inert mass: ". . . il semble qu'il suffit que Dieu veuille qu'il y ait de la matière, afin que non seulement elle existe, mais aussi afin qu'elle existe en repos." (*Recherche*, Bk. 6, Pt. 2, Ch. 9, L. ii, p. 279.) As we saw in Chapter I, however, already at this time Malebranche had made important advances beyond Descartes by claiming that hardness could not be attributed to rest, for rest was no positive force, but merely the privation of motion. Furthermore, despite the above statement in the *Recherche*, in his early correspondence with Liebnitz, about 1672-1675, Malebranche seems to deny that concretely existing matter can be conceived to be inert. He seems to be saying that while extension is indeed the essence of matter, still movement is inseparable from and indeed derivative from the very existence of matter. (*Correspondance de Malebranche et de Liebnitz*, pp.

355-65, Cousin edition; O. C. xviii, pp. 96-104. *Cf. Recherche*, Bk. 3, Ch. 1, Sec. 1, L. i, pp. 214-15.)

In any case and far more importantly, at the time of the *Recherche* Malebranche had unambiguously committed himself to the philosophical distinction between essence and existence. Accordingly, it may be said that at a very early date he was, on the metaphysical level, equipped with the required philosophical tool for the eventual revamping of Cartesian science. By having made the important separation between essence and existence, he was thereafter enabled to identify existential matter with pure turbulent process. See above, Chapter I, note 147.

140. Malebranche, *Entretiens sur la métaphysique*, Dial. 8, Sec. 2, Ginsberg, p. 204.

141. *Ibid.*, Sec. 4, Ginsberg, p. 207.

142. *Ibid.*, Sec. 8, Ginsberg, p. 212.

143. *Ibid.*, Sec. 7, Ginsberg, p. 210.

144. *Ibid.*, Sec. 6, Ginsberg, p. 209.

145. Descartes, *Reply to Objections I*, H. R. ii, p. 15.

146. Ginsberg, *Preface*, p. 48.

147. *Ibid.*, p. 58.

148. *E.g.*, Church, *Study*, pp. 106-10 and 129.

149. Ginsberg, *Preface*, p. 49.

150. *Ibid.*, pp. 48-9.

151. *Cf.* Spinoza, *Ethics*, Pt. 1, Prop. 15.

152. *Ibid.*, Pt. 2, Def. 2.

153. *Ibid.*, Pt. 3, Props. 6 and 7, my ital.

154. Malebranche, *Entretiens sur la métaphysique*, Dial. 9, Sec. 2, p. 227.

155. Brunschvicg, *Spinoza*, pp. 349-57.

156. Gilson, *Being*, p. 161.

157. *Ibid.*, p. 162.

158. *Ibid.*, p. 166.

159. *Ibid.*, pp. 184-5.

160. *Ibid.*, pp. 175-6.

161. Gilson, *Medieval Philosophy*, pp. 140-1.

162. Gouhier, *Philosophie de Malebranche*, pp. 192-3. Malebranche's

biographer André also observes that Malebranche held that not all Thomists were disciples of Thomas. (*Vie du R. P. Malebranche*, pp. 93-4.) Cf. Malebranche's expression: "il y a Thomistes & Thomistes." (*Prémotion*, O. C. xvi, p. 77.)

163. Augustine, *Confessions*, Bk. 1, Sec. 2.

164. *Ibid.*, Sec. 3.

165. *Ibid.*, Sec. 6.

166. Malebranche, *Entretiens sur la métaphysique*, Dial. 8, Secs. 4 and 5, Ginsberg, pp. 207-9.

167. Malebranche, *Recherche*, Appendice, L. iii, pp. 298-300. Prost, *Atomisme et occasionalisme*, p. 127 and note, points out that La Forge identified the immensity of God with His omnipotence and that He sought to repel pantheism by equating His immensity with His power.

168. Gilson, *Medieval Philosophy*, p. 141.

169. a) Ginsberg says that Occasionalism leads to Spinozism and reduces creatures to non-entities. (*Preface*, p. 57.)

b) Arnauld, the Jansenist, says Occasionalism deprives man of freedom and reduces him to a beast. (Arnauld, *Réflexions philosophiques*, I, ch. ix, p. 254, Oeuvres, *Edition de Lausanne*, 1775 à 1783, vol. XXXIX, cited by Gouhier, *Philosophie de Malebranche*, p. 200, n. 1.) For Bouillier, Malebranche gives God all reality and activity, and reduces the creature to wax. (Bouillier, *Histoire*, Vol. 2, pp. 60-1, 111 and 113.)

c) Blampignon and Ollé-Laprune accuse Malebranche of being a Jansenist. He is a fatalist who deprives man of all power and of all causality. (Blampignon, *Etude*, p. 173; cf. p. 180. Ollé-Laprune, *Malebranche*, Vol. 1, pp. 316, 319, 338 ff., 356, etc.)

d) Since Malebranche insists on free will, he is accused by Laporte and Arnauld of being a "pure Molinist," *i.e.*, one who believes that man achieves salvation entirely through his own merits and by his own natural forces. For the Molinist God cooperates with man, but man alone initiates and *commences* his salvation. (See Gouhier, *op. cit.*, pp. 194 and 200-2.)

e) Gueroult (*Malebranche*, Vol. 2) is another who condemns the alleged radical impotence of secondary causes (*e.g.*, pp. 227, 232, 238-9), although he comes close to seeing the power of occasional causes in *disposing* or *determining* the general laws (p. 234) and their close connection with Malebranche's conception of creation by divine will.

Says Malebranche, wearily: ". . . Je suis Janséniste selon les uns; et je suis Moliniste selon les autres, et cela sans que ni les uns, ni les autres, se veuillent donner la peine d'examiner les ouvrages sur lesquels ils prononcent." (Letter of July 29, 1708, *Correspondance inédite*, p. 24; cited by Gouhier, *op. cit.*, p. 203, who concludes: "Malebranche est d'abord Malebranche." O. C. xix, pp. 789-90.)

170. Gilson, *Medieval Philosophy*, pp. 69 and 71.

171. Malebranche, *Méditations chrétiennes*, Med. 5, Sec. 6, p. 78, Gouhier edition, or O. C. x, pp. 48-9; *Entretiens sur la métaphysique*, Dial. 7, Sec. 11, Ginsberg, p. 190.

172. Malebranche, *Recherche*, Bk. 6, Pt. 2, Ch. 3, L. ii, p. 201.

173. *Ibid.*, p. 204.

174. *Ibid.*, p. 203, my ital.

175. *Ibid.*, Ecl. 15, L. iii, pp. 129-30.

176. In the *Conversations chrétiennes*, Malebranche denies a plethora of deities or creative powers, because the result would be chaos for science. A multiplicity of intelligences could not agree to produce so remarkable an order as we find in nature. (Dial. 1, p. 16 and note 1, Bridet edition; O. C. iv, pp. 21-2.)

177. Malebranche, *Méditations chrétiennes*, Med. 6, Sec. 6, pp. 99-100, Gouhier edition; O. C. x, p. 60.

178. *Ibid.*, Med. 5, Sec. 4, p. 76, Gouhier edition; O. C. x, p. 47; my ital. *Cf. Recherche*, Bk. 6, Pt. 2, Ch. 3, L. ii, p. 200 and *ibid.*, Ch. 4, L. ii, p. 222; *Entretiens sur la métaphysique*, Dial. 7, Sec. 2, Ginsberg, p. 179.

179. Again, I am compelled to disagree with Church. He writes that it would be tempting to suppose that when Malebranche claims that perception fails to disclose necessity among events, he is simply condemning sensible experience. He might be saying: ". . . only that perception affords no ground from which to demonstrate as true the belief that the same cause has always the same effect." (*Study*, p. 96.) But Church decides that this is impossible, for when Malebranche examines the idea of extension and finds no efficacy therein, Malebranche is thus openly acknowledging that for reason too power, efficacy and necessity are meaningless. (Pp. 96-7.)

I have already shown that, on the contrary, power is not meaningless for Malebranche. In truth, Malebranche condemns perception only—reason does find in God's nature the ground for believing (not indeed in necessity, but) in the contingent regularity or uniformity of nature. Malebranche, moreover, does not use the idea of extension to show that power is meaningless, but only to indicate that power is not derivative from essence. See below, present section, (c) The Occasional Cause.

180. Gilson, *Being*, p. 103.

181. *Ibid.*, p. 106.

182. Malebranche, *Recherche*, Ecl. 15, L. iii, p. 123.

183. *Ibid.*, p. 124.

184. *Ibid.*, p. 125.

185. *Ibid.*

186. *Ibid.*, pp. 123-7.

187. In a "fragment" published by Vidgrain, which refers to Ecl. 15, Malebranche clearly shows that cre-ation is the basic issue in his attack on secondary causes: "Les termes de ברא et de עשה qui marquent davantage la cause efficiente se disent de Dieu dans le 1er ch. de la Genèse, alors qu'il est dit: 'Que la terre produise et les eaux' '*producat terra herbam*,' il y a תדשא דשא qui signifie proprement '*terra herbescat herbam*' et ישרצו שרץ qui signifie 'reptile reptet,' comme 'volatile volitet' עוף יעופף etc., ce qui marque que Dieu n'a point donné de prétendue force pour produire." (*Fragments et correspondance*, p. 20. See note 2. O. C. xvii-1, p. 539. [Note variations in Hebraic orthography in O. C.] Also see Gouhier, *Vocation*, pp. 43-4, and *Recherche*, Ecl. 15, L. iii, pp. 141-4.)

188. See above, note 162.

189. Malebranche, *Recherche*, Ecl. 15, L. iii, p. 147, note c. Malebranche's reference reads: "Sol et homo generant hominem. Arist. phys. Ausc. I, 2, c. 2. Voyez *Saint Thomas sur ce texte*." Which text of St. Thomas Malebranche has in mind, he does not say. He may be referring to Chapter LXIX of the *Contra gentiles* (Bk. 3, Pt. 1, p. 171). If so, it may at first glance appear as if in reproving Aristotle directly, Malebranche is subtly condemning Aquinas indirectly. For in this chapter Aquinas comes staunchly to the defense of the action of secondary causes.

We must note, first of all, however, that Aristotle's statement is not used by Aquinas to establish the power of creatures, but merely to illustrate this point: in putrefaction, the action of the sun suffices to engender animals, although ordinarily production requires in addition a univocal agent, for the souls of higher animals "are not produced otherwise than by seed: hence Aristotle says that *man and the sun generate man*." (P. 171.) Malebranche, it goes without saying, believes neither in production by putrefaction nor in the principle that animals have souls. Nevertheless, he uses the Aristotelian statement in a wholly different context from that of Thomas, namely, to refute, not the action of creatures, but their alleged (a) creative action, (b) independent action, or (c) action derivative from essence.

Furthermore, it is noteworthy that in this fifteenth Eclaircissement Malebranche nowhere opposes any of the really significant arguments given by Thomas in Chapter LXIX in favor of the action of creatures. To be sure, Malebranche takes a firm stand against qualities, virtues, forms; but if his target were Aquinas rather than Suarezians, then why did he neglect to consider those important demonstrations? The answer, I believe, is simple. An impartial analysis of Thomas' text would show that all his major reasons for supporting the efficacy of creatures are in perfect accord with Malebranchianism.

In this Chapter LXIX, Thomas argues that we are not to "withdraw from natural things their proper actions" (part of title) because secondary causes are required to explain: (1) the diversity of effects, (2) their unity and regularity, (3) generalizations in science, (4) the similarity of creatures to God (since creatures are analogues of God's being, they must also be like Him in the point of acting), (5) the goodness, wisdom and omnipotence of God. In addition, it is important to note that in this very chapter Aquinas opposes Platonic abstractionism and insists that it is not forms as such that make things be or in virtue of which they act, but that they are and act in virtue of their existence (pp. 169-70).

Now Malebranche's doctrine of "occasional" causes to whom God communicates His power through His general will is in complete accord with the first three points. (See below, "(c) The Occasional Cause.") And his doctrines of God as Being, of the immensity of God, and of the distinction between essence and exist-

ence, in my opinion, assert the fourth and fifth points.

190. *Ibid.*, pp. 128-9.

191. *Ibid.*, p. 130. *Cf. Fragments et correspondance*, p. 29; O. C. xvii-1, p. 544.

192. Gilson, *Being*, p. 164, and *Discours*, pp. 340-1.

193. Malebranche, *Méditations chrétiennes*, Med. 5, Sec. 7, pp. 78-9, Gouhier edition; O. C. x, p. 49.

194. Malebranche, *Entretiens sur la métaphysique*, Dial. 7, Sec. 8, Ginsberg, p. 187, my ital.

195. Malebranche, *Recherche*, Ecl. 15, L. iii, p. 148.

196. *Ibid.*, p. 146.

197. *Ibid.*, p. 148.

198. *Ibid.*, p. 149.

199. *Ibid.*, p. 146.

200. Malebranche, 2e *Lettre en réponse au livre 1er des Réflexions*, Ch. 1, p. 147. Cited by Gouhier, *Vocation*, p. 118, n. 2.

Gouhier maintains that Malebranche's true adversaries in the fifteenth Eclaircissement are not those who attribute real efficacy to secondary causes, but rather the partisans of the theory of *divine concourse* (*op. cit.*, pp. 116-20). This doctrine asserts that when the creature acts, God simultaneously concurs with it. In theology this meant that God cooperates with the creature in the work of salvation: the creature acts by a power of its own; man begins and God comes to his aid. (Malebranche, *Recherche*, Ecl. 1, L. iii, p. 13. See Gouhier, *Philosophie de Malebranche*, Pt. 2, Chs. 3 and 4.) For Malebranche, however, the notion of such divine concourse is unintelligible (*Recherche*, Bk. 3, Pt. 2, Ch. 6, L. i, p. 250), for since true power is the power to create and to conserve, it is God who really begins salvation by giving His grace, and it is the creature that cooperates with God in accepting or rejecting the grace that is offered. This power to act or to consent belongs to the human will and constitutes its freedom. It is not a creative power, but it is nonetheless active.

201. Malebranche, *Recherche*, Ecl. 15, L. iii, p. 136.

202. *Ibid.*, p. 152.

203. *Ibid.*, p. 156.

204. Malebranche, *Méditations chrétiennes*, Med. 5, Sec. 5, p. 77, Gouhier edition; O. C. x, p. 48.

205. Malebranche, *Recherche*, Bk. 6, Pt. 2, Ch. 3, L. ii, pp. 200-1.

206. *Ibid.*, p. 202. *Cf. Méditations chrétiennes*, Med. 6, Sec. 11, pp. 104-7, Gouhier edition; O. C. x, pp. 62-3.

207. Malebranche, *Recherche*, Bk. 6, Pt. 2, Ch. 3, L. ii, p. 202, and *Méditations chrétiennes*, Med. 6, Sec. 11.

208. Church, *Study*, p. 99.

209. Mr. Church refuses to note that all his references in Malebranche to the inefficacy of the will involve a discussion of the true and principal cause, that is, creation.

210. Malebranche, *Méditations chrétiennes*, Med. 6, Sec. 14, p. 109, Gouhier edition; O. C. x, pp. 64-5.

211. Gilson, *Medieval Philosophy*, p. 71.

212. *Ibid.*, p. 72.

213. *Ibid.*, p. 90, my ital. *Cf.* p. 89.

214. *Ibid.*, pp. 96 and 100-1. *Cf. Being*, pp. 184-5.

215. Malebranche, *Conversations*, Dial. 6, pp. 154-5, Bridet edition; O. C. iv, p. 134.

216. Pascal, *Thoughts*, p. 258, n. 2.

217. Lovejoy, *Great Chain*, Ch. 3.

218. Malebranche, *Recherche*, Bk. 4, Ch. 6, Secs. 1-3, especially L. ii, p. 28.

219. Malebranche, *Entretiens sur la métaphysique*, Dial. 7, Sec. 14, Ginsberg, p. 196.

220. Malebranche, *Méditations chrétiennes*, Prière, pp. 7-8, Gouhier edition; O. C. x, pp. 9-10. *Cf.* André, *La vie du R. P. Malebranche*, p. 216.

221. Malebranche, *Conversations*, Dial. 2, pp. 61-2, Bridet edition; O. C. iv, p. 58.

222. Malebranche, *Entretiens sur la métaphysique*, Dial. 7, Sec. 3, Ginsberg, p. 182.

223. *Ibid.*, Sec. 1, Ginsberg, p. 178, my ital.

224. *Ibid.*, Sec. 7, Ginsberg, p. 186.

225. Descartes, *Meditations*, Med. 3, p. 168. *Cf. Reply to Objections II*, Axiom 2, H. R. ii, p. 56. *Principles*, Pt. 1, Prin. 21, in the Latin, speaks of conservation explicitly as a reproduction. (A. T. viii, p. 13. See Gilson, *Discours*, p. 340.)

226. Malebranche, *Recherche*, Bk. 1, Ch. 8, Sec. 2, L. i, p. 42. See Chapter I, Section I, above, Malebranche's relational theory of space and time.

227. Malebranche, *Entretiens sur la métaphysique*, Dial. 7, Sec. 7, Ginsberg, p. 186.

228. *Ibid.*, Sec. 8, Ginsberg, pp. 186-7.

229. *Ibid.*, Dial. 8, Sec. 5, Ginsberg, p. 209. *Cf. Correspondance avec Mairan*, p. 140, Moreau edition; O. C. xix, p. 886.

230. Dial. 7, Sec. 10, Fontana i, pp. 153-4, my ital. Ginsberg (Ginsberg, p. 189) errs in translating "si ce n'est que Dieu accomode . . ." as "if it is God alone who adapts . . ."

231. Malebranche, *Méditations chrétiennes*, Med. 5, Secs. 14 and 15, pp. 86-7, Gouhier edition; O. C. x, pp. 53-4.

232. *Ibid.*

233. Church, *Study*, p. 102.

234. Malebranche, *Entretiens sur la métaphysique*, Dial. 7, Sec. 11, Ginsberg, p. 191. *Cf. Méditations chrétiennes*, Med. 5, Sec. 17, p. 89, Gouhier edition; O. C. x, pp. 54-5.

235. *Ibid.*, Med. 9, Secs. 6 and 7, pp. 170-1, Gouhier edition; O. C. x, p. 98.

236. *Ibid.*

237. *Ibid.*, Med. 6, Sec. 5, p. 97, Gouhier; O. C. x, p. 58; my ital.

238. Malebranche, *Entretiens sur la métaphysique*, Dial. 7, Sec. 12, Ginsberg, p. 193, my ital.

239. *Ibid.*, Dial. 10, Sec. 16, Ginsberg, pp. 269-70.

240. Malebranche, *Méditations chrétiennes*, Med. 5, Sec. 15, p. 87, Gouhier edition; O. C. x, p. 54. *Cf. Entretiens sur la métaphysique*, Dial. 7, Sec. 14, Ginsberg, p. 196. Also compare *Prémotion*, O. C. xvi, p. 55: "Car ce n'est que par l'établissement des Loix naturelles, que Dieu communique la puissance aux causes secondes, puisqu'il fait tout en toutes choses."

241. Malebranche, *Méditations chrétiennes*, Med. 5, Sec. 17, p. 89, Gouhier edition; O. C. x, pp. 54-5.

242. *Ibid.*, p. 90, Gouhier; O. C., p. 55.

243. Malebranche, *Recherche*, Bk. 6, Pt. 2, Ch. 3, L. ii, p. 201.

244. *Ibid.*, p. 202.

245. *Ibid.*, Ecl. 15, L. iii, p. 139.

246. Malebranche, *Entretiens sur la métaphysique*, Dial. 7, Sec. 13, Ginsberg, p. 195. *Cf. Méditations chrétiennes*, Med. 5, Sec. 19, p. 92, Gouhier edition or O. C. x, p. 56, and *Recherche*, Ecl. 15, L. iii, pp. 149-50. With respect to the last reference, note especially p. 150, where Malebranche says: ". . . Non que les créatures aient par *elles-mêmes* aucune action efficace, mais parce que la puissance de Dieu leur est en quelque sorte *communiquée* par les lois naturelles que Dieu a établies en leur faveur." (My italics.)

247. Church, *Study*, p. 94.

248. Malebranche, *Méditations chrétiennes*, Med. 5, Sec. 5.

249. *Ibid.*, Sec. 18, p. 90, Gouhier edition; O. C. x, p. 55.

250. *Ibid.*, Med. 6, Sec. 5, p. 97, Gouhier edition; O. C. x, p. 59. Translation of Church, *Study*, p. 94.

251. Church, *Study*, pp. 112-13.

252. Malebranche, *Nature et grâce*, Disc. 2, Pt. 1, Art. 3. Quoted from Church, *Study*, pp. 113-14.

253. Malebranche, *Recherche*, Bk. 6, Pt. 2, Ch. 3, L. ii, p. 201. *Cf. Méditations chrétiennes*, Med. 5, Sec. 15.

254. Church, *Study*, p. 103.

255. *Ibid.*, p. 114.

256. Gilson, *Medieval Philosophy*, p. 90.

257. Malebranche, *Recherche*, Bk. 6, Pt. 2, Ch. 3, L. ii, p. 203.

Norman Kemp Smith points out that while Descartes in his metaphysics speaks of motion as a mode of extension, in his physics he really conceives them as distinct in nature and origin. As such, they are *"equally substantial,* since they are equally ingenerable out of nothing, and equally indestructible." (*Studies*, pp. 69-70.) Unlike the Greeks, says Smith, for whom the difference in natural phenomena are due to differences in matter, for Descartes, "Matter becomes the mere vehicle of motion, and motion the all-important reality." And since motion possesses an equalitarian status with matter, Descartes, concludes Smith, really lands, not in a dualism, but in a trinitarianism, one of whose elements mediates between the other two. Motion is not mental, yet like mind is unextended, immaterial and active.

Thus Descartes really has two views of motion, depending on whether he regards it geometrically or dynamically. From the geometric point of view motion as a mode is simply a change of position or transference from place to place. So regarded, motion cannot be viewed as itself transferable or communicable, any more than a body's figure can be. As a physicist he regards movement as the active dynamic power that impels and moves. Descartes vacillates between these two views of motion, according to Kemp Smith. Now it is important to get clear on the reasons for this vacillation, for doing this will throw light on Malebranche.

First of all, Descartes as physicist has to have a dynamic view of motion. Since for him matter is homogeneous, since the differences among natural phenomena cannot be ascribed to differences in atoms or elements, movement is, as Spinoza pointed out, a necessary prerequisite to account for the varieties of things.

Had Descartes clung to the geometric view of motion as locomotion, he would have faced two alternatives, neither of which he could adopt. "Either, first, motion being as untransferable as figure, he would have had to ascribe to each particular body the power of creating new motion (in the dynamic sense) in other bodies on impact. Or, secondly, he would have been forced to admit that body is incapable of acting on body, and that therefore God is the sole Mover." (*Ibid.*, pp. 75-6.) To avoid the unpleasant alternatives, continues Smith, Descartes seeks refuge in an ambiguous inconsistency. He continues to treat movement as a mysterious unknown entity, distinct both from God, its creator, and the matter into which it is insinuated and in which it resides like salt in water.

Now, says Smith, when Descartes is taken to task on these ambiguities and inconsistencies, the alternative that he frankly adopts in his reply to More is that of extreme Occasionalism. There he admits, first, that motion as locomotion is not transferable; second, that in speaking of the constancy of motion he is referring to movement in the dynamic sense; third, that movement in the dynamic sense comes directly from God upon the impact of bodies, and not from the bodies. And, adds Descartes, the reason for his failing to make his position clear in his published writings is a fear of vulgar misinterpretation. To make God the active mover might suggest that He is the soul of the world united to matter.

Now the question that I wish to raise is whether the Occasionalism in Descartes is indeed that Occasionalism developed by Malebranche. At first sight it would appear so. It even appears as if Malebranche were led to Descartes' brand of Occasionalism by the same tensions and ambiguities

that are characteristic of Descartes' philosophy. For Malebranche too seems to offer two views of motion— that of the geometer when he speaks of motion as a mode of extension and as change of position, and that of the physicist, when he regards movement as the supreme force for the generation and corruption of natural phenomena. And like Descartes, but with absolute candor and boldness, he declares that God alone is the moving force of bodies.

Nevertheless, my view with regard to Malebranche's Occasionalism is this —while as a mathematician and geometer he is employing concepts pertinent to Descartes, nevertheless as metaphysicians, they are far apart. Descartes' metaphysics is founded on the level of essence and moves within that framework. Malebranche's metaphysics is grounded on God as Being and Creator. Accordingly, the type of Occasionalism implicit in Descartes is not that developed by Malebranche, however much the two may on the surface resemble each other. When Descartes suggests that God is the sole mover or dynamic force in matter, his matter is an inert, passive extension actually existing. Hence it is no wonder that he is afraid that the vulgar will construe God as the soul of the world and as extended. But Malebranche moves on the plane of God as Being and Creator. He is insistent, as Descartes is not, on the distinction between essence and existence. He is emphatic, as Spinoza is not, on the principle of creation and on the need for distinguishing between intelligible or ideal extension and material or actually concrete extension. The concrete, existing body is no ideal bit of geometry. As inert, it is an ideal essence only. It becomes actual only when existence is added to or conferred upon it through and by the creative will of God. Now to me it appears that this doctrine makes sense only if we maintain that to receive existence by God's creative will is to receive or to participate in that very will. It is to become an embodiment of His will. Hence for a body to exist is to become endowed with dynamic power, with movement in the physical sense. And this is consistent with Malebranche's reform of Cartesian physics and his own statement that God creates occasional causes by communicating His power to them. At the same time, while the occasional cause communicates movement, it is God alone who can enable the second body to receive motion and keep it.

For a very different interpretation of Cartesian physics, see Gueroult, *L'idée de force*, especially pp. 4, 5, 7, 31, 115-16, 128.

258. Church, *Study*, pp. 104-5.

259. Malebranche, *Avis*, p. 112, Le Moine edition; O. C. xv, p. 52.

260. Malebranche, *Nature et grâce*, Dernier Ecl., O. C. v, p. 205. *Cf.* Gilson, *Aquinas*, p. 194: "in the sensible world causes and effects follow with perfect regularity . . . It is therefore evident that the nature of the effect produced is inseparately bound up with the nature of the producing cause. Now it is this constancy in the relation of natural effects to secondary causes which makes it impossible to assume that the power of God simply takes their place; for if the action of God *were not diversified in accordance with the different beings in which it operates*, neither would the effects be diversified in the same manner as the things themselves, and the result would be that anything whatever would produce anything whatever. The existence of laws of nature consequently renders it impossible to suppose that God has created beings deprived of causality." (My ital.)

261. Malebranche, *Méditations chrétiennes*, Med. 6, Sec. 11, p. 106, Gouhier edition; O. C. x, p. 63. Since genesis, Malebranche declares, God no longer acts immediately by Him-

self but "par les créatures en conséquence de la puissance qu'il leur a donnée." (*Réponse aux Réflexions*, Recueil . . . , III, David, 1709 edition, p. 251; cited by Gueroults. *Malebranche*, Vol. 2, p. 241.)

262. Malebranche, *Entretiens sur la métaphysique*, Dial. 7, Sec. 10, pp. 189-90.

263. *Ibid.*, Dial. 10, Ginsberg, p. 251.

264. Church, *Study*, pp. 111-13.

265. *Ibid.*

266. Malebranche, *Recherche*, Appendice, L. iii, p. 300.

267. Labbas, *L'idée de science*, Ch. 2, pp. 62 ff.

268. *Ibid.*, pp. 79-80.

269. *Ibid.*, pp. 27, 37, 41.

270. While the foregoing interpretation of Labbas is sound, there are serious omissions in his further treatment of Occasionalism. Malebranche's theory of occasional causality is even more original than Labbas realizes. First of all, Labbas goes too far when he asserts that Malebranche definitely renounces altogether the ancient conception of a cause as a principle of intelligible explanation. (*Ibid.*, p. 42.) Malebranche, unlike Bacon or Descartes, reintroduces finality into his philosophy. True, he declares, as we saw, final causes are "assez inutile" in physics. (*Conversations*, Dial. 3, p. 64, Bridet edition; O. C. iv, p. 60.) But they are not altogether useless, for in the *Entretiens sur la métaphysique*, he argues on the basis of observation that the eyes are made to see, and it is on the basis of observed finality that he rejects Descartes' theory of the mechanical origin of organized life.

In the second place, the whole theory of occasional or natural causes rests on the metaphysical principle of the existence of a necessary cause at the base of the universe. God exists necessarily, and between His will and the world there is an essential connection. It is true that his view of God is not that of an essence that involves existence and that between God's will and nature there is no logical necessity. Nevertheless it cannot be said that Malebranche renounces the notion of a cause as a principle of intelligible explanation. His entire polemic against the attribution of power to secondary causes and his insistence on the absence of necessity between occasional causes rest on the notion that true efficacy is derivative from a creative will and that creation is both meaningful and immediately knowable. In so far as Malebranche goes to God as Being and Will, he is indeed departing from ancient Greek abstractionism or essentialism, but not from the view that there is a principle or sufficient reason that renders the world intelligible.

Now, because Labbas neglects the profound role of Being in Malebranche's philosophy as well as his distinction between essence and existence, he does not explore fully the role of the occasional cause. He sees well enough that for Malebranche cause and effect is more than a haphazard conjunction or concomitancy. But why is it such? It is not enough to answer: because it depends on God's decrees; for the application of those general laws is determined by the occasional cause. Thus the occasional cause is more than it is for Hume; it is more than a self-contained matter of fact. The occasional cause acts in so far as it exists. The laws, which are expressions of God's will, empower or communicate their efficacy to the occasional cause by being immanent in its existence. "Without the occasional cause, there could be no general law." (*Entretiens sur la métaphysique*, Dial. 10, Sec. 16, Ginsberg, p. 269.) The law is thus descriptive of the actual behavior and power of the natural cause. The occasional cause is regulated in its existential behavior by laws, but it is the active *to be* of the occasional cause

that determines the exemplification and application of laws. Existence is the principle of individuation. Hence, scientific laws require observation and experimentation because, however regular, in a very real sense they are dependent upon the activity of concrete matters of fact.

271. Church, *Study*, p. 114.

272. Ginsberg, *Preface*, p. 58. Bouillier, *Histoire*, Vol. 2, p. 113, Blampignon, *Etude*, pp. 163 and 178.

273. Church, *Study*, p. 114-15.

274. Malebranche, *Méditations chrétiennes*, Med. 5, Sec. 19, p. 92, Gouhier edition; O. C. x, p. 56. *Cf. Entretiens sur la métaphysique*, Dial. 7, Sec. 13, Ginsberg, p. 195.

275. Malebranche, *L'Amour de Dieu*, pp. 81-2, 86, 91-99, 107, and 312-14, note to p. 107; *Conversations*, Dial. 3, pp. 87-91, Bridet edition or O. C. iv, pp. 78-82; and consult Gouhier, *Malebranche*, pp. 58-9, 132-40, and 144-60.

276. Arnauld, *Défense contre Malebranche*, Letter to Roucy, p. 464.

277. Gouhier, *Philosophie de Malebranche*, Pt. 2.

278. See above, note 275. Also, *cf.* André, *La vie du R. P. Malebranche*, pp. 251 and 259.

279. Church, *Study*, p. 115.

280. Malebranche, *Entretiens sur la métaphysique*, Dials. 10 and 11, *passim.*

281. Malebranche, *Recherche*, Ecl. 1, L. iii, p. 13.

282. Malebranche, *Réponse à la Dissertation*, Ch. 14, Sec. 2, Recueil ii, pp. 446-7. *Cf. Entretiens sur la métaphysique*, Dial. 12, Sec. 17, Ginsberg, pp. 317-19.

283. Brunschvicg, *Expérience et causalité*, p. 244: "En opposition au dogmatisme de la causalité, la doctrine de Malebranche nous était, dans la première partie de notre ouvrage, apparue sous son aspect *négatif*. Vue de l'intérieur de la science, elle reprend son aspect *positif* et, il est

permis d'ajouter cette fois, *positiviste.* Si le positivisme implique ces deux conditions: d'une part l'élimination systématique de toute spéculation sur la cause en tant que cause, d'autre part la définition des lois comme relation de fonction entre coefficients expérimentalement attribués aux phénomènes, il est exact, en effet, de dire que l'*occasionalisme* de Malebranche, c'est déjà le positivisme sous une forme que l'on pourrait dire définitive." *Cf.* Mouy, *Physique cartésienne,* p. 318 and n. 2, Labbas, *L'idée de science,* pp. 79-80.

284. Lalande, *Vocabulaire de la philosophie,* Vol. 2, p. 909.

285. Malebranche, *Entretiens sur la métaphysique,* Dial. 7, Sec. 11, Ginsberg, p. 191.

286. *Ibid.,* Sec. 13, Ginsberg, p. 195, my italics. Note that italicizing "active" in the phrase "active qualities" rather than italicizing "qualities" would reflect the conventional inter-

pretation of Malebranche's Occasionalism. Italicizing both "active" and "qualities" suggests essentialism—Spinoza's 'active essence,' a position which Malebranche is of course repudiating.

287. Malebranche, *Méditations chrétiennes,* Med. 6, Sec. 5, p. 97, Gouhier edition; O. C. x, p. 58.

288. Cited from *In Metaphys.,* Bk. 5, Lect. 1, by Gilson, *Medieval Philosophy,* p. 90. *Cf.* Aquinas, *Contra gentiles,* Bk. 3, Ch. 69, p. 172.

289. Perry, *Puritanism and Democracy,* p. 82.

290. Gilson, *Medieval Philosophy,* p. 141.

291. *Ibid.,* pp. 139 ff.

292. *Ibid.* p. 141.

293. Malebranche, *Entretiens sur la métaphysique,* Dial. 13, Sec. 9, Ginsberg, p. 337.

294. Moreau, *Malebranche et le Spinozisme,* p. 91.

295. *Ibid.,* p. 85.

CHAPTER V. THE SELF

1. Descartes, *Search,* H. R. i, p. 323.

2. *Ibid.,* pp. 324-5.

3. Descartes, *Meditations,* Med. 2, H. R. i, p. 153.

4. Descartes, *Reply to Objections II,* Arguments Demonstrating the Existence of God . . . , H. R. ii, p. 52.

5. Descartes, *Principles,* Pt. 1, Prin. 9, H. R. i, p. 222.

6. Church, *Study,* pp. 43-4.

7. Descartes, *Principles,* Pt. 1, Prin. 53, H. R. i, p. 240, my ital.

8. Descartes, *Meditations,* Med. 6, H. R. i, p. 186. See *ibid.,* p. 190.

9. *Ibid.,* Med. 2, H. R. i, p. 155.

10. Balz, *Cartesian Studies,* p. 174.

11. *Ibid.*

12. *Ibid.,* p. 95.

13. Church, *Study,* p. 44.

14. Malebranche, *Recherche,* Bk. 3, Pt. 1, Ch. 1, Sec. 1, L. i, p. 214.

15. *Ibid.,* pp. 214-15, my ital.

16. E.g., Malebranche, *Traité de morale,* Pt. 1, Ch. 3, Secs. 14-16, pp. 31-4.

17. Church, *Study,* p. 44.

18. *Ibid.,* p. 45. *Cf.* Gueroult, *Malebranche,* Vol. 3, pp. 43-5.

19. Church, *Study,* p. 44.

20. *Ibid.,* pp. 48-9.

21. Malebranche, *Recherche,* Ecl. 11, L. iii, p. 99; *cf.* Church, *Study,* p. 49.

22. Church, *Study,* pp. 49-50.

23. *Ibid.,* pp. 50 and 52.

24. *Ibid.,* pp. 50-53.

25. "The *sentiment intérieur* is an experience; it is sensuous, as is any feeling; and the awareness of pure spirit is no experience of sensuous consciousness. Pure spirit is actually present in meditation and prayer. For the reason that conscious states are exhausted by images, sensations, passions, and volitions, this presence of the Word is not a presence in or to any modification of the soul." (*Ibid.,* p. 53.)

26. *Ibid.* *Cf.* Callot, *Problèmes du cartésianisme*, "Un Paralogisme de la philosophie de Malebranche: La Connaissance de l'Ame," pp. 190-204.

27. Malebranche, *Recherche*, Bk. 3, Pt. 1, Ch. 1, Sec. 1, L. i, p. 215.

28. *Ibid.*

29. *Ibid.* For a dissenting view on the relations between willing and thought and extension and movement, see Gueroult, *L'idée de force*, pp. 122-3.

30. Malebranche, *Recherche*, Bk. 3, Pt. 1, Ch. 1, Sec. 2, L. i, p. 217.

31. *Ibid.*, Sec. 1, L. i, p. 215.

32. Gilson, *Discours*, p. 304.

33. Malebranche, *Recherche*, Ecl. 10, L. iii, p. 75; *Réponse à Régis*, Ch. 2, L. iii, p. 243 or O. C. xvii-1, p. 280. *Cf. Recherche*, Bk. 5, Ch. 1, L. ii, p. 78.

34. *Ibid.*, Bk. 3, Pt. 1, Ch. 1, Sec. 3, L. i, p. 219.

35. *Ibid.*, Pt. 2, Ch. 1, Sec. 1, L. i, p. 235, "pure intellections" and "conceptions," my ital.

36. See above, Introduction.

37. See Gouhier, *Vocation*, p. 59, notes 1 and 3.

38. Malebranche, *Entretiens sur la métaphysique*, Dial. 1, Sec. 1, Ginsberg, p. 72; *cf.* Cuvillier edition, p. 64.

39. Descartes to Elizabeth, June 28, 1643, A. T. iii, p. 691.

40. See Gilson, *Augustin*, pp. 56-61.

41. Lewis, *L'Individualité selon Descartes*, Ch. 4.

42. Descartes, *Rules*, Rule 12, see H. R. i, p. 43.

43. Descartes, *Meditations*, Med. 3, H. R. i, pp. 165 and 170.

44. Hence, I cannot accept Mlle. Lewis' statement that Descartes' *je pense donc je suis* is not ontological in character. (Lewis, *L'Individualité selon Descartes*, p. 108.) True, Descartes' thinking self depends upon God for its existence and conservation; it does not exist *per se*. However, since Descartes, as Mlle. Lewis admits (pp. 82-4), denies a real distinction between essence and existence, what God does in creation is actualize the essence that is Descartes. Hence it remains true that the *cogito* expresses an essence that makes *Descartes* to be, and is therefore to that extent ontological in character.

45. Burtt, *Foundations of Physics*, p. 57.

46. Descartes, *Principles*, Pt. 1, Prin. 32.

47. Malebranche, *Recherche*, Bk. 3, Pt. 2, Ch. 1, Sec. 1, L. i, p. 235.

48. *Ibid.*, Bk. 1, Ch. 4, L. i, pp. 18-19. In the first edition this passage ended with the words: "et toutes ses pensées comme ses inclinations naturelles, ses passions et ses perceptions." After the first edition this was made to read: "et généralement toutes ses pensées lorsqu'elle les connaît par la réflexion qu'elle fait sur soi."

49. *Ibid.*, Bk. 4, Ch. 11, Sec. 3, L. ii, p. 61.

50. Church, *Study*, p. 52.

51. Malebranche, *Recherche*, Bk. 3, Pt. 2, Ch. 7, Sec. 4, L. i, pp. 257-8.

52. *Ibid.*, Ecl. 11, L. iii, pp. 98-9.

53. *Ibid.*, p. 99.

54. *Ibid.*

55. *Ibid.*

56. Church, *Study*, p. 49.

57. Malebranche, *Recherche*, Bk. 6, Pt. 2, Ch. 6, L. ii, p. 239, my ital. *Cf. ibid.*, Ecl. 1, L. iii, p. 10.

58. *Ibid.*, Ecl. 11, L. iii, p. 100.

59. Malebranche, *Correspondance inédite*, p. 32, Blampignon edition; O. C. xix, pp. 564-5.

60. Church, *Study*, p. 52.

61. *Objections V*, H. R. ii, p. 150.

62. Malebranche, *Recherche*, Ecl. 11, L. iii, p. 101.

63. Descartes, *Reply to Objections IV*, H. R. ii, pp. 101-2.

64. *Ibid. III*, H. R. ii, p. 63 and *ibid. V*, H. R. ii, p. 211.

65. Malebranche, *Recherche*, Ecl. 11, L. iii, p. 103.

66. Malebranche, *Méditations chrétiennes*, Med. 9, Sec. 22.

67. Malebranche, *Recherche*, Ecl. 11, L. iii, p. 102.

68. *Ibid.*

69. Malebranche, *Entretiens sur la métaphysique*, Dial. 3, Sec. 7, Ginsberg, pp. 102-3.

70. Augustine, *Confessions*, Bk. 10, Secs. 16 and 17, Sheed, pp. 185-6, my ital.

71. *Ibid.*, Sec. 11, Sheed, p. 182.

72. *Ibid.*, Bk. 11, Sec. 23, Loeb, p. 262 and Sec. 28, Loeb, pp. 276 and 278. *Cf.* Gilson, *Augustin*, pp. 253-5.

73. See Gilson, *Augustin*, pp. 135-9.

74. Augustine, *Confessions*, Bk. 13, Sec. 9, Loeb, p. 390. *Cf.* Gilson, *Augustin*, pp. 174-5.

75. Malebranche, *Recherche*, Bk. 6, Pt. 2, Ch. 5, L. ii, p. 236.

76. *Ibid.*, Ch. 7, L. ii, p. 257. Gueroult notes (*Malebranche*, Vol. 1, pp. 148-9) how much greater is the affinity of Malebranche's views on the self, *i.e.*, our lack of knowledge of the soul, to Augustinianism and to Thomism than to Cartesianism. With respect to Thomas, Gueroult points out that "il professe que nous ne pouvons connaître directement que l'existence de l'âme, non son essence." (Gueroult cites *Sum. theol.*, Iᵃ, qu. 79, a. 7; qu. 87, a. 1, 2; qu. 88, a. 1, 3; *De Veritate*, X, 8, ad Resp.; *De anima*, III, ad 4ᵐ.)

77. Malebranche, *Traité de morale*, Pt. 1, Ch. 5, Sec. 17, p. 55.

78. Malebranche, *Recherche*, Ecl. 1, L. iii, p. 10, my ital. *Cf. Prémotion*, O. C. xvi, p. 38.

79. Brunschvicg, *Spinoza*, p. 289; *cf.* p. 253.

80. *E.g.*, Gilson, *Medieval Philosophy*, pp. 57 and 89.

81. See Lewis, *L'Individualité selon Descartes*, p. 96.

82. Malebranche, *Recherche*, Bk. 6, Pt. 2, Ch. 6, L. ii, p. 239. See above, passage to which note 57 refers.

83. *Ibid.*, Bk. 2, Pt. 1, Ch. 1, Sec. 3, L. i, p. 96.

84. Malebranche, *Traité de morale*, Pt. 2, Ch. 5, Sec. 1, p. 177. This, I understand, is an Augustinian doctrine. (Gilson, *Medieval Philosophy*, pp. 225-8.)

85. Malebranche, *Traité de morale*, Pt. 2, Ch. 5, Sec. 4, p. 178.

86. Malebranche, *Recherche*, Ecl. 2, L. iii, p. 18. *Cf. ibid.*, Bk. 5, Ch. 1, L. ii, p. 78.
Gueroult maintains that Malebranche's theory of knowledge asserts complete passivity on the part of the knowing subject. Be it sensible perception or pure conception, "la connaissance est *passion.*" (Malebranche, Vol. 1, pp. 155-6.) Gueroult neglects, however, the active role of the will and attention as the occasional cause for obtaining knowledge. This is all the more paradoxical, since he devotes considerable analysis to *attention.* (*Cf. ibid.*, Vol. 3, pp. 150 ff.) One can only comment that he makes an illegitimate bifurcation of willing from knowing in Malebranche.
Connell (*La passivité*) poses the question, why did Malebranche sustain the strange doctrine that the understanding is passive? He rightly concludes that the doctrine rests on Malebranche's interpretation of Descartes' *cogito*—that passivity could not have been eliminated from Malebranche's system without violating the very foundations of his doctrine, namely, that thought is the essence of the soul. Connell fails to note, however, how, building on these very cartesian origins, Malebranche redresses the balance by placing activity in the will and in attention as the occasional cause for eliciting ideas to the understanding.
While Anita Fritz (*Berkeley's Self*) also insists upon the passivity of the understanding, she does, on the other hand, speak of the will's role as an escape from passivity on the part of the soul. But, she claims, "the leeway granted is slight," because the freedom of the will "to act in relation to

any particular content of understanding [is] a negative sort of freedom, consisting in the ability to withhold rather than in the ability to do anything." This capacity to suspend judgment, she insists, is even further restricted by the fact that "having so suspended judgment one must wait *to be convinced* . . . The decision is not a function of will." Whence she concludes that, for Malebranche, "man is for the most part, if not wholly, determined to will as he does and that his will as well as the realization of his capacity to perceive, imagine, remember and reason are passive responses to the action of God." (Pp. 556-7.)

Several comments are in order. In the first place, the capacity to withhold judgment is by no means a mincing or slight process, but involves an intense and even agonizing effort to abstain from yielding assent. Granted, moreover, that it does not *produce* anything (in Malebranche's sense that the withholding of judgment is an immanent act and not productive of anything positive), nonetheless it is not so negative as it appears to Fritz, for it rests upon an anterior positive choice not to choose. Finally, Anita Fritz fails to take into account the painstaking act of attention as the natural prayer of the soul, with its subtle dialectic of searching, sifting, filtering, examining and continuously probing, until the final truth is found. Of course, culminating this active work of the will's attention (which, it must be remembered, is the occasional cause that finally elicits the truth) is the revelation of the truth itself, which then naturally forces itself upon the mind as being there. Then indeed, as Malebranche acknowledges (Letter to Jaquemet, December, 1690, O. C. xix, pp. 566-7), does the will's freedom become destroyed, for then attention is wholly at rest, the will becomes polarized as it were, rivetted or attached to the truth—it then no longer needs to prolong the search or to withhold assent. *Cf.* Disc. III, Art. 32, *Nature et grâce*, O. C. v, pp. 140-1. On Malebranche's doctrine of divine and human freedom and their close affinity to the views of St. Thomas, see Laporte, *La liberté*, entire.

As for Dr. Fritz's suggestive comparison between Berkeley and Malebranche on the activity of the self, there is some difficulty in her treatment of Berkeley's crucial doctrine of 'notions.' She unfortunately construes notions to be contents of the mind, rather than intentional acts. "Representative, meaningful mental entities," she asserts, "must appear in some guise for Berkeley. If all ideas were the non-referential and extended particulars familiar to us as 'things,' then Berkeley's remarks concerning souls and God would be meaningless . . . In the face of such a situation Berkeley introduced 'notions.' " (P. 563.) That Fritz accurately focusses the central issues on the nature of notions is very much to be praised. But that notions are third, entitative, representative *things* between the self and perceived reality is erroneous. Therefore Fritz's tentative suggestion that ". . . in notions Berkeley does seem to recognize the existence of something at least similar to Malebranche's general ideas . . ." is highly dubious. For an analysis of notions as immanent yet external, direct or immediate spiritual activity, see S. Rome's *Berkeley's Conceptualism*. It is there argued that Berkeley admits abstract conceiving in his middle period without rescinding his arguments against abstract ideas. (P. 685.)

87. Malebranche, *Traité de morale*, Pt. 2, Ch. 5, Sec. 4, p. 179; *Recherche*, Appendice, L. iii, pp. 299-300.

88. Pascal, *Thoughts*, Chap. 22, Wight, p. 333 and Chap. 21, Wight, p. 328.

89. Malebranche, *Entretiens sur la*

métaphysique, Dial. 7, Sec. 16, Ginsberg, pp. 199-200.

90. Malebranche, *Traité de morale,* Pt. 2, Ch. 5, Sec. 4, p. 179.

91. Malebranche, *Recherche,* Bk. 4, Ch. 11, Sec. 3, L. ii, p. 61. See above, passage to which note 49 refers.

92. Church, *Study,* p. 52.

93. Cousin, *Procès-verbal,* pp. 110-12. *Cf.* Malebranche's statement in *Prémotion* (O. C. xvi, pp. 130-1):

La nature des esprits est simple & indivisible. On le croit assez: car le sentiment interieur m'apprend, & à tous ceux qui font reflexion sur ce qui se passe en eux-mêmes, que c'est mon unique MOI, ma même, unique & indivisible substance, qui connoît & qui veut, qui a de la joye & de la tristesse, & plusieurs sensations differentes dans le même temps. Un homme donc, qui ne pourroit ou ne voudroit pas reflechir sur ce qui se passe en lui-même, auroit-il raison de juger, que ce qui pense en nous, ne peut pas être la même chose, que ce qui veut, & que ce qui sent en nous. Auroit-il raison de croire, que son ame n'est pas une seule substance simple & indivisible, mais un amas confus de plusieurs substances differentes; à cause que n'ayant pas une idée claire de l'ame, on ne peut ny connoître, ny par consequent expliquer clairement ce que c'est que cette substance, qui n'est pas distinguée de nous-mêmes, & comment elle est toute entiere, & intelligente & voulante. Si on en avoit une idée claire, on la connoîtroit aussi clairement qu'on la sent vivement. Mais quoique nous ne puissions nous sentir qu'en nous mêmes: nous ne comprendrons jamais clairement ce que nous sommes, jusqu'à ce que Dieu manifeste à l'ame l'idée claire ou l'archetype, sur lequel il l'a formée; care il n'y a que de telles idées qui puissent par elles mêmes éclairer les intelligences.

94. Church, *Study,* p. 53.

95. Goheen, *Matter and Form,* p. 99.

96. *Ibid.,* pp. 100 ff., especially p. 105.

97. Novaro, *Malebranche,* pp. 75-6. Novaro interprets Malebranche's account of the soul in an idealistic manner:

Malebranche macht als Philosoph die Seele, von seinem Glauben abgesehen, zu dem blossen Inbegriff der Bewusstseinzustände. . . . Er fasst die Seele als das subjective actuelle Denken auf, das Ich bleibt für ihn bloss eine leere vereinigende Form der Bewusstseinserscheinungen, bloss ein Pol, zu dem ein jeder Phänomen eine Beziehung hat. *Das Bewusstsein ist bloss das Subjectivwerden des objectiven Gedankens. . . . Die Seele ist sozusagen ein Brennpunkt, in welchem der objective Gedanke sich zum Selbstbewusstsein erhebt.* (*Ibid.,* my ital.)

Novaro's erroneous interpretation of the soul rests on his initial misconception of the nature of Malebranche's God. Although he rightly recognizes the notion of being to be "den Gipfel" of Malebranche's thought (p. 11), his thesis is that in Malebranche's philosophy, "Idealismus und Pantheismus sind die zwei Hauptmerkmale derselben und er sucht umsonst Hülfe im Glauben." (P. v. *Cf.* pp. 78, 82, and 91.) Here we have but another example of those critics who refuse to treat Malebranche's Christianity on its own merits!

98. Malebranche, *Conversations,* Dial. 3, pp. 87 ff., Bridet edition, or O. C. iv, pp. 78 ff.; *Recherche,* Préface, L. i, pp. vii-viii and xi-xii; *ibid.,* Bk. 3, Pt. 1, Ch. 4, Sec. 1, L. i, pp. 228-9; *ibid.,* Bk. 4, Ch. 1, Secs. 2-4, L. ii, pp, 2-4; and *ibid.,* Bk. 5, Ch. 1, L. ii, p. 77 and Ch. 5, L. ii, p. 107.

Malebranche's singular concept of *attention* has been accorded a refreshing and reverent study by Pierre Blanchard in his *L'attention à Dieu*. By focussing upon attention as the central element of Malebranche's method and the cornerstone of his metaphysics, Blanchard succeeds in illuminating the unified character of Malebranche's philosophy. Thus he writes:

> Son univers intérieur est celui de l'harmonie conquise mais réelle, harmonie de l'expérience et de la raison, de la raison et de la volonté, de l'intelligence et de la foi, de la nature et de la grâce, du temps et de l'éternité, harmonie de la science et de la métaphysique, de la métaphysique et de la mystique, de la théologie et de la philosophie. (P. 230.)

Unfortunately, Blanchard too falls into the familiar conventional error: he too condemns occasionalism as "the negator of all true causality." (P. 222.) Hence, he concludes, occasionalism is unacceptable for defining the structure and action of man and his intersubjective relations. (*Ibid.*) Malebranche is the prisoner of a closed system, he declares. (P. 226.) Strangely, Blanchard calls our attention to a crucial passage in *Prémotion* in which Malebranche declares that although God is the unique efficacious cause of all modalities and of all real changes, "je soutiens & j'ai toûjours soutenu, que l'ame étoit l'unique cause de ses actes, c'est-à-dire de ses déterminations libres. . . . J'ai toûjours soûtenu que l'ame étoit active: mais que ses actes ne produisoient rien de physic . . ." (*Prémotion*, O. C. xvi, pp. 40-1.) Commenting on this passage, Blanchard says: Burdened by the consequences of his principles, pushed to conclusions he cannot admit, Malebranche often accords man in practice that which he has withheld from him in theory. (*Op. cit.*, p. 239.)

It has been my contention, of course, that no such diremption between theory and practice obtains.

There never was the need to wait for Maine de Biran, as Blanchard proclaims, to reestablish human causality and to rectify the error of Malebranche. (*Ibid.*)

99. *Ibid.*, Ecl. 1, L. iii, p. 4, my ital.

100. *Ibid.*, pp. 4-7. *Cf. Conversations*, Dial. 3, p. 91, Bridet edition; O. C. iv, pp. 81-2.

101. Malebranche, *Recherche*, Bk. 3, Pt. 1, Ch. 4, Secs. 1 and 2, L. i, pp. 228-9; *ibid.*, Bk. 4, Ch. 2, Secs. 1 and 2, L. ii, pp. 5-6; *ibid.*, Ch. 5, Sec. 1, L. ii, p. 23 and note 2; *ibid.*, Bk. 5, Ch. 1, L. ii, p. 77. *Cf. Prémotion*, O. C. xvi, pp. 46-50, 65-6.

102. Malebranche, *Recherche*, Bk. 3, Pt. 2, Ch. 8, Sec. 1, L. i, p. 260; *ibid.*, Bk. 6, Pt. 1, Ch. 5, L. ii, p. 182.

103. Descartes, *Meditations*, Med. 4, H. R. i, pp. 174-5.

104. Le Moine in his book *Vérités éternelles* claims that (a) Malebranche's theory of knowledge *implicitly* implicates (b) a "mental dynamism" (p. 233), that (c) paradoxically resembles that of Aquinas and Aristotle (p. 234), and thus (d) betrays a "profound vice and hidden contradiction" (p. 235) in Malebranche's epistemology.

Le Moine's interpretation is correct but only partially so, and for this reason is too significant to be left unexamined. His claim is almost but not quite true, for his evidence is inadequate; and therefore the net result is profoundly misleading, to the point of distortion. Why, we may ask, is this dynamism merely implicit? The answer, according to Le Moine, lies in the official or overt manner in which Malebranche treats the intellect, namely, as doing nothing but passively fixing its gaze upon God and therein beholding ideas through arrested attention. "Et c'est là justement le rôle de cette attention dont l'étude tient une place si considérable dans la psychologie telle que la comprend Malebranche, mais qui est conçue par lui comme l'attitude de l'esprit qui s'oriente vers lui [God] de façon à le voir, mieux peut-être, qui simplement met tout en œuvre pour ne pas être détourné de lui par les créatures. Il est nécessaire de faire apparaître nettement ce rôle de l'attention tel que le conçoit Malebranche, rôle purement passif: l'esprit se met en état de réceptivité complète: c'est tout." (P. 217.)

Le Moine thus assumes that for Malebranche attention requires no active element. The evidence he cites for this assumption is this: (i) In the *Entretiens sur la métaphysique,* Theodore declares that reason always speaks, but for lack of attention Aristes cannot hear it. (P. 217.) How this proves that the attention necessary for listening is something passive, I cannot see. (ii) The second bit of evidence (pp. 217-18) is from *Conversations* where attention is described as the "prière naturelle que nous faisons à la vérité intérieure, afin qu'elle se découvre à nous."—But the fact that knowledge is a gratuitous gift or reward granted to the mind through prayerful attention does not prove that attention is passive. All it shows is that attention does not create ideas and hence is not a *true* cause. As an occasional cause attention may be (and indeed is) a most laborious effort, that through its struggle elicits the reward or discovery of truth. (iii) The final bit of evidence for a passive attention is this: Malebranche describes judgment and reasoning as no more than the perception of relations. "Connaître," says Le Moine, "c'est donc purement et simplement percevoir; et le rôle de l'attention, développé dans ce chapitre et les suivants, n'est autre que de mettre l'esprit en état de voir, en veillant à supprimer tout ce que pourrait l'en empêcher." (P. 218.)—Still, this does not prove that the attention required to suppress disturbances and to put the mind in

a position of discovering the truth is passive.

From these bits of evidence it follows, says Le Moine, that the mind does nothing and God does all. (P. 219.) Nevertheless, some pages later on we find Le Moine asserting that in reality Malebranche does implicitly assume an activity on the part of the mind, for his description of what is involved in intellectual labor presupposes such activity. When Malebranche recommends to his disciples the exercise of logical rules and the employment of reflection and analysis, and above all when he stresses the importance of making "quelque effort d'esprit"—is he not admitting activity? (P. 230.) M. Le Moine is correct in reaching this conclusion, but it does not prove that there is any contradiction or "self-betrayal" (p. 230) on Malebranche's part. As Le Moine properly observes, it would be easy to multiply texts and analyses on this point, for Malebranche never once denied that attention and prayer, which are operations of the will, demand a most profound effort and activity. What Le Moine does not see, however, is that all that Malebranche ever did deny is that this activity or dynamism is *creative.* Hence there is nothing hidden or implicit or vicious about his mental dynamism.

But Le Moine now develops a bizarre view of this dynamism. He makes these claims: (1) Relations for Malebranche "ne sont 'rien de réel' "; only ideas are real (p. 231); (2) therefore relations "don't exist outside the mind that contemplates them" (p. 232); (3) therefore the mind, through an "active intervention," "establishes by its labor and its personal faculties" the relations that it contemplates (p. 231); and (4) therefore this contradicts the view of judgment and reasoning as no more than passive awareness of relations of relations (p. 232). Thus Le Moine reduces Malebranche to a form of conceptualism: relations are dependent for their reality on the mind's inventive thinking of them and thus making them. Yet Le Moine is not too clear, for he also speaks of this positive mental activity as simply one of discovery (P. 233).

Now it is entirely harmonious with Malebranche's thought to speak of discovering the truth through attention as a positive mental activity. But on what grounds can Le Moine make the reality of relations dependent on a mental construction? How may he say that they exist only in the mind that contemplates them? Does not Malebranche explicitly affirm that judgment is the perception of a relation between ideas and that reasoning is the awareness of relations among relations? Does he not say that the truth of $2 \times 2 = 4$ consists in apprehending the *real* relation of equality? And does he not say that this true relation is independent of any one's perceiving it?

Le Moine admits all this, but to him these statements appear to contradict those passages wherein Malebranche declares that relations are unreal. Hence Le Moine concludes that relations exist only in the mind. What then are these passages in which relations are said to be *unreal?* Le Moine calls attention to one in the *Recherche,* and to one in the dialogue between a Christian and a Chinese Philosopher. In the latter work (pp. 69-70, Le Moine edition; O. C. xv, pp. 19-20) Malebranche affirms: "Otez les idées, vous ôtez les vérités, car il est évident que les vérités ne sont que les rapports qui sont entre les idées. . . . Quel genre d'être est-ce, quelle réalité trouvez-vous dans un rapport, ou un souverain rapport? Si un corps est double d'un autre je conçois qu'il a plus de réalité. Mais ôtez la réalité des corps, vous ôtez leur rapport. Le rapport qui est entre les corps, n'est donc dans le fond que les corps mêmes." But this passage does not show that relations are unreal; still less that they exist in

the mind or that the mind gives them reality by thinking of, attending to, or discovering them. It merely affirms that there can be no relations without terms. Even if we assume that Malebranche reduces relations to an adjectival status, it still does not make them exist only in the mind. Moreover, Le Moine admits that for Malebranche truth, which is a relation, is no arbitrary construction of the mind. By describing relations as being in the mind, he cannot mean, then, that they are merely useful fictions or distinctions of reason. Whatever the ontological status of a relation may be, whether it is a property of ideas or an ultimate metaphysical category, by no stretch of the imagination can it be said that the equality between 2×2 and 4 is real only for a mind that thinks of it. It may take great effort to discover the twentieth decimal place of π, but as for James, so for Malebranche, that truth is there whether or not there is any mind to perceive it; and, as we saw, even God is obliged to admit it. Neither human nor divine awareness "establishes" the relation. Le Moine is right when he declares that it takes a positive effort to discover the relation of agreement between two ideas; but he is wrong in the further assertion that "la vérité n'existe que lorsque l'esprit voit le rapport," (*Vérités éternelles,* pp. 233-4), or that it is the result of an inventive intelligence (p. 235). The being of the relation does not depend for Malebranche on its being seen or found. The *finding* of truth results from the mind's effort, for this effort is the occasional cause that provokes the appearance of the truth. It makes the truth or the relation appear or reveal itself.

As for the passage from the *Recherche,* that, far from supporting, flatly contradicts Le Moine's position. "Nous pensons donc que les vérités, même celles qui sont éternelles, comme que deux fois deux font quatre, ne sont pas seulement des êtres absolus, tant s'en faut que nous croyons qu'elles soient Dieu même. Car il est visible que cette vérité ne consiste que dans un rapport d'égalité, qui est entre deux fois deux et quatre. Ainsi nous ne disons pas que nous voyons Dieu en voyant les vérités, comme le dit saint Augustin, mais en voyant les *idées* de ces vérités: car les idées sont réelles, mais l'égalité entre les idées, qui est la vérité, n'est rien de réel. Quand par exemple, on dit que du drap que l'on mesure à trois aunes, le drap et les aunes sont réels. Mais l'égalité entre trois aunes et le drap n'est point un être réel; ce n'est qu'un rapport qui se trouve entre les trois aunes et le drap. Lorsqu'on dit que deux fois deux font quatre, les idées des nombres sont réelles, mais l'égalité qui est entre eux n'est qu'un rapport. Ainsi selon notre sentiment, nous voyons Dieu lorsque nous voyons des vérités éternelles: non que ces vérités soient Dieu, mais parce que les idées dont ces vérités dépendent sont en Dieu; peut-être même que saint Augustin l'a entendu ainsi." (*Recherche*, Bk. 3, Pt. 2, Ch. 6, L. i, p. 253.) Manifestly, this passage denies the reality of relations as terms or things. But this simply means that relations have the sort of ontological status that befits them, namely, to be relations. It does not reduce them to adjectival properties of things; it merely declares that without terms relations would vanish.

Hence, there is no contradiction between these passages and Malebranche's theory of truth as an infinitely complex continuum of relations of relations. In attention the mind is indeed active as the occasional cause. It reflects, compares, analyzes; it exercises effort to *find* the exact relations that do obtain. But this effort does not create the relations, and the triumph of its effort is to find and see and thus become illumined by the relations that are there.

Accordingly Le Moine is right to this extent: The knowing process does indeed involve a mental activity, inasmuch as attention and the effort of will are integral to knowledge, from beginning to end. The seeking after truth commences with an act of attention and of volition. As Malebranche says, the will commands the understanding. Effort, attention, concentration on what is given to perception is the *terminus a quo* for knowledge. This effort consists in comparing, reflecting, analyzing, and removing or eliminating the irrelevant and superfluous. It is thus an active process of discrimination and selection, comparable to experimentation in science. But Malebranche is no positivist. Experimental operations are a guide to truth. After nature has been vexed and hounded, or after prayerful searching and attending, the relations among things or ideas are then beheld. The intellect then beholds or intuits clearly and distinctly and the will acquiesces to or accepts what is thus beheld. This consent is again an act, an act of commitment or devotion to what is given. This final affirmation is the terminal point in which the knowing process culminates.

To summarize: I agree with Le Moine that there is mental dynamism in Malebranche's system in so far as the will is engaged in knowledge. I disagree that this activity of the will involves a vicious contradiction, because I further disagree that this activity of the will is ever constructive or creative of the relations. It finds them, and they are really real—really real relations.

CHAPTER VI. SENSE, FAITH AND THE EXTERNAL WORLD

1. Church, *Study*, p. 203; Novaro, *Malebranche*, pp. 87-9.

2. Fritz, *Malebranche and Berkeley*, p. 60.

3. *Ibid.*, pp. 62 ff.

4. Malebranche, *Entretiens sur la métaphysique*, Dial. 14, Sec. 4, Ginsberg, p. 355; Dial. 6, Sec. 2, Ginsberg, p. 163; and Dial. 9, Sec. 11, Ginsberg, p. 243; *Méditations chrétiennes*, Med. 3, Secs. 4 and 5.

5. *E.g.*, Malebranche, *Recherche*, Bk. 3, Pt. 2, Ch. 6, L. i, p. 248, and Appendice, L. iii, p. 299.

6. Fritz, *Malebranche and Berkeley*, pp. 64 ff.

7. Malebranche, *Recherche*, Bk. 1, Ch. 1, Sec. 1, L. i, p. 3; Bk. 3, Pt. 2, Ch. 5, L. i, p. 247; Ecl. 6, L. iii, pp. 28-9.

8. Fritz, *Malebranche and Berkeley*, pp. 71 and 78-80.

9. Berkeley, *Commonplace Book*, Entry 429, Luce and Jessop i, p. 53.

10. Berkeley, *Principles*, Prin. 98.

11. Berkeley, To Johnson, Nov. 25, 1729, Luce and Jessop ii, pp. 280-1.

12. *Ibid.*, March 24, 1730, Luce & Jessop ii, p. 292. In the *Commonplace Book* he comments. "Malbranch does not prove that the figures & extensions exist not w^n the are not perceiv'd. Consequently he does not prove nor can it be prov'd on his principles, that ye sorts are the work of the mind & onely in the mind." Entry 288, Luce and Jessop i, p. 35.

13. Fritz, *Malebranche and Berkeley*, p. 63. Mrs. Fritz interprets Malebranche's Diety either in a Spinozistic sense or else in Berkeley's sense that God is pure Spirit. (*Ibid.*, pp. 69-70.) She forgets that for Malebranche God is first and foremost the act of being. As a result of this misinterpretation, she does not realize (p. 66) that while for Malebranche God is the *true* cause of all things in the sense of Creator, this in no way deprives the occasional cause of being active and instrumental in the governance of things.

14. Mrs. Fritz also asserts that inasmuch as matter is wholly unlike God or finite minds, being by nature extended, divisible, and thus lacking in unity, for this reason too its existence is superfluous. (P. 68.) Here she ignores the role of existence in Malebranche's thought; it is existence that puts a limit on divisibility and gives unity to matter. But she uncritically assumes that for Malebranche, essence and existence are identical (p. 69), thus ignoring his contrary declarations to Mairan. Having overlooked this vital distinction between essence and existence, she then naturally tends to assume that created existing matter is no more than appearance or presentation of pure ideas to minds. Whence immaterialism ought to follow. (P. 70.)

15. Church, *Study*, p. 31. For a recent, critical, and detailed appraisal of Malebranche's key notion of natural judgment, see Father John R. Klopke's *Natural Judgment*. The author examines the many intellectual vicissitudes which befall and entrap the 'natural judgment' from its initial appearance in the first edition of the *Recherche* throughout the consequent writings of Malebranche. He concludes: "It is extremely difficult to accommodate Malebranche's further explanations of sensory perception with the initial description of it as natural judgment." There is "no master key which puts all of Malebranche's thought into coherence." (P. 360.)

16. Church, *Study*, p. 39.

17. *Ibid.*, p. 33, my ital.

18. *Ibid.*, p. 37, my ital.

19. *Ibid.*, pp. 37-8, my ital.

20. *Ibid.*, p. 38, my ital.

21. *Ibid.*

22. *Ibid.*, p. 39.

23. *Ibid.*, my ital.

24. *Ibid.*, pp. 226-7.

25. *Ibid.*, pp. 216-17.

26. Malebranche, *Recherche*, Bk. 1, Ch. 7, Schrecker edition, pp. 89-90 and notes.

27. *Ibid.*, Bk. 3, Pt. 2, Ch. 6, L. i, p. 253.

28. Church, *Study*, pp. 131-2.

29. Malebranche, *Recherche*, Bk. 1, Chs. 6-9, *passim*.

30. *Ibid.*, Bk. 1, Ch. 2, Sec. 1, L. i, pp. 7-8. *Cf. ibid.*, Ch. 7, Sec. 4, L. i, p. 37.

31. *Ibid.*, p. 38, my ital.

32. Malebranche, *Réponse à Régis*, Ch. 1, L. iii, p. 234; O. C. xvii-1, p. 265.

33. Church, *Study*, p. 41.

34. Malebranche, *Recherche*, Bk. 1, Ch. 8, Sec. 2, L. i, pp. 41-3.

35. Malebranche, *Entretiens sur la métaphysique*, Dial. 4, Sec. 8, Ginsberg, pp. 126-7.

36. Malebranche, *Recherche*, Bk. 3, Pt. 2, Ch. 6, L. i, p. 253.

37. "Sur la nature des idées. Dans lequel j'explique *comment* on voit en Dieu *toutes* choses, les vérités et les lois éternelles." *Ibid.*, Ecl. 10, L. iii, p. 74, my ital.

38. *Ibid.*, p. 84.

39. *Ibid.*, p. 85.

40. *Ibid.*

41. *Ibid.*, p. 91.

42. *Ibid.*

43. *Ibid.*, pp. 92-3.

44. *Ibid.*, p. 92.

45. Bacon, *Advancement of Learning*, Scribner, p. 137. See note 17, Chapter II.

46. Malebranche, *Recherche*, Ecl. 10, L. iii, p. 91.

47. Church, *Study*, p. 141.

48. *Ibid.*, p. 140.

49. Gouhier, *Philosophie de Malebranche*, pp. 382-90.

50. Church, *Study*, p. 188.

51. *Cf. ibid.*, pp. 140 and 205. See Arnauld, *Vraies et fausses idées*, Ch. 15, pp. 131-7, and Malebranche, *Réponse au Livre des vraies, etc.*, Chs. 13, 15 and 17, *passim*.

52. Arnauld, *Vraies et fausses idées*, Chs. 15 and 16, *passim*.

53. "Comment comprendre que nous apercevions des figures intelligibles sur cette étendue uniforme, infinie, où rien n'est figuré. Comment y découper telle ou telle figure, si déjà par devers nous, nous n'en avons pas le patron et le modèle? Ou si ce n'est pas nous qui limitons, qui découpons l'étendue, si c'est l'étendue intelligible elle-même qui s'applique à notre esprit, sous telle ou telle limite, quelle est la raison de cette limite? Comment l'étendue intelligible se circonscrit-elle à notre regard en cercle ou en carré, sans cesser de nous apparaître comme infinie? Quoi de plus obscur et de plus chimérique que toutes ces imaginations pour concilier, avec l'uniformité de l'étendue intelligible, la variété infinie de nos perceptions sensibles! Enfin, si l'étendue intelligible, avec le sentiment, suffit à nous donner tous les spectacles et toutes les impressions due monde extérieur, si nous ne sommes réelement en rapport qu'avec ce monde intelligible, à quoi bon supposer l'existence d'un monde réel, et quoi de plus contraire à ce grand principe de la simplicité des voies, sans cesse invoqué par Malebranche?" Bouillier, *Histoire*, Vol. 2, p. 99.

54. Moreau points out (*Malebranche et le Spinozisme*, pp. 77-8) that there is an ambiguity in Malebranche's treatment of Intelligible Extension. When he speaks of "nombres nombrants" and intelligible figures, Malebranche uses intelligible in the sense of *definite* or *determinate:* definite relations, definite forms. But when he talks of intelligible parts contained in a uniform homogeneous intelligible extension, then intelligible means the *virtual, indefinite potential, i.e.*, of extension as a field of indefinite possibilities, of infinite elements, and of infinite divisibility. This second aspect Moreau compares to Plato's Receptacle; the former to Plato's Forms. Had Malebranche dissociated the two meanings and rendered ideas into intelligible constructions, his thought would have culminated in idealism. But the realism of the ideas as archetypes kept him from immaterialism; it was not simply religious faith. Moreau is right but I should like to add to

his observations the following. Malebranche could not have made Intelligible Extension into a Platonic Receptacle divorced from ideas, without also violating his empirical method and his ontology of Being. Had he made the divorce, his God would have become a Platonic Demiurge, not the Creator, and his universe would have become existenceless, abstract, not concrete. The forms would have become those active essences against which he rebelled; existence would have become reduced to the Suarezian actualization of an essence and his entire distinction between essence and existence would have vanished. Thus by retaining the plurality and reality of ideas as definite aspects of Intelligible Extension, as archetypes in a God who is Being, Malebranche escapes both essentialism and immaterialism.

55. Malebranche, *Recherche*, Ecl. 10, L. iii, p. 92.

56. Malebranche, *Réponse au Livre des vraies, etc.*, Ch. 13, Secs. 3-9, pp. 355-7; *Recherche*, Ecl. 10, L. iii, pp. 91-2; *Réponse à Régis*, Ch. 2, L. iii, p. 244, or O. C. xvii-1, pp. 281-2.

57. Malebranche, *Réponse à Régis*, *ibid.*, and L., p. 249, or O. C., pp. 289-90. *Cf. Recherche*, Ecl. 10, p. 85.

58. Malebranche, *Entretiens sur la métaphysique*, Dial. 6, Sec. 3, p. 165.

59. Church, *Study*, p. 204.

60. Malebranche, *Recherche*, Ecl. 2, L. iii, p. 18.

61. To Arnauld, Malebranche wrote that he too rejects those superfluous representative entities that Arnauld attributed to him (*Réponse au Livre de vraies, etc.*, Ch. 10, Sec. 8, p. 342), and he takes Arnauld to task for not realizing that the problem regarding ideas is not one concerning sense perception but is one concerning universals: ". . . La question n'est pas de *l'origine*, mais de la *nature* des idées des choses matérielles." (*Ibid.*, Ch. 17, Sec. 5, p. 382.)

62. In the course of his controversy with Arnauld, Malebranche said that colors are seen *here* and *there*. For Malebranche, these positions are intelligible, not material, for colors are modifications of soul, and soul is where its modifications are. (Cited by Church, *Study*, pp. 200-1.) For, if soul and its colors were at material positions, then Malebranche would have had to say that the soul was extended.

Church feels that Malebranche's doctrine leads to paradox. He asks (*ibid.*, p. 202) how, if colors are seen in intelligible positions, do we know what material spread-out-ness is?

However, Church ignores the fact that ideal extension does not keep us from *understanding* what actual spread-out-ness means. All that Malebranche is asserting is that the ideal meaning or essence is vast but not itself spatial, just as the idea of a circle is an algebraic meaning that is not itself figured, although it means a spatial figure.

Church argues further that actual spread-out-ness must be given in sense perception and that this requirement raises the dilemma that *either* the seen spatial landscape is not an intelligible spread, since "nothing at all can be spread out in an abstract idea," *or else* the spatial character of a landscape is an illusory appearance. (Pp. 202-3.)

The answer to Church is this. While metaphysically sensations of color may be conjoined with ideal meanings, this does not necessarily prevent us from being aware of *actual* material figure. Malebranche declares that: "Those spaces which you see are only intelligible spaces which do not occupy any place. For the spaces which you *see* are quite different from the material spaces which you *survey*." (*Entretiens sur la métaphysique*, Dial. 4, Sec. 10, Ginsberg, p. 128, my ital.) Sensations are attached to ideal distances and to ideal figures; but at the same time Malebranche tells us that we can survey or notice or discern material spaces, ". . . The sensations that we have of colour . . . are of use to us in distinguishing objects rather than in uniting ourselves to or separating ourselves from them. It is to the objects that we refer these sensations . . ." (*Ibid.*, Dial. 12, Sec. 2, p. 300.) It is clear that for Malebranche, in perception the mind is directed towards grasping the ideality of the object perceived; this nevertheless does not prevent us from beholding a real physical "spread-out-ness." And the reason why he stresses the unity between mind and intelligible content is that in perception there is a gap between knower and known on the level of existents. In knowledge or in perception, we may know intimately the ideal character of the object, but we never become confluent with the thing's actual material existence.

Once again we must distinguish between the epistemic and ontological issues. Epistemically we apprehend ideal meanings; ontologically our sensations are joined to those ideal meanings; but at the same time there is, through these sensations, an intuitive sensuous awareness or judgment of an actually figured or localized extension.

Perhaps, in the end, Malebranche's solution of this perceptual problem will not be acceptable to the contemporary reader. But criticism must go far deeper than Church has gone, namely, to the metaphysical foundations of the system, before it cuts against Malebranche. And if criticism goes that far, then it is hardly worthwhile to direct it against *Malebranche* alone rather than against a fairly large number of metaphysicians with a variety of systems.

63. Church, *Study*, p. 228.

64. Malebranche, *Recherche*, Bk. 1, Ch. 10, L. i, p. 53.

65. *Ibid.*, Chs. 6-9, *passim*.

66. *Ibid.*, Ch. 10, L. i, p. 53.

67. Malebranche, *Entretiens sur la*

métaphysique, Dial. 6, Sec. 6, Ginsberg, p. 168.

68. Church, *Study*, p. 202.

69. *Ibid.*, p. 229.

70. *Ibid.*, p. 230.

71. Malebranche, *Réponse au Livre des vraies, etc.*, Ch. 10, Sec. 8, p. 342.

72. Wolfson, *Philo*, Vol. 1, pp. 239-40 and 326-7.

73. Malebranche, *Recherche*, Bk. 3, Pt. 2, Ch. 1, Sec. 1, L. i, p. 234.

74. Malebranche, *Contre la prévention*. Cited from Church, *Study*, pp. 180-1.

75. Church, *Study*, p. 238.

76. Malebranche, *Recherche*, Bk. 1, Ch. 7, Sec. 1, L. i, p. 37.

77. Malebranche, *Entretiens sur la métaphysique*, Dial. 5, Sec. 7, Ginsberg, p. 150. *Cf. Recherche*, Bk. 1, Chs. 6 and 7.

78. Church, *Study*, pp. 231-2.

79. Malebranche, *Recherche*, Bk. 1, Ch. 6, Sec. 1, L. i, p. 31, my ital. Malebranche continues: "De ce que Dieu nous fait avoir une telle idée sensible de grandeur, lorsqu'une toise est devant nos yeux, il ne s'ensuit pas que cette toise *n'ait que* l'étendue qui nous est représentée par cette idée." (My ital.)

80. Malebranche, *Entretiens sur la métaphysique*, Dial. 12, Sec. 3, Ginsberg, p. 301.

81. Church, *Study*, pp. 229-30.

82. Malebranche, *Recherche*, Ecl. 6, L. iii, p. 32.

83. *Ibid.*, p. 31.

84. *Ibid.*, p. 32. "Dieu ne tire sa lumière que de lui-même, il ne voit le monde matériel que dans le monde intelligible qu'il renferme, et dans la connaissance qu'il a de ses volontés qui donnent actuellement l'existence et le mouvement à toutes choses." (P. 30.)

85. *Ibid.*, p. 30.

86. Malebranche, *Réponse au Livre des vraies, etc.*, Ch. 26, Secs. 1-2, pp. 443-4.

87. Malebranche, *Entretiens sur la*

métaphysique, Dial. 6, Sec. 3, Ginsberg, p. 165.

88. *Ibid.*, Sec. 4, Ginsberg, pp. 166-7.

89. *Ibid.*, Dial. 6, Sec. 6, Ginsberg, p. 168.

90. *Ibid.*, Secs. 3 to 7.

91. *Ibid.*, Dial. 4, Sec. 15, Ginsberg, pp. 132-3.

92. *Ibid.*, Sec. 18, Ginsberg, p. 136.

93. Malebranche, *Recherche*, Bk. 1, Ch. 5.

94. *Ibid.*, Ch. 3, Sec. 2, L. i, p. 17. ". . . Parce qu'il arrive ordinairement que plusieurs, jointes ensembles, ont autant de force pour convaincre que des démonstrations très évidentes."

95. *Ibid.*, Ecl. 6, L. iii, p. 31.

96. Malebranche, *Entretiens sur la métaphysique*, Dial. 6, Sec. 7, Ginsberg, p. 171, my ital. Ginsberg mistranslates "Je ne suis pas porté invinciblement à croire qu'il est . . ." as "I am inevitably led to believe that it exists." Cuvillier has a typographical error in this sentence. (Fontana i, p. 135; Cuvillier i, p. 192.) I have corrected Ginsberg.

97. Church, *Study*, pp. 237-8.

98. Malebranche, *Recherche*, Bk. 5, Ch. 2, L. ii, p. 83.

99. Malebranche, *Entretiens sur la métaphysique*, Dial. 13, Sec. 9, Ginsberg, pp. 337-8.

100. Church, *Study*, pp. 235-6.

101. Malebranche, *Entretiens sur la métaphysique*, Dial. 6, Sec. 7, Ginsberg, p. 170, my ital.

102. *Ibid.*, pp. 170-1.

103. Malebranche, *Recherche*, Bk. 6, Pt. 1, Ch. 5, L. ii, p. 183.

104. *Ibid.*

105. *Ibid.*, Bk. 3, Pt. 2, Ch. 9, Sec. 1, L. i, p. 268.

106. *Ibid.*, Sec. 3, L. i, p. 269.

107. Malebranche, *Entretiens sur la métaphysique*, Dial. 6, Sec. 8, Ginsberg, pp. 171-2. *Cf.* Gueroult, *Descartes*, Vol. 2, pp. 118-22, 156, and 165, note, for differences between Descartes' and Malebranche's proofs for the existence of the external world

and for their respective attitudes toward that world.

108. Arnauld, *Vraies et fausses idées*, Ch. 28, p. 260; Church, *Study*, p. 109; Blampignon, *Etude*, p. 143.

109. See title of Descartes' *Search*.

110. Descartes, *Principles*, Pt. 4, Prins. 206 and 207, H. R. i, pp. 301-2. What Descartes has to say to P. Dinet in a letter of 1642 must not pass unnoticed: ". . . ce serait une espèce d'impieté d'appréhender que les vérités découvertes en la philosophie fussent contrairent à celles de la foi. Et même j'avance hardiment que notre religion ne nous enseigne rien qui ne se puisse expliquer aussi facilement ou même avec plus de facilité, suivant mes principes, que suivant ceux qui sont communément reçus . . . (A. T. vii, p. 581; cited by Vidgrain, *Le christianisme*, p. 76.)

111. Malebranche, *Recherche*, Bk. 2, Pt. 2, Ch. 5, L. i, p. 156.

112. *Ibid.*, Ch. 3, Sec. 2, L. i, p. 150.

113. *Ibid.*, Ch. 5, L. i, p. 157, my ital.

114. *Ibid.*, Ch. 3, Sec. 2, L. i, p. 150.

115. Bacon, *Novum Organum*, Vol. 1, Aph. 65; Malebranche, *Recherche*, Bk. 2, Pt. 2, Ch. 8, Sec. 3, L. i, p. 170.

116. Malebranche, *ibid.*, pp. 170-1.

117. *Ibid.*, Bk. 1, Ch. 3, Sec. 2, L. i, p. 16.

118. Delbos, *Etude*, pp. 24, 26 and 31.

119. Malebranche, *Recherche*, Préface pour servir de réponse à la Critique du premier volume, L. ii, pp. 307-8.

120. Malebranche, *Fragments et correspondance*, p. 15, Vidgrain edition; O. C. xvii-1, p. 548.

121. Malebranche, *Recherche*, Bk. 4, Ch. 6, Sec. 2, L. ii, p. 27.

122. *Ibid.*, Bk. 6, Pt. 2, Ch. 6, L. ii, p. 241

123. *Ibid.*, pp. 246-7.

124. Delbos, *Etude*, p. 32.

125. Malebranche, *Entretiens sur*

la métaphysique, Dial. 13, Secs. 7 and 8, Ginsberg, pp. 333 and 335.

126. Delbos, *Etude*, p. 42.

127. Le Moine, *Vérités éternelles*, pp. 244-5.

128. Malebranche, *Fragments et correspondance*, pp. 15-16, Vidgrain edition; O. C. xvii-1, pp. 548-9.

129. Malebranche, *Correspondance avec Mairan*, p. 143, Moreau edition; O. C. xix, p. 888.

130. Malebranche. *Entretiens sur la métaphysique*, Dial. 14, Sec. 13, Ginsberg, p. 370.

131. Malebranche declared to the Jesuit Louis de la Ville (Le Valois): ". . . la liberté de philosopher ou de raisonner sur des notions communes, ne doit point être ôtée aux hommes. C'est un droit qui leur est naturel comme celui de respirer." André, *Vie du R. P. Malebranche*, p. 68; *Polémique avec Le Valois*, O. C. xvii-1, p. 524.

132. Vidgrain, *Christianisme*, p. 84.

133. Malebranche, *Recherche*, Bk. 6, Pt. 2, Ch. 6, L. ii, p. 246.

134. *Ibid.*, Pt. 1, Ch. 3, L. ii, p. 168, my ital.

135. *Ibid.*, Bk. 5, Ch. 5, L. ii, p. 111.

136. Malebranche, *Conversations*, Dial. 4, pp. 121-2, Bridet edition; O. C. iv, p. 106.

137. Delbos, *Etude*, p. 33.

138. Malebranche, *Conversations*, Dial. 5, pp. 143-4, Bridet edition; O. C. iv, p. 126.

139. Malebranche, *Entretiens sur la métaphysique*, Dial. 4, Sec. 17, Ginsberg, p. 134.

140. Malebranche, *Nature et grâce*, Ecl. 3, No. 26, O. C. v, pp. 187-8.

141. Vidgrain, *Christianisme*, p. 152.

142. Malebranche, *Entretiens sur la métaphysique*, Dial. 6, Sec. 8, Ginsberg, pp. 171-2.

143. Malebranche, *Recherche*, Bk. 6, Pt. 2, Ch. 6, L. ii, pp. 246-7.

144. Malebranche, *Entretiens sur la métaphysique*, Dial. 6, Sec. 2, Ginsberg, pp. 163-4.

Brunschvicg observes (*Progrès de la conscience*, Vol. 1, p. 201):

Si le Verbe qui est pure immanence à l'Unité divine, si le *Logos* des 'philosophes et savants,' ne l'a point contenté, ce n'est point du tout parce que Malebranche aurait d'avance infléchi son système vers les vérités de foi aux quelles il veut aboutir, c'est tout au contraire parce que les difficultés proprement philosophiques ne lui paraissent susceptibles de solution que dans la mesure où les vérités de la foi viennent les éclaircir.

145. This summary is based on *ibid.*, Dials. 13 and 14, *passim*.

146. *Ibid.*, Dial. 13, Sec. 12, Ginsberg, p. 348.

147. *Cf.* Gouhier, *Vocation*, pp. 37-48, for the relation between Malebranche and Simon.

148. Malebranche, *Conversations*, Dial. 6, pp. 156 ff., Bridet edition; O. C. iv, pp. 136 ff.

149. Malebranche, *Entretiens sur la métaphysique*, Dial. 14, Sec. 3, Ginsberg, p. 353.

150. *Ibid.*, Sec. 4, Ginsberg, pp. 355-6.

151. *Ibid.*, Sec. 13, Fontana ii, p. 351.

152. Malebranche, *Traité de morale*, Pt. 1, Ch. 2, Sec. 13, p. 23.

153. Malebranche, *Entretiens sur la métaphysique*, Dial. 6, Sec. 1, Ginsberg, pp. 160-3.

154. Malebranche, *Traité de morale*, Pt. 1, Ch. 2, Sec. 11, p. 20.

155. Malebranche, *Méditations chrétiennes*, Med. 4, Sec. 15, pp. 71-2, Gouhier edition; O. C. x, pp. 44-5.

156. Malebranche, *Recherche*, Bk. 6, Pt. 2, Conclusion, L. ii, pp. 296-7.

157. Malebranche, *Prémotion*, Sec. 8, p. 383a; cited by Gouhier, *Vocation*, p. 150; O. C. xvi, p. 26. *Dieu* substituted for *lui* of original.

158. Malebranche, *Nature et grâce*,

Disc. 2, Pt. 17, p. 355; cited by Gouhier, *Vocation*, p. 152.

159. Malebranche, *Conversations*, Avertissements, pp. xxi-xxiii, Bridet edition; O. C. iv, pp. 4-5.

160. Malebranche, *Entretiens sur la métaphysique*, Dial. 14, Sec. 13, Ginsberg, p. 370. Léon Brunschvicg asserts: "L'importance historique du malebranchisme, c'est qu'il est le premier système, peut-être le seul, où le dogme chrétien soit mis directement en connexion avec une philosophie de l'esprit, de la raison et de la vérité, qui ne cherche d'aucune manière à ruser avec l'esprit, avec la raison, avec la vérité . . ." (*Progrès de la conscience*, Vol. 1, p. 209.)

Author Index

[421]

Author Index

Subject Index

[425]

and communicating activity, 178; *eminent,* 382; employed by Descartes, 102; *final,* rejected by Descartes, 42-45, 48, 364-367; maintained to guarantee intercourse between Being and beings, 183-185; for Leibnitz, useful in consideration of physical phenomena, 364; necessary for religion, 391; *immanent,* maintained by Spinoza, 183; Spinoza's immanence rejected, as not allowing contingency, 183; *occasional* (*see* Creatures), a speculation—occasional cause, in so far as it exists, acts, 190, 403, 413; active analogue of God's power, through the Incarnation, 191; dependent on conservation as continuous creation: duration a continuum—conservation sustains continuously enduring finite existence—self-subsistence of creatures—conservation sustains movement of bodies, 223-224; in what sense creatures act, 225; motion of bodies stems from their act of existence, 226; communicates motion acting in accordance with God's laws, 227, 283, 398, 402-403; activity of, dependent on God's conserving and creating power, 228, 236, 402; intended to produce diversity of effects, 229, 283; why natural causes are called occasional causes, 230; creatures possess power, 230; cannot create existence, 231; God's instrument, 231; "true" causality not meaningless though inaccessible to perception, 233, 397; perceived through sense perception, 233; antecedent and consequence, and causality, 235; not inconsistent with divine power, 236; creatures embodiments of God's will, 237; function of the formal order, 238; bodies, acts of existence, 239; vehicle through which divine efficacy is expressed, 239, 283, 398, 402; power of, acquired from act of existence, 240; so far as it exists, is active, 361, 403; behavior and power of described by laws, 403; *true* (*see* Creatures), "true cause," 162-182; foundation of experimental method, 167;

cause between which and its effects the mind perceives a necessary connection, 169, 177, 211, 233-234; God is only true cause, 169, 173, 175-176, 190, 209-210, 214-215, 225; must be apprehended "par simple vue," 172, 174; implicative of, not equivalent to, logical necessity, 179; necessary connection with effect surpasses human comprehension, 390; meaningful, 397; and secondary causes, 397-399.

"Celui qui est"—*see* God, God is Being.

Certainty (*see* Essences—and Knowledge, God—Knowledge of, Ideas, Mathematics—Certainty in, Number, Truth—Necessary, Vision in God): yielded by intelligible ideas, 67; innate ideas and Descartes, 86-116; Cartesian condition of, 103; inaccessible if ideas belong to finite minds, 109; not guaranteed by divine veracity, 114; based on realm of immutable ideas, 117-118, 124; of Spinoza, rational, apodictic, 123.

Christ, incarnation of: realization of divine glory, 187; sanctifies nature, 189, 191, 391; would have occurred without Adam's fall, 189; Christ as man, occasional cause of grace, 189-190; temporal beginning of God's glory, 189; indispensable for metaphysics, 191; satisfies reason in demonstrating connection between finite and infinite, 324.

"Cogito" of Descartes: existence of thought cannot be doubted, 244; does not imply self-consciousness as central to definition of mind, 245; immediate awareness of the self, 255; prototype of clear and distinct knowledge, 255; ontological character of, 405.

Conception: central role of, in treatment of ideas, 58-60; conceptualism of Descartes rejected, 75-76, 382-383; Vision in God solves problems arising in Descartes' conceptualism, 118; conceptual essences in perception, 286; sense perception involves pure ideas, 291.

[427]

ence in God, 137, 199, 210, 268; distinct from existence in creatures, 164-165, 172, 195, 197-199, 202, 206, 242, 275, 282.

Essences (*see* Ideas, Intelligible Extension, Sense Perception, Universals, Vision in God): *characteristics of*, universal, 96, 120; immutable, 96, 120, 128, 133, 138; necessary, 120; eternal, 125, 128, 196; uncaused, 128, 133, 138; have super-essential import, 130, 143; contrasted with Santayana's, 130; unified, 99, 139-140; constitute an intelligible extension, 292-299; *existential import of*, are not creatures, 128-129; aspects of existence, 142; do not reveal existence of things, 172; concretization of, is creation, 191; the tradition of essentialism, 193; for Spinoza, not distinguished from concrete things, 196; *and God*, in God, 131, 143; archetypal attributes of God, 133; expressions of the infinite, 139; dependent on Being, 144, 415; concretization of, entails participation in Divine Being, 208; in God are the essences of external objects, 309; *and knowledge*, as objects of knowledge, 66-67; not dependent on being perceived or conceived, 91; self-identical for every intelligence, 120; guarantee rational certainty, 120; connote and denote themselves, 131; of Santayana, acquire symbolic reference to fact, 131; knowledge of, is Vision in God, 171; have reference beyond themselves, 172; known by light and clear ideas, 292; are not images, 383; *relations of*, essences and essences, eternal and immutable, 29; essences and existents, contingent, 29.

Essentialism: error of Scholastic physics—forms reified into entities and therefore into efficient agents, 163; essence and existence identified in Aristotle, 164; identified in Descartes, 192; the tradition of essentialism, 193; Malebranche distinguishes existence and essence, 195; correspondence with Dortous de Mairan, 195; essentialism in Spinoza and exist-

ence in Malebranche, 195-198; did Malebranche understand Spinoza's God?, 198.

Existence: for Descartes, greatest perfection, 49; for Descartes, not distinct from essence, 128, 193, 213, 268; no logical necessity between essence and existence, 130, 172, 195, 198-199, 305-306; identical with essence in God, 137, 199, 210, 268; prior to essence, 158; identified with essence in Aristotle, 164; distinct from essence in creatures, 164-165, 172, 195, 197-199, 202, 206, 242, 275, 282; contingent in creatures, 166; necessary in God, 166; possible only if we think of God, 177; added to essence in process of creation, 192, 201, 204, 275, 282-283, 380; the tradition of essentialism, 193; principle of individuation, 198-201, 296; limits infinite divisibility of essence, 200, 413; and the immensity of God, 209-220; conjoint with movement, 201, 226; participation in Divine Being, 208-209; not reducible to or derivable from essence, 213; allows action and stability, 242; for Berkeley, is "percipi" or "percipere," 281; revelation of, through sense, 298; natural revelations of external existence, 299-305; accessible but not wholly penetrable, 310.

Existents (*see* Cause, Causality, Creation, Creatures, Efficacy, God—Will of, Power): relations among, contingent, 29; necessarily connected with God, 175; created by God alone, 176; activity, potency, and will, 209; knowledge of, 292, 299; how changing existents seen in divine essence, 293; how we see existents in God, 298; subject to change, 369; must be created in accordance with principle of rationality, 280, 392.

Experiment (*see* Faith, Hypothesis, Scientific Method): function of, as understood by Descartes and Bacon, 21; indispensable to scientific method, 29, 31, 40; species of demands made to author of nature, 30-31; link with reason, sought by Bacon, 31; abuses of, 32; confirmation of abstract reasoning, 39-40; reveals will of God, 40, 235; abandoned by Descartes, 41, 363; for Bacon, reveals Forms, 59; validation of perception, 305; and experience, for Descartes, 357; frequency theory of color and experiments on light, 359.

Extension (*see* Immaterialism): for Descartes and Malebranche, essence of all bodies, 44, 192-193, 208, 226, 282, 380; man's indubitable knowledge of, 123; for Descartes, can be conceived as infinitely divisible and apart from its modes, 193; and motion and existence, 199; continuum of inexhaustible and infinitely divisible parts, 200; for Spinoza, parallel to thought, 257; conceived as independently existing, 284; limit of, is figure, 293; *idea of,* most clear and evident, 27, 72; for Descartes, innate, 61; objective reality and a priori certainty of, fundamental problem for Descartes, 72; immutable, 72; *intelligible—see* Intelligible Extension, Faith.

External World: chapter vi, 279-330; existence of bodies neither demonstrable nor necessary, 305; the sixth Eclaircissement: distinction between essence and existence precludes demonstration of existence, 306—natural revelation of the existence of creatures, 308; perceptual evidence for the existence of the external world, 310-317; how we encounter existence in sense perception, 310; no disproof of external existence—probable evidence for it, 312; existence of, rendered certain by faith, 324-325; existence of, for Leibnitz, truth of reason, 361; existence of, historic fact, 361; differences between Descartes and Malebranche concerning, 417.

Faith (*see* External World, Sense Perception, Senses): explains relation between finite and infinite, 187-188; chapter vi, 279-330; for Descartes, independent of reason, 318; for Descartes, could not be source or guide to knowledge, 318; and reason, not bifurcated, 318, 321-327; not sup-

portable by evidence, 319-320; rests on knowledge of God, 321; contents of, may be illumined by reason, 321, 329; wisdom speaks in two ways, 322; function of, analogous to sense in science—to embody truth concretely and to lead to intelligence, 323; possesses two sorts of intelligibility, 323; sense communicates but does not confirm, 324; renders existence of external world certain, 324-325; reason, not sense, confirms revelations of, 325; will elevate man to enlightenment, 326; philosophy and scripture, reason and authority of Church, in fundamental accord, 326; infallibility of the Church, 326; justified by reason, 328; what if conflict arises between faith and reason?, 328; strengthens intelligence, 329; synthesis of faith, reason, and experimental evidence, 329, 419; solves philosophical perplexities, 330, 418; for Descartes, philosophical truths not contrary to, 417.

Feeling (*see* Self, Sense Perception, Soul, Will): inseparable from thought, 251-253.

Forms, of Bacon: immanent in nature, 21, 40, 59; nature-engendering natures of things, 59, 168; are real essences, 59; confined and determined by matter, 370-371.

Geometry: essentially algebra, 10-17; science of relationships, 10; images of, embody intelligible meaning, 10-11, 13; sensibility and reason, 12; exact knowledge relational, 12; truths consist in real relations, 13; arithmetic and algebra superior to, 14; conceiving infinity, 14; truth, system of infinitely complex relations, 15-16.

God: *activity of,* wills to reveal the ideas He contains, 118; does not will truths, 121; possessed knowledge of ideas before creating matter, 129; for Descartes, creator of inert matter which He subsequently influences, 192; communicates His power to creatures, 241; *attributes of,* for Descartes, attributes simple and indis-

187; activity, 192; contains Intelligible Extension, 196, 202, 293; for Spinoza, essence involves existence, 204; traditional views of, threatened in seventeenth century, 220-221; three-personed deity, 270-271; immanent in creatures, 302; not reducible to sphere of abstract truth, 383-384; nameable but indefinable, 385; *will of,* experienced in search for truth, 135; not connected to its effects by necessity, 171; cause of our conception of ideas, 176; for Descartes, separate and self-contained existent, 179; existence of world depends on, 179; expressed in maximum heterogeneity, 209; animates and vivifies all things, 215; determines relativity of perceptions, 292; consulted by God in His awareness of change and existence, 296, 307, 416.

God is Being: chapter iii, 120-160; Christian God unique, 135; Christian God is Being, 135; God more than a realm of essences, 136; Christian ontological realism, 136; Malebranche, a Christian ontological realist, 137; rejection of philosophy of creative essence, 138; God as supra-essential, 139; Augustinian formulation of, 140; God of Exodus, 141; essence, existence, and being, 142; Being, creativity, and the glory of God, 161-191; Spinoza's cardinal error, 195-200, 382-383, 395.

Hypothesis (*see* Cause—True, Experiment, Scientific Method): nature of experimental hypothesis, 35-41; for Descartes, explanatory principle sufficient to save the phenomena, 35-37; for Descartes, true cause based on observation and experiment, 36-37; for Boyle and Newton, "verae causae," 36-37; "verae causae" sought by Malebranche, 36-38; consequent reform in Cartesian physics, 38-41, 360-361.

Ideas: order of issues in treatment of, 63-68, 415; refer intrinsically to existence, 129-134; vision of, accompanied by vision of power, 134-135; *clear and distinct,* basis of Descartes' physics, 43; three kinds of, the soul, God, extension, for Descartes, 72; indubitable, for Spinoza, 358; dominate physics, but do not constitute it, 359; for Descartes, can alone present the nature of things, 372; have exact relations, 378; *and God,* not related to creative will or thought of God, 57, 123-124, 126; universal archetypes in God, 60, 379; identified with being of God, 122, 129; objects for God's thought, 126; not exhaustive of God, 129-130; afford a priori knowledge of concrete things to God, 129; non-created status of, attests God's existence, 157; participate in Being, 157; aspects of intelligible extension, embodied in objects, 296; *innate,* for Descartes, implanted in the mind by God, 41, 87; make man the measure of truth, 61; rejection of, 75, 89-91, 93, 98-119, 144, 154, 290; Malebranche's "equitable" separation of act and object in Descartes, 86 ff., 374; conceiving infinity, 89; selecting correct ideas from the magazine of innate ideas, 90; God supplies concepts as needed—difficulties over infinite relations, 91; Gouhier holds Malebranche not in significant disagreement with Descartes' innatism, 91; infinity and the magazine hypothesis, 92; we can conceive, but not comprehend the infinite, 97; Descartes cannot admit actually infinite ideas, 98; organic unity of the infinite, 99; hard to attribute to mind an idea possessing exteriority, 107; finite mind not hospitable receptacle of immutable real ideas, 108; Descartes' subjectivism renders universality inaccessible, 108; opposites of contingent states of mind conceivable, 108; innate ideas based on anthropologism, 109; vindication of Descartes' ego-centrism, 365; for Descartes, man's gaze should be averted from super-natural to natural, 366-367; comprehension of, 372; *intelligible character of,* ideas as universals, 58-68; central role of conception, 58-60; averts radical skepticism by assuming reality of intelligible ideas, 62; problem of perception subsequent to problem of nature of intelligible ideas, 65; knowledge of universals goal of Malebranche's epistemology, 66; intelligible ideas yield certainty and generality, 67; how Malebranche treats intelligible ideas, 68; ideas are not thoughts, but immutable objects of thought—universality, immutability, infinity, 118; Vision in God solves problems arising in Descartes' conceptualism—more truly rational, more truly objective, affords a true a-priorism, 118-119; *and mind,* immediate objects of thought, 63-64; copy theory of, rejected, 68; for Descartes and Malebranche, idea any object of which the mind thinks, 70; not dependent on being conceived or thought by the mind, 86, 115, 124; innate ideas and Descartes, 86-116; for Descartes, ideas are modifications of mind, 100, 132-133; not modifications of mind, 100-107; infinite ideas and ideas of infinity, 101; exteriority, 102; ideas as modifications reduces knowledge to mere opinion, 103, destroys universality, 104, precludes immutability, 104, and makes strict demonstration impossible, 105; *nature of,* universals, 58-68, 104-105, 108, 117-118, 376; Descartes' pure ideas are essences or universals, 70; Malebranche's "intelligible ideas," 70; ideas are real beings, for Descartes, 71; possess distinct properties, 73; require an efficient cause, for Descartes, 75; are abstracted copies of external objects, for peripatetics, 77; impressed species, denied, 78-81, 86, 373; creation "ex nihilo," denied, 82; creativity denied—assumes a priori model, 83 ff., 376; innate ideas and Descartes, 86-116; homogeneous, for Descartes, 87-88; are spiritual entities, for Descartes, 93; contain properties of their objects in spiritual form, for Descartes, 93-94, 97; immutable, for Descartes and Malebranche, 103-104, 108, 115-118; identification

theory of, makes demonstration impossible, 105-106; belong to infinite minds, for Descartes, 109; are arbitrarily created, for Descartes, 109; constitute a single eternal, infinite, universal reason, 117-118; potentiality for actualization, 129; existential referents, 130; perfections in which creatures may participate, 130; implicit referents to power, 130; archetypes of which the world is participant, 154, 304; uncreated, 176; ideas and notions, for Berkeley, 407; *reality of,* maintained, 62, 71-72, 75, 82; questioned by Descartes, 62; considered twofold by Descartes, 71-72; *relationships among,* are eternal and immutable, 13, 29; *as representatives,* does "representative" necessarily mean duplication?, 64; how cartesian ideas "represent," 93-96; cartesian ideas spiritually contain what they objectify, 93; objective properties of ideas must characterize Descartes' ideas, 94; nominalistic tendencies in Descartes, 94; insistence on real universals, 95-96; knowledge of the existence of external objects, 299; alleged copy theory, 300; erroneous apprehension of essences no evidence for a copy theory in veridical perception, 302; how ideas "represent" in veridical perception, 303; are pure essences too pure for sense perception?, 304; bodies become knowable only when grasped in their essence, 370; representative ideas rejected, 415; *theories of,* first alternative: physical impression, 77-81; second alternative: mind creates ideas, 82-86; third alternative: ideas as innate, 89-100, 107-109; fourth alternative: ideas as mind's own modifications, 100-107; general critique of arbitrary origination of ideas, 109-116; fifth alternative: vision in God, 116-119.

Idols (*see* Doubt): Baconian doctrine of, intended to eradicate dogmatism, 61.

Immaterialism: is immaterialism inevitable for Malebranche?, 279; Berkeley's twofold immaterialism, 281; the issue: independent reality

things as isolated realities, 16; deserve distrust, not wholesale condemnation, 62; for Descartes, do not give direct access to existential objects, 63; reasons for distrust of, 63; cannot reveal unaided inner mechanisms of nature, 168; cannot reveal unaided true power, 218; for Spinoza, limited and inadequate, 363; intelligible extension comprehensible apart from sense, 394, 414.

"Sentiment intérieur"—*see* Self.

"Simple vue"—*see* God, God is Being.

Skepticism (*see* Doubt, Senses): provisional and therapeutic, 61; Descartes' radical antecedent skepticism does not result in certainty, 61; averted by assuming the reality of intelligible ideas, 62.

Soul (*see* Mind, Self, Will): perceives objects in three ways, 60; one and indivisible, 71, 408; for Medievals, produces own ideas in response to external stimuli, 82; lacks creative power, 86; for Cartesians, requires only itself to understand objects, 100; cannot simultaneously exhibit an infinite number of states, 101; nature of, not easily knowable, 258-267; not revealed to be distinct substance by introspection, 264; union of, with God, that of distinct existence, 275.

Substance: for Descartes, that which can be conceived by itself, 102; multiplicity of, denied by Spinoza, 204; multiplicity of, affirmed by Malebranche, 195-209.

Termism: maintained by Berkeley, 94-95.

Thought (*see* Mind, Self, Soul, Will): for Descartes and Malebranche, not equivalent to physical movements, 69; for Descartes and Malebranche, includes all mental operations, 69, 244, 246; pure intellection is acquaintance, 69; pure thought the principal attribute of mind, 243-254; for Descartes, nature of, self-evidently clear, 244; for Descartes and Malebranche, essence of mind, 245, 252-253; capacity to grasp universal meanings, 246; intellectual thought and existential thought, 255-267; for Descartes, act and content identified, 256; act and content distinguished, 256, 258.

Time: for Descartes, independent instants, 223; infinitely compact continuum, 223; not absolute, 287.

Truth: Descartes' efforts to guarantee, 41-54; a priori, mathematical truth for Descartes, 72; certainty and reality of mathematics, 72; a priori universals assumed, 73; problem of continued existence of truth, for Descartes, 148, 367-369, 385; *attainment of*, only through intuition, 21; entails removal of prejudices and a good method, 25, 57; immanent within experience, 25-35; search for, an experience of causal power, 134; entails personal effort, 277, 411; *created*, for Descartes, preserves the omnipotence and unicity of God, 45 —incomprehensibility of the infinite, 47—eliminates final causes, 48—requires us to conceive infinity as indefinite, 48; rejected, 109 ff., 378; God's arbitrary will, and certainty, 109; Malebranche contra Descartes: the immutability of God's will no guarantee of certainty, 110—our assurance of God's veracity founded on obscure ideas, 112—divine veracity conflicts with divine power, 114—idea of veracious God a finite idea, 115—Descartes' alleged errors and their consequences, 116; Descartes' correspondence re, 365-367; rejection in tenth Eclaircissement, 378; *and God*, identical for man and God, 92, 124; for Descartes, dependent on God's will, 111, 121; necessary truths are necessary for God, 120; how truths can be necessary for God, 121; independent of God's will, 121-123; imposed on the divine mind, 121, 126; moderate conceptualism of God's thought for Scholasticism, 122; God no conceptualist for Malebranche; an interpretation, 123; *in natural revelation*, sensations cause errors by affecting our acts of attention, 310; despite the fact of error, veridical perception continues to depend on natural revelation, 311; theory of error itself depends on truth as revelation, 314; source of error: diminished attention, 315; Adam had truth because he could resist error, 316; finitude necessarily implies error, 317; degrees of truth, 317; *nature of,* for Descartes, lies in quantitative relations, 9; consists of real relations, 13, 315, 411; system of infinitely complex relations, 15, 21, 26, 119, 412; necessary and contingent distinguished, 29, 167; intrinsic necessity of, 113; uncreated, 119; holds for all minds, 123; content of, in realm of pure ideas, 124; independent of causal efficacy, 125; continued existence of, 148; error nothing, 316; error limited aspect of truth, 316-317; truth its own index, 316-317; not dependent on human or divine awareness, 411; *necessary,* certainty of, 120; universality of, 120; reality of, 369; not entitative, 384.

Turbulence: relevance to contemporary physics, 354, 360; existential matter identified with, 395.

Understanding: distorts the nature of things, 40-41; passive function of, to perceive, 60; guides and regulates imagination, 84; for Spinoza, needs no preliminary purification, 358; *pure understanding alone,* can grasp truths of mathematics, 13; can apprehend spiritual objects, 60; for Descartes and Malebranche, exercises cognitive function of thought, 69; for Descartes and Malebranche, has intelligible ideas as its objects, 70-71; can fully apprehend what is presented to sense, 85, 313.

Universals (*see* Essences, God—Nature of, Ideas, Intelligible Extension, Knowledge, Sense Perception, Vision in God, Word): ideas as, 58-68; must be grasped "in re," 63; present in perception, 63, 85; goal of epistemology is knowledge of universals, 66; a priori existence of, assumed by Descartes and Malebranche, 73-74, 86-87; not reducible to confused

assemblages of sensuous images, 80; genetic account of, cannot afford certainty, 86; form a single, interconnected infinite continuum, 99; exist without being perceived, 282; intelligible extension, 292-299; known by intellection, 298; not fabricated, 373-374, 413.

Vision in God: chapter ii, 55-119; also 129, 133, 292, 298, 387; fifth alternative theory of ideas, 116-119; provides foundation for certainty, 118, 165; demonstrates dependence of minds on God, 119; distinguished from Vision of God, 158, 171, 388-389; knowledge of essences, 171.

Vision of God—*see* God, God is Being.

Will (*see* Attention, Mind, Self, Soul): active principle in mind, which is seat of error and truth, 60, 406-407; movement toward or repose in what is right, 125; is not a "true" cause, 162, 218-219; capacity to choose sustained by God, 237, 277, 398-399; constrained to seek God, 237, 270, 274-275; inseparable from thought, 251-253; ascent to God, an act of, 266; freely commits itself to accept natural revelation, 313; occasional cause for obtaining knowledge, 406; active or passive?, 408-410.

Word (*see* Christ—Incarnation of): God obliged to honor and to follow, 120-126, 170-171, 383; gives no idea of power, contingency, or the future, 169-170; realm of essence and representative of creatures, 169-171, 383; identical with God's wisdom, 171-172, 383; distinct from divine Will, 172; speaks in two ways—the light of nature and the light of faith, 322; became incarnate to render men wise, 322-323; engendered when God knows Himself, 383; consubstantial with, and necessary emanation from, God the Father, 383, 388-389; vision of God through Word more than Vision in God, 388-389; contains the whole of God's substance, 389.